Lady Mary Wortley Montagu
From a miniature by C. F. Zincke, 1738

THE

COMPLETE LETTERS

OF

Lady Mary
Wortley Montagu

EDITED BY

ROBERT HALSBAND

VOLUME II

1721–1751

OXFORD

AT THE CLARENDON PRESS

1966

Oxford University Press, Ely House, London W. 1

GLASGOW NEW YORK TORONTO MELBOURNE WELLINGTON
CAPE TOWN SALISBURY IBADAN NAIROBI LUSAKA ADDIS ABABA
BOMBAY CALCUTTA MADRAS KARACHI LAHORE DACCA
KUALA LUMPUR HONG KONG

PRINTED IN GREAT BRITAIN

CONTENTS

LIST OF PLATES

INTRODUCTION TO VOLUME II

LETTERS 1721–1751

IN the whole range of Lady Mary's correspondence, the letters to her sister the Countess of Mar (from 1721 to 1727) are unequalled for concentrated and sustained brilliance. With Hogarthian clarity and pungency they bring to life the *beau monde* during the latter half of George the First's reign. Since her sister, who lived in Paris, suffered from melancholia (which deepened into insanity in 1728) and she herself felt the pangs of growing old, she spiced her letters with wit to amuse and cynicism to console. The original manuscripts of these letters have been divided between two collections— Lord Bute's, with about two-thirds, and Lord Harrowby's, with about one-third (and copies of the others). They all appear now for the first time from both collections in a complete, accurate, and unbowdlerized text.

Lady Mary began to write to the Countess of Pomfret in 1738,[1] shortly before Lady Pomfret, who had held a post at Court, moved to the Continent; she found her a sympathetic recipient for political and personal gossip as well as for more general notions about marriage. After she herself went abroad in 1739 she continued to confide in Lady Pomfret, who encouraged her eloquent and clever commentary. Since the manuscripts of these letters evidently do not survive, the first printed text (of 1837) has been reprinted here.

In the Countess of Oxford, Lady Mary enjoyed a friend towards whom she felt great affection and gratitude. Her rather formal letters, beginning in 1744,[2] show how she could adapt her courtliness to a dull, estimable woman. For the first time Lady Oxford's side of the correspondence has been used, mainly in the annotations.

---

[1] Printed below, pp. 118 ff.   [2] Below, pp. 325 ff.

ix

After she moved abroad Lady Mary's most frequent correspondent was her husband. Her letters to him[1] record her experiences and observations as she travelled through France into Italy, where she settled for almost a year in Venice. After visiting Florence, Rome, Naples, Genoa, Turin, and Geneva, she stayed in Chambéry for a winter, and then settled in the Papal city of Avignon for four years. In 1746 she moved to the Venetian province of Brescia, where she made her home for ten years. Aside from documenting her life as a tourist and as an expatriate, these letters deal with the career of her son, who achieved eminence in his own right as a rogue and an eccentric.

Lady Mary's letters to her daughter the Countess of Bute start in 1746,[2] and continue until her return to London fifteen years later. It is her most copious and felicitous correspondence, particularly during the years when she lived near Brescia and also visited the Italian lakes, which at that time were virtually unknown to English tourists. The subject-matter of these letters is, like the landscapes she depicts, pleasantly diversified: domestic activities of her strenuous retirement, advice on the education of her granddaughters, criticism of new books sent to her from England, and philosophical ruminations as she faced old age.

Of her entirely new letters in this volume there are two important correspondences,[3] which reveal new aspects of her personality and epistolary art. Her letters to Francesco Algarotti, the Italian poet and savant, begin in 1736,[4] while they were both in London, and continue until 1741, when they were finally reunited in Italy. Their rendezvous there, which had been her main motive for leaving England, put an end to her romantic fantasy. These love-letters, in French and English, are unique for her in their extravagant passion and rhetoric. Their survival and gradual discovery make a fascinating story.[5] Since Algarotti's heirs did not follow the polite custom of returning private letters to the families

---

[1] Below, pp. 140 ff.
[2] Below, pp. 366 ff.
[3] For a third, Lord Hervey's letters to LM, see p. 84, n. 2. (List of abbreviations is on p. xiii below.)

[4] Below, pp. 101 ff. Their correspondence was resumed in 1756, after a lapse of fifteen years (vol. iii).
[5] Details in Halsband, *LM*, pp. 290–1.

of the correspondents, the letters remained in Italy. (Undoubtedly they would have been destroyed if returned to Lady Bute.) Later, through the good offices of Byron, a collection of Algarotti's letters including six of Lady Mary's was bought by John Murray, the publisher. In 1837 they were generously loaned to Lord Wharncliffe, Lady Mary's descendant, for possible use in the second edition of her letters and works, but he politely declined to print them. Twenty-four of her letters to Algarotti, remaining together, were seen in Venice in 1850, and then dropped out of sight until they came up for auction in London in 1938, when they were bought for the Bodleian Library.

The other newly discovered correspondence in this volume is that with Mme Chiara Michiel, *née* Bragadin, a Venetian lady.[1] They are witty, debonair, and gracious. Written in fluent if ungrammatical French, they kept alive a warm friendship that endured to the end of Lady Mary's life. After having been misplaced among the Bute Manuscripts for two hundred years, this correspondence has only recently come to light.

PREVIOUS EDITIONS[2]

1803

The Works of the Right Honourable Lady Mary Wortley Montagu, Including Her Correspondence, Poems, and Essays . . . [ed. James Dallaway] . . . 1803.

1837

The Letters and Works of Lady Mary Wortley Montagu. Edited by Her Great Grandson Lord Wharncliffe . . . 1837.

1861

The Letters and Works of Lady Mary Wortley Montagu. Edited by Her Great-Grandson Lord Wharncliffe. Third Edition, With Additions and Corrections. . . . By W. Moy Thomas. . . . MDCCCLXI.

1887

The Letters and Works [of 1861]. New Edition, Revised. (Bohn's Standard Library) 1887.

[1] Below, pp. 217 ff.   [2] For detailed descriptions, see vol. i, pp. xviii–xix.

MANUSCRIPT OWNERS

The following own letters, to or from Lady Mary, printed in the text of this volume: Archivio di Stato, Venice (1), the Bodleian Library, Oxford (18), the British Museum (8), the Marquess of Bute (66), the Editor (1), the University of Geneva (3), the Earl of Harrowby (237), Harvard University (1), the Historical Society of Pennsylvania (1), Mrs. Donald F. Hyde (1), the Pierpont Morgan Library (1), Sir John Murray (4), the National Trust, Ickworth (14), the Duke of Portland (1), Princeton University (1), the Royal College of Surgeons, London (3), the Scottish Record Office (4), the Victoria and Albert Museum (1), the Victoria Art Gallery, Bath (2), Wellesley College (1), the Earl of Wharncliffe (37), Professor Ralph M. Williams (1).

SHORT TITLES AND OTHER ABBREVIATIONS

All dates in England before 1752 are given in Old Style (O.S.) and on the Continent in New Style (N.S.), eleven days later.

All references to Lady Mary's published letters and works are cited by the dates of the editions (described on the previous page).

The following standard biographical works and peerages have been used but will not be cited unless for a particular reason: ENGLISH—Collins; *DNB*; G. E. Cokayne, *Complete Baronetage*, 1900–9; GEC *Peerage*; FRENCH—F.-A. A. de La Chenaye-Desbois, *Dictionnaire de la noblesse*, 3rd ed., 1863–76; J. C. F. Hoefer, *Nouvelle Biographie générale*, 1853–70; H. Jougla de Morenas, *Grand Armorial de France*, 1934–49; J. F. Michaud, *Biographie universelle ancienne et moderne*, [1870–3]; GERMAN—*ADB*; C. von Wurzbach, *Biographisches Lexikon*, 1856–91; ITALIAN—G. B. Crollalanza, *Dizionario storico-blasonico*, 1886–90; P. Litta, *Famiglie celebri di Italia*, 1819–1902; V. Spreti, *Enciclopedia storico-nobiliare italiana*, 1928–35; ECCLESIASTICAL—C. Eubel, *Hierarchia Catholica*, 1901–58.

Standard encyclopaedias likewise have been used but will not generally be cited.

ADB	*Allgemeine Deutsche Biographie*, 1875–1912.
Add MS	Additional Manuscripts, British Museum.
Berkhout MS	Owned by Jonkheer Frans Teding van Berkhout.
BM	British Museum.
Bod.	Bodleian Library, Oxford.
Bristol MS	Owned by the National Trust, Ickworth, Suffolk.
Bute MS	Owned by the Marquess of Bute; at Mount Stuart, Isle of Bute.
Collins	Arthur Collins, *Peerage of England*, ed. Sir Egerton Brydges, 1812.
Delany, *Corr.*	Mrs. Mary Delany, *Autobiography and Correspondence*, ed. Lady Llanover, 1861.
DNB	*Dictionary of National Biography.*
Eg MS	Egerton Manuscripts, British Museum.
Egmont, *Diary*	Historical Manuscripts Commission, *Diary of Viscount Percival afterwards First Earl of Egmont*, 1920–3.
Finch MS	Owned by Major J. R. Hanbury; on deposit in the Leicestershire Record Office.
GEC *Peerage*	G. E. Cokayne, *The Complete Peerage*, ed. V. Gibbs *et al.*, 1910–59.
H MS	Owned by the Harrowby Manuscripts Trust; at Sandon Hall, Stafford.
Halsband, *LM*	Robert Halsband, *The Life of Lady Mary Wortley Montagu*, 1956.
Harley MS	Owned by the Duke of Portland; on deposit at the British Museum.
Hertford–Pomfret, *Corr.*	*Correspondence between Frances, Countess of Hartford, and Henrietta Louisa, Countess of Pomfret*, 1805.
Hervey, *Memoirs*	John, Lord Hervey, *Some Materials Towards Memoirs of the Reign of King George II*, ed. R. Sedgwick, 1931.
HMC	Historical Manuscripts Commission Reports.
Isenburg	W. K. von Isenburg, *Stammtafeln zur Geschichte der europäischen Staaten*, revised ed., 1958–61.
LM	Lady Mary Wortley Montagu.

Manvers MS	At the University of Nottingham.
Mar and Kellie MS	At the Scottish Record Office, Edinburgh.
Mellerstain MS	Owned by the Earl of Haddington; at Mellerstain, Berwickshire.
Monson MS	Owned by Lord Monson; at South Carlton, Lincoln.
MS	Manuscript *or* Manuscripts.
Murray MS	Owned by Sir John Murray, London.
OED	*Oxford English Dictionary.*
P.C.C.	Prerogative Court of Canterbury (wills), Somerset House.
Pope, *Corr.*	Alexander Pope, *Correspondence*, ed. G. Sherburn, 1956.
Prior, *Works*	Matthew Prior, *Literary Works*, ed. H. B. Wright and M. K. Spears, 1959.
PRO	Public Record Office, London.
Repertorium	F. Hausmann, *Repertorium der diplomatischen Vertreter aller Länder*, 1936–50.
SP	State Papers, Public Record Office.
W	Edward Wortley Montagu, senior.
W MS	Wortley Manuscripts (vols. i–viii: Harrowby MS, vols. 74–81).
Walpole, *Corr.*	Horace Walpole, *Correspondence*, ed. W. S. Lewis *et al.*, 1937– .
Wh MS	Wharncliffe Muniments, owned by the Earl of Wharncliffe; on deposit in the Sheffield Central Library.

INDEX OF CORRESPONDENTS
AND LETTERS IN VOLUME II

[Symbols of first publication given in vol. i, p. xxiii]

¹ Its correct chronological place is in vol. iii, p. 13.

[1] In John Wilson Croker's edition of Hervey, *Memoirs of George II* (1848).

[1] In Joseph Hunter, *South Yorkshire* (1831).

[1] In Owen Ruffhead, *Life of Pope* (1769).

To Lady Mar[1] [*March 1721*]

From the Tranquil and easy Scituation in which you left me (Dear Sister) I am reduce'd to that of the highest degree of vexation, which I need not set out to You better than by the plain matter of Fact, which I heartily wish I had told you long since; and nothing hinder'd me but a certain mauvaise honte, which you are reasonable enough to forgive as very natural, thô not very excusable where there is nothing to be asham'd of, since I can only accuse my selfe of too much good nature, or at worst too much credulity, thô I beleive there was never more pains taken to deceive any body. In short, a person, whose name is not necessary because you know it,[2] took all so⟨rt⟩ of methods during allmost 2 year to persuade me that there never was so extrodinary an attachment (or what you please to call it) as they had for me. This ended in coming over to make me a visit,[3] against my will, and as was pretended, very much against their Interest. I cannot deny I was very silly in giving the least credit to this stuff, but if people are so silly, you'l own tis natural for any body that is good natur'd to pity and be glad to serve a person they beleive unhappy upon their account. It came into my head, out of a high point of Generosity (for which I wish my selfe hang'd), to do this creature all the good I possibly could since twas impossible to make them happy their own way. I advis'd him very strenuously to sell out of the Subscription, and in compliance to my advice he did so, and in less than 2 days saw he had done very prudently.[4]

After a piece of service of this Nature I thought I could

---

[1] Frances Pierrepont (1690–1761) m. (1714) 6th Earl of Mar. In England since the early summer of 1720, she left on 9 Jan. 1721 to rejoin her exiled husband in Paris (*Post Boy*, 10–12 Jan.).

[2] Nicolas-François Rémond (b. 1676), who had introduced himself by letter to LM in 1718, when she was still in Constantinople (see i. 395). She probably

saw him in Paris in Sept. 1718, on her way home to England, after which they resumed their correspondence. Eight of his letters to her survive (for extracts see vol. i); hers to him do not.

[3] At the time of the South Sea Bubble, May 1720 (see i. 451, n. 2).

[4] His initial investment of £2,000 had yielded a profit of £840 (see i. 451, n. 4).

more decently press his departure, which his follys made me think necessary for me. He took leave of me with so many tears and grimaces (which I can't imagine how he could counterfeit) as realy mov'd my Compassion, and I had much ado to keep to my first resolution of exacting his Absence, which he swore would be his Death. I told him that there was no other way in the world I would not be glad to serve him in, but that his extravagancys made it utterly impossible for me to keep him company. He said that he would put into my hands the money I had won for him, and desir'd me to improve it, saying that if he had enough to buy a small estate and retire from the world, 'twas all the happyness he hop'd for in it.[1] I represented to him that if he had so little money as he said, 'twas ridiculous to hazard it all. He reply'd that twas too little to be of any value, and he would either have it double or quit. After many objections on my side, and replys on his, I was so weak to be overcome by his intreaties, and flatter'd my selfe also that I was doing a very heroic Action in trying to make a man's fortune thô I did not care for his addresses.

He left me with these Imaginations, and my first care was to employ his money to the best Advantage. I laid it all out in stock, the General discourse and private intelligence then scatter'd about being of a great rise. You may remember it was 2 or 3 days before the 4th Subscription,[2] and you were with me when I paid away the money to Mr. Binfield.[3] I thought I had manag'd prodigious well in selling out the said stock the day after the shutting the books, for a small profit, to Cox and Cleeve, Goldsmiths, of very good reputation. When the Opening of the books came, my Men went off,[4] leaving the stock upon my hands, which was allready sunk from near 900 to 400. I immediately writ him word of this misfortune, with the Sincere Sorrow natural to have upon such an Occasion, and ask'd his opinion as to the selling the stock remaining in. He made me no answer to this part of

---

[1] Before he came to England Rémond had written to LM that he wanted only 'une jolie terre . . . une petite maison. . . . Que puis je desirer davantage ?' ([c. 12/1 Feb. 1720], W MS iv. 220).

[2] Pope, for example, had advised her to buy, two days before it opened on 24 Aug. 1720 (see i. 452, n. 5).

[3] Not identified.

[4] The bankruptcy of Cox and Cleave, goldsmiths and bankers, was reported in the *London Gazette* of 8 Nov. 1720.

my Letter, but a long Eloquent Oration of miserys of Another Nature. I attributed this Silence to his disinterested neglect of his money, but however resolv'd to make no more steps in his busynesse without direct orders, after having been so unlucky. This occasion'd many Letters to no purpose, but the very post after you left London I receiv'd a Letter from him in which he told me that he had discover'd all my tricks, that he was convince'd I had all his money remaining untouch'd, and he would have it again or he would print all my Letters to him, which thô God knows very innocent in the main, yet may admit of ill constructions, besides the monstrousness of being expos'd in such a manner. I hear from other people that he is Lyar enough to publish that I have borrow'd the money of him,[1] thô I have a note under his hand by which he desires me to employ it in the Funds, and acquits me of being answerable for the Losses that may happen. At the same time, I have attestations and wittnesses of the Bargains I made, so that nothing can be clearer than my Integrity in this busynesse, but that does not hinder me from being in the utmost terror for the consequences (as you may easily guess) of his villainy, the very Story of which appears so monstrous to me, I can hardly beleive my selfe while I write it, thô I omit (not to tire you) a thousand aggravating Circumstances.

I can not forgive my selfe the folly of ever regarding one word he said, and I see now that his Lyes have made ⟨me⟩ wrong several of my Acquaintance, and you amongst the rest, for having said (as he told me) horrid things against me to him. 'Tis long since, that your behaviour has acquitted you in my opinion, but I thought I ought not to mention, to hurt him with you, what was perhaps more misunderstanding or mistake than a design'd Lye; but he has very amply explain'd his Character to me. What is very pleasant is that but 2 posts before, I receiv'd a Letter from him full of higher flights than ever. I beg your pardon, Dear Sister,

[1] Pope put this gossip into his 1728 *Dunciad*:

(Whence hapless Monsieur much complains at Paris
Of wrongs from Duchesses and Lady Mary's)   (Book II, ll. 127–8).

In 1735 Pope added a note: 'This passage was thought to allude to a famous Lady who cheated a French wit of 5000 pounds in the South-Sea year. But the Author meant it . . . of all Whores and Cheats under the name of Ladies.'

for this tedious account, but you see how necessary 'tis for
me to get my Letters from this Mad Man. Perhaps the best
way is by fair means; at least they ought to be first try'd. I
would have you then, my Dear Sister, try to make the wretch
sensible of the Truth of what I advance, without asking for
the Letters, which I have allready ask'd for. Perhaps you may
make him asham'd of his infamous proceedings by talking of
me without takeing notice that you know of his Threats, only
of my Dealings. I take this method to be the most likely to
work upon him.

I beg you would send me a full and true account of this
detestable affair enclosed to Mrs. Murry.[1]

If I had not been the most unlucky creature in the world,
his letter would have come while you were here, that I might
have show'd you both his Note and the other people's. I
knew he was discontented, but was far from imagining a
possibillity of this thing. I give you a great deal of trouble,
but you see I shall owe you the highest Obligation if you can
serve me. The very endeavouring of it is a tye upon me to
serve you the rest of my Life without reserve and with
Eternal Gratitude.

Text W MS iv. 3–8   *Address* A Madame Madme La Comtesse
de Mar

To Lady Mar [*May 1721*]

I give you many thanks (my Dear Sister) for the trouble
you have given your selfe in my affair, but am afraid 'tis
not yet effectual. I must beg you to let him know I am now
at Twictnam, and that who ever has his procuration may
come here on divers pretences, but must by no means go

[1] Griselda Murray (1692–1759), legal-
ly separated from her husband Alexander
Murray of Stanhope (d.1743) since 1714,
lived with her parents, Lady Griselda
and George Baillie. She occasionally
entertained LM at dinner (e.g. Feb.
1719, Lady G. Baillie, *Household Book*,
1692–1733, ed. R. Scott-Moncrieff,
1911, p. 290); and John Gay put her at
LM's side the next year in his poem
celebrating Pope's return from Homeric
Greece (*Additions to Pope*, [ed. G.
Steevens], 1776, i. 97).

to my House at London.[1] I wonder you can think Lady
Stafford[2] has not writ to him. She shew'd me a long plain
letter to him several months ago; as a Demonstration he
receiv'd it, I saw his answer. 'Tis true she treated him with
the contempt he deserv'd, and told him she would never give
her selfe the trouble of writeing again to so despicable a
wretch. She is willing to do yet farther and write to the Duke
of Villeroi[3] about it if I think it proper. R[émond] does nothing
but lie, and either does not or will not understand what is
said to him. You will forgive me troubling you so often with
this busyness. The Importance of it is the best excuse; in
short

　　　　　—'tis joy or sorrow, peace or Strife,
　　　　　'Tis all the colour of remaining Life.[4]

I can foresee nothing else to make ⟨me⟩ unhappy, and I
beleive shall take care another time not to involve my selfe
in difficulties by an overplus of Heroic Generosity.

　　I am, Dear Sister, ever yours with the utmost Esteem and
affection. If I get over this cursed affair, my stile may enliven.

Text W MS iv. 11–12　　　*Address* A Madme Madme La Comtesse
de Mar

To Lady Mar [*June 1721*]

　　I have just receiv'd your Letter of May 30th, and am surpriz'd since You own the receit of my Letter that you give
me not the least hint concerning the busynesse that I writ so

　　[1] After their return from Turkey the
Wortley Montagus rented a house in the
Piazza of Covent Garden, paying an
annual rent of £125 (Wh MS 508). It
had been occupied by Lord Stamford,
who died 31 Jan. 1720, and must have
been large since it paid higher rates than
any other house there (Rate Books, Westminster Public Library). With Pope's
encouragement and assistance they had
also rented a house in Twickenham,
probably from Sir Godfrey Kneller, the
painter, and moved there in June 1719

(Pope, *Corr.* ii. 6–7, 12).
　　[2] Born Claude-Charlotte de Gramont,
and widow of the 10th Earl of Stafford,
she had come to England in Jan. 1720
with an introduction from Rémond to
LM (see i. 447).
　　[3] François de Neufville (1644–1730),
duc de Villeroi, retired from a military
career but very active in Court life.
Rémond had boasted to LM of Villeroi's
interest in him (4 Sept./24 Aug. [1720],
W MS iv. 230).
　　[4] Prior, *Solomon* (*Works*, i. 339).

earnestly to you about. Till that is over, I am as little capable of hearing or repeating News as I should be if my house was on Fire. I am sure a good deal must be in Your power. The hurting of me can be no way his Interest. I am ready to assign or deliver the money for £500 stock to who ever he will Name, if he will send my Letters into Lady Stafford's hands, which, were he sincere in his offer of burning 'em, he would readily do. Instead of that, he has writ a Letter to Mr. W[ortley] to inform him of the whole affair. Luckily for me, the person he has sent it to assures me it shall never be deliver'd, but I am not the less oblig'd to his good Intentions. For God's sake do something to set my Mind at ease from this busyness, and then I will not fail to write you regular accounts of all your Acquaintance. Mr. Strickland[1] has had a prodigy of good Fortune befalln him, which I suppose you have heard of.

My little Commission is hardly worth speaking of. If you have not allready laid out that small Summ in St. Cloud ware,[2] I had rather have it in plain Lutestring[3] of any Colour. Lady Stafford desires you would buy one Suit of minunet[4] for head and ruffles at Boileau's.

Text W MS iv. 17–18   *Address* A Madme Madame la Comtesse de Mar

To Lady Mar [*c. 7 July 1721*]

I send you, Dear Sister, by Lady Lansdown[5] this Letter accompany'd with the only present that ever was sent me by that Monster.[6] I beg you to return it immediately. I am told he is preparing to come to London. Let him know that 'tis not at all necessary for receiving money or examining my

[1] Possibly William Strickland, M.P. (*c.* 1686–1735).

[2] A porcelain made in this town near Paris.

[3] A fine non-lustrous taffeta.

[4] Mignonette: a light, fine lace used for head-dresses.

[5] Mary Villiers (d. 1735), da. of 1st Earl of Jersey, m. (1711) 1st Baron Lansdown. After his imprisonment in London from 1715 to 1717 for Jacobite activity, he lived in Paris, and Lady Lansdown frequently travelled between the two capitals.

[6] Rémond. The present was evidently a cup, mentioned at the end of the letter.

Accounts; he has nothing to do but to send a Letter of attorney to who he pleases (without exception) and I will readily deliver up what I have in my hands, and his presence will not obtain one farthing more. His design (then) can only be to expose my Letters here. I desire you would assure him that my first step shall be to acquaint my Lord Stair[1] with all his obligations to him as soon as I hear he is in London, and if he dares to give me farther trouble I shall take care to have him rewarded in a stronger manner than he expects. There is nothing more true than this, and I solemnly swear that if all the credit or money that I have in the World can do it, either for Freindship or hire, I shall not fail to have him us'd as he deserves; and since I know his Journey can only be design'd to expose me, I shall not value what noise is made. Perhaps you may prevent it; I leave you to judge of the most proper method. 'Tis certain no time should be lost. Fear is his predominant passion, and I beleive you may fright him from coming hither, where he will certainly find a reception very disagreable to him.

Lady Lansdown does not go till Tuesday.[2] I have left the Cup with her, and 3 guineas to be laid out in plain Lutestring.

Text W MS iv. 1–2   *Address* To The Countesse of Mar

To Lady Mar [*July 1721*]

I am now at Twict'nam. 'Tis impossible to tell you (Dear Sister) what agonys I suffer every post day. My Health realy suffers so much from my Fears that I have reason to apprehend the worst Consequences. If that Monster acted on the least principles of reason, I should have nothing to fear, since 'tis certain that after he has expos'd me, he will get nothing by it. Mr. Wortley can do nothing for his Satisfaction I am not willing to do my selfe. I desire not the least indulgence of any kind. Let him put his affair into the

[1] John Dalrymple (1673–1747), 2nd Earl of Stair. As Ambassador in Paris (1715 to 1720), he had used Rémond in political intrigues (see i. 396, n. 2). Stair was spending the summer of 1721 in Kensington for his health (John M. Graham, *Annals and Corr. of the Earls of Stair*, 1875, ii. 160).

[2] She left for Paris on Friday, 14 July (*Daily Post*, 18 July 1721).

hands of any Lawyer whatever; I am willing to submit to any Examination. 'Tis impossible to make a fairer offer than this is. Whoever he employs may come to me hither on several pretences. I desire nothing from him but that he would send no Letters nor Messages to my House at London, where Mr. Wortley now is. I am come hither in hopes of benefit from the Air, but I carry my distemper about me, in an Anguish of Mind that visibly decays my body every Day. I am too melancholy to talk of any other Subject. Let me beg you, Dear Sister, to take some Care of this Affair, and think you have it in your power to do more than save the Life of a Sister that loves you.

Text W MS iv. 21–22   *Address* A Madme Madme La Comtesse de Mar

To Lady Mar [*c. 15 July 1721*]

I wish to see you, Dear Sister, more than ever I did in my Life. A thousand things pass before my Eyes that would afford me infinite pleasure in your Conversation and that are lost for want of such a Freind to talk 'em over. Lechmere is to be Lord Hungerford.[1] But the most considerable Incident that has happen'd a good while was the ardent affection that Mrs. Harvey and her dear spouse took to me.[2] They visited me twice or thrice a day, and were perpetually cooing in my rooms. I was complaisant a great while, but (as you know) my Talent has never lain much that way. I grew at last so weary of those Birds of Paradice, I fled to Twictnam as much to avoid their persecution as for my own Health, which is still in a declineing way. I fancy the Bath would be a good Remedy, but my affairs lye so oddly I cannot easily resolve upon it.

If you please, Dear Sister, to buy 20 yards of the Lute-string I have bespoke—Black—and send it by the first

[1] Nicholas Lechmere (1675–1727) was created Baron Lechmere on 4 Sept. 1721.

[2] John Hervey (1696–1743), 2nd son of 1st Earl of Bristol, m. (April 1720) Mary Lepell (1700–68), a Maid of Honour to the Princess of Wales. Both were noted for their good looks. He later became one of LM's closest friends.

Oppertunity; I suppose you know we are in mourning for Lady Pierrepont.[1] Lady Loudoun and Lady Stair are in my Neighbourhood.[2] The first of those Ladies is on the brink of Scotland for Life. She says she does not care; to say truth, I see no very lively Reasons why she should.

I am affectionately Yours.

Text Bute MS   *Address* A Madme Madme La Comtesse de Mar

To Lady Mar [*July 1721*]

I cannot enough thank you (Dear Sister) for the trouble you give your selfe in my Affairs, thô I am still so unhappy to find your care very ineffectual. I have actually in my present possession a formal Letter directed to M. W[ortley] to acquaint him with the whole busynesse. You may imagine the inevitable eternal misfortunes it would have thrown me into had it been deliver'd by the person to whom it was intrusted. I wish you would make him sensible of the Infamy of this proceeding, which can no way in the world turn to his advantage. Did I refuse giving the strictest account, or had I not the clearest demonstration in my hands of the truth and sincerity with which I acted, there might be some temptation to this basenesse, but all he can expect by informing M. W[ortley] is to hear him repeat the same things I assert. He will not retreive one farthing, and I am for ever miserable.

I beg no more of him than to direct any person, Man or Woman, either Lawyer, Broker, or person of Quality, to examine me; and as soon as he has sent ⟨the⟩ proper Authority to discharge me on enquiry, I am ready to be examin'd. I think no offer can be fairer from any person whatsoever. His conduct towards me is so infamous that I am inform'd I might prosecute him by Law if he was here, he demanding

[1] Lucy, widow since 1715 of LM's great-uncle, Gervase, Lord Pierrepont, died 8 July 1721. (See i. 208, n. 2.)

[2] The two ladies were closely related. Margaret Dalrymple (1684–1779), Lord Stair's sister, m. (1700) 3rd Earl of Loudoun. Eleanor Campbell (d. 1759), Lord Loudoun's sister, m. (1708) Lord Stair. He was house-hunting near Hampton Court, while living in Kensington (John M. Graham, *Annals and Corr. of the Earls of Stair* 1875, ii. 160.)

the whole Summ as a debt from Mr. Wortley, at the same time I have a note under his hand, sign'd, to prove the Contrary. I beg with the utmost earnestness that you would make him sensible of his Error. I beleive tis very necessary to say something to fright him. I am perswaded if he was talk'd to in a stile of that kind, he would not dare to attempt to ruin me. I have a great Inclination to write seriously to your Lord about it.[1] Since I desire to determine this affair in the fairest and the clearest manner, I am not at all afraid of makeing any body acquainted with it, and if I did not fear makeing Mr. Wortley uneasy (who is the only pe⟨rson⟩ from whom I would conceal it) all the transactions should have been long since enroll'd in Chancery. I have allready taken care to have the Broker's depositions taken before a Lawyer of Reputation and Merit.[2] I deny giving him no Satisfaction; and after that offer I think there is no Man of honnour that would refuse signifying to him that as 'tis all he can desire, so if he persists in doing me an injury he may repent it. You know how far 'tis proper to take this Method. I say nothing of the uneasyness I am under; 'tis far beyond any Expression. My obligation would be proportionable to any body that would deliver me from it, and I should not think it paid by all the services of my Life.

Text W MS iv. 19–20

To Lady Mar [*c. 11 Aug. 1721*]

Dear Sister,

I give you ten thousand thanks for the trouble you have given your selfe. I hope you will continue to take some care of my affairs, because I do not hear they are finish'd and can not yet get rid of my Fears. You have not told me that you have receiv'd what I sent you by Lady Lansdown, as also 3 guineas that she took for you, one of which I beg you would lay out in the same narrow minunet that you sent ⟨Mrs.⟩ Murray, and send it me by the fi⟨rst⟩ Oppertunity

[1] John Erskine (1675–1732), attainted Earl of Mar, He had been a leader of the Jacobite rebellion of 1715.
[2] Isaac Delpeche.

for the use of my Daughter, who is very much your Humble servant, and grows a little Woman.

I suppose you know our Sister Gower[1] has lain in, in the country, of a Son.[2] The Dutchess of K[ingston][3] is preparing for the Bath. I live in a sort of Solitude that wants very little of being just what I would have it. Lady J. Wharton is to be marry'd to Mr. Holt,[4] which I am sorry for, to see a young Woman that I realy think one of the agreablest Girls upon Earth so vilely misplac'd; but where are people match'd! I suppose we shall all come right in Heaven, as in a Country Dance, thô hands are strangly given and taken while they are in motion, at last all meet their partners when the Jig is done.

Text Bute MS   *Address* A Madme Madme la Comtesse de Mar

To Lady Mar [*Aug. 1721*]

Dear Sister,

Having this occasion I would not omit writeing, thô I have receiv'd no Answer to my 2 last. The Bearer is well Acquainted with my affair, thô not from me, till he mention'd it to me first, having heard it from those to whom R[émond] had told it, with all the False Colours he pleas'd to lay on. I shew'd him the formal Commission I had to employ the Money, and all the Broker's testimonys taken before Delpeeke with his Certificate.[5] Your remonstrances have hitherto had so little Effect that R[émond] will neither send a Letter of Attorney to examine my Accounts, or let me be in peace. I receiv'd a Letter from him but 2 posts since, in which he renews his threats except I send him the

[1] Evelyn Pierrepont (1691–1727) m. (1712) 2nd Baron Gower.

[2] Granville Leveson-Gower (d. 1803), later 1st Marquess of Stafford, was born on 4 Aug. 1721 at Trentham, Staffs.

[3] LM's stepmother since 1714 (see i. 215, n. 2).

[4] Lady Jane (1706–1761), elder da. of 1st Marquess of Wharton. In a note to this letter Horace Walpole wrote: 'Lady Jane was remarkably like Lord Cobham [1675–1749], her mother Lady Wharton's lover' (*Corr.* xxxiv. 256). She married John Holt (d. 1729) two years later (Lady Jane Coke, *Letters to Mrs. Eyre*, ed. Mrs. A. Rathborne, 1899, pp. xv–xvi, xxi).

[5] Isaac Delpeche, described as an eminent notary to the Bank of England, died in 1736 (*London Mag.*, p. 339).

whole summ, which is as much in my power as it is to send a million. I can easily comprehend that he may be asham'd to send a procuration, which must convince the world of all the Lies he has told. For my part, I am so willing to be rid of the plague of hearing from him, I desire no better than to restore him with all Expedition the money I have in my hands, but I will not do it without a general Acquittance in due form, not to have fresh Demands every time he wants money. If he thinks that he has a larger sum to receive than I offer, why does he not name a procurator to examine me? If he is content with that sumn, I only insist on the Acquittance for my own Safety. I am ready to send it him, with full License to tell as many Lies as he pleases afterwards.

I am weary of troubling you with Repetitions which cannot be more disagreable to you than they are to me. I have had, and still have, so much vexation with this execrable affair tis impossible to describe it. I had rather talk to you of any thing else, but it fills my whole head.

I am still at Twict'nam, where I pass my time in great Indolence and sweetness. Mr. W[ortley] is at this present in Yorkshire. My fair Companion[1] puts me oft in mind of our Thorsby[2] Conversations. We read and walk together, and I am more happy in her than any thing else could make me except your conversation.

Text W MS iv. 15–16

To Lady Mar 6 *Sept.* [*1721*]

Twictnm, Sept. 6.

I have just receiv'd your Letter, Dear Sister. I am extreme sensible of your goodness, which I beg you to continue. I am very glad to hear of the good Health of your Family, and should be only more so to be a witness of it, which I am not without some hopes of.

[1] This may be Maria (1702–38), da. of Thomas Skerrett, merchant; later second wife of Sir Robert Walpole. According to LM's granddaughter they met about 1720 (Lady Louisa Stuart, 'Supplement to the Anecdotes', Wh MS 439). They became intimate friends.

[2] The Duke of Kingston's seat in Notts. (see i. 3).

My time is melted away here in allmost perpetual Consorts.[1] I do not presume to judge, but I'll assure you I am a very hearty as well as humble Admirer. I have taken my little thread satin Beauty[2] into the house with me. She is allow'd by Bononcini[3] to have the finest Voice he ever heard in England. He and Mrs. Robinson[4] and Senesino[5] lodge in this village and sup often with me, and this easy indolent Life would make me the happiest thing in the world if I had not this execrable affair still hanging over my head. I have consulted my Lawyer and he says I cannot with safety to my selfe deposite the money I have receiv'd into other hands without the express order of R[émond], and he is so unreasonable that he will neither send a procuration to examine my Accounts or any order for me to transfer his stock into another Name. I am heartily weary of the Trust which has given me so much trouble, and can never think my selfe safe till I am quite got rid of it. Rather than be plagu'd any longer with the odious keeping, I am willing to abandonn my Letters to his Discretion. I desire nothing more of him than an Order to place his money in other hands, which methinks should not be so hard to obtain since he is so disatisfy'd with my management, but he seems to be bent to torment me, and will not even touch his money because I beg it of him. I wish you would represent these things to him. For my own part, I live in so much uneasyness about it that I am sometimes weary of Life it selfe.

Mrs. Stoner[6] will be a good person to send things by. I would have no black silk, having bought here.

Text W MS iv. 13–14

[1] 'I very much envy you your Musical Company', Pope wrote to LM on 15 Sept. 1721 (*Corr*. ii. 82).

[2] She is mentioned in Pope's letter as 'the Young Lady with you'; and may be the 'fair Companion' of LM's previous letter.

[3] Giovanni Bononcini (1670–?1755) came to London in 1720 to compose for the Royal Academy of Music. Among the many fashionable subscribers to his *Cantate e duetti* (1721) were LM for one copy and W for five (MS note, BM).

[4] Anastasia Robinson (d. 1755),

prima donna, was closely associated with Bononcini; it was said that she haunted him (letter from Atterbury, 1722, Pope, *Corr*. ii. 123). In Jan. 1722 she and Senesino sang in his opera *Crispo*, and the next month in *Griselda*.

[5] Francesco Bernardi (d. *c.* 1750), famous *castrato* singer known as Senesino, sang for the Royal Academy of Music from 1720 to 1728.

[6] Probably Winifred Roper (d. 1722), da. of 5th Baron Teynham, m. (1705) Thomas Stonor, who had a house at Twickenham (Pope, *Corr*. i. 417).

To Lady Mar [*Dec. 1721*]

I cannot forbear (Dear Sister) accusing you of unkindness that you take so little care of a business of the last consequence to me. R[émond] writ to me some time ago to say if I would immediately send him £2,000 Sterling, he would send me an acquittance. As this was sending him several hundreds out of my own pocket, I absolutely refus'd it, and in return I have just receiv'd a threatening Letter to print I know not what Stuff against me. I am too well acquainted with the world (of which poor Mrs. Murray's affair is a fatal instance) not to know that the most groundless Accusation is allways of ill Consequence to a Woman,[1] besides the cruel misfortunes it may bring upon me in my own family. If you have any compassion either for me or my innocent children I am sure you will try to prevent it. The thing is too serious to be delaid. I think (to say nothing either of blood or affection) ⟨your⟩ Humanity and Christianity are interested in my preservation. I am sure I can answer for my hearty Gratitude and everlasting Acknowledgment of a service much more important than that of saving my Life.[2]

Text W MS iv. 9–10   *Address* A Madme Madme la Comtesse de Mar

[1] Mrs. Griselda Murray (see above, p. 4) had been the centre of a scandal. On 14 Oct. Arthur Gray, a footman in her father's house, entered her bedroom early in the morning and attempted to rape her, but she drove him off. He was caught a few hours later. The weekly newspapers embellished their account of the case with jokes and verse (*Weekly Journal or Saturday's Post* and *Weekly Journal or British Gazetteer*, 21 Oct. 1721); and an anonymous printed ballad entitled *Virtue in Danger* (copy in the Huntington Library) helped spread the scandal. At his trial, on 7 Dec., the footman accused Mrs. Murray of going to bed with her friend the Rev. Gilbert Burnet (1690–1726), son of the Bishop, whom she admitted entertaining, though decorously, after her family retired for the night (letter from Lady Binning to Lady Mary Howard, 9 Dec. 1721, Mellerstain MS). Arthur Gray, sentenced to be hanged, was instead pardoned and transported to New England (*Daily Journal*, 18 Jan. 1722). A report of the trial is given in *Select Trials*, 1742, i. 97–102.

[2] This is the last mention of Rémond's persecution in LM's surviving letters, described by Horace Walpole as 'dismal lamentations and frights' (*Corr.* xx. 281). Rémond's extant letters, all written before 1721, were read and endorsed by W—who could understand the financial muddle, having been appointed, on 4 Jan. 1721, to the parliamentary committee to investigate the South Sea Bubble (Rich. Chandler, *Hist. and Proc. of the H. of C.*, 1742–4, vi. 229). He even

To Lady Mar [*April 1722*]

I have had no Answer (Dear Sister) to a long letter that I
writ to you a month ago, but however I shall continue leting
you know (de temps en temps) what passes in this corner of
the world till you tell me 'tis disagreable. I shall say little of
the Death of our Great Minister[1] because the news papers
say so much. I suppose the same faithfull Historians give
you regular Accounts of the Growth and spreading of the
Innoculation of the small pox, which is become allmost a
General practise, attended with great success.[2] I pass my
time in a small snug set of dear Intimates, and go very little
into the Grand Monde, which has allways had my hearty
contempt. I see sometimes Mr. Congreve, and very seldom
Mr. Pope,[3] who continues to embellish his House at
Twict'nam. He has made a subterrenean Grotto, which he
has furnish'd with Looking Glass, and they tell me it has a
very good Effect.[4] I here send you some verses address'd to
Mr. Gay, who writ him a congratulatory Letter on the
Finishing his House.[5] I stiffle'd them here, and I beg they
may dye the same Death at Paris, and never go farther than
your Closet.

> Ah Freind, tis true (This Truth you Lovers know),
> ⟨In⟩ vain my Structures rise, my Gardens Grow,

made a modest profit himself, in Oct.
1722, on some shares of South Sea stock
(Child and Co., Ledger no. 18, 1718–31,
f. 158).

[1] Probably Charles Spencer (*c.* 1674–
1722), 3rd Earl of Sunderland, who died
suddenly on 19 April. He had resigned
in April 1721 as First Lord of the
Treasury.

[2] This 'success' in April 1722 came
from the inoculation of the two younger
daughters of the Prince of Wales, and of the
Lord Bathurst's six children, and of the
Duke of Dorset's eldest son (*Daily Journal*, 24, 25 April; *London Journal*, 28
April 1722).

[3] A few months later, however, LM
apparently saw him so often in Twick-

enham that Mrs. Murray's mother
gossiped: 'She and Pope keeps so close
yonder that they are a talk to the whole
town' (14 July 1722, Mellerstain MS).

[4] Pope's famous grotto was still quite
new. In July 1722 he asked William
Broome to come and see the 'grotto you
have heard so poetical an account of'
(*Corr.* ii. 125). Some years later, LM
mentioned a few details of the grotto in
her satire 'The Court of Dullness' (W
MS viii; printed 1803, v. 161).

[5] In 1715–16 LM had been closely
allied with Gay and Pope in the poetic
confederacy that produced the *Court
Poems* of 1716 (Halsband, *LM*, pp.
49–50). Gay's 'Letter' is not known.

> In vain Fair Thames refflects the double Scenes
> Of hanging Mountains and of Slopeing Greens;
> Joy lives not here, to happier seats it flys,
> And only dwells where W——— casts her Eyes.
> What is the Gay Parterre, the chequer'd shade,
> The morning Bower, the Evening Colonnade,
> But soft recesses of uneasy Minds,
> To sigh unheard in to the passing Winds?
> So the struck Deer in some sequester'd part
> Ly's down to dye, the Arrow at his Heart,
> There, stretch'd unseen in Coverts hid from Day,
> Bleeds drop by drop, and pants his Life away.[1]

My paper is done, and I will only put you [in] mind of my Lutestring, which I beg you will send me plain, of what colour you please.

Text Bute MS   *Address* A Madme Madme la Commtesse de Mar.

To Lady Mar [*June 1722*]

Dear Sister,

I have writ you so many Letters which you say you have not receiv'd, that I suppose you won't receive this; however, I will acquit my selfe to my own Conscience as a good Christian ought to do. I am sure I can never be realy wanting in any Expression of affection to you, to whom I can never forget what I owe in many Respects.

Our Mutual Acquaintance are exceedingly dispers'd, and I am engag'd in a new set, whose ways would not be entertaining to you since you know not the people. Mrs. Murray is still at Castle Howard.[2] I am at Twict'nm where there is

---

[1] Pope sent the last eight lines of this verse, with a few changes, to Judith Cowper on 5 Nov. [1722] (*Corr.* ii. 142). The entire poem is printed in his *Minor Poems*, ed. N. Ault and J. Butt, 1954, pp. 225–6.

[2] Mrs. Murray, still smarting from the unpleasant notoriety of the previous autumn, spent the spring and summer visiting Lord Carlisle's family in York-shire (Mellerstain MS). An unsigned, unidentified, gossipy letter, written from Castle Howard on 21 June 1722 and addressed to 'My Dear Sister', was apparently sent to Lady Mar in Paris (HMC *Townshend MSS*, 1887, p. 190). But there is no evidence as to whether LM (or her other sister Lady Gower) visited Castle Howard at this time. In style the letter is unlike LM.

PLATE 2

Letter of Lady Mary Wortley Montagu to Frances, Countess of Mar, [April 1722]

Bute MSS

(at this time) more Company than at London. That poor Soul Mrs. Johnson is return'd into our Neighbourhood,[1] and sent to me to carry her to Richmond Court to morrow,[2] but I begg'd to be excus'd. She's still in sad pickle, I think. Mr. and Madam Harvey are at Lord Bristol's.[3] A propos of that Family, the Countesse is come out a new Creature: she has left off the dull Occupations of Hazard and Bassette,[4] ⟨and⟩ is grown Young, blooming, Coquette and Galante; and to shew she is fully sensible of the errors of her past Life, and resolv'd to make up for time mispent, she has 2 Lovers at a time, and is equally, wickedly talk'd of for the Gentile Coll[onel] Cotton[5] and the supperfine Mr. Braddocks.[6] Now I think this the greatest compliment in Nature to her own Lord, since tis plain that when she will be false to him, she is forc'd to take 2 men in his stead, and that no one Mortal has merit enough to make up for him.

Poor Lady Gage is parting from her Discreet Spouse[7] for a meer triffle. She had a mind to take the Air this Spring in a new Yatcht (which Lord Hillsborrough[8] built for many good

[1] Catherine, da. of 2nd Baron Poulett, m. (1696) James Johnston. A former Secretary of State for Scotland, he had retired to Orleans House in Twickenham. Walpole's comment on 'That poor Soul' was: 'Wife of Secretary Johnson. She had been married to an Irish gentleman with whom she was in love; but he proving to have another wife, she went mad, and afterwards married old Johnson . . .' (*Corr.* xxxiv. 260).

[2] The Prince and Princess of Wales left London on 3 June to pass the summer at Richmond (*Daily Journal*, 4 June 1722).

[3] John Hervey (1665–1751), 1st Earl of Bristol, had a house in St. James's Square.

[4] Lady Bristol's addiction to cards is evident from her letters (e.g. John Hervey, *Letter-Books*, 1894, i. 362). LM named her Cardelia in 'The Basset-Table,' one of the *Court Poems* (1716).

[5] Colonel Stanhope Cotton (Charles Dalton, *George the First's Army 1714–1727*, 1910–12, ii. 296) had been Deputy-Governor of Gibraltar. At

Bath Lady Bristol wrote to her husband how 'kind and civil' he was to her (*Letter-Books*, ii. 170). 'The ladies are all so fond of him', one of Mrs. Howard's friends wrote in 1721, 'that I believe he must take to his bed soon' (Henrietta, Countess of Suffolk, *Letters 1712–1767*, ed. J. W. Croker, 1824, i. 74). He died at Bath, after a long illness, in Dec. 1725 (*Mist's Weekly Journal*, 11 Dec.).

[6] General Braddock, Walpole surmised (*Corr.* xxxiv. 260), meaning Edward Braddock (1695–1755), appointed major-general 1754. Walpole also gossiped that as a young man Braddock was kept by a Mrs. Upton (ibid. xx. 492–3).

[7] Benedicta Maria Theresa Hall (d. 1749) m. (*c*. 1717) Thomas (d. 1754), 1st Viscount Gage. Hervey calls him 'a petulant, silly, busy, meddling, profligate fellow' (*Memoirs*, i. 265).

[8] Trevor Hill (1693–1742), 1st Viscount. Thomas Hearne describes him in 1725 as very handsome, wanton, and immodest (*Remarks and Collections*, 1885–1921, viii. 406).

uses, and which has been the Scene of much pleasure and pain). She ⟨went⟩ in companny with his Lordship, Fabrice,[1] ⟨Mr.⟩ Cook,[2] Lady Litchfield and her Sister[3] as far as Greenwich, and from thence as far as the buoy of the Nore, when to the great Surprize of all the good Company, who thought it impossible the wind should not be as fair to bring them back as it was to carry 'em thither, they found there was no possibillity of returning that Night. Lady Gage, in all the concern of a good wife, desir'd her Lord might be inform'd of her safety, and that she was no way blamable in staying out all Night. Fabrice writ a most galant Letter to Lord Gage, concluding that Mr. Cook presented his humble service to him, and let him know (in case of necessity) Lady Margaret[4] was in town; but ⟨his Lordship, not liking the change, I suppose,⟩[5] carry'd the Letter strait to the ⟨King's⟩ Majesty, who not being at Leisure to give him Audience, he sent it ⟨in open⟩ by Mahomet,[6] thô 'tis hard to guess what sort of redress he intended to petition for, the Nature of the Thing being such, that had he complain'd he was no Cuckold, his Majesty (at least) might have prevail'd that some of his Court might confer that dignity upon him, but if he was, neither King, Council, nor the 2 houses of Parliament could make it null and of none Effect. This public Rupture is succeeded by a treaty of Separation, and here is all the Scandal that is uppermost in my Head.

Dear Sister, I should be glad to contribute any way to

---

[1] John Lewis von Fabrice (*c.* 1678–*c.* 1733), Hanoverian Privy Councillor, George I's confidential secretary (Louis Melville, *The First George*, 1909, ii. 144, n. 1). On 3 July 1722 Hervey mentions 'Fabrice's Assembly and gowing by water' as the only pleasures of the moment (Bristol MS, ii. 155).

[2] Thomas Coke (1697–1759), later 1st Earl of Leicester. Egmont wrote that half a year after his marriage (in 1718) he resumed his debaucheries (*Diary*, ii. 392–3).

[3] Frances (1698–1769), da. of Sir John Hales, m. (before 1718) 2nd Earl of Lichfield. Hearne (in 1727) describes her as a very virtuous woman, but his information came from her brother (ix.

268). Her sister is not identified.

[4] Lady Margaret Tufton (1700–75), da. of 6th Earl of Thanet, m. (1718) Thomas Coke.

[5] This passage in the torn MS is supplied from a copy (W MS iv. 40), and the following two insertions from 1803, iii. 126.

[6] Lewis Maximilian Mahomet (d. 1726), *valet de chambre* to the King, who had captured him in 1685 in the war against the Turks. He was reputed to have great influence at Court (*Polit. State of G.B.*, 1726, p. 509; James Caulfield, *Portraits, Memoirs, and Characters*, 1819–20, ii. 124–5). Pope calls him 'honest Mah'met' (*Epistle to a Lady: Of the Characters of Women*, line 198).

your Entertainment and am very sorry you seem to stand in so much need of it. I am ever Yours.

I wish you would think of my Lutestring, for I'm in terrible want of Linings.

Text Bute MS   *Address* To The Countess of Mar

To Lady Mar [*July 1722*]

Dear Sister,

I am surpriz'd at your Silence, which has been very long, and I'm sure is very tedious to me. I have writ 3 times. One of my Letters I know you receiv'd long since, for Charles Churchill told me so at the Opera.[1] At this Instant I am at Twictnam. Mr. Wortley has purchas'd the small habitation where you saw me.[2] We propose to make some small alterations; that and the Education of my Daughter are my cheife Amusements. I hope yours[3] is well, et ne fait que croitre et embellir.

I beg you would let me hear soon from you, and particularly if the approaching Coronation[4] at Paris raises the price of Diamonds. I have some to sell and cannot dispose of 'em here. I am afraid you have quite forgot my plain Lutestring, which I am in great want of, and I can hardly think you can miss of oppertunitys to send it. At this Dead Season 'tis impossible to entertain you with news, and yet more Impossible (with my dullness) to entertain you without it. The Kindest thing I can do is to bring my Letter to a speedy conclusion. I wish I had some better way of shewing how

[1] Col. Charles Churchill, M.P. (*c.* 1679–1745), illegitimate son of Gen. Charles Churchill (brother to the Duke of Marlborough). He had been in Paris in May (*London Journal*, 9 June 1722). The previous year in Paris he had 'gallanted' Lady Mar to the opera (*Jacobite Court at Rome 1719*, ed. H. Taylor, 1938, p. 207).

[2] This house, rented in 1719, stood next to Twickenham Heath, and was later called Saville House (R. S. Cobbett, *Memorials of Twickenham*, 1872, p. 353).

[3] Lady Frances Erskine (*c.* 1715–76).

[4] Louis XV was crowned at Reims on 25/14 Oct. 1722.

sincerely I am yours. I am sure I never will slip any Occasion of convinceing you of it.

Text Bute MS   *Address* To The Rt Honble The Countesse of Mar

To Lady Mar [*25 Dec. 1722*]

I have writ you at least five and forty Letters, dear Sister, without receiving any Answer, and resolv'd not to confide in posthouse Fidelity any more, being firmly persuaded that they never came to your hands, or you would not refuse one Line to let me know how you do, which is and ever will be of great Importance to me.

The freshest news in Town is the Fatal Accident happen'd 3 nights ago to a very pritty young Fellow,[1] Brother to Lord Finch, who was drinking with a dearly beloved Drab whom you may have heard of, by the name of Sally Salisbury.[2] In a jealous pique, she stabb'd him to the heart with a Knife. He fell down dead immediately, but a Surgeon being call'd for, and the Knife drawn out of his body, he open'd his Eyes, and his first words were to beg her to be freinds with him, and Kiss'd her. She has since staid by his bed side till last night, when he begg'd her to fly, for he thought he could not live;[3] and she has taken his advice, and perhaps will honnour you with her Residence at Paris.

Adeiu, Dear Sister. I send you along with this Letter the Count of Caÿlus,[4] who if you do not know allready, you will thank me for introduceing to you. He is a Frenchman and

[1] John Finch (1692–1763), brother of Daniel (1689–1769), later 8th Earl of Winchilsea; he was a lawyer and (in 1724) M.P. The crime occurred on 22 Dec. (1861, i. 463, n. 2).

[2] Sarah Pridden alias Salisbury (1690–1724), a notorious prostitute. Her dispute with Finch was over his giving an opera ticket to her sister, which she insisted was for the purpose of seducing the girl. In her anger she seized a knife from a waiter and wounded him (James Caulfield,

Portraits, Memoirs, and Characters, 1819–20, ii. 151–3).

[3] When tried for assault with intent to murder she was found guilty only of the first part, fined £100 and sentenced to one year in prison—where she died (*London Journal*, 27 April, 4 May 1723, 15 Feb. 1724).

[4] Anne-Claude, comte de Caylus (1692–1765), archaeologist and man of letters. He had been in England since Nov. 1722.

no Fop, which besides the Curiosity of it is one of the prittyest things in the World.[1]

Since you find it so difficult to send me the Lutestring that I ask'd for, I beg you would lay out my Money in a night-gown, ready made.[2] There can be no di⟨fficulty⟩ in sending that by the first person that comes over. I shall like it the better for your having worn it one Day, and then it may be answer'd for that 'tis not new. If this is also impossible, pray return me my money, deducting for the minunet which I have receiv'd.

Text Bute MS   *Address* A Ma Sœur

To Lady Mar [*c. 2 April 1723*]

Dear Sister,

I am now so far recover'd of the Dangerous illness which I had when I receiv'd your Letter that I hope I may think of being once more a Woman of this World. But I know not how to convey this Letter to you. I intend to send it to Mrs. Murray.[3] I have a great many reasons to beleive the present direction you have given me a very bad one, especially since you say that you never receiv'd one of the number of Letters that I really have sent you.

I suppose the public prints (if no body else) have inform'd you of the sudden death of poor Lady D[owager] Gower,[4] which has made a large addition to Lord Gower's[5] fortune, and utterly ruin'd Mrs. Proby's,[6] who is now in very deplorable Circumstances. I see Mrs. Murray so seldom, I can give little account of her, but I suppose her House is the

[1] He had been to Constantinople in the suite of the French Ambassador, Bonnac, but had left in Nov. 1716, a few months before LM's arrival there. His description of the journey, 'Voyage à Constantinople', is printed in the *Gazette des beaux-arts*, 1938.

[2] LM means a dressing-gown or *négligé* (rather than an evening gown).

[3] Probably Mrs. Griselda Murray

(see above, p. 4).

[4] Catherine, widow of 1st Baron Gower, and mother-in-law of LM's sister Evelyn. She died on 7 March 1723. LM had tried to buy South Sea stock for her in June 1720 (see i. 450).

[5] John Leveson-Gower (1694–1754), 2nd Baron.

[6] Gower's sister Jane (d.1726) m.(1720) John Proby, M.P. (*c.* 1689–1762).

same place it us'd to be. Operas flourish more than ever,[1] and I have been in a tract of going every time. The people I live most with are none of your Acquaintance, the D[uchess] of Montagu excepted, who I continue to see often.[2] Her Daughter Belle is at this instant in the Paradisal state of receiving visits every day from a passionate Lover who is her first Love, who she thinks the finest Gentleman in Europe, and is besides that Duke of Manchester.[3] Her Mama and I often laugh and sigh refflecting on her Felicity, the Consummation of which will be in a fortnight. In the mean time they are permitted to be alone together every day and all the Day. These are lawfull matters that one may talk of, but Letters are so surely open'd, I dare say nothing to you either of our Intreigues[4] or Duels, both which would afford great matter of Mirth and Speculation.

Adieu, Dear Sister. Pray don't forget the Nightgown and let it be what you please.

Text Bute MS   *Address* [*struck out*]

To Lady Mar [*May 1723*]

Dear Sister,

I have writ to you twice since I receiv'd yours in Answer to that I sent by Mr. de Caÿlus, but I beleive none that I send by the post ever come to your hands, nor ever will, while they are directed to Mr. Waters, for reasons that you may easily guess.[5] I wish you would give me a safer direction.

[1] On 26 March, when Handel's *Otho* played as a benefit for Francesca Cuzzoni, more than £700 was taken in; some of the nobility were said to have paid her 50 guineas for a ticket (*London Stage 1660–1800*, Part 2, ed. E. L. Avery, 1960, ii. 716).

[2] Mary Churchill (1689–1751), da. of the Duke of Marlborough, m. (1705) 2nd Duke of Montagu.

[3] Isabella Montagu (d. 1786) m. (16 April 1723) William Montagu (1700–39), 2nd Duke of Manchester.

The marriage turned out to be unhappy (Delany, *Corr.* ii. 62; iv. 452).

[4] The aftermath of the Jacobite plot referred to in the next letter.

[5] George Waters (d. 1752), a banker in Paris, was closely connected with the Jacobites (Richard Hayes, *Biog. Dict. of Irishmen in France*, 1949, p. 315). Hence letters to him would be intercepted. Lord Mar received letters under an assumed name 'chez Monsr Waters, banquier', in the Rue Dauphine (HMC *Townshend MSS*, 1887, p. 190).

Tis very seldom I can have the oppertunity of a private Messenger, and tis very often that I have a mind to write to my dear Sister. If you have not heard of the D[uches]s of Montagu's intended Journey, you will be surpriz'd at your manner of receiving this, since I send it by one of her Servants. She does not design to see any body or any thing at Paris, and talks of going from Monpellier to Italy.[1] I have a tender esteem for her, and am heartily concern'd to lose her Conversation, yet I cannot condemn her Resolution.

I am yet in this wicked Town but propose to leave it as soon as the Parliament rises.[2] Mrs. Murray and all her satellites have so seldom falln in my Way I can say little about 'em. Your old Freind Mrs. Louther[3] is still fair and young and in pale pink every night in the parks; but after being highly in favour, poor I am in utter disgrace without my being able to guess wherefore, except she fancy'd me the Author or Abettor of 2 vile ballads written on her Dying Adventure, which I am so innocent of, I never saw.[4] A propos of Ballads, a most delightfull one is said or sung in most houses about our dearly beloved Plot, which has been laid firstly to Pope and secondly to me, when God knows we have neither of us Wit enough to make it.[5]

Mrs. Hervey lies in of a Female child.[6] Lady Rich is happy in dear Sir Robert's absence[7] and the polite Mr. Holt's return to his allegiance, who thô in a treaty of Marriage with one of the prittyest Girls in Town (Lady J[ane]

---

[1] She left England soon after 11 May for Montpellier (*London Journal*, 11 May 1723).

[2] The session ended 27 May 1723.

[3] Jane Lowther (d. 1752), sister of 3rd Viscount Lonsdale.

[4] The title of one of the ballads, as printed many years later and attributed to LM, summarizes the adventure: 'On a Lady mistaking a Dy[e]ing Trader for a Dying Lover' (*Additions to Pope*, [ed. G. Steevens], 1776, i. 173–5). It was also attributed to LM by the 2nd Lord Oxford (BM Harley MS 7316, ff. 167–8). The second 'vile' ballad may be the anonymous one printed in the *Weekly Journal or British Gazetteer* of 16 Dec. 1727.

[5] This Jacobite plot was headed by Francis Atterbury, Bishop of Rochester, who was imprisoned in Aug. 1722, and impeached in March 1723. The ballad may have been Swift's 'Upon the Horrid Plot discovered by Harlequin the Bishop of Rochester's French Dog' (1861, i. 466, n. 4).

[6] Lepell (d. 1780), da. of John and Mary Hervey, b. 15 April 1723 (John Hervey, *Diary 1688–1742*, 1894, p. 73).

[7] Sir Robert Rich (1685–1768) had left for Ireland to join his regiment on 6 April (*British Journal*, 13 April 1723; cited 1861, i. 466, n. 6). He m. (*c.* 1710) Elizabeth Griffith (1692–1773), a vivacious partner in LM's friendship with Pope (see i. 269, n. 2).

Wharton)¹ appears better with her than ever. Lady B[etty]
Manners is on the brink of matrimony with a Yorkshire Mr.
Monckton of £3,000 per Annum.² Tis a match of the Young
Dutchesse's makeing³ and, as she thinks, matter of great
Triumph over the 2 Coquet Beauties, who can get no body to
have and to hold. They are decay'd to a piteous degree, and so
neglected that they are grown constant and particular to the
2 uglyest fellows in London.⁴ Mrs. ⟨Poultney conde⟩scends
to be publickly kept by the noble Earl of Cadogan; whether
Mr. Poultney has a pad nag deducted out of the ⟨profits⟩
for his share I can't tell, but he appears very well satisfy'd
with it.⁵ This is (I think) the whole state of Love. As to
that of Wit, it splits it selfe into ten thousand Branches.
Poets encrease and multiply to that Stupendous degree, you
see 'em at every turn, even in Embrodier'd Coats and pink
colour'd Top knots. Makeing verses is allmost as common as
takeing snuff, and God can tell what miserable stuff people
carry about in their pockets and offer to all their Acquaintance, and you know one can't refuse reading and takeing a
pinch. This is a very great greivance, and so particularly
shocking to me, that I think our wise Lawgivers should take
it into consideration, and appoint a Fast-day to beseech
Heaven to put a stop to this Epidemical Disease, as they did
last year for the Plague with great success.⁶

Dear Sister, Adieu. I have been very free in this letter
because I think I am sure of its going safe. I wish my Night

¹ Their engagement (see above, p.
11) finally ended in marriage on 3 July
1723.
² Lady Elizabeth Manners (*c.* 1709–
30), da. of 2nd Duke of Rutland, and
about fourteen at this time, m. (n.d.)
John Monckton (1695–1751), later 1st
Viscount Galway.
³ The young Duchess was Bridget
Sutton (1699–1734), who m. (1717) the
Marquess of Granby, later 3rd Duke of
Rutland. The widows of the 1st and 2nd
Dukes were still alive.
⁴ Lady Elizabeth's older sisters: Lady
Catherine Manners (1701–80) m. (1726)
Henry Pelham (1695 ?–1754), politician
(see below, p. 79); and Lady Frances
m. (1732) Richard Arundel, M.P.

(*c.* 1696–1758).
⁵ Margaret (1699–1763), da. of
Benjamin Tichborne, m. (1717) Daniel
Pulteney (1684–1731), Whig politician.
(The wife of his cousin William
Pulteney, later 1st Earl of Bath, was an
heiress, who would not need to be kept.) A
'pad nag' or road-horse was appropriate
payment from William (1672–1726),
1st Earl Cadogan, who was a cavalry
officer.
⁶ In England a fast day against the
plague raging in France was decreed for
8 Dec. 1721; and a day of thanksgiving
celebrated on 25 April 1723 (*Hist.
Register*, vi. *sub* 24 Oct. 1721; Thomas
Hearne, *Remarks and Collections*, 1885–
1921, viii. 69).

gown may do the same. I only chuse that as most convenient to you; but if it was equally so, I had rather the money was ⟨laid out in⟩ plain Lutestring, if you could send me 8 yards ⟨at a time of⟩ different colours, designing it for li⟨nings; but if⟩ this scheme is impracticable, send me ⟨a night Gown à la⟩ mode.[1]

Text Bute MS

To Lady Mar [*June 1723*]

Dear Sister,

I sent you a long letter by the Dutchess of Montagu and (thô I have had no Answer) I cannot resolve to leave London without writeing another.

I go to morrow to Twictnam where I am occupy'd in some Alterations of my House and Gardens. I beleive I have told you, we bought it last year, and there is some sort of pleasure in shewing one's own fancy upon one's own Ground. If you please to send my Nightgown to Mr. Hughes, an English Banker at Paris, directed for Madame Cantillon,[2] it will come safe to my Hands. She is a new Neighbour of mine, having a very Handsome House in the Piazza,[3] and her selfe eclipses most of our London Beautys. You know how fond we are of Noveltys; besides that, she is realy very pritty, does not want understanding, and I have a thousand commoditys in her Acquaintance. Mrs. D'avenant is return'd from Genoa, and I have the pleasure of an agreable Intimacy with her.[4] So much for my Acquaintance.

Lady Biny has innoculated both her children, and is big

---

[1] MS torn; insertions from a copy (W MS iv. 36).

[2] Mary Anne Mahony or O'Mahony (d. 1751), da. of an Irish merchant in France, m. (1722) Richard Cantillon (1680–1734), banker and economist (Richard Hayes, *Biog. Dict. of Irishmen in France*, 1949, p. 25). Five letters from her to LM in 1732–3 are W MS iv.

158–67.

[3] Covent Garden.

[4] On 19 March Frances Davenant arrived in London (*Daily Journal*, 25 March). Her husband, Henry Molins Davenant, had been Envoy to Genoa 1714–22; they had entertained the Wortley Montagus there in 1718 (see i. 428).

with child her selfe.[1] The Operation is not yet over, but I beleive they will do very well. Since that Experiment has not yet had any ill effect, the whole Town are doing the same thing, and I am so much pull'd about and solicited to visit people,[2] that I am forc'd to ⟨run⟩ into the Country to hide my selfe.

There is a ridiculous marriage on the point of conclusion that diverts me much. You know Lady Mary Sanderson; she is makeing over her discreet person and £1,500 a year jointure to the tempting Embrace of the noble Earl of Pembroke, ag'd 73.[3]

Text Bute MS   *Address* A Madme Madme La Comtesse de Mar

To Lady Mar [*July 1723*]

Dear Sister,

I have receiv'd by Lady Lansdown the very pritty Nightgown you sent me.[4] I give you many thanks for it, but I should have thought it much more valuable if it had been accompany'd with a Letter. I can hardly persuade my selfe you have receiv'd all mine, and yet can never spare time from the pleasures of Paris to answer one of 'em.

I am sorry to inform you of the Death of our Nephew my Sister Gower's Son of the small Pox.[5] I think she has a great deal of reason to regret it, in consideration of the offer I made her 2 year together of takeing the child home to my House, where I would have innoculated him with the same Care and

[1] Rachel (1696–1773), da. of George Baillie, m. (1717) Charles Hamilton, Lord Binning. Her children were Grisell Hamilton (b. 6 April 1719), Thomas (b. 23 Oct. 1720), later 7th Earl of Haddington, and George (b. 24 June 1723) (Lady G. Baillie, *Household Book 1692–1733*, ed. R. Scott-Moncrieff, 1911, p. xxix).

[2] LM's interest in smallpox inoculation had been aroused in Turkey, where she had it performed on her son in March 1718 (see i. 339, 392).

[3] This gossip was not true. Lady Mary Saunderson, sister of 1st Earl Castleton, apparently did not marry; in 1734 she was very ill (HMC *Townshend MSS*, 1887, p. 244) and probably died. Thomas Herbert (1656–1733), 8th Earl of Pembroke, m. (1725) as his third wife Mary (d. 1749), da. of 1st Viscount Howe.

[4] Lady Lansdown (see above, p. 6) arrived in London shortly before 29 June 1723 (*London Journal*).

[5] John Leveson-Gower, aged ten, died 15 July 1723.

safety I did my own.[1] I know nobody that has hitherto repented the Operation thô it has been very troublesome to some Fools who had rather be sick by the Doctors' Prescriptions than in Health in Rebellion to the College.[2]

I am at present at Twict'nam, which is become so fashionable and the Neighbourhood so much enlarg'd that 'tis more like Tunbridge or the Bath than a Country Retreat. Adieu, Dear Sister. I shall write you longer letters when I am sure you receive 'em, but it realy takes off very much from the pleasure of correspondance when I have no Assurance of their coming to your Hands. Pray let me know if this does, and beleive me ever Affectionately Yours.

Text Bute MS   *Address* A Madme Madme La Comtesse de Mar

To Alexander Pope [*Aug. 1723*][3]

As I carefully return'd your Arcadia without damage, I hope you will trust me with a volume of Shakespear's plays,[4] which I shall take the same care to restore.

Text Add MS 4809, f. 85

[1] In April 1721 LM engaged Charles Maitland (1668–1748), who had been surgeon on the Embassy, to inoculate her daughter; he published his report of it in the *Account of Inoculating the Small Pox*, 1722 (2nd ed. 1723).
[2] LM wrote an essay describing the operation and attacking those physicians who opposed it; her piece, with its strictures softened, was published in *The Flying-Post* of 11–13 Sept. 1722. For her connexion with the inoculation controversy see article by R. Halsband in the *Journal of the Hist. of Medicine*, viii., 1953, pp. 390–405; Halsband, *LM*, pp. 109–12; and Genevieve Miller, *The Adoption of Inoculation for Smallpox in England and France*, 1957, pp. 70–80.
[3] This letter is among the assorted scraps of paper, most of them backs of letters received, that 'Paper-sparing'

Pope used for drafts of his translation of Homer, and its position there makes July or Aug. 1723 a likely date (Pope, *Corr.* ii. 194, n. 1). This and the following letter were first identified by R. Halsband in *Philological Quarterly*, xxix, 1950, pp. 349–52. They had been printed in *Supplemental Vol. to the Works of Pope*, 1825, pp. 42, 176, but wrongly ascribed.
[4] In 1739, when LM's library was listed to be sent abroad, she owned a copy of Sir Philip Sidney's *Arcadia* and of Shakespeare, both in folio (Wh MS 135). She probably kept them in her London house, and so in Twickenham borrowed from her neighbour Pope. Her granddaughter found in her library 'Theobald's edition of Shakspeare [1734], manifestly much read' (Stuart, 1861, i. 110).

To Alexander Pope [*Oct. 1723*][1]

Friday night

If you are not well enough to come hither, I will be with you to morrow morning, having something particular to say to You.[2]

Text Add MS 4809, f. 106

To Lady Mar [*Oct. 1723*]

I have allready writ you so many Letters (dear Sister) that if I thought you had silently receiv'd them all, I don't know whither I should trouble you with any more, but I flatter my selfe that they have most of 'em miscarry'd. I had rather have my Labours lost than accuse you of unkindness. I send this by Lady Lansdowne,[3] who I hope will have no curiosity to open my Letter, since she will find in it that I never saw any thing so miserably alter'd in my Life. I realy did not know her:

> So must the fairest face appear
> When Youth and years are flown,[4]
> So sinks the pride of the Parterre
> When something over blown.

My Daughter makes such a noise in the room, 'tis impossible to go on in this Heroic style. I hope yours is in great bloom of Beauty. I fancy to my selfe we shall have the pleasure of seeing them Co-Toasts of the next Age. I don't

---

[1] Like the previous letter, this may be roughly dated from its position in the Homer MS (Pope, *Corr.* ii. 204).

[2] This and the preceding brief letter are the last surviving tokens of friendship between Pope and LM. For reasons not clearly documented they became estranged at some time before 1728, when he openly attacked her in the *Dunciad* (see Halsband, *LM*, pp. 130–2).

[3] On 1 Oct. 1723 Lady Lansdown was to 'set out speedily for Paris' (*Daily Journal*).

[4] Two lines in the third stanza of the ballad 'William and Mary' by David Mallet. It was first published in Edinburgh in Allen Ramsay's *Jenny and Meggy*, 1723 (G. F. Sleigh in *The Library*, 5th series, viii, 1953, pp. 121–3); or perhaps LM saw a manuscript copy.

at all doubt but they will outshine all the little Auroras of this, for there never was such a parcel of ugly Girls as reign at present. In recompence they are very kind, and the Men very mercifull, and content in this dearth of Charms with the poorest Stuff in the World. This you'd beleive had I but time to tell you the tender Loves of Lady Rumney and Lord Carmichil.[1] They are so fond it does one's heart good to see 'em. There are some other peices of Scandal not unentertaining, particularly the Earl of Stair and Lady M. Howard,[2] who being your Acquaintance I thought would be some Comfort to you. The Town improves daily. All people seem to make the best of the Talent God has given 'em. The Race of Roxburghs, Thanets, and Suffolks are utterly extinct,[3] and every thing appears with that edifying plain dealing that I may say in the words of the Psalmist, there is no Sin in Isarel [*sic*].

[*Postscript*] I have allready thank'd you for my Nightgown, but tis so pritty it will bear being twice thank'd for.

Text Bute MS   *Address* To The Countesse of Mar

To Lady Mar [*Oct. 1723*]

Dear Sister,
    I am heartily sorry to have the pleasure of hearing from you lessen'd by your Complaints of uneasyness, which I

---

[1] Elizabeth (1692–1750), da. of Sir Cloudesley Shovel, m. (1708) Robert Marsham (d. 1724), Baron Romney. John, Lord Carmichael (1701–67), later 3rd Earl of Hyndford, married her in 1732 but, according to Walpole, 'used her very ill' (*Corr.* xxxiv, 257).

[2] Lady Mary (d. 1786), da. of 3rd Earl of Carlisle.

[3] Mary Finch (1677–1718), da. of 2nd Earl of Nottingham, and widow of 2nd Marquess of Halifax, m. (1708) 1st Duke of Roxburgh. LM had depicted her as Roxana, a censorious prude, in her town eclogue 'The Drawing-Room',

one of the *Court Poems* (1716); and Mary, Countess Cowper, describes her similarly in her *Diary* (ed. S. Cowper, 2nd ed., 1865, p. 46).

Catharine Cavendish (1665–1712), da. of 2nd Duke of Newcastle, m. (1684) 6th Earl of Thanet.

By Lady Suffolk, LM probably means Anne Montagu (1660-1720), da. of 3rd Earl of Manchester, m. (1682) 3rd Earl of Suffolk. She had shown unusual devotion to her elderly husband (GEC, xii. i. 469, n. *f*)—which may have seemed a form of prudery.

wish with all my soul I was capable of releiving either by my Letters or any other way. My Life passes in a kind of Indolence, which is now and then awaken'd by agreable moments, but pleasures are transitory and the Ground work of every thing in England stupidity, which is certainly owing to the coldness of this Vile Climate. I envy you the Serene Air of Paris, as well as many other conveniencys. Here, what between the Things one can't do and the Things one must not do, the Time but dully lingers on, thô I make as good a shift as any of my Neighbours.

To my great Greife some of my best Freinds have been extreme ill, and in general Death and Sickness have never been more frequent than now. You may imagine poor Galantry droops, and except in the Elysian Shades of Richmond There is no such thing as Love or Pleasure. Tis said there is a fair Lady retir'd for having taken too much on't.[1] For my part they are not at all cook'd to my taste, and I have very little share in the Diversions there, which except season'd with Wit or at least Vivacity will not go down with me, who have not altogether so voracious an Appetite as I once had. I intend, however, to shine and be fine on the birth night, and review the Figures there. My poor Freind the young D[uchess] of Marlbrô I'm afraid has expos'd her selfe to a most violent Ridicule; she is as much embarrass'd with the loss of her big belly, and as much asham'd of it, as ever Dairy Maid was with the getting one.[2]

I desire you would say something very pretty to your

---

[1] This may refer to Mrs. Henrietta Howard (*c*. 1688–1767), later Countess of Suffolk, mistress of the Prince of Wales; she was at this time engaged in a passionate epistolary affair with Lord Peterborough (Lady Suffolk, *Letters 1712–1767*, ed. J. W. Croker, 1824, i. 126–74). In July [1723] Pope expected to find Peterborough visiting her at Richmond (Pope, *Corr*. ii. 178 and n. 1); but since Peterborough was at this time keeping Anastasia Robinson (as mistress or wife), his ardour toward Mrs. Howard may have been entirely political.

[2] Henrietta, Countess of Godolphin,

da. of the Duke of Marlborough, succeeded to her father's title in 1722. Her pregnancy was reported in the newspapers as early as 17 Aug. 1723 (*London Journal*); and she gave birth to a daughter on 23 Nov. The Duchess had not had a child for twenty years, and 'there has been more work about her great belly than ever was heard of before' (Katherine Scrase to Thomas Pelham, 3 Dec. [1723], Add MS 33,085, f. 104). The child had been fathered by William Congreve, the Duchess's lover for many years (John C. Hodges, *William Congreve the Man*, 1941, pp. 116–17).

Daughter in my name. Notwithstanding the great Gulph that is at present between us, I hope to wait on her to an Opera one time or other.

[*Postscript*] I suppose you know our uncle Fielding is dead.[1] I regret him prodigiously.

Text Bute MS   *Address* To The Countesse of Mar

To Lady Mar *31 Oct.* [*1723*]

Oct. 31.

I write to you at this time piping hot from the Birth night,[2] my Brain warm'd with all the Agreable Ideas that fine Cloths, fine Gentlemen, brisk Tunes and lively dances can raise there. 'Tis to be hop'd that my Letter will entertain you; at least you will certainly have the freshest Account of all passages on that Glorious day. First, you must know that I led up the ball, which you'll stare at; but what's more, I think in my Conscience I made one of the best figures there. To say truth, people are grown so extravagantly ugly that we old Beautys are force'd to come out on show days to keep the Court in Countenance. I saw Mrs Murray there, through whose hands this Epistle is to be convey'd. I don't know whither she'll make the same Complaint to you that I do. Mrs. West[3] was with her, who is a great Prude, having but 2 lovers at a Time; I think those are Lord Haddingtoun[4] and Mr. Lindsay,[5] the one for use, the one for show.

The World improves in one virtue to a violent degree— I mean plain dealing. Hipocricy being (as the Scripture

---

[1] William Feilding died at Epsom on 22 Sept. (*London Journal*, 28 Sept. 1723).

[2] The Prince and Princess of Wales returned to Leicester House from Richmond on 26 Oct. to celebrate his birthday on the 30th with a splendid ball (*Daily Journal*, 23 Oct.; *Polit. State of G.B.*, 1723, p. 454).

[3] This may be the lady of whom Mrs. Delany wrote (in 1732): 'Poor Mrs.

West! there's an end of her beauty and vanity; the illness she had before her death I hope was of service to her' (*Corr.* i. 364).

[4] Thomas Hamilton (1680–1735), 6th Earl of Haddington; his son Lord Binning was married to Mrs. Murray's younger sister.

[5] Possibly James Lindsay (1691–1768), later 5th Earl of Balcarres.

declares) a damnable Sin, I hope our publicans and Sinners will be sav'd by the open profession of the contrary virtue. I was told by a very good Author, who is deep in the secret, that at this very minute there is a bill cooking up at a Hunting Seat in Norfolk to have Not taken out of the Commandments and clap'd into the Creed the Ensuing session of Parliament. This bold attempt for the Liberty of the subject is wholly projected by Mr. Walpole, who propos'd it to the Secret Committee in his Parlor.[1] Will: Yonge seconded it, and answer'd for all his Acquaintance voteing right to a man. Doddington[2] very gravely objected that the obstinancy of Human Nature was such that he fear'd when they had possitive Commandments so to do, perhaps people would not commit adultery and bear False Wittness against their Neighbours with the readyness and Cheerfullness they do at present. This Objection seem'd to sink deep into the minds of the greatest Politicians at the Board; and I don't know whither the bill won't be dropped, thô tis certain it might be carry'd with great Ease, the world being intirely revenue du bagatelle, and Honnour, Virtue, Reputation etc., which we used to hear of in our Nursery, is as much laid aside and forgotten as crumple'd Riband. To speak plainly, I am very sorry for the forlorn state of Matrimony, which is as much ridicul'd by our Young Ladys as it us'd to be by young fellows; in short, both Sexes have found the Inconveniencys of it, and the Apellation of Rake is as genteel in a Woman as a Man of Quality. 'Tis no Scandal to say, Misse —— the maid of Honnour looks very well now she's up again, and poor Biddy Noel[3] has never been quite well since her last Flux. You may Imagine we marry'd Women look very silly; we have nothing to excuse our selves but that twas done a great while ago and we were very young when we did it.

This is the General state of Affairs; as to particulars, if you have any Curiosity for things of that kind, you have

---

[1] Sir Robert Walpole was entertaining a hunting party of his political cronies in Oct. 1723; and while the magnificent Houghton Hall, Norfolk, was being built he continued to occupy the old house (J. H. Plumb, *Walpole: The King's Minister*, 1960, p. 81 and n. 2).

[2] William Yonge (d. 1755) and George Bubb Dodington (1691–1762) were politicians and wits.

[3] Bridget (d. 1729), da. of John Noel, married the next year (see below, p. 46).

nothing to do but to ask me Questions and they shall be answer'd to the best of my understanding, my Time never being pass'd more agreably than when I am doing something obliging to you. This is Truth in spite of all the Beaux, Wits, and witlings in Great Brittain.

Text Bute MS

To Mrs. Barbara Calthorpe[1] 7 *Dec.* [*1723*][2]

London, Dec. 7.

My Knight Errantry is at an end, and I beleive I shall hence forward think freeing of Galley Slaves and knocking down Windmils more Laudable undertakeings than the Defence of any Woman's Reputation whatever. To say Truth, I have never had any great Esteem for the gennerality of the fair Sex, and my only Consolation for being of that Gender has been the assurance it gave me of never being marry'd to any one amongst them.[3] But I own at present I am so much out of Humour with the Actions of Lady Holderness that I never was so heartily asham'd of my Petticoats before.[4] You know, I suppose, that by this discreet match[5]

[1] Barbara Yelverton (1691 ?–1724), da. of 1st Viscount Longueville, and widow since 1720 of Reynolds Calthorpe, M.P. Her brother, 1st Earl of Sussex, held a post at Court as Lord of the Bedchamber.

[2] Printed by Dallaway (1803, i. 132–3) but dated 1709 and addressed to Anne Wortley; corrected in 1837.

[3] LM repeated this in a collection of maxims: 'I am never pleas'd to think I am not a Man but when I think I can never be marry'd to a Woman' (MS Commonplace Book, f. 3, Fisher Library, University of Sydney). Many years later it was repeated by Samuel Richardson in *Sir Charles Grandison* (LM to Lady Bute, 20 Oct. [1755]).

[4] Frederica (1688–1751), da. of 3rd

Duke of Schomberg, m. (1715) 3rd Earl of Holdernesse (d. 1722). LM had greatly esteemed Holdernesse (see i. 42, 232).

[5] Lady Holdernesse m. (18 June 1724) Benjamin Mildmay (1672–1756), brother and heir of Lord FitzWalter, whom he succeeded in 1728. The newspapers announced their engagement as early as 28 Nov. 1723 (*Daily Journal*). Others besides LM thought it 'an odd match for so discreet a person as she has been always esteemed' (Helen S. Hughes, *The Gentle Hertford*, 1940, p. 86). The Duchess of Montagu called it 'the nastyest thing I ever heard in my life. There is nothing in my Lord Rotchester's verses that makes one more ashamed' (to LM, 6 Jan. [1724], W MS iv. 204).

she renounces the care of her Children,[1] and I am laugh'd
at by all my Acquaintance for my Faith in her Honnour and
Understanding. My only Refuge is the Sincere Hope that
she is out of her senses, and takeing her selfe for Queen of
Sheba and Mr. Mildmay for King Solomon. I don't think it
quite so ridiculous. But the Men, you may well imagine, are
not so charitable, and they agree in the Kind Refflexion that
nothing hinders Women from playing the Fool but not
having it in their power.[2] The many Instances that are to be
found to support this opinion ought to make the Few reasonable more valu'd—but where are the Reasonable Ladys?

Dear Madam, come to Town that I may have the Honnour
of saying there is one in St. James' Place.

Text W MS v. 2–3   *Address* To The Honble Mrs Calthorpe at
Elvetham near Hartford Bridge Hampshire   *Postmark* MT   7 DE

From Edward Young[3] [*Feb. 1724*]

Madam,
    The more I think of your criticisms, the more I feel the just force
of them: I will alter which are alterable; those that are not I beg you
to make a secret of, and to make an experiment on the sagacity of the
town, which I think may possibly overlook what you have observed,
for the players and Mr. Dodington,[4] neither of whom were backward
in finding fault, or careless in attention, took no notice of the flaw in
D[emetrius]'s honour, or Erixene's conduct, and I would fain have
their blindness continue till my business is done; the players are fond

---

[1] Robert Darcy (1718–78), 4th Earl
of Holdernesse, and Lady Caroline (*c.*
1719–78), who m. (1735) the Earl of
Ancram. Her dowry was £20,000. Lady
Holdernesse did not, in fact, renounce
the care of her children: the Court of
Chancery decided that they should
remain with her until 'riper of years',
and then if anything appeared wanting
in their education the trustees could
apply again (*Daily Journal*, 11 Feb.
1725).

[2] LM frequently expresses this view,
particularly in *The Nonsense of Common-*

Sense of 24 Jan. 1738 (ed. R. Halsband,
1947, pp. 24–28; also 1861, ii. 414–18).

[3] The poet (1683–1765), famous for
his *Night Thoughts* (1742–5). In this
letter he discusses his verse tragedy *The
Brothers*, not produced until 1753.

[4] As a persistent patron-hunter Young
at this time attached himself to George
Bubb Dodington; he dated his letters
from Dodington's houses in Covent
Garden and Chiswick in Nov. and Dec.
1724 (Richard E. Tickell, *Thomas
Tickell*, 1931, pp. 104, 105).

of it, and as it has been said on a point of a little more importance, *si populus vult decipi, decipiatur.*[1] I am, madam, Your most obedient and most humble servant.

[*Postscript*] Madam,—Your alteration in the fifth act will be of exceeding advantage in more views than one.[2] I will wait on your ladyship with it as soon as I have done it, which will be, I believe, Monday morning. But that I'm satisfied you want no inducement to assist me as much as you can, I should add that I have more depending on the success of this particular piece than your ladyship imagines.

Friday noon.

Text 1861, ii. 13–14[3]

From Edward Young [*Feb. 1724*]

Madam,

A great cold and a little intemperance has given me such a face as I am ashamed to show, though I much want to talk with your ladyship. For my theatrical measures are broken; Mariamne brought its author above 1500*l.*,[4] The Captives above 1000*l.*,[5] and Edwin, now in

---

[1] 'If the people wish to be deceived, let them be deceived.' This is a variant of the remark supposed to have been uttered by Carlo Caraffa (d. 1561) when he observed the profound reverence which greeted his entry into Paris as Cardinal Legate in 1556 (W. F. H. King, *Classical and Foreign Quotations*, 3rd ed., 1904, § 2210).

[2] In LM's alteration Erixene, the heroine, instead of waiting for news to be brought, descends into the dungeon where Demetrius awaits his death (W. Thomas, *Le Poète Edward Young*, 1901, p. 305). In his satire 'On Women' (1727) Young set down a composite portrait of the lovely Daphne which contains several hints of LM, e.g.

With legs tost high on her Sophee she sits,

Vouchsafing audience to contending Wits;

Of each performance she's the final test;

One Act read o'er, she prophesies the rest. . . .

(*Love of Fame*, 3rd ed., 1730, p. 91).

Young had dedicated his previous play, *The Revenge* (1721), to the Duke of Wharton, who had suggested 'the most beautiful incident' in it (Dedication). When printed many years later, *The Brothers* bore no dedication.

[3] Formerly Harrowby MS; sold at Sotheby's on 25 July 1903 as lot 577.

[4] *Mariamne* by Elijah Fenton (1683–1730) was produced at Lincoln's Inn Fields on 22 Feb. 1723. It played seventeen nights that season, its author having four benefits. Although a newspaper had predicted that he would get more than £1,000, the receipts for his benefit nights came to £671 (*London Stage 1660–1800*, Part 2, ed. E. L. Avery, 1960, ii. 711–28 *passim*).

[5] John Gay's *The Captives* opened on

rehearsal, has already, before acting, brought its author above 1000*l.*[1]
Mine, when acted, will not more than pay for the paper on which it is
written; but the moment I get abroad I will wait on your ladyship, and
explain further. Only this at present, for the reason mentioned, I am
determined to suppress my play for this season at least.[2] The concern
you showed for its success is my apology for this account, which were
otherwise very impertinent. I am, madam, Your ladyship's much
obliged And most obedient humble servant.

Text 1861, ii. 11[3]

To Lady Mar [*March 1724*]

I do verily beleive (Dear Sister) that this is the 12th, if not
the 13th Letter I have writ since I had the pleasure of hearing
from you, and tis an uncomfortable thing to have precious
time spent and one's wit neglected in this manner. Sometimes I think you are falln into that utter Indifference for all
things on this side the Water, that you have no more curiosity
for the Affairs of London than for those of Pekin; and if that
be the Case tis downright impertinent to trouble you with
news, but I cannot cast off the affectionate concern I have
for my dear Sister, and consequently must put you in mind
of me whenever I have an opertunity.

The bearer of this Epistle is our Cousin,[4] and a consummate
puppy as you'l perceive at first sight. His shoulder-knot
last birthday made many a pritty Gentleman's Heart ake
with Envy, and his addresses have made Misse Howard

15 Jan. 1724 with high expectations of
its success, but Gay may have paid 30
guineas himself to coax a fifth night's
performance. The £1,000 mentioned by
Young must have been a rumour or a
subscription from Gay's friends (Pope,
Corr. ii. 216; William H. Irving, *John
Gay*, 1940, pp. 201–2).

[1] *Edwin: A Tragedy* by George Jeffreys (1678–1755) was produced on 24
Feb. 1724. In print it was dedicated to
the Duke of Montagu, who may have
rewarded its author.

[2] Young contemplated Holy Orders
for the 'prudential Motive' of an appointment from the Lord Lieutenant of
Ireland; in Aug. he was determined to
prepare for it immediately, and in Dec.
he was ordained (Richard E. Tickell,
Thomas Tickell, 1931, pp. 102–6).

[3] Formerly Harrowby MS; sold at
Sotheby's on 25 July 1903 as lot 578.

[4] Henry Vane (*c.* 1705–58), eldest
son of 2nd Baron Barnard. His great-
grandmother was Grace, da. of the
Hon. William Pierrepont.

the happyest of her Highnesse's honnourable virgins,[1] besides the Glory of thrusting the Earl of deLorain from the post he held in her Affections.[2] But his Relations are so ill bred to be quite Insensible of the Honnour arising from this Conquest, and fearing that so much Galantry may conclude in Captivity for Life pack him off to you, where tis to be hop'd there is no such killing Fair as Misse Howard.

I made a sort of Resolution at the beginning of my Letter not to trouble with the mention of what passes here, since you receive it with so much coldness, but I find tis impossible to forbear telling the metamorphosis of some of your Acquaintance, which appear as wondrous to me as any in Ovid. Could one beleive that Lady Holdernesse is a Beauty and in Love? and that Mrs. Robinson is at the same time a prude and a kept Mistriss? and these things in spite of Nature and Fortune. The first of these Ladys is tenderly attach'd to the polite Mr. Mildmay, and sunk in all the Joys of happy Love notwithstanding she wants the use of her 2 hands by a Rheumatism, and he has an arm that he can't move. I wish I could send you the particulars of this Amour, which seems to me as curious as that between 2 Oysters, and as well worthy the serious Enquiry of the Naturalists. The 2nd Heroine has engag'd halfe the Town in Arms from the Nicety of her virtue, which was not able to bear the too near approach of Senesino in the Opera,[3] and her Condescention in accepting of Lord Peterborrough for a Champion,[4] who has signaliz'd both his Love and Courage upon this occasion in as many instances as ever D[on] Quixote did for Dulcinea. Poor Senesino like a vanquish'd Giant was forc'd to confess upon his knees that Anastasia was a non pareil of virtue and of Beauty.[5] Lord Stanhope, as dwarf to the said Giant, jok'd of

[1] Mary (1700–44), da. of Charles Howard, was appointed Maid of Honour to the Princess of Wales in Feb. 1721 (*Daily Post*, 11 Feb.). In his *Memoirs* Hervey praises her beauty but not her morals or sense (ii. 491).

[2] She m. (1726) Henry Scott (1676–1730), 1st Earl of Delorain.

[3] Senesino and Anastasia Robinson continued to appear together until the end of the season in June.

[4] Charles Mordaunt (*c.* 1658–1735), 3rd Earl of Peterborough and a great military hero. About 1723 he took a house for Miss Robinson and her sister near his own villa; and she retired from the stage after June 1724. Just before his death he acknowledged her as his wife, stating that they had been secretly married for many years.

[5] Jonathan Swift had also heard of this incident: 'Ld Peterborows Gallantry

his side, and was challeng'd for his pains.[1] Lord Delawar[2] was Lord Peterborrough's second; my Lady miscarry'd. The Whole Town divided into partys on this important point. Innumerable have been the disorders between the 2 sexes on so great an Account, besides halfe the House of Peers being put under Arrest. By the Providence of Heaven and the wise Cares of his Majesty no bloodshed ensu'd. However, things are now tolerably accomodated, and the Fair Lady rides through the Town in Triumph in the shineing Berlin of her Hero, not to reckon the Essential advantage of £100 per month which (tis said) he allows her.

In General, never was Galantry in so elevated a Figure as it is at present. 20 very pritty fellows (the Duke of Wharton[3] being President and cheif director) have form'd themselves into a committee of Galantry. They call themselves Schemers, and meet regularly 3 times a week to consult on Galant Schemes for the advancement of that branch of Happyness which the vulgar call Whoring. Viscount Hillsborrough[4] (who I verily beleive compensates in the sight of God for his indirect acquirement of riches by his public spirited distribution of them, as much as ever Cardinal Wolsey did by his Foundation of Colleges) has turn'd his house, one of the handsomest in Hannover Square, into an Edifice apropriated to this use. He open'd on Ash Wednesday by the best contriv'd Entertainment in the World, and the only remedy against spleen and vapours occasion'd by the Formality of that day, which still subsists amongst other rags of Popery not yet rooted out.

The Schemers were all sworn to several Articles absolutely necessary for the promotion of public good and the

---

is exactly of a Size with the whole Tenor of his Life, onely in complyance to his Age he seeks to make a Noise without the Fatigue of travelling. . . .' (13 Feb. 1724, *Corr.*, ed H. Williams, 1963–5, iii. 6–7).

[1] Philip Stanhope (1694–1773), later famous as Earl of Chesterfield. He was notably short in stature; and he had a 'propensity to ridicule, in which he indulged himself with infinite humour and no distinction, and with inexhaust-

ible spirits and no discretion' (Hervey, *Memoirs*, i. 71). Senesino was a *castrato* singer of 'majestic figure'.

[2] John West (1693–1766), 7th Baron (later 1st Earl) De La Warr, lieutenant-colonel of the Horse Guards. He was 'long, lank, awkward' (ibid. ii. 549).

[3] Philip Wharton (1698–1731), 1st Duke, and notorious for his brilliance, instability, and profligacy.

[4] For Lord Hillsborough, see above, p. 17.

conservation of peace in private Familys: 1st, that every member should come at the hour of 6 mask'd in a Domine, leading in the then predominant Lady of his affections mask'd likewise; 2ndly, that no member should presume, by peeping, squeaking, staring or any other impertinence, to discover his brother's incognita, who should remain wholly and solely his, without any molestation soever, to his use for that night being; 3rdly, no member should dare to introduce any Lady who did not appear sometimes barefac'd at the drawing-room, Lord Strafford's,[1] etc; 4thly and lastly, that if by Accident or the Lady's indiscretion her name should chance to be discover'd by one or more of the Schemers, that name should remain sacred and as unspeakable as the name of the Deity amongst the Jews.

You may imagine such wholsome Laws brought all the best Company to this polite Assembly; add to these the Inducement of good Music, Fine Liquors, a splendid Supper, and the best punch you ever tasted. But you'l ask, how could they sup without shewing their faces? You must know the very Garrets were clean'd and lighted out at this Solemnity. The whole Company ⟨view'd the supper, which was large enough to⟩[2] suffer every fair one to point to what she thought most delightfull to be convey'd to her respective apartment. Those who were yet in the state of probation, and scrupul'd too much happyness in this world for fear of its being deducted in the Next, had screens set round little neat Tables in the public rooms, which were as inviolate (but to the partners) as Walls of Adamant. You may imagine there were few of this latter Class, and tis to be hop'd that good Examples and the Indefatigable endeavors of the Schemers (who spare no pains in carrying on the good cause) will lessen them daily. These Galantrys are continu'd every Wednesday during Lent, and I won't ask your pardon for this long Account of 'em since I consider the duty of a true English Woman is to do what Honnour she can to her native Country, and that it would be a Sin against the pious Love I bear the Land of my Nativity to confine the renown due to the

---

[1] Thomas Wentworth (1672–1739), 1st Earl of Strafford. Swift thought him 'infinitely proud, & wholly illiterate' (1712, *Journal to Stella*, ed. H. Williams, 1948, ii. 489).

[2] From a copy (W MS iv. 54).

Schemers[1] within the small extent of this little Isleland, which ought to be spread where ever Men can sigh or Women wish. Tis true they have the Envy and Curses of the old and ugly of both Sexes, and a general persecution from all old Women, but this is no more than all Reformations must expect in their beginning, and what the Christian Church suffer'd in a remarkable manner at its first blaze. You may easily beleive, The whole Generation of Fathers, Mothers, and Husbands raise as great a Clamour against this new institution as the pagan preists did of old against the light of the Gospel, and for the same reasons, since it strikes at the very foundation of their Authority, which Authority is built on grosse impositions upon Mankind.[2]

Text Bute MS

To Lady Mar [*April 1724*]

The enclos'd, as you will very well perceive, was writ to be sent by Mr. Vane, but he was posted off a day sooner than I expected, and it was left upon my hands, since which time the Schemers got hold of it amongst 'em, and I had much ado to get it from 'em. I have also had a delightfull letter from you to let me know you are coming over,[3] and I am advis'd not to write; but you having not nam'd that Time (which is expected with the utmost impatience by me and many more), I am determin'd to send my Epistle, but trouble you with no farther Account thô you will find here a thousand new and consequently amusing Scenes.

---

[1] They are called 'gallant schemers' by Lady Elizabeth Hastings, who names as members the Duke of Wharton, Lord Hillsborough, Sir George Oxenden, and Edward Thompson (24 June [?1724], HMC *Hastings MSS*, ed. F. Bickley, iii, 1934, pp. 1–2). They are listed as a 'Hell Fire Club' by Robert J. Allen, *The Clubs of Augustan London*, 1933, pp. 122–3.

[2] Previous editions have omitted two passages from this letter.

[3] Lady Mar arrived in London on 19 May (*Daily Post*, 25 May 1724).

Among our Acquaintance things strangly are carry'd:
Lord Tenham is shot,[1] Mr. Strickland is marry'd,[2]
⟨Lady⟩ Harvey with child,[3] and her Husband is dying,[4]
. . . ⟨ ? ⟩ has left playing and crying,[5]
. . .[6] ⟨Mrs.⟩ Cook so bright and so gay
. . . ⟨ ? ⟩ Church vault this many a day.

Text Bute MS

To Lady Mar [*c. 12 Nov. 1724*][7]

I am heartily sorry, Dear Sister, for all that displeases you, and for this time admit of your excuses for Silence,[8] but I give you warning c'est pour la derniere fois. To say truth, they don't seem very reasonable; what ever keeps one at home naturally enclines one to write, especially when you can give a Freind so much pleasure as your Letters allways do me.

Miss Skerret staid all the remainder of the Summer with me,[9] and we are now come to Town, where variety of things

[1] Henry Roper, 8th Baron Teynham, had committed suicide 16 May 1723. The verse is based on Prior's *Down-Hall*, stanzas xviii, xix (*Works*, i. 553).

[2] Possibly William Strickland (*c.* 1686–1735), later 4th Baronet; he m.(n.d.) Catharine, da. of Sir Jeremy Sambrooke.

[3] Augustus John Hervey (d. 1779), later 3rd Earl of Bristol, b. 19 May 1724. On the death of Carr, Lord Hervey (on 14 Nov. 1723), his courtesy title had passed to his half-brother John.

[4] Lord Hervey suffered from atrocious ill health, as he himself detailed it (*Memoirs*, Appendix II).

[5] No doubt Lord Hervey's mother, Lady Bristol—of whom a friend at Bath (in 1721) observed that 'she cries every post-day for an hour, because the earl has not come; she dries up her tears about twelve, to play upon the walks, and an hour sooner, if any body gives a breakfast. . . .' (Henrietta, Countess of Suffolk, *Letters 1712–1767*, ed. J. W. Croker, 1824, i. 76–77).

[6] The edge of the paper is torn away.

[7] Lady Mar had been in England to settle her financial affairs. By an agreement signed on 30 May 1724 Lord Mar's sequestered estates were taken over by his brother James Erskine, Lord Grange, with the provision that he pay Lady Mar an annual rent of £1,000 and her daughter's dowry of £10,000 (Eg MS 3530, f. 56). On 28 Aug. Lady Mar left London to return to Paris with her daughter (*Daily Journal*, 31 Aug. 1724).

[8] Lady Mar's excuses are in her letter of 10 Nov./30 Oct. (W MS iv. 112–13): 'You think me a strange creature I'm sure for being so long without writeing to you. All I can say is Lazyness, Stupidity and ill humour have taken such hold upon me that I write to nobody nor have Spirrits to go any where. Perhaps a letter from you may contribute to my Cure.' She then goes on to tell about her debts, increased by the devaluation of the French livre, and about the dullness of Paris.

[9] Maria Skerrett (see above, p. 12) had by this time become Sir Robert

happen every day. Sophia[1] and I have an immortal Quarrel, which thô I resolve never to forgive, I can hardly forbear laughing at. An Acquaintance of mine is marry'd who I wish very well to. Sophia has been pleas'd on this Occasion to write the most Infamous ballad that ever was writ, where both the bride and bridegroom are intollerably maul'd, especially the last, who is complemented with the hopes of Cuckoldom and 40 other things equally obliging. Sophia has distributed this ballad in such a manner as to make it pass for mine, on purpose to pique the poor Innocent Soul of the new marry'd man, whom I should be the last of creatures to abuse. I know not how to clear my selfe of this vile Imputation without a train of Consequences I have no mind to fall into.—In the mean time Sophia enjoys the pleasure of heartily plaguing both me and that person.

Now the Money is so high at Paris I wish you would be so good to enquire for what I could sell a Di'mond, clean and thick, Indian Cut, weighing 39 grains strong. Your quick Answer to this would be very kind. If it is as I like, perhaps I may pass the Xmas Holidays at Paris.

Adieu, Dear Sister.

The new Opera is execrable.[2]

Text Bute MS   *Address* A Madme Madame de Mar

To Lady Mar [*Dec. 1724*]

I am heartily sorry (Dear Sister), without any affectation, for any uneasyness that you suffer, let the Cause be what it will, and wish it was in my power to give you some more

Walpole's mistress, perhaps through LM's good offices (J. H. Plumb, *Walpole: The King's Minister*, 1960, p. 113). When he read this letter Horace Walpole noted that Miss Skerrett often lived with LM (*Corr.* xxxiv. 256). Elsewhere he called her LM's *élève* (ibid. xiv. 245). (He also called her LM's relative, though no evidence supports it.)

[1] The Duke of Wharton. LM and

her sister had evidently agreed on this cypher for the Duke, whose Jacobite intrigues would make mention of his name suspect in a letter sent by post.

[2] On 31 Oct. Handel's *Tamerlane*, with Cuzzoni and Senesino, opened the season of the Royal Academy of Music at the King's Theatre (*London Stage 1660–1800*, Part 2, ed. E. L. Avery, 1960, ii. 792).

Essential mark of it than unavailing Pity. But I am not so
fortunate, and till a fit Occasion of disposing of some superfluous Di'monds,[1] I shall remain in this sinfull Sea Cole
Town; and all that remains for me to do to shew my willing-
ness (at least) to divert you, is to send you faithfull Accounts
of what passes amongst your Acquaintance in this part of the
World. Madam de Broglio[2] makes a great Noise, but tis
only from the frequency and Quantity of her pissing, which
she does not fail to do at least ten times a day amongst a
cloud of Wittnesses.[3]

> One would think her daughter of a River,
> As I heard Mr. Mirmont[4] tell,
> And the best Commendation that he could give her
> Was that she made Water excellent well.
> With a fa la la etc.[5]

My Lord Clare attracts the Eyes of all the Ladys, and
gains all the Hearts of those who have no other way of
disposing of them but through their Eyes.[6] I have din'd
with him twice, and had he been dumb I beleive I should
have been in the Number of his admirers, but he lessen'd
his Beauty every time he spoke, till he left him selfe as few
charms as Mr. Vane, thô I confess his outside very like Mrs.
Duncomb,[7] but that the lovely lines are softer there, with
wit and spirit, and improv'd by Learning.

[1] In her letter of 29/18 Nov., a melancholy recital of unhappiness, Lady Mar
wrote: '. . . I know this is the worst time
to think of selling any thing here. Money
is so Scarce that I question whether any
body cou'd be found to buy such a
diamond as you speak of. Ev'ry thing is
very dear, which makes people retrench
their expence to what is absolutely necessary, and jewells you know cannot be
comprehended under that head; but I
hope that won't hinder you from makeing your trip' (W MS iv. 114–15).

[2] Thérèse Gilette de Grandville m.
(1716) François Marie II, duc de
Broglie (1671–1745), who had come to
England in June 1724 as French Am-
bassador; she followed in Aug. (*Daily
Journal*, 19 June; *Daily Post*, 8 Aug.
1724). Mme de Broglie was 'une rude
Malouine, à la langue bien pendue, qui

semble avoir été active et grande maî-
tresse de maison' (Jean La Varende, *Les
Broglie*, 1950, p. 51).

[3] She gave birth to a son on 25 Nov.
(*Polit. State of G.B.*, 1724, p. 530);
hence her visitors. (He d. 12 Dec.)

[4] Armand de Bourbon, marquis de
Miremont (1655–1732), a Huguenot
refugee. According to Hervey, he was
later kept at Court by Queen Caroline
only to amuse the King (*Memoirs*, i.
261).

[5] Previous editions have omitted the
ribald verse with its explanation.

[6] Charles O'Brien (1699–1761), Viscount Clare; Mrs. Delany considered
him 'a gay flattering audacious Frenchman', silly and excessively vain of his
person (*Corr.* i. 93, 95).

[7] This may be the Mrs. Duncombe
(d. 1751) described by Mrs. Delany as

The Duke of Wharton has brought his Dutchess to Town, and is fond of her to Distraction, in order to break the Hearts of all the other Women that have any claim upon his.[1] Besides the Family Dutys that he pretends to perform o' nights, he has public devotions twice o' day and assists at them in person with exemplary Devotion; and there is nothing pleasanter than the remarks of some pious Ladys on the Conversion of so great a Sinner. For my own part, I have some Cotterys where wit and pleasure reign, and I should not fail to amuse my selfe tolerably enough but for the Damn'd, damn'd Quality of growing older and older every day, and my present Joys are made imperfect by fears of the Future.

Text Bute MS   *Address* A Madme Madme de Mar

To Lady Mar [*Jan. 1725*]

Dear Sister,

I am extreamly sorry for your Indisposition, and did not wait for a Letter to write to you, but my Lord Clare has been going every day this 3 weeks, and I intended to charge him with a packet. Nobody ever had such ineffectual charms as his Lordship. Beauty and money are equally ill bestow'd when a fool has the keeping of them; they are incapable of Happyness and every blessing turns useless in their hands.

You advise a change of taste, which I confess I have no Notion of. I may (with Time) change my persuit, for the same reason that I may feed upon Butcher's meat when I am not able to purchase greater Delicates, but I am sure I shall never forget the flavour of Gibier. In the mean time I divert my selfe passably enough and take care to improve as much as possible that stock of Vanity and Credulity that Heaven

very sensible, wise, and worthy (ibid. i. 499; iii. 59).

[1] The Duke m. (1715) Martha (c. 1700–26), da. of Maj.-Gen. Richard Holmes. They had been estranged. Lady Bristol also remarked on the 'extra-ordinary joyning' of the couple, whose happiness was confirmed to her by the young Duchess herself (28 Nov. 1724, John Hervey, *Letter-Books*, 1894, ii. 377).

in its mercy has furnish'd me with, being sensible that to those two Qualitys (simple as they appear) all the Pleasures of Life are owing.

My Sister Gower is in Town on the point of Lying in. I see every Body but converse with nobody but des Amis choisies. In the first Rank of these are Lady Stafford[1] and dear Molly Skerret, both of which have now the Additional merit of being old acquaintance and never having given me any reason to complain of either of 'em. I pass some days with the Dutchess of Montagu, who might be a reigning Beauty if she pleas'd. I see the whole Town every Sunday, and select a few that I retain to Supper. In short, if Life could be allways what it is, I beleive I have so much Humility in my temper, I could be contented without any thing better this two or three hundred year, but alas!

> Dullness and wrinkles and disease must come,
> And Age and Death's irrevocable Doom.

Text Bute MS   *Address* A Madme Madme de Mar

To Lady Mar [*Feb. 1725*]

I beleive you have by this time, Dear Sister, receiv'd my Letter from the Hand of that Thing my Lord Clare. However, I love you well enough to write again in hopes you will Answer my Letters one time or other.

All our Acquaintance are run mad; they do such things, such monstrous and stupendous things! Lady Harvey and Lady Bristol have quarrell'd in such a polite manner that they have given one another all the Titles so liberally bestow'd amongst the Ladys at Billingsgate.[2] Sophia and I have been quite reconcil'd and are now quite broke, and I beleive not likely to piece up again. Ned Thompson is as happy as

[1] LM had known Lady Stafford since 1720.

[2] Lady Bristol had an irascible temper, and was occasionally on bad terms with her daughter-in-law (John Hervey, *Letter-Books*, 1894, ii. 325, 377). For her part, Lady Hervey found that 'vast civility, much coolness, and great distance, are not only the best preservatives, but the only acquirers of that lady's good graces' (Oct. [1725], Henrietta, Countess of Suffolk, *Letters 1712–1767*, ed. J. W. Croker, 1824, i. 194).

the Money and charms of Belle Dunch can make him, and a miserable Dog for all that.[1] Public places flourish more than ever; we have Assemblys for every day in the week, besides Court, Operas, and Masquerades. With Youth and Money 'tis certainly possible to be very well diverted in spite of Malice and ill Nature, thô they are more and more powerfull every day. For my part, as it is my establish'd Opinion That this Globe of ours is no better than a Holland Cheese and the Walkers about in it Mites, I possess my Mind in patience, let what will happen, and should feel tolerably easy thô a great Rat came and eat halfe of it up.

My Sister Gower has got a 6th Daughter[2] by the Grace of God, and is as merry as if nothing had happen'd. My poor Love Mr. Cook has fought and been disarm'd by J. Stapleton on a National Quarrel;[3] in short he was born to conquer nothing in England, that's certain, and has good Luck neither with our Ladys nor Gentlemen. B. Noel is come out Lady Milsington,[4] to the Encourragment and consolation of all the Coquets about Town, and they make hast to be as infamous as possible in order to make their fortunes.—

I have this moment receiv'd from Mrs. Pelling[5] a very pritty Cap for my Girl. I give you many thanks for the trouble you have had in sending it, and desire you would be so good to send the other things when you have opper-

---

[1] Edward Thompson, M.P. (1697–1742), one of the Schemers, m. (6 Feb. 1725) Arabella, da. of Edmund Dunch. The previous summer he had been 'full of raptures of his queen of hearts, as he calls her' (HMC *Hastings MSS*, iii, 1934, p. 2), but the outcome of the marriage was not so happy. In June [1727] Edward Young reported that 'Tompson of York has rusticated his Lady for Gallantrys' (Richard E. Tickell, *Thomas Tickell*, 1931, p. 131). According to Hervey, Mrs. Thompson was seduced by her brother-in-law Sir George Oxenden (also a Schemer), separated from her husband, and died in childbed (*Memoirs*, iii. 741). LM wrote a pathetic elegy on her death (1861, ii. 484–5).

[2] Evelyn Leveson-Gower (26 Jan. 1725–63), later Countess of Upper Ossory. It was her daughter-in-law who loaned Horace Walpole these letters to read, and at her request he wrote the notes in the Fitzpatrick MS, printed in Walpole, *Corr.* xxxiv, Appendix 9.

[3] In the duel, which took place about 5 Feb. 1725, M. Cooke, a captain of dragoons attached to the French Embassy, was wounded (1861, i. 481, n. 4). His opponent was probably John Stapylton (c. 1684–1733), who succeeded to his father's baronetcy in 1727.

[4] Bridget Noel (see above, p. 32) m. (20 Nov. 1724) Viscount Milsington, son of 1st Earl of Portmore.

[5] Possibly married or related to the Rev. John Pelling (1669–1750), rector of St. Anne's, Westminster (*Gentleman's Mag.*, 1750, p. 139).

tunity. I have another favour to ask, that you would make my Compliments to our English Embassador when you see him.[1] I have a constancy in my Nature that makes me allways remember my old Freinds.

Text Bute MS

From Henrietta, Duchess of Marlborough
11 [*March 1725*]

When I sent to you yesterday, Dear Madam, to tell you the Musick was to be here to night[2] you were with my Lord Dochester; therefore this comes only to beg if you have been there to day or do intend to go, that you will not come here.[3] I am ever your most obedient servant,

Marlborough.

Thursday the 11th

Text W MS iv. 189   *End. by W* Hen. Dutchess of Marlborough

To Lady Mar [*c. 20 March 1725*]

Dear Sister,

Having a few momentory Spirits, I take pen in hand, thô tis impossible to have tenderness for you without having spleen upon reading your Letter, which will I hope be receiv'd as a Lawfull excuse for the Dullness of the Following Lines, and I plead (as I beleive has been done upon other Occasions) I should please you better if I lov'd you less.

My Lord Carlton has left this transitory World,[4] and

[1] Sir Robert's brother Horatio Walpole (1678–1757), diplomatist, was in Paris as Ambassador Extraordinary (D. B. Horn, *Brit. Dipl. Rep. 1689–1789*, 1932, pp. 17–18).

[2] The Duchess was fanatically fond of music, patronized Bononcini, and gave great concerts in her house in St. James's.

[3] LM's nephew, the Marquess of Dorchester, had been inoculated for smallpox on 27 Feb. at his grandfather's house in Arlington Street (see below, p. 49); hence the Duchess fears that her own infant daughter may be exposed to infection if LM comes to her house.

[4] Henry Boyle (M.P. 1689), 1st Baron Carleton, died 14 March 1725.

dispos'd of his Estate as he did of his time, between Lady Clarendon and the Dutchess of Queensbury. Jewells to a great value he has given, as he did his Affections, first to the Mother and then to the Daughter.[1] He was taken ill in my Company at a Consort at the D[uchess] of Marlbrô's,[2] and dy'd 2 days after, holding the fair Dutchesse by the hand, and being fed at the same time with a fine fat chicken, thus dying, as he liv'd, indulging his Pleasures. Your Freind Lady A. Bateman[3] (every body being acquainted with her affair) is grown discreet, and no body talks of it now but his family, who are violently pique'd at his refusing a great Fortune. Lady Gainsborrough has stoln poor Lord Shaftsbury, ag'd 14, and chain'd him for Life to her Daughter upon pretence of having been in love with her several years.[4] But Lady Harvey makes the Top Figure in Town, and is so good as to shew twice a week at the Drawing room and twice more at the Opera for the Entertainment of the Public. As for my selfe, having nothing to say I say nothing. I insensibly dwindle into a Spectatress and lead a kind of—as it were—[5]

I wish you here ev'ry day, and see in the mean time Lady Stafford, the D[uchess] of Montagu and Miss Skerret, and realy speak to allmost no body else, thô I walk about every where. Adieu, Dear Sister. If my Letters could be any Consolation to you I should think my time best spent in writeing. When you buy the Triffles that I desir'd of you, I fancy Mr. Walpole will be so good to give you oppertunity of sending

---

[1] As LM explains in her letter of 1 March [1754], Jane Leveson-Gower (1670–1725) who m. (1692) Lord Hyde, later 4th Earl of Clarendon, had been Carleton's mistress, and one of their daughters was the famous beauty Catherine Hyde (1701–77) who m. (1720) 3rd Duke of Queensberry. Carleton, who died unmarried, actually left the Duchess a life interest in his estates in Wiltshire and Oxfordshire as well as £5,000, and to her mother all his diamond and ruby rings. The largest share of his estate, however, went to his nephew the 3rd Earl of Burlington (Violet Biddulph, *Kitty, Duchess of Queensberry*, 1935, pp. 29–30).

[2] LM had thus accepted the Duchess's conditional invitation of 11 March.

[3] Lady Anne Spencer (d. 1769), granddaughter of the Duke of Marlborough, m. (1720) William, later 1st Viscount Bateman.

[4] Dorothy Manners (1681–1739), da. of 1st Duke of Rutland, was widow of 3rd Earl of Gainsborough. Her daughter Susanna Noel (d. 1758) m. (12 March 1725) Anthony Ashley Cooper (d.1771), 4th Earl of Shaftesbury. Both were 14 at the time; and soon after the wedding he returned to his studies at Oxford (*Daily Journal*, 30 March 1725).

[5] This phrase is from Prior's 'An Epitaph' (*Works*, i. 462).

them without trouble if you make it your request and tell him they are for me.

Text Bute MS   *Address* A Madme Madme de Mar

To Lady Mar [*March 1725*]

Dear Sister,

My Eyes are very bad to Day from having been such a Beast to sit up late last night. However, I will write to enquire after your Health tho at the Expence of my own.

I forget whither I told you Lord Dorchester[1] and our Sister Carolina[2] have been Innoculated and are perfectly well after it.[3] I saw her Grace the D[uchess] of Kingston yesterday, who told me that she heard from you last post, and that you have been ill but are recover'd. My Father is going to the Bath, Sir Wm Wyndham is dying of a Fistula,[4] Lady Darlington and Lady Mohun are packing up for the next World,[5] and the rest of our Acquaintance playing the Fool in this, a l'ordinaire. Amongst the rest a very odd Whim is enter'd the little Head of Mrs. Murray. Do you know that she won't visit me this Winter? I, according to the usual Integrity of my Heart and Simplicity of my Manners, with great Naïveté desir'd to explain with her upon the Subject, and she answer'd that she was convince'd that I had made the Ballad upon her, and was resolv'd never to speak to me

[1] Evelyn Pierrepont (1712–73), only son of LM's brother, on whose death in 1713 he was styled Lord Kingston; in 1715 he assumed the title of his grandfather the Marquess of Dorchester, when the latter was advanced to the Dukedom of Kingston. He became (1726) the 2nd Duke of Kingston.

[2] Lady Caroline Pierrepont (d. 1753), LM's half-sister, born on 23 July 1716 (Eg MS 3531). Her other half-sister, Lady Anne (b. 1 Feb. 1721), died in 1739—of smallpox (*Daily Advertiser*, 17 May 1739).

[3] On 27 Feb. both Dorchester and Lady Caroline were inoculated at the

Duke's house in Arlington Street (*Daily Post*, 3 March 1725).

[4] Lady Bristol also reported Sir William Wyndham 'in great danger' (1 April 1725, John Hervey, *Letter-Books*, 1894, ii. 389), but he lived until 1740.

[5] Sophia Charlotte von Kielmann-segge (1675–1725), one of George I's mistresses, cr. (1722) Countess of Darlington, died on 20 April. She had corresponded with LM during the Turkish Embassy (see i. 345). Elizabeth, widow of 4th Baron Mohun (killed in a duel in 1712), died on 15 May 1725.

again. I answer'd (which was true) that I utterly defy'd her
to have any one single proofe of my making it, without being
able to get any thing from her but repetitions that she knew
it.[1] I can't suppose that any thing you have said[2] should
occasion this Rupture, and the Reputation of a Quarrel
is allways so ridiculous on both sides that you would oblige
me in mentioning it to her, for tis now at that pritty pass she
won't curtsie to me where ever she meets me, which is super-
latively silly (if she realy knew it) after a suspension of
Resentment for two year together.

To turn the Discourse on something more Amusing, we
had a Masquerade last night, where I did not fail to triffle
away a few hours agreably enough, and fell into Company
with a quite new Man that has a great deal of wit joyn'd to
a Diabolical person. Tis my Lord Irwin, who tis impossible
to love and impossible not to be entertain'd with.[3] That
Species are the most Innocent part of the creation, et ne
laisse pas de faire plaisir. I wish all Mankind were of that
Class.

Dear Sister, I would give the World to converse with you,
maïs Helas! the Sea is between us.

Text Bute MS

[1] The ballad about the attempted
rape on Mrs. Murray was *Virtue in
Danger* (see above, p. 14). If LM in
fact wrote the ballad she never acknowledged her authorship, as she did an
'Epistle from Arthur Gray to Mrs.
Murray', which she copied into her
album of verse (H MS vol. 255); the
latter is a serious, pathetic plea from the
unhappy footman in prison (1861, ii.
478–80). In the opinion of the hard-
headed Sarah, Duchess of Marlborough,
Mrs. Murray would have done much
better to have concealed the incident
from the beginning, and in general such
episodes were worthy of being celebrated
in ballads (*Letters of a Grandmother
1732–1735*, ed. G. S. Thomson, [1943],
p. 74: her comment made in 1732).

[2] The most curious fact about Mrs.
Murray's resentment has not been commented on, not even by the editor of
Lady Suffolk's letters (J. W. Croker),
who castigates LM for writing the inde-
cent ballad. 'We have here an excellent
new ballad', Lady Lansdown wrote to
Lady Suffolk from Paris, 'sent from
England by the lady herself [Mrs.
Murray] to her dear friend L. M. [Lady
Mar]. Pray be so good as to let me know
who is named for the author' (5 Dec.
[1721], Suffolk, *Letters*, 1824, i. 84–85;
original letter Add MS 22,627, f. 70).

[3] Arthur Ingram (1689-1736), 6th
Viscount Irwin or Irvine. He never
married.

To Lady Mar [*May 1725*]

Dear Sister,

I take this Occasion of writeing to you, thô I have receiv'd no Answer to my last, but tis allways most agreable to me to write when I have the Conveniency of a private hand to convey my Letter, thô I have no dispositions to politiquer. But I have such a complication of things both in my Head and Heart that I do not very well know what I do; and if I can't settle my Brains, your next News of me will be that I am lock'd up by my Relations. In the mean time I lock my selfe up and keep my Distraction as private as possible. The most facetious part of the History is that my Distemper is of such a Nature, I know not whither to laugh or cry at it. I am glad and sorry, and smiling and sad—but this is too long an account of so whimsical a being. I give my selfe sometimes admirable advice but I am incapable of taking it.

Mr. Baily you know is dismiss'd the Treasury,[1] and consol'd with a pension of equal value. Your acquaintance D[on] Rodrigue has had a small accident befalln him:[2] Mr. Annesley found him in bed with his Wife, prosecuted, and brought a bill of Divorce into Parliament.[3] Those Things grow more

[1] George Baillie (1664–1738), Mrs. Murray's father, a Lord of the Treasury since 1717 (*London Gazette*, 9–12 April 1717). As early as July 1723 he felt that his post was in jeopardy (HMC *Polwarth MSS*, iii, 1931, p. 282); but according to Mrs. Murray he resigned against the entreaties of his friends and even of the King (*Mem. of the Lives and Characters of George Baillie and of Lady Grisell Baillie*, 1822, p. 25).

[2] José Rodrigo y Villalpando (d. 1741), Chamberlain at the Court of Spain, had been in Paris in Nov. 1721 to arrange the engagement, later broken, between Louis XV and the Spanish Infanta (Saint-Simon, *Mémoires*, ed. A. de Boislisle, 1879-1930, xxxviii. 348–9 and n. 1). Whether he or a son was now in London is uncertain.

[3] On 26 April Francis Annesley (d. 1740) brought into the House of Lords a bill to dissolve his marriage with Elizabeth Sutton for 'unlawful Familiarity and adulterous Conversation with one Don Roderigo. . . .'; on 4 May the bill was passed (*Journals of the House of Lords*, xxii. 520, 527, 530). A correspondent of the Earl of Oxford described the debate: 'The Bishop of Peterborough made the House good sport, he said it was incredible that a Christian woman should lie with a Jew, but being told that Roderigo was a Christian he said O! if it was so then what he had to object to this bill was that the petitioner's wife was an infamous woman before his marriage to her and he took her as such; he was answered by the Bishop of London' (HMC *Portland MSS*, vi, 1901, p. 2).

fashionable every day, and in a little while won't be at all Scandalous. The best Expedient for the public and to prevent the Expence of private familys would be a genneral Act of Divorceing all the people of England. You know, those that pleas'd might marry over again, and it would save the Reputations of several Ladys that are now in peril of being expos'd every day.

I saw Horace the other Day, who is a good creature. He returns soon to France,[1] and I will engage him to take care of any pacquet that you design for me.

Text Bute MS   *Address* A Madme Madme de Mar

To Lady Mar [*c. 10 June 1725*]

I can't help being very sorry for your Sake to hear that you persist in your Design of retiring,[2] thô as to my own part I have no view of conversing with you where you now are, and 90 leagues is but a small addition to the Distance between us. London never was more Gay than it is at present but—I dont know how—I would fain be 10 years younger. I love Flattery so well I could fain have some circumstances of probabillity added to it that I might swallow it with Comfort. The reigning Dutchess of Marlbrô has Entertain'd the Town with Consorts of Bononcini's Composition very often, but she and I are not in that degree of Freindship to have me often Invited. We continu to see one another like 2 people that are resolv'd to hate with Civillity.

Sophia is going to Aix la Chappelle and from thence to Paris.[3] I dare swear she'll endeavor to get acquainted with you. We are broke to an irremediable degree. Various are the

[1] Horatio Walpole, in London since 11 May (*Daily Post*, 14 May), was preparing to return to Paris on 1 June (*Daily Journal*), but apparently did not go until July (*Daily Courant*, 31 July, cited 1861, i. 487, n. 2).

[2] Although Lord Mar had planned in March to move to 'some distant part of France', in April he took instead a house at Fontainebleau for the summer (Folkstone Williams, *Mem. and Corr. of Francis Atterbury*, 1869, ii. 79, 124).

[3] Newspapers reported that the Duke of Wharton—LM used 'Sophia' as his cipher the year before—had gone to Aix-la-Chapelle 'to use the Waters' (*Daily Journal*, 19 June 1725). He never returned to England.

persecutions I have endur'd from her this Winter, in all which I remain Neuter, and shall certainly go to Heaven from the passive meekness of my temper. Lady Lansdown is in that sort of figure here no body cares to appear with her.[1] Madame Villette has been the Favourite of the Town, and by a natural Transition is become the aversion.[2] She has now no body attach'd to her suitte but the vivacious Lord Bathurst, with whom I have been well and ill ten times within this two months; we now hardly speak to one another.[3]

I wish you would lay out part of my Money in a made up Mantua and petticoat of Rat de St. Maur. It will be no trouble to you to send a thing of that nature by the first travelling Lady.

I give you many thanks for the good offices you promise me with regard to Mrs. Murray, and I shall think my selfe sincerely oblig'd to you, as I allready am on many accounts. Tis very disagreable in her to go about behaving and talking as she does, and very silly into the Bargain. I am ever affectionately Yours.

Text Bute MS

To Lady Mar [*July 1725*]

I am now at the same distance from London that you are from Paris, and could fall into solitary Amusements with a good deal of Taste, but I resist it as a Temptation of Satan, and rather turn my Endeavors to make the World as agreable to me as I can, which is the true Philosophy; that of despising it is of no use but to hasten wrinkles. I ride a good deal,

[1] Lady Lansdown had arrived from Paris in May of the previous year (*Daily Journal*, 22 May 1724). For Mrs. Delany's opinion of her character, see below, p. 81, n. 1.

[2] Marie Claire des Champs (1675–1750), widow of the marquis de Villette, m. (1720) the attainted Viscount Bolingbroke, who had fled to France after the failure of the 1715 Jacobite rebellion.

She had been in England since May 1724 (*Daily Journal*, 25 May 1724). At Court she displeased the King by talking too much and disrespectfully (GEC *Peerage sub* Bolingbroke).

[3] Allen Bathurst (1684–1775), 1st Baron, was a friend of Bolingbroke and of Pope. Five years later Bathurst characterized himself as an unchangeable admirer of LM's (Pope, *Corr.* iii. 134).

and have got a Horse superior to any two legg'd animal, he being without a fault.[1] I work like an angel, I receive visits upon Idle days, and shade my Life as I do my Tent stitch,[2] that is, make as easy Transitions as I can from Busyness to Pleasure. The one would be too flaring and gaudy without some dark Shades of 'tother, and if I work'd all together in the grave Colours, you know 'twould be quite Dismal. Miss Skerret is in the house with me, and Lady Stafford has taken a Lodging at Richmond. As their ages are different and both agreable in their kind, I laugh with one or reason with 'tother as I happen to be in a gay or serious humour,[3] and I mannage my Freinds with such a strong yet with a gentle hand that they are both willing to do whatever I've a mind to.

My daughter presents her duty to you, and service to Lady Francesse, who is growing to Womanhood a pace. I long to see her and you, and am not destitute of wandering designs to that Purpose.

Text Bute MS   *Address* A Madme Madme de Mar

To Lady Mar [*Aug. 1725*]

Dear Sister,

I think this is the first time of my Life that a Letter of yours has lain by me 2 posts unanswer'd. You'l wonder to hear that short silence is occasion'd by not having a moment unemploy'd at Twictnam, but I pass many hours on Horse-back, and I'll assure you ride stag hunting, which I know you stare to hear of. I have arriv'd to vast courrage and skill that way, and am as well pleas'd with it as with the Acquisition of a new sense. His Royal Highness hunts in Richmond Park, and I make one of the Beau monde in his Train.[4] I

---

[1] 'As to your Manner of living at Twickenham,' Lord Hervey wrote, 'I entirely disapprove it; Nature never design'd you to perform the offices of a Groom and a Nursery-Maid' (28 Oct. [1727], MS at Victoria Art Gallery, Bath).

[2] Embroidery done on a frame.

[3] In Lady Hervey's opinion, Lady Stafford 'had as much humour and as much good sense as I ever met with in any creature' (*Letters*, 1821, p. 179).

[4] At the beginning of June the Prince and Princess of Wales had moved to Richmond for the summer (*Daily Journal*, 8 June 1725).

desire you after this Account not to name the Word old Woman to me any more; I approach to 15 nearer than I did 10 year ago, and am in hopes to improve ev'ry year in Health and Vivacity. Lord Bolingbroke is return'd to England[1] and is to do the Honnours at an assembly at Lord Berkeley's[2] the ensuing Winter, but the most surprizing News is Lord Bathurst's assiduous Court to their Royal Highnesses,[3] which fills the Coffee houses with profound Speculations. But I, who smell a Rat at a considerable Distance, do beleive in private that Mrs. Howard and his Lordship have a Freindship that borders upon the Tender.

> 'And tho in Historys, learn'd Ignorance
> 'Attributes all to Cunning or to chance,
> 'Love in that Grave Disguise does often smile,
> 'Knowing the cause was kindness all the while.'[4]

I am in hopes your King of France behaves better than our Duke of Bedford, who by the care of a pious Mother certainly preserv'd his Virginity to his marriage bed, where he was so much disapointed in his fair Bride (who thô his own Inclination could not bestow on him those expressless Raptures he had figur'd to himselfe) that he allready Pukes at the very name of her, and determines to let his Estate go to his Brother, rather than go through the filthy Drudgery of getting an Heir to it.[5] N.B. This is true History

[1] Henry St. John (1678–1751), 1st Viscount Bolingbroke. Although partially pardoned in 1723, he hoped to have all his rights and privileges restored. On 5 May 1725 the House of Commons passed a bill allowing him to own property in England but not to sit in either House (Rich. Chandler, *Hist. and Proc. of the H. of C.*, 1742–4, vi. 344–5). On 29 May newspapers announced that he had arrived incognito from Paris (*London Journal*).

[2] James Berkeley (d. 1736), 3rd Earl, First Lord of the Admiralty, had zealously espoused Bolingbroke's cause. He was dismissed by Sir Robert Walpole in 1727.

[3] A newspaper reported, on 14 Aug. 1725, that he had 'been lately to pay his Court to his Royal Highness at Rich-

mond, and was received with particular Marks of Esteem' (*Mist's Weekly Journal*).

[4] On occasion Bathurst, unaccompanied by his wife, visited Mrs. Howard at Marble Hill, her house at Twickenham (Pope, *Corr.* ii. 298–9). When Walpole annotated this passage he wrote that their friendship was 'merely political'; (*Corr.* xxxiv. 259). The verse is from John Sheffield, Duke of Buckingham's 'The Rapture', *Works*, 1726, p. 95.

[5] Louis XV m. (5 Sept. 25 Aug. 1725) Marie Leszczynska, da. of the King of Poland. After the marriage the bride's father was informed, 'le mari a donné pendant la nuit à sa femme sept preuves de sa tendresse' (Pierre Richard, *La Vie privée de Louis XV*, 1954, pp. 54–55).

Wriothesley Russell (1708–32), 3rd

and I think the most extrodinary has happen'd in this last age. This comes of living till sixteen without a competent knowledge either of practical or speculative Anatomy, and litterally thinking fine Ladys compos'd of Lillys and Roses. A propos of the best red and white to be had for money, Lady Harvey is more Delightfull than ever, and such a Politician that if people were not blind to Merit she would govern the Nation. Mrs. Murray has got a new Lover of the most accomplish'd Mr. Doddington.—So far for the progress of Love. That of Wit has taken a very odd Course and is making the Tour of Ireland, from whence we have pacquets of Ballads, songs, petitions, panegyricks etc. So powerfull is the Influence of Lord Carteret's Wit and my Lady's Beauty,[1] the Irish Rhime that never Rhime'd before.[2]

Adeiu, Dear Sister. I take a sincere part in all that relates to you, and am ever yours. I beg as the last favour that you would make some small Enquiry and let me know the minute Lord Finch[3] is at Paris.

Text Bute MS   *Address* A Madme Madame de Mar

To Lady Mar [*Sept. 1725*]

I writ to you very lately (my dear Sister) but ridiculous things happening, I cannot help (as far as in me lies) sharing all my Pleasures with you. I own I enjoy vast delight in the Folly of Mankind, and God be prais'd that is an inexhaustible Source of Entertainment. You may remember I mention'd in my last some Suspicions of my own in Relation to

Duke of Bedford, m. (April 1725) Anne Egerton (d. 1762), da. of 1st Duke of Bridgewater. They had no children; and he was succeeded by his brother John (1710–71). Their 'pious Mother': Elizabeth Howland (1682–1724), m. (1695) 2nd Duke of Bedford.

[1] John (1690–1763), 2nd Baron Carteret, later Earl Granville, Lord Lieutenant of Ireland 1724–30, m. (1710) Frances (1694–1743), da. of Sir Robert Worsley. He was handsome, learned, and witty; she was musical, exceedingly

beautiful, and agreeable. Walpole described her as 'very handsome, but an idiot' (*Corr.* xxxiv. 259).

[2] In Dublin and London, the publication in June 1725 of Ambrose Philips's poems stimulated many clever parodies, nearly all of them coarse (Philips, *Poems*, ed. M. G. Segar, 1937, pp. xlv, 181–2). Philips was in Ireland as secretary to the Archbishop of Armagh, and in his verse celebrated Carteret's young daughters, among others.

[3] Daniel, later 8th Earl of Winchilsea.

[Lord] Bat[hurst], which I realy never mention'd (for 50 reasons) to any one what ever, but as there is never smoke without some Fire, there is very rarely Fire without some smoke. These smother'd Flames (thô admirably cover'd, with whole heaps of Politics laid over 'em) were at length seen, felt, heard and understood, and the Fair Lady given to understand by her Commanding Officer that if she serv'd under other Colours she must expect to have her pay re-trench'd, upon which the Good Lord was dismiss'd, and has not attended in the drawing room since.[1] You know one cannot help laughing when one sees him next, and I own I long for that pleasurable moment.

I am sorry for another of our Acquaintance whose follys (for it is not possible to avoid that word) are not of a kind to give Mirth to those that wish her well. The discreet and sober Lady Lechmere[2] has lost such Furious summs at the Bath that 'tis question'd whether all the sweetness that the Waters can put into my Lord's blood can make him endure it,[3] particularly £700 at one sitting, which is aggravated with many astonishing Circumstances. This is as odd to me as Lord Tenham's shooting himselfe, and another Demonstration of the latent Fire that lyes under cold Countenances. We wild Girls allways make your prudent Wives and mothers.

I hear some near Relations of ours are at Paris who I think you are not acquainted with. I mean Lord Denbeigh and his Dutch Lady, who I am very certain is the Produce of some French Valet-de-chambre. She is entertaining enough

——extreamly Gay,
Loves Music, Company and play.[4]

I suppose you'l see her.

Text Bute MS   *Address* A Madme Madme de Mar

[1] From about the middle of Sept. Bathurst spent more than a month on a 'Northern Expedition' of visiting, as far as Castle Howard near York (*Wentworth Papers 1705–1739*, ed. J. J. Cartwright, 1883, p. 455).

[2] Elizabeth Howard (d. 1739), da. of 3rd Earl of Carlisle, m. (1718) Nicholas Lechmere, later 1st Baron.

[3] Lechmere arrived in Bath at the end of Aug. (*Mist's Weekly Journal*, cited 1861, i. 491, n. 2).

[4] William Feilding (1697–1755), 5th Earl of Denbigh, LM's 1st cousin, m. (c. 1718) Isabella (1693–1769), da. of Peter de Jonge, burgomaster of Utrecht. She was a clever and entertaining woman, as her letters show (HMC *Denbigh MSS*, v, 1911, pp. 116–69). Verse from Prior, 'Hans Carvel' (*Works*, i. 184).

From Henrietta, Duchess of Marlborough [*1725*]

I am sure you wont dislike to have Mr. Congreve tomorrow, if you can get him, for he is like all good things, hard to come at. And 'tho I shant add to the Company, I have witt enough not to Spoyle it, which, you must allow, is being tolarable. What hour woud you have me come?

Text W MS iv. 185–6   *Address* To Lady Mary Wortly Montague. *End. by W* Henrietta Ds of Marborough

To Lady Mar [*c. 3 Feb. 1726*]

It is very true, dear Sister, that if I writ to you a full account of all that passes, my Letters would be both frequent and volumnious [*sic*]. This sinfull Town is very populous, and my own affairs very much in a Hurry, but the same things that afford me much matter give me very little time, and I am hardly at Leisure to make observations, much less to write them down. But the melancholy Catastrophe of poor Lady Lechmere is too extrodinary not [to] attract the attention of ev'ry body. After having play'd away her Reputation and fortune, she has poison'd her selfe—this is the Effect of prudence![1] All Indiscreet people live and flourish. Mrs. Murray has retreiv'd his Grace,[2] and being reconcil'd to the Temporal, has renounce'd the Spiritual. Her Freind Lady Harvey by aiming too high[3] has falln very low, and is reduce'd

---

[1] Lady Lechmere had piled up gambling debts estimated at £5,000 and £10,000, and her husband refused to pay more than he was compelled to. Her attempted suicide was the talk of London early in Feb. 1726 (HMC *Portland MSS*, vii, 1901, pp. 421–2). Walpole's annotation is succinct: 'She took laudanum, but told it immediately, and was saved by a vomit' (*Corr.* xxxiv. 259).
[2] In *Virtue in Danger*, the ballad about the attempted rape by a footman (see above, p. 14, n. 1), the fifth stanza describes Mrs. Murray asleep:

While the poor Lady, nothing dreamt, Or, dreamt it was His Grace.

When Walpole read this in his copy of *Additions to Pope*, 1776, i. 177, he named the 'Duke of Athol' (*Huntington Library Quarterly*, i, 1938, p. 482). If accurate, he supports LM's remark; he points to James Murray (1690–1764), 2nd Duke of Atholl.

[3] Walpole's comment, when he read this letter, was: 'George I made love to her, but she certainly did not yield' (*Corr.* xxxiv. 259).

to trying to persuade folks she has an Intrigue, and gets no body to beleive her, the man in Question taking a great deal of pains to clear him selfe of the scandal.[1] Her Chelsea Grace of Rutland is marry'd to an attorney;[2] there's prudence for you![3] 'Tis a strange thing that Women can't converse with a Lawyer, a parson, nor a man midwife without putting them all to the same use, as if one could not sign a deed, say one's prayers, or take physic without doing you know what after it. This Instinct is so odd, I am sometimes apt to think we were made to no other end. If that's true, Lord ha' mercy upon me; to be sure, I shall broil in the next world for living in the neglect of a known duty in this.

Text Bute MS   *Address* A Madme Madme de Mar

From Jean-Baptiste Rousseau[4] *23/12 Feb. 1726*

A Brusselles, le 23 fevrier 1726

Il est vrai, Madame, que j'ai profité le plus qu'il m'a esté possible du hasard qui m'a fait trouver ici une amie digne de Vous. Personne ne se connoît mieux en merite que Madame de Cantillon,[5] et il seroit bien difficile que le Votre echapât aux conversations qu'on a avec elle. Je ne puis païer d'assez de reconnoissance la bonté qu'elle a eüe de ne

---

[1] According to Charles Hanbury Williams, Lady Hervey was 'Incapable of love . . . . Her total, real indifference to mankind has hindered her ever having a lover' (Hervey, *Memoirs*, i. xvii).

[2] Lucy (1685–1751), widow of 2nd Duke of Rutland, lived in Chelsea (*Wentworth Papers 1712–1739*, ed. J. J. Cartwright, 1883, p. 499). A correspondent of Lord Oxford, passing on the same gossip, named the attorney: '. . . Mr. P. Walters is to be married to the Duchess Dowager of Rutland. . . .' (1 Feb. 1726, HMC *Portland MSS*, vi, 1901, p. 10). Peter Walters (1662–1745), eminent as a usurer, acquired an immense fortune. The rumoured marriage did not take place.

[3] In previous editions the letter ends here.

[4] French poet (1671–1741). Banished from France for his libellous satires, he lived in Vienna from 1715 to 1722, as Prince Eugene's secretary. LM met him there on her journey to Constantinople in 1716. (Pope wrote to her 'By what I have seen of Mons. Rousseau's Works, I should envy you his conversation': *Corr.* i. 385). From Adrianople she corresponded with him through the French Ambassador (23 April 1717, Ministère des Affaires Étrangères, Constantinople, vol. 57, f. 154). Rousseau visited England for about six months in 1723 (Henry A. Grubbs, *Jean-Baptiste Rousseau*, 1941, pp. 153–5), and LM no doubt saw him there. She owned a copy of his *Œuvres* (1712), now in Lord Harrowby's collection.

[5] See above, p. 25.

point m'oublier et de vous faire souvenir des sentimens de respect et d'admiration que j'ai conservez pour vous. J'ai pensé perdre, depuis votre lettre venüe, le seul ami de ce Païs ci qui les partage avec moi; le Duc d'Aremberg[1] a esté attaqué Dimanche passé d'une pleuresie qui a mis sa vie en danger. Il est beaucoup mieux depuis hier, et je suis chargé de vous assurer de sa part que personne ne vous honore autant que lui.

Les changemens arrivez en votre Cour n'ont rien qui me surprenne, et ne m'affligeroient même que mediocrement si j'estois sur que mes Amis scaissent faire un bon usage de ce que le vulgaire appelle disgrace.[2] Deplacer un Courtisan de son poste est lui rendre la liberté, et il me semble que quand on a païé son tribut au Public et établi suffisament sa fortune et sa reputation, on ne devroit plus songer qu'a jouïr en paix du fruit de ses peines et a se reposer sur ses trophées. Pour moi, je regarde les hommes en faveur comme les Lacedemoniens regardoient les gens Grecs, et a les bien examiner la pluspart sont plus dignez de pitié que d'envie. On nous fait esperer que la Faustina[3] passera par ici ce Carême avant de se rendre a Londres. Je suis persuadé qu'elle reveillera le goût des Anglois pour l'opera. On parle de grands changemens a la Cour de France.[4] Votre Spectateur auroit de quoi s'exercer si les manieres de politique estoient de son ressort comme celles de morale.

Adieu, Madame; si vous conservez quelque pitié pour un homme qui se trouve exilé partout ou vous n'estes pas, daignez me donner quelque fois des nouvelles de votre santé et de celle de vostre charmante amie, que je prens la liberté de saluer ici. Personne au monde n'est avec autant de respect que je le suis, Madame, Votre tres humble et tres obéissant Serviteur,

Rousseau.[5]

Text W MS iv. 235–6   *End. by* W Mr Ruisseau

[1] Léopold de Ligne (1690–1754), duc d'Aremberg, a Marshal in the Imperial Army, and described by Saint-Simon as 'un des plus grands seigneurs de Flandres' (*Mémoires*, ed. G. Truc, 1954–61, vi. 414). His patronage may have been a reason for Rousseau's decision to settle in Brussels in the spring of 1725, when he took a lodging near the Hôtel d'Aremberg (Grubbs, pp. 163, 167).

[2] After William Pulteney was dismissed by Walpole in 1725, he became the active head of the Opposition. Other disgruntled politicians joined the growing but unsuccessful faction.

[3] Faustina Bordoni (1700–81), a leading *prima donna*. She was 'discovered' by Handel in Vienna and brought to London, where she made her début in his *Alessandro* on 5 May 1726. Hervey compared her gift for singing with LM's for writing (to LM, 12 Oct. [N.S., 1729], Bristol MS ii. 37).

[4] See below, p. 66, n. 3.

[5] Translated in Appendix I below.

From Edward Young *1 March 1726*

Madam,

I have seen Mr. Savage, who is exstreamly sensible of the Honour your Ladyship did him by me.[1] You was I find too modest in your opinion of the present you pleasd to make him, if Mr. Savage may be allowd to be a judge in the case.[2] I'm obligd to go down tomorrow to *Wicomb Election* which is on Thursday.[3] As soon as I return I will wait on your Ladyship with the trifle you pleasd to ask, which I had done before but I have been and still am in all the uneasiness a Cold can give. I am, Madam, with great esteem, Your Ladyship's most Obedient and Obligd Humble Servant,

                                                               E. Young.

March the 1st 1725/6.

Text MS owned by Professor Ralph M. Williams

To Lady Mar 7 *March* [*1726*]

                                                    March 7, O.S.

Dear Sister,

This Letter will be in a very different style from that which I hope you receiv'd last post. I have now to tell you the surprizing Death of my Father,[4] and a great deal of surprizing management of the people about him, which I leave

[1] In Feb. 1726 Richard Savage (d. 1743) dedicated to LM his *Miscellaneous Poems* (Clarence Tracy, *The Artificial Bastard: Savage*, 1953, p. 76). His fulsome dedication, besides praising her person, soul, wit, and verses, states that he did not have the honour to be known to her; it was probably Young who made the arrangement. Dr. Johnson's opinion of this dedication was that Savage 'flatters without reserve, and, to confess the truth, with very little art' (*Lives of the Poets*, ed. G. B. Hill, 1905, ii. 343). Savage showed his gratitude more disinterestedly in his poem *The Wanderer* (1729), where he praises 'Fair *Wortley*'s angel-Accent, Eyes, and

Mind' (v. 72).

[2] The customary fee for a dedication was 20 guineas (Swift, *Corr.*, ed. H. Williams, 1963–5, iii. 267). Perhaps LM gave more.

[3] Young was to be at the Wycombe election on 3 March as chaplain to George Bubb Dodington, who was managing it for Walpole; and for this political service Young was rewarded in May with a pension of £200 (C. E. Crawford in *Mod. Lang. Notes*, lx, 1945, pp. 459–61; Richard E. Tickell, *Thomas Tickell*, 1931, p. 123).

[4] The Duke of Kingston died 5 March 1726 at his house in Arlington Street.

informing you till another time, being now under some Hurry of Spirits my selfe. I am unfeignedly sorry that I cannot send word of a considerable Legacy for your selfe.[1] I suppose the Trustees[2] will as soon as possible send you a Copy of the Will. If you would have an abstract of it, Mr. Wortley will take care to get it for you.

I am affectionately Yours.

Text Bute MS   *Address* A Madme Madme de Mar

From Lady Gower[3] to Lady Mar *15 April* [*1726*]

London, Ap'l 15

Dear Sister,

I wou'd have writ to you some time ago, but Lord Erskine[4] told me you had been ill, so my Lord Mar had not acquanted you with my poor Father's Death. To be sure, the Shock must be very great to you when ever you heard it, as indeed t'was to us all here, being so sudden. Tis to no purpose now to relate particulers but only renewing our greif. I can't forbare telling you the Du[che]ss has behaved very oddly in indeavouring to get the Gairdianship of the young Duke and his sister, contaray to her Husband's Will,[5] but the boy when he was 14[6] confermed the trustees his Grandfather left, so that ended all disputes, and Lady Fanny is to Live with my Aunt Cheyne. There is a vast number of things that has happend, and some people's behaveier so extrodenary in this malencholy business that t'wou'd be great eaise of

---

[1] Lady Mar and her heirs were bequeathed the income of the Duke's estates in Lincolnshire, with several stipulations including one that they reside in England. The Duke's will, drawn in 1725, is P.C.C. Romney, f. 90; a copy is Eg MS 3531. (In both will and copy Lady Mar is misnamed Catherine.)

[2] The Duke's brother-in-law, William (1657–1728), 2nd Lord Cheyne; John Monson (1693–1748), later 1st Baron; and Thomas Bennett or Bennet, probably the Master of the High Court of Chancery who d. 1764 (*London Mag.*, p. 382).

[3] Although this letter has always been printed as LM's, it is not in her

hand, style, or spelling. On the MS is a note by Lady Louisa Stuart: 'Is it not Lady Gower's [writing]?' And the editor of the HMC *Fifth Report* (1876, p. 620) lists the MS letter as 'apparently from Lady Gower'.

[4] Thomas, Lord Erskine (1707–66), Lady Mar's stepson.

[5] Although the Duke's will appointed his wife guardian of their two young daughters, he recommended to his 'said Executors and Trustees to take Care of the Education' of his grandson and successor and of his granddaughter Lady Frances Pierrepont (1713–95).

[6] On 3 April 1726.

mind if I could tell it you, but I must not venter to speak too freely in a letter.

Pray let me hear from you soon, for I long to know how you do. I am but in an uneasey way my self, for I've been confined this fourteenight to one flouir after my useiall maner.[1] I can send you no news, for I see very few people and have hardly been any where since I came to Town. Adieu.

Text Bute MS   *Address* To the Countess of Mar

To Lady Mar [*22 April 1726*]

I receiv'd Yours, dear sister, this minute, and I am very sorry both for your past illness and affliction, thô au bout de compte, I don't know why filial piety should exceed fatherly fondness. So much by way of Consolation. As to the management at that time, I do verily beleive if my good Aunt and Sister had been less fools and my dear Mother-in-law[2] less mercenary, things might have had a turn more to your advantage, and mine too.[3] When we meet I will tell you many Circumstances, which would be tedious in a Letter. I could not get my Sister Gower to joyn to act with me, and Mama and I were in an actual scold when my poor Father expir'd.[4] She has shewn a hardness of Heart upon this Occasion that would appear incredible to any body not capable of it themselves. The addition to her joynture is (one way or other) £2,000 per annum, so Her good Grace remains a passable rich Widow,[5] and is allready presented by the Town with variety of young Husbands, but I beleive her constitution is not good enough to let her Amorous Inclinations get the better of her Covetous.

Mrs. Murray is in open Wars with me, in such a manner

[1] Lady Gower, who bred regularly, bore a son, Richard Leveson-Gower (d. 1753), on 30 April 1726 (Collins, ii. 449).

[2] Lady Cheyne, Lady Gower, and the widowed Duchess of Kingston.

[3] LM was left, besides £200 for mourning clothes, £6,000 in trust, which yielded £300 a year; and the principal was to go, after her death, to her daughter. For the later history of the legacy, see below, p. 117, n. 1.

[4] The Duke died at about five o'clock in the afternoon (Eg MS 3531).

[5] Her jointure, according to the trustees' accounts, actually came to about £3,800 a year (MS El 10638, 10667, Huntington Library).

as makes her very ridiculous without doing me much harm,[1] my moderation having a very bright pretence of shewing it selfe. Firstly she was pleas'd to attack me in very Billingsgate language at a Masquerade, where she was as visible as ever she was in her own Cloaths. I had the temper not only to keep Silence my selfe, but enjoyn'd it to the person with me, who would have been very glad to have shown his great skill in souseing upon that occasion. She endeavor'd to sweeten him by very exorbitant praises of his person, which might even have been mistaken for making Love from a Woman of less celebrated virtue, and concluded her Oration with pious Warnings to him to avoid the conversation of one so unworthy his regard as my selfe, who to her certain knowledge lov'd another man. This last Article, I own, pique'd me more than all her preceding Civilitys. The Gentleman she address'd her selfe to had a very slight acquaintance with me, and might possibly go away in the opinion that she had been confidante in some very notorious affair of mine. However, I made her no answer at that Time, but you may imagine I laid up these things in my Heart; and the first assembly I had the honour to meet her at, with a meek tone of voice ask'd her how I had deserv'd so much abuse at her hands, which I assur'd her I would never return. She deny'd it in the spirit of Lying, and in the spirit of folly own'd it at length. I contented my selfe with telling her she was very ill advis'd, and thus we parted.

But 2 days ago, when Sir G[odfrey] K[neller]'s pictures were to be sold, she went to my Sister Gower and very civilly ask'd if she intended to bid for your picture, assuring her that if she did, she would not offer at purchasing it.[2] You know Crimp and Quadrille incapacitate that poor Soul from ever buying any thing. But she told me this circumstance, and I expected the same civility from Mrs. Murray, having

[1] Mrs. Murray suspected LM of being the author of the embarrassing ballad *Virtue in Danger* (see above, p. 14, n. 1).

[2] When Kneller died, in Nov. 1723, he left some 800 unfinished pictures, which his assistant Edward Byng completed and sold in conjunction with Lady Kneller (Lord Killanin, *Sir Godfrey Kneller*, 1948, p. 30). A three-day sale of those not claimed began on 18 April; lot 339, the portrait of Lady Mar, was sold on the 20th (*A Catalogue of all the Remaining Works of the Late Sir Godfrey Kneller, Bart . . .*, 1726). Kneller had painted an earlier portrait of Lady Mar, in 1715 (Killanin, p. 88).

no way provok'd her to the contrary. But she not only came to the Auction, but with all possible spite bid up the picture thô I told her that if you pleas'd to have it I would gladly part with it to you, thô to no other person. This had no effect upon her, nor her Malice any more on me than the loss of ten guineas extrodinary which I paid upon her Account. The picture is in my possession, and at your service if you please to have it. She went to the masquerade a few nights afterwards, and had the good sense to tell people there that she was very unhappy in not meeting me, being come there on purpose to abuse me. What profit or pleasure she has in these ways I cannot find out. This I know, that Revenge has so few joys for me, I shall never lose so much time as to undertake it.

Text Bute MS   *Address* A Madame Madame de Mar

To Lady Mar [*May 1726*]

All I had to say to you was that my F[ather] realy express'd a great deal of kindness to me at last, and even ⟨?⟩ desire of talking to me, which my Lady Dutchess would not permit, nor my Aunt and Sister shew any thing but a servile complaisance to her. This is the abstract of what you desire to know, and is now quite useless. —Tis over and better to be forgot than remember'd. The Duke of Kingston has hitherto had so ill an Education tis hard to make any Judgment of him. He has Spirit but I fear will never have his father's good Sense. As young Noblemen go, tis possible he may make a good figure amongst them.

Wars and rumours of Wars make all the conversation at present.[1] The tumbling of the stocks one way or other influences most people's affairs.[2] For my own part, I have no concern there or any where but hearty prayers that what relates to my selfe may ever be exactly as it is now. The

---

[1] The breach between England and Spain made war seem imminent.

[2] The market had begun to fall in March; on the 22nd Pope wrote to Lord Oxford, 'We shall all be undone in the Stocks' (*Corr.* ii. 372).

Mutability of Sublunary things is the only melancholy Refflection I have to make on my own Account. I am in perfect
Health and hear it said I look better than ever I did in my
Life, which is one of those Lyes one is allways glad to hear.
However, in this dear minute, in this golden Now, I am
tenderly touch'd at your Misfortunes, and can never call
my selfe quite happy till you are so.

My Daughter makes her complements to yours, but has
not yet receiv'd the Letter Lord Areskine[1] said he had for
her.

Adieu, Dearest Sister.

Text Bute MS   *Address* A Madme Madame de Mar

To Lady Mar [*June 1726*]

Dear Sister,

I cannot possitively fix a time for my waiting on you at
Paris, but I do verily beleive I shall make a trip thither
sooner or later. This Town improves in Gaity ev'ry day. The
young people are younger than they us'd to be, and all the
Old are grown Young. Nothing is talk'd of but Entertainments of Galantry by Land and Water, and we insensibly
begin to taste all the Joys of Arbitrary Power. Politics are no
more; no body pretends to wince or Kick under their Burdens,
but we go on cheerfully with our Bells at our Ears, orna-
mented with Ribands and highly contented with our present condition.

So much for the general state of the Nation.—The last
pleasure that fell in my way was Madam Sevigny's Letters;[2]
very pretty they are, but I assert without the least vanity that
mine will be full as entertaining 40 years hence. I advise you
therefore to put none of 'em to the use of Wast paper. You
say nothing to me of the change of your Ministry.[3] I thank
you for your silence on that Subject; I don't remember my

---

[1] Lord Erskine, Lady Mar's stepson.
[2] On 1 June they were advertised as
'just imported' (1861, i. 499, n. 1).
[3] The duc de Bourbon was dismissed
on 31 May [O.S.], and replaced by
Louis XV's former tutor, the Abbé
Fleury.

selfe ever child enough to be concern'd who reign'd in any part of the Earth. I am more touch'd at the Death of poor Miss Chiswell, who is carry'd off by the Small Pox.[1] I am so oddly made that I never forget the tendernesses contracted in my Infancy, and I think of my past play fellow with a concern that few people feel for their present favourites. After giving you Melancholy by this Tragedy, tis but reasonable I should conclude with a farce, that I may not leave you in ill humour. I have so good an Opinion of your taste to beleive Arlequin in person will never make you laugh so much as the Earl of Stairs's furious passion for Lady Walpole, aged 14 and some months.[2] Mrs. Murry undertook to bring the busyness to bear, and provided the oppertunity (a great Ingredient you'l say), but the young Lady prov'd skittish. She did not only turn this Heroic Flame into present ridicule, but expos'd all his generous Sentiments to divert her Husband and Father-in-law. His Lordship is gone to Scotland;[3] and if there was any body wicked enough to write upon it, Here is a subject worthy the pen of the best Ballad maker in Grubstreet.

Text Bute MS

From Jean-Baptiste Rousseau 6 *July*/25 *June 1726*

A Brusselles, le 6 Juillet 1726.

Rien n'est plus humiliant pour moi, Madame, que la modestie avec laquelle vous me parlez de vous, et si j'estois homme a me piquer d'ecrire de belles lettres, je serois confondu par le peu de cas que vous paroissez faire des votres. Mais qu'arriveroit-il dela? Je ne vous ecrirois plus et par consequent point de reponse, et alors il faudroit bientost retomber dans la létargie d'ou vous m'avez retiré. Que Dieu m'a fait une belle grace de me guerir de la Vanité, et de l'entestement

[1] Sarah Chiswell was LM's friend in Nottingham to whom she had addressed the Embassy letter on inoculation (i. 337–40).

[2] Margaret Rolle (1709–81), a great heiress, m. (1724) Sir Robert Walpole's eldest son, Robert (*c.* 1701–51), Baron Walpole. She was actually aged 17 and some months. Her gallantries in later years were commented on by LM and more sharply by her unloving brother-in-law Horace.

[3] Stair, who had been in London since Jan., left for his seat in Scotland on or shortly before 4 June (*London Journal*).

du bel esprit! Il y a longtems que je n'y pretens plus, mais je pretens encore un peu au merite du discernement, et sur ce pied la vous me permettrez, s'il vous plaist, Madame, de vous admirer toujours quelque chose que vous fassiez pour me séduire. Ma foi est inebranlable, et Je persisterai dans ma Religion jusqu'au martyre inclusivement.

Je comprens en quel sens vous estes si indifferente pour les nouvelles qui font l'attention du commun des hommes. Quand les Rois faisoient des folies, les Grecs qui en portoient la peine avoient raison de s'en inquieter. Pour nous a qui elles ne font ni chaud ni froid, nous aurions grand tort de nous couroucer contre un Spectacle qui n'est fait que pour notre amusement. L'allusion du Chevalier Falstaff, que Je me suis fait expliquer, ⟨?⟩ me fait connoitre le bon usage que vous savez en faire, et Je suis persuadé que c'est sur ce pied la que vous considerez toutes les autres Pieces de Theatre qui se representent dans les differentes cours de la partie du monde que nous habitons.

La sagesse y perdroit trop si tout le monde estoit sage. L'extravagance est son aliment et les fous sont ses pourvoïeurs. L'evaporation et la tristesse sont deux extremitez qui lui sont egalement opposées, et je ne saurois mieux vous prouver cette verité, Madame, que par le petit apologue avec lequel Je vais finir cette lettre.

La Folie, s'estant mise en teste de voïager, partit un jour de France et vint aborder en Angleterre. Elle y trouva le Bon Sens, et l'etonnement que leur causa une rencontre si nouvelle pour eux fut suivi d'une curiosité qui les porta a lier connoissance. Ils ne furent pas longtems sans s'appercevoir que chacun d'eux avoit un merite qui manquoit a l'autre. Les voila unis d'une amitié qui reconvertit bientost en amour. Ils se marient; et de cette Alliance, plus raisonable que celle d'Hanover,[1] naquit la Sagesse, dont la perfection consiste dans la reünion des bonnes qualitez du Pere et de la mere, qui, melangées selon les regles d'une proportion discrete, forment en elle cette raison enjoüée qui fait les veritables Philosophes.

Monsieur le Duc d'Aremberg part dans cinq ou six jours pour Paris, ou il voudroit fort que vous fussiez encore Ambassadrice. Pour moi, Madame, Je ne souhaite rien tant au monde que de pouvoir vous convaincre du respectueux attachement avec lequel Je vous suis devoüé pour jamais.

Text W MS iv. 237–8   *End. by W* Mr Ruisseau

[1] The Treaty of Hanover, on 3 Sept. 1725, between England, France, and Prussia.

To Lady Mar [*c. 15 July 1726*]

Dear Sister,

I am very glad to hear you mention meeting at London. We are much mistaken here as to our Ideas of Paris; to hear Galantry has deserted it sounds as extrodinary to me as a want of Ice in Green land. We have nothing but ugly faces in this Country, but more Lovers than ever. There is but three pretty Men in England and they are all in love with me at this present writeing. This will amaze you extreamly, but if you were to see the reigning Girls at present, I'll assure you there is very little difference between them and old Women.

I have been embourbé in Family affairs for this last fortnight. Lady F. Pierrepont having £400 per annum for her maintenance has awaken'd the consciences of halfe her Relations to take care of her Education, and (excepting my selfe) they have all been squabbling about her, and squabble to this day.[1] My Sister Gower carrys her off to morrow morning to Staffordshire.[2] The Lyes, Twattles, and contrivances about this affair are innumerable. I should pity the poor Girl if I saw she pity'd her selfe. The Duke of Kingston is in France, but is not to go to your capital.[3] So much for that Branch of

[1] Besides the £400 for Lady Frances's maintenance and education, £200 was allotted for clothes, and £20 for the 'Receiver's salary' (Trustees' minutes, Eg MS 3530, f. 34). On 5 July Thomas Bennett informed his co-trustee John Monson of the squabble about the girl's custody, which he thought might have to be put before the Lord Chancellor; and this, he wrote, was feared by Lady Cheyne, who wanted to assume full charge. 'I hear,' he continued, 'Lady Francis has told some of her friends as a great secret, that she had rather live with Lady Torrington than any of them [her relations]. Lady Mary Wortley has just sent to me to shew me Lady Torrington's Letter in which she sais she will take Lady Francis' (Monson MS, vol. cx). Lady Torrington (d. 1735), widow of 1st Baron, was actually a distant relation,

born Anne Pierrepont (a great-grand-daughter of Robert, 1st Earl of Kingston).

[2] Lady Frances had been staying with Lady Cheyne (her grand-aunt); on 28 June Lord Cheyne applied to Monson for permission to send her to visit Lady Gower at Trentham for the summer (Monson MS, vol. xiv).

[3] The Duke arrived in Boulogne on 11 July O.S. with an entourage of tutor, Peter Platel; physician, Nathan Hickman; and three servants (ibid.). His stay abroad, lasting ten years, is discussed in G. E. Mingay, *English Landed Society in the Eighteenth Century*, 1963, pp. 138–40. Platel's and Hickman's letters to Lord Cheyne are in the Huntington Library (MS El 10824–10858), and those from Hickman to Monson are now among the Monson MS.

your Family. My blessed offspring has allready made a great noise in the World. That young Rake my Son took to his Heels 'tother day and transported his person to Oxford, being in his own opinion thoroughly qualify'd for the university.[1] After a good deal of search we found and reduc'd him much against his Will to the humble condition of a School boy. It happens very luckily that the Sobriety and Discretion is of my Daughter's side. I am sorry the Uglyness is so too, for my Son grows extream handsome.

I don't hear much of Mrs. Murray's dispair on the death of poor Gebby,[2] and I saw her dance at a ball where I was, 2 days before his death. I have a vast many pleasantrys to tell you, and some that would make your Hair stand an end with wonder. Adieu, Dear Sister, conservez moi l'honneur de vostre Amitie, et croyez que je suis toute a vous.

Text Bute MS

From Henrietta, Duchess of Marlborough [? *1726*]

I give you a thousand thanks, Dear Madam, for your plentiful provision; nothing can add to your goodness but letting me see you to morrow Evening. I wou'd wait on you, but will tell you the reason when I have the Honour to see you, which is allways a most inexpressible pleasure to your Ladyship's most obedient.

Sat. Even. 8 a cl.

Forgive this, but you gave me leave, nay commanded. Let me know if I shall be so happy tomorrow.

Text W MS iv. 187–8   *Address* To the Rt Honble the Lady Ma. Wortely.   *End. by W* Hen. Dutchess of Marlborough

[1] Edward Wortley Montagu, junior, was thus beginning his career as an eccentric. After the family's return from Turkey he had been placed in Westminster School, which W had attended. A fictitious account of his earlier escapades and of his activities at Oxford is uncritically included in Jonathan Curling, *Edward Wortley Montagu 1713–1776*, 1954, p. 38.

[2] Gilbert Burnet (d. 17 June 1726), Chaplain to the King since 1718. He had been accused (in 1721) of being Mrs. Murray's lover (see above, p. 14, n. 1)

To Lady Mar [*Nov. 1726*]

I am very sorry (dear Sister) for your ill Health, but hope
it is so entirely past that you have by this Time forgot it. I
never was better in my Life, nor ever past my hours more
agreably. I ride between London and Twictnam perpetually
and have little societies quite to my Taste, and that is saying
every thing. I leave the great World to Girls that know no
better, and do not think one bit the worse of my selfe for
having outliv'd a certain Giddyness which is sometimes
excusable but never pleasing. Depend upon it, tis only the
Spleen that gives you those Ideas; you may have many
delightfull days to come, and there is nothing more silly than
to be too wise to be happy.

> If to be sad is to be wise,
> I do most heartily despise
> Whatever Socrates has said
> Or Tully writ or Montaigne read.

So much for Philosophy—
    What do you say to Pelham's marriage?[1] There's Flame!
there's Constancy! If I could not employ my time better I
would write the History of their Loves in 12 Tomes. Lord
Harvey should dye in her Arms like the poor King of
Assyria; she should be sometimes carry'd off by Troops of
Masques and at other times block'd up in the strong castles
of the Bagnio, but her honour should allways remain Inviolate by the strength of her own virtu and the freindship of
the Enchantress Mrs. Murray, till her happy Nuptials with
her faithfull Cyrus.[2]—Tis a thousand pitys I have not time for
these vivacitys. Here is a book come out, that all our people
of taste run mad about. Tis no less than the united Work of
a dignify'd clergyman, an Eminent Physician, and the first
poet of the Age, and very wonderfull it is, God knows.[3] Great

---

[1] Henry Pelham, possibly Lady
Catherine Manners's lover three years
earlier (see above, p. 24), finally married
her on 17 Oct. 1726. Verse adapted from
Prior's *Alma* (*Works*, i. 516).

[2] Mlle de Scudéry's romance *Arata-*

mène ou le Grand Cyrus in 10 vols.

[3] *Gulliver's Travels* was published
28 Oct. 1726. In June, Edward Young
had made a similar guess as to its authorship: 'Pope, Swift & Arbuthnot are
coming abroad in a triple Alliance of

Eloquence have they employ'd to prove themselves Beasts, and show such a veneration for Horses that since the Essex Quaker no body has appear'd so passionately devoted to that species;[1] and to say truth, they talk of a stable with so much warmth and Affection I can't help suspecting some very powerfull Motive at the bottom of it.

Text Bute MS   *Address* A Madme Madame de Mar

To Lady Mar [*March 1727*]

I am very sorry, dear Sister, that you are in so melancholy a way, but I hope a return to Paris[2] will revive your Spirits. I had much rather have said London, but I do not presume upon so much happyness.

I was last night at the play en famille in the most literal Sense. My Sister Gower dragg'd me thither in Company of all our children with Lady F. Pierrepont at their Head. My 3rd Niece Luson, Jenny by name, will come out an Errant Beauty;[3] she is realy like the Dutchess of Queensborrough. As for news, the last Wedding is that of Peg Pelham, and I have, I think, never seen so comfortable a prospect of Happyness. According to all appearance she can not fail of being a Widow in 6 weeks at farthest, and accordingly she has been so good a Huswife to line her wedding cloaths with black.[4] Assemblys rage in this part of the World. There is not a street in Town free from 'em and some spirited Ladys goe to seven in a Night. You need not question but Love and Play flourish under these encourragments. I now and then peep upon these things with the same coldness I would do

Wit' (Richard E. Tickell, *Thomas Tickell*, 1931, p. 130). John Gay wrote to Swift of the publication: 'From the highest to the lowest it is universally read, from the Cabinet-council to the Nursery' (17 Nov., Swift, *Corr.*, ed. H. Williams, 1963–5, iii. 182).

[1] LM here refers to 'News from Colchester. Or, A Proper new Ballad of certain Carnal Passages betwixt a Quaker and a Colt, at Horsly near Col-chester, in Essex'[1659]by John Denham (*Poems and Translations*, 5th ed., 1709, pp. 105–10).

[2] From Chatton (see below, p. 76), about 90 miles south of Paris.

[3] Jane Leveson-Gower (d. 1737).

[4] Margaret (d. 1758), da. of 1st Baron Pelham, m. (16 March 1727) Sir John Shelley (1692–1771). Since he was only 35 years old, LM may imply that he was ill at this time.

on a moving Picture;[1] I laugh at some of the motions, wonder at others etc., and then retire to the elected Few that have Ears and hear, but mouths they have and speak not. One of these chosen, to my great Sorrow, will soon be at Paris; I mean Lady Stafford, who talks of removing next April. She promises to return, but I had rather she did not go.

Text Bute MS   *Address* A Madame Madame de Mar

To Lady Mar [*April 1727*]

My Lady Stafford set out towards France this morning, and has carry'd halfe the pleasures of my Life along with her. I am more stupid then I can describe, and am as full of moral Refflections as either Cambray or Pascal.[2] I think of nothing but the nothingness of the good things of this world, the Transitoryness of its Joys, the pungency of its sorrows, and many discoverys that have been made this three thousand years and committed to print ever since the first erecting of Presses. I advise you as the best thing you can do that day, let it happen [when] it will, to visit Lady Stafford. She has the goodness to carry with her a trueborn English Woman, who is neither good nor bad nor capable of being either, Lady Phil Prat by name, of the Hamilton Family, and who will be glad of your Acquaintance, and you can never be sorry for hers.[3]

Peace or War, cross or Pile, makes all the conversation.[4] The Town never was fuller, and God be prais'd some people

[1] 'Moving pictures' had been shown in London since at least 1709. Swift attended one in 1713; and from 1716 for more than thirty years a more elaborate kind, synchronized with sound, was being exhibited (*Notes & Queries*, clxxxviii, 1945, pp. 38–39).

[2] Francois de la Mothe Fénelon, Archbishop of Cambrai; Blaise Pascal (1623–62).

[3] Lady Philippa Hamilton (d. 1767), da. of 6th Earl of Abercorn, m. (*c.* 1720) Benjamin Pratt, D.D. She was bitterly satirized by Swift after her elderly husband's death in 1721 ('The Progress of

Marriage', *Poems*, ed. H. Williams, 1937, i. 289–95). In Lady Stafford's opinion, after the two ladies parted company: 'outre qu'elle est sotte comme vous le sçavez, elle est fausse et le contrepied de la raison en toute chose' (to LM, [June 1727], W MS iv. 256).

[4] 'The Dispute about a War or no War still continues', Swift wrote from London on 13 May (*Corr.*, ed. H. Williams, 1963–5, iii. 207). War against Spain, an ally of Austria, was threatened. (Cross and pile means head and tail of a coin.)

brille in it who brille'd 20 years ago. My Cousin Butler[1] is of that Number, who is just what she was in all respects when she inhabited Bond street. The sprouts of this age are such green wither'd things, tis a great comfort to us grown up people. I except my own daughter, who is to be the ornament of the ensuing Court. I beg you would exact from Lady Stafford a particular of her perffections, which would sound suspected from my Hand. At the same time I must do justice to a little twig belonging to my Sister Gower. Miss Jenny is like the Dutchess of Queensbury both in face and spirit. A propos of family affairs, I had allmost forgot our dear and Aimable Cousin Lady Denbiegh,[2] who has blaz'd out all this Winter. She has brought with her from Paris cart loads of Riband, surprizing fashions, and a complexion of the last Edition, which naturally attracts all the she and he fools in London, and accordingly she is surrounded with a little Court of both, and keeps a Sunday Assembly to shew she has learnt to play at cards on that day. Lady F. Fielding is realy the prittyest Woman in Town and has sense enough to make one's heart ake to see her surrounded with such fools as her Relations are.[3]

The Man in England that gives the greatest pleasure and the greatest pain is a Youth of Royal blood, with all his Grandmother's beauty, Wit, and good Qualitys;[4] in short, he is Nell Guin in person with the Sex alter'd, and occasions such fracas amongst the Ladys of Galantry that it passes [belief]. You'l stare to hear of her Grace of Cleveland at the Head of them.[5] If I was poetical I would tell you:

> The God of Love, enrag'd to see
> The Nymph despise his Flame,
> At Dice and cards mispend her Nights
> And slight a nobler Game;

---

[1] Not identified.

[2] Married to LM's cousin, 5th Earl (see above, p. 57).

[3] Youngest sister of 5th Earl of Denbigh, Lady Frances (d. 1734) m. (1729) Daniel Finch, later 8th Earl of Winchilsea.

[4] Lord Sidney Beauclerk (1702–44) was a son of 1st Duke of St. Albans, Charles II's bastard son by Nell Gwyn.

'Very handsome, but no wit' was Walpole's note (*Corr.* xxxiv. 258).

[5] Anne Pulteney (1663–1746) m. (1694) 2nd Duke of Cleveland (1662–1730), another bastard son of Charles II by Barbara Villiers. Since the Duchess was a relation by marriage of Lord Sidney, and their ages were 63 and 25, the comparison to Phaedra and Hippolytus at the end of the letter is apt.

For the Neglect of offers past
And Pride in days of yore,
He kindles up a Fire at last
That burns her at threescore.

A polish'd white is smoothly spread
Where whilom wrinkles lay,
And glowing with an artfull red
She ogles at the Play.

Along the Mall she softly sails
In White and Silver drest,
Her neck expos'd to eastern Gales,
And Jewells on her breast.

Her children banish'd, Age forgot,
Lord Sidney is her care,
And, what is much a happier lot,
Has hopes to be her Heir.

This is all true History thô it is dogrell Rhime. In good
earnest, she has turn'd Lady Grace and Family[1] out o'
doors to make room for him, and there he lies like leafe Gold
upon a pill. There never was so violent and so indiscreet a
passion. Lady Stafford says, nothing was ever like it since
Phedra and Hipolitus.—Lord ha' mercy upon us; see what
we may all come to!

Text Bute MS   *Address* A Madme Madme de Mar

To Lady Mar [*May 1727*]

Dear Sister,
    I writ to you some time ago a Long letter which I per-
ceive never came to your hands—very provokeing—It was
certainly a chef d'œvre of a Letter and worth any of the
Sevigny's or the Grignan's,[2] cramm'd with news; and I can't
find in my heart to say much in this because I beleive there

---

[1] Lady Grace Fitzroy (1697–1763), her daughter, m. (1725) Henry Vane, later 1st Earl of Darlington. They had an infant son, Henry (1726–92).
[2] The previous year LM had read Mme de Sévigné's letters (see above, p. 66). In the very rare 1725 edition, the letters had been preceded by a single short one from her daughter, the comtesse, to comte de Grignan.

is some fault in the direction. As soon as I hear you have receiv'd this, you shall have a full and true account of the affairs of this Island. My own are in the utmost prosperity—

Add but Eternity, you make it Heaven.

I shall come to Paris this summer without fail, and endeavor to pull you out o' your melancholys.

Text Bute MS   *Address* A Madme Madme de Mar a Chatton

To Lady Mar [*May 1727*]

Dear Sister,

I was very glad to hear from you, thô there were some things in your Letters very monstrous and shocking. I wonder with what Conscience you can talk to me of your being an old Woman; I beg I may hear no more on't. For my part I pretend to be as young as ever, and realy am as young as needs to be, to all Intents and purposes. I attribute all this to your living so long at Chatton,¹ and fancy a week at Paris will correct such wild Imaginations and set things in a better light. My cure for lowness of Spirits is not drinking nasty Water but galloping all day, and a moderate Glass of Champaign at Night in good Company; and I beleive this regimen closely follow'd is one of the most wholsom that can be prescrib'd, and may save one a world of filthy doses and more filthy Doctors' fees at the Year's end.

I rid to Twictnam last night, and after so long a stay in Town am not sorry to find my selfe in my Garden. Our Neighbourhood is something improv'd by the removal of some old Maids, and the arrival of some fine Gentlemen, amongst which are Lord Middleton and Sir J. Gifford, who are perhaps your Acquaintance.² ⟨They⟩ live with their aunt Lady Westmorland,³ and we endeavor to make the Country

¹ Soon after Lady Stafford arrived in Paris, she wrote to LM: 'Madame vostre soeur m'a fait l'honneur de me venir voir; elle m'a assuré qu'elle ne s'ennuioit point a Chaton' (W MS iv. 246).

² John (1683–1746), 3rd Earl of Middleton; his sister's son was Sir John Gifford (b. 1704) (GEC *Peerage*, *sub*

Middleton). They were Jacobite sympathizers.

³ Dorothy Brudenell (1647–1740), da. of 2nd Earl of Cardigan, m. 3rd Earl of Westmorland (d. 1691). She lived in Twickenham in a house adjoining LM's (Walpole, *Corr.* xxxiv. 260).

agreable to one another. Dr. Swift and Johny Gay are at Pope's, and their Conjunction has produce'd a Ballad[1] which if no body else has sent you I will, being never better pleas'd than when I am endeavoring to amuse my Dear Sister.

Text Bute MS   *Address* A Madame Madame de Mar

To Lady Mar [*23 June 1727*][2]

I am allways pleas'd to hear from You (Dear Sister), particularly when you tell me you are well. I beleive you'l find upon the whole my Sense is right, that Air, Exercise and Company are the best med'cines, and Physic and Retirement good for nothing but to break Hearts and spoil Constitutions.

I was glad to hear Mr. Remond's History from you, thô the newspaper had given it me en gros and my Lady Stafford in detail some time before.[3] I will tell you in return, as well as I can, what happens amongst our Acquaintance here. To begin with family affairs: the Dutchess of Kingston grunts on as usual, and I fear will put us in black Bombazine soon, which is a real greife to me. My dear Aunt Cheyne makes all the money she can of Lady Francesse, and I fear will carry

---

[1] Swift arrived in England at the end of April, and stayed with Pope at Twickenham then and in May (Pope, *Corr.* ii. 430, 435). The ballad referred to is difficult if not impossible to identify: it could have been 'The Capon's Tale' (Pope, *Minor Poems*, ed. N. Ault and J. Butt, 1954, pp. 256–8); or, as Moy Thomas suggests (1861, i. 506, n. 5), 'A Ballad on Quadrille'; or, finally, a ballad never printed.

[2] Dated by the beginning of next letter.

[3] Rémond's 'History' was probably that of his engagement to be married to the daughter of a jeweller, mentioned by Saint-Simon (*Mémoires*, ed. G. Truc, 1954–61, vi. 303). Lady Stafford, writing from Paris, relates it without mentioning Rémond by name: 'J'ay esté charmée de ce que vous me mandez de la fiancée. C'est une chose tout a fait Comique que cet amour. Le frère [Toussaint Rémond de Saint-Mard (1682–1757)] de l'amant a dit hier qu'il estoit fort mallade et qu'il avoit deffendu qu'on luy ecrivit ny qu'on luy parlait d'affaires. C'est, sans doutte, pour s'occuper entièrement de sa belle passion. . . .' (W MS iv. 246). His later career is obscure. From 1736 to 1740 he conducted a literary correspondence with Président Bouhier, whose editor treats him more favourably than Saint-Simon does (Emmanuel de Broglie, *Les Portefeuilles du président Bouhier*, 1896, pp. 256–69).

on those Politics to the last point, thô the Girl is such a fool, tis no great matter.[1] I am going within this halfe hour to call her to Court.

Our poor Cousins the Fieldings are grown yet poorer by the loss of all the little money they had, which in their Infinite wisdom they put into the hands of a rogueish Broker who has fairly walk'd off with it.

The most diverting story about Town at present is in relation to Edgecombe,[2] thô youre not knowing the people concern'd as well as I do will, I fear, hinder you from being so much entertain'd by it. I can't tell whither you know a Tall, musical, silly, ugly thing, niece to Lady Essex Roberts, who is call'd Miss Leigh.[3] She went a few days ago to visit Mrs. Betty Titchburne, Lady Sunderland's sister,[4] who lives in the House with her, and was deny'd at the door; but with the true manners of a great Fool told the porter that if his Lady was at home she was very positive she would be very glad to see her. Upon which she was shew'd up stairs to Miss Titchburne, who was ready to drop down at the sight of her, and could not help asking her in a grave way how she got in, being deny'd to every mortal, intending to pass the Evening in devout preparations. Miss Liegh [*sic*] said she had sent away her chair and servants with intent of staying till 9 o' clock. There was then no Remedy and she was ask'd to sit down, but had not been there a quarter of an hour when she heard a violent rap at the door, and somebody vehemently run up stairs. Miss Titchburne seem'd much surprizd and said she beleiv'd it was Mr. Edgcombe, and was quite amaz'd how he took it into his Head to visit her. During these Excuses, enter Edgcombe, who appear'd frighted at the sight of a third person. Miss Titchburne told him almost at his Entrance that the Lady he saw there was

---

[1] LM's daughter contradicted this opinion of her cousin, Lady Frances Pierrepont, who, she thought, had good sense but was uncommonly timid (1861, i. 509, n. 2).

[2] Richard Edgcumbe (1680–1758), later 1st Baron, politician.

[3] Elizabeth (d. 1734), da. of Col. Legh of Cheshire; Lady Essex Robartes

(d. 2 Jan. 1727) was her mother's sister. Walpole describes Miss Legh as 'a virtuosa, a musician, a madwoman', who was in love with Handel and wore his picture, along with the Pretender's, on her breast (*Corr.* xxxiv. 258).

[4] Elizabeth Tichborne (d. 1752); her sister Judith (*c.* 1702–49) m. (1717) 3rd Earl of Sunderland (d. 1722).

a perfect mistriss of music, and as he passionately lov'd it she thought she could not oblige him more than by desiring her to play. Miss Leigh very willingly sat to the Harpsicord, upon which her Audience decamp'd to the Bed Chamber, and left her to play over 3 or 4 lessons to her selfe. They return'd, and made what excuses they could, but said very frankly they had not heard her performance and begg'd her to begin again, which she comply'd with, and gave them the opertunity of a second retirement. Miss Leigh was by this time all Fire and Flame to see her heavenly Harmony thus slighted, and when they return'd told them she did not understand playing to an empty room. Mr. Edgecombe begg'd ten thousand pardons, and said if she would play Godi,[1] it was a Tune he dy'd to hear, and it would be an Obligation he should never forget. She made answer, she would do him a much greater Obligation by her Absence, which she suppos'd was all that was wanting at that Time, and run down stairs in a great Fury, to publish as fast as she could, and was so indefatigable in this pious design that in 4 and twenty hours all the people in Town had heard the story,[2] and poor Edgcombe met with nothing where ever he went but complements about his third Tune, which is reckon'd very handsome in a Lover past forty.

My Lady Sunderland could not avoid hearing this Galant History, and 3 days after invited Miss Leigh to dinner, where in the presence of her Sister and all the servants in waiting, she told her she was very sorry she had been so rudely treated in her House; that it was very true Mr. Edgecombe had been a perpetual Companion of her sister's this 2 year, and she thought it high time he should explain himselfe; and she expected her sister should act in this matter as discreetly as Lady K. Pelham had done in the like case, who she heard had given Mr. Pelham 4 months to resolve in, and after that he was either to marry or lose her for ever.[3] Sir Robert Sutton intterupted her by saying that he never doubted the Honour of Mr. Edgecombe and was persuaded

---

[1] The aria 'Gode l'alma' in Handel's opera *Ottone* (performed in 1723, revived in Feb.–March 1726 and April 1727) (Otto E. Deutsch, *Handel*, [1955], pp. 151, 193, 207).

[2] Previous editions have omitted the rest of this sentence.

[3] See above, p. 71 and n. 1.

79

he could have no ill design in his Family.[1] The Affair stands thus, and Edgecombe has 4 months to provide him selfe elsewhere, during which time he has free egress and regress, and tis seriously the opinion of many that a wedding will in good earnest be brought about by this admirable Conduct.[2]

I send you a novell instead of a Letter, but as it is in your power to shorten it when you please by reading no farther than you like, I will make no Excuses for the length of it.

Text Bute MS   *Address* A Madme Madme de Mar

To Lady Mar [*28 June 1727*]

I had writ you a long letter, dear Sister, and only wanted sealing it, when I was intterupted by a summons to my sister Gower's, whom I never left since. She lasted from Friday till Tuesday and dy'd about 8 o' clock, in such a manner as has made an Impression on me not easily shaken off.[3] We are now but two in the World, and it ought to endear us to one another. I am sure whatever I can serve my poor Nieces and Nephews in, shall not be wanting on my Part. I won't trouble you with melancholy circumstances; you may easily imagine the affliction of Lord Gower and Lady Cheyne.[4] I hope you will not let melancholy hurt your own Health, which is truly dear to your affectionate sister.[5]

Text Bute MS   *Address* A Madme Madme La Comtesse de Mar

[1] Sutton (1671–1746), M.P., retired diplomatist, m. (1724) Lady Sunderland.

[2] Walpole noted that many people thought they were already married (*Corr.* xxxiv. 258). But Edgcumbe, a widower since 1721, never remarried.

[3] Lady Gower, who had given birth to a daughter (Diana, d. 1737) on 31 May, died on 27 June (*Daily Post*, 3, 28 June 1727).

[4] By a request in her grandmother's

will Lady Gower had been brought up by her aunt Lady Cheyne.

[5] Lady Stafford in turn tried to console LM: 'Madame, je ne doute point que vous n'en ayez esté un peu triste. Cela est bien pitoyable de perdre la vie par jouer a cadrille, mais aussy il faut considerer qu'elle ne perd que ce plaisir la, et que c'est tout ce qu'elle auroit fait dans ce monde si elle y estoit restée plus longtems' ([July 1727], W MS iv. 242).

To Lady Mar [*July 1727*]

You see, Dear Sister, that I answer your Letters as soon as I receive them, and if mine can give you any Consolation or Amusement you need never want 'em. I desire you would not continue greiving your selfe. Of all sorrows those we pay to the Dead are most vain, and as I have no good Opinion of Sorrow in general, I think no sort of it worth cherrishing.

I suppose you have heard how good Lady Lansdowne has pass'd her Time here; she has liv'd publickly with Lord Dunmore,[1]

> Fam'd for their Loves, their mutual happy Loves.

You'l wonder perhaps to hear Lord Gower is a topping Courtier, and that there is not one Tory left in England.[2] There are some circumstances extreamly risible in these affairs, but not so proper to be communicated by Letter, and I will in humble way return to my Domestics. I hear my Niece your Daughter is a very fine young Lady, and I wish you Joy of it as one of the greatest blessings in Life. My Girl gives me a great prospect of satisfaction, but my young Rogue of a Son is the most ungovernable little Rake that ever plaid Truant.[3]

If I was inclinable to lay worldly matters to Heart, I could write a Quire of complaints about it, so you see no body is quite happy, thô tis pretty much my Nature to console upon all occasions. I advise you to do the same as the only remedy

---

[1] While her husband remained in France Lady Lansdown continued to make long visits to England; she was there from the spring of 1726 to Aug. 1727 (Eliz. Handasyde, *Granville the Polite*, 1933, pp. 223–4). In Mrs. Delany's opinion, she was handsome, gay, and fond of admiration; and 'the libertine manners of France accomplished what her own nature was too prone to' (*Corr.* i. 81–82). John Murray (1685–1752), 2nd Earl of Dunmore, a military man, never married. In 1729 they were still living together (Handasyde, p. 225).

[2] After the death of George I in June, the Tory Opposition scrambled to support Walpole, who had unexpectedly been retained by George II as chief Minister. Gower had flirted with the Jacobites; in June 1727 he kissed the royal hand (C. D. Realey, *Early Opposition to Sir Robert Walpole*, 1931, p. 219). In his dictionary Dr. Johnson almost put *Gower* as the definition of *Renegado* (Boswell, *Life of Johnson*, ed. G. B. Hill and L. F. Powell, 1934, i. 296).

[3] On 13 July he again ran away from Westminster School (see next page).

against the inevitable vexations of this vile Life, which in my conscience I think affords disagreable things to the highest ranks and comforts to the very lowest, so that upon the whole, things are more equally dispos'd amongst the sons of Adam than they are generally thought to be. You see my Philosophy is not altogether so Lugubre as yours. I am so far from avoiding Company, I resolve never to live without; and when I am no longer an Actor upon this stage (by the way, I talk of twenty years hence at soonest), as a Spectator I may laugh at the farcical Actions that will doubtless be then represented, Nature being exceeding provident in providing Fools and Coxcombs in all Ages, who are the greatest preservatives against the Spleen that I ever could find out. I say all these things for your Edification. I shall conclude my consolatory Espistle with one rule that I have found very conducing to Health of Body and Mind. As soon as you wake in the morning, lift up your Eyes and consider seriously what will best divert you that Day. Your Imagination being then refresh'd by sleep will certainly put in your mind some party of pleasure, which if you execute with prudence will disperse those melancholy vapours which are the foundation of all Distempers.

Text Bute MS   *Address* A Madame Madame La Comtesse de Mar

To Lady Mar [*Aug. 1727*]

My Cousin is going to Paris, and I will not let her go without a Letter for you, my dear Sister, thô I never was in a worse humour for writeing. I am vex'd to the blood by my young Rogue of a Son, who has contriv'd at his age to make himselfe the Talk of the whole Nation. He is gone Knight Erranting God knows where, and hitherto 'tis impossible to find him.[1] You may judge of my uneasyness by what your

[1] An advertisement in the *Daily Journal* offered a reward of £20 for information leading to the finding of a boy about 14, with inoculation scars on both arms, who had run away on 13 July, and who had either gone on board a ship or hired himself out to a tradesman or labourer. 'If the Boy will return of himself, he shall be kindly received, and put to Sea, if he desires it' (18 Aug.; *Daily Post*, 19 Aug., and *Mist's Weekly Journal*, 9 Sept. 1727). He had actually

own would be if dear Lady Fanny was lost. Nothing that ever happen'd to me has touch'd me ⟨so⟩ much. I can hardly speak or write of it with tolerable temper, and I own it has chang'd mine to that degree I have a mind to cross the Water to try what Effect a new Heaven and a new Earth will have upon my Spirit. If I take this Resolution you shall hear in a few posts. There can be no situation in Life in which the conversation of my dear only Sister will not administer some comfort to me.

Text Bute MS　　*Address* To The Countesse ⟨of Mar⟩

To Lady Mar [*Sept. 1727*]

This is a vile World, dear Sister, and I can easily comprehend that whither one is at Paris or London one is stiffled with a certain mixture of Fool and Knave that most people are compos'd of. I would have patience with a parcel of polite Rascals, or your downright honest Fools. But Father Adam shines through his whole progeny; he first eat the Apple like a sot and then turn'd Informer like a Scoundrel.[1] —So much for our inside. Then our outward is so liable to uglyness and distempers that we are perpetually plagu'd with feeling our own Decays and seeing other people's—yet six pennorth of common sense divided amongst a whole Nation would make our Lives roul away glib enough. But then we make laws and we follow customs; by the first we cut off our own pleasures, and by the second we are answerable for the faults and extravagancys of others. All these things and 500 more convince me (as I have the most profound Adoration for the Author of Nature) that we are here in an Actual state of punishment. I am satisfy'd I have been damn'd ever since I was born, and in submission to divine

shipped on a military transport bound for Gibraltar, but after being taunted by the crew for boasting of his birth, he had confessed his identity to the captain (told by the captain's grandson to 1st Lord Wharncliffe, Wh MS 439). In

Dec. he was sent home from Gibraltar under the care of Lord Forbes, a commander in the Royal Navy (*London Journal*, 6 Jan. 1728).
[1] Previous editions have omitted the second half of this sentence.

Justice don't at all doubt but I deserv'd it in some præexistent state. I am very willing to soften the Word damn'd and hope I am only in Purgatory, and that after whining and grunting here a certain number of years I shall be translated to some more happy sphere, where Virtue will be natural and custom reasonable, that is, in short, where common Sense will reign.

I grow very devout, as you see, and place all my hopes in the next Life, being totally persuaded of the nothingness of this. Don't you remember how miserable we were in the little parlor at Thorsby? We thought marrying would put us at once into possession of all we wanted; then came being with Child etc., and you see what comes of being with Child.

Tho' after all I am still of Opinion that 'tis extreamly silly to submit to ill Fortune; one should pluck up a Spirit, and live upon Cordials when one can have no other Nourishment. These are my present Endeavors, and I run about thô I have 5,000 pins and needles running into my Heart.[1] I try to console with a small Damsel who is at present every thing that I like, but alas, she is yet in a white Frock. At 14 she may run away with the Butler. There's one of the Blessed consequences of great Disapointment; you are not only hurt by the Thing present, but it cuts off all future hopes and makes your very Expectations melancholy. Quel vie!

Text Bute MS *Address* A Madme Madme La Comtesse de Mar

From Lord Hervey[2] *8 Oct.* [1727]

Bath, Oct'r the 8th

I had too much Pleasure in recieving your Ladyship's Commands to have any merit in obeying them, and should be very insincere if I pretended that my Inclination to converse with you could ever be a second motive to my doing it. I came to this Place but yesterday, from

[1] On 5 Sept. the *Daily Journal* reported LM as 'dangerously ill'.
[2] Of the correspondence between Hervey and LM only his side remains (except for some brief verse by her)—a total of forty-five letters, from 1727 until 1743. After his death in that year his eldest son sealed up LM's letters and returned them to her; she probably destroyed them (Stuart, 1861, i. 95–96).

which you may imagine I am not yet sufficiently qualify'd to execute the Commission you gave me, which was to send you a List of the Sojourners and Inmates of this Place; but there is so universal an affinity and resemblance among these individuals that a small Paragraph will serve amply to illustrate what you have to depend upon. The D[uches]s of Marlborough, Congreve, and Lady Rich are the only People whose Faces I know, whose Names I ever heard, or who I believe have any Names belonging to them. [*Passage omitted*]

Text MS at Victoria Art Gallery, Bath   *End. by W* Ld Hervey from Bath

To Lady Mar [*Oct. 1727*]

I cannot deny but I was very well diverted the Coronation Day.[1] I saw the procession much at my Ease in a House I fill'd with my own Company, and then got into the Hall without any trouble, where it was very entertaining to Observe the variety of airs that all meant the same thing, the Business of every walker there being to conceal Vanity and gain Admiration. For these purposes some languish'd and others strutted, but a visible Satisfaction was diffused over every countenance as soon as the Coronet was clapp'd on the Head. But she that drew the greatest Number of Eyes was indisputably the Countess of Orkney.[2] She exposed behind a mixture of Fat and Wrinkles, and before a considerable pair of Bubbys a good deal withered, a great Belly that preceeded her; add to this the inimitable roll of her Eyes, and her Grey Hair which by good Fortune stood directly upright, and 'tis impossible to immagine a more Delightfull Spectacle. She had embellish'd all this with a great deal of Magnificence which made her as big again as usual, and I shou'd have thought her one of the largest things of God's

---

[1] George II was crowned on 11 Oct.
[2] Elizabeth (d. 1733), da. of Sir Edward Villiers, m. (1695) Lord George Hamilton (d. 1737), later Earl of Orkney. She had been mistress of William III, for her wisdom rather than non-existent physical charms. Walpole told a famous anecdote about her: 'Lady Dorchester [mistress of James II] meeting her and the Duchess of Portsmouth [mistress of Charles II] in King George's Drawing-Room, said, "Who would have thought we three whores should have met here?"' (*Corr.* xxxiv. 260).

making if my Lady St. John[1] had not display'd all her Charms that day. The poor Dutchess of Montross[2] Crep'd along with a Dozen of black Snakes playing round her Face; and my Lady Portland (who is fall'n away since her dismission from Court)[3] represented very finely an Egyptian Mummy embroider'd over with Hieroglyphics. In General I could not perceive but the Old were as well pleas'd as the Young, and I (who dread growing Wise more than any thing in the World) was overjoy'd to observe one can never outlive one's Vanity.

I have never received the long Letter you talk of, and am afraid you have only fancy'd that you writ it.

Adieu, my Dear Sister. I am affectionately Yours.[4]

Text W MS iv. 110–11 (copy)[5]

From Lord Hervey *28 Oct.* [*1727*]

Bath, Oct'r the 28th

Your Suspicions with regard to the D[uches]s of Marlborough are utterly groundless; she neither knew to whom I was writing, nor that I ever had the Pleasure of a Letter from you in my Life. The Speech you had cook'd up for her was delightfull, exactly her Style, and word for word what she would infallibly have say'd had she been in the Situation you suposed. How far I made free with your Letter I will nakedly confess; I read two or three things to her out of it relating to the Coronation, but, upon my Honour, without giving the least Hint

[1] Angelica Pelissary (*c.* 1667–1736) m. (1687) Henry, later 1st Viscount St. John, Lord Bolingbroke's father.

[2] Christian Carnegie (d. 1744), da. of 3rd Earl of Northesk, m. (1702) 1st Duke of Montrose. She was a great friend of Mrs. Murray and her family.

[3] Jane Martha Temple (1672–1751) m. (1700) 1st Earl of Portland (d. 1709). In April 1718 she had been appointed governess of the Prince of Wales's children after George I had taken custody of them because of his quarrel with his son. News of her discharge, after the Prince's accession, appeared in newspapers in Sept. (*Whitehall Evening Post*, 26–28 Sept. 1727).

[4] Lady Mar's melancholy worsened; in Nov. 1727 Atterbury wrote from Paris that she was dangerously ill (Folkstone Williams, *Mem. and Corr. of Francis Atterbury*, 1869, ii. 107). She arrived in London in March 1728 'so disorder'd in her Head,' one newspaper reported, 'that it's believed she'll scarce ever recover her Senses' (*London Evening Post*, 2–5 March 1728). For a detailed account of the squabble about her custody and maintenance, see Halsband, *LM*, pp. 133–5.

[5] The original, formerly among the Bute MS, has been removed from its album; a summary of its contents is on the mounting leaf.

from whence it came, and by a thing she say'd three Days afterwards, I found she guess'd Lord Chesterfield to be my Correspondent. If I went farther in this Step than you would have me, give me absolution upon my Confession of my Fault and I'll give you my Word never to repeat it. This Preliminary article settled, I beg for the future our Commerce may be without any restraint, that you would allow me the Liberty of communicating my thoughts naturally, and that you would conclude your-self safe in doing so to me, 'till I cease to have the least grain of natural, gratefull, or political Honesty in my whole Composition. [*Passage omitted*]

Text MS at Victoria Art Gallery, Bath   *Address* To The Rt Honble the Lady Mary Wortley Montague in Covent Garden London *Postmark* 30 oc   *End. by W* Ld Hervey from Bath

From Lord Hervey 7 *Nov.* [*1727*]

Bath, Nov. the 7th

[*Passage omitted*] You always speak and write agreably, but give me leave to tell you, even You never putt Words so prettyly together as in your last Letter. That Rapidity of Imagination, those lively Images, that Strength of Expression, and that Justness of Sentiment: in short, that Union of every thing that strikes at first, and pleases still more upon Examination (a Happyness so peculiar to your-self) was never more evident than in what I am now to thank you for. You desire me to read with the same Spirit you write, an Injunction which you must be a great Loser or I a great Gainer before it will be in my Power to obey. All I can assure you in answer to it is that if you write with as great a disposition to entertain as I have to be entertain'd whenever I see your Hand upon Paper, you must be much more Solicitous to please than People generally are where the Success is so little uncertain.

[*Passage omitted*] I would now answer that Part of your Letter where you speak of your-self; but there is something so outré in the false Modesty of it that one is as much embarass'd how to behave upon it as one is with Lady Burlington's[1] Civility, who from affecting the Character of an affable Woman of Quality accosts you always in that of a cringing House-Maid. You carry your humility with regard to your Age to full as absurd a Pitch as she does hers as to place; and you

---

[1] Dorothy Saville (1699–1758), da. of 2nd Marquess of Halifax, m. (1721) 3rd Earl of Burlington.

must know I should not think your pretending to be young enough to take a Pleasure in dressing Babys to be one Bitt more extravagant than that grave assertion of your being too old for a Man to find any in undressing you: they are different extreams, but, like all extreams, equally distant from Truth and equally ridiculous. I grant you the affectation of being older than one is, is a more uncommon one than the reverse, but that does not make it less Affectation; and I should be just as ready to laugh and think you mad if I mett you visiting about the Town with Spectacles and Crutches as if I found you running up and down your own House with a Rattle and a Go-Cart. [*Passage omitted*]

Text Bristol MS, ii. 59–60, 62–63

From Lord Monson[1] *14 July* [*1728*]

Madam,

I received the honour of your Ladyship's letter by the last post, and it will be ever with the utmost regret that I excuse my self from paying a ready obedience to your Ladyship's commands, but as I am entirely unacquainted with the nature of the trust your Ladyship proposes to me,[2] and am already engaged in severall others, which give me full employment, I am very unwilling to concern my Self with any farther trusts at present. And as Your Ladyship is desirous to name a Trustee against whom Lord Grange[3] can take no exception, I should think any other Body would be more proper than my self, for as I did my self the honour to wait on your Ladyship into Court, Lord Grange may look upon me as one that has concern'd him self in the Affair, and except against it.[4] I Shall be in town in two or three days and will then wait on your Ladyship, being with the greatest respect, Madam, Your Ladyship's Most obedient and most humble Servant,

Monson.

Broxborne,[5] July 14th

Text W MS iv. 202–3 *End. by W* Ld Monson

[1] John Monson (a trustee of LM's father's estate), Bart. 1727, cr. Baron in May 1728.

[2] LM had evidently asked Monson to serve as a trustee for Lady Mar, who—two days before—had been adjudged insane (PRO C 211, E 16: report of lunacy inquisition).

[3] James Erskine (1679–1754), Lord Mar's brother, called by his Scottish judicial title. He was the representative of the Erskine family in the struggle to secure Lady Mar's custody and income. In June (1728) he had attempted to take her to Scotland secretly, but was thwarted by LM and the law ('Affidavit Ja: Erskine', Mar and Kellie MS 574).

[4] About a week later the Court of Chancery awarded custody of Lady Mar to LM (*Daily Post*, 23 July 1728).

[5] Monson's seat in Hertfordshire.

From Lord Mar *19/8 Nov. 1728*

Paris, Novemb. 19th. 1728.

Madam,

As soon as I had your last, about two months ago, I wrote a full answer which I hoped would be to your satisfaction, but having heard nothing from you since, I fear it has miscarried as I find Letters 'twixt this and London frequently do. The reason of my not writing to your Ladyship since, has been that I thought I had reason to expect every post to have accounts of my pardon's being past, when hearing from me would be less inconvenient and of more use.[1]

[Passage omitted]

... should the pardon continue to be stop'd, It will unavoidably throw your poor sister's affairs, and mine and those of my whole family, into such confusion as may be their entire ruin. I must therefor beg of you, Madam, to be so good to contribute all you can to remove all difficulties and to help forwarding the passing of my pardon. This friendship I hope I may expect of one to whom I have the honour to be so nearly allied, and also that you will use your endeavours with Mr. Wortley to do the same, which will be a very great obligation and never to be forgot by me or my family, and I shall be very glad to owe this (as the Dutch Gazette had it) to my wife's relations.

I see by the news papers that Dr. Hale is dead, and his having attended your distrest Sister made it give me great concern.[2] I beg to know from your Ladyship who now attends her in his place. I am sure you would take care to have it one of the best, but 'tis some satisfaction to know who that is. Let me intreat you too to inform me of the condition she is now in, and what hopes there is of her recovery, on which depends all the happiness and comfort of my life.

I will not trouble you farther at this time, but I'll be in hopes in [*sic*] hearing something agreable soon from you, and I am, Madam, your most obedient and most humble servant.

Adieu.

---

[1] Since he had outwardly severed connexions with the Jacobites in 1725, Lord Mar continually attempted to secure a pardon from the King and permission to return to England. On 5 Sept., in fact, the King had granted him a pardon but with no provision for his return to England (*Polit. State of G.B.*, 1728, p. 278).

[2] Richard Hale (1670–26 Sept. 1728), physician to Bethlehem Hospital. In treating insanity, he was one of the first to use 'moral means and sedatives . . . to lessen the restraints and cruelty then so generally practised' (MS Roll, Royal Soc. of Physicians).

I hope the way I am to send this will prove surer than that by which the last went.

Text Mar and Kellie MS 614 (copy)   *End.* Not subscribed. Copy, to Lady Mary Wortley. Paris. Novbr 19. 1728.

To Lord Islay[1] *20 Feb.* [*1729*]

I receiv'd the enclos'd from my Solicitor last night, by which I apprehend that the Lawyers on each side have not yet met. I am not supriz'd when Men so much loaded with Busyness are slow, but I am amaz'd my Lord Grange should so far misrepresent things to your Lordship as to talk above a week ago of my demands when even the affair had not been mention'd, and I remain in the same Opinion of being contented to demand no more of him than £500 per Annum.[2] I beg your Lordship's pardon for this trouble, but could not help taking this oppertunity of shewing you with what Integrity things are acted on the part of, My Lord, your oblig'd humble Servant,

M. W. M.

Feb. 20.

Text Mar and Kellie MS 632   *Address* To The Rt Honble The Earl of Ilay

From Wortley *27 July 1729*

As I mentioned to you in my last, I found your letter here, and had another since dated the 20th from Twickenham. If I did not mention the first it was an oversight. I am now prepared to leave this place

[1] Archibald Campbell (1682–1761), 1st Earl of Islay, later 3rd Duke of Argyll, had been trained as a lawyer. In the opinion of LM's granddaughter he was 'cool, shrewd, penetrating, argumentative—an able man of business' (Lady Louisa Stuart, *Selections from Her Manuscripts*, ed. J. Home, 1899, p. 15). He lived at Whitton Park, Twickenham. LM was dealing with him in the case of Lady Mar's custody, probably because he was Lord Justice General of Scotland.

[2] Articles of Agreement were finally signed on 9 June 1729 that LM should continue to have custody of her sister, with £500 a year allowed for maintenance, of which an accounting would have to be made (Mar and Kellie MS 636).

tomorrow and hope to be at the Lodge[1] by the end of this week. My stay in Wensladale will only be 2 or 3 days.

We hear no news here but of the gaietys of my two partners, Sir H. Liddel[2] and Mr. Bowes,[3] who are so much taken up with feasting and Balls that I have had a good deal of difficulty to get them to settle to business. Lord Scarborough[4] is at Lumley Castle, about six miles off, and entertained us one day very magnificently.

Newcastle, 27 July 1729.

There were at a ball here last week no less than 5 ladies the poorest of which had above £20,000, and the richest above £50,000; I believe I might say £80,000.

Text W MS i. 108–9   *Address* To Lady Mary Wortley at Twickenham Middlesex by London Frank Edw. Wortley.   *Postmark* 30 IV

To John Arbuthnot[5] [*Oct. 1729*][6]

Sir,

Since I saw you, I have made some enquirys, and heard more of the story you was so kind to mention to me. I am told Pope has had the surprizing Impudence to assert he can bring the Lampoon when he pleases to produce it, under my own hand.[7] I desire he be made to keep to this offer; if he is so skillful in Counterfeiting Hands I suppose he will not confine that great Talent to the gratifying his Malice, but

---

[1] Wharncliffe Lodge at Wortley, Yorks. W's father, who lived there, had died in 1727.

[2] Sir Henry Liddell (1708–84), M.P. 1734–47, later 1st Baron Ravensworth. Horace Walpole calls him 'one of the warmest and honestest Whigs in England' (*Mem. of George II*, 1822, i. 265).

[3] See below, p. 169, n. 2.

[4] Richard Lumley (c. 1688–1740), 2nd Earl.

[5] Physician and wit (1667–1735); he remained on friendly terms with both LM and Pope even after their falling out.

[6] This letter should perhaps be placed after the following one.

[7] This and the following letter probably refer to the verse satire *One Epistle to Mr. A. Pope*. Although not published until April 1730, it was advertised as early as Feb. 1729 (Robert W. Rogers, *Major Satires of Pope*, 1955, p. 139). The poem, which must have been circulated in manuscript, praises 'Lady M. W. M.' in a footnote (p. 12) as one who had not escaped Pope's detraction, referring to the 1728 *Miscellanies* and the *Dunciad*. In a letter to a friend on 13 Sept., Pope had accused LM of libelling him (*Corr.* iii. 53); perhaps he had *One Epistle* in mind.

take some occasion to encrease his fortune by the same Method, and I may hope (by such practises) to see him exalted according to his merit, which no body will rejoyce at more than my selfe.

I beg of you, Sir (as an act of Justice), to endeavour to set the Truth in an open Light, and then I leave to your Judgment the Character of those who have attempted to hurt mine in so barbarous a maner. I can assure you (in particular) you nam'd a Lady to me (as abus'd in this Libel) whose name I never heard before;[1] and as I never had any acquaintance with Dr Swift, am an utter stranger to all his affairs, and even his person, which I never saw to my knowledge; and am now convinc'd the whole is a contrivance of Pope's to blast the Reputation of one who never injur'd him. I am not more sensible of his injustice than I am, Sir, of the candor, Generosity, and good sense I have found in you, which has oblig'd me to be with a very uncommon warmth your real Freind,[2] and I heartily wish for an opertunity of shewing I am so more effectually than by subscribing my selfe your very humble servant,

M. Wortley Montagu.

Text MS at Royal College of Surgeons, London

To John Arbuthnot 17 *Oct.* [*1729*]

Sir,

I have this minute receiv'd your Letter, and cannot remember I ever was so much surpriz'd in my Life, The whole contents of it being matter of astonishment. I give you sincere and hearty thanks for your Intelligence and the obliging manner of it. I have ever valu'd you as a Gentleman both of sense and merit, and will joyn with you in any method you

---

[1] The final passage in *One Epistle* charges that Vanessa 'yielded up her charms' to Swift. This referred to his friendship with Esther Vanhomrigh (*c.* 1688–1723), which had been exposed in his *Cadenus and Vanessa* (1726).
[2] She had first written 'humble Servant'.

can contrive to prevent or punish the authors of so horrid a villainy.¹ I am with much Esteem Your Humble Servant,

M. Wortley M.

Oct. 17.

Text MS at Royal College of Surgeons, London

From Henry Fielding² *4 Sept.* [*1730*]³

I hope your Ladyship will honour the Scenes which I presume to lay before you with your Perusal. As they are written on a Model I never yet attempted, I am exceedingly anxious least they should find less Mercy from you than my lighter Productions. It will be a slight compensation to the Modern Husband, that your Ladyship's Censure will defend him from the Possibility of any other Reproof, Since your least approbation will always give me a Pleasure infinitely superiour to the loudest Applauses of a theatre.⁴ For whatever has past your Judgment may, I think, without any Imputation of Immodesty, refer Want of Success to Want of Judgment in an Audience.⁵ I shall do my self the Honour of waiting on your Ladyship at Twickenham next Monday to receive my Sentence,⁶ and am, Madam, with the most devoted Respect, Your Ladyship's most obedient, most humble Servant,

London, 7br 4   Henry ffielding.

Text Facsimile, 1803, i. 107; MS fragment in Forster Coll., Victoria and Albert Museum

¹ The joint authors of *One Epistle* were Leonard Welsted and James Moore Smythe (Welsted, *Works*, ed. J. Nichols, 1787, p. 186). After the poem was printed Pope designated Moore Smythe and some others unnamed as its authors (*Corr.* iii. 106, 113–14).

² LM's second cousin (1707–54) by descent from 3rd Earl of Denbigh, he had begun his career in 1728 with *Love in Several Masques*, which he dedicated to her. After an interlude of studying law in Leyden, he had resumed his initial career as a playwright.

³ In Sept. 1730 *The Craftsman* reported (inaccurately) that Fielding's comedy *The Modern Husband* would be produced shortly (Charles B. Woods in *PMLA* (Pub. of Mod. Lang. Assoc.), lii, 1937, p. 362.)

⁴ Up to this point the letter is printed from the facsimile, the rest from MS.

⁵ The play treats of a husband so corrupt that he tries to persuade his own wife to have an affair with a wealthy nobleman. When produced, in Feb. 1732, it drew and shocked audiences. It was dedicated to Sir Robert Walpole, who—Fielding's biographer writes—probably accepted it out of friendship to LM (Wilbur L. Cross, *History of Henry Fielding*, 1918, i. 120–1).

⁶ Many years later Fielding acknowledged that a lady of the first rank [LM] had approved of the character of the young lady of quality [Lady Charlotte Gaywit] although the audience, largely made up of clerks and apprentices, had called her unnatural (*Tom Jones*, Book viii, Chap. i; Cross, i. 120).

From Charles de Montesquieu[1] *11 March 1731*

J'ai l'honeur, Madame, de vous demander une grace; C'est de vouloir envoyer a Lincoln In Filds de lundi en huit 22 du mois autant de vos amis que vous pouriez. C'est pour le benefit de Mll Sallé.[2] Elle m'a esté beaucoup recomandee par Monsieur de Fontenelle[3] et madame la Marquise de Lambert,[4] et de plus Milady Staffort la protege. Come elle est fort sage persone ne lui a obligation. Vous me ferez donc, Madame, un vray plaisir si vous voulez vous interesser pour elle. J'ay l'honneur d'estre avec toutte sorte de respect votre tres humble et tres obeissant serviteur,[5] Madame:

Montesquieu.

a Londres, Ce 11 mars 1731

Text W MS vi. 282–3   *End. by W* Montesquieu.

To Lady Frances Erskine[6] *11 Dec. 1731*

I am very sorry your Ladyship did not receive a long Letter that I wrote to you in answer to your last, giving a full account of my unhappy Sister. She is now much better than

[1] The baron de Montesquieu (1689–1755), already famous as the author of *Lettres persanes* (1721), arrived in London Nov. 1729, and remained in England until May 1731. Since records of his sojourn are very sparse, this letter is of some importance (Robert Shackleton, *Montesquieu*, 1961, Chap. vi; 'Montesquieu's Correspondence,' *French Studies*, xii, 1958, pp. 325–6). It is translated in the Appendix below.

[2] Marie Sallé (1707–56), on leave from the Paris opera, appeared at Lincoln's Inn Fields in 1730–31 (Émile Dacier, *Une Danseuse de l'Opéra sous Louis XV...*, 1909, pp. 61–71). Although she danced on Monday, 22 March, her own benefit 'By His Majesty's Command' took place on Thursday the 25th. *The Cheats of Scapin* by Otway was performed to a crowded house, and the King and Queen with other members of the Royal Family attended (*London Stage 1660–1800*, Part 3, ed. A. H.

Scouten, 1961, p. 124–5).

[3] Bernard de Fontenelle (1657–1757), venerable littérateur, recommended the dancer, praising her for her virtue (Montesquieu, *Corr.*, ed. F. Gebelin, 1914, i. 283).

[4] Anne-Thérèse de Courcelles (1647–1733) m. (1666) the marquis de Lambert; she maintained a famous *salon* frequented by Fontenelle, her intimate friend.

[5] Probably between 1734 and 1738, Montesquieu read a French essay by LM about marriage, and copied out three brief excerpts ('Spicilège' 576, *Œuvres complètes*, ed. R. Caillois, 1956–8, ii. 1373–4; LM's 'Sur la Maxime de M. de Rochefoucault', 1861, ii. 422, 424). And in 1746, when she was in the south of France, she told a mutual friend of her very favourable opinion of Montesquieu (Halsband, *LM*, pp. 233–4; Shackleton in *French Studies*, p. 333).

[6] Lady Mar's daughter, whose sym-

she was at that time, having in some measure recover'd the
Ruffle she was then under, but is very far from being in a
Condition to undertake a Journey, of which she her selfe is
so sensible that I beleive nothing but down right Force
could prevail upon her to begin one.[1] Quiet and Regularity
is all that can be done for her in her present state of Health,
and (however I may have been misrepresented)[2] I am conscious to my selfe that it is my utmost endeavor to contribute
what I can to make her easy. She has drank the Spa waters
but was oblig'd to leave them off by disagreing with her
Distemper. As to Mrs. Peeling's[3] seeing her, I must repeat
what I said in my last Letter, that she has much disoblig'd
my Aunt Cheyne by confidently asserting you were in the
House when you had actualling [*sic*] left London, and has
industriously spread so many base Lyes concerning me, it
will be my own fault if I put it in her power to tell any more,
and I can truly assert my Sister never asks for her, and I
beleive has entirely forgot her.

I am sincerely sorry for the ill situation of my Lord your
Father's affairs,[4] and if it Lyes in my power to do him any
service, will not fail on all occasions to shew my selfe, Dear
Madam, Your affectionate Aunt and humble servant,

M. W. Montagu.

Dec. 11 O.S. 1731

My Daughter is your humble servant and very sorry to
be at this distance from you.

Text MS now owned by the Editor   *Address* A Miledi Miledi

pathies were with her father's family,
lived with him at Aix-la-Chapelle. She
was in correspondence with Lady Mar,
having received a letter from her which
she answered on 22 Dec. N.S. 1731 (Mar
and Kellie MS).

[1] In April 1731 Lord Grange, Lord
Mar's brother, had come to London
from Edinburgh for the purpose of
having Lady Mar declared sane (*Mis-
cellany of the Spalding Club*, 1846, iii.
4–8). He then hoped—as a friend of his
wrote—to 'bring her down to Scotland,
for the advantage of the family' (Robert
Wodrow, *Analecta*, 1842–3, iv. 227). But

Lady Mar remained in LM's custody.

[2] LM must mean malicious gossip
about her treatment of Lady Mar; such
a report Lady Lechmere had heard from
Lord Mar the year before, and then put
in a letter to Lady (formerly Mrs.)
Murray on 20 Dec. N.S. 1730 (Mellerstain MS).

[3] Probably the same person mentioned above, p. 46.

[4] In spite of his efforts, Mar had not
been able to win permission to return to
England. He was besides heavily in debt
(Francis Atterbury, *Epistolary Corr.*,
[ed. J. Nichols], 1783–90, v. 143).

Francesse Ereskine chez miLord Mar A Aix La Chappelle par Rotterdam   *Postmark* 14 DE   *End.* Recd at Aix La Chapelle Jany the 3d n.s. 1731/2

From Henry Fielding [*Feb. 1732*]

Madam,

I have presum'd to send your Ladyship a Copy of the Play[1] which you did me the Honour of reading three Acts of last spring, and hope it may meet as light a Censure from your Ladyship's Judgment as then; for while your Goodness permits me (what I esteem the greatest and indeed only Happiness of my Life) to offer my unworthy Performances to your Perusal, it will be entirely from your Sentence that they will be regarded or disesteem'd by Me. I shall do my self the Honour of calling at your Ladyship's Door to morrow at eleven, which if it be at an improper Hour, I beg to know from your servant what other time will be more convenient. I am with the greatest Respect and Gratitude, Madam, Your Ladyship's most obedient, Most devoted humble servant,

Henry ffielding.

Wednesday Evening.

Text MS at Harvard University   *Address* To The Rt honble the
Lady Mary Wortley Mountague   *End. by W* H. F.

To Lady Frances Erskine [*June 1732*]

. . . anent Lord Mar's death[2] and Lady Mar's illness—written while Lady Mar was in her care—[3]

Text Summary in 19th-century hand; album among Mar and Kellie MS

---

[1] Probably *The Modern Husband,* staged and published in Feb. 1732. For LM's earlier connexion with it, see above, p. 93.

[2] In May 1732 at Aix-la-Chapelle.

[3] Lady Mar was still in the custody of LM and W at the end of 1736, when he urged LM to relinquish it to her daughter and other trustees ([*c.* 7 Nov. 1736], W MS i. 146–7).

From Lord Peterborough [*Feb. 1733*]

Madame,

I was very unwilling to have my name Made use of in an affair in which I had noe concern, and therefore would not engage my self to speak to Mr. Pope, but he coming to my house the moment you went away, I gave him as exact an account as I could of our conversation. He said to me what I had taken the Liberty to say to you, that he wonderd how the Town could apply those Lines to any but some noted common woeman, that he should yett be more surprised if you should take them to your self.[1] He named to me fower remarkable poetesses and scribblers, Mrs. Centlivre, Mrs. Haywood, Mrs. Manly and Mrs. Been, Ladies famous indeed in their generation, and some of them Esteemed to have given very unfortunate favours to their Friends, assuring me that such only were the objects of his satire.[2]

I hope this assurance will prevent your further mistake, and any ill consequences. Upon so odd a Subject I have nothing more to add. Your Ladyship's most humble and obedient servant,

Peterborow.

Text Eg MS 1949, ff. 5–6   *Address* For the Lady Mary Wortley

From Giles Jacob[3] *11 June 1733*

Islington, 11th June 1733.

My Lady,

In my Letter of Thanks that I sent to your Ladyship about a week ago for your favourable Acceptance of my Collection of Letters under the Title of the Mirrour,[4] I desired You would be pleas'd to

[1] On 15 Feb. Pope had published his first imitation of Horace's satires (II. i); it had one couplet aimed at LM: 'From furious *Sappho* scarce a milder Fate [than poisoning or hanging], / P–x'd by her Love, or libell'd by her Hate.'

[2] Susannah Centlivre (1667 ?–1723), dramatist; Eliza Haywood (1693 ?–1756), novelist; Mary de la Rivière Manley (1663–89), novelist and miscellaneous writer; and Aphra Behn (1640–89), dramatist and novelist. Aside from its caustic tone, the disingenuousness of this letter is evident from

the fact that three of these four were no longer alive.

[3] (1686–1744), a diligent compiler, particularly of legal works. He had been noticed in the *Dunciad* as the 'Scourge of Grammar' and 'Blunderbuss of Law'.

[4] On 10 May 1733 he published *The Mirrour; or, Letters Satyrical, Panegyrical, Serious and Humorous* (Robert W. Rogers, *Major Satires of Pope*, 1955, p. 143). It consists of twenty letters, addressed by initials to fellow victims of Pope's satire, and on a variety of topics, many of them attacks on Pope.

communicate to me any Letter or other Composition as You Should think fit concerning Mr. Pope, to be inserted in a Second Edition of the above Pamphlet;[1] but I quite forgot to mention how You might convey the Same to me, which is the occasion of my giving your Ladyship this Trouble, and further to Send You the following rude Epigram which I have lately writ on Pope, comparing him as a Satirist with the famous Dryden.

Epigram.
Dryden's just Satire rightly Others blam'd;
But Pope's Scurrility Himself has Damn'd.

If this or my former Letter be thought worthy of an Answer, please to direct to me at my Country Lodgings, at Mrs. Jones's in Rufford's Buildings beyond the Church in Islington.

I am, My Lady, Your Ladyship's most Obedient, Humble Servant,

G. Jacob.

Text W MS iv. 178   *End. by W* Mr Jacob   11 June 1733.

To Lord Hervey [*30 Oct.* (?) *1734*]

Letter to Lord Hervey from Twict'nam wrote on the King's Birthday.

Twict'nam,

Where I enjoy in Contemplative chamber
'Lutes, Lawrels, seas of Milk, and ships of Amber.'[2]

Through shineing Crouds you now make way
With slideing Bow and gilded Key,[3]
While wrap'd in Spleen and easy Chair
For all this Pomp so small my Care
I scarce remember who are there.
Yet in Brocade I can suppose
The Potent Knight whose Belly goes
At least a Yard before his Nose,[4]

[1] Evidently a second edition never appeared.

[2] From Thomas Otway, *Venice Preserv'd* (1682), Act V.

[3] Since 1730 Hervey had been Vice-Chamberlain of the Royal Household, with a golden key as his badge of office.

[4] Walpole's obesity was a frequent butt of satirists, and also of friends like Queen Caroline—who was herself fat.

And Majesty with sweeping Train,
That does so many Yards contain,
Superior to her waiting Nymphs,
As Lobster to attendant Shrimps.
   I do not ask one Word of News
Which country Damsels much amuse,
If a new batch of Lords appears
After a Tour of halfe six years
With Foreign Airs to grace the Nation
(The Maids of Honor's admiration),
Whose bright Improvements give Surprize
To their own Lady Mothers' Eyes.
Improvements! such as Colts might show,
Were Mares so mad to let them go,
Their Limbs perhaps a little stronger,
Their Mains and Tails grown something longer.
I would not hear of Ball-room Scuffles
Or what new Whims adorn the Ruffles;
I leave to my Ingenious Neighbours
To criticise on Birthday Labours.[1]
   This meek Epistle comes to tell
On Monday I in Town shall dwell,
Where if you please to condescend
In Candish Square[2] to see your Freind
I shall disclose to you alone
Such thoughts as n'ere were thought upon.

Text H MS vol. 256; printed inaccurately in 1803, v. 207–8

To John Arbuthnot *3 Jan.* [*1735*]

Sir,
   I have perus'd the last Lampoon of your ingenious Freind, and am not surpriz'd you did not find me out under the name of Sapho,[3] because there is nothing I ever heard in our characters or circumstances to make a paralell, but as the

---

[1] In 1734 the Birthday Ode by Colley Cibber, Poet Laureate, was particularly ridiculed because it was a near replica of the previous year's effusion.

[2] In 1731 the Wortley Montagus moved from Covent Garden to a house in Cavendish Square, a newly developed residential quarter (Rate Books, Marylebone Town Hall).

[3] In the *Epistle to Arbuthnot*, pub. 2 Jan. 1735, Pope had mentioned Sappho as a dangerous female wit.

Town (except you who know better) generally suppose Pope means me whenever he mentions that name, I cannot help takeing notice of the terrible malice he bears against the Lady signify'd by that name, which appears to be irritated by supposing her writer of the verses to the Imitator of Horace.[1] Now I can assure him they were wrote (without my knowledge) by a Gentleman of great merit, whom I very much esteem, who he will never guess, and who, if he did know, he durst not attack; but I own the design was so well meant, and so excellently executed, that I cannot be sorry they were written.

I wish you would advise poor Pope to turn to some more honest livelihood than libelling. I know he will alledge in his excuse that he must write to eat, and he is now grown sensible that nobody will buy his verses except their curiosity is pique'd to it to see what is said of their Acquaintance, but I think this method of Gain so exceeding vile that it admits of no excuse at all. Can any thing be more detestable than his abuseing poor Moor scarse cold in his Grave, when it is plain he kept back his Poem while he liv'd for fear he should beat him for it?[2] This is shocking to me thô of a man I never spoke to, and hardly knew by sight; but I am seriously concern'd at the worse scandal he has heap'd on Mr. Congreve, who was my Freind, and whom I am oblig'd to Justify because I can do it on my own knowledge, and which is yet farther, being witness of it from those who were then often with me, that he was so far from loveing Pope's Rhyme, both that and his Conversation were perpetual jokes to him, exceeding despicable in his opinion, and he has often made us laugh in talking of them, being particularly pleasant on that subject.[3] As to Pope's being born of Honest Parents, I verily beleive it, and will add one praise to his mother's character, that (thô I only knew her very old) she allways

---

[1] The *Verses to the Imitator of Horace,* published on 8 March 1733, was a bludgeoning attack on Pope. It was written by LM and Lord Hervey (who had been ridiculed by Pope for his versifying); and although the exact share of the two collaborators is not known, Hervey took the initiative of preparing a second edition, which was not published (Bristol MS).

[2] James Moore Smythe, co-author of *One Epistle to Pope,* had died the previous October; he is mentioned several times in the *Epistle to Arbuthnot,* though not with any severity.

[3] The 'worse scandal' about Congreve in the *Epistle to Arbuthnot* was that he had loved Pope's poetry (line 138).

appear'd to me to have much better sense than himselfe.[1] I desire, Sir, as a favour, that you would shew this Letter to Pope and you will very much oblige, Sir, your humble servant,

M. W. Montagu.

Jan. 3rd

Text MS at Royal College of Surgeons, London *Address* To Dr. Arbuthnott

To Francesco Algarotti[2] [*April 1736*]

Monday night

My Lady Stafford and my selfe waited for you three Hours. Three Hours of expectation is no small Tryal of Patience, and I beleive some of your Martyrs have been canoniz'd for suffering less. If you have repentance enough to be enclin'd to ask pardon you may obtain it by comeing here to morrow at 7 o' clock.

Let me have a line of answer.

Text Bod. MS Don. c. 56, f. 17 *Address* To The Marquis[3] of Algarotti

[1] Pope's parents were Alexander (1646–1717) and Editha (1642–1733), *née* Turner.

[2] Born in Venice, Algarotti (1712–64) studied science and belles-lettres at the University of Bologna with brilliant and precocious success. After visiting Rome, he made his way to Paris in 1735, and then spent six weeks at Cirey with Voltaire and Mme du Châtelet, transposing Newton's *Optics* into a set of graceful dialogues. He reached London in March 1736 with introductions to learned men—he was soon elected to the Royal Society and to the Society of Antiquaries—and to people at Court, including Lord Hervey (Ida Treat,

Francesco Algarotti, 1913, pp. 24 ff.). LM's impassioned letters to Algarotti, which outline a newly discovered episode of her life, are printed here in full for the first time.

[3] The title was a social courtesy (paid also by Voltaire in 1735); Algarotti's father had been a merchant (Treat, p. 24). In 1741 the snobbish French Ambassador to Turin, the marquis de Saint-Nectaire, reported scornfully that 'il est fils d'un libraire et neveu d'un apoticaire ayant actuellement leurs boutiques a Venise' (Ministère des Affaires Étrangères, Sardaigne, vol. 202, f. 61).

To Francesco Algarotti [*May 1736*]

If it be true you have any Inclination to see me, it will be in your power to morrow at 7 o' clock. I will expect you if I hear nothing from you to the contrary. C'est une terrible Caresme que j'attends apres cette petite Carnaval.

Text Bod. MS Don. c. 56, f. 19   *Address* A Monsieur Monsieur le marquis d'Algarotti

To Lord Strafford[1] *17 July* [*1736*]

My Lord,

I am ashamed to give your Lordship so much trouble about this triffle after all the good nature and Generosity you have shew'd on this subject, but it seems you forgot the name of your petitioner, which is Elizabeth White.[2] The vacancy has now happen'd but she is refus'd admittance except your Lordship gives her name under your hand. I beg you would be so good to enclose a note to that purpose to me, and I hope you will have no farther trouble on this affair, but the obligation shall be ever gratefully remember'd and acknowledg'd by, My Lord, Your Lordship's most obedient humble servant,

M. W. Montagu.

July 17.

Text Add MS 22,222, ff. 97–98   *End. by Strafford* Ly Mary Wortley   July the 12th: [*sic*] 1736

To Lord Strafford *29 July 1736*

My Lord,

You know how to do the most obliging thing in the most obliging manner. In telling me that I have given you pleasure, you do not only take from me the shame of being

[1] The 1st Earl (see above, p. 39).   [2] Not identified.

troublesome, but have found a way to make me pleas'd with my selfe, since I never can employ my time more to my own satisfaction than in showing your Lordship that I am with the utmost gratitude and esteem, my Lord, Your Lordship's most obedient Humble servant,

M. W. Montagu.

1736 July 29

Text Add MS 22,222, ff. 99–100[1]   *End. by Strafford* Ly Mary Wortly   July the 29th 1736

To Francesco Algarotti [*Aug. 1736*][2]

Je ne sçai plus de quel façon vous écrire. Mes sentimens sont trop vif; je ne sçaurois les expliquer ni les cacher. Il faut estre touché d'un entousiasme pareil au mien pour souffrir mes Lettres. J'en voye toute la folie sans la possibil- lité de me corriger. La seul Idée de vous revoir m'a donnée un Saississment en lisant vostre Lettre, que m'a quasi fait évanouir. Qu'est devenu cet Indifference philosophe qui a fait la Gloire et la tranquillité de mes jours passée? J'ai l'ai perdu pour le retrouver jamais, et si cette passion est guerri, je prevoye rien qu'un ennui mortel.—Pardonnez l'extra- vagance que vous avez fait naitre, et venez me voir.[3]

Text Bod. MS Don. c. 56, f. 63

To Francesco Algarotti [*Sept. 1736*][4]

Qu'on est timide quand on aime! J'ai peur de vous offenser en vous envoyant ce billet quoique mon intention est de vous faire plaisir. Enfin je suis si folle en tout ce que vous regarde que je ne suis pas seure de mes propres pensées. Ma

---

[1] Printed in *Wentworth Papers 1705–1739*, ed. J. J. Cartwright, 1883, p. 524.
[2] By mid-Aug. 1736 Algarotti had decided to return to Italy, and informed his friends of his imminent departure (Hervey to Algarotti, 14 Aug. 1736, Murray MS). He left on 6 Sept. (Earl of

Ilchester, *Lord Hervey and His Friends 1726–38*, 1950, p. 249).
[3] LM's letters in French to Algarotti are translated in the Appendix below.
[4] This brief, ardent, letter probably expresses LM's feelings immediately after Algarotti's departure.

raison murmure tout bas de sottises de mon cœur sans avoir la force de les detruire. Je suis dechiré de mille mouvemens differens, que vous importe tres peu, et je ne sçai pourquoy je vous en fais la confidence. Tout ce qui est certain, c'est que ⟨je⟩ vous aimeray toute ma vie malgre vos caprices et ma raison.

Text Bod. MS Don. c. 56, f. 27   *Address* A Monsieur Monsieur Algarotti chez Mr Robert Baigneur[1] dans la Rûe de la Seine Paris *Postmark* SH

To Francesco Algarotti [*10 Sept. 1736*]

Vendredi, minuit passé

Nox erat; et placidum carpebant fessa soporem
corpora per terras, sylvæque et sæva quierant
Æquora: cum medio volvuntur sidera lapsu:
cum tacet omnis ager: percudes [*sic*], pictæque volucres,
Quæque lacus latè liquidos, quæque aspera dumis
Rura tenent, somno positæ sub nocte silenti,
Lenibant curas, et corda oblita laborum.
At non infelix animi Phœnissa, nec unquam
solvitur in somnos, oculisve aut pectore noctem
accipit. Ingeminant curæ, rursusque resurgens
sævit amor—[2]

Je suis mille fois plus a plaindre que la triste Didon, et j'ai mille fois plus des raisons de me donner la mort. Mais comme jusqu'ici je n'ai pas imité sa conduitte, je croi que je vivray ou par poltronerie ou par force d'esprit. Je me suis jetté a la tête d'un étranger tout comme elle, mais au lieu de crier parjure et perfide quand mon petit Ænée temoigne qu'il a envie de me quitter, j'ÿ donne les mains par un sentiment de

[1] Hervey also sent a letter to Algarotti at 'Monsieur Robert le Baigneur' (9 Oct./28 Sept. [1736], Murray MS).

[2] 'It was night, and over the earth weary creatures were tasting peaceful slumber; the woods and wild seas had sunk to rest—the hour when stars roll midway in their gliding course, when all the land is still, and beasts and gay birds, both they that far and near haunt the limpid lakes, and they that dwell in fields of tangled brakes, couched in sleep beneath the silent night, [and with hearts forgetful of toil, laid aside their troubles]. But not so the soul-racked Phoenician queen; she never sinks to sleep, nor draws the night into eyes or heart. Her pangs redouble, and her love, swelling up, surges afresh' (*Aeneid*, iv. 522–32; transl.—except seventh line— Loeb Library).

PLATE 3

Francesco Algarotti

From drawings by Jonathan Richardson, senior, 19 Aug. 1736

Generosité dont Virgile n'a pas crû les femmes capable. En verité je me scai bon gré d'un desinterresment si extrodinaire, et vous devez estre contente d'etre aimé d'une façon si singuliere. L'amour pur dont parle si eloquemment Mr. de Cambrai[1] n'est pas si parfait que la mienne, et j'ai une devotion pour vous plus zelé qu'aucun des adorateurs de la Vierge a jamais eû pour elle. Je croi que tous ces messeiurs ont eû un peu de vanité dans leur devoûement, où ils ont esperé des grandes recompenses de leurs oraisons. Me voici en oraison a vous sans esperance que vous m'en teniez le moindre comte, et je passe des heures entiere en mon Cabinet absorbé dans la contemplation de vos perfections. Je me souvienne de moindre de vos paroles, vos enfances, vos folies, jusqu'a vos impertinences mesme; tout me plait en vous, et je vous trouve si different de la reste de genre humain (qui ont l'insolence pourtant de se croire de la mesme species) qu'il m'étonne pas que vous avez inspiré des sentimens que jusqu'ici ont été inspiré à personne.—

    C'est peut estre du mauvais françois que j'écrive, mais comme mes lettres sont entre vos mains de bruler le moment qu'elles vous ennuient, j'écris tout ce que me vient a la tête. Je n'ai pas la vanité d'oser esperer vous plaire; je n'ai nulle but que de me satisfaire en te disant que je t'aime,—et qui vous aimera pas ? Je priay Mademoiselle——a souper hier au soir. Nous avons bû a vostre santé, et elle disoit naïvement qu'elle n'avoit jamais rien vû de si aimable que vous.[2] Je ne repondois pas, mais ces peu de paroles me l'ont rendu d'une conversation si charmante que je retenois la pauvre fille jusqu'a deux heures apres minuit, sans parler d'avantage de vous, mais contente d'être avec une personne qui vous avoit vû—quel plaisir bisarre! Il faut avoir le Cœur occupé d'une forte passion, pour être touché des bagatelles qui parroissent aux autres si peu important. Ma raison me fait voir tout l'extravagance, et mon Cœur me fait sentir toute l'importance. Foible Raison! qui choque ma passion et ne le détruit

---

[1] 'On peut aimer Dieu d'un amour qui est une charité pure, et sans aucun mélange du motif de l'intérêt propre' (Fénelon, 'Explication des maximes des saints sur la vie intérieure', 1697, *Œuvres*, 1835, ii. 6).

[2] Algarotti's contemporaries agreed that 'his most pronounced characteristic was the desire to please—at the cost, if need be, of being "all things to all men"' (Francis Haskell, *Patrons and Painters*, 1963, p. 360).

pas, et qui me fait voir inutilement toute la folie d'aimer au point que j'aime sans esperance de retour. Vous etiez pourtant fasché de partir; je l'ai vû dans vos yeux, et il n'avoit point d'affectation dans le chagrin qui a paru en vostre air. Je me flatte pas sur l'impossible; ce n'estoit pas moi que vous etiez fasché de quitter, mais seurement vous etiez fasché de quitter Londres. J'aurois donc pû vous retenir, et c'estoit une fausse delicatesse qui m'a empeché de vous faire la proposition, et j'ai donc perdu, par mauvaise honte, crainte, et generosité mal placé, toute le plaisir de ma vie.—

Je ne sçai si vous comprenez rien a ce Galimatias, mais croyez que vous possedez en moi l'ami le plus parfait et l'amante la plus passioné. J'aurois été ravy que la nature m'avoit permis de me borner a cet premier titre; j'enrage d'avoir été fait pour porter des juppes.

> Why was my haughty Soul to Woman joyn'd?
> Why this soft sex impos'd upon my Mind?
> Even this extravagance which now I send
> Were meritorious in the name of Freind.
> Thee I might follow, thee my Lovely Guide,⎫
> Charm'd with thy voice, and ever by thy side,⎬
> Nor Land, nor sea, our common way divide. ⎭
>   How much these golden Wishes are in Vain!
> I dream to pleasure, but I wake to pain.

Voici la 2nd lettre que j'ecris. Ce le seul plaisir que me reste. Que cet triste plaisir est mélé d'amertumes!

Text MS in Hyde Collection[1]

To Francesco Algarotti *20 Sept.* [*1736*]

Sept. 20. V.S.

Est-il possible que je n'ai pas de vos nouvelles? Il me semble que vous m'avez promis de m'écrire de Calais. Je ne songe qu'a cela, et en attendant tout m'ennuye, tout me deplait, et je suis dans un état qui feroit pitié aux Gens meme qui me haïssent le plus. Il me ⟨paroist⟩ qu'il devoit vous moins couter de m'écrire trois ou quatre lignes que de passer autant d'heures dans ma conversation. Philosophiquement,

---

[1] Letter listed and verse printed in *R. B. Adam Library* (1929), iii. 174.

un commerce des lettres avec moi devoit vous faire un es-
pecee de Plaisir. Vous verrez (ce qu'on n'a pas vûe jusqu'ici)
le fidele portrait d'un Cœur de femme sans detour ou de-
guisement, peint au naturel, qui se donne pour ce qu'elle est,
et qui ne vous cache ni vous farde rien. Mes foiblesses et
mes emportemens doivent attirer au moins vostre curiosité en
vous presentant la vraie disection d'une Ame femelle. On dit
que Montagne plait par cette naiveté qui decouvre jusqu'a
ses defauts,[1] et j'ai cette merite si je n'ai point d'autres
aupres de vous. Il n'est pas donc possible que mes lettres
vous ennuyent au point que vous y renoncer si brusque-
ment.

Ce seroit bien pis si quelque malheur vous etiez arrivé.—
On n'a pas parlé des tempettes ni des vaissaux perdu.—Il
faut m'en éclaircir a quelque prix que cela soit.—Je veux
voir milord Harvey; il auroit eû de vos nouvelles.[2] Tout
ingrat que vous étes, j'aurois un moment de plaisir en sachant
que vous étes heureusement arrivé a Paris, ou vous vous
moqueriez de mes lettres aupres de quelque belle Parrisi-
enne. N'importe, je vous écrira toujours, pour vous faire
plaisir si vous m'aimez, ou pour vous faire enrager si vous
voulez m'oublier. Que je suis malheureuse! et qu'un coup
de Foudre dans ce moment me seroit un coup de Grace!

Voici le quatrieme Lettre que je vous envoye. Vous devez
estre bien ennuyé des mes plaintes, mais suis-je en droit de
menager vostre repos quand vous avez si peu de soin du
mien?[3]

Text Eg MS 23, ff. 233–4   *Address* A Monsieur Monsieur Algarotti
[*struck out*] chez Robert Baigneur dans la Rue de Seine Paris [*in
another hand*] A Venize   *Postmark* VR

[1] Montaigne had expressed this intention in 'Au lecteur' (*Œuvres complètes*,
ed. A. Thibaudet and M. Rat, 1962,
p. 9), for which Voltaire praised him in
his 'Remarques sur les Pensées de M.
Pascal' (*Lettres philosophiques*, 1734, ed.
G. Lanson, 1909, ii. 216–17).

[2] She had already written to
Hervey, who answered, 'The Body
you speak of has not mention'd you in
his Letters to me. He knows I have

seen you by the first of mine to him, in
which I say'd, without any other Com-
ent, that I was to see you next day'
(n.d., Bristol MS, ii. 5).

[3] Unwittingly or not, LM here sug-
gests the couplet from Pope's 1728
Dunciad (i. 91–92):
While pensive Poets painful vigils keep,
Sleepless themselves to give their readers
sleep.

To Francesco Algarotti [*c. 29 Sept. 1736*]

Your Letter came in very good time to save the small remains of my understanding. Your silence had so far disturb'd it, that not able to bear the perplexity of my own Imaginations, I sent Lord H[ervey] word I should be glad to speak to him.[1] You may beleive (with his politeness) I saw him soon after, and then I was in allmost as much difficulty to draw from him what I had a mind to know; that is, whither you were arriv'd safe at Paris? The Question was very short, but the way to make it very hard, and in short I said nothing of what I had a mind to know, and all he could collect from my conversation was that I was very near if not quite distracted. He told me very plainly that after so much neglect as I had shewn him he could not fancy I would honnour him with a message, except I had something to demand of him that I thought of importance to my selfe, and very generously made me all sort of offers of Services and assurances of obeying my commands, reasonable or unreasonable. This speech, which was meant to give me courrage to explain my selfe, made it quite impossible for me to do it. I refflected I could not now ask him this Question with an air of Indifference, since he allready thought nothing but the last necessity would make me ask him any Question at all, and I was reduce'd to confess I had something of consequence to impart but could not prevail on my selfe to do it that day, and postpone'd my Enquiry to another.[2] I receiv'd your Letter the Day following, and have now nothing farther to demand of him.

I shall go to morrow (late as it is in the year) to my Country House, where I intend to bury my selfe for at least 3 months.

---

[1] Hervey had answered her on [18 Sept.]: 'It is not strange that any body who labours as much as you do to be unintelligible should be misunderstood, but if you will send me word what hour to night I may see you, I will call upon you for better information, if it be but for a minute, to show you that at least it is not willfully (as you say) that I misunderstand' (Bristol MS, ii. 15).

[2] Hervey sent Algarotti a long and caustic account of how he had at first evaded LM's attempt to see him, and then of her painful, extended, and unsuccessful interview with him (9 Oct./28 Sept. [1736], Murray MS; partially printed in Halsband, *LM*, p. 160).

People tell me that I am going to a Wilderness, because they don't know that I am leaveing one, and 'tis all one to me whether I see Beasts cover'd with their natural Hides, or Embrodierys; they are equally unconversible. You have taken from me not only the taste but the sufferance of those I see, but in recompence you have made me very entertaining to my selfe, and there are some moments when I am happy enough to think over the past till I totally forget the present.

> —Vixi: cras vel atrâ
> nube polum pater occupato,
> vel sole puro: non tamen irritum
> quodcumque retro est, efficiet, neque
> diffinget infectumque reddet,
> quod fugiens semel hora vexit.[1]

My picture is doing.

Text Eg MS 23, ff. 235–6   *Address* A Monsieur Monsieur Algarotti à Venise   *End.* avec le compliments de Busenello.[2]

To Francesco Algarotti *21 Oct.* [*1736*]

If you realy had wrote to me from Lyons, I think tis impossible I should not have receiv'd your Letter. Must not I then from thence conclude—? I will conclude nothing. If possible I will hope you think of me, thô I have no ground for that Hope but a consciousness how much I deserve it from you—I could talk long upon this subject. There is not a moment that does not add to the obligations you have to me, if you can be oblig'd by the tenderest wishes and by the softest remembrance. I am now in the Country where I chuse to see nothing but trees since I cannot see the only Object dear to my Heart and Lovely to my Eyes. 'Tis with

---

[1] 'I have lived to-day; to-morrow let the Father fill the heaven with murky clouds, or radiant sunshine! Yet will he not render vain whatever now is past, nor will he alter and undo what once the fleeting hour has brought' (Horace, *Odes*, III. xxix. 43–48; transl. Loeb Library).

[2] Giacomo Busenello, Venetian Resident in London from Aug. 1736 to July 1737 (*Repertorium*, ii. 414). LM sent her letter to Algarotti this way because, like Hervey, she had no Italian address for him.

difficulty that I restrain my pen from falling into the extravagancys of Poetry, which indeed are only fit to attempt the
expressing my thoughts of you or to you. But I am very
little sure of this ever reaching your Hands. I have no way
of sending it but by your wise Resident, who perhaps will
take little care of it, and till I know you have receiv'd my last,
which was sent this way, I want spirits to write.

If you have any degree of regard for me you will let me
have the pleasure of hearing from you (the only pleasure 'tis
possible for me to taste in your Absence). If you have none,
I should not trouble you with my Letters, nor ever will tire
you with complaints of a neglect which, perhaps, proceeds
from a cause we can neither of us remedy. Only beleive this
serious protestation (you may beleive it since there is no
appearance of deceit in it), that the Impression you have made
on my Heart can never leave it while I have life enough to
feel a warmth in it.

Oct. 21. O.S.

Since I wrote what is above, I have seen Lord Hervey at
Court (where I have never been till yesterday) and he told me
he has had a Letter from you.[1] And you can find no time to
send a few lines to one that can receive no other Happyness
in your absence!

Text Eg MS 23, ff. 237–8   *Address* A Monsieur Monsieur
Algarotti [*in another hand*][2] Cale Stella S. Gio: e Paolo à Venise.

To Francesco Algarotti [*Dec. 1736*]

I have sent you so many verses, this shall wait on you in
the Form of plain prose. My picture went last, wrapp'd up in
poetry without Fiction. I could be angry at your haste in
restoreing a Triffle that, if you ever intend to see me again,
might have been time enough deliver'd to my own hand. If
you seriously wish to see me, it will certainly happen; if your

---

[1] Hervey had received a letter from
Paris on 24 Sept.; another came from
Turin on 30 Oct. In his answer to the

latter, he begged Algarotti to write
more often (Murray MS).
[2] Probably the Venetian Resident's.

affairs do not permit your return to England, mine shall be arrang'd in such a manner as I may come to Italy. This sounds extrodinary, and yet is not so when you consider the impression you have made on a Heart that is capable of receiveing no other. My thoughts of you are such as exceed the strongest Panegyric that the vainest Man upon Earth ever wish'd to hear made of him selfe, and all conversations since I lost yours are so insipid to me that I prefer my closet meditations to all the amusements of a populous Town or crouded Court.

I shall endeavor to obey all your commands because they are yours, but I have so little correspondance and yet less faith in Doctors of all degrees that I know not who to apply to for your old Relation. I only know in General many people here have Cataracts, and none are cur'd but by couching, which is a manual operation.[1]

You may spare the recommendation of remembring you. You are ever present to my thoughts, and halfe those aspirations to the B. V. would deserve her personal appearance to encourrage so sincere a Votary.

Let me know when you receive my picture. Write to me, and beleive when ever you do it you are bestowing the only happyness I can be sensible of in your Absence.[2]

Text Bod. MS Don. c. 56, ff. 54–55   *Address* A Monsieur Monsieur Algarotti.

From Lord Hervey *18 June 1737*

Ickworth Park,[3] June 18. 1737.

You can not imagine how much I felt my-self obliged to you for remembering me at this Distance of Place and Time, and showing you

[1] Inserting a needle through the membrane of the eye and displacing the cataract below the axis of vision. By 1710 it was being successfully performed (OED).

[2] The next letter from LM to Algarotti is dated 24 Feb. [1738], more than a year later. During 1737 she may have written letters to him which have been lost; or he may have discouraged the correspondence with her (as with Hervey and with Mme du Châtelet) because he was occupied in preparing his Newtonian dialogues for publication.

[3] The Earl of Bristol's seat in Suffolk, near Bury St. Edmunds.

desired to entertain me. If you succeed as well in every thing you desire, *blessed art thou among Women*,[1] for you will never meet with any disappointment. I have often say'd to you and of You, that there is a charming Speciality in your way of thinking, and a Nostrum in your manner of expressing your-self, that hits my thinking Constitution beyond any Medcine I ever took for Spleen, Solitude, or Ennui in my Life.

But for God's sake how can you talk so like a canting Seneca of the Purity of Air and the Quiet of Retirement raising one's Imagination? You might as well talk of Water-Gruel raising one's Spirits, or my Lady Key's[2] raising any thing else. My Imagination is never so much raised as in the midst of ridiculous Objects; and if you would own fair, I'll be hang'd if your Imagination ever work'd half so well, or so fast, in the Solitude of Twickenham or the Purity of Country Air as it has in a Drawing-room and the Impurity of the Smoak of London. As for the Beautyfull Scenes and the pleasing Verdure of Country Prospects, when People talk of the Pleasures these things exhibit to them I always either think they lye egregiously or have a most execrable taste; and look upon them with just the same degree of Admiration that I should on any body in London who told me they had been extreamly happy the whole Day and prodigiously well entertain'd because they had pass'd it in a Room hung with Green Damask. [*Passage omitted*]

Text Bristol MS ii. 53–54

To Lord Hervey [*c. 20 June 1737*]

Conclusion of a Letter to Lord H—— giving an Account of the Death of Mr. Hedges[3] Treasurer to his *R.H.*

——This is wrote with Tears,
Tears for our loss, it is not his I mourn,
Who past all Care sleeps in his peace-full Urn;
Or crown'd with Roses in Elysian Groves
With bright Ophelia now renews his Loves;

---

[1] Luke, i. 28.
[2] Possibly Anne (d. 1740), da. of Sir Samuel Marow, who m. (1690) Sir Arthur Kaye.
[3] John Hedges (*c.*1689–20 June 1737),

M.P., Treasurer to the Prince of Wales. Hervey, in his *Memoirs*, writes that he and Hedges composed ballads and songs for the Prince of Wales, who passed them off as his own (i. 309).

Where Purer Light and happier Feasts they share
With Ovid, Congreve, Sapho, Delawar,[1]
Perhaps with Pity at a distance view
The Paths poor Poets militant persue.

Text H MS vol. 256   *End. by LM* Answer'd by Lord H——y.

From Lord Hervey *23 June 1737*

Ickworth Park, June 23. 1737.

[*Passage omitted*] The News of poor Hedges's Death and your Coments upon it enlarg'd and *raised my Imagination*, as you call it, more than any Leisure, or the reality of the finest Landskips Claude Lorain ever painted, could do in seven Years: nothing, I own, affects my mind much but human Creatures, and Black and White.

Why doest thou ignorantly mourn his Fate,
And wish his scanty Lease a longer Date?
His [*sic*] gone, his Honors green upon his Brow,
The Lover's Myrtle and the Poet's Bough;
Unwasted yet to Ashes either Fire,
Nor dwindled into Dotage from Desire.
In the full Vigor of his Blood and Mind
He drank of Life, and left the Dregs behind:
Exempt from all th' Infirmitys of Age,
Nor doom'd to totter on Life's latest Stage
(Where many breath, tho they no longer live,
And all worth living for, despised, survive):
Sure too the Reccord of his Fame to save,
For Lady Mary writes upon his Grave.[2] [*Passage omitted*]

Text Bristol MS ii. 57–58

[1] Probably Charlotte MacCarthy (1701–35), da. of 4th Earl of Clancarty, who m. (1721) Baron, later Earl, De La Warr (see iii. 187).

[2] Hervey also sent these verses to Algarotti (Earl of Ilchester, *Lord Hervey and His Friends 1726–38*, 1950, p. 272).

To [James Roberts][1] [*c. 14 Dec. 1737*]

I ⟨?⟩ paper[2] was printed for next ⟨?⟩ sure the author will remain ⟨?⟩ and I ⟨?⟩ you will return me the originals.
Let me have half a dozen saturday morn.

Text W MS vii. 143

To [James Roberts] [*15 Feb. 1738*]

Wednesday night[3]
I desire I may see you to morrow Evening if possible, having many matters to communicate. I can not be at home Friday.

Text W MS vii. 247

To Francesco Algarotti[4] *24 Feb.* [*1738*]

There needs only your absence to make any place disagreable to me, but at present we have a complication of every

---

[1] An eminent printer, Roberts (d. 1754) had published earlier works by LM: his name appears on the title page of her *Court Poems* (1716), though Edmund Curll had been responsible for it; he and Dodd are listed on the title page of the 1719 *Letter* from Constantinople; and in 1733 he and Dodd published, on successive days, the *Verses to the Imitator of Horace*. More personally, the newspaper advertisements for LM's runaway son (in 1727) stated that the reward for his recovery would be paid by Roberts, to whom any letters about the boy were to be directed.

[2] This letter, parts of which were irrecoverably obliterated by LM, is written on the same sheet as the essay issued on 16 Dec. 1737 as No. I of *The Nonsense of Common-Sense*, her anonymous periodical, published by J. Roberts. Its essays are mainly devoted to feminism and social satire; they also support Walpole's Ministry by attacking *Common Sense*, the Opposition's paper (*The Nonsense of Common-Sense 1737–38*, ed. R. Halsband, 1947).

[3] This letter is written on the same sheet as the essay published on 21 Feb. 1738 as No. VIII of *The Nonsense of Common-Sense*. No. IX, on 14 March, was apparently the last one published.

[4] During 1737, while he stayed in Milan preparing his Newtonian dialogues for publication, Algarotti neglected his friends in England. Hervey complained in July that his previous two letters had not been answered. 'I enquire

thing in London that is contrary to my Inclination: Noise, croud, Division, and allmost an impossibillity of keeping entirely clear of the Infection. Thô my mind is too well fill'd with soft remembrances to be penetrable to the rough impressions of Faction and Nonsense,[1] yet my Ears are daily wounded with epidemic madness, and my person expos'd to the Rheumes and disorders incident to this watry climate. I am forc'd to remember this by a cursed tooth ach that endeavors to torment me at this very moment, but your Idea shall give me stoicism enough to resist it. This is doing a great deal, but you cannot expect me to carry it so far as to be entertaining in my present scituation. 'Tis enough that you can make me insensible either to pain or politics, but I must necessarily be dull when the Sun and you are both so distant from me; may the spring bring a return of both.

> You, Lovely Youth, shall my Apollo prove,
> Adorn my Verse, and tune my soul to Love.

Feb. 24. O.S.

Text Bod. MS Don. c. 56, ff. 33–34   *Address* A Monsieur Monsieur Algarotti [*in another hand*] Francois Venetia. S. Gio: e Paolo. Calle Ca' Stella

To Francesco Algarotti[2] *15 June* [*1738*]

Il y a plus d'un mois que je n'ai entendu de vos nouvelles; pourtant je me presse de repondre a vostre lettre par le premier ordinaire apres que je le reçois. Je comprends assez la sottise de cette conduitte, mais c'est un plaisir que je ne sçaurois me refuser. Il me semble que la Fortune m'en refuse

often of Lady Mary what she knows of you; sometimes she says she hears from you, sometimes that she does not. Which is true I know not' (29/18 July 1737, Murray MS). In Dec. 1737 the dialogues were published in Milan as *Il Newtonianismo per le dame*.

[1] These references to politics hint at LM's published periodical essays.

[2] In the spring of 1738 Algarotti, whose family fortunes had declined, intended to return to England to take advantage of his well-placed friends there, as he told his brother. He set out from Milan with an enchanting young friend, but instead of travelling directly to Paris, began a leisurely tour of Provence (Ida Treat, *Francesco Algarotti*, 1913, pp. 64–67).

assez, sans que je prens la peine de me querreller moi mesme.
Je m'abbandonne donc a mon penchant et me rappelle tous
mes aimables chimeres au mepris de tout ce que m'environne,
et je veux me laisser aller a la douce illusion que me repre-
sente que vous pensez quelque fois a moi, toute éloigné que
vous ettes, et tout incertain que je suis quand je vous verray.
C'est la seule Idée que puisse me plaire. J'avoue je suis surpris de me trouver des Sentimens si extrodinaire. J'ai un
Cœur fait pour entretenir un Sylphe, et si vous etiez un de
ces intteligences qui lisse dans le fonds de l'ame, vous seriez
charmé de voir le mien si rempli de tendresse delicate et
desintteressé.

Serieusement, si vos affaires mettoient de l'impossibillité
dans vostre dessein de venir en Angleterre, et que j'etois bien
persuadé que je vous ferois un vrai plaisir de me retirer a
Venise, je ne balanceray pas de m'etablir dans les états de la
Seignorie pour le reste de ma vie, je vous l'asseure de bonne
foi. C'est assez vous dire que je suis tout a vous.

Jun. [? Jan. 1739] 15. V.S.

Text Bod. MS Don. c. 56, ff. 30–31   *Address* A Monsieur Monsieur
Algarotti chez Mr Robert Baigneur dans la Rûe de la Seine Paris
Postmark SH

To Francesco Algarotti *11 July* [*1738*]

Est il possible que vous croyez que j'ai receu la plus
aimable Lettre qui a jamais été ecrit, de vostre part, sans y
repondre? Non; vous n'en croyez rien, et vous me cachez que
vous avez receû deux de mes Lettres depuis la vostre de
Milan, pour excuser vostre silence. Je vous pardonne cet
artifice, comme je vous pardonne touttes choses, en faveur
d'un merite et des graces aussi singuliere que les vostres.
J'ai été la Penelope de vostre absence, negligant tous les
objets que je voyez pour m'entretenir sans cesse des charmes
d'un fugitif dont je ne sçavois pas mesme la demeure, et me
doutoit quelque fois de l'existence. Malgre ces cruelles
incertitudes, cet cher souvenir faisoit le seul plaisir de ma

vie. Jugez donc de vostre Injustice quand vous m'accusez ⟨?⟩ vous avoir oublié. J'ai lû, j'ai relû et je relirai vostre livre. Je trouverai toujours des beautez nouvelles; aucune des agremens m'echape.[1] Vous seriez trop heureux de trouver mon goût et mes sentimens dans une personne qui touchera vostre Inclination.

> 'How often have I wish'd some other Cæsar,
> 'Great as the first, and as the second young,
> 'Would court my Love to be refus'd for you?'[2]

This is a serious, solemn truth, as extrodinary as it sounds. The Enthusiasm you have infected me with is as violent as ever; and as (you know) the Human Vanity makes food out of every thing, there are some moments in which I value my selfe for so uncommon a way of thinking, and a Heart capable of an Impression not to be destroy'd, or even lessen'd, by Absence or accidents. While I ⟨?live⟩ I am and will be yours.

> This outward Form submits to Nature's power,
> Thus far can Fortune, but she can no more;[3]
> Unchang'd my Heart retains the living Fire
> Which only can with the last breath expire.

Juillet 11. V.S.

Text Bod. MS Don. c. 56, ff. 22–23   *Address* A Monsieur Monsieur Algarotti chez Mr Robert Baigneur dans la Rûe de la Seine Paris. *Postmark* SH

To Francesco Algarotti *24 July* [*1738*]

Je ne pouvois pas m'empecher de vous faire reponse le premier moment que j'ai receû vostre lettre, quoi que j'ai peur que vous n'etes pas encore a Paris, et peutestre Mr. Robert se donneroit pas la peine de vous le garder. Je suis assez accoutumé a perdre des Lettres aupres de vous; pourtant je ne sçaurois me consoler de deux que j'ai addressé a

---

[1] LM wrote commendatory verses in English which were printed, together with others, in later editions of the dialogues, beginning 1739.

[2] Dryden's *All for Love* (1678), Act II, Scene i.

[3] Couplet adapted from Prior's *Solomon* (*Works*, i. 339).

Milan que vous dittes que vous n'avez pas receû. Vostre indifference, vostre oubli mesme (tout cruel qu'il est), m'est plus supportable que vostre Injustice. Je ne sçaurois souffrir un moment que vous me croyiez capable de n'etre pas toute ma vie occupé de vous. Non; vous ne me connoisez point. J'ai une constance et une probité qui doivent tenir lieu des charmes et d'agremens; et malgre la promptitude avec laquelle vous m'avez plû, je suis assez difficile à plaire, et par consequence incapable de changer d'objet de mon attachement.

J'écris dans une mauvaise humeur, horrible par la crainte que vous n'auriez pas ma lettre. Voici la seconde que j'ai addressé a Paris. Quand je suis seure que vous l'auriez receû, je vous parlerois plus longtemps, mais jamais avec plus de tendresse et de sincerité.

Juillet 24 V.S.

Text Bod. MS Don. c. 56, ff. 24–25   *Address* A Monsieur Monsieur Algarotti chez Mr Robert Baigneur dans la Rûe de la Seine Paris *Postmark* ⟨?⟩

To Lady Pomfret[1] *26 July 1738*

I hope, dear madam, you find at least some amusement in your travels, and though I cannot wish you to forget those friends in England, who will never forget you, yet I should be pleased to hear you were so far entertained as to take off all anxiety from your mind.[2] I know you are capable of many

---

[1] Here begins an important series of letters. Henrietta Louisa (1698-1761), da. of 2nd Baron Jeffreys, m. (1720) Thomas Fermor (1698–1753), later 1st Earl of Pomfret. She had been Lady of the Bedchamber to the late Queen Caroline, and her husband Master of the Horse. Probably on account of his debts (Egmont, *Diary*, ii. 489) they moved to the Continent with two of their daughters, leaving London on 8 July 1738. Lady Pomfret had met LM at an auc-

tion, as she noted in her diary (Finch MS).

[2] In Abbeville Lady Pomfret, who had written to LM on 23/12 July, confided to her diary that LM's 'Wit and Charming Conversation, join'd to the most obliging Friendship she has in a great many Instances show'd to me at a time when she cou'd not propose even the return of my passing some Hours with her, has engaged me extreamly to her.' She wrote to LM again on 27/16 July.

pleasures that the herd of mankind are insensible of; and wherever you go I do not doubt you will find some people, that will know how to taste the happiness of your conversation. We are as much blinded in England by politicks and views of interest, as we are by mists and fogs, and 'tis necessary to have a very uncommon constitution not to be tainted with the distempers of our climate. I confess myself very much infected with the epidemical dulness; yet as 'tis natural to excuse one's own faults as much as possible, I am apt to flatter myself that my stupidity is rather accidental than real; at least I am sure that I want no vivacity when I think of my Lady Pomfret, and that it is with the warmest inclination as well as the highest esteem that I am ever affectionately yours,

M. W. M.

July 26, O.S. 1738.[1]

Here is no alteration since you left us except in the weather, and I would not entertain you with the journal of the thermometer. I hope to hear soon from you.[2]

Text 1837, ii. 205–6[3]

To Francesco Algarotti *20/9 Aug.* [*1738*]

Je perds patience. C'en est une grande preuve que je hazarde de vous écrire par une voye qui me deplaist infiniment. J'ai vous addressé deux Lettres a Milan et deux autres chez Mr. Robert, sans entendre parler de vous. Je n'ose entrer en detail de mes sentimens. Imaginez ce que j'ai a vous dire, accablée comme je suis de vostre silence.

20 Aoust. N.S.

Text Murray MS

[1] On 17/6 Aug. Lady Pomfret received a letter from LM, almost certainly this one (Finch MS).
[2] Lady Pomfret wrote to her from Paris on 23/12 Aug. (ibid.).
[3] The original manuscripts of this correspondence are untraced. In 1834 they were lent to Lord Wharncliffe by Sir Henry Campbell, whose father, Alexander Campbell of Cawdor, had married a daughter of LM's niece Lady Frances (Pierrepont) Meadows.

To Lady Pomfret [*Aug. 1738*]

I am afraid so quick a return of thanks will frighten your ladyship from a continuance of this correspondence, but I cannot help gratifying myself in saying something, yet I dare not say half I think of your delightful letter; though nobody but myself could read it and call any thing complimental that could be said of it.

'Tis as impossible to send an equivalent out of this stupid town as it would be to return a present of the fruits of Provence out of Lapland. We have no news, no trade, no sun, and even our fools are all gone to play at Tunbridge; and those that remain are only miserable invalids, who talk of nothing but infirmities and remedies; as ladies who are on the point of encreasing the world, who speak of only nurses and midwives. I do not believe either Cervantes or Rabelais would be able to raise one moment's mirth from such subjects; and I acquit myself of writing stupidly from this place; as I should do Mr. Chloe if he was condemned to furnish an entertainment out of rotten turnips and artichokes run to seed.[1]

I was in this part of my letter when young Vaillant[2] arrived at my door, with a very pretty box in the name of Lady Pomfret: there needed nothing to keep up my regard for you; yet I am deeply touched at every mark of your attention. I believe he thought me very unreasonable, for I insisted on it that he had also a letter. Let me entreat to hear often from you. If I had the utmost indifference for you, I should think your letters the greatest pleasure of my life; and if you deputed Lady Vane to write for you, I could find a joy in reading her nonsense,[3] if it informed me of your health.

---

[1] Monsieur Chloé, whose name is variously spelled, was a famous chef employed by the Duke of Newcastle. He is mentioned by Horace Walpole and Chesterfield; also in J. Jean Hecht, *Continental and Colonial Servants in Eighteenth Century England,* Smith College Studies in History, xl, 1954, p. 26.

[2] Probably Paul Vaillant (1715–

1802), whose grandfather founded the well-known publishing house (John Nichols, *Lit. Anecdotes of the 18th Century*, 1812–15, iii. 309, n.).

[3] Frances Anne (*c.* 1715–88), da. of Francis Hawes, and widow of Lord William Hamilton, m. (1735) 2nd Viscount Vane. Her immorality was notorious. When she later published her

Judge then how important it is to me to hear from you, and with what sincere attachment I am ever yours.[1]

I suppose your ladyship knows your friend Mr. West is in the happy state of honeymoon.[2]

Text 1837, ii. 206–7

To Lady Pomfret [*Sept. 1738*][3]

1738.

I begin to think you are grown weary of so dull a correspondent. 'Tis a long time since I sent my last letter, which was full of acknowledgments for your obliging token and entertaining letter. I am impatient to hear how you like the place you are settled in, for settled I am told you are, though I was not informed exactly where, only that it is not far from Paris;[4] which I am very glad of, being persuaded you will find it much more pleasant, and every way as convenient as any of those distant provinces you talked of. I suppose it is no news to you that Lady Betty Finch is married to Mr. Murray. People are divided in their opinions, as they commonly are, on the prudence of her choice. I am among those who think, *tout bien compté*, she has happily disposed of her person.[5] Lord Townshend is spitting up his lungs at the

scandalous 'Memoirs of a Lady of Quality' in 1751, LM considered them too well written to be by her (see iii. 2–3).

[1] On 20/9 Sept. Lady Pomfret received LM's letter 'full of Wit and Tenderness that Charms more than one can express; either is engaging, but when they are joyn'd they are not to be resisted nor discribed' (Finch MS).

[2] James West (1704 ?–72), politican and antiquary, m. (15 Aug. 1738) Sarah (d. 1799), only daughter of Sir Thomas Stephens, with a dowry of £30,000 (*Gentleman's Mag.*, 1738, p. 435).

[3] On 5 [4] Oct./23 Sept. Lady Pomfret noted in her diary that she received this letter (Finch MS).

[4] At the beginning of Sept. Lady Pomfret and her family settled in Monts on the Seine, which she described as 'a small but very pretty village' (Hertford, *Corr*. i. 3).

[5] William Murray (1705–93), son of 5th Viscount Stormont, was by now a successful barrister; he became Chief Justice of the King's Bench and 1st Earl of Mansfield. He m. (20 Sept. 1738) Lady Elizabeth Finch (1704–84), da. of 7th Earl of Winchilsea. Hervey's comment was: 'sotte marriage de chaque côté' (to Henry Fox, 12 Sept. [1738], BM Holland House MS, xciii).

Gravel-pits,[1] and his charming lady[2] diverting herself with daily rambles in town. She has made a new friendship which is very delightful; I mean with Madame Pulteney,[3] and they hunt in couples from tea-drinking 'till midnight.

I won't trouble you with politicks, though the vicissitudes and conjectures are various. Lady Sundon drags on a miserable life;[4] it is now said she has a cancerous humour in her throat; which if true is so dismal a prospect, as would force compassion from her greatest enemies. I moralize in my own dressing-room on the events I behold, and pity those who are more concerned in them than myself; but I think of dear Lady Pomfret in a very different manner than I do of princes and potentates, and am warmly interested in every thing that regards her. Let me beg then to hear soon from you; and, if you will honour me so far, let me have a particular account how you pass your time. You can have no pleasure in which I shall not share, nor no uneasiness in which I shall not suffer; but I hope there is no reason to apprehend any; and that you are now in the perfect enjoyment of uninterrupted tranquillity, and have already forgot all the fogs and spleen of England. However, remember your less happy friends that feel the pain of your absence; and always number amongst them, Your faithful, &c. &c.

Text 1837, ii. 207–9

[1] Charles (1700–64), 3rd Viscount Townshend. He had been reported as being very ill at the end of Aug. (*Daily Advertiser*, 31 Aug.). Because of its gravel-pits Kensington was considered salubrious.

[2] Etheldreda (or Audrey) Harrison (1708–88) m. (1723) Lord Townshend; she was notorious for her loose morals and racy wit.

[3] LM may mean the widow of Daniel (see above, p. 24), but more probably Anna Maria Gumley (1697–1758), who m. (1714) William Pulteney, later 1st Earl of Bath. Hervey mentions her vanity and coquetry (*Memoirs*, i. 8).

[4] Charlotte Dyve (b. 1661) m. (before 1714) William Clayton, later 1st Baron Sundon. She had been taken ill in July (*Daily Advertiser*, 8 July), but lived until Jan. 1742. As confidante and Woman of the Bedchamber to Queen Caroline she had been a person of consequence. The Pomfrets had cultivated her friendship, as can be seen in Lady Pomfret's letters to her (Add MS 20,104, ff. 126–79); and they were said to have bribed her with a pair of diamond earrings to procure Lord Pomfret his post as Master of the Horse (H. Walpole, *Reminiscences*, ed. P. Toynbee, 1924, pp. 90–91).

To Lady Pomfret [*Oct. 1738*][1]

1738.

Yesterday was very fortunate to me; it brought two of your ladyship's letters. I will not speak my thoughts of them, but must insist once for all that you lay aside all those phrases of *tiring me, ashamed of your dulness,* &c. &c. I can't help when I read them either doubting your sincerity, or fearing you have a worse opinion of my judgment than I desire you should have. Spare me those disagreeable reflections; and be assured, if I hated you, I should read your letters with pleasure; and that I love you enough to be charmed with hearing from you, though you knew not how to spell.

The delightful description of your retirement makes me wish to partake it with you; but I have been so much accustomed to wish in vain, that I dare not flatter myself with so pleasing an idea. We are wrapt up in fogs, and consequential stupidity; which encreases so visibly, we want but little of the state of petrifaction which was said to befall an African town. However there remains still some lively people amongst us that play the fool with great alacrity. Lady Sophia Keppel has declared her worthy choice of the amiable Captain Thomas.[2] Poor Lady Frances Montagu is on the point of renouncing the pomps and vanities of this world, and confining herself to rural shades with Sir Roger Burgoyne,[3] whose mansion-house will, I believe, perfectly resemble Mr. Sullen's; but, as we are in dead peace, I am afraid there is no hope of a French count to enliven her solitude.[4] It is reported a much greater, fairer lady is going to be disposed of to a much worse retreat, at least I should think so.[5] 'Tis terrible to be the fifth

[1] Received by Lady Pomfret on 22/11 Oct. (Finch MS).

[2] Lady Sophia Keppel (1711–73), da. of 1st Earl of Albemarle, m. Capt., later Gen., John Thomas. He was one of her father's aides-de-camp (Earl of Albemarle, *Fifty Years of My Life,* 2nd ed., 1876, i. 49).

[3] Lady Frances (d. 1788), da. of 1st Earl of Halifax, m. (1 Jan. 1739) Sir Roger (c. 1710–80), of Sutton Park, Bedfordshire. Lady Hertford sent a very romantic account of their courtship to Lady Pomfret on 18 Oct. (*Corr.* i. 18–19).

[4] Referring to *The Beaux' Stratagem* (1707) by George Farquhar.

[5] Princess Mary (1723–72), da. of George II, m. (19 May 1740) Prince-Elector Frederick II of Hesse-Kassel (1720–85).

in rank after having been the first; but such is the hard condition of our sex: women and priests never know where they shall eat their bread.

All the polite and the gallant are either gone or preparing for the Bath. You may suppose Lady Hervey would not fail appearing there; where I am told she has made a marvellous union with the Duchess of Manchester, and writes from thence that she is charmed with her grace's sweetness of temper.[1] The Duchess of Richmond declares a design of passing the winter at Goodwood,[2] where she has had a succession of olios of company. It is said very gravely that this loss to the town is occasioned by the suspension of operas.[3] We have no less than fifty-three French strollers arrived to supply their place;[4] and Monsieur de Cambis[5] goes about with great solemnity, negociating to do them service. These are the most important events that are come to my knowledge; perhaps I should remember some more serious if I was so happy as to be with you. I am very glad to hear of the return of Lady Sophia's health and beauty.[6] My dear Lady Pomfret has on all occasions my warmest wishes; and the truest esteem and affection of Your faithful, &c. &c.

Text 1837, ii. 210–12

[1] The Duchess of Manchester (see above, p. 22), whose marriage had been unhappy, was described by Hervey as savagely ferocious (to LM, 18 Nov. [1727], Bristol MS i. 67–68).

[2] Sarah (1706–51), da. of 1st Earl Cadogan, m. (1719) Charles Lennox, later 2nd Duke of Richmond. His seat was Goodwood, in Sussex.

[3] In July Heidegger had announced the cancellation of the opera for the ensuing season because of poor subscriptions (*London Stage 1660–1800*, Part 3, ed. A. H. Scouten, 1961, p. 725).

[4] A company of seventy French players had arrived in London at the end of Sept. (*Daily Advertiser*, 27 Sept., 4 Oct. 1738). When they opened at the Haymarket on 9 Oct. the audience rioted and would not let them finish (*London Stage 1660–1800*, Part 3, pp. 735–6).

[5] Louis-Dominique, comte de Cambis (1669–1740), French Ambassador since Sept. 1737.

[6] Lady Sophia Fermor (1721–45), Lady Pomfret's eldest daughter, was universally praised as a great beauty. In Aug. and Sept. 1738 she suffered from a bad cold and high fever—as Lady Pomfret records in her diary (Finch MS).

To Lady Pomfret [*Oct. 1738*]

1738.

There are some moments when I have so great an inclination to converse with dear Lady Pomfret, that I want but little of galloping to Paris to sit with you one afternoon; which would very well pay me for my journey. Though this correspondence has every charm in it to make a correspondence agreeable, yet I have still a thousand things to say and hear, which cannot be communicated at this distance. Our mobs grow very horrible; here are a vast number of legs and arms that only want a head to make a very formidable body.[1] But while we readers of history are, perhaps, refining too much, the happier part of our sex are more usefully employed in preparation for the birth-day, where I hear Lady Pembroke[2] is to shine in a particular manner, and Lady Cowper to exhibit some new devices worthy of her genius.[3]

The Bath is the present scene of gallantry and magnificence, where many caresses are bestowed, not from admiration of the present, but from spite to the absent.[4] The most remarkable circumstance I hear is a coolness in the Earl of Chesterfield, which occasions much speculation; it must be disagreeable to play an under-part in a second-rate theatre.[5] To me that have always been an humble spectator, it appears

[1] On 11 Oct., when the King's Coronation was celebrated, mobs in London rioted (*Daily Advertiser*, 13 Oct. 1738).

[2] The widowed Lady Pembroke (see above, p. 26, n. 3) m. (1735) Col. the Hon. John Mordaunt (1709 ?–1767).

[3] Henrietta de Auverquerque (d. 1747), da. of 1st Earl of Grantham, m. (1732) 2nd Earl Cowper. At the King's Birthday, celebrated on 30 Oct., Lady Cowper made her appearance at Court 'in a rich Suit of embroider'd Cloth, done by the ingenious Mrs. Nicolaus' (*Daily Advertiser*, 1 Nov. 1738). In the opinion of the Dowager Duchess of Marlborough, she was lucky to be married to Lord Cowper 'for it is certain she has no great title to sense from either side of her family, and had but £10,000'

(*Letters of a Grandmother 1732–1735*, ed. G. S. Thomson, [1943], p. 47).

[4] Since 1737, on the occasion of the Princess of Wales's lying-in, the King had been estranged from the Prince (in the fashion followed by the Hanoverian monarchs), and the political Opposition naturally gravitated around the heir. The Prince and Princess left London on 19 Oct. (Hertford–Pomfret, *Corr.* i. 20), to avoid the birthday celebration there.

[5] Chesterfield, a leader of the Opposition, had gone to Bath in Sept. for the restoration of his health, seriously impaired during the two previous months, and he remained there until Nov. (*Letters*, ed. B. Dobrée, 1932, ii. 330, 336).

odd, to see so few desirous to quit the stage, though time and infirmities have disabled them from making a tolerable figure there. Our drama is at present carried on by such whimsical management, I am half inclined to think we shall shortly have no plays at all. I begin to be of opinion that the new northern actress has very good sense; she hardly appears at all, and by that conduct almost wears out the disapprobation of the publick.[1] I believe you are already tired with this long dissertation on so trifling a subject; I wish I could enliven my letter with some account of literature; but wit and pleasure are no more, and people play the fool with great impunity, being very sure there is not spirit enough left in the nation to set their follies in a ridiculous light. Pamphlets are the sole productions of our modern authors, and those profoundly stupid. To you that enjoy a purer air, and meet at least with vivacity whenever you meet company, this may appear extraordinary; but recollect, dear madam, in what condition you left us; and you will easily believe to what state we are fallen. I know nothing lively but what I feel in my own heart, and that only in what relates to your ladyship; in other respects I partake of the contagion, as you will plainly see by these presents; but I am ever, with the utmost affection, Yours, &c. &c.

Text 1837, ii. 212–14

To Lady Pomfret [*Nov. 1738*]

1738.

I should take your ladyship's question (whether I should always desire your friendship) very unkindly, if I was in the least disposed to quarrel with you; it is very much doubting

[1] Amalie-Sophie von Wendt (1704–65) m. (1727) Gottlieb von Wallmoden. At Hanover she attracted the King's fancy in 1735, and he frequently visited her there. After the Queen's death she was brought to England in June 1738. Tactful and discreet, she did not meddle in politics. She was created Countess of Yarmouth in 1740.

both my understanding and morals,—two very tender points. But I am more concerned for your opinion of the last than the other, being persuaded 'tis easier for you to forgive an involuntary error of the head than a levity in the mind, of which (give me leave to say) I am utterly incapable; and you must give me very great proofs of my being troublesome before you will be able to get rid of me. I passed two very agreeable evenings last week with Lady Bell Finch;[1] we had the mutual pleasure of talking of you, and joined in very sincere wishes for your company.

The reason of Lord Morpeth's[2] leaving Caen are variously told; I believe Lady Carlisle[3] is persuaded he was not properly used there; I hear he is with his father at Venice. The whole seems odd; but it is not possible to know the true motives of people's conduct in their families; which may be very reasonable, when it does not appear so.

Here are some few births, but neither marriages or burials worth mentioning. Lady Townshend has entertained the Bath with a variety of lively scenes; and Lady Harriet Herbert furnished the tea-tables here with fresh tattle for this last fortnight.[4] I was one of the first informed of her adventure by Lady Gage,[5] who was told that morning by a priest, that she had desired him to marry her the next day to Beard, who sings in the farces at Drury-lane.[6] He refused her that good office, and immediately told Lady Gage, who (having been unfortunate in her friends) was frighted at this affair and asked my advice. I told her honestly, that since the lady was capable of such amours, I did not doubt if this was broke off she would bestow her person and fortune on some hackney-coachman or chairman; and that I really saw no method of saving *her* from ruin, and her *family* from dishonour, but by poisoning her; and offered to be at the expence of the arsenic, and even to administer it with my own hands,

---

[1] Lady Isabella (d. 1771), da. of 7th Earl of Winchilsea, Lady of the Bedchamber to Princess Amelia.

[2] Charles Howard (1719–41), heir of Henry (1693–1758), 4th Earl of Carlisle.

[3] Frances Spencer (d. 1742), da. of 2nd Earl of Sunderland, m. (1717) the future 4th Earl.

[4] Lady Henrietta (1717–53), da. of

1st Earl Waldegrave, Ambassador to France, m. (1734) Lord Edward Herbert, son of 2nd Marquess of Powis; he died the same year.

[5] See above, p. 17, n. 7.

[6] John Beard (1716?–91), actor and singer, then beginning his career. His moral and social qualities were generally commended.

if she would invite her to drink tea with her that evening.
But on her not approving that method, she sent to Lady
Montacute,[1] Mrs. Dunch,[2] and all the relations within the
reach of messengers. They carried Lady Harriet to Twickenham; though I told them it was a bad air for girls.[3] She is
since returned to London, and some people believe her
married; others, that he is too much intimidated by Mr.
Waldegrave's threats[4] to dare to go through the ceremony;
but the secret is now publick, and in what manner it will
conclude I know not.[5] Her relations have certainly no reason
to be amazed at her constitution; but are violently surprized
at the mixture of devotion that forces her to have recourse to
the church in her necessities; which has not been the road
taken by the matrons of her family.[6] Such examples are
very detrimental to our whole sex; and are apt to influence
the other into a belief that we are unfit to manage either
liberty or money.[7] These melancholy reflections make me
incapable of a lively conclusion to my letter; you must accept

[1] Mary Herbert (d. 1744), da. of 1st
Marquess of Powis (hence Lady Henrietta's aunt by marriage) and widow of
4th Viscount Montagu.

[2] Elizabeth (1672–1761), da. of
Charles Godfrey and Arabella Churchill, and widow of Edmund Dunch
(1657–1719), was doubly related to Lady
Henrietta: her half-sister was Lady Henrietta's grandmother; and her aunt
Godfrey had married John Waldegrave,
Lady Henrietta's grand-uncle (A. L.
Rowse, *The Early Churchills*, 1956,
p. 134). The Dowager Duchess of Marlborough had a very high opinion of her
judgement, disposition, and easy good
breeding (*Letters of a Grandmother
1732–1735*, ed. G. S. Thomson, [1943],
p. 146).

[3] LM is no doubt thinking of her
own disobedient daughter and niece:
Mary Wortley Montagu married the
3rd Earl of Bute in 1736 against her
parents' wishes—though with their
final, reluctant consent; and Lady
Frances Pierrepont had eloped with
Philip Meadows in 1734.

[4] The younger of Lady Henrietta's
two brothers, John Waldegrave (1718–

84), later 3rd Earl. (The elder was styled
Viscount Chewton.) In his *Diary* Egmont gossiped that 'Her brother, an
Ensign in the Guards, told her that her
lover had the pox, and that she would be
disappointed of the only thing she married him for, which was her lust; for
that he would continue to lie every
night with the player that brought them
together, and give her no solace. But
there is no prudence below the girdle'
(iii. 4).

[5] The marriage took place on 8 Jan.
1739. Although the *London Mag.* (p. 49)
put her jointure at £800 a year, Egmont
wrote that it was £600 depleted by two-
thirds.

[6] Her grandmother, wife of 1st Baron
Waldegrave, had been the illegitimate
daughter of James II by his mistress
Arabella Churchill, and as a widow at
the exiled Court of Saint-Germain had
been ordered into a convent because she
was pregnant, and would not name her
lover (Philippe de Dangeau, *Journal*,
ed. F. de Conches, 1860, v. 134).

[7] LM had expressed this idea in No.
VI of *The Nonsense of Common-Sense* on
24 Jan. 1738.

of a very sincere one in the assurance that I am, dear madam, Inviolably yours, &c.

Text 1837, ii. 217–19

To Francesco Algarotti [*Nov. 1738*][1]

Je suis trop touché par vos mannieres d'agir avec moi. Qu'avez vous vû de si desobligeante dans ma derniere Lettre? Plût au dieu que je recevray des parreiles marques de vostre attachment pour moi! Mais je ne suis pas fait pour inspirer la tendresse que je suis capable de sentir, et j'ai tort de m'offenser. Vous avez trop d'esprit pour avoir besoin d'explication. Si vous voulez me querreller, c'est parce que vous le voulez. Vous ne sçavez que trop que vous etes le seul objet du monde qui me plaist. J'ai tout fait jusqu'a cette heure pour vous le prouver, et je serois toujours de mesme pour vous; et j'ai si peu d'Idee de trouver rien autre agreable, je voudrois de tout mon cœur, si je perds l'esperance de vous voir, perdre la vie dans le mesme Instant.

Text Murray MS   *Address* Monsieur Algarotti chez Mr. Robert Baigneur dans la Rûe de la Seine Paris

To Lady Pomfret [*Nov. 1738*][2]

1738.

I will say nothing of your complaints of your own dulness; I should say something very rough if I did; 'tis impossible to reconcile them to the sincerity that I am willing to flatter myself I find in the other parts of your letter. 'Tis impossible you should not be conscious that such letters as

---

[1] During the summer of 1738 Algarotti remained in the south of France, mainly in Carcassonne and Toulouse, and in Sept. finally reached Paris (Ida

Treat, *Francesco Algarotti*, 1913, p. 67).

[2] Received by Lady Pomfret on 6 Dec./25 Nov. (Finch MS).

yours want not the trimmings of news, which are only necessary to the plain Spitalfields'[1] style, beginning with *hoping you are in good health*, and concluding *pray believe me to be*, &c. &c. You give me all the pleasure of an agreeable author; and I really wish you had leisure to give me all the length too, and that all your letters were to come to me in twelve tomes. You will stare at this impudent wish; but you know imagination has no bounds; and 'tis harder for me to be content with a moderate quantity of your writing, than it was for any South Sea director to resolve to get no more. This is a strange way of giving thanks, however 'tis the clearest proof of my tasting my happiness in your correspondence, to beg so earnestly not only the continuance but the encrease of it.

I hear of a new lady-errant, who is set forth to seek adventures at Paris, attended by her enchanter. These are Mrs. Bromley[2] and Anthony Henley,[3] who, I am told, declares very gallantly that he designs to oblige her to sell her large jointure, to furnish money for his *menus plaisirs*. This is the freshest news from the Island of Love. Amongst those bound for the golden coast (which are far more numerous), there arise every day new events. The Duchess of Northumberland's will raises a great bustle among those branches of the royal blood.[4] She has left a young niece,[5] very pretty, lively enough, just fifteen, to the care of Captain Cole,[6] who was director of Lady Bernard.[7] The girl has 300*l.* per annum allowed for her maintenance, but is never to touch her fortune till she marries, which she is not to do without his

[1] A parish in the east of London, inhabited by weavers.

[2] Widow of William Bromley (1699?-1737), politician. According to Egmont, she was the daughter of a physician named Throckmorton, and had a dowry of £30,000; and soon after her marriage cuckolded her husband, who had her 'put away' in Jan. 1736 (*Diary*, ii. 218, 367).

[3] Henley (d. 1748), politician, m. (1728) Lady Elizabeth (d. 1745), da. of 3rd Earl of Berkeley. In 1732 his wife's relations tried to have their marriage dissolved because of his monstrous,

homicidal treatment of her (HMC *Carlisle MSS*, 1897, p. 93).

[4] Mary Dutton (d. 27 Aug. 1738) m. (1715) 1st Duke of Northumberland, bastard son of Charles II by Lady Castlemaine. He d. 1716, childless. Her will is P.C.C. Brodrepp, f. 220.

[5] Grace Parsons, da. of Sir William Parsons and Frances Dutton. As late as 1744 she had not married and 'continues to behave very right' (Lady Oxford to LM, 3 March 1744, O.S., Harley MS).

[6] John Merick Cole, one of the three executors.

[7] Not identified.

consent; and if she dies without issue, her twenty thousand pounds to be divided between the children of the Duchess of St. Albans[1] and Lord Litchfield.[2] The heirs-at-law contest the fantastical will, and the present tittle tattle of visits turns upon the subject.

Lord Townshend has renewed his lease of life by his French journey,[3] and is at present situated in his house in Grosvenor-street in perfect health. My good lady is coming from the Bath to meet him with the joy you may imagine.[4] Kitty Edwin has been the companion of his [her] pleasures there. The alliance seems firmer than ever between them after their Tunbridge battles, which served for the entertainment of the publick.[5] The secret cause is variously guessed at; but it is certain Lady Townshend came into the great room gently behind her friend, and tapping her on the shoulder with her fan, said aloud, *I know where, how, and who*. These mysterious words drew the attention of all the company, and had such an effect upon poor Kitty, she was carried to her lodgings in strong hystericks. However, by the intercession of prudent mediators peace was concluded; and if the conduct of these heroines was considered in a true light, perhaps it might serve for an example even to higher powers, by shewing that the surest method to obtain a lasting and honourable peace, is to begin with vigorous war.[6] But

---

[1] Diana de Vere (d. 1742), da. of 20th Earl of Oxford and widow of 1st Duke of St. Albans, son of Charles II by Nell Gwyn. She had eight sons, but the will designates two of her granddaughters: Lady Diana (d. 1766) and Caroline Beauclerk (d. 1769).

[2] George Henry Lee (1690–1743), 2nd Earl of Lichfield. His mother was a daughter of Charles II by Lady Castlemaine. The will names his two youngest daughters: Harriet (1726–52) and Anne (c. 1731–1802).

[3] At the beginning of Oct. he had set out for Aix-la-Chapelle, and Lady Townshend for Bath (*Daily Advertiser*, 4 Oct. 1738).

[4] Egmont's gossip was that when Lady Townshend was at Bath, 'being observed to have too great familiarity with one Brown, a gamester, and one Lindsey, an ensign of the Guards, my Lord's friends advised him thereof, whereupon he returned to England; but she, instead of coming up to town to meet him, stayed at Bath till she heard he was gone to his estate in Bedfordshire, and then she left Bath for London' (22 Dec. 1738, *Diary*, ii. 514–15).

[5] Catherine Edwin (d. before 1777) was a granddaughter of 3rd Earl of Manchester (John G. Nichols, *Herald and Genealogist*, 1863–74, vi. 58). Her quarrels with Lady Townshend in Tunbridge Wells the previous summer had occasioned much talk and some very scandalous lampoons (Hertford–Pomfret, *Corr.* i. 5).

[6] Here LM, like the political Opposition, advocates vigorous measures

leaving these reflections, which are above my capacity, permit me to repeat my desire of hearing often from you. Your
letters would be my greatest pleasure if I had flourished in
the first years of Henry the Eighth's court; judge then how
welcome they are to me in the present desolate state of this
deserted town of London. Yours, &c.

Text 1837, ii. 214–17

To Francesco Algarotti *8 Jan.* [*1739*]

J'ai juré de ne plus vous ecrire jusqu'a j'entends de vos
nouvelles. On a beau jurer quand l'Inclination entraine. Je
suis horriblement sotte pourtant de me laisser entrainer par
cet Demon, pendant que vous m'oubliez devant les yeux de
quelque Idole de Parisienne peint et doré, qui reçoit (peutestre insensiblement) des hommages qui feront tout mon
bonheur. Je ne veux plus me repaitre de chimeres, et j'entere-
rois infailliblement dans mon triste bon sens si vous ne me
fournissez pas bientost nouvelle mattiere des visions deli-
cieuses par une petite aimable Lettre.

Jan. 8. V.S.

Text Bod. MS Don. c. 56, f. 61

To Lady Pomfret [*Jan. 1739*]

Amidst the shining gallantries of the French court, I know
not how you will receive a stupid letter from these regions of
dulness, where even our ridiculous actions (which are very
frequent, I confess) have a certain air of formality that
hinders them from being risible, at the same time that they
are absurd. I think Lady Anne Lumley's marriage may be
reckoned into this number, who is going to espouse with

against Spain, which she had deplored in No. III of *The Nonsense of Common-
Sense*. Or perhaps she is being ironical.

great gravity a younger brother of Sir Thomas Frankland's.[1] There are great struggles and many candidates for her place. Lady Anne Montagu, daughter to Lord Halifax,[2] is one of them; and Lady Charlotte Rich, Lady Betty Herbert,[3] and the incomparable Lady Bateman are her competitors.[4]

I saw Mrs. Bridgeman[5] the other day, who is much pleased with a letter she has had the honour to receive from your ladyship: she broke out, '*Really Lady Pomfret writes finely!*' I very readily joined in her opinion; she continued, '*Oh, so neat, no interlineations, and such proper distances!*' This manner of praising your style made me reflect on the necessity of attention to trifles, if one would please in general, a rule terribly neglected by me formerly; yet it is certain that some men are as much struck with the careless twist of a tippet, as others are by a pair of fine eyes.

Lady Vane is returned hither[6] in company with Lord Berkeley, and went with him in publick to Cranford, where

[1] Lady Anne (d. 1740), da. of 1st Earl of Scarborough, was Lady of the Bedchamber to Princess Amelia and Princess Caroline at £300 p.a. On 26 Jan. 1739 she asked leave to give up her post (Delany, *Corr.* ii. 32). She m. (19 Feb.) Frederic Meinhardt Frankland (*c.* 1694–1768), M.P. and barrister, brother of Sir Thomas Frankland (d. 1747). She was then between 40 and 50, ugly, and fat (Egmont, *Diary*, iii. 72). The marriage was worse than absurd: in June her husband insisted on a separation because he had taken an intense aversion to her, having 'parted beds with her before she had been three weeks married, and on all occasions behaved towards her with the utmost cruelty' (Hertford–Pomfret, *Corr.* i. 113). His reason, it has been elsewhere stated, was her attending Methodist meetings (Henrietta Keddie, *The Countess of Huntingdon and Her Circle*, 1907, p. 21).

[2] Lady Anne (d. 1766), da. of George Montagu (d. 1739), 2nd Earl of Halifax; she succeeded Lady Anne Lumley, who was her aunt.

[3] Lady Charlotte Rich (1713–91), da. of 29th Earl of Warwick; Lady Eliza-

beth Herbert (d. ?1745), da. of 8th Earl of Pembroke.

[4] Lady Bateman (see above, p. 48, n. 3) had recently separated from her husband, and was rumoured about to be appointed (Egmont, *Diary*, ii. 514; Hertford–Pomfret, *Corr.* i. 49).

[5] This lady (d. 1742) was probably related to the family of Sir Orlando Bridgeman. She was a widow, and a neighbour of LM's in Cavendish Square (John G. Nichols, *Herald and Genealogist*, 1863–74, iv. 143).

[6] Lady Vane (see above, p. 120, n. 3) had deserted her husband in Paris in 1736 to run off with the Hon. Sewallis Shirley, and in Jan. 1737 her husband advertised in the newspapers offering a reward of £100 for her return (HMC *Portland MSS*, vi, 1901, p. 63; *Wentworth Papers 1705-1739*, ed. J. J. Cartwright, 1883, p. 531). 'Lord Vane was said to be Impotent,' Horace Walpole wrote, 'yet at any time woud give his Wife great Sums to return to Him, which as soon as She had got, She always ran away again' (MS *Poems and Other Peices* [*sic*], p. 33; owned by Mr. W. S. Lewis, Farmington, Connecticut).

they remain as happy as love and youth can make them.[1] I am told that though she does not pique herself upon fidelity to any one man (which is but a narrow way of thinking), she boasts that she has always been true to her nation, and, notwithstanding foreign attacks, has always reserved her charms for the use of her own countrymen.[2] I forget you are at Paris, and 'tis not polite to trouble you with such long scrawls as might perhaps be supportable at Monts; but you must give me leave to add, that I am, with a true sense of your merit, for ever your's, in the largest extent of that expression.

Text 1837, ii. 219–21

To Francesco Algarotti[3] [*Feb. 1739*]

Vous me rendez justice en croyant je suis de toute façon sincere avec vous. Je le suis naturellement avec tout le monde; et en recompence d'agremens que vous ne trouverois point, vous trouverois toujours une bonne foi la plus rare et la plus parfaitte.

Vous pouvez croire que je suis beaucoup plus content de faciliter vostre retour que vostre depart, quoique j'avoue que je tremble et ma philosophie m'abbandonne quand je songe que je vous verray peutestre cherchant d'autres attachments,—

Mais laissons ces Refflections; je veux m'aveugler la dessus. Je ne sçai pas trop bien comment m'y prendre pour vous envoyer un billet de change. Je croi que le meilleur moyen est que vous tirez pour la ditte somme sur Mr. Tribble in Litchfield street near Soho Square.[4] Il est mon Joüallier, et j'ai bonne opinion de sa discretion, quoi que je ne connois

[1] Augustus (1716–55), 4th Earl of Berkeley; Cranford Park, Middlesex, was one of his houses. In Nov. 1741 Lady Vane was still living with him (Walpole, *Corr.* xvii. 210).

[2] Lady Vane said the same thing: 'Soon after my appearance in Paris, I was favoured with the addresses of several French lovers; but I never had any taste for foreigners' ('Memoirs of a Lady of Quality', in Smollet's *Adventures of Peregrine Pickle*, 1751, iii. 215).

[3] Still in Paris, Algarotti needed financial assistance to get to England, as this letter indicates.

[4] John Trible, jeweller at this address after 1726 (Ambrose Heal, *The London Goldsmiths 1200–1800*, 1935, p. 257).

aucune preuve. Quand je vous verrois, je vous dirois bien des choses.

Text Murray MS

To Lady Pomfret [*March 1739*]

1738 [*sic*].

I am so well acquainted with the lady you mention, that I am not surprized at any proof of her want of judgment; she is one of those who has passed upon the world vivacity in the place of understanding; for me, who think with Boileau

Rien n'est beau que le vrai, le vrai seul est aimable,[1]

I have always thought those geniuses much inferior to the plain sense of a cook-maid, who can make a good pudding and keep the kitchen in good order.

Here is no news to be sent you from this place, which has been for this fortnight and still continues overwhelmed with politicks, and which are of so mysterious a nature, one ought to have some of the gifts of Lilly or Partridge[2] to be able to write about them; and I leave all those dissertations to those distinguished mortals who are endowed with the talent of divination; though I am at present the only one of my sex who seems to be of that opinion, the ladies having shewn their zeal and appetite for knowledge in a most glorious manner. At the last warm debate in the House of Lords,[3] it was unanimously resolved there should be no crowd of unnecessary auditors;[4] consequently the fair sex were excluded, and the gallery destined to the sole use of the House of Commons. Notwithstanding which determination, a tribe of

---

[1] Epistle ix, 'L'Éloge du vrai', line 43.

[2] William Lilly (1602–81), astrologer and almanac-maker; John Partridge (1644–1715), cobbler turned almanac-maker, satirized by Swift.

[3] The debate, on 1 March 1739—thanking the King for the Convention of El Prado with Spain—was long and bitter, with the Opposition protesting

that Spanish depredations on English shipping should be vigorously fought; but the Ministry won by a majority of 21 (*Hist. and Proc. of the House of Lords*, 1742–3, vi. 181).

[4] The House had decided in May 1738 to exclude strangers of whatever degree (A. S. Turberville, *The House of Lords in the XVIIIth Century*, 1927, p.14; LM's account is discussed on p. 238).

dames resolved to shew on this occasion, that neither men
nor laws could resist them. These heroines were Lady
Huntingdon, the Duchess of Queensbury, the Duchess of
Ancaster, Lady Westmoreland, Lady Cobham, Lady Charlotte Edwin, Lady Archibald Hamilton and her daughter,
Mrs. Scott, and Mrs. Pendarvis, and Lady Frances Saunderson.[1] I am thus particular in their names, since I look upon
them to be the boldest assertors, and most resigned sufferers
for liberty, I ever read of. They presented themselves at the
door at nine o'clock in the morning, where Sir William
Saunderson[2] respectfully informed them the [Lord] Chancellor[3] had made an order against their admittance. The
Duchess of Queensbury, as head of the squadron, pished at
the ill-breeding of a mere lawyer, and desired him to let them
up stairs privately. After some modest refusals he swore by
G—— he would not let them in. Her grace, with a noble
warmth, answered, by G—— they would come in, in spite
of the Chancellor and the whole House. This being reported,
the Peers resolved to starve them out; an order was made
that the doors should not be opened till they had raised their
siege.

These Amazons now shewed themselves qualified for the
duty even of foot-soldiers; they stood there till five in the
afternoon, without either sustenance or evacuation, every
now and then playing vollies of thumps, kicks, and raps,
against the door, with so much violence that the speakers in
the House were scarce heard. When the Lords were not to be
conquered by this, the two Duchesses (very well apprized of
the use of stratagems in war) commanded a dead silence of
half an hour; and the Chancellor, who thought this a certain

[1] Selina Shirley (1707–91) m. (1728)
9th Earl of Huntingdon; the Duchess of
Queensberry (see above, p. 48, n. 1),
who had quarrelled with the King in
1728; Albinia Farrington (d. 1745) m.
(1705) 1st Duke of Ancaster (d. 1723);
Mary Cavendish (1700–78) m. (1716)
7th Earl of Westmorland; Anne Halsey
(d. 1760), wife of 1st Viscount Cobham;
Lady Charlotte (1703–77), da. of 1st
Duke of Hamilton, m. (1736) Charles
Edwin; Jane Hamilton (d. 1752), da. of
6th Earl of Abercorn, m. (1719) Lord

Archibald Hamilton; her daughter,
Elizabeth (1720–1800); Mrs. Scott, not
identified; Mary Granville (1700–88)
m. (1718) Alexander Pendarves (d.
1725) and m. (1743) Patrick Delany;
Lady Frances Hamilton (d. 1772), da.
of 1st Earl of Orkney, m. (1724) Thomas
Lumley-Saunderson.

[2] Sir William (1692–1754), Yeoman
Usher of the Black Rod.

[3] Philip Yorke (1690–1764), Baron,
later Earl of, Hardwicke.

proof of their absence, (the Commons also being very impatient to enter) gave order for the opening of the door; upon which they all rushed in, pushed aside their competitors, and placed themselves in the front rows of the gallery. They stayed there till after eleven, when the House rose; and during the debate gave applause, and showed marks of dislike, not only by smiles and winks (which have always been allowed in these cases), but by noisy laughs and apparent contempts; which is supposed the true reason why poor Lord Hervey spoke miserably.[1] I beg your pardon, dear madam, for this long relation; but 'tis impossible to be short on so copious a subject; and you must own this action very well worthy of record, and I think not to be paralleled in any history, ancient or modern.[2] I look so little in my own eyes (who was at that time ingloriously sitting over a tea-table),[3] I hardly dare subscribe myself even, Yours.

Text 1837, ii. 221–4

To Francesco Algarotti *12 March* [*1739*]

Que vous etes injuste, et que vous me connoisez mal! Mais est vous obligé de me connoitre? Vous m'avez trop peu veû,

[1] In reporting the debate, a month later, Lord Orrery wrote: 'Lord Hervey, who has been ill ever since (occasioned by too violent a Fitt of Eloquence) spoke nicely and was full of Peace, Plenty and Sugar-Plumbs' (*Orrery Papers*, ed. Countess of Cork and Orrery, 1903, i. 256).

[2] After telling her correspondent that seventeen ladies made up the raiding party, Mrs. Pendarves continued: '... We bore the buffets of a stinking crowd from half an hour after ten till five in the afternoon, without moving an inch from our places, only see-sawing about as the motion of the multitude forced us. At last our committee resolved to adjourn to the coffee-house of the Court of Requests, where debates began, how we were to proceed? it was agreed amongst us to address Sir Charles Dalton [Gentleman Usher of the Black Rod] for admittance. The address was presented, and an answer returned, that "whilst *one lady* remained in the passage to the gallery, the door *should not* be opened for the members of the House of Commons;" so we generously gave them the liberty of taking their places. As soon as the door was opened they all rushed in, and we followed; some of them had the gallantry to *give us their places*, and with violent squeezing, and such a resolution as hardly was ever met with, we riggled ourselves into seats' (Delany, *Corr.* ii. 44–45). Although Egmont attended the debate, which he says lasted nine hours, he does not mention any disturbance (*Diary*, iii. 29).

[3] LM did not join the ladies for a better reason: she was a friend and journalistic supporter of Walpole's.

mais pourtant il me semble qu'une tendresse a l'épreuve de l'absence et de la silence doit produire plus de confiance. Ay-je pû imaginer que la proposition que j'ai vous a fait devoit vous offenser? N'importe; vous serez servi a vostre manniere. Je vous envoye le billet d'echange comme vous le souhaittez. Je m'exprime peut estre mal, mais mon Cœur me reproche rien que des Foiblesses dont vous me devez de la reconnoisance.[1]

Voici le billet dans la forme qu'on me dit est requise. Je l'aurois mieux aimé d'un autre façon.

Mars 12. V.S.

J'ai receû vostre Lettre hier.

Text Bod. MS Don. c. 56, f. 60

To Lady Pomfret [*9 May 1739*]

It is with great pleasure, dear madam, that I hear from you, after a silence that appeared very long to me. Nothing can be more agreeable or more obliging than your letter. I can give you no greater proof of the impression it made on me than letting you know that you have given me so great an inclination to see Italy once more, that I have serious thoughts of setting out the latter end of this summer. And what the remembrance of all the charms of music, sculpture, painting, architecture, and even the sun itself could not do, the knowledge that Lady Pomfret is there has effected; and I already figure to myself the charms of the brightest conversation in the brightest climate. We have nothing here but clouds and perpetual rains, nor no news but deaths and sickness. Lord Halifax died this morning, and I am really touched for the melancholy situation of his numerous family.[2] A loss more

---

[1] LM may have been thinking of this transaction when she wrote to her daughter, on 30 May [1756], of the impossibility of buying affection (iii. 108).

[2] The 2nd Earl of Halifax d. 9 May 1739. Egmont called him 'a squanderer of his money, so that it is said his daugh-ters will have very small fortunes. . . . He was a great improver of ground, a good companion, loved horse-racing, and kept a mistress' (*Diary*, iii. 59). Of his seven daughters five were still unmarried. His possessions were auctioned in July (see below, p. 190).

peculiarly my own is that of poor Lady Stafford, whose last remains of life I am daily watching with a fruitless sorrow. I believe a very few months, perhaps weeks, will part us for ever.[1] You who have a heart capable of friendship may imagine to what a degree I am shocked at such a separation, which so much disorders my thoughts, as renders me unfit to entertain myself or any others. This reflection must shorten my letter. In you I hope to repair the loss of her, and when we meet I am persuaded there will not be many regrets sent to England by, dear madam, Your faithful and affectionate, &c.

May 2 [*sic*], O. S. 1739.

Text 1837, ii. 224–5

To Francesco Algarotti[2] *16 July* [*1739*]

Je pars pour vous chercher. C'est n'est pas necessaire d'accompagner une telle preuve d'un Attachment éternelle d'une broderie de parolles. Je vous donne rendezvous a Venise. J'avois dessin de vous trouver en chemin faisant, mais je croi que c'est plus discret, et mesme plus certain, d'attendre vous voir a la fin de mon pelerinage. C'est a vous a exaucer mes vœux et me fair oublier tous mes fatigues et mes chagrins.

Ne m'écrivez plus a Londres. Je n'ÿ serois pas, et une Lettre trouvé pourroit avoir des suittes tres facheuses.

Juillet 16. V.S.

Je hazarde cette Lettre par une autre voye, n'etant pas seure que vous avez receû celle que j'a addressé a Mr. Rondeau.[3] J'espere qu'il n'est pas necessaire de vous prier de ne pas rester a Londres, en cas que vous y arrivez.

[1] She died on 14 May 1739. Her last years had not been happy; Montesquieu, who mentions her dangerous wit, wrote: 'Elle étoit dans le désespoir de la vieillesse' (*Œuvres complètes*, ed. R. Caillois, 1956–8, i. 1326).

[2] Algarotti had arrived in London at the end of March, and stayed with a succession of friends, including Hervey; then on 10 May he had sailed for St. Petersburg as the guest of Lord Balti-more, emissary to the Russian Court for the marriage of Princess Anne of Mecklenburgh, the Czarina's niece, to the Prince of Brunswick-Wolfenbüttel. They arrived at Kronstadt on 20 June O.S. (21 June 1739, SP 91/23).

[3] Claudius Rondeau (d. 16 Oct. 1739), Minister Resident in St. Petersburg since 1731 (D. B. Horn, *Brit. Dipl. Rep. 1689–1789*, 1932, p. 113).

Text Bod. MS Don. c. 56, ff. 51–52   *Address*[1] A Monsieur Monsieur Algarotti chez Mons Rondeau   Resident de sa majesté Britanique à Petersbourg

To Francesco Algarotti [*24 July 1739*]

Enfin je pars demain avec la Resolution d'un homme bien persuadé de sa Religion et contente de sa conscience, rempli de foye et d'esperance. Je laisse mes amis pleurant ma perte et franche le pas hardiment pour un autre monde. Si je vous trouve tel que vous m'avez juré, je trouve les champs élissée et la Felicité au de la de l'imagination; si—Mais je ne veux plus douter, et du moins je veux joüir de mes esperances. Si vous voulez me recompenser tout ce que je sacrifie, hatez vous me trouver a Venise, ou je presserai mon arrivé autant qu'il m'est possible.

Text Bod. MS Don. c. 56, f. 66   *Address* A Monsieur Monsieur Algarotti

To Wortley [*25 July 1739*]

Dartford

I staid an hour with the Dutchess of Montagu,[2] and am arriv'd here at 12 o'clock, less fatigued than I expected. I should be very glad to hear you are well. If you write to me to be left at the post house at Dover, I suppose I may have your Letter before I leave that place.

Text W MS i. 311   *End. by W* ⟨L.⟩ M. 25 July from Dartford. Ad 26th.

---

[1] Probably in Hervey's hand.
[2] At Blackheath—on the Dover road between London and Dartford—where the Duchess had a house (*Daily Journal*, 5 June 1724; Henry S. Richardson, *Greenwich: Its History*, 1834, p. 89).

To Wortley *26 July* [*1739*]

July 26.

I am safely arriv'd at Dover without any accident and have born the Journey very well. I have follow'd your Direction in sending for Mr. Hall,[1] who has been very civil. By his advice I have hir'd a Boat for 5 guineas; otherwise I must have gone in the night, which he councell'd me not to do. The Wind is fair, and I hope to be in Calais to morrow. I cannot say I am well, but I think not worse for my Journey.

Text W MS i. 312   *End. by W* L. M. 26 July 1739. From Dover has hired a Ship.

To Wortley *7 Aug./27 July* [*1739*]

I am safely arriv'd at Calais, and found my selfe better on ship board than I have been this six months, not in the least sick, thô we had a very high sea, as you may imagine, since we came over in 2 hours 3 quarters. My servants behav'd very well, and Mary not in the least afraid, but said she would be drowned very willingly with my Ladyship.[2]

They ask me here extravagant prizes for Chaises, of which there is great choice, both French and Italian. I have at last bought one f⟨or⟩ 14 guineas of a man[3] which Mr. Hall recommended to me. ⟨My⟩ things have been examin'd and seal'd at the custom House. They took from me 2 pound of Snuff, but did not open my Jewel boxes, which they let pass on my Word, being things belonging to my Dress. I set out early to morrow. I am very impatient to hear from you; I could not stay for the post at Dover for fear of loseing the Tide.

I beg you would be so good to order Mr. Kent[4] to pack up

---

[1] Probably Richard Halls, who may have been attached to the customs at Dover (1861, ii. 41, n. 1).

[2] William and Mary Turner, who accompanied LM, stayed abroad with her for five years (see below, p. 324).

[3] Francia (see below, p. 156).

[4] Thomas Kent, evidently W's secretary (W to LM, [13 Aug. 1739], W MS i. 112).

my side saddle and all the Tackling belonging to it, in a Box to be sent with my other things.[1] If (as I hope) I recover my Health abroad so much as to ride, I can get none I shall like so well.

July 27

Text W MS i. 313–14   *Address* To Edwd Wortley Esqr in Cavendish Square London   *Postmark* 1 AV   *End. by W* L.M. 27 July 1739. Arrival at Calais The side saddle.

To Wortley *11 Aug./31 July* [*1739*]

Laon, July 31.

This is the first oppertunity I have had of writeing, having continu'd my Journey without stopping any where to this place. I set out again to morrow for Dijon, which I hope to reach in 4 or 5 days by small Journeys, which I find agrees best with me. I receiv'd your pacquets at Boulogne,[2] where I supp'd with Mrs. Bradshaw,[3] who seems in good Health but is situate in the uglyest Town I ever saw. We have had continual cold Rains, and been oblig'd to have fires in several Inns, notwithstanding which I think both my Health and Spirits much mended; but the Weather has determin'd my road southward. I hope to find a fine climate in Burgundy. I am now too much tir'd to write a long letter, but will not fail to do it from Dijon.

Text W MS i. 315   *End. by W* L.M. 31 July 1739 From Laon.

To Wortley *18 Aug.* [*1739*]

Dijon, August 18 N.S.

I am at length arriv'd here very safe and without any bad accident, and so much mended in my Health that I am

---

[1] It was sent to her in the spring along with her other baggage (W to LM, 25 March 1740, W MS i. 117).

[2] In a letter to W on 8 Aug./28 July Richard Halls wrote, 'Her ladyship in-

tending to stay two or three days at Boulogne, she desires me to send those letters after her' (1861, ii. 42, n. 2).

[3] Not identified.

surpriz'd at it. France is so much improvd it is not to be known to be the same Country we pass'd through 20 year ago. Every thing I see speaks in praise of Cardinal Fleury;[1] the roads are all mended and the greatest part of them pav'd as well as the streets of Paris, planted on both sides like the roads in Holland, and such good care taken against Robbers that you may cross the Country with your purse in your Hand. But as to travelling incognito, I may as well walk incognito in the Pall Mall; there is not any Town in France where there is not English, Scotch or Irish Familys establish'd, and I have met with people that have seen me (thô often such as I do not remember to have seen) in every Town I have pass'd through. And I think the farther I go the more acquaintance I meet; here is in this Town no less than 16 English familys of Fashion. Lord Mansel[2] lodges in the House with me, and a Daughter of Lord Bathurst's (Mrs. Whichcote)[3] is in the same street. The Duke of Rutland[4] is gone from hence some time ago, which Lady Peterborrough[5] told me at St. Omers, which was one reason determin'd me to come here, thinking to be quiet, but I find it is impossible, and that will make me leave the place after the return of this post. The French are more chang'd than their roads; instead of pale yellow Faces wrapp'd up in Blankets as we saw them,[6] the Villages are all fill'd with fresh colour'd lusty peasants, in good Cloath and clean Linnen. It is incredible, the Air of plenty and content that is over the whole Country.

I hope to hear as soon as possible that you are in good Health.[7]

Text W MS i. 316–17   *Address* To Edwd Wortley Esqr at his

---

[1] In No. IX of *The Nonsense of Common-Sense* (14 March 1738) LM praised Fleury, Louis XV's chief minister from 1726 to 1743, as 'a Blessing to his Country, who makes her Greatness and neglects his own' (ed. 1947, p. 42).

[2] Thomas (1719–44), 2nd Baron Mansell. Egmont considered him a 'good natured youth' (*Diary*, iii. 283).

[3] Frances, eldest daughter of Bathurst, m. (1738) James Whitshed, M.P. LM probably confused the name with that of her girlhood friend Mary Banks

(d. 1726), who m. (1717) Sir Francis Whichcote.

[4] John Manners (1696–1779), 3rd Duke.

[5] Probably Mary Cox (d. 1755), m. (before 1735) the future 4th Earl of Peterborough, rather than Anastasia Robinson, widow of the 3rd Earl (d. 1735).

[6] In 1718 (i. 438).

[7] W received this letter on 26/15 Aug. and answered it the following day (W to LM, W MS i. 113, 114).

House in Cavendish Square London Angleterre   *Postmark* AV 15
End. by W L.M. 18 Aug. 1739. Acct of her journey To Dijon.

To Wortley 27 *Aug.* [*1739*]

Dijon, Aug't 27. N.S.

This is a very agreable Town, and I find the air agree[s] with me extreamly. Here is a great deal of good Company, and I meet with more civillitys than I had any reason to expect. I should like to pass the Winter here if it was not for the expence, but it is utterly impossible for me to live decently within my allowance. I have been entertain'd by all the considerable people, French and English, and can have no excuse for not returning it but being on the road. The lodgings are excessive dear, and every thing in proportion.

Lord Mansel has been so particularly obliging to me, that if you see him, or Mrs. Blackwood,[1] his mother, I think it would be proper for you to give him thanks. I did not mention it in my last Letter, because I thought you might be alarm'd, and I hope'd it would be over before I wrote again, as it now is, but I was then in some difficultys. I beleive I told you in my last I accidentally met Lady Peterborrough at St. Omers by going to the same Inn where she lodg'd. We supp'd together, and in discourse I told her I had brought guineas with me from England. She assur'd me they would not pass without a loss, and in going from Flanders to France if I was search'd all Foreign Money might be seiz'd. She offer'd me the assistance of her Banker, whom she immediately sent for. He confirm'd what she said, but told me he would give me a Bill on Mr. Waters[2] at Paris which would be paid at sight in any Town in France. Not knowing how to do better, I accepted of this expedient, only reserving in money what was necessary for my Journey to Dijon, which was at an end as soon as I arriv'd here. I gave my Bill the

[1] Anne (d. 1741), da. of Sir Cloudesley Shovel, m. (1718) Robert Mansell (d. 1723); she later m. John Blackwood.

[2] Banker (see above, p. 22, n. 5). W sent letters through him (W to LM, W MS i. 113).

next morning to my Landlord to carry to the cheif Banker of the Town. He came back very Blank saying the Banker knew neither Mr. Waters nor the person who had drawn upon him, and that he could advance no money till the return of Letters from Paris, which would be at least eight days. I suppose Lord Mansel heard of this disapointment by the Land Lord, and without mentioning it to me, went immediately himselfe to the Banker and pass'd his word for what ever Summ I pleas'd to take up, and then came to wait on me, and told me with great respect what he had done, and desir'd me to ⟨make⟩ use of his credit. Thô I am sensible he acted ⟨only⟩ by the Direction of his Governor,[1] who came ⟨with⟩ him to see me, and is a very reasonable man, ⟨yet⟩ I think it deserves some acknowledgment, thô I ⟨did⟩[2] not judge it fit to make use of it, chuseing rather to live a few days upon Trust. My Bill was accepted at Paris, and paid me here last Sunday.

I think now of moving very soon, but am yet undetermin'd as to my place of Residence. I receive as many different councels as I see people. What I would avoid is the crouds of English which are spread all over France. A Daughter of Lord Bathurst's is here (Mrs. Whichcote) and has entertain'd me.

Text MS at Wellesley College   *Address* To Edwd Wortley Esqr at his House in Cavendish Square London Angleterre   *Postmark* ⟨?⟩ 22 *End. by W* Ad   L.M. 27 Aug. N.S. from Dijon.   Ad 23 Aug.   The Dearness at Dijon.

From Lord Hervey *28/17 Aug. 1739*

Kensington,[3] Aug. 28/17, 1739

I recieved a Letter from you yesterday from Dijon, the third I have to thank you for since I lost one of the most agreable acquaintance I ever made, and England one of the most distinguish'd Inhabitants it ever produced; and tho I know my Letter can not set out these four

---

[1] Dr. John Clephane (d. 1758), phycian (Mansell to LM, 18/7 July [1740], W MS iv. 181–2; Walpole, *Corr.* xvii. 63).

[2] Words in brackets restored from

first printing of letter in *Cat. of Alfred Morrison Coll.*, 1883–92, iv. 286.

[3] As Vice-Chamberlain Hervey was apparently with the Court at Kensington Palace.

Days, yet I feel such an impatience to write to you that I can not resist indulging it. Your sending me a direction at last, makes me feel the same eagerness to write that I fancy People who have been long gag'd feel to talk; and like those who love talking imeasurably, I fear I shall as little consider the pleasure you are likely to have in reading, as they do what their Audience has in hearing. In the first place I must chide you for the Festivity of your first Letter; it was a sort of Insult to one who you knew was lamenting your Departure, to show you thought you had left nothing behind you worth lamenting . . . [*Passage omitted*] As to your proposing to me to follow you, unless you could give me the same motive[1] that you have for jolting in Post-Chaises and lying in dirty Inns, I do not see I should get much by taking your Advice; if I could make my-self a Bigot, I would certainly walk bare-foot, let my Beard grow, lye upon Straw by night, and wear a woollen Shirt by day. But to what purpose should I renounce my false Gods, as you call them, unless I could change them for a true one; and may I not just as well bend my Knee to an Oinion or a Monkey where I am, as put on a Turban or make a Pilgrimage to Mecca, unless I could at the same time believe the Alcoran and have Faith in Mahomet? For You, who not only credit his Doctrine but are to enjoy his Paridise upon Earth, You are in the right to take the Pilgrim's Staff in your Hand, and travel with Shells upon your Garment; but I, who should have nothing but the journey for my Pains, may as well stay at home, not forgetting (according to the Custom of the Country you at present inhabit) to throw up an ejaculation for the Soul of my departed Friend, and that the Purgatory you are to pass through before you enter the Gates of that Heaven your Piety deserves, may not be of long duration.

[*Passage in verse omitted*]

But to return from Verse and Fancy to prose and Busyness, I must ask if you have no Codicil to ad to your last Will, which you left with me when you departed this Life and took your Flight to another World? You will see by the inclosed that I have hitherto been a carefull Executor.[2] [*Passage omitted*]

Text Bristol MS ii. 73–76

[1] Her rendezvous in Venice with Algarotti.
[2] He probably enclosed a letter from

Algarotti, who was then returning from St. Petersburg through the German States.

To Wortley *1 Sept.* [*1739*]

Lions, Sept. 1. N.S.

I am now arriv'd at this place, where I find the same reasons for not staying that I did at Dijon, and am persuaded I shall find them in every Town in France,[1] which makes me resolve for Turin, where I shall set out to morrow morn:, and hope to be unknown and live at as little expence as I please. I have bargain'd to be carry'd there, my selfe and servants, for 12 louis, which is the cheapest I could get.[2]

I desire to know whither I am to make use of the credit you have given me on Mr. Waters, or whither you will send me a bill. If it be the last, I desire it may be sent to Mess. Martin Bellandi Amatis and Comp. at Turin, and your Letters directed to them. I have not yet heard from you, but I have taken care to have any Letters that come to Dijon sent after me thither.

I hasten to cross the Alps, being told that the rains very often fall in this month, which will make the passage more disagreable. I will write again as soon as I arrive at Turin.

Text W MS i. 318–19   *Address* To Edwd Wortley Esqr at his House in Cavendish Square London Angleterre   *Postmark* ⟨?⟩ 3 *End. by* W L.M. 1 Sept. 1739   from Lyons   Abt Money   Ad 6 Sept.[3]

To Francesco Algarotti [*c. 6 Sept. 1739*]

Me voici aux pieds des Alpes, et demain je franche le pas qui doit me conduire en Italie. Je me recommande a vous dans tous les perils comme Don Quichotte a sa Dulcinée, et je n'ai pas l'imagination moins échauffée que lui. Rien

[1] A month later Thomas Gray counted almost thirty English at Lyons (13 Oct., *Corr.*, ed. P. Toynbee and L. Whibley, 1935, i. 122).
[2] The silver louis (or *écu*) was worth

4*s.* 6*d.* in 1704 (*OED*).
[3] W usually repeats LM's New Style dates (with the year), and adds the Old Style dates of his answers.

m'effraye, rien me dissipe un moment; recueilli en moi mesme, ni les fatigues de la poste ni les plaisirs qu'on m'a proposé dans les villes m'ont distrait un instant de la douce contemplation ou je suis plongé.

> Such soft Ideas all my pains beguile,
> The Alps are levell'd, and the Desarts smile.
> These pendant Rocks and ever during snow,
> These rolling Torrents that eternal Flow:
> Amidst this Chaos that around me lyes,
> I only hear your voice, and see your Eyes.

Text Bod. MS Don. c. 56, f. 67

To Wortley *10 Sept.* [*1739*]

Turin, Sept. 10.

I am now, thank God, happily past the Alps.[1] I beleive I wrote to you that I had met English of my Acquaintance in every Town in France; this fortune continu'd to the last, for at Pont Beau Voisin I met Lord Carlisle,[2] who was in the Inn when I arriv'd, and immediately came to offer me his Room, his Cook to dress my Supper (he himselfe having supp'd before I came in) and all sort of civillitys. We pass'd the Evening together and had a great deal of Discourse. He said he lik'd Rome so well that he should not have left it so soon but on the Account of Lord Morpeth, who was so ill there that he was not yet recover'd and now carry'd in a Litter. His Distemper has been the Bloody Flux, which return'd upon him in the Mountains with so much violence, they had been kept 3 weeks at a miserable village. He is still so weak I did not see him.[3]

My Lord Carlisle told me that next to Rome the best place to stay in Ittaly is without contradiction Venice; that the Impertinence of the little Sovereigns in other Countrys is intolerable. I have no Objection to his Advice but the Fear

[1] LM and W had passed over them about twenty years before (i. 434–5).
[2] The 4th Earl (see above, p. 127).
[3] Lord Morpeth died Aug. 1741 of consumption, though gossip attributed his death to 'the venereal distemper which he caught in Italy and kept secret so long that it proved at last incurable' (HMC *Twelfth Report*, Part ix, 1891, p. 204).

of the Air not agreeing with me, thô my Journey has now so
far establish'd my Health that I have lost all my bad Sym-
ptoms, and am ready to think I could even bear the damps of
London. I will therefore venture to try, and if I find Venice
too cold or moist (which I am more afraid of) I can remove
very easily, thô I resolve against Rome, on an Account you
may guess. My Lord Carlisle said he thought me in the right,
that it is very hard to avoid meeting a certain person,[1] and
there are so many little dirty Spys that write any Lye comes
into their Heads, that the doing it may be dangerous. I have
receiv'd a Letter from Lady Pomfret that she is leaving
Sienna[2] and intends for Venice, which is another Inducement
⟨to me⟩ to go there; but the cheife is the hopes of living as
quiet and as private as I please, which hitherto I have found
impossible. The English Resident here, Mr. Villette,[3] came
to wait on me the very night of my arrival, to my great surprise. I found the Intteligence came from the King of
Sardinia's[4] officers who were at Pont Voisin, and had learnt
my name from Lord Carlisle's servants. I have been oblig'd
to excuse my going to Court on having no Court dress, and
saying I intended to leave the Town in a few days. However,
I have not been able to avoid the visits that have been made
to me.

Text W MS i. 320–1   *Address* To Edwd Wortley Esqr in Cavendish Square London Angleterre   *Postmark* DE TURIN SE ⟨?⟩   *End. by*
W L.M.   10 Sept. N.S. 1739.   From Turin.

To Lady Pomfret *11 Sept. 1739*

Turin, September 11, N.S. 1739.

I am now, dear madam, in a country where I may soon
hope for the pleasure of seeing you; but in taking your advice
I see I have taken the wrong road to have that happiness
soon; and I am out of patience to find that, after passing the

---

[1] The Old Pretender, James Edward,
who maintained his court in Rome.

[2] Lady Pomfret remained in Sienna
until mid-December, when she moved
to Florence (Finch MS).

[3] Arthur Villettes (*c.* 1702–76), at
Turin as Secretary (1734–41) and then
Resident (1741–9) (D. B. Horn, *Brit.
Dipl. Rep. 1689–1789*, 1932, p. 124).

[4] Charles Emanuel III (1701–73).

Alps, we have the Apennines between us; besides the new-invented difficulties of passing from this country to Bologna, occasioned by their foolish quarantines. I will not entertain you with my road adventures 'till we meet. But I cannot help mentioning the most agreeable of them, which was seeing at Lyons the most beautiful and the best behaved young man I ever saw. I am sure your ladyship must know I mean my Lord Lempster.[1] He did me the honour of coming to visit me several times; accompanied me to the opera; and, in short, I am indebted to him for many civilities, besides the pleasure of seeing so amiable a figure. If I had the honour of all my relations much at heart, I should, however, have been mortified at seeing his contrast in the person of my cousin Lord Fielding,[2] who is at the same academy.

I met Lord Carlisle at Pont Beauvoisin, who had been confined in the mountains three weeks in a miserable village, on the account of his son's health, who is still so ill that he can travel in no way but in a litter. I enquired after your ladyship, as I cannot help doing so of every body that I think may have seen you. He told me that he had not had that advantage, but he was informed that you intended leaving Sienna, and would certainly pass the carnival at Venice; which determines me to go thither, where I beg you would direct your next letter, enclosed to Mr. Brown, the English consul there.[3]

It is impossible to express to you the satisfaction I feel in the hopes of passing our time together, remote from the nonsense of our own country, and present to the only happiness this world can afford, a mutual friendship and esteem; which I flatter myself your partiality gives me, and which is paid to you with the utmost justice by, dear madam, Your faithful, &c. &c.[4]

Text 1837, ii. 225–7

[1] George Fermor (1722–85), later 2nd Earl of Pomfret, eldest son of Lady Pomfret. He attended an academy in Lyons. Later in life he became eccentric, vicious, extravagant, and perhaps mad.

[2] Basil Feilding (1719–1800), later 6th Earl of Denbigh. (LM was cousin to his father.) In 1736–7 his mother had asked her friends for advice about his education (HMC *Denbigh MSS*, 1911, pp. 126, 200, 202, 208).

[3] Niel Browne (*c.* 1660–1740).

[4] On 21 Sept. Lady Pomfret, in Sienna, received a letter from LM, probably this one (Finch MS).

To Wortley 25 Sept. [1739]

Venice, Sept. 25

I am at length happily arriv'd here, I thank God. I wish it had been my original Plan, which would have sav'd me some money and fatigue, thô I have not much reason to regret the last, since I am convince'd it has greatly contributed to the Restoration of my Health. I have met nothing disagreable in my Journey but too much company. I find (contrary to the rest of the World) I did not think my selfe so considerable as I am, for I verily beleive if one of the Pyramids of Ægypt had travell'd, it could not have been more follow'd, and if I had receiv'd all the visits that have been intended me, I should have stop'd at least a year in every Town I came through.

I lik'd Milan so well that if I had not desir'd all my Letters to be directed hither, I think I should have been tempted to stay there. One of the pleasures I found there was the Borromean Library, where all strangers have free access, and not only so, but Liberty on giving a Note for it to take any printed Book home with them. I saw several curious Manuscripts there.[1] And as a proofe of my recovery I went up to the very top of the Dome of the great church without any assistance.[2] I am now in a Lodging on the great canal. Lady Pomfret is not yet arriv'd, but I expect her very soon, and if the Air does not disagree with me I intend seeing the Carnival here. I hope your Health continues, and that I shall hear from you very soon.

I think I have been a very good Huswife to come thus far

[1] The Ambrosiana, founded in 1609 by Cardinal Frederic Borromeo, was considered the best library in Italy next to the Vatican (Thomas Nugent, *The Grand Tour*, 3rd ed., 1778, iii. 147). It was praised by Charles de Brosses, who visited it in July 1739, for being open every day and evening and for displaying unusually handsome and ancient manuscripts (*Lettres familières sur l'Italie*, ed. Y. Bezard, 1931, i. 99). Other travellers praised its liberal access; but David Garrick (in 1763) quoted its Latin inscription forbidding the removal of any books or manuscripts (*Journal... France and Italy*, ed. G. W. Stone, 1939, pp. 16–17, 47); and Edward Gibbon (in 1764) remarked that books could be used only in the library (*Journey from Geneva to Rome*, ed. G. A. Bonnard, 1961, p. 50).

[2] Climbing to the top of the cathedral tower was a customary activity of travellers (Nugent, iii. 146; de Brosses, i. 91; Gibbon, p. 47).

on the money I carry'd out with me, but you may be sure I am very near the end of it. I desire you would send me a bill of exchange enclos'd in your next Letter, directed to be left at the Consul Mr. Brown's at Venice; he is the only person I have seen here. He tells me our old Freind Grimani[1] is procurator of St. Marc and will come to see me as soon as he hears of my Arrival.

Text W MS i. 322–3   *Address* To Edwd Wortley Esqr in Cavendish Square London Angleterre   *Postmark* oc 5   *End. by W* L.M. 25 Sept. 1739   Rec. 5 Oct.   from Venice.   Ad 9 Oct.   Desires a bill.

To Wortley [*1 Oct. 1739*]

The procurator of St. Marc has been to see me. I found him something fatter, but in as good Health and spirits as ever I saw him at Vienna. He has offer'd me all the services in his power, and says he will bring the most agreable Venetian Ladys to wait on me. He talk'd a great while of you with large proffessions of regard and Esteem. The Abbé Conté[2] has been with me, in much better Health than I knew him at London; and if one was to Judge by the old people here, this air cannot be unwholsome. Our English Consul, who has resided, as he says, this 40 years, is as chearfull an old Man as ever I saw. I have had visits from the French, Imperial, Neapolitan, and Spanish Ambassador and his Lady.[3] This last enquir'd first of the Consul if their visit would [be] agreable to me. I beleive you will think me in the right to answer that as a stranger I desir'd to be thought quite neutral in all national Quarrels, and should be pleas'd with the Honour of their Company.[4]

[1] Pietro Grimani (1677–1752), Venetian Ambassador in London 1710–13 and in Vienna 1715–20. He was elected Doge in 1741.

[2] Antonio Conti (1677–1749). LM had met him in London in 1715, and corresponded with him 1717–18.

[3] French Ambassador, Charles-François, comte de Froulay (1683–1744); Imperial, Prince Luigi Antonio Pio (d. 1755); Neapolitan, Don José Baeza y Vincentello (d. 1770), Count of Cantillana; Spanish, Luis Reggio e Branciforte (c. 1675–1757), Prince of Campoflorido (*Repertorium*, ii. 132, 88, 241, 395). The Spanish Ambassadress was Caterina Gravina e Gravina (c. 1680–1747), daughter of the Prince of Palagonia.

[4] England, on bad terms with Spain, did not declare war until 30/19 Oct. 1739,

As far as I can yet Judge, this Town is likely to be the most agreable, and the quietest place I can fix in. If you think so, I should be glad you would send my things hither: 3 boxes of my Books,[1] my papers and Bureau No. 1, my Work No. 2, a Box of my china, and the Box of my Dressing plate which is at Mr. Child's,[2] and a small empty Book case No. 4 —in all, 8 boxes.[3] I am told there is now in the River Thames the Ship Tygress, Capt. Petre master,[4] who is a Relation of Lord Petre's[5] and a man of an extrodinary good Character, that his ship is an extreme good one, of 30 Guns and well mann'd, capable of resisting a privateer and therefore not likely to be attack'd, and is bound directly to Venice. This is a happy oppertunity and should not be slipp'd, especially since I am told that even at Leghorn I should have trouble with my Books, which would be all examin'd by the Inquisition; and here care will be taken that I may receive them without any Impediment.

I hope you continue your good Health in spite of our Climate; it is now Spring here.

Sept. 31 [*sic*].

I think my things should be sent before the French fit out privateers, which, if the Intelligence here is worth minding, may be very soon. I forgot to mention a Box of Snuff[6] and the Hair Trunk of my Cloaths. If this ship does not put in to Venice, the consul will take care that my Goods shall be put on a Dutch ship and consign'd hither.

Text W MS i. 324–5   *Address* To Edwd Wortley Esqr in Cavendish

[1] They are listed, by an unknown hand, in a document headed by W: 'Catalogue [of] Lady Mary Wortley's books Packed up to be sent Abroad July 1739' (Wh MS 135). The great number and variety of books are summarized in Halsband, *LM*, p. 180.

[2] Probably Samuel Child (d. 1752), of the London banking firm (F. G. H. Price, *The Marygold by Temple Bar*, 1902, p. 31).

[3] When W sent LM her baggage the following spring he listed the contents of thirteen cases—the eight mentioned here, the two at the end of this letter, and

three additional ones: one of clothes and her saddle, and two containing two chairs each (25 March 1740, draft, W MS i. 117–18).

[4] John Petre, listed at his death (*c.* 1750) as captain of another ship (Joseph Jackson Howard and H. F. Burke, *Genealogical Collections of R. C. Families of England*, i, 1887, p. 45).

[5] Robert (1713–42), 8th Baron Petre, of a prominent Catholic family, and conspicuous for his learning and virtuous behaviour.

[6] LM's snuff had been confiscated at Calais (see above, p. 141).

Square London Angleterre   *End. by W* L.M. 31 Sept. from Venice.
Recd 9 Oct.   Ad 7 Nov. [*Summary*]¹

To Lady Pomfret *10 Oct.* [*1739*]

Venice, Oct. 10, N.S.

I did not answer dear Lady Pomfret's letter the moment I
had received it,² from a very ridiculous reason, which was
however a very serious impediment; a gnat had saluted one
of my eyes so roughly, that it was for two days absolutely
sealed down: it is now quite well; and the first use I make of
it is to give thanks for your kind thoughts of me, which I
wish I knew how to deserve.

I like this place extremely, and am of opinion you would
do so too: as to cheapness, I think 'tis impossible to find any
part of Europe where both the laws and customs are so con-
trived purposely to avoid expences of all sorts; and here is a
universal liberty that is certainly one of the greatest *agrémens*
in life. We have foreign ambassadors from all parts of the
world, who have all visited me. I have received visits from
many of the noble Venetian ladies; and upon the whole I am
very much at my ease here. If I was writing to Lady Sophia,³
I would tell her of the comedies and operas which are every
night, at very low prices; but I believe even you will agree
with me that they are ordered to be as convenient as possible,
every mortal going in a mask, and consequently no trouble
in dressing, or forms of any kind. I should be very glad to
see Rome, which was my first intention (I mean next to
seeing yourself); but am deterred from it by reasons that are
put into my head by all sorts of people that speak to me of it.
There are innumerable little dirty spies about all English;
and I have so often had the ill-fortune to have false witness
borne against me, I fear my star on this occasion. I still hope
you will come to Venice; where you will see a great town,
very different from any other you ever saw, and a manner of

¹ W's summaries, which are often
lengthy, will usually be omitted here-
after.

² Lady Pomfret, in Sienna, had sent
a letter on 23 Sept. (Finch MS).

³ Lady Pomfret's eldest daughter.

living that will be quite new to you. Let me endeavour to tempt you by naming another motive; you will find a sincere friend, who will try the utmost of her power to render the place agreeable to you; it can never be thoroughly so to me 'till I have the happiness of seeing Lady Pomfret, being ever, in the strictest sense of that phrase, Yours, &c.[1]

Text 1837, ii. 227–8

To Wortley *14 Oct.* [*1739*]

Venice, Oct. 14

I find my selfe very well here; I am visited by the most considerable people of the Town, and all the foreign Ministers, who have most of them made great Entertainments for me. I din'd yesterday at the Spanish Ambassador's,[2] who even surpass'd the French in magnificence. He met me at the Hall door, and the Lady at the stair Head, to conduct me through the long Apartment. In short, they could not have shewn me more Honors if I had been an Ambassadresse. She desir'd me to think my selfe Patrona del casa, and offer'd me all the Services in her power, to wait on me where I pleas'd etc. They have the finest Palace in Venice. What is very convenient, I hear it is not at all expected I should make any Dinners, it not being the Fashion for any body to do it here but the foreign Ministers, and I find I can live here very genteely on my Allowance. I have allready a very agreable general Acquaintance, thô when I came, here was no one I had ever seen in my Life but the Cav. Grimani and the Abbé Conti; I must do them Justice to say they have taken pains to be obliging to me. The procurator brought his Niece (who is at the Head of his Family)[3] to wait on me, and they invited me to reside with them at their Palace on the Brent, but I did not think it proper to accept of it. He also introduced to me the Signora Pisani Mocenigo, who is the most

[1] On 19 Oct. Lady Pomfret received a letter from LM, probably this one.
[2] Prince of Campoflorido.
[3] Grimani was a bachelor. His 'niece' was probably Francesca Giustinian, who m. (1719) Pietro Grimani, his nephew (Andrea da Mosto, *I Dogi di Venezia nella vita . . . privata*, 1960, pp. 487, 488).

considerable Lady here.[1] The Nuncio[2] is particularly Civil
to me; he has been several times to see me, and has offer'd
me the use of his Box at the Opera.[3] I have many others at
my service, and in short tis impossible for a stranger to be
better receiv'd than I am. Here are no English except a
Mr. Bertie[4] and his Governour, who arriv'd 2 days ago and
who intends but a short stay.

I hope you are in good Health, and that I shall hear of it
before you can receive this Letter.

Text W MS i. 326–7   *Address* To Edwd Wortley Esqr in Cavendish
Square London Angleterre   *Postmark* OC 22   *End. by W* L.M.
14 Oct. 1739   From Venice   Ad 7 Nov.

To Wortley *15 Oct.* [*1739*]

Oct. 15, Venice

I have this day receiv'd 5 letters from you by Mr. Waters.
I did not apprehend that you intended to direct to him,
which was the reason I never wrote to him till I receiv'd your
Letter directed to Dijon, which also came late to my Hands. I
will answer them all in order as well as I can. As to takeing
the pacquet boat to my selfe, it was done to avoid a night
passage, which Mr. Hall told me I must otherwaies suffer;
and for the price of the Chaise, thô it appear'd to me very
dear, I can assure you it was the cheapest in all Calais. There
was not one at the post house, thô I saw above 40 there, that
they would sell under 18 guineas, and the common price
ask'd was 25. For a fine one lin'd with velvet etc. they ask'd
me 58. I bought mine at a private House call'd Mr. Francia's,[5] who pretended to sell me a penyworth. If you make an

[1] Pisana Corner (d. 1769) m. (5 Oct.
1739) Cav. Giovanni Alvise Mocenigo,
procurator of San Marco, elected Doge
in 1763 (Pompeo Molmenti, *La Dogar-
essa di Venezia*, 1884, pp. 346, 361).

[2] Giovanni Francesco Stoppani (1695–
1774), Papal representative in Venice
from July 1739 to 1743.

[3] 'Boxes in the Theatres are esteemed
of such Consequence here, that they are
allowed to the Ambassadors by the

Government, who place on the doors the
arms of the Crouns they serve' (James
Gray, British Resident in Venice, to
Duke of Newcastle, 9 June 1747, SP
99/65).

[4] Possibly Norreys Bertie (1718–66),
M.P. 1743–54 (J. Foster, *Alumni Oxon.
1715–1886*, i. 102).

[5] Francis Lewis Francia (b. 1675) or
his son George, merchants in Calais
(Marcus Lipton, 'Francis Francia—the

Enquiry you will find all I say to be truth. I have kept an exact Journal of my travels and all the accidents I have met with.[1]

You guess right that I was advis'd at Boulogne what road to take to Dijon, by an English Gentleman in the French service who I met at Mrs. Bradshaw's; his name Capt. Cokely.[2] I went from thence, as I have inform'd you in a former letter, to St. Omers, then to Arras and Perone, Laon, Reins, Challons sur Marne, and Dijon. There is no going by Water from thence, the River Soan not being navigable till Challons sur Sone. I took Water there for Lyons, but found it very disagreable and not much cheaper than the post. When I went my selfe to fetch my Money from Mr. P.,[3] I gave nothing to his Clerk; when he brought it to me I made him a present.

I had wrote to Holland, but I see my Letter was not receiv'd when he wrote to me. I have this post very near copy'd your Letter to him.[4] I have desir'd him to direct for me recommended to Mr. Waters at Paris, being willing to conceal from him where I am, least he should be extravagant enough to come to me. As to the papers of which you send me copys, I know no use they are of, and should all be burnt. No. 5 was, as you thought, a receit for the Terine that I had mislaid.

The Nuncio told me last night that his letters from England say Sir R. W. is dying; if be true, I suppose he is now dead.[5] Let me know if you would have me write the news I meet with here. I hear a great many reports, this place being very nouvelliste.

My chaise lasted me to Brescia, where it broke down, and

Jacobite Jew' in *Jewish Hist. Soc. of England*, xi, 1928, pp. 190–205).

[1] LM outlines her journey in such detail because of W's request: 'If you mention a few of the great towns you have passed I shall see the whole journey . . . I wish, if it be easy, you would be exact and clear in your facts' ([13 Aug. 1739], W MS i. 112). Her journals were destroyed in 1794 by Lady Bute (Lady Louisa Stuart, 1861, i. 64).

[2] Neither is identified.

[3] Possibly M. Pontsainpierre, a

banker at Lyons in 1716 (HMC *Stuart Papers*, ii, 1904, p. 468).

[4] LM clearly refers to her son. After his escapades as a runaway from school, his career is undocumented (Jonathan Curling, *Edward Wortley Montagu*, 1954, pp. 45–49). He had lived on the Continent at least since 1732; and since 1737 in Ysselstein, Holland—where he was protected from his creditors. He was forbidden to write directly to W.

[5] Walpole, who suffered from the gout and the stone, lived until 1745.

I was forc'd to hire another to Padoua. From thence I came by Water, in a Burcello which cost me but 2 sequins.¹ I have receiv'd this day one hundred pounds from Mr. Waters. I have now 5 sequins left of the money I carry'd out and no debt, which I think is not being an ill manager.

Text W MS i. 328–9   *Address* To Edwd Wortley Esqr in Cavendish Square London Angleterre   *Postmark* OC 25   *End. by W* L.M. 15 Oct. 1739   from Venice   Ad 7 Nov.

To Wortley *1 Nov.* [*1739*]

I never had my Health better than I have in this Climate, thô it is now cold. But here is a constant clear sun and instead of the dampness I aprehended the air is particulary dry, which I beleive my constitution requir'd. I have a general acquaintance that are very civil and obliging to me, thô I never saw any of them in my Life (except the Abbé Conti and Grimani). I have never wrote you any news, being persuaded that all Letters are open'd at the post office, but, if you would have me, I will inform you of all I hear amongst the Foreign Ministers. I think it a long time since I have had a Letter from you.

November 1, N.S.

Text W MS i. 330–1   *Address* To Edward Wortley Esqr in Cavendish Square London Angleterre   *Postmark* NO 10   *End. by W* Venice   L.M.   1 Nov. 1739   Recd 12 Nov.   Ad 22

To Lady Pomfret *6 Nov.* [*1739*]

Venice, Nov. 6.

It was with the greatest pleasure I read dear Lady Pomfret's letter half an hour ago:² I cannot too soon give thanks for the delightful hopes you give me of seeing you here; and, to say truth, my gratitude is even painful to me 'till I try to express some part of it.

¹ In Venetian, a *burcelo* was a small, slow boat. A sequin (*zecchino*) was a gold coin current all over Italy, and worth about ten shillings.
² Lady Pomfret had written to her on 28 Oct. (Finch MS).

Upon my word, I have spoke my real thoughts in relation to Venice; but I will be more particular in my description, least you should find the same reason of complaint you have hitherto experienced. It is impossible to give any rule for the agreeableness of conversation; but here is so great a variety, I think 'tis impossible not to find some to suit every taste. Here are foreign ministers from all parts of the world, who, as they have no court to employ their hours, are overjoyed to enter into commerce with any stranger of distinction. As I am the only lady here at present, I can assure you I am courted, as if I was the only one in the world. As to all the conveniences of life, they are to be had at very easy rates; and for those that love publick places, here are two playhouses and two operas constantly performed every night, at exceeding low prices. But you will have no reason to examine that article, no more than myself; all the ambassadors having boxes appointed them, and I have every one of their keys at my service, not only for my own person, but whoever I please to carry or send. I do not make much use of this privilege, to their great astonishment. It is the fashion for the greatest ladies to walk the streets, which are admirably paved; and a mask, price sixpence, with a little cloak, and the head of a domino, the genteel dress to carry you every where. The greatest equipage is a gondola, that holds eight persons, and is the price of an English chair. And it is so much the established fashion for every body to live their own way, that nothing is more ridiculous than censuring the actions of another. This would be terrible in London, where we have little other diversion; but for me, who never found any pleasure in malice, I bless my destiny that has conducted me to a part where people are better employed than in talking of the affairs of their acquaintance. It is at present excessive cold (which is the only thing I have to find fault with); but in recompence we have a clear bright sun, and fogs and factions things unheard of in this climate. In short, if you come, and like the way of living as well as I do, there can be nothing to be added to the happiness of, dearest madam, Your faithful, &c.[1]

Text 1837, ii. 228–30

[1] On 24 Nov. Lady Pomfret received a letter, probably this one, from LM (ibid.).

From Lord Hervey *13/2 Nov. 1739*

St. James's, Nov. 2. 1739. O.S.

I left the Bath to my infinite Satisfaction last Week, but little expected to be so well entertain'd upon the Road as I found my-self. [*Passage omitted*] I left one of my Footmen to bring my Letters after me, and at Sandy Lane he brought me yours dated from Venice the 14 of last Month, where in the first Place I was glad to hear you was settled so much to your Satisfaction, and in the next that the distance of time and Country had not weaken'd the Partiality with which you used to think of a constant Admirer and very faithfull Friend. Your Descriptions of Venice are delightfull. Cagnioletti[1] never drew any Views of it half so amusing; I prefer your mezzotintos to all the Arts of his colouring: and I am as well acquainted with all the foreign ministers residing at Venice from your half-Sheet of Paper, as if I had pass'd half my Life in their Company. . . . [*Passage omitted*]

Our Friend is in London; he dined with me to day.[2] I did not say I had hear'd from you, because you gave me no Directions to do so; and when ever I am afray'd to err whatever I do, I generally prefer tacite to loquacious Errors, as they are easier corrected, and their Consequences not so dangerous. Whatever Instructions you send I will ex[e]cute, but do not let them be too delicate or too refined; I am no more made to be Plenipotentiary with such Comissions than any of the Embassadors at present from any of the Princes in Europe. . . . [*Passage in verse and prose omitted*]

Text Bristol MS ii. 77–79

To Wortley *20 Nov.* [*1739*]

Venice, Nov. 20.

I have wrote to you so often without receiving any answer that I am quite in pain about it. I thought directing to me at Venice would be sufficient, but perhaps Letters address'd in that manner may have miscarry'd. Pray send your next

[1] Antonio Canale or Canaletto (1697–1768). Although he did not visit England until 1746, his popularity among English collectors began in the 1720's.

[2] Algarotti had returned to England (by way of Rheinsburg and Hamburg) shortly before 10 Oct./29 Sept., when Hervey wrote from Bath to welcome him to London (Murray MS).

PLATE 4

Henrietta, Countess of Pomfret
From a bust attributed to G. B. Guelfi

recommended to Mr. Brown, the English Consul here; I am told that is the securest Direction.

I have made several agreable Acquaintance, thô they are all strangers except Grimani and the Abbé Conti. Thô we are at War with Spain, the Spanish Ambassadresse is one of my best Freinds.[1] I write you no farther particulars, having done it in many Letters, and I do not know on what subjects you desire I should write.

Text W MS i. 332   *End. by W* Recd 8 Decr. [*Summary*]

To Lady Pomfret [*Dec. 1739*][2]

Venice.

You have put me to a very difficult choice, yet, when I consider we are both in Italy, and yet do not see one another, I am astonished at the capriciousness of my fortune. My affairs are so uncertain, I can answer for nothing that is future. I have taken some pains to put the inclination for travelling into Mr. Wortley's head, and was so much afraid he should change his mind, that I hastened before him in order (at least) to secure my journey. He proposed following me in six weeks, his business requiring his presence at Newcastle. Since that, the change of scene that has happened in England has made his friends persuade him to attend parliament this sessions: so that what his inclinations, which must govern mine, will be next spring, I cannot absolutely foresee. For my own part, I like my own situation so well that it will be a displeasure to me to change it. To postpone such a conversation as your's a whole twelvemonth is a terrible appearance; on the other hand, I would not follow the example of the first of our sex, and sacrifice for a present pleasure a more lasting happiness. In short, I can determine nothing on this

[1] The Princess of Campoflorido. When the young Dutch patrician Jan Teding van Berkhout (1713–66) was brought to the house of the Spanish Ambassador and his wife by their son, he met there LM, the Nuncio, and two Venetian ladies (18 May 1740, MS diary, quoted in Halsband, *LM*, p. 194).

[2] Lady Pomfret received a letter from LM on 14 Dec. (Finch MS).

subject. When you are at Florence,[1] we may debate it over again.—I had letters last post from England that informed me we lodged in a house together. I think it is the first lie I ever heard invented that I wished a solemn truth.

The Prince of Saxony[2] is expected here in a few days, and has taken a palace exactly over against my house.[3] As I had the honour to be particularly well acquainted (if one may use that phrase) with his mother[4] when I was at Vienna, I believe I cannot be dispensed with from appearing at the conversations which I hear he intends to hold: which is some mortification to me who am wrapt up among my books with antiquarians and virtuosi. I shall be very impatient for the return to this letter, hoping to hear something more determined of your resolutions; which will in a great measure form those of, dear madam, Your ladyship's most faithful, &c.

Text 1837, ii. 230–1

To Wortley *11 Dec.* [*1739*]

Venice, Dec. 11.

It was with great pleasure I receiv'd your letter halfe an hour ago; having not heard any thing so long, I was in great pain for your health. I was also pleas'd to hear of your Daughter's, thô I cannot say the manner of it was obliging to me. I beleive she is the first that ever took the Liberty of sending a Letter to a Mother open.[5] I can see through the

1 Between 14 and 20 Dec. Lady Pomfret moved from Sienna to Florence, and lodged in the via Guicciardini (ibid.).

2 Frederick Christian (1722–63), son of Augustus III, Elector of Saxony and King of Poland.

3 On 24 Oct. the French Ambassador wrote, 'Miledy Mery Montaigu cherche a louer un Palais, et a vû tous les Ministères étrangers' (Archives des Affaires Étrangères, Venise, vol. 198, f. 308). The house she rented was on the Grand Canal (see below, p. 184).

4 Marie Josefa, da. of Joseph I (see i. 267), m. (1719) Augustus III.

5 LM had been on bad terms with her daughter since 1736, when the girl had disobediently married the young, handsome, but impoverished Earl of Bute. LM's attitude is reflected in a letter from her brother-in-law Lord Gower: 'I was very much concern'd to hear your daughter had given you so much uneasiness, and surpriz'd to find she had fixt upon an husband that had not your approbation. I hope by her future conduct she will attone for her past, and that her choice will prove more happy than you and Mr. Wortley expect' (11 Sept. 1736, W MS iv. 174). Still, in

Scotch Artifice of the Design in it, which is by making you Wittness of the fine things she is pleas'd to say, to convince you (as she thinks) that she has never fail'd in her Respect to me, in case I had made any Complaint.—It is rubbing a Wound to talk on this Subject; she has been the passion of my Life, and in a great measure the cause of all my ill Health.[1]

I am as agreably here as any stranger in my Circumstances can possibly be, and indeed a Repetition of all the Civillitys I have receiv'd would sound more like Vanity than Truth. I am sensible I owe a great part of them to Grimani, who is in the first Esteem and Authority in this Republic, and as he takes pains to appear my Freind, his Relations and allys of both Sexes (which are the most considerable people here) endeavor to oblige me in all sort of ways. The Carnaval is expected to be more brillant than common from the great concourse of Noble strangers. The Princesse of Holstein[2] and the Prince of Wolfembutel (nephew to the Empress)[3] are allready arriv'd, and the Electoral Prince of Saxony expected next Week. If my Age and Humour permitted me much pleasure in public Amusements, here are a great variety of them. I take as little share of them as I can,

> Frui paratis, et valido mihi,
> Latoe dones, et precor integra
> cum mente, nec turpem senectam
> degere, nec cithara carentem.[4]

You see I have got a Horace, which is borrow'd of the Consul, who is a good Scholar; but I am very impatient for my own Books.

Here is enclos'd Mr. Child's Note for my dressing Plate, which I forgot to leave with you.[5]

1738 LM stood as godmother to Lady Bute's first child (*General Eve. Post*, 18–21 Feb. 1738).

[1] This paragraph, except for the first sentence, has been omitted by previous editors.

[2] Anna Caroline (1707–69), Countess Orzelska, natural daughter of Augustus the Strong, Elector of Saxony and King of Poland, m. (1730) and divorced (1733) the Duke of Holstein (Isenburg, i. 92). On 24 Oct. the French Ambassador reported her arrival in Venice.

[3] Charles I (1713–80), Prince of Wolfenbüttel. His mother's sister, the Empress Elisabeth, was consort to Charles VI (Isenburg, i. 72, 73).

[4] 'Grant me, O Latona's son, to be content with what I have, and, sound of body and of mind, to pass an old age lacking neither honour nor the lyre' (Horace, *Odes*, I, xxxi; transl. Loeb Library).

[5] W had written to her, on 7 Nov., that Childs the bankers would not give him her 'Plate-trunk' to send unless they had her note for it (W MS i. 115).

Y⟨ou do⟩ not seem desirous to hear news, which makes me not trouble you with any.

I could wish when you send my things you would be so good to send me the Covers of the cushions that were us'd at Constantinople. The additional weight to the Baggage will be very small. I do not think they can be of any service to you, and they would be usefull to me, being in fashion here. They were put into the Box that was left open, where the Furniture of my dressing room was put.

Text W MS i. 333–4 *Address* To Edwd Wortley Esqr at his House in Cavendish Square London Angleterre *Postmark* DE 20 P *End. by W* L.M. 11 Dec. 1739. La. Bute. Covers for Cushions. Ad 21 Dec.

To Francesco Algarotti[1] *24 Dec.* [*1739*]

Dec. 24 S.N.

J'ay de la peine a croire que tous mes lettres, que j'ai envoyé par differents routes, vous ont manqué; mais même quand cela auroit arrivé, il me semble encore plus extrodinaire que vous pouviez imaginer que je coure le monde pour voir des carnivals et des Fêtes. Vous devez vous souvenir que vous etes convenu avec moi de vivre dans les états de Venise, et je ne peus pas deviner aucune nouvelle Raison pour vous detourner de ce dessein. J'ai rangé tous mes affaires sur cet plan, et il n'est pas possible que je va a Paris, quand mesme j'aurois un Envie, que je suis tres eloigné d'avoir.

J'ai assez fait pour prouver le desir de passer ma vie avec vous. Il est seure que si je ne suis pas capable de faire vostre bonheur vous ne pouvez pas faire le mien. Je ne pretends pas vous gener.

J'ai receû ici beaucoup plus des civilittez et même honneurs que je ne merite; et je menerai une vie assez douce s'il elle n'etoit troublé par le souvenir d'un ingrat qui m'a oublié dans un Exil qu'il a causé.

Text Bod. MS Don. c. 56, f. 69

[1] From Sept. 1739 to June 1740 Algarotti remained in England.

To Wortley *24 Dec.* [*1739*]

I receiv'd yours of the 22nd Nov. with a great deal of pleasure as it brought me news of your Health. I made your Compliments in the best manner I could to the Procurator,[1] who returns them with a great appearance of cordiality. He behaves to me with the utmost Freindship and does every thing in his power to make this Country agreable to me. I am very quiet here, and I think can live more decently on my allowance than in any other Town. If the air continues to agree with me I do not design to leave it.

Here are no English at present but Lord Granby,[2] who arriv'd 2 days ago. He has been to see me with his Governor Mr. Hewet.[3] Lady Pomfret has been stopp'd by the illness of one of her Daughters, but I expect her very soon.[4]

Dec. 24.

Text W MS i. 335   *End. by W* L.M. 24 Dec. 1739   Recd 5 Jan. Ad 10 Janry.

To Wortley *5 Jan.* [*1740*] /*25 Dec.* [*1739*]

Dec. 25 O.S.

I receiv'd yours yesterday dated Dec. 7. I find my Health very well here notwithstanding the cold, which is very sharp, but the sun shines as clear as at midsummer.

I am treated here with more distinction than I could possibly expect. I went to see the Ceremony of High Mass celebrated by the Doge on Xmas Eve. He appointed a Gallery for me and the Prince of Wolfembutel where no other person was admitted but those of our Company; a greater Complement could not have been paid me if I had been a Sovereign Princess. The Doge's Niece[5] (he having no Lady) met me at

[1] Pietro Grimani.

[2] John Manners (1721–70), Marquess of Granby, heir to 3rd Duke of Rutland, and famous in later life as a military commander.

[3] William Hewett of Stretton Magna, Leics. (Walter E. Manners, *Some Ac-* *count of John Manners Marquis of Gran-by*, 1899, p. 9, n.).

[4] On 9 Oct. Lady Pomfret 'had no thoughts of removing [from Sienna] till after Christmas' (Hertford, *Corr.* i. 139).

[5] Alvise Pisani (1664–1741), Doge (1735), had been a widower since 1729

the Palace Gate and led me through the Palace to the Church of St. Mark, where the Ceremony was perform'd in the pomp you know,[1] and we were not oblig'd to any Act of adoration.

The Electoral Prince of Saxony is here in Public and makes a prodigious expence. His Governour is Count Wackerbart,[2] Son to that Madam Wackerbart with whom I was so intimate at Vienna,[3] on which account he shews me particular civillitys and obliges his Pupil to do the same. I was last night at an Entertainment made for him by the Signora Pisani Mocenigo[4] (which was one of the finest I ever saw), and he desir'd me to sit next to him in a great chair. In short, I have all the reason that can be to be satisfy'd with my treatment in this Town, and I am glad I met Lord Carlisle, who directed me hither.

I have receiv'd Sir. F. Ch.'s[5] bill dated Oct. 11, which I certify'd to him some time ago. I have not yet had any for the Xmas Quarter.

I have so little correspondance at London, I should be pleas'd to hear from you whatever happens amongst my Acquaintance. I am sorry for Mr. Pelham's misfortune,[6] thô tis long since that I have look'd upon the Hopes of continuing a Family as one of the vainest of mortal Projects.

> 'Tho Solomon with a thousand Wives
> To get a wise successor strives,
> But one, and he a Fool, survives.

The Procurator of St. Mark[7] has desir'd his complements to you whenever I write.

Text W MS i. 336–7   *Address* To Edwd Wortley Esqr in Cavendish Square London Angleterre   *Postmark* IA 15   *End. by W* L.M. 25 Dec. O.S.   recd 15 Jan. 1739/40   Xmas Quarter Ad 25 Jan.

(Andrea da Mosto, *I Dogi di Venezia*, 1939, pp. 295–6). His niece was Isabella Pisani.

[1] W must have seen it while travelling in Italy with Joseph Addison, who was in Venice in Jan. 1700 (Addison, *Letters*, ed. W. Graham, 1941, p. 408).

[2] Josef Anton Gabaleon (d. 1761), Count von Wackerbarth-Salmour, had previously held diplomatic appointments for Saxony.

[3] LM had written to her from Turkey in 1717 (see i. 344).

[4] See above, p. 156, n. 1.

[5] Sir Francis Child (1684?–1740), head of the banking firm.

[6] Henry Pelham's two young sons died suddenly on 27 Nov. 1739.

[7] Pietro Grimani.

From Lord Hervey *11 Jan.1740/31 Dec. 1739*

St. James's, Dec. 31. O.S. 1739

By the size of my Paper you see I am sat down with Malice prepense to inflict a long Letter upon you. . . . [*Passage omitted*] But before I proceed I must clear up and State the Account of the Letters which have already pass'd between us unmention'd by either. You wrote me one from Turin which you say I never acknowledg'd, and I wrote you one from the Bath which you never spoke of. Since that I recieved a short one from Venice in which you say'd you had written Volumes to me without recieving any answer, and which put me into so ill a humour that I was half resolved to write no more, when another came to dispell the melancholly occasion'd by its Predecessor.

I do not wonder in the least at the distinctions shown you at Venice . . . [*Passage omitted*] . . . where Arts flourish, Sciences are cultivated, Conversation is tasted, and Wit distinguished, that You should be sought is no more an Object of wonder than that an English Guinea should be taken for its intrinsic Value in a Country where the Metal was known tho the Coin was not. [*Passage omitted*] I had written thus far when our Friend[1] came into the Room. I did not tell ⟨him⟩ to whom I was writing, and as you decline giving me any Directions for my Conduct, am at a Loss to know what sort of Conduct I should hold; but as those who are uncertain what is right to do, always do best when they do least, so I determine to steer my Course by that negative Compas as directly as I can, and shall not tell ⟨him⟩ what I really believe, which is that as ⟨a Venetian⟩ when you was at London made you forget every Englishman, so a Piedmonteze at Venice will make you forget every Venetian. [*Passage omitted*]

Text Bristol MS ii. 81–84   *Address* A Madame Madame de Montagu chez Monsr Brown Consul Anglois a Venise (par Amsterdam)   *Postmark* ⟨?⟩

From Wortley *12/1 Jan. [1740]*

1 Jan.
[*Passage omitted*]

Tho you have asked me 2 or 3 times whether I desired to have any news sent,[2] I made no reply till now because I had not found a way to

---

[1] Undoubtedly Francesco Algarotti. To disguise Hervey's allusion, LM later added an *s* to *Friend*, and obliterated the other words indicated in this passage. Hervey alone shared her secret.

[2] See above, pp. 157, 158.

send a letter by some passenger into Holland which coud not easily fall into the hands of any one that woud open it.

When you send any news I desire it may be directed thus:

> To Mr. Charles Atkinson, Merchant,
> at Mr. Francis Horton in Lee-Street,
> Red Lyon-Square, Holbourn.

This is not Mr. H[orton][1] that you know, but an acquaintance of his who will not open the letter. It is best the letter should not be writ in your own hand but your maid's, or some merchantlike hand. I shall know it comes by your direction if you mention the receipt of one of this date. I keep a copy of this. I think you are not in a likely place for intelligence, but it is possible you may have some worth sending between this and the Spring.

If you said I have this or that from a Frenchman, a Roman, etc., I should ghess from what hand it came. But if you should mean any new person, you should mention him in a letter directed to me some posts before.

If I coud have any good intelligence from abroad it might be of use to me in many respects. Trifles, I think, (tho they relate to foreign Courts) may safely enough be writ in those directed to me, if the authors woud not be concealed.[2]

[Passage omitted]

Text W MS i. 158–9 (draft)   *End. by W* To L.M. 1 Jan.   Sent to Holland by Mr. H.

To Wortley *21 Jan.* [*1740*]

I am sorry your Daughter continues troubling you concerning me. She cannot beleive, after her behaviour to me the last time she was in Town, that it is possible to persuade me of any real Affection, and all beside is an affectation that is better left off now Decency no longer exacts it. I am not only conscious of having in every point perform'd my Duty to her, but with a tenderness and Freindship that is not commonly found, and I may say with truth that as even from her Infancy I have made her a Companion and Wittness of my

---

[1] Not identified.
[2] LM sent W a letter full of political intelligence on 31 May 1740 (now lost) and another on 11 April [1741].

Actions, she owes me not only the regard due to a Parent, but the Esteem that ought to be paid to a blameless Conduct and the gratitude that is shown by every honest mind to a valuable Freind. I will say no more on this Subject, which is shocking to me and cannot be agreable to you. If you desire it, I will write a Letter to her enclos'd in my next to you, not knowing how to direct to Lord B[ute]'s Agent. I had rather drop the Correspondance, being very incapable of dissembling. She need take no notice of it to the World, and I shall never be ask'd here whither I hear from her or no.

The noble Venetian Ladys live now very much after the manner of the French, and visit all Strangers of Quality. They come to me sometimes in the morning and sometimes in the afternoon, as my Acquaintance us'd to do at London. Many of them keep assemblys where they are very glad to see Foreigners of Distinction. I have introduce'd Lord Granby to them as a Relation of mine[1] at the Request of his Governour; and he now visits several at their Toilets, where I beleive he is very welcome, being a figure not unlike Mr. Bows,[2] thô but 19 year old. They do not converse with Ambassadors out of masque, and they ask at my door if any are with me, and if they hear there are, they send me a complement that they will defer their visits to another time. The foreign Ministers do the same thing, and thus they avoid meeting; but at their Balls, where masques are allways admitted, I have seen them converse very freely with them.[3]

I have never plaid at any Game since I came here. They have Cards at their assemblys, but I do not even understand the figures and have no Inclination to learn. My House is properly a meeting of Litterati; the Procurator Grimani seldom fails coming when I am at home, and the Abbé Conti never. Here are some Ladys who place themselves in that Rank. I do not go often to the Opera, thô I have many Boxes at my Service, and cannot allways refuse the pressing Invitations of the Ladys that will carry me thither. The Signora Grimani, Niece of the procurator, the Isabella Pisani, Niece

---

[1] Through his ancestor the 8th Earl of Rutland, whose mother, Grace Pierrepont, was sister of 1st Earl of Kingston.

[2] Perhaps George Bowes of Gibside

(1701–60), M.P. for Durham, and associated with W in coal-mining.

[3] By law Venetian patricians were forbidden to converse with foreign ministers.

of the Doge, the procuratessa Pisani Mocenigo,[1] the Corn-
eli⟨a⟩ Tepoli,[2] the Clara Michielli,[3] the procuratessa Fosca-
⟨rini⟩,[4] the Justiniani Gradinego,[5] and the Livia Moro,[6] are
all intimate with me. I sup⟨pose⟩ you know these are the first
Familys here.

January 21. N.S.   Your last letter was without date.

Text W MS i. 338–9   *Address* To Edwd Wortley Esqr in Cavendish
Square London Angleterre   *Postmark* FE 1   *End. by* W L. M.
21 Jan. 1739/40   Rec. 2 Feb.   Ad 4 Feb.

To Wortley 25 *Jan.* [*1740*]

Jan. 25.

I wrote to you last post, but as I do not know whither I was
particular enough in answering all the Questions you ask'd
me, I add the Following Account, which I do not wonder will
surprise you, since both the Procurator Grimani and the
Abbé Conti tell me often that this last twenty year has so far
chang'd the Customs of Venice that they hardly know it for
the same Country. Here are several foreign Ladys of Quality,
I mean Germans and from other parts of Ittaly, here not
being one French Woman. They are all well receiv'd by the
Gentil Donnas, who make a vanity in Introduceing them to
the assemblys and other public diversions, thô all those Ladys
as well as my selfe go frequently to the Princesse of Campo
Florida's (the Spanish Ambasadresse's) assembly. She is in a
very particular manner obliging to me, and is, I realy think,

---

[1] These three ladies have already
been mentioned.

[2] Cornelia Mocenigo m. (1721)
Francesco Tiepolo.

[3] Chiara (d. 1780), da. of Daniele
Bragadin, m. (1726) Antonio Michiel
(Archivio di Stato, Venice). She became
and remained LM's most intimate
Italian friend.

[4] Eleonora Loredan m. (1694) Nicolò
Foscarini, later Procurator (ibid.).
Charles de Brosses wrote in Aug. 1739

that he had attended a '*conversation* chez
la procuratesse Foscarini, maison d'une
richesse immense, et femme très gracieuse
d'ailleurs' (*Lettres familières sur l'Italie*,
ed. Y. Bezard, 1931, i. 189).

[5] Giustiniana Morosini (b. 1705) m.
(1719) Girolamo Gradinego (Archivio
parrocchiale di S. Tomà; Archivio di
Stato, Venice).

[6] Livia Marcello m. (1738) Giovanni
Moro (Archivio di Stato, Venice).

one of the best sort of Women I ever knew.[1] The Neapolitan
(thô he has been here some months)[2] makes his public Entry
to day, which I am to go see about an hour hence. He gives
a great Entertainment at Night, where all the noble Venetians
of both Sexes will be in Masque. I am engag'd to go with the
Signora Justiniani Gradinego, who is one of the first Ladys
here. The Prince of Saxony has invited me to come into his
Box at the Opera, but I have not yet accepted of it, he
having allways the 4 Ladys with him that are wives to the
4 Senators deputed to do the Honors of Venice; and I am
afraid they should think I interfere with them in the Honor
of his conversation, which they are very fond of, and have
behav'd very coldly to some other noble Venetian Ladys that
have taken the Liberty of his Box. I will be directed in this
(as I am in all public matters) by the Procurator Grimani,—
my Letter is shorten'd by the arrival of the Signora.

I have receiv'd my Xmas Quarter, for which I thank you.

Text W MS i. 340–1   *Address* To Edwd Wortley Esqr at his House
in Cavendish Square London Angleterre   *Postmark* FE 1   *End. by*
W L.M. 25 Jan   recd 2 Feb 1739/40   Ad 4 Feb

To Wortley *15 Feb.* [*1740*]

In Obedience to you,[3] I have wrote the enclos'd, in which
I have kept within the bounds of Truth, since it is certain
that whatever reason I have to complain of my Daughter's
behaviour, I shall allways wish her well, and if it was in my
power to give her any solid mark of it I would do it, and shall
ever be of that Opinion. I wrote sometime since to my Son
desiring him to send his Letters to Mr. Waters at Paris, who
will forward them where ever I am. I think all Letters are
open'd, and I hear other people make the same Complaint.

[1] The French Ambassador also
thought highly of her: 'C'est une tres
bonne femme, et fort polie' (27 Feb.
1740, Ministère des Affaires Étrangères,
Venise, vol. 99). At the French Court
the duc de Luynes was struck by her
noble air, though she was short, fat, and
ugly. He noted that she had never
learned French, and spoke Spanish and
Italian badly (*Mémoires sur la cour de
Louis XV*, 1860–5, iii. 227; viii. 246).

[2] The Count of Cantillana had been
in Venice since June 1738 (*Repertorium*,
ii. 241).

[3] W had asked her 'To correspond
with Daughter and Son' (memorandum,
21/10 Jan., W MS i. 115).

The Duke of Rutland[1] has wrote a very handsome Letter to thank me for the Civillitys I have shewn his Son.[2]

Here has been great Entertainments made by all the Ambassadors for the Prince of Saxony, where I could not avoid appearing, He haveing been obliging to me even in a surprizing manner, thô I have been but once in his Box at the opera after many Invitations. The Senate has deputed 4 of their Principal members to do the Honors of the Republic. He has 3 Boxes made into one in the midst of the Theatre, which is finely illuminated, hung with crimson velvet, richly trim'd with gold lace and fringe, and has a magnificent Collation there every night. He has allways several noble Ladys with him when ever he has been at any of these Balls and Serenatas. He is seated between me and the Spanish Ambassadresse; indeed the Distinctions shew'd me here are very far above what I could expect. The Signora Justiniani Gradinego made a great Supper for me this Carnival,[3] which I am told was what never done before for any Stranger. She only invited 5 Ladys of my Acquaintance and 10 of the cheife Senators.

I am of opinion you would very much repent your Son's removal to France;[4] there is no part of it without English or Irish, and the first bad Councellor he meets he will return to all his Former Follys.

Feb. 15

Text W MS i. 342–3   *Address* To Edwd Wortley Esqr at His House in Cavendish Square London Angleterre   *Postmark* MR 5   *End. by* *W* L.M. 15 Feb. 1739/40.   Recd 5 Mar.   Ad 7 Mar

To Lady Pomfret [*Feb. 1740*][5]

I cannot help being offended to find that you think it necessary to make an excuse for the desire that you so

---

[1] John Manners (1696–1779), 3rd Duke, generally esteemed for his goodness and parental affection.

[2] Lord Granby.

[3] The Carnival, begun on St. Ste-

phen's Day (26 Dec.), would last until Lent (2 March).

[4] From Holland.

[5] Lady Pomfret received a letter from LM on 2 March (Finch MS).

obligingly expressed of seeing me. Do not think me so taste-
less or so ungrateful not to be sensible of all the goodness
you have shewn me. I prefer one hour of your conversation to
all the raree-shows that have ever been exhibited. But little
circumstances commonly overrule both our interests and
our inclinations. Though I believe, if the weather and roads
permitted, I should even now break through them all, to
gratify myself with waiting on you; however I hope [for] that
happiness in a few weeks; and in the mean time must go
through a course of conversations, concerts, balls, &c. I envy
you a more reasonable way of passing your time. It is but a
very small quantity that is allowed us by nature, and yet how
much of that little is squandered. I am determined to be a
better housewife for the future; and not to be cheated out of
so many irretrievable hours, that might be laid out to better
advantage.

I could pity the Duchess of Manchester, though I believe
'tis a sensation she is incapable of feeling for any body, and
I do not doubt it is her pride that is chiefly shocked on this
occasion; but as that is a very tender part, and she having
always possessed a double portion of it, I am persuaded she
is very miserable.[1] I am surprized at the different way of
acting I find in Italy, where, though the sun gives more
warmth to the passions, they are all managed with a sort of
discretion that there is never any public *eclât*, though there
are ten thousand publick engagements; which is so different
from what I had always heard and read, that I am convinced
either the manners of the country are wonderfully changed,
or travellers have always related what they have imagined,
and not what they saw; as I found at Constantinople, where,
instead of the imprisonment in which I fancied all the ladies
languished, I saw them running about in veils from morning
to night.[2]

'Till I can see you, dear madam, let me hear from you as
often as possible, and do not think your favours thrown away
upon a stupid heart; it is sincerely devoted to your service,

---

[1] The Duchess of Manchester, a
widow since 21 Oct. 1739, had been
unhappily married. She was engaged to
marry the 2nd Earl of Scarborough

when, on 29 Jan. 1740, he committed
suicide.

[2] LM describes this in her Embassy
letters (i. 328, 406).

with as much attachment as ever. I can part with all other pretensions, but I must be angry if you are in this point unjust to Your faithful servant, &c. &c.

Text 1837, ii. 238–40

To Lady Pomfret [*Feb. 1740*][1]

I must begin my letter, dear madam, with asking pardon for the peevishness of my last. I confess I was piqued at yours, and you should not wonder I am a little tender on that point. To suspect me of want of desire to see you, is accusing at once both my taste and my sincerity; and you will allow that all the world are sensible upon these subjects. But you have now given me an occasion to thank you, in sending me the most agreeable young man I have seen in my travels.[2] I wish it was in my power to be of use to him; but what little services I am able to do him, I shall not fail of performing with great pleasure. I have already received a very considerable one from him in a conversation where you was the subject, and I had the satisfaction of hearing him talk of you in a manner that agreed with my own way of thinking. I wish I could tell you that I set out for Florence next week; but the winter is yet so severe, and by all report, even that of your friends, the roads so bad, it is impossible to think of it.

We are now in the midst of carnival amusements, which are more than usual, for the entertainment of the Electoral Prince of Saxony, and I am obliged to live in a hurry very inconsistent with philosophy, and extreme different from the life I projected to lead. But 'tis long since I have been of Prior's opinion, who, I think, somewhere compares us to cards, who are but played with, do not play.[3] At least such has been my destiny from my youth upwards; and neither

---

[1] Date suggested by mention of the 'peevishness' of her last letter and the 'more than usual' carnival amusements.

[2] Charles-Juste, Prince de Beauvau (1720–93); his father Prince de Craon was head of the Council of Regency that governed Tuscany. Under the date

21 Jan. 1740 Lady Pomfret wrote in her journal: 'Prince Beauvoir [*sic*] went to Venice. I gave him a letter to Lady M. Wortley' (Finch MS).

[3] Prior, *Alma*, 1718, ii. 234–40 (*Works*, i. 491).

Dr. Clarke or Lady Sundon could ever convince me that I was a free agent;[1] for I have always been disposed of more by little accidents, than either my own inclinations or interest. I believe that affairs of the greatest importance are carried the same way. I seriously assure you (as I have done before), I wish nothing more than your conversation; and am downright enraged that I can appoint no time for that happiness; which however I hope will not be long delayed, and is impatiently waited for by, dear madam, Your ladyship's, &c.

Text 1837, ii. 232–3

To Francesco Algarotti *12 March* [*1740*]

Pourquoi si peu de Sincerité? Est-il possible que vous pourriez dire que vous m'avez fait des remonstrances contre l'Italie? Au contraire, j'ai encore une de vos lettres, dans laquelle vous m'asseurez que en quelque ville que je m'etablirois vous ne manquerois pas de vous rendre, et j'ai choisi Venice comme celle que vous convenoit le plus. Vous sçavez que le moindre de vos desirs m'auroit determiné pour le Japon mesme. La Provence ou le Languedoc m'auroit parfaitement plû, et épargné beaucoup des Fatigues et Depenses. Rappellez, s'il vous plaist, les Conversations que nous avons eû ensemble, et vous avoura que je devois croire, naturellement, que le voyage que j'ai fait etoit celui qui m'approchoit le plus de vous. Geneve est toujours rempli des Anglois, par consequent peu propre pour mon Sejour, l'Hollande encore moins par rapport au voisinage.

Je suis domicilé ici ou j'ai trouvé des agremens aux quelles je n'ai point de tout attendu. Le Procurator Grimani (dont vous sçavez sans doute le merite et le poids) est si fort de mes Amis qu'il s'est piqué de me rendre Venise agreable. Je suis recherché par tout ce qu'il y a ici de plus considerable des Dames et des Seigneurs. Enfin je me trouve miraculeusement beaucoup plus a mon aise qu'a Londres. Il est seure que je quitterois une seconde fois toutes les commoditez de ma vie

---

[1] The churchman Samuel Clarke (1675–1729) was considered deistical by the orthodox; Lady Sundon had been his great friend.

pour faire le bonheur de la vostre si j'etois persuadé que j'ÿ
été necessaire. Soyez assez honnete homme pour penser
serieusement la dessus. Consultez vostre Cœur; s'il vous dit
que vous seriez heureux aupres de moi, je sacrifie tout pour
cela. Ce n'est plus un sacrifice; vostre Amitie et vostre conversation feront les delices de ma vie. Il n'est pas possible
que nous vivons dans la mesme maison, mais vous pouriez
loger pres de chez moi et me voir tous les jours si vous
voudriez. Dit moi naivement vos pensées. S'il est vrai que le
gout vous determine a choisir ce plan, je retournerois en
France et m'établirois en quelque ville de province ou nous
pourrions vivre en Tranquillité.

Mars 12. N.S.

Text Bod. MS Don. c. 56, ff. 71–72   *Address* A Monsieur Monsieur
Algarotti

To Lady Pomfret [*March 1740*][1]

I cannot deny your ladyship's letter gave me a great deal
of pleasure; but you have seasoned it with a great deal of
pain, in the conclusion (after the many agreeable things you
have said to me) that you are not entirely satisfied with me:
you will not throw our separation on ill fortune; and I will
not renew the conversation of the fallen angels in Milton,
who in contesting on predestination and free-will, we are
told, 'They of the vain dispute could know no end.'[2] Yet I
know that neither my pleasures, my passions, nor my
interests, have ever disposed of me, so much as little accidents, which, whether from chance or destiny, have always
determined my choice. Here is weather for example, which,
to the shame of all almanacks, keeps on the depth of winter
in the beginning of spring; and makes it as much impossible
for me to pass the mountains of Bologna, as it would be to
wait on you in another planet, if you had taken up your residence in Venus or Mercury. However, I am fully determined

[1] On 24 March Lady Pomfret received a letter from LM (Finch MS).

[2] A paraphrase of *Paradise Lost*, ii.
558–61.

to give myself that happiness; but when is out of my power to decide.

You may imagine, apart from the gratitude I owe you and the inclination I feel for you, that I am impatient to hear good sense pronounced in my native tongue, having only heard my language out of the mouths of boys and governors for these five months. Here are inundations of them broke in upon us this carnival, and my apartment must be their refuge, the greater part of them having kept an inviolable fidelity to the languages their nurses taught them. Their whole business abroad (as far as I can perceive) being to buy new cloaths, in which they shine in some obscure coffee-house, where they are sure of meeting only one another; and after the important conquest of some waiting gentlewoman of an opera Queen, who perhaps they remember as long as they live, return to England excellent judges of men and manners. I find the spirit of patriotism so strong in me every time I see them, that I look on them as the greatest blockheads in nature; and, to say truth, the compound of booby and *petit maître* makes up a very odd sort of animal. I hope we shall live to talk all these things over, and ten thousand more, which I reserve till the hour of meeting; which that it may soon arrive is the zealous wish of Your ever faithful, &c. &c.

Text 1837, ii. 233–5

To Wortley *16 March* [*1740*]

I am very sorry that my mistake gave you any trouble; it arose from my takeing the two Letters of Exchange to be first and second for the same Summ. I shall be more carefull for the Future. As to the March Quarter, you know there is £45 due to me on my Interest money.[1] Not to embarrass

[1] This interest, £180 a year, came from the legacy of £6,000 from her father in 1726. At first the trustees allowed her £300 a year (Eg MS 3527, f. 8; Manvers MS 4349), but then when —as directed in the will—they invested in South Sea annuities (in Dec. 1728) the income fell to £160 (receipt of 22 May 1729, Monson MS, xxv, no. 1). In July 1731 LM tried to have the annuities converted to a more profitable investment; and permission of the Court of Chancery was obtained, but with restrictions that displeased her (Monson MS, cx, nos. 73, 74; xiv, nos. 91, 99, 104, 113, 122). Eventually the greater

Child with Fractions, I think it would be best to take the 2 years for this Summ, which makes £90. The other £10 may be taken out of the 3rd year, I then receiveing (if I live to see it) but £30. I mention this as what I think will look best for you, and be most convenient for me, I having allready receiv'd the £100 upon Credit from Mr. Waters, and it is all I have taken, or foresee I shall have occasion to take. I make no Expences but what are absolutely necessary, and what I am persuaded you would approve.

Lord Scarborrough's terrible History is publickly known. I am of Opinion his Engagement with that Lady was not the cause but sign of his being mad.[1] Count Wackerbarth talk'd to me of it last night at the Assembly, which is 3 times o' week for the Entertainment of the Prince of Saxony, at the Expence of the Senate, who gave him the most magnificent Ball I ever saw, in the great Theatre on Shrove Tuesday. I could not avoid going there with a set of Noble Ladys. I was led in by the Procurator G[rimani] and plac'd next the Prince by his own direction. I was told since that the Princess of Holstein took it ill, and, as she is marry'd into a Sovereign House, I think she had reason; but he affects giving her some mortifications in return of many that the present King and Queen[2] have receiv'd from her when she was all powerfull in the reign of the late King of Poland.[3]

I was but once at the Ridotto[4] during the whole Carnival. A Regata is intended after Easter for the Prince, which is said to be one of the finest shows in the World, and never given since the King of Denmark was here, which is 30 year ago.[5] Many English and others of all Nations are expected

part was invested in a mortgage (see below, p. 199).

[1] Scarborough had shot himself shortly before his intended marriage to the Duchess of Manchester. From England Lady Hertford sent Lady Pomfret a full account of the tragedy (4 Feb., *Corr.* i. 188–9). As to the cause of his suicide, there were three theories: his illness, his imminent marriage, or his realization that the Duchess had betrayed his confidence by passing on a state secret to her grandmother the Dowager Duchess of Marlborough

(Edith Milner, *Records of the Lumleys of Lumley Castle*, 1904, pp. 166–71). In 1737 he was thought to be insane (Hervey, *Memoirs*, iii. 750).

[2] Augustus III and Marie Josefa.

[3] Augustus the Strong.

[4] See below, p. 455, n. 3.

[5] Frederick IV had visited Venice from Dec. 1708 to March 1709, his principal object being the amusements of the carnival (P. H. Mallet, *Histoire de Dannemarc*, 3rd ed., 1788, ix. 318; Pompeo Molmenti, *Venice*, transl. H. F. Brown, 1908, III, i. 110).

to come to see it. Lord Shrewsbury[1] is arriv'd in company with Prince Beauveau; they ⟨cam⟩e to see me as soon as they arriv'd, as all ⟨str⟩angers do.

I am glad if my Letters can be any amusement to you, and will not fail to let you know all that passes. I am sorry for the badness of my Ink; the Consul tells me it is the best to be had, but it is realy very bad.

None of the canals have been froze here, thô we have had some sharp weather. It is now so warm most people have left off Fires, thô I have not. Several Ladys have invited me to their Palaces for some time in the Summer, but I beleive I shall not accept of their Invitations.

March 16.

Text W MS i. 344–5   *Address* To Edwd Wortley Esqr in Cavendish Square London Angleterre   *Postmark* MR 21   *End. by* W L.M. 16 Mar 1739/40   Recd 21 Mar.   ad 25.

To Wortley *29 March* [*1740*]

March 29.

I send you the enclos'd, which came to me the Last post, to shew you that my Bill of Credit is of no farther use to me; and if you think it proper I should have one, Mr. Child should send one on his Correspondant here, thô I do not foresee any occasion I shall have for it. I think Mr. Waters seems dissatisfy'd with my Letters being directed to him. Those he mentions were from my Son, pretty much in the usual Style. He desires to leave the Town where he now is[2] because he says there is no Temptation to Riot, and he would shew how able he is to resist it. I answer him this post, and shall endeavor mildly to shew him the necessity of being easy in his present situation.

Lord Granby leaves this place to morrow to set out for Constantinople; the Prince of Saxony stays till the 2nd of May. In the mean time there are Entertainments given him almost every day of one sort or other, and a Regata prepareing,

---

[1] George Talbot (1719–87), 14th Earl.   [2] Ysselstein in Holland.

which is expected by all Strangers with great Impatience. He went to see the Arsenal 3 days ago, waited on by a Numerous Nobillity of both Sexes; the Bucentaur[1] was adorn'd and launch'd, a magnificent collation given, and we sail'd a little way in it. I was in company with the Signora Justiniani Gradinego and Signora Marina Erizzo.[2] As you have been at Venice, there is no occasion of describeing those Things to you. There was 2 Canons founded in his presence, and a Galley built and launch'd in an Hour's time. Last night there was a Consort of voices and Instruments at the Hospital of the Incurabili,[3] where there are 2 Girls that in the Opinion of all people excel either Faustina or Cuzoni;[4] but you know they are never permitted to sing on any Theatre.

Lord FitzWilliams[5] is expected in this Town to night on his Return to England, as I am told. The Prince's Behaviour is very obliging to all and in no part of it liable to censure, thô I think there is nothing to be said in praise of his Genius. I suppose you know he has been lame from his Birth, and is carry'd about in a chair, thô a Beautifull B⟨oy⟩ from the Waste upwards.[6] It is said his Family design him for the Church, he haveing 4 Brothers who are fine children.[7]

The Weather is now very fine. We have had none of the Canals Frozen in the coldest part of the winter, but the mountains are still cover'd with Snow.

Your last letters have said nothing of my Baggage. If there is danger of its being taken by the privateers, I had rather it staid in England, and I would go into the Southern

[1] The gorgeously decorated boat used for the official Venetian ceremonies on Ascension Day.

[2] Marina Gradinego m. (1739) Battista Erizzo (Archivio di Stato, Venice).

[3] One of the four musical conservatories in Venice. Charles Burney, who visited it in 1770, found it 'difficult to avoid hyperboles': the girls were 'absolute nightingales' (*Musical Tours in Europe*, ed. P. A. Scholes, 1959, i. 112, 116–17, 126–7).

[4] Faustina Bordoni had sung in London 1726–8 in rivalry with Francesca Cuzzoni (1700–70), who sang there 1723–8 and 1734–5.

[5] William Fitzwilliam (1720–56), 3rd Earl.

[6] Prince Frederick Christian was described (about 1747) by Sir Charles Hanbury Williams, British Envoy in Dresden, as a helpless cripple, of very weak intellect but 'civil, good, and well-tempered' (*Works*, 1822, ii. 216–17).

[7] The Prince's next brother, Franz Xaver (1730–1806), was their mother's favourite, and she tried to persuade Frederick Christian to go into orders so that his brother might succeed their father (ibid. ii. 218). But the Prince married in 1747, and had seven children.

part of France, where it might be convey'd to me without Hazard, than risque the loss of it. If there is a probabillity of a Rupture with France, I can go to Avignon.[1]

Text W MS i. 346–7   *Address* To Edwd Wortley Esqr at his House in Cavendish Square London   *Postmark* AP 3   *End. by W* recd 3 Apr. [*Summary*] Ad 8 Apr.

To Lady Pomfret [*April 1740*][2]

Upon my word, dear madam, I seriously intend myself the happiness of being with you this summer; but it cannot be till then; while the Prince of Saxony stays here I am engaged not to move; not upon his account, as you may very well imagine, but here are many entertainments given, and to be given him by the publick, which it would be disobliging to my friends here to run away from; and I have received so many civilities from the first people here, I cannot refuse them the complaisance of passing the feast of the Ascension in their company, though 'tis a real violence to my inclination to be so long deprived of your's, of which I know the value, and may say, that I am just to you from judgment as well as pleased with you from taste. I envy nothing more to Lady Walpole than your conversation, though I am glad you have met with her's.[3]

Have you not reasoned much on the surprizing conclusion of Lord Scarborough? I confess I look upon his engagement with the Duchess, not as the cause, but sign, that he was mad. I could wish for some authentic account of her behaviour on this occasion. I do not doubt she shines in it, as she has done in every other part of her life. I am almost inclined to

---

[1] Papal territory at this time, and hence a haven of peace.

[2] On 13 April Lady Pomfret received a letter from LM (Finch MS).

[3] Margaret, Lady Walpole (see above, p. 67). On unfriendly terms with her husband, she had been living on the Continent since 1734, and was now settled in Florence. To Lady Pomfret she seemed 'very well-bred and entertaining. She has shewn me great civilities' (3 Jan. 1740, Hertford, *Corr.* i. 175).

superstition on this accident; and think it a judgment for the death of a poor silly soul, that you know he caused some years ago.[1]

I had a visit yesterday from a Greek called Cantacuzena,[2] who had the honour to see your ladyship, as he says, often at Florence, and gave me the pleasure of speaking of you in the manner I think. Prince Beauveau and Lord Shrewsbury intend to leave us in a few days for the Conclave.[3] We expect after it a fresh cargo of English; but, God be praised, I hear of no ladies among them: Mrs. Lethuilier[4] was the last that gave comedies in this town, and she had made her exit before I came; which I look upon as a great blessing. I have nothing to complain of here but too much diversion, as it is called; and which literally diverts me from amusements much more agreeable. I can hardly believe it is me dressed up at balls, and stalking about at assemblies; and should not be so much surprized at suffering any of Ovid's transformations, having more disposition, as I thought, to harden into stone or timber, than to be enlivened into these tumultuary entertainments, where I am amazed to find myself, seated by a sovereign prince, after travelling a thousand miles to establish myself in the bosom of a republic, with a design to lose all memory of kings and courts. Won't you admire the force of destiny? I remember my contracting an intimacy with a girl in a village, as the most distant thing on earth from power and politics. Fortune tosses her up (in a double sense), and

---

[1] The 'poor silly soul' was Rachel Baynton (1695–1722), who m. (1711) Lord Kingston (d. 1713), LM's only brother. As a widow Lady Kingston had lived openly with Scarborough. When LM's granddaughter Lady Louisa Stuart read this passage she wrote to her nephew and co-editor, 'I would not rip up old scandal in my note about the widow lady Kingston and Lord Scarborough. . . . She had two sons by Lord S. whom he called *Lumley Kingston* to the great indignation of her husband's family; and she died in childbed. The poor woman was so very weak and foolish that like the servant-maids she thought herself *as good as married* to him, yet she had so much feeling that

when his having no such intentions flashed upon her, it literally broke her heart; she became speechless and died the next day. Lady Frances Medows [her daughter] could remember having been taught to call him Papa Scarborough' (to the Rev. Dr. Stuart Corbett, 7 Sept. 1834, Wh MS 439).

[2] Not identified.

[3] To choose a successor to Clement XII, who had died on 6 Feb. By 16 April, Shrewsbury reached Rome (Walpole, *Corr.* xvii. 4).

[4] Probably Margaret Sloper (1708–53), who m. (1726) Smart Lethieullier, antiquary (John Nichols, *Lit. Anecdotes of the 18th Century*, 1812–15, v. 370, n.).

I am embroiled in a thousand affairs that I had resolved to avoid as long as I lived.[1] Say what you please, madam, we are pushed about by a superior hand, and there is some pre-destination, as well as a great deal of free-will, in my being Faithfully yours, &c.

Text 1837, ii. 235–8

To Wortley *10 April* [*1740*]

I hope my things will come safe since they are put on Board,[2] but I own I am in some pain about them, hearing of so many English Vessells taken; it is possible I may hear more than is true.

I should be very glad you made what compliments you think proper to those that enquire after me.

The Prince of Saxony continues here at least a month longer, and consequently the Entertainments which are given him; thô there are no Operas during this Lent season, yet there are Consorts once o' week and assemblys Sundays, Tuesdays and Thursdays. I am forc'd on a greater share of them than suits my Inclination, but my Acquaintance encreasing amongst the Venetian Ladys, I cannot avoid some complyance as due to the Civillitys I receive from them.

Ap. 10.

Text W MS i. 348–9   *Address* To Edwd Wortley Esqr in Caven-dish Square London Angleterre   *Postmark* AP 20   *End. by W* L.M. 10 Apr. 1740.   Recd 21 Apr.   Ad 16 May.

---

[1] LM refers to Maria Skerrett, Sir Robert Walpole's mistress, who married him in 1738, soon after the death of his first wife, and died herself the same year. She had been generally esteemed, and although she was sometimes accused by Walpole's enemies of influencing him, there is no evidence of it. The only known political embroilment of LM with Walpole was her writing *The Non-* *sense of Common-Sense*, 1737–8 (ed. R. Halsband, 1947, pp. xviii–xix).

[2] On 3 March [O.S.] her baggage had been put aboard the *St. Quintin*, Captain John Barker—as W informed her on 7 March (his memorandum, W MS i. 115). On 25 March W sent her a long letter with a detailed bill of lading and elaborate explanations and instructions (copy, W MS i. 117–18).

To Wortley *19 April* [*1740*]

I receiv'd yours of January 1[1] but yesterday, for which reason I think it useless to answer it at present, but if I find any occasion shall not fail to follow your orders.

Lord Granby is set out on his Journey for Constantinople. Lord Fitzwilliams arriv'd here 3 days ago; he came to see me the next day, as all the English do, who are much surpriz'd at the Civillitys and Familiarity with which I am with the noble Ladys. Every body tells me 'tis what never was done but to my selfe, and I own I have a little Vanity in it, because the French Ambassador[2] told me when I first came that thô the Procurator Grimani might persuade them to visit me, he defy'd me to enter into any sort of Intimacy with them; instead of which, they call me out allmost every day on some diversion or other, and are desirous to have me in all their partys of pleasure. I am invited to morrow to the Foscarini's to Dinner, which is to be follow'd by a Consort and a Ball, where I shall be the only Stranger, thô here is at present a great Number come to see the Regata, which is fix'd for the 29th of this month, N.S.[3] I shall see it at the Procurator Grimani's, where there will be a great Entertainment that Day. My own House is very well situated to see it, being on the Grand Canal, but I would not refuse him and his Niece since they seem desirous of my Company, and I shall oblige some other Ladys with my Windows; they are hir'd at a great Rate to see the Shew. I suppose you know the nature of it, but if it will be any amusement I will send you a particular description.[4]

Ap. 19. N.S.

Text W MS i. 350–1   *Address* To Edwd Wortley Esqr in Cavendish Square London Angleterre   *Postmark* AP 28   *End. by W* Recd 28 Apr.   Ad 2 May. [*Summary*]

[1] Extract printed above, pp. 167–8.
[2] Comte de Froulay.
[3] It was actually held on 4 May.
[4] She sent it on 1 June [1740].

To Wortley *29 April* [*1740*]

I have made no use of my Credit but for £100 at my first arrival here before I had receiv'd any Letters either from you or Child, nor never intend to do it, being sensible of the disadvantage of it.

The last news I have heard is that Spinola, whom we knew at Vienna, is likely to be elected Pope. I am told he still remembers me.[1] Lord Mansel is arriv'd here, and Lord FitzWilliams gone. I endeavor to shew the first what Civillitys I can in return for those I receiv'd from him at Djion [*sic*].[2] It is very much in my power to oblige any strangers by introduceing them into the best Company, where they could not be known without me. The Prince of Saxony stays here till after the Ascension.

Ap. 29. N.S.

Text W MS i. 352   *End. by W* Recd 3 May. [*Summary*] Ad 16 May

To Wortley *12 May* [*1740*]

May 12. N.S.

I receiv'd a Letter from you Yesterday without date.[3] I am very sorry I explain my selfe so ill; I never intend it, and endeavor to write as plain as I can. I have taken up no more money since the first £100 soon after my arrival here, before I had receiv'd any Letters from England. I have receiv'd nothing yet for the March quarter; this is all I think necessary to be said on that subject.

I will obey your Orders in Relation to your Son, thô I

---

[1] Giorgio Spinola (1667–1739), Papal envoy to Vienna 1713–20 (*Repertorium*, ii. 261), was now dead. But Cardinal Giambattista Spinola (1681–1753) took part in the conclave (Gaetano Moroni, *Dizionario di erudizione storico-ecclesiastica*, 1840–61, lxviii. 298). According to Ludwig von Pastor, who also confuses the two prelates, Spinola was pro-

posed the second week of the conclave but had little backing (*The History of the Popes*, transl. E. F. Peeler, 1938–53, xxxv. 12).

[2] See above, pp. 144–5.

[3] W's dated memorandum (19/8 April): 'Son how to remove. Tell him of £300 a year remittances. 245 [for LM] due on 25 Jan.' (W MS i. 115).

should not have given that advice; it is as much as Edge-combe[1] allows his, whose behavior (thô very bad) has not been so despicable as ours. You will find people enough to exhort you to pay his debts. I know Gibson's way of talking,[2] and I also know that if his wisdom had been hearken'd to, your Son would have run out £5 or 6,000 and been at this time just where he is. I have answer'd his Letters and will write again this post touching his allowance. As to his removal, it is so much against my Opinion that I shall say nothing of it till I have farther orders. I can perceive by his Letters he is in the same folly of thinking he can make a figure, and imagines that your immense Riches will furnish him with all the fine things he has a fancy for. His offering to marry while his Wife is alive is a proofe of his way of thinking.[3]

Lord Mansel is here and intends to stay the Ascension. He is the most zealous patriot I ever knew, and thô his own Master, has no vice or Extravagance. I have introduce'd him to the Ladys of my acquaintance (who are now very numerous) in return for the Civillitys I receiv'd from him at Dijon. He will soon be in England. If Mrs. Blackwood[4] falls in your way, I could wish you would tell her (which is truth) that I have seen no young man in my travells with so reasonable a conduct.

The War seems to kindle on all sides, but if it be true (as I am told from a very good hand) that the German Councils are entirely influenced by the F[rench], our alliance is very small and very dear bought.[5]

I would be more particular if I had a safe direction. I will write at length by the first man I can depend on that goes strait to England.

[1] Richard Edgcumbe, later 1st Baron. His elder son Richard (1716–61), mentioned here, won a reputation as wit, rake, and gambler.

[2] John Gibson (d. 1762) was an agent of W's in charge of his son.

[3] While still under age [before 1734] Montagu married 'a woman of very low degree, considerably older than himself. . . . he forsook her in a few weeks, and never sought to see her again,

though her life lasted nearly as long as his own' (Stuart, 1861, i. 111). Very little is known of her except her name, Sally, and her profession, washerwoman (Jonathan Curling, *Edward Wortley Montagu*, 1954, p. 46).

[4] Mansell's mother (see above, p. 144).

[5] By undermining England's alliance with the German States, France would weaken English power in her current war with Spain.

Text W MS i. 353–4   *Address* To Edwd Wortley Esqr in Cavendish Square London Angleterre   *Postmark* MA 22   *End. by W* Recd 22 May. [*Summary*] Ad 27 May.

To Lady Pomfret *17 May* [*1740*]

Venice, May 17.

I had the happiness of a letter from your ladyship a few days since,[1] and yesterday the pleasure of talking of you with Sir Henry Englefield.[2] He tells me you are still in ice and snow at Florence, and we are very little better at Venice, where we remain in the state of warming beds and sitting by fire-sides. I begin to be of opinion that the sun is grown old; it is certain he does not ogle with so much spirit as he used to do, or our planet has made some slip unperceived by the mathematicians. For my own part, who am more passionately fond of Phœbus than ever Clymene[3] was, I have some thoughts of removing into Africa, that I may feel him once more before I die; which I shall do as surely as your olive-trees, if I have much longer to sigh for his absence. In the mean time I am tied here as long as the Prince of Saxony, which is an uncertain term, but I think will not be long after the Ascension;[4] and then I intend myself the pleasure of waiting on you, where I will listen to all your reproaches, hoping you will do the same to my excuses, and that the balance will come out in my favour: though I could wish you rather here, having a strong notion Venice is more agreeable than Florence, as freedom is more eligible than slavery; and I have an insuperable aversion to courts, or the shadows of them, be they in what shapes they will.

I send you no description of the regatta, not doubting you have been wearied with the printed one. It was really a

<hr>

[1] Sent on 7 May (Finch MS).

[2] Englefield (d. 1780) also visited LM on 20 May, accompanied by Lord Mansell and by van Berkhout.

[3] Mother of Phaethon.

[4] Thursday (26 May), the day of the famous ceremony of marriage between the Republic and the Adriatic Sea. LM witnessed it, as we know not from her letters but from the diary of van Berkhout, one of her companions on that day (summarized in Halsband, *LM*, p. 195).

magnificent show, as ever was exhibited since the galley of
Cleopatra. Instead of her Majesty we had some hundreds of
Cleopatras in the windows and balconys. The operas and
masks begin next Wednesday, and we persevere in gallantries
and raree-shows, in the midst of wars and rumours of wars
that surround us. I may, however, assure you with an
English plainness, these things can at most but attract my
eyes, while (as the song says) you engage my heart; which I
hope to convince you of when I am so happy as to tell you by
word of mouth that I am Sincerely and faithfully yours, &c.[1]

Text 1837, ii. 240–1

From Wortley [*27/16 May 1740*][2]

It is with concern that I trouble you upon so melancholy a subject
as our Son. Mr. Gibson is convinced by his Letters that he is able to
live within his present allowance, and others think him not so weak as
we suppose him. I therefore think it necessary he shou'd remove, but
the difficulty is how to dispose of him. He is, I fear, too weak to
conceal himselfe any where, and I am assured by my Lord Middleton[3]
and by Mr. Drummond[4] who was many years a Banker at Amsterdam,
that no one is protected in France or Holland against Bills of Exchange
or Bonds, and I do not know in what Country he can be safe out of a
privileged place. Mr. Drummond thinks an English man may be safe
in Avignon because the Pope will take no notice of what has passed in
England. It is probable that most of the Foreign Ministers and merchants at Venice can inform you how far any one may be safe in the
countries from which they come.

He writes word he will not stir from the place where he is in or go
to any other without your leave or mine. And I think you are absolutely safe against his coming near you, because you coud hardly keep
him out of a Jail if you woud, and coud easily get him confined any
where but in England. You will do well to assure him his allowance

---

[1] On 25 May Lady Pomfret received
a letter from LM (Finch MS).

[2] Dated from LM's answer, on 17
June.

[3] Probably Alan Brodrick (1702–
47), 2nd Viscount Midleton, admitted

to the Inner Temple (1721), a Commis-
sioner of the Customs (1727–30).

[4] Probably of the firm of Andrew
Drummond (1687–1769), London gold-
smith (F. G. H. Price, *A Handbook of
London Bankers*, 1890–1, p. 55).

will be stopped as soon as it is known he comes nearer to you than you allow him to do. He is weak enough to desire his Debts may be paid, tho no one can ghess whether they are nearer to £1,000 or £100,000, and he has behaved himselfe so that no one ought to give the least Credit to what he says or writes. You will say to him what you think proper on that head. His business is to make it appear plainly that he can act with more prudence than a downright Idiot, and that is what shoud be replied to the greatest part of what he writes.

[Passage omitted]

I have absolutely refused taking the least notice of him or meddling in his affairs, and have desired he will apply to no one but you. I will give you my opinion from time to time when you woud have it, and can desire Mr. G[ibson], who corresponds with him, to write ⟨if⟩ you woud have him. The Germans can tell you whether a Debtor may be protected at Aix la Chapelle or Francfort. What he begs is to be tried where there is much Company. For my part, I foresee it is likely he will again go into the hands of Sharpers, or worse is possible. But the place he is in is too private unless he were governed there, and I think he will go without leave if he cannot get it.

[Passage omitted]

You will do well to let him know how likely it is that he will be confined for his life if once he gets into a Jail, since no ⟨one⟩ will be weak enough to pay his Debts. He ought not to entertain a thought of satisfying his Creditors any way but out of his allowance, be it greater or less. It is his business to shew it is proper to trust him with the increase I proposed to make, about which I suppose you have writ to him. *[Passage omitted]*

Text W MS i. 116 (copy, not by W)

To Wortley *1 June* [*1740*]

June 1.

I wrote you a long letter yesterday, which I sent by a private hand, who will see it safely deliver'd.[1]

It is impossible to be better treated, I may even say more courted, than I am here. I am very glad of your good Fortune at London. You may remember I have allways told you that it is

[1] It must have contained political intelligence. She sent it by Lord Mansell, as she states on 28 June; and Mansell informed her that he had left it at W's house (18/7 July, W MS iv. 181-2).

in your power to make the first figure in the House of Commons.[1] As to the Bill, I perfectly remember the paying of it, which you may easily beleive when you enquire that all auction bills are paid at farthest within 8 days after the sale. The date of this is March 1st, and I did not leave London till July 25, and in that time have been at many other auctions, particularly Lord Halifax's,[2] which was a small time before my Journey. This is not the first of Cock's mistakes;[3] he is famous for makeing them, which are (he says) the fault of his servants.

You seem to mention the Regata in a manner as if you would be pleas'd with a Description of it.[4] It is a race of Boats; they are accompany'd by vessells which they call Piotes and Bichones, that are built at the Expence of the nobles and strangers that have a mind to display their magnificence. They are a sort of Machines, adorn'd with all that sculpture and gilding can do to make a shineing appearance. Several of them cost £1,000 sterling and I beleive none less than 500. They are row'd by Gondoliers dress'd in rich Habits suitable to what they represent. There was enough of them to look like a little Fleet, and I own I never saw a finer sight. It would be too long to describe every one in particular; I shall only name the principal. The Signora Pisani Mocenigo's represented the chariot of the night, drawn by 4 sea Horses, and showing the rising of the moon accompany'd with stars, the statues on each side representing the hours to the number of 24, row'd by Gondoliers in rich Liveries, which were chang'd 3 times, all of equal richness; and the decorations chang'd also to the dawn of Aurora and the midday Sun, the statues being new dress'd every time, the first in green, the 2nd time

[1] W's good fortune may have had something to do with the parliamentary decline of Walpole, whom he had opposed since 1719. Or he may have been an active (though unmentioned) partisan of the Act for 'preventing the wilful and malicious Destruction of Collieries and Coal-works', which received the Royal Assent on 29 April 1740 (*Journ. of H. of C.*, xxiii. 529).

[2] He had died on 9 May 1739 (see above, p. 138).

[3] Christopher Cock (d. 1748) had auction rooms in the Piazza of Covent Garden (*Gentleman's Mag.*, 1748, p. 572; H. B. Wheatley, *London Past and Present*, 1891, iii. 84).

[4] W's memorandum of his letter of 13/2 May contains the word 'Ragatta' (W MS i. 115). LM also wrote a description, no longer extant, which she allowed Lady Pomfret to copy at Florence in Sept. 1740 (Hertford, *Corr.* ii. 83–87).

red, and the last blue, all equally lac'd with silver, there being 3 Races. Signor Soranzo represented the Kingdom of Poland with all the provinces and Rivers in that Dominions, with a consort of the best instrumental music in rich Polish Habits; the painting and gilding were exquisite in their kinds. Signor [Simoni] Contarini's Piote shew'd the Liberal Arts; Apollo was seated on the stern upon Mount Parnasso, Pegasus behind, and the muses seated round him. Opposite was a figure representing painting, with Fame blowing her Trumpet, and on each side Sculpture and music in their proper dresses. The Procurator Foscarini's was the chariot of Flora, guided by Cupids and adorn'd with all sorts of Flowers, rose trees, etc.

Signor Julio Contarini represented the Triumphs of Valour; Victory was on the Stern, and all the Ornaments warlike Trophys of every kind. Signor Correri's was the Adriatic Sea receiving into her Arms the Hope of Saxony. Signor Alvisio Mocenigo's was the Garden of Hesperides. The whole Fable was represented by different Statues. Signor Querini had the chariot of Venus drawn by Doves, so well done they seem'd realy to fly upon the water; the Loves and Graces attended her.

Signor Paul Dona had the chariot of Diana, who appear'd Hunting in a large wood, the trees, hounds, Stag, and Nymphs all done naturally, the Gondoliers dress'd like peasants attending the chase, and Endimion lying under a large Tree gazing on the Goddess.

Signor Angelo Labbia represented Poland crowning of Saxony, waited on by the Virtues and subject provinces. Signor Angelo Molino was Neptune waited on by the Rivers. Signor Vicenzo Morosini's Piote shew'd the Triumphs of Peace, discord being chain'd at her Feet, and she surrounded with the Pleasures, etc.

I beleive you are allready weary of this description, which can give you but a very imperfect Idea of the show,[1] but I must say one word of the Bichones, which are less vessels, quite open, some representing Gardens, others apartments, all the oars being gilt either with Gold or Silver, and the

---

[1] A brief account of the regatta, which took place on 4 May, is printed   in *La Storia dell'anno MDCCXL*, Amsterdam [Venice].

Gondoliers' Liverys either velvet or rich silk with a profusion
of Lace fringe and Embrodiery. I saw this show at the Procurator Grimani's house, which was near the place where the
Prizes were deliver'd. There was a great assembly invited on
the same Occasion, which were all nobly entertain'd.

I can get no better Ink here, thô I have try'd several times,
and it is a great vexation to me to want it.

Text W MS i. 355–6

To Lady Pomfret *4 June* [*1740*]

June 4th.

I have this moment received the most agreeable and
most obliging letter I ever read in my life; I mean your ladyship's of the 28th May. I ought to take post to-morrow
morning to thank you in person, but the possibilities are
wanting. Here is a new unforeseen, impertinent impediment
rose up, in vulgar English called a big belly. I hope you
won't think it my own; but my dear chambermaid, the only
English female belonging to me, was pleased to honour me
last night with the confidence that she expects to lie-in every
day; which my negligence and her loose gown has hindered
me from perceiving till now; though I have been told to-day
by ten visitors that all the town knew it except myself. Here
am I locked up this month at Venice for her sweet sake, and
consequently going to hate it heartily; but it is not possible
for me to travel alone, or trust an Italian with the care of my
jewels, &c. The creature is married to an English servant of
mine, so there is no indecency in keeping her, but a great
deal of inconveniency.[1]

I beg your pardon, dear madam, for this ridiculous detail
of my domesticks, but it is at present the only thing that
stops my journey, the Prince of Saxony's being fixed for the
tenth of this month. You cannot know me so little as to suppose the pleasure of making my court, determined me to stay
as long as he did. I freely confess a very great esteem, and even
friendship for his governor,[2] whose civilities to me have been

[1] See next letter.   [2] Count Wackerbarth (see above, p. 166).

192

so great, I must have been very stupid, as well as ungrateful, if I could have thought they deserved no return; and he exacted this promise from me at a time when neither he nor I thought he could stay above half the time he has done. This friendship of ours is attended with such peculiar circumstances as make it as free from all possibility of a reproach, as a fancy your ladyship may take, for aught I know, to the Venus de Medici; he being in some sense as immoveable as she, and equally incapable, by the duties of his cursed place, to leave the post he is in, even for one moment. I go there to visit him behind the Prince's chair, which is his grate;[1] where we converse in English (which he speaks perfectly well), and he has the pleasure of talking to me with a freedom, that he does not use to any other. You may easily imagine the consolation this is to him; and you have so good a heart, that I am sure you must be sensible of the pleasure I find in giving any to a man of so extraordinary a character both for virtue and understanding. This is the true history of my stay here, which shall be as short as these *remoras*[2] will permit, being ever, &c.[3]

Text 1837, ii. 241–3

To Wortley *17 June* [*1740*]

June 17. N.S.

I have just receiv'd yours of the 16 of May.[4] I have been told that my Son has several considerable Debts in Italy, particularly at this Place, but as he kept himselfe altogether in low Company he did not pass for my Son. The P[rocurator] G[rimani] ask'd me once if a young man that was here was of your Family, bearing the same name. I said slightly I knew nothing of him, and he reply'd that he had allways suppos'd from his behaviour that he was some sharper that had assum'd that name to get credit. I was glad to have it pass over in this manner to avoid being daily dunn'd by his

[1] As in a convent.
[2] Delays.
[3] Lady Pomfret received a letter,

probably this one, from LM on 15 June (Finch MS).
[4] Extracts printed above, pp. 188–9.

Creditors. He run away from hence and went to Florence, where, being receiv'd by Mr. Man,[1] he had more oppertunity of running in Debt and exposing himselfe. I am sorry he has parted with his Woman, being persuaded he will fall into worse Hands. I have try'd to know from the Consul whither there is any priveleg'd place from Debt, but I hear of none. If he should come where I am, I know no remedy but running away my selfe. To undertake to confine him would bring me into a great deal of trouble and unavoidable Scandal. I know very well how fair he can make his own Story, and how difficult it would be at this distance to prove past facts.

Mr. Mackensie,[2] younger Brother to Lord Bute, is here at present. He is a very well behav'd Youth; he makes great court to me, and I have shew'd him as many Civillitys as are in my power.

I hope I shall have the £245 at midsummer;[3] not being to be receiv'd till 3 months after date, you may be sure I shall want it at that time, notwithstanding I mannage as well as I can with Decency.

The Prince of Saxony is gone, and many people retiring to their Country Houses; the Heat is not yet at all troublesome.

I am a good deal vex'd at a foolish Accident that has happen'd in my small Family. Mrs. Mary is downlying of a big belly which she has conceal'd till now. William[4] and she say they were marry'd before they left London. I know no remedy but Patience, thô you must be sensible both of the Inconvenience and Expence of it. There is no dependance on a Fool, which is her case. She allways lay in my Room on the road, and eat with me even here, till I saw her Eyes so fix'd upon him all the time he waited I thought it to no purpose to keep them asunder, and it seems they were wedded before they begun the Journey.

---

[1] After two years as chargé d'affaires in Florence, Horace Mann (1701–86) was appointed British Resident in April 1740.

[2] James Stuart (1719?–1800), Bute's only brother, assumed the name Mackenzie on inheriting (in 1723) the estates of his great-grandfather. He became LM's friend and correspondent.

[3] Evidently W had agreed to give LM an annual income of £800 in addition to the 'interest money' from the trust left to her by her father.

[4] Turner.

Text W MS i. 357–8   *Address* To Edwd Wortley Esqr in Cavendish Square London Angleterre   *Postmark* ⟨?⟩   *End. by W* [*Summary*] Rec'd 20 June.   Ad 24 June.

From Lord Hervey *21/10 June 1740*

Tho I am quite weary, dear Madam, of writing so many Letters,
which by every one you favor me with, I find are never recieved, yet
I can not help endeavouring at least to let you know I have convey'd
that to Sir R[obert] W[alpole] inclosed to me,[1] as you order'd me,
and he has desired me to thank you for your Remembrance of him,
and the offer you make of opening a farther Correspondence; but as
the Subject of that Correspondence must depend on the Prince of
[Saxony] remaining where you are, and on a more secure Canal than
the comon Post being found out for this Negociation, the Difficultys
of adjusting the last Point, and the design of soon removing the Prince
of [Saxony] to another Place, has induced Sir R. W. to confine his
answer to you to the Thanks I have already mention'd, and to ordering
me to let you know he thinks him-self obliged to you for the trouble
you have taken and for that you are ready to give your-self, and is
sorry things are so circumstanced as not to allow him the Pleasure
of continuing a Comerce which, if it had not been for the Obstacles
I have mention'd, would in every Light have been so agreable to him.[2]
I act so inconsiderable a Part in this affair that it would be impertinent
in me to add any thing farther from my-self than my being ever
Yours.

June 10/21 1740.

Direct for me in Grosvenor Street.[3]

I am at present in great Affliction for the Loss of my Friend
Algarotti, who left England last Friday for the Court of Berlin on a
Sumons he recieved from the new King of Prussia, and a very kind
one, under his own Hand, before he had been five Days on the throne.[4]

Text Bristol MS ii. 95

[1] LM used Hervey as a channel to the
Prime Minister because he was Walpole's
chief ally in the House of Lords, and had
been appointed Lord Privy Seal on
1 May 1740.

[2] For LM's opinion of Walpole's
rejection, see below, p. 323. She engaged
in other political activity in Venice by
asking Walpole to resume diplomatic

relations with the Republic (see below,
p. 334, n. 2).

[3] On resigning as Vice-Chamberlain,
Hervey had to give up his apartment in
St. James's Palace.

[4] On his way back from St. Petersburg the previous autumn Algarotti
had stayed eight days at Rheinsberg, the
court of Crown Prince Frederick of

To Lady Pomfret [*June 1740*]¹

I send you this letter by so agreeable a companion, that I think it a very considerable present. He will tell you that he has pressed me very much to set out for Florence immediately, and I have the greatest inclination in the world to do it; but, as I have already said, I am but too well convinced that all things are relative, and mankind was not made to follow their own inclinations. I have pushed as fair for liberty as any one; I have most philosophically thrown off all the chains of custom and subjection; and also rooted out of my heart all seeds of ambition and avarice. In such a state, if freedom could be found, that lot would sure be mine; yet certain atoms of attraction and repulsion keep me still in suspence;² and I cannot absolutely set the day of my departure, though I very sincerely wish for it, and have one reason more than usual: this town being at present infested with English, who torment me as much as the frogs and lice did the palace of Pharaoh, and are surprized that I will not suffer them to skip about my house from morning till night; me, that never opened my doors to such sort of animals in England. I wish I knew a corner of the world inaccessible to petit-maîtres and fine ladies. I verily believed when I left London I should choose my own company for the remainder of my days; which I find more difficult to do abroad than at home; and with humility I sighing own,

> Some stronger power eludes the sickly will,
> Dashes my rising hope with certain ill;
> And makes me with reflective trouble see,
> That all is destin'd that I fancy'd free.³

I have talked to this purpose with the bearer of this letter: you may talk with him on any subject, for though our acquaintance has been very short, it has been long enough to

Prussia. In the following months, while they corresponded, their friendship deepened. Immediately after his father's death (31 May 1740), Frederick summoned Algarotti to join him.

¹ On 29 June Lady Pomfret received a letter from LM (Finch MS).

² Undoubtedly LM was waiting for Algarotti to answer her proposal of 12 March (pp. 175–6 above).

³ Prior's *Solomon* (*Works*, i. 378).

shew me that he has an understanding that will be agreeable
in what light he pleases to shew it.

Text 1837, ii. 243–5

To Wortley *28 June* [*1740*]

June 28. N.S.

I have wrote to my Son according to your order and to the
purpose you design. I have sent you a letter by Lord Mansel,
in which you will find a full answer to yours of Jan. 1, and
something that will much surprize you.

I do not know of any account that needs ajusting between
us, being very well satisfy'd with it as it now stands. You
have told me that you receiv'd the 6th the 122.10. from Mr.
Perkins,[1] which was to pay you for the 100 advance'd to me
the 20th of July. The Letter in which you mention this is
without date.

The reason of my hastening out of France was being told
every where that a War was likely to be soon declar'd, and I
was afraid of being forc'd to pass the mountains in bad
Weather if I did [not] make use of the present season.

Since I wrote this Letter I hear the Consul[2] is dead
suddenly. He was near 80 years of age, and much esteem'd;
he had resided here 40 year. I desire you would direct your
next to the Care of Mr. Smith, merchant, here.[3]

Text W MS i. 359–60 *Address* To Edwd Wortley Esqr in Cavendish
Square London Angleterre *Postmark* 1Y 4 *End. by W* Recd 4 July.
[*Summary*] This is an answer to mine of 27 May. Ad 10 July.

To Lady Pomfret *29 June* [*1740*]

Your ladyship's letter[4] (which I have this minute received)
would have been the most agreeable thing in the world, if it
had been directed to another; but I can no more be charmed

---

[1] Not identified.
[2] Niel Browne d. 29 June (K. T. Parker, *Drawings of Canaletto at Windsor Castle,* 1948, p. 13).
[3] Joseph Smith (*c.* 1675–1770), art collector, appointed Consul in 1744.
[4] Sent 18 June (Finch MS).

with it than a duellist can admire the skill by which he is mortally wounded. With all the respect I owe you, I cannot forbear saying, that no woman living ever reproached another with less reason than you do me at present. You can't possibly suspect I have got my chambermaid with child myself for a pretence to stay here. This is a crime of which all mankind will acquit me; and if she had any such malicious design in conceiving, I can assure you she had no orders from me; but, as the song says,

> 'Tis e'en but a folly to flounce;
> 'Tis done, and it cannot be holp.

As soon as she is able to travel, I will certainly set out, notwithstanding the information of your popish priest. There's another thing; how can you pin your faith upon the sleeve of one of those gentlemen, against the assurances given you by a daughter of the Church of England? After this, you are obliged to me that I do not suspect he can persuade you into a belief in all the miracles in the Legend.[1] All quarrelling apart, if neither death nor sickness intervene, you will certainly see me at Florence. I talk of you every day at present with Mr. Mackenzie, who is a very pretty youth, much enchanted by the charms of Lady Sophia, who, I hear from all hands, so far outshines all the Florentine beauties, that none of them dare appear before her. I shall take great pleasure in being spectatress of her triumphs; but yet more in your ladyship's conversation, which was never more earnestly desired by any one than it is at this time by, dearest madam, Yours, &c.

Venice, June 29th.

Text 1837, ii. 245–6

To Francesco Algarotti [*July 1740*][2]

. . . Voila l'amusement que je me suis donne dans vostre absence. J'ai peur que vostre grande visite est destiné a une

---

[1] The Golden Legend, a thirteenth-century collection of saints' lives.

[2] This undated fragment seems to express LM's mood after she had received the news of Algarotti's splendid summons to the Court of Berlin.

grande sotte. En ce cas la, je vous verray tard. Mais j'attend-
rois avec tant de patience et de soumission¹ qui doivent
meriter des recompenses extrodinaire.

Text Murray MS

To Wortley *19 July* [*1740*]

July 19.

I have not yet receiv'd the £245 and it will inconvenience
me very much if it be long delay'd. As to the £100 you
advance'd, I suppose you forgot to blot it out when you
receiv'd it. As to the regularity of the future payments of my
Mortgage, I then told you that as Sir Marmaduke begun to
be dilatory in his payments, he might probably continue so,
and you made answer that should make no alteration in the
payment of my allowance, which should be regular whatever
happen'd.²

I shall set out for Florence in a few days. Be pleas'd to
direct your next chez Madame La Comtesse de Pomfret,
Pairesse d'Angleterre, a Florence.

Text W MS i. 361–2   *Address* To Edwd Wortley Esqr in Cavendish Square London Angleterre   *Postmark* IY 24

To Lady Pomfret [*July 1740*]³

To convince you of my sincere impatience to see you,
though my waiting gentlewoman is not yet brought to bed,
I am determined to set out the last day of this month, whether
she is able to accompany me or not. I hope for one month's

---

¹ The frequency of LM's letters to
Algarotti can be gauged from Hervey's
remark to him: 'I send you inclosed
another Letter from Sapho; they seem to
me like Sancho's Geese and Banco's
Kings, as if there was no End of them'
(3 Oct./22 Sept. 1740, Murray MS).

² In 1731 LM invested part of the

legacy from her father in a mortgage
from Sir Marmaduke Gresham (1700–
41) of Titsey, Surrey (Monson MS,
xiv, no. 104). For the earlier history of
this legacy, see above, p. 177, n. 1).

³ On 27 July Lady Pomfret received
a letter from LM, probably this one
(Finch MS).

happiness with you at Florence; and if you then remove to Rome, I will wait on you thither, and shall find double pleasure in every fine thing I see in your company. You see, whatever acquaintance I have made at Venice, I am ready to sacrifice them to your's. I have already desired my London correspondents to address their letters to your palace,[1] and am Most faithfully yours, &c.

Text 1837, ii. 246

To Wortley *25* [*July 1740*]

I give you many thanks for the Bill of £245 which I receiv'd last post and came very oportunely, I designing for Florence (on the pressing Invitations of Lady Pomfret) next week. If my things sail'd the time you mention,[2] they will be soon at Leghorn, and it will be convenient for me to be at Florence, from whence (if I find it necessary) I can easily go to take care of them.

I enclose to you my Letter to my Daughter, she having given me no other Direction. I wrote a long one to her some days ago to be carry'd by Mr. Mackensie, who then intended to leave this place the next day, but he now says his time of setting out is uncertain, and my Letter still lyes on my table. I beleive he has got a mistrisse here who ⟨is⟩ likely to lead him a long dance. He is a very pretty Youth with a turn of Head very like his Uncle Islay.[3] I have wrote such Letters to your Son as I think answers your Intentions.

I expect Lady Pomfret will press me to go with her to see Rome; I have no thoughts of doing it, but should be glad of your opinion of such a Journey.

Venice, June [*sic*] 25. N.S.

[1] After three months in lodgings, Lady Pomfret and her family moved, on 19 March 1740, into the Palazzo Ridolfi, a large house with extensive gardens (Finch MS; Hertford, *Corr.* i. 227–31). It is today called Palazzo Stiozzi-Ridolfi, 75 via della Scala (Walthar Limburger, *Die Gebäude von Florenz*, 1910, pp. 163–4).

[2] On 5 April/25 March W informed her that the *St. Quintin*, carrying her baggage, was not likely to sail in less than a fortnight (W MS i. 118).

[3] Lord Islay, a shrewd lawyer and man of business (see above, p. 90).

Text W MS i. 363–4   *Address* To Edwd Wortley Esqr at his House in Cavendish Square London Angleterre   *Postmark* IY 31   *End. by W* Ad L.M. 25 July 1740. [*Summary*] Recd 31 July.

From Edward Wortley Montagu, junior, *1 Aug. 1740*

Madam,

I have been honour'd with Your Ladyship's and am infinitely oblig'd to my Father and You for Your extream goodness in entending to encrease my allowance;[1] it is so much the more agreable to me as being a certain sign my conduct since here has not been displeasing to You, and I assure You I shall always search all means of testifying to You my Gratitude for this Your great tenderness and of rendring my self more and more worthy of Your Affection, ⟨and⟩ as I am persuaded nothing can acquire me that so soon as a stea⟨dy⟩ course of Sober and Prudent conduct, I am absolutely deter⟨mined⟩ never to follow any but the strictest rules of Virtue and Honour.

As I am very sensible how much my former conduct must render me suspect, my whole thoughts are continualy employ'd in searching some efficacious way of persuading You of the sincerity of my Reformation, and have att length fallen upon one which will not leave You the least room to doubt of me and therefore humbly beg Your Ladyship will be so good as to permitt me to pursue it. Some days past, Lord Strafford[2] past through Utrecht and told me Your Ladyship was not expected in England in less than three or four years; if so, I should be infinitely oblig'd to You if You would permitt me to have the honour of accompanying You whilst abroad. You would then be a witness of my whole conduct and I should have no occasion for any allowance att all since every thing would be att Your Ladyship's disposal. I can [not] express to You with how deep a sense of Gratitude I should be touched if You would be pleasd to grant me this favour; You would by it put it into my own power to convince You of my sincerity by my attachment to You and by obeying the least of Your orders, and it would be out of the power of my enemies to misrepresent my behaviour or misinterprett my actions. I should have the Happiness of being continualy near so tender a Mother, and the Satisfaction of having it in my power (by searching with the greatest zele every thing that could give Your Ladyship the least pleasure) to shew You with how much

---

[1] His allowance of £300 a year was to be increased by £50 (W to LM, 15/4 Sept. 1740, W MS i. 119).

[2] William Wentworth (1722–91), 2nd Earl of Strafford, then on the Grand Tour.

tenderness I am, Madam, Your Ladyship's Most dutiful son and humble servant,

Edwd Wortley.

Ysselstein, ce: 1er: Aoust: 1740. N.S.

Text W MS iii. 1–2   *Address* To The right Honble Lady Mary Wortley

To Lady Pomfret *12 Aug.* [*1740*]

Aug. 12, N.S.

I am going to give your ladyship a very dangerous proof of my zealous desire of seeing you. I intend to set out to-morrow morning, though I have a very swelled face; attended by a damsel who has lain in but sixteen days. I hope after this expedition you will never more call in doubt how much I am, dearest madam, Yours, &c.

Text 1837, ii. 247

To Lady Pomfret *16 Aug.* [*1740*]

Bologna, Aug. 16.

I am thus far arrived towards the promised land, where I expect to see your ladyship; but shall stay here a day or two to prepare myself for the dreadful passage of the Apennines. In the mean time I have taken the liberty to direct two trunks and a box to your palace. The post is just going out,[1] and hinders me from saying more than that I am Ever yours.

Text 1837, ii. 247

To the Countess of —— [*Aug. 1740*]

[*A spurious letter, dated from Florence, printed 1767 (see i. xviii) pp. 37–55; 1861, ii. 70–75*]

---

[1] On 17 Aug. Lady Pomfret received two letters from LM (Finch MS).

To Wortley *3 Sept.* [*1740*]

Florence, Sept. 3. N.S.

I arriv'd safe here some days ago,[1] after passing the terrible Appenines, which I realy think more disagreable than the Alps. I am lodg'd with Lady Pomfret, to whose House I desire you would direct for me. All the people of Quality have been to see me,[2] and I have allready visited the Venus of Medicis,[3] who answers the Description I have often heard you make of her.

I send you the enclos'd from your Son[4] to shew you what simple projects he is capable of, but as he appears in the Intention of being submissive, I hope the Letter I shall write to him this post will prevent his coming near me.

I intend to go my selfe to take care of my things as soon as I hear the Ship is arriv'd at Leghorn.

I hope your Health continues and am impatient to hear from you.

I have allready thank'd you for the money I receiv'd at Venice.

Text W MS i. 366   *End. by W* L.M. 3 Sept. 1740 from Florence directed to the Lodge.[5] [*Summary*] Rec'd 19 Sept. Ad 23.

To Wortley *11* [*Sept. 1740*]

Florence, Aug't [*sic*] 11.

This is a very fine Town, and I am much amus'd with visiting the Gallery,[6] which I do not doubt you remember too well to need any Description of. Lord and Lady Pomfret take pains to make the place agreable to me,[1] and I have been visited by the greatest part of the people of Quality. Here is an Opera, which I have heard twice,[2] but it is not so fine, neither for voices or Decorations, as that at Venice.

I am very willing to be at Leghorn when my things arrive, which I fear will hinder my visiting Rome this season except they come sooner than is gennerally expected. If I could go from thence to Sea by [*sic*] Naples with safety, I should prefer it to a Land Journey, which I am told is very difficult, and that it is impossible I should stay there long, the people being entirely unsociable. I do not desire much company, but would not confine my selfe to a place where I could get none.

I have wrote to your Daughter directed to Scotland this post.[3]

Text W MS i. 365   *End. by* *W* L.M. 11 Sept. 1740. [*Summary*] Recd 24 Sept. Ad 6 Oct.

To Wortley 6 *Oct.* [*1740*]

I see plainly that my Son's desiring to stay where he now is,[4] is a Trick, to which I suppose he is advis'd by some of the Sharpers he corresponds with, and encourag'd to it by Gibson. I don't mean that Gibson has any part in it, but his silly flattery and writeing to him how fond you are of him etc., I guess may persuade him, than [*sic*] rather than you will suffer him to remain where he is, you will comply with all his extravagant demands. I have heard G[ibson] talk to him in my presence in that style, even when he was persuing

---

[1] Their daughter confirms this in a letter to a friend: 'All the news I can tell your Ladyship is that we are so happy as to enjoy my Lady Mary Wortley's conversation at present. She arriv'd here from Venice a week past and does us the honour to accept of an Apartment in our house' (Lady Sophia Fermor to Lady Noel Somerset, 28 Aug. 1740, Finch MS).

[2] On 4 Sept. Lady Pomfret 'went for the first time to the Comick Opera', and on the 11th again to the opera (Finch MS).

[3] Lady Bute lived with her husband at Mount Stuart on the Isle of Bute.

[4] On 15/4 Sept. W wrote to LM that their son had informed Gibson that he wished to stay where he was because travelling was expensive; and W added, 'My opinion is that some other woman or the Thieves engage him to stay where he is least nothing shoud come from him when he removes' (W MS i. 119–20).

his Ruin in the worst manner, and was very angry with me that I would not set a gloss on his Actions to you, saying it was a Duty of a Christian to make a father and a Son well together. I made answer I thought the first Duty was Truth, and I would disguise nothing; and indeed I am now of opinion (as I was then) that it is to no purpose to set him free, since in a halfe a year's time (what ever is pretended of his Reformation) he would be as deeply in debt as before. He has said nothing of his Italian debts,[1] which are both here and at Venice.

I see so little sincerity that I cannot help thinking he is again falln into plotting against himselfe either with his old Acquaintance or some new ones that are as bad. However it is, I think 'tis lucky he desires to stay where he is. I suppose you have before this receiv'd mine in which I enclos'd one from him, where he makes me a proposal of a very different nature, perhaps with a design to make me great offers in case I can prevail with you to leave him all your Estate; thô if he remembers in what manner I receiv'd his first proposal of that sort, if he had common sense he would not renew it. But he is so easily led by people that know neither you nor me that I can not be surpriz'd at any of his Projects.

I have wrote some time since to Mr. Child to remit the Midsummer Quarter to Legorn. I set out for Rome in a few Days; it may be remitted to me thither from Leghorn. I have desir'd Mr. Man, the English Resident here, to take care of my Letters, and I beg you would direct your next recommended to him.

There is great outcries here amongst the Merchants.[2]

Oct. 6. N.S.

Text W MS i. 367–8   *Address* To Edwd Wortley Esqr in Cavendish Square London Angleterre   *Postmark* OC 15   *End. by W* [*Summary*] Recd 15 Oct. Ad 23 Oct.

1 W's letter (ibid.) contained a list of Montagu's debts.

2 In her war with Spain, England was blockading the Italian ports.

To Francesco Algarotti *11 Oct.* [*1740*]

Je vous écrirai peu de choses parceque je crains que vous ne reçevrai pas ma Lettre. Je ne veux pas croire que vous ne vouliez pas y repondre. Faittes moi le plaisir de sçavoir vos Resolutions.[1] J'ai quitté Venise et suis prete d'aller ou vous voudrez. J'attens vos ordres pour regler ma vie. Songez y qu'il y a longtemps que je suis indecis, et qu'il est asseurement temps de me determiner.

Oct. 11. N.S.

Addressez vostre Lettre a la Recommendation du Resident d'Angleterre a Florence. Je quitte cette ville pour faire une petite tour, en attendant de vos nouvelles.

Text Bod. MS Don. c. 56, f. 64

To Wortley *22 Oct.* [*1740*]

Rome, Oct'r 22. N.S.

I arriv'd here in good Health 3 days ago;[2] this is the first post day. I have taken a lodging for a month, which is (as they tell me) but a short time to take a view of all the Antiquitys etc. that are to be seen. From hence I propose to set out for Naples; I am told by every body that I shall not find it agreable to reside in. I expect Lady Pomfret's family here in a few days. It is Summer here, and I left Winter at Florence, the Snows having begun to fall on the mountains.

I shall probably see the Ceremony of the new Pope's[3] taking possession of the Vatican, which is said to be the finest that is ever perform'd at Rome.

I have no news to send from hence; if you would have me

---

[1] Since his summons to Berlin Algarotti had remained close to the new Prussian King, and he impatiently awaited more substantial rewards than intimate friendship. 'Mais soyez toujours rond et sincère,' Frederick wrote to him, echoing LM's plea ([autumn 1740],

Frederick, *Œuvres*, ed. J. D. E. Preuss, 1846–57, xviii. 19).

[2] LM left Florence on 16 Oct. (Finch MS).

[3] Prospero Lambertini (1675–1758), Benedict XIV, elected 17 Aug., did not take possession until April 1741.

speak to any particular point, I beg you would let me know it, and I will give you the best Information I am able.

Be pleas'd to continu directing to Mr. Man, the English Resi⟨dent⟩ at Florence. He will take care to send my Letters where ever I am.

Text W MS i. 369–70   *Address* To Edwd Wortley Esqr in Cavendish Square London Angleterre par Venise   *Postmark* NO 7   *End. by W* [*Summary*] Ad 20 Nov. Recd 8 Nov.

To Lady Pomfret *22 Oct.* [*1740*]

Oct. 22, N.S.

Dear Madam,

I flatter myself that your ladyship's goodness will give you some pleasure in hearing that I am safely arrived at Rome. It was a violent transition from your palace and company to be locked up all day with my chambermaid, and sleep at night in a hovel; but my whole life has been in the Pindaric style. I am at present settled in the lodging Sir Francis Dashwood[1] recommended to me. I liked that Mr. Boughton[2] mentioned to me (which had been Sir Bourchier Wray's)[3] much better; 'tis two zechins per month cheaper, and at least twenty more agreeable; but the landlord would not let it, for a very pleasant reason. It seems your gallant knight used to lie with his wife; and as he had no hopes I would do the same, he resolves to reserve his house for some young man. The only charm belonging to my present habitation is the cieling, which is finer than that of the gallery, being all painted by the proper hand of Zucchero, in perfect good preservation.[4]

[1] (1708–81), later Baron Le Despencer, famous as a rake. LM had seen him in Florence, where he visited and dined at Lady Pomfret's (Finch MS).

[2] This 'Mr. Boughton'—who dined at Lady Pomfret's, where LM had met him —must have been Richard (b. 1708), second son of Sir William Boughton; he was abroad for the recovery of his health, and died at Lyons (W. Betham, *Baronetage*, 1801–5, i. 419–20; J. Foster, *Alumni Oxon. 1715–1886*, i. 136).

[3] Another visitor at Lady Pomfret's had been Sir Bourchier Wrey (1714–84), 'a very foolish knight' according to Horace Walpole (*Corr.* xix. 224).

[4] Probably LM stayed in the house built by the 16th-century painter Federico Zuccaro, famous for his frescoes. Early in the 18th century the Palazzo Zuccari was turned into an inn (*locanda*) and occupied mostly by scholars and artists (Werner Körte, *Der Palazzo Zuccari in Rom*, 1935, p. 53).

I pay as much for this small apartment as your ladyship does for your magnificent palace; 'tis true I have a garden as large as your dressing-room. I walked last night two hours in that of Borghese, which is one of the most delightful I ever saw. I have diverted myself with a plain discovery of the persons concerned in the letter that was dropped in the Opera House. This is all the news I know, and I will not tire you with my thanks for the many civilities for which I am obliged to your ladyship; but I shall ever be highly sensible of them, and can never be other than, dear madam, your ladyship's Most faithful humble servant.[1]

Text 1837, ii. 247–8

To Wortley *1 Nov.* [*1740*]

Rome, Nov. 1. N.S.

I have now been here a week, and am very well diverted with viewing the fine Buildings, paintings, and antiquitys. I have neither made nor receiv'd one visit, nor sent word to any body of my arrival on purpose to avoid Interruptions of that sort.

The Weather is so fine that I walk every Evening in a different Beautifull Garden, and I own I am charm'd with what I see of this Town, thô there yet remains a great deal more to be seen. I propose making a stay of [a] Month, which shall be entirely taken up in that Employment, and then I will remove to Naples to avoid, if possible, feeling the Winter.

I do not trouble you with any Descriptions, since you have been here, and I suppose very well remember every thing that is worth remembering, but if you would have me speak to any particular point, I will give you the best Information [that] is in my power.

Direct your next Letter to Mons. Belloni, Banquier a Rome.[2] He will take care to deliver it to me either here or

---

1 Lady Pomfret received a letter from LM on 25 Oct. (Finch MS).

2 Gerolamo Bellóni (d. 1761), economist and banker.

at Naples. Letters are very apt to miscarry, especially those to this place.

Text W MS i. 371–2   *Address* To Edwd Wortley Esqr in Cavendish Square London Angleterre par Venezia   *Postmark* NO 17   *End. by W* [*Summary*] Ad 20 Nov.   Recd 17 Nov.

To Lady Pomfret *11 Nov.* [*1740*]

Nov. 11, Rome.

I received the honour of your ladyship's letter[1] but last night. I perceive all letters are stopped. Two that you enclosed are from dear Mr. Mackenzie, pressing with the most friendly solicitude my return to Venice, and begging me to let him meet me at Bologna. I am amazed at the good-nature of that youth. I could not wish a child of my own a more affectionate behaviour than he has shewn to me; and that inducement is added to many others to incline me to Venice; but——. I intend for Naples next week; but as my stay there will not exceed fifteen days, I shall be again here before it is possible for you to arrive; where I wish you for your own sake. Here are entertainments for all tastes; and whatever notions I had of the magnificence of Rome, I can assure you it has surpassed all my ideas of it. I am sincerely concerned for Mr. Boughton, and wish the air of Pisa may recover his health. I shall very readily tell your ladyship all I guess about the said letter. An English lady called Mrs. D'Arcie[2] (what D'Arcie I can't imagine) lodged in the house where I now am, and Sir Francis Dashwood was every day with her; she went from hence, by the way of Florence, to England. Putting this together, I supposed her the person concerned. This is all I know. You may see that I have no other advantage from this discovery but the bare satisfaction of my curiosity. The Abbé Niccolini[3] arrived last night; I believe

---

[1] Sent on 1 Nov. (Finch MS).
[2] Not identified.
[3] Antonio Niccolini, marchese di Ponsacco (1701–69), Florentine ecclesiastic and man of letters. A later traveller found him 'particularly obliging and attached to the *English*' (John, Earl of Cork and Orrery, *Letters from Italy*, 1774, p. 111, n.).

I shall see him this evening. Here are yet no English of your acquaintance, except Lord Elcho.[1] I am told Lord Lincoln[2] has taken a large house, and intends to keep a table, &c.

The life I now lead is very different from what you fancy. I go to bed every night at ten, run about all the morning among the antiquities, and walk every evening in a different beautiful villa; where if amongst the fountains I could find the waters of Lethe, I should be completely happy.

> Like a deer that is wounded I bleed and run on,
> And fain I my torment would hide.
> But alas! 'tis in vain, for wherever I run
> The bloody dart sticks in my side,

and I carry the serpent that poisons the paradise I am in.[3] I beg your pardon (dear madam) for this impertinent account of myself; you ought to forgive it, since you would not be troubled with it, if I did not depend upon it, that your friendship for me interests you in all my concerns; though I can no way merit it but by the sincerity with which I am, &c.

Text 1837, ii. 249–50

To Wortley *12 Nov.* [*1740*]

Nov. 12. N.S.

I receiv'd this morning Mr. Child's bill on Gott and How for 200. I intend not to take it up till I go to Leghorn, where I design to go to receive my things, which Mr. Man writes me word are daily expected. I shall set out for Naples on next Friday. I do not doubt liking the Situation, but by all the Information I can get, it will be every way improper for my

---

[1] David Wemyss (1721–87), styled Lord Elcho. On the Grand Tour, he reached Rome on 25 Oct. 1740, and stayed for six months during which time he became an ardent Jacobite (Evan Charteris, *A Short Account of the Affairs of Scotland by Lord Elcho*, 1907, pp. 19, 29; Paul Chamley, *Documents relatifs à Sir James Steuart*, 1965, pp. 96–99).

[2] Henry Fiennes-Clinton (1720–94), 9th Earl of Lincoln and later 2nd Duke of Newcastle.

[3] The cause of LM's anguish (if any) must have been Algarotti, still in Berlin, where he was recovering from what Frederick euphemistically called 'des blessures de Cythère' (*Œuvres*, ed. J. D. E. Preuss, 1846–57, xviii. 22, 26).

Residence, and I propose no longer stay there than is necessary to see what is curious. I have been very diligent in viewing every thing here, making no Acquaintance, that I might have no Interuption. Here is a statue of Antinous lately found,[1] which is said to be equal to any in Rome, and is to be sold; perhaps the Duke of Bedford might be glad to hear of it.[2] I do not hear of one valuable Picture that is to be purchas'd.

It has been this last week as dark and rainy as ever I saw it in England.

Your Letter of Sept. 23rd came to me but this Day. I perceive Letters are stop'd and perus'd more carefully than ever, which hinders my writeing any of the Reports I hear; some of them are very extrodinary. The Emperor's Ambassador here has taken the character of the Queen of Bohemia's and as such presented his Credentials, which have been receiv'd.[3]

I wrote to you the last post very fully as to what concerns my Son. I intend to write again to my Daughter, thô I have had no answer to my last.

Text W MS i. 373–4   *Address* To Edwd Wortley Esqr in Cavendish Square London Angleterre   *Postmark* ROME NO 26   *End. by W* [*Summary*] Recd 26 Nov.   Ad 28.

To Wortley *23 Nov.* [*1740*]

Naples, Nov. 23. N.S.

I arriv'd here last night after a very disagreable Journey. I would not in my last give you any Account of the present

[1] Cardinal Alessandro Albani's excavation of Hadrian's villa at Tivoli, begun in 1738, yielded several important statues of Antinous (Lorentz Dietrichson, *Antinoos: eine kunstarchäologische Untersuchung*, 1884, p. 117).

[2] John Russell (1710–71), 4th Duke, m. (1737) LM's niece Gertrude Leveson-Gower. He became a member of the Society of Dilettanti in 1742.

[3] After Charles VI died, on 20 Oct. 1740, his daughter Maria Theresa succeeded not as Empress but as Queen of Hungary. Josef Count von Thun (d. 1763), who had been Imperial Ambassador since Dec. 1739, then terminated his appointment. But he was not appointed Austrian Ambassador to the Papacy until April 1743 (*Repertorium,* ii. 73, 255).

state of Rome, knowing all Letters are open'd there, but I
cannot help mentioning what is more curious than all the
Antiquitys, which is that there is litterally no money in the
whole Town, where they follow Mr. Law's System[1] and live
wholly upon Paper. Belloni, who is the greatest Banker not
only of Rome but all Italy, furnish'd me with 50 sequins,
which he solemnly swore was all the money he had in the
House. They go to market with paper, pay the Lodgings with
paper, and, in short, there is no Specie to be seen, which
raises the prices of every thing to the utmost extravagance,
no body knowing what to ask for their goods. It ⟨is sa⟩id the
Present Pope (who has a very good character)[2] has declar'd
he will endeavor a remedy, thô it is very difficult to find one.
He was bred a Lawyer and has pass'd the greatest part of his
Life in that proffession, and is so sensible of the misery of the
State that he is reported to have said that he never thought
himselfe in want till since his Elevation. He has no Relations
that he takes any Notice of. The Country belonging to him
which I have past is allmost uninhabited, and in a poverty
beyond what I ever saw. The Kingdom of Naples appears
gay and Flourishing, and the Town so crouded with people
that I have with great difficulty got a very sorry Lodging.

Text W MS i. 375–6   *Address* To Edward Wortley Esqr in Cavendish Square London Angleterre   *Postmark* ROME ⟨?⟩   *End. by W*
[*Summary*] Recd 12 Dec.   Ad 23 Dec.

To Lady Pomfret 25 *Nov.* [*1740*]

Naples, Nov. 25, N.S.

Here I am arrived at length, after a most disagreeable
journey. I bought a chaise at Rome, which cost me twenty-
five good English pounds; and had the pleasure of being laid
low in it the very second day after I set out. I had the marvellous good luck to escape with life and limbs; but my

---

[1] John Law (1671–1729) was the
financial wizard who had inflated the
Mississippi Bubble in France.
[2] Benedict XIV was universally es-

teemed; Lady Pomfret's opinion—'a
very reasonable good sort of man'—was
typical (Hertford, *Corr.* ii. 189).

delightful chaise broke all to pieces, and I was forced to stay a whole day in a hovel, while it was tacked together in such a manner as would serve to drag me hither. To say truth, this accident has very much palled my appetite for travelling.

I was last night at the opera, which is far the finest in Italy;[1] it was the Queen's birth-night;[2] the whole house was illuminated, and the court in its greatest splendour. Mrs. Allen[3] is very well behaved, and (*entre nous*) her lover one of the prettiest men I ever saw in any country;[4] but all is managed with the strictest decency. I have been diverted both at Rome and here with Lady W[alpole]'s memoirs. The consul[5] told me that when she first came here she was in the full fury of her passion for Mr. Sturgis.[6] He went once to take the air in a coach with them, and her ladyship was so violent, he protested he had a great mind to have alighted and walked home on foot, rather than have been a spectator. I could not help laughing when I remembered our disputes.[7]

I am informed here are many pretty houses to be had, and I own I have half a mind to send orders for my goods to be brought hither; but fixing is a point of such importance, it deserves to be well considered. I am now sitting comfortably without a fire, and a soft winter is an article of consequence. It is possible there may be as many intrigues here as in other places; but there is an outward decency that I am pleased

[1] The newly built San Carlo had been open only since Nov. 1738, and its splendour was generally admired (Harold Acton, *The Bourbons of Naples*, 1956, pp. 33–38).

[2] Marie Amalie (1724–60), da. of Augustus III, Elector of Saxony and King of Poland, m. (1738) Charles III, King of the Two Sicilies, and son of Philip V of Spain.

[3] Catherine, da. of Sir John Shadwell, former physician to George II; she m. (1737) Edward Allen, British Consul in Naples (HMC *Denbigh MSS*, 1911, p. 215; Thomas Shadwell, *Complete Works*, ed. M. Summers, 1927, i, facing page ccliv).

[4] Probably he was mentioned when Lady Sophia Fermor wrote to a friend that LM's only acquaintances in Naples

were 'the Consul and his Wife and a Mr. Cantillion' (to Lady Anne [?], [1 Jan. 1741], Finch MS).

[5] Edward Allen, consul from at least 1734 (Acton, pp. 31–32) until 1753 or later (Augustus Hervey, *Journal 1746–1759*, ed. D. H. Erskine, 1953, p. 137).

[6] Samuel Sturgis (*c.* 1701–43), Lady Walpole's lover; they had gone abroad together (Walpole, *Corr.* xvii. 70, n. 14).

[7] In Florence, as Lady Pomfret's diary records, the three ladies had spent some time together. Horace Walpole, after observing them, wrote of LM: 'She laughs at my Lady Walpole, scolds my Lady Pomfret, and is laughed at by the whole town' (*Letters*, ed. Mrs. P. Toynbee, 1903, i. 84). LM later remembered her friendship with Lady Walpole (p. 486 below).

with; and by what I see of the Neapolitans (contrary to their common character), they appear to me a better sort of people than the Romans, or (if you will give me leave to say it) the Florentines. There seems some tincture of Spanish honour amongst them; and in favour of that I can forgive a little Spanish formality.[1] However, I have yet determined nothing; but wherever I am, I shall be, dear madam, faithfully yours &c.

Text, 1837, ii. 250–2

To Wortley 6 *Dec. 1740*

Naples, Dec. 6. N.S. 1740

I heard last night the good news of the arrival of the Ship on which my things are loaded, at Leghorn. It would be easy to have them convey'd hither, and I like the Climate extreamly, which is now so soft I am actually sitting without any want of a Fire. I do not find the people so savage as they were represented to me. I have receiv'd visits from several of the principal Ladys, and I think I could meet with as much company here as I desire, but here is one article both disagreable and incommodious, which is the Grandeur of the Equipages. 2 Coaches, 2 running footmen, 4 other footmen, a Gentleman usher, and 2 pages are as necessary here as the attendance of a single Servant is at London. All the Spanish customs are observ'd very rigorously. I could content my selfe with all of them except this. But I see plainly, from my own Observation as well as Intteligence, that it is not to be dispens'd with, which I am heartily vex'd at.

The affairs of Europe are now so uncertain,[2] it appears reasonable to me to wait a little before I fix my Residence, that I may not find my selfe in the Theatre of War, which is

---

[1] In Naples the ostentation of Spanish punctilio was noticed by other visitors— among them, by Charles de Brosses (*Lettres familières sur l'Italie*, ed. Y. Bezard, 1931, i. 422) and Augustus Hervey (*Journal 1746–1759*, ed. D. H. Erskine, 1953, p. 140).

[2] England's war with Spain was in progress; and the War of the Austrian Succession was imminent: Frederick II of Prussia invaded Silesia on 16 Dec. 1740.

threaten'd on all sides. I hope you have the continuation of your Health; mine is very well establish'd at present.

Text W MS i. 377–8   *Address* To Edward Wortley Esqr in Cavendish Square London Angleterre   *Postmark* ROME IA 6   *End. by W* [*Summary*] Recd 6 Jan.   Ad 16 Jan.

To Wortley *12 Dec.* [*1740*]

Naples, Dec. 12 N.S.

I have receiv'd halfe an hour ago 2 Letters from you, the one dated Oct'r the 6th, the other the 23rd. I am surpriz'd you have receiv'd none from me during the whole Month of Aug't, having wrote several, but I perceive all Letters are stopp'd and many lost. I gave my Daughter a Direction to me long since, but as far as I can find she has never receiv'd neither that nor another which I directed to her in Scotland.

The Town lately discover'd[1] is at Portice, about 3 mile from this place. Since the first discovery no care has been taken, and the ground falln in that the present passage to it is, as I am told by every body, extreme dangerous, and of some time no body ventures into it. I have been assur'd by some English Gentlemen that were let down into it the last year that the whole account given in the news papers is litterally true. Probably great Curiositys might be found there, but there has been no expence made either by proping the Ground or clearing a way into it, and as the Earth falls in daily, it will possibly be soon stopp'd up as it was before.[2]

I wrote to you last post a particular account of my reasons for not chuseing my Residence here, thô the air is very agreable to me and I see I could have as much company as I desire. But I am persuaded the climate is much chang'd since you knew it; the Weather is now very moist and misty, and

[1] Herculaneum. In his letter of 3 Nov./23 Oct. (W MS i. 121) W asked LM for details about the newly excavated town he had read of.

[2] The official excavation of Herculaneum had been under way since the autumn of 1738. The site had been inspected in June 1740 by Horace Walpole (*Corr.* xiii. 222–4) and his travelling companion Thomas Gray (*Corr.*, ed. P. Toynbee and L. Whibley, 1935, i. 163–4).

has been so for a long time. However, it is much softer than in any other place I know.

I desire you would direct to Mons. Belloni, Banker at Rome; he will forward your Letters where ever I am. The present uncertain Situation of affairs all over Europe makes every correspondance precarious.

I am sorry to trouble you with the Enclos'd to my Daughter, but as she seems concern'd for not hearing from me, and I have reason to fear that no Letter directed to her in Scotland will arrive safe, I send her these few Lines.

Text W MS i. 379–80   *Address* To Edwd Wortley Esqr in Cavendish Square London   *Postmark* ROME IA 6   *End. by W* [*Summary*] Recd 6 Jan.   Ad 16 Jan.

To Wortley *27 Dec.* [*1740*]

I did not write to you last post, hoping to have been able to have given you an account in this of every thing I had observ'd at Portice, but I have not yet obtain'd the King's License, which must be had before I can be admitted to see the Pictures and fragments of statues which have been found there, and has been hitherto delaid on various pretences, it being at present a very singular favor. They say that some English carry'd a Painter with them the last year to copy the Pictures, which renders it more difficult at present to get leave to see them. I have taken all possible pains to get information of this Subterrean Building, and am told 'tis the remains of the ancient City of Hercolana,[1] and by what I can collect there was a Theatre entire with all the Scenes and ancient Decorations. They have broke it to pieces by digging irregularly.[2] I hope in a few days to get permission to go, and will then give you the exactest Description I am capable of.

I have receiv'd no letters this 3 weeks, which does not

[1] For an account of the early excavations of Herculaneum, see Niccolò Marcello Venuti, *Descrizione delle prime scoperte dell'antica città d'Ercolano* (1748) and Charles Waldstein and Leonard Shoobridge, *Herculaneum Past Present and Future* (1908).

[2] Venuti also criticizes the excavation of the theatre (p. 76).

surprize me, thô it displeases me very much, hearing the same complaint made by every body. Mount Vesuvio is much diminish'd, as I am generally told, since the last great Irruption, which was 4 years ago.

The Court here is very magnificent and all the customs entirely Spanish. The new Opera House built by this King is the largest in Europe. I hear a great deal of news, true or false, but cannot communicate it at this time. I hope my next Letter will be more particular.

Naples, Dec. 27. N.S.

Text W MS i. 381–2   *Address* To Edwd Wortley Esqr in Cavendish Square London Angleterre   *Postmark* ROME IA 15   *End. by* W
[*Summary*] Rec. 15 Jan.   Ad 16 Jan.

To Mme Chiara Michiel[1] 28 *Dec.* [*1740*]

Je ne sçaurois temoigner trop tôt (ma chere Madame) ma reconnoisance pour une Lettre aussi obligeante et aussi aimable que celle que j'ai eû l'honneur de recevoir de vous. Elle m'auroit fait plaisir par son agrement quand elle auroit été addressé a une autre personne; jugez donc à quel point je suis touché des marques de vos bontez pour moi, qui me sent aucune merite que celui d'etre tres sensible au vostre, qu'asseurement je ne fais que partager avec tous ceux qui ont le bonheur de vous approcher. Je suis ravÿ que Mons. Mackinsie[2] soit de ce nombre; il n'est pas indigne de vostre distinction. Je n'ai jamais connu un esprit mieux fait ni un Cœur mieux placé. Je n'oublirai jamais l'offre qu'il m'a fait de venir a ma rencontre jusqu' a Boulogne si je voulois retourner a Venise.[3] Je serois trop heureuse si je pouvois trouver un occasion de lui preuver l'estime que je fais de son attention pour moi. En attendant, je vous la recommande,

[1] Here begins a new correspondence (35 letters from, 5 to, LM) with a Venetian lady whom LM had known for almost a year (see above, p. 170). Van Berkhout described Mme Michiel as 'dame fort belle et gracieuse, et qui parloit fort bien le françois. Son mari venoit d'etre nommé ambassadeur a la cour d'Espagne, et il est un des douze premieres maisons de la Republique' (28 May 1740, MS diary).

[2] Lord Bute's brother. During the summer LM had seen him in Venice (see above, p. 194).

[3] On 11 Nov. 1740 LM had written to Lady Pomfret of Mackenzie's kind offer.

Madame; vous voyez que j'ose me fier a vous pour payer mes dettes, et je suis persuadé que je me tromperois pas dans la confiance que j'ai en vostre bonté. En effet ce n'est que les femmes laides et les têtes foibles qu'on doit craindre, et vous possedez trop des graces pour en manquer de la Generosité.[1] Veritablement je ne trouve aucune defaut a ce Monsieur qu'un peu trop de Jeunesse; il me semble qu'on peut pardonner ce joli defaut, qu'en [i.e. quand] ce n'est seroit qu'en consideration qu'il s'en corrigera que trop rapidement.

Quoique je trouvois plusieurs personnes aimable dans ce Païs ici, je suis sur le point d'en sortir. Ma presence est absolument necessaire aupres de mon Baggage,[2] que je ne ferai transporter qu'au leiu ou je fixerois mon sejour; et il m'est impossible de faire mon salut dans une Monarchie, tant je trouve des occasions de murmurer contre la Providence qui le souffre sur la terre. Je ne doute pas, Madame, que vous n'aÿez souvent remercié Dieu de l'avantage de vostre naissance, mais quand vous serois établi dans une Cour, j'en repons que vous en seriez si sensible au Bonheur de l'Independance que vous en feriez journellement des actions de Graces. Je voye ici le pauvre Prince di Accia[3] quasi dans un esclavage aussi dur que celui du Comte de Wackerbarth,[4] obligé de se lever a la pointe de jour, quelque temps qu'il fasse, pour marcher 3 ou 4 lieus pour partager avec le Roi la Gloire de masacrer des Beccassines.[5] Ce travail n'a point d'intermission que les Dimanches, qu'il dit qu'il attend avec plus d'impatience que le plus pauvre Artisan. Voici pourtant les faveurs dont les princes comble leur bien aimez. Je ne vous parle point de l'interieur du Palais, que vous verrez a Madrid, dont celui ci n'est que la Miniature.[6]———

[1] Twenty-five years later, when Mme Michiel was 'a little advanced in years' but still 'gay, lively, *appétissante*', she extended her generosity to another young Scotsman—James Boswell (*Boswell on the Grand Tour: Italy, Corsica, and France*, ed. F. Brady and F. A. Pottle, 1955, pp. 10, 94, 95, 98).

[2] At Leghorn, where the ship carrying her baggage had arrived.

[3] Don Stefano Reggio, Prince Iaci (c. 1715–90)—son of Prince of Campo-

florido, Spanish Ambassador to Venice —was Gentleman of the Bedchamber to Charles III in Naples.

[4] Governor to the Prince of Saxony (see above, pp. 166, 192–3).

[5] The King had a 'mania for hunting' (Harold Acton, *The Bourbons of Naples*, 1956, p. 47).

[6] Mme Michiel's husband, Antonio, was Venetian Ambassador to Spain from Oct. 1741 to Aug. 1744 (*Repertorium*, ii. 416).

Ma Lettre devient trop longue, et il n'est pas juste qu'en recompense du plaisir que la vostre m'a donné, je vous tûe par une Lecture ennuyante. Adieu, ma tres chere Madame; soyez asseuré qu'en tout Païs ou ma Destiné m'entraineroit, vous aurez toujours une personne entierement devoué a vostre service, et je serois toute ma vie de V[otre] E[xcellence] La tres humble et tres Obeissante Servante,

M. W. de Montagu.

Addressez vostre lettre recommandé a Mons. Goldsworthy,[1] Consul d'Angleterre a Livourne.[2] Dec. 28.

Text Bute MS   *Address* A S. E. La Signora Chiara Michielli Bragadini a Venezia.

From Lord Bute[3] *11 Jan. 1741/31 Dec. 1740*

Madam,

Lady Bute has desir'd Me to lett Your Ladyship know that after a few days Ilness She was safely deliver'd of a Son about ten last Night. Both her Self and the Infant are as well as can possibly be Expected.[4] She begs You would accept her Compliments, and that You would give her humble Duty to Lady Marr. She intends to write to Your Ladyship the Minute her strength shall suffer her.

I am, Madam, with great Respect, Your Ladyship's Most Devoted and Most humble Servant,

Bute.

Mountstewart,[5] Dec. 31, 1740

Text Bute MS

[1] Burrington Goldsworthy (1705–74), consul at Leghorn 1736–54 (Warren H. Smith, *Originals Abroad*, 1952, pp. 18, 63, 73).

[2] LM's letters to Mme Michiel, all of them in French, are translated in the Appendix below.

[3] John Stuart (1713–92), 3rd Earl of Bute, m. (1736) Mary Wortley Montagu.

[4] This child, christened Edward, died a year later (see below, p. 271).

[5] Mount Stuart, the family seat at Rothesay, Isle of Bute.

To Wortley *13 Jan.* [*1741*]

Jan. 13. N.S., Rome.

I return'd hither last night after six weeks stay at Naples; great part of that time was vainly taken up in endeavoring to satisfy your Curiosity and my own in Relation to the late discover'd Town of Hercolana. I waited 8 days in hopes of permission to see the pictures and other Raritys taken from thence which are preserv'd in the King's Palace at Portice;[1] but I found it was to no purpose, his Majesty keeping the Key in his own Cabinet, which he would not part with, thô the Prince di Zathia [*sic*] (who is one of his favourites) I beleive very sincerely try'd his Interest to obtain it for me. He is Son to the Spanish Ambassador I knew at Venice, and both he and his Lady loaded me with Civillitys at Naples.[2] The Court in General is more barbarous than any of the ancient Goths; one proofe of it, amongst many others, was melting down a Beautifull Copper Statu of a vestal, found in this new Ruin, to make Medalions for the late Solemn Christening.[3]

The whole Court follow the Spanish Customs and Politics. I could say a good deal on this Subject if I thought my Letter would come safe to your Hands. The apprehension it may not, hinders my answering another enquiry you make concerning a Family here,[4] of which indeed I can say little, avoiding all commerce with those that frequent it. Here are some young English travellers; amongst them, Lord Strafford behaves himselfe realy very modestly and genteely, and has lost the pertness he acquir'd in his mother's assembly.[5]

---

[1] Thomas Gray, Walpole's companion, wrote: 'The work is unhappily under the direction of Spaniards, people of no taste or erudition, so that the workmen dig, as chance directs them, wherever they find the ground easiest to work without any certain view. . . . the principal paintings, & Statues . . . have been convey'd to the Palace, & there we went to see them' ('Notes of Travel,' *Gray and His Friends,* ed. D. C. Tovey, 1890, pp. 253–4, 255).

[2] Prince Iaci m. (15 June 1740) Jeanne-Romaine de la Châtre (1726–43), da. of comte de Nançay. She arrived in Naples in Sept., when she was made a Lady of Honour to Queen Marie Amalie.

[3] The Queen had borne a daughter on 6 Sept. 1740 (Isenburg, ii. 50).

[4] That of the Pretender.

[5] When Lady Pomfret met Strafford in Florence a month later, her opinion

Lord Lincoln appears to have Spirit and sense,[1] and proffesses great abhorrence of all measures destructive to the Liberty of his Country. I do not know how far the young Men may be corrupted on their Return, but the Majority of those I have seen have seem'd strongly in the same Sentiment.[2]

Lady Newburgh's[3] eldest Daughter,[4] who I beleive you may have seen at L[ady] Westmorland's,[5] is marry'd to Count Mahony, who is in great Figure at Naples. She was extreme obliging to me; they made a fine Entertainment for me, carry'd me to the Opera, and was civil to me to the utmost of their power. If you should happen to see Mrs. Bulkely[6] I wish you would make her some Compliment upon it.

I receiv'd this day yours of the 20th and 28th of November.

Text W MS ii. 1–2   *Address* To Edwd Wortley Esqr in Cavendish Square London Angleterre par Venezia   *Postmark* IA 29   *End. by W* [*Summary*] Ad 23 Feb. Recd 30 Jan.

was that he 'talks very well, and is well bred' (Hertford, *Corr.* ii. 277). His mother was Anne Johnson (1684–1754), who m. (1711) 1st Earl. Once when LM called on her, in 1734, Lady Strafford wrote that 'she had no news, and I was sadly tired of her before she went' (*Wentworth Papers 1705–1739*, ed. J. J. Cartwright, 1883, p. 501).

[1] Lady Pomfret also found him 'a very lively, sensible young man' (Hertford, *Corr.* ii. 160). On 21 Jan. he wrote to his uncle the Duke of Newcastle about meeting the extraordinary LM: 'I am so happy as to be mightily in my kinswoman's good graces, for you must know she claims a relation, which I own I did not in the least suspect' (Add MS 33,065, f. 392). He was related to her through their common ancestor 'Wise' William Pierrepont.

[2] LM repeated this sentiment to Lincoln's tutor, Joseph Spence. After quoting a line from Addison's *Cato*: 'O Liberty! O Virtue! O my Country!' she

told him that 'she travelled because she could not bear to see the distresses of her country' (*Anecdotes*, ed. J. M. Osborn, 1966, § LM 19). Spence reported their extended conversations fully in his letters to his mother (Eg MS 2234, ff. 247–52; summarized in Halsband, *LM*, pp. 210–11).

[3] Charlotte Maria Livingston, Countess of Newburgh (1694–1755).

[4] Lady Anne Clifford (1715–93) m. (1739) James Joseph Mahony (1699–1757), Count Mahony in the Neapolitan service (Edwin B. Livingston, *The Livingstons of Callendar*, 1920, p. 201; S. T. McCarthy, *Three Kerry Families*, [?1923], pp. 28, 30).

[5] See above, p. 76.

[6] Born Mary Anne Mahony, widow of Richard Cantillon (see above, p. 25), she m. (1736) Francis Bulkeley (1686–1756) of the French army (HMC *Denbigh MSS*, 1911, p. 120; Walpole, *Corr.* xviii. 429, n. 6).

To Lady Pomfret *20 Jan.* [*1741*]

Rome, January 20, N.S.

This is the fourth letter I have wrote to your ladyship, since I had the honour of hearing from you. I own I am much mortified at it. I do not doubt my letters have miscarried, for I cannot believe your silence proceeds from any other cause. In the mean time I must suffer greatly in your opinion if you think me stupid or ungrateful enough to neglect a correspondence which is every way so advantageous to me. I am returned from Naples, where I was much tempted to fix my residence, both from the charms of the climate, and the many civilities I met with. Some considerations made me decline it; and since my arrival here I have received such pressing and obliging letters from my friends at Venice, I can hardly resist my inclination to go thither. I am ashamed of my irresolution, but I own I am still undetermined. You see I confess to you all my weakness. My baggage is arrived at Leghorn; and, wherever I turn myself afterwards, it is necessary for me to go thither to give some orders concerning it; I only wait for the moon-light to begin my journey.[1]

I see all the English here every day, and amongst them Lord Lincoln, who is really, I think, very deserving, and appears to have both spirit and understanding. They all expect your ladyship's family here before the end of the carnival. I wish my affairs would permit me to stay till that time, if it be true you intend coming, otherwise the shows give me very little curiosity. The Abbé Niccolini is very obliging to me, but I fear his interest is not sufficient to do the service to my friend, that I endeavour with all my heart;[2]

---

[1] Lady Pomfret's daughter gossiped about LM: 'She has a ship full of her goods arrived at Leghorn, which is the reason of her setting out from Rome for that place, that she may order what is to be done with them. She design'd to set up her standard in Italy when first she came abroad, if things went to her mind, but as I fancy they have not, and that tho her ship has brought fine goods enough to adorn any Italian house, the principal piece of Furniture would be wanting, I'm of opinion she will lay aside the thoughts of settling abroad, and return to England to spend the rest of her days with old and odd Mr. Wortley' (Lady Sophia Fermor to Mrs. Wallop, 21/10 Feb. 1741, Finch MS).

[2] Antonio Niccolini, whom LM mentioned on 11 Nov. [1740], was an influential Florentine.

though I've little hopes of success from what the Venetian ambassador[1] told me last night.[2] I had last post a great deal of news from England, but as I suppose you had the same, I do not trouble you with the repetition. I hope all your family continue in health and beauty.

I am ever, dear madam, your ladyship's, &c.

Text 1837, ii. 252–3

To Wortley *4 Feb.* [*1741*]

Rome, Feb. 4. N.S.

I receiv'd this post yours of Dec. 23 O.S. and at the same time one from your Son which is very absurd. He still proffesses obedience, but seems to think it reasonable you should get him chose in the next Parliament.[3] I have wrote to him, representing to him in mild but very plain terms his true condition, and telling him how creditable it would be to him to set apart some of his allowance towards making his Creditors easy. The rest of my Letter was as near as I could what I thought you would have me say. I have also wrote a Letter to my Daughter directed to Scotland; I beg you would mention it when you write, least it should have miscarry'd.

I am not surpriz'd at Lady F[rances] Ereskine's marriage;[4]

---

[1] Francesco Venier (b. 1700) (Archivio di Stato, Venice). He was Venetian Ambassador in Rome from 13 Oct. 1740 to 1743 (*Repertorium*, ii. 415). When van Berkhout called on LM in Venice he found at her house 'le Procurateur Grimani et le Chevalier Vesnier, qui passent pour deux bonnes têtes de la Republique' (5 June 1740, MS diary).

[2] In Dec. 1740 Algarotti had finally been rewarded by Frederick of Prussia —with the title of Count and a diplomatic mission to the Court of Savoy in Turin. But what he wanted, as he wrote in Feb. to his brother, was to be named Prussian Ambassador to Venice (Ida

Treat, *Francesco Algarotti*, 1913, p. 115). Hence LM's endeavours 'to do the service to my friend' may concern him, if not Lady Pomfret (see below pp. 230–1).

[3] As a Member of Parliament Montagu would be able to return to England with immunity from arrest for his debts.

[4] Lady Mar's daughter married her cousin James Erskine (1713–85), 3rd son of James Erskine of Grange (who gave up his judicial title upon resigning from the Scottish Bench in 1734). The marriage must have taken place shortly before 30 Sept. 1740, when the Duchess of Bedford, Lady Frances's cousin, wrote to congratulate her (Mar and Kellie MS).

she had allways a false cunning which generally ends in the ruin of those that have it; but I am amaz'd at Mr. Ereskine's Impudence in pretending to be ignorant of it. I have receiv'd a Letter from my poor Sister in which she calls it a Match of her making, which would be a very plain proofe of her Lunacy if there was no other.

I hope you have before this time my Letter in which I inform'd you of the arrival of my goods at Leghorne.

Text W MS ii. 3–4   *Address* To Edwd Wortley Esqr in Cavendish Square London Angleterre   *Postmark* FE 23   *End. by W* [*Summary*] Ad 19 Mar.   Recd 23 Feb.

To Lady Mar *14 Feb.* [*1741*]

Dear Sister,
The letter you sent to Venice never came to my Hands, and this (which I receiv'd yesterday)[1] is the first I have had from you. I am now in a place where I hear you spoke of with a great deal of regard, and remember'd with a real Esteem.[2] I wish you all Happyness, and the same to Lady F[rances] Ereskine. If I knew any Method of serving her, I should ever be ready to do it, being (dear Sister) with a most sincere affection, faithfully Yours,

M. W. Montagu.

Rome, Feb. 14. N.S.

Be pleas'd to direct recommandé a Signor Belloni, Banquier a Rome.

Text Bute MS   *Address* To The Rt Honble The Countess Dowager of Mar at Weston Northamptonshire by way of London Angleterre *Postmark* MR 3

---

[1] LM apparently received it earlier, for she mentions it in the previous letter.
[2] In Nov. 1718 Lady Mar had gone to the Pretender's court in Rome, and stayed for about a year (*Stuart Papers at Windsor*, ed. A. and H. Taylor, [1939], pp. 53–59).

To Lady Pomfret 15 Feb. [1741]

Your ladyship's letters are so concise, I suppose you neither expected or desired a quick return to them; however I could not let slip this opportunity of assuring you that you have still in being a very sincere (though perhaps insignificant) humble servant. If you could know all my behaviour here, you would be thoroughly convinced of this truth, and of my endeavours to serve you. I was not at all surprized at the sight of Mr. Sturgis; he has the very face of a lover kicked out of doors; and I pity his good heart, at the same time I despise his want of spirit. I confess I am amazed (with your uncommon understanding) that you are capable of drawing such false consequences. Because I tell you another woman has a very agreeable lover, you conclude I am in love with him myself;[1] when God knows I have not seen one man since I left you, that has affected me otherwise than if he had been carved in marble. Some figures have been good, others have been ill made; and all equally indifferent to me.

The news I have heard from London is, Lady Margaret Hastings having disposed of herself to a poor wandering methodist;[2] Lady Lucy Manners being engaged to Mr. Pawlet;[3] Miss Henshaw married to Captain Strickland;[4] and Lady Carnarvon[5] receiving the honourable addresses of Sir Thomas Robinson;[6] here is a great heap of our sex's folly.

[1] Samuel Sturgis was Lady Walpole's lover. Later Lady Pomfret's son reported a conversation with LM who passionately defended 'poor Sturgis' as 'too Sensible a Man to Love a Woman who treated him so ill' (19 April [1741], Finch MS; quoted in Halsband, *LM*, p. 214). Or LM may mean Cantillion (above, p. 213).

[2] Lady Margaret (1700–68), youngest da. of 7th Earl of Huntingdon, did not marry Benjamin Ingham (1712–72) until 12 Nov. 1741, though their marriage was gossiped about in London as early as May 1740 (Hertford, *Corr.* i. 234; HMC *Hastings MSS*, iii, 1934, p. 31). He had spent about a year in Georgia with the Wesley brothers. Her sister-in-law, Selina, Countess of Hunt-

ingdon, famous for evangelical work, was her convert (D. M. Stenton, *The English Woman in History*, 1957, pp. 283–4).

[3] Lady Lucy (1717–88), da. of 2nd Duke of Rutland, m. (28 Oct. 1742) 2nd Duke of Montrose. Probably Vere (1710–88), third son of 1st Earl Poulett.

[4] Katherine, da. of Edward Henshaw, m. (n.d.) William Strickland (d. 1788).

[5] Catherine Tollemache (c. 1684–1754), da. of 3rd Earl of Dysart, and widow since 1727 of the Marquess of Carnarvon, inherited enormous riches at her mother's death in 1740; but she did not remarry (C. H. Collins Baker and Muriel I. Baker, *James Brydges First Duke of Chandos*, 1949, p. 245).

[6] Sir Thomas (1700?–77) m. (1728) Lady Lechmere (d. 1739). His extrava-

I intend setting out for Leghorn the next Sunday, and from thence I am yet undetermined. What is very pleasant, I have met two men exactly in the same circumstances. The one is Prince Couteau (brother to the Princess of Campo Florida), who has abandoned his country on being disgusted with his wife;[1] and the other a Genoese Abbé, who has both wit and learning in a very ugly form, and who on a disagreeable adventure is resolved never to return to Genoa.[2] We often talk over every town in Europe, and find some objection or other to every one of them.

If it would suit your conveniency to see me at Sienna, I would stop there to receive that pleasure.[3]

Rome, February 15th.

Text 1837, ii. 254–5

To Wortley *18 Feb.* [*1741*]

Feb. 18. N.S., Rome.

I receiv'd the last bill of exchange yesterday, for which I return you thanks. I shall set out to morrow for Leghorn to receive it and to look after my things.

I have seen all that is curious in this Town, of which I shall send you some description after I have left it. I have wrote to you 2 or 3 letters relateing to the new discover'd Town of Hercolana, which I hope you have receiv'd.

The Weather is now very fine. I had the good Luck to escape the great Inundation by my stay at Naples.[4]

gance had pushed him into great debt, and in 1742 he accepted the governorship of the Barbadoes where he later remarried.

[1] Princess of Campoflorido's brother was Michele Gravina e Gravina, Prince of Comitini; his wife, Marianna Massa e Valguarnera. He did not permanently abandon his country (Sicily), for he occupied political offices in Palermo from 1749 to 1769. His name is garbled by either LM or the unknown transcriber of the text.

[2] Horace Walpole (in Florence) gossipped to Lord Lincoln about LM: 'I hear there is a Genoese abbé declared her cicisbeo in all the forms; poor man!' (31 Jan. 1741, *Corr.* xxx. 11).

[3] On her way from Florence to Rome Lady Pomfret planned to stop for a day at Sienna. But she did not leave Florence until 13 March (Hertford, *Corr.* ii. 277, 284), by which time LM had reached Leghorn.

[4] At the beginning of Dec. 1740 Rome suffered severe floods, including the

I shall say no more at present, being in some hurry prepareing for my Journey.

Text W MS ii. 5   *End. by W* [*Summary*] Recd 3 Mar.

To Wortley 25 *Feb.* [*1741*]

Leghorn, Feb. 25. N.S.

I arriv'd here last night, and have receiv'd this morning the bill of 905 dollars odd money.[1]

I shall be a little more particular in my Accounts from hence than I durst be from Rome, where all the Letters are open'd and often stopp'd. I hope you had mine relateing to the Antiquitys in Naples. I shall now say something of the Court of Rome. The first minister, Cardinal Valenti,[2] has one of the best characters I ever heard, thô of no great Birth, and has made his Fortune by an attachment to the Dutchess of Salviati.[3] The present Pope is very much belov'd, and seems desirous to ease the people and deliver them out of the miserable poverty they are reduce'd to. I will send you the history of his Elevation as I had it from a very good hand, if it will be any amusement to you.

I never saw the Chevalier during my whole stay at Rome. I saw his 2 Sons at a public Ball in Masque;[4] they were very richly adorn'd with Jewells. The eldest seems thoughtless enough, and is realy not unlike Mr. Littleton in his Shape and air.[5] The youngest is very well made, dances finely, and

overflowing of the Tiber, because of heavy continuous rain (Walpole, *Corr.* xxx. 3).

[1] At the rate of $45 for £10 (W to LM, 25 March 1740 [O.S.], W MS i. 117), this amount would be LM's quarterly allowance of £245 minus £45 to be applied to her loan of £100. Her annual allowance was evidently £800 from W, plus the 'interest money' from her father's legacy (see above, p. 177).

[2] Silvio Valenti Gonzaga (1690–1756), Cardinal 1738, Secretary of State 1740 (Ludwig von Pastor, *The*

History of the Popes, transl. E. F. Peeler, 1938–53, xxxv. 43).

[3] Anna Boncompagni (1696–1752) m. (1717) Gianvincenzo Salviati, Duke of Giuliano, whose family was prominent in the Church (Litta; Spreti; cf. Walpole, *Corr.* xvii. 4, n. 14).

[4] The Chevalier de St. George, as James Edward was called, and his sons: Charles Edward (1720–88) and Henry Benedict (1725–1807).

[5] George Lyttelton (1709–73), later 1st Baron, was—as described by Hervey —extremely tall and thin his face ugly, his person ill made, and his carriage

has an ingenuous Countenance; he is but 14 years of age.[1]
The family live very splendidly, yet pay every body and
(where ever they get it) are certainly in no want of money. I
heard at Rome the true tragical history of the Princess
Sobieski,[2] which is very different from what was said at
London. The Pope Clement the 12 was commonly suppos'd
her Lover, and she us'd to go about publickly in his state
Coach to the great Scandal of the people.[3] Her Husband's
mistrisse[4] spirited him up to resent it so far that he left Rome
upon it, and she retir'd to a Convent where she destroy'd
her selfe.[5]

The English Travellers at Rome behave in general very
discreetly. I have reason to speak well of them since they were
all exceeding obliging to me.[6] It may sound a little vain to
say it, but they realy paid a regular Court to me, as if I had
been their Queen, and their Governors told me that the desire
of my aprobation had a very great Influence on their conduct.
While I staid, there was neither Gameing or any sort of
Extravagance; I us'd to preach to them very freely, and they

awkward (*Memoirs*, ii. 387–8); and
Chesterfield, a close friend, described
him in similar terms (*Letters*, ed. B.
Dobrée, 1932, iv. 1402–3). 'Bonnie'
Prince Charles was tall and thin, but
also very charming in manners and con-
versation (Charles Petrie, *The Jacobite
Movement*, 1959, p. 332). Charles de
Brosses described him as 'aimable, polis
et gracieux' though of 'un esprit médi-
ocre' (*Lettres familières sur l'Italie*, ed. Y.
Bezard, 1931, ii. 89).

[1] Thomas Gray had seen the sons at
another ball: 'They are good fine boys,
especially the younger, who has the more
spirit of the two' (July 1740, *Corr.*, ed.
P. Toynbee and L. Whibley, 1935, i.
166).

[2] James Edward m. (1719) Clemen-
tina (d. 1735), da. of Prince James
Sobieski; in 1725 they quarrelled and
she entered a nunnery for two years,
after which they were more or less
reconciled.

[3] Lorenzo Corsini (1652–1740), Pope
Clement XII (1730), had tried to reconcile the Pretender and his wife after their

quarrel (*The Lockhart Papers*, 1817, ii.
254). He had once lent her his litter for
returning to Rome from the country
(Lesley Lewis, *Connoisseurs and Secret
Agents in Eighteenth Century Rome*, 1961,
pp. 80–81).

[4] Marjory Murray, da. of 5th Viscount Stormont, m. (1715) Col. John
Hay of Cromlix (1691–1740), son of 7th
Earl Kinnoul; he was Secretary of State
to the Pretender 1725–7. She was handsome and coquettish, and commonly
believed to be the Pretender's mistress
(and thus the cause of his wife's jealousy),
but this was not so (*Lockhart Papers*, ii.
340). The Pretender was melancholy
rather than unfaithful (Petrie, pp. 308–9).

[5] As a staunch anti-Jacobite LM was
not reluctant to pass on this sort of
sensational rumour.

[6] Lady Pomfret's daughter confirmed
this about LM in Rome: 'she sups and
dines with the English, and I hear diverts
them very well, adapting her conversation and humour to their taste' (to
Mrs. Wallop, 21/10 Feb. 1741, Finch
MS).

all thank'd ⟨me for⟩ it. I shall stay some time in this Town, where I expect Lady Pomfret.

I think I have answer'd every particular you seem'd curious about. If there be any other point you would have me speak of, I will be as exact as I can.

Direct recommandé a Monsieur Jackson,[1] negotiant Anglois a Livourne.

Text W MS ii. 6–7　　*Address* To Edward Wortley Esqr in Cavendish Square London Angleterre　　*Postmark* MR 11　　*End. by W* [*Summary*] Ad 19 Mar.　Recd 11 Mar.

To Mme Chiara Michiel 25 *Feb.* [*1741*]

Livourne, Feb. 25.

Je suis arrivé ici hier au soir, ou j'ai eû l'honneur de trouver vostre aimable Lettre. Je ne veux pas tarder un moment de vous marquer ma reconnoisance, quoi que je suis tout entouré de ballots, et embarrassé des comptes des marchands etc. Malgres toutes les choses obligeante que vous me dittes, il faut que je vous reproche la defense que vous me faittes de m'etendre sur vos Louanges. Vous voulez donc, Madame, me priver de mon plus sensible plaisir, mais vous avez beau faire, et je veux dire de bien de vous par tout, mesme quand vous devrez enrager.

Je suis ravÿ que Mons. Mackinsie se rende digne de vos bontez; et franchement je croi avoir passé ma vie dans des prejugez vulgaire a l'égard des personnes de son age. J'avois des Preventions qu'ils etoient tous des étourdis qu'on faisoit tres bien d'éviter, ce que j'ai toujours fait, jusque mes voiages m'ont forcé de les pratiquer; et je vous asseure que j'en ai trouvé parmi eux de la bonne Foi et de l'honneur, qui est assez rare ailleurs, et naturellement cela doit éstre ainsi. Il y a peu des Gens douée d'une vertu assez forte pour se conserver dans le commerce du monde; les Jeunes personnes ont encore une reste de sincerité, ce que, joint aux maximes d'un Education noble, leur rendent plus estimable que ceux

[1] George Jackson (d. 1764), merchant (*Gentleman's Mag.*, p. 46).

d'un age avancé, qui sont ordinairement corrompu par des mauvaises Exemples. Vous voyez que ce n'est pas mon éloge que je fais; pour vous, Madame, vous joüisez de cette saison Brillante ou l'esprit est meürie sans que la figure en a souffert. Je voudrois que le Ciel fit un miracle en vostre faveur, et que vous pourriez éstre telle que vous ettes, deux ou trois cents anns a venir.

Je ne sçai ce que mon destin ambulante veut de moi; de façon ou d'autre le Cœur me dit que nous nous reverrons. Je viens de Rome, que j'ai vû dans tous ses charmes durant les derniers jours du Carnival, mais les Brodeurs et les Baigneurs perdent leur peines a travailler sur leurs personnes. Peutestre c'est une Grace que St. Pierre accorde a l'etat de l'Eglige [*sic*], mais je n'ai jamais vû des visages si formé pour inspirer la chasteté. En effet la ville est si peu peuplée qu'on comprend qu'elle ne dure que par pur devoir conjugalle.

Permettez moi, Madame, de vous prier de faire des complimens tres vifs et tres sincere a Mons. le Procurator Grimani de ma part; et soyez persuadé qu'en tout païs ou je serois, je suis invio[l]ablement, Ma tres chere Madame, de V. E. La tres humble et tres Obeissante Servante,

M. W. Montagu.

Text Bute MS   *Address* A S. E. La Signora Chiara Michielli Bragadini a Venetia.

To Lady Pomfret 3 *March* [1741]

I am extremely sorry (dear madam) that things have turned out so unluckily to hinder me the pleasure of your conversation; I really believed Lord Strafford intended to go straight to Florence, instead of which he has been at Leghorn, Pisa, and Lucca, which has occasioned these mistakes. When you arrive at Rome, I am persuaded you will be convinced of my endeavours to serve you; and I'm very positive nothing but ill management can hinder that affair from succeeding. I own it will require some skill from the opposition it is like to meet with. I am now expecting every hour to be summoned on board,¹ or I would take a trip to Florence to inform you of every thing. I am sorry you seem to doubt the benignity of your stars; pray trust to mine, which (though of little use to myself) have never failed of showering some good fortune where I wished it, as I do most sincerely to you, being, dear madam, Faithfully yours,

M.W.M.

Leghorn, March the 3rd.

Text 1837, ii. 255–6

To Wortley *17 March* [*1741*]

Turin, March 17. N.S.

I arriv'd here last night, after very bad roads. I hope you have receiv'd my Letters relateing to the Town of Hercolana, which, thô perhaps not very satisfactory, are all Truth. Sir John Shadwell² can know nothing concerning it; the discovery of it happen'd six months after he had left Naples. You know he is famous for Romanceing.

I left Rome realy from being too much courted there, since I found that (in spite of all my Caution) if I had staid it had been impossible for me to escape suspicions I no way deserv'd, and the Spys are so numerous and such foolish rogues, a small matter would have serv'd for accusation.³ I will be more particular on this Subject the first Oppertunity I find of sending a Letter by a safe hand.

Text W MS ii. 8   *End. by W* [*Summary*] Recd 27 Mar. Ad 6 Apr.

¹ She was apparently waiting to board the *Dragon,* a sixty-gun ship of the Mediterranean fleet under Capt. Curtis Barnet, which sailed from Leghorn on 5 March, and after 'hard gales' and squalls reached Genoa the next day (Walpole, *Corr.* xxi. 473; PRO Ad 51/274).

² Retired physician (1671–1747), whose daughter was married to the British Consul in Naples (see above, p. 213, n. 3). His wife had seen LM in Venice (Eliz. Montagu, *Corr. 1720–1761,* ed. E. J. Climenson, 1906, i. 50); and with his family he returned to England in July 1740 (Mansell to LM, 18/7 July 1740, W MS iv. 181).

³ Of Jacobite intrigue.

From Lord Hervey 31/20 *March 1741*

Grosvenor-Street, March 31/20. 1741

Dear Madam,

I have just recieved a Letter from You dated from Turin, which gave me the double Pleasure of finding you desire to contribute to mine, and are in a way of promoting your own; and tho all Retrospects are mere Vanity, as most present Views are Vexation of Spirit, yet I can not help saying a few Words by way of Solution to the Riddle of our writing constantly to one another without corresponding. As I knew nothing of your leaving Florence, I wrote twice thither, directing my Letters to Lady Pomfret, when perhaps you were three or four hundred Miles off; and just after I complain'd of You in my Letter to Mons'r Alg[arotti], I recieved one from you dated from Naples, which I answer'd directed to Rome. . . . [*Passage omitted*]

Pray tell your—*Friend*,[1] that Cicero is publish'd and that I have sent him this Work in two large Vols. in quarto,[2] by Lord Hindford to Berlin, who set out last Week.[3] Continue to direct for me in Grosvenor-Street, and do not send your Letters in the Office-Paquet. Adieu. I am in great haste but will write again soon and never lose any Oportunity of telling you how ardently I wish to be remember'd by you with some Affection, or how gratefully and warmly I ever think of You.

[*Passage omitted*]

Text Bristol MS ii. 97–98

[1] After one and a half years of anxious anticipation LM was now in the same city as Algarotti. He had arrived in Turin on 28 Jan. as Frederick of Prussia's unofficial emissary to the Court of Savoy. He planned to rent an apartment because, he told the French Ambassador, the noise of an inn would keep him from sleeping (4 Feb. 1741, Ministère des Affaires Étrangères, Sardaigne, vol. 202, f. 61). His attitude towards LM can be judged from his remark to his brother that their meeting in Turin was one of the most curious episodes in his strange life ('e questa non è una delle men curiose epoche della vita mia, assai per altro singolare': 25 March 1741, MS in Biblioteca di Treviso).

[2] *The Life of Cicero* by Conyers Middleton, published in Feb. 1741, was dedicated to Lord Hervey; among its subscribers were Algarotti and LM.

[3] John Carmichael, 3rd Earl of Hyndford, appointed Envoy to Prussia. He received his instructions on 21 March and arrived in Berlin 27 April 1741 (D. B. Horn, *Brit. Dipl. Rep. 1689–1789*, 1932, p. 107).

To Wortley 7 *April* [*1741*]

Turin, Ap. 7.

I receiv'd this day yours of Jan. 29th and Feb. 23.

Mr. Mackinsie (Brother to Lord Bute) arriv'd here last night on his road to England. He intends to stay but few days here, and I will send by him a long letter in which I will answer particularly all you desire to know. I beleive he may not be able to leave this place so soon as he designs; it now snows very hard, and if it continues the roads will be impassable. I am at present in debate whither to fix at Genoa, Venice or Geneva;[1] there are some things which I am told of this last that encline me very much to it; I mean the easy expence and, as I hear, the Beauty of the Country. Be pleas'd to order my next bill hither; I shall probably stay till that time.

Text W MS ii. 9   *End. by W* [*Summary*] Ad 23 Apr.   Recd 13 Apr.

To Wortley *11 April* [*1741*]

I take this opertunity of writeing to you on many Subjects in a freer manner than I durst do by the post, knowing that all letters are open'd, both here and in other places, which occasions them to be often lost, beside other Inconveniencies that may happen.

The English Politics is the general Jest of all the nations I have pass'd through, and even those who profit by our Follys cannot help laughing at our Notorious Blunders, thô they are all persuaded that the Minister does not act from Weakness but Corruption, and that the Spanish Gold

[1] In Lady Pomfret's opinion, LM was 'wandering about Italy and for ought I know out of it to find some place where she may have six friends to pass the Evenings with her. As her Merit is uncommon perhaps she may find in Bundles what most people long before the[y] Arrive at her Years give over the hopes of finding single' (to Lady Evelyn, Rome, 29 April 1741, Finch MS).

influences his measures.[1] I had a long discourse with Count Mahony[2] on this Subject, who said very freely that halfe the Ships sent to the coast of Naples that have lain Idle in our Ports last Summer would have frighted the Queen of Spain[3] into a Submission to whatever terms we thought proper to impose. The people, who are loaded with Taxes, hate the Spanish Government, of which I had daily proofes, hearing them curse the English for bringing their King[4] to them, when ever they saw any of our Nation. But I am not much surpriz'd at the Ignorance of our Ministers after seeing what Creatures they employ to send them Intelligence; (except Mr. Villette at this Court)[5] there is not one that has common sense. I say this without prejudice, all of them having been as civil and serviceable to me as they could. I was told at Rome, and convince'd of it by Circumstances, that there has been great endeavors to raise up a sham plot. The person who told it me was an English Antiquarian[6] who said he had been offer'd any Money to send accusations. The Truth is, he had carry'd a Letter wrote by Mr. Mann from Florence to that purpose to him, which he shew'd in the English Palace. However, I beleive he is a Spy, and made use of that Stratagem to gain credit.

This Court makes great preparations for War. The King is certainly no bright Genius, but has great natural Humanity. His Minister, who has absolute power, is generally allow'd to have sense.[7] As a proofe of it, he is not hated as the generallity of ministers are. I have seen neither of them, not going to Court because I will not be at the trouble and expence of the Dress, which is the same as at Vienna. I sent my Excuse by Mr. Villette, as I hear is commonly practis'd by Ladys that are only Passengers. I have had a great number

---

[1] Peace-loving Sir Robert Walpole, nearing the end of his long reign of power, did not wage war against Spain with enough energy, according to the Opposition.

[2] See above, p. 221.

[3] Elizabeth Farnese (1692–1766) m. (1714) Philip V.

[4] Charles III, King of the Two Sicilies, was Elizabeth's son.

[5] See above, p. 149.

[6] Mark Parker (*c.* 1698–1775), an English Catholic in Rome, who combined the profession of spying with that of guiding English tourists (Walpole, *Corr.* xvii. 81–82 and n. 30).

[7] Charles Emanuel III of Savoy entered the War of the Austrian Succession the following year, on the side of Austria. His minister was Carlo Vincenzo Ferrero di Roasio, marchese d'Ormea (1680–1745).

of visitors, the Nobillity piqueing themselves on Civillity
to Strangers. The Weather is still exceeding cold, and I do
not intend to move till I have the prospect of a pleasant
Journey.

Ap. 11. N.S.

Text W MS ii. 10–11   *Address* To Edwd Wortley Esqr   *End. by*
W L.M. 11 Apr. 1741 from Turin by Mr Mackenzie.   Ad 21 May.

To Mme Chiara Michiel *15 April* [*1741*]

Madame,

J'ai receu par Monsieur Mackinsie l'aimable Lettre que
vous m'avez fait l'honneur de m'écrire. Le pauvre Garçon
est parti hier, tout penetrée du chagrin de quitter l'Italie. Il
a soupé avec moi, nous avons bû a vostre santé, et il m'a
recommandé plus de dix fois de vous dire de sa part tout ce
que la Reconnoisance et l'admiration pouvoit produire. Il
a veritablement le meilleur Cœur que j'ai jamais connu, et je
suis fort content de son Goût, puis qu'il m'asseure n'avoir
jamais rien vû de si charmante et si estimable que vous.

Je suis tres flatté du Souvenir dont Mons. le Procurator
Grimani m'a honoré. Jusqu'ici mes voiages m'ont rien offert
qui valent mes amis de Venise, mais vous le quittez, Madame,
et vous enlevez avec vous un tres grand parti des agremens
que j'ai y trouvé. Je'n doute pas que vous trouverois en tout
Païs des personnes sensible a vostre merite; mais j'ose
ajouter que vos Adorateurs de Londres seront plus digne de
vous que ceux de Madrid. La Beauté est le vraie Language
universelle; on rendra justice a la vostre par tout, mais vous
avez mille graces qui échaperont aux Espagnols et qui
charmeront les Anglais. Apres vingt annees de sejour chez
nous, il vous restera de quoi effacer toutes les Beautez de
l'Espagne. Vostre Senat (dont le sage Oeconomie fait
l'admiration de l'Europe) devoit penser serieusement a
cette affaire; il me semble que c'est une depense aussi

inutile que s'ils envoyoit cent mille hommes en garnison dans l'Isle de Corfu.

Adieu, Madame. J'étois en train de vous ennuyer encore longtemps; heureusement pour vous, des visites, triste pour moi, m'oblige a vous dire a la hâte que je suis inviolablement, Madame, de Vostre Excellence La tres humble et tres Obeissante Servante,

M. W. de Montagu.

Ap. 15, Turin

Text Bute MS   *Address* A S. E. La Signora La Signora Chiara Michielli Bragadini a Venise.

From Lord Hervey *2 May/21 April 1741*

Grosvenor-Street, May 2/April 21. 1741

[Passage omitted]

I want much to know if the Friend[1] who inserted a Paragraph in your two last Letters has recieved one I wrote to him about a fortnight ago, concieved in terms which, if it is fallen into any Hands but his own, I am sure will not be understood, but which I long much to have an answer to from him; tho I whilst I am writing to him or to you, I feel my-self so cramp'd by prudential Views that it not only takes away the Freedom and Pleasure I should otherwise have in talking to you on Paper, but mortifys my Vanity to the last degree in making me the dullest and dryest of all Correspondents where I had rather even be quite forgotten than remember'd on such terms. . . . *[Passage omitted]*

All you say of Reason and Philosophy I aprove extreamly, and have long thought that Humankind possess that boasted Gift in so perverse and worse than useless a Degree, that the best thing Any-Body can do by it is to renounce it, and with the same Valediction that the Queen of Sweeden renounced her Crown, non mi bisogna e non mi basta.[2]

Text Bristol MS ii. 100–2   *Address* (par Paris) A Madame Madame de Montagu chez Monsr Vilette Ministre de sa Majesté Britanique à Turin   *Postmark* TR

[1] Algarotti. And in writing to him, Hervey sent a message to LM: 'Adieu, my best respects and wishes attend your delightfull Companion' (29/18 May 1741, Murray MS).

[2] Queen Christina (d. 1689), who abdicated in 1654, later struck a medal with this motto above a terrestrial globe (Sven Stolpe, *Från Stoicism till Mystik*, 1959, p. 113).

To Francesco Algarotti [*May 1741*][1]

Oui, je passerois le matin a vous écrire quand vous devriez enrager. Je me suis mis a mepriser vostre mépris, et sur ce pied la je ne veux plus me contraindre. Dans le tems (de sotte memoire) que j'ai eû un goût effrené pour vous, l'envie de vous plaire (quoi que je compris toute l'impossibilité) et la peur de vous ennuyer m'éttouffoit quasi la voix quand je vous parlay, et par plus forte raison m'arrettoit la main cinq cens fois par jour quand j'ai pris la plume pour vous écrire. À l'heure qu'il est, ce n'est plus cela. Je vous a étudié, et si bien étudiée, que le Chevalier Newton n'a pas disecté les raions du Soleil avec plus d'exactitude que j'ai dechiffré les sentimens de vostre ame.[2] Vos yeux m'ont servi de Prism pour demeler les Idées dans vostre esprit. J'ÿ ay regardois avec une si grande Aplication, je me suis presqu'aveuglée (car ces prisms sont fort éblöüissante). J'ai vû que vostre ame est rempli de mille belles imaginations mais tout ensemble ne forme que de l'indifference. Il est vrai que separement, mettez cet Indifference (par exemple) en sept parties, sur des objets a des certains distances, on verroit le gout le plus vif, les sentimens les plus fin, l'imagination la plus delicat etc. Chaqu'une de ces qualitez sont réelement en vous. Sur les manuscripts, sur les statues, sur les Tableaux, les vers, le vin, la conversation, on vous trouveroit toujours du gout, de la Delicatesse, et de la vivacité. Pourquoi donc est ce que je ne trouve que de la grossierité et de l'indifference? Ce que je suis assez épais pour n'exciter rien de mieux, et je voye si clairment la nature de vostre ame que j'ai tout autant de Desespoir de le toucher que Mr. Newton avoit d'augmenter ses decouvertes par des Telescopes, que par leur propres Qualités dissipent et changent les raions de la Lumiere.[3]

Text Bod. MS Don. c. 56, ff. 57–58

[1] This undated letter fits an occasion when LM was not far from Algarotti, had known him for a long time, and was suffering a disagreeable disillusion in him. Yet the physical properties of the letter (paper, ink, pen) are similar to those of her letters to him before she went abroad—and so on that evidence it may date from the spring of 1739, and its tone of disillusion be interpreted as a lapse from the intense ardour which drove her across the Alps to meet him.

[2] Here LM alludes to Algarotti's graceful dialogues, *Il Newtonianismo per le dame* (1737)——based on the *Optics*.

[3] Algarotti's diplomatic mission to

To Wortley *31 May* [*1741*]

Genoa, May 31 N.S.

I came here last night, where I intend either to fix, or to put my Baggage (which is all here) in order to move by land, which it cannot do as it is pack'd at present. The present discourse of the designs on Italy makes it necessary for me to determine very soon, and not possible for me to reside in the King of Naples' Dominions or any of the disputed States. I desire that the next money you intend for me may not be sent till I let you know where I shall stay; going through many hands makes a considerable abatement.

I hope you receiv'd my long letter by Mr. Mackensie. I dare write no News but when I have the opertunity of sending it by a private hand.

Text W MS ii. 12–13   *Address* To Edwd Wortley Esqr in Cavendish Square London Angleterre par Paris   *Postmark* IV 3   *End. by* W [*Summary*] Recd 3 June   14 days coming.   Ad 22 June.

To [Lord Hervey] [? *June*] *1741*

The conclusion of a Letter to a Freind[1] wrote 1741[2] from Italy

> But happy you, from the Contagion free,
> Throû all her Vails can Human Nature see;
> Calm you refflect amidst the Frantic Scene
> On the low views of those mistaken men,
> Who lose the short invaluable Hour
> Through Dirt persuing Schemes of distant Power,

Turin was a failure, for he could not enlist Charles Emanuel III on the Prussian side in the War of the Austrian Succession. Recalled by Frederick, he left for Berlin on 17 May (A. Neri, 'F. Algarotti, diplomatico', *Archivio storico italiano*, xviii, 1886, p. 252). His departure apparently interrupted his correspondence with LM—which was resumed fifteen years later (see iii. 117).

[1] The friend to whom LM habitually addressed verse was Hervey.

[2] Possibly this is LM's answer to Hervey's letter of 27/16 May 1741 from Ickworth Park, in which he extols—in prose and verse—the pleasure of philosophic retirement in the country (Bristol MS ii. 103–6).

Whose best Enjoyments never pay the chase,
But melt like Snow, within the warm Embrace.
Beleive me, Freind (for such indeed are you,
Dear to my Heart and to my Int'rest true),
Too much already have you thrown away,
Too long sustain'd the labour of the Day.
Enjoy the Remnant of declineing Light,
Nor wait for Rest, till overwhelm'd in Night.
By present Pleasure, pay the Pains are past,
Forget all Systems, and indulge your Taste.

To the Same[1]

Where ever Fortune points my Destin'd Way,
If my Capricious Stars ordain my Stay
In Gilded Palace or in Rural Scene;
While Breath shall animate this frail Machine,
My Heart sincere, which never Flatt'ry knew,
Shall consecrate its warmest Sighs to you.

A Monarch compass'd by a Suppliant Croud,
Prompt to obey, and in his Praises loud,[2]
Amongst those thousands on his Smiles depend,
Perhaps has no disinterested Freind.

Text H MS vol. 256; printed inaccurately in 1803, v. 210–11

To Wortley *17 June* [*1741*]

Genoa, June 17. N.S.

I have taken a House here for the remainder of the Summer, which I have been induce'd to by a fine Situation on the Sea, which is allways the pleasantest, and I beleive the wholesomest in a warm climate. Most of the Ladys here have been to visit me.

I suppose you have receiv'd my letter in which I gave you thanks for the encrease of my allowance,[3] but I wish the next

[1] LM transcribed this epistolary verse immediately after 'The conclusion of a Letter to a Freind wrote 1741'.
[2] This couplet adapted from Prior's

Solomon (*Works*, i. 369, 370).
[3] On 30/19 March W informed her: 'I shall hence forward make up your interest money (which may not

Quarter would be sent payable at sight; the last was 3 months after date, so that I have not yet receiv'd it.

Be pleas'd to direct recommandé a Mons. Birtles, Consul Britanique a Gènnes.[1]

Text W MS ii. 14   *End. by W* [*Summary*] Recd 24 June.   Ad 25.

From Lord Hervey *22/11 June 1741*

Grosvenor Street, June 11/22, 1741

I have now, to my great Shame and to my great Pleasure, two Letters to thank you for; the one dated from Turin near a very disagreable Epoque of your Life,[2] and the other from Genoa, which I recieved this Morning; and I am in the most eager expectation of a third which you tell me is coming by my Son,[3] as I expect there to find your thoughts (charming in any dress but most so undress'd) stript of that useless Load of covering in which you are forced to wrap them when they come by the Post, and that like the coverings of the eastern Women when they go in public, are at once a Constraint and Encumberance to the Wearer, and cursed by those whose View they intercept and whose curiosity they disapoint. [*Passage omitted*]

As to your present Situation, on which you say you would ask my Advice if I was nearer, and follow it, it is impossible on ⟨?⟩ Subject you mean that Solomon and Socrates together could give you any so good as what you may give your-self. In the ⟨?⟩ where People's Pleasure and Interest clash foreign counsel may be of great use, but on the present Occasion as you have nothing but your Pleasure to consider, your own Breast must be your best Cabinet-Council, your Passions, Affections and Inclinations must compose it, and your Heart be the President of it. But as for its not being material because late in your Life, I am so far from saying what you supose I would say, that I think it the more material; the less one has left the more industrious

improperly be reckon'd your Pin-money) £300 a year, and instead of remitting 242.10. at Midsummer, shall remit you 250 and the like sum at Xmas. As this was not done the last Xmas, I shall remit you 250 for this L[ady] Day [25 March].... As you have been travelling about, the addition at this time may not be unreasonable' (W MS i. 122). With these increases LM's annual income was £1,100.

[1] John Birtles (d. ?1765), Consul at Genoa 1740–60 (Walpole, *Corr*. xvii. 92, n. 7).

[2] Her meeting with Algarotti.

[3] George William Hervey (1721–75), later 2nd Earl of Bristol. He had been studying abroad since 1738.

one should be to manage and improve it; and if I knew I was to dye at eight a Clock and lay uneasy, I would get up and have my Bed made at half an hour seven. Adieu, and for your *Oh where is now the soft etc.* I answer from Ovid.

> Intrat amor mentes Usu; dediscitur Usu [. . . .]
> Successore novo vincitur omnis Amor.[1]

[Passage omitted]

Text Bristol MS ii. 107–10   *Address* (par Paris) A Madame Madame de Montagu chez Monsr Vilette Ministre de sa Majesté Britannique à Turin   *Postmark* TR

From Lord Hervey 6 *July*/25 *June 1741*

June 25. 1741.

I have at last recieved your long expected Letter by my Son, and two more from Genoa, the one by a Courier, the other by the Post. They all came in the Compass of five Days, and consequently brought me a greater Share of Pleasure than I have generally been used to in as many Weeks. As to the ⟨first⟩, I assure you I have talk'd (with regard to the Court you therein mention) exactly the same Language this whole Sumer, and have made my-self hoarse with inculcating what you so iudiciously observe, assuring all I converse with on these Subjects, that one Map of Europe is worth all the Refinements of Tacitus, the Maxims of Machiavel and the whole Corps Diplomatique, when we are deliberating upon the Measures this Country ought to pursue,[2] and the Policy that ought to guide those who advise the Crown either in the Cabinet or the Parliament; but as almost every thing is call'd by an improper Name, so what is generally stiled Comon-Sense is in reality so uncomon, that when I say 3 and 2 make five, the answer I generally meet with from most of my Acquaintance is either that they believe I mistake, or at best that my Proposition requires consideration. *[Passage omitted]*

I will get the Books you desire and send them to You by the first Oportunity, but they are really fitter for the Kitten you mention than for you, for tho the tearing the Leaves may give that happy playfull animal some Entertainment, it is as morally impossible that the reading them should give you any, as it is for me to fancy the Black-berry

[1] 'By practice love comes into the mind, by practice love is unlearnt; all love is vanquished by a succeeding love' (*Remedia Amoris,* lines 503, 462; transl. adapted from Loeb Library).

[2] In the War of the Austrian Succession: whether to support or disavow the Pragmatic Sanction.

Bushes in Ickworth Park are as fragrant as the Orange-trees in your Salon at Genoa.

There is no Resolution yet taken in the Genoese affair.[1]

Text Bristol MS ii. 111–12

To Mme Chiara Michiel 6 *July* [*1741*]

Excellenza,

J'espere (ma tres chere Madame) que vous etes heureusement arrivé a Madrid, ou je ne doubte pas que vous brilliez de toutes façons. Je suis établi pour cette été a Gènnes, ou je trouvois un assez beau Palais, dans une Situation charmante, dont la vûe de la mer et la terre paroissent fait pour entretenir les Reveries. Les Dames sont fort poli, et m'ont fait toutes les civilitez possible. Veritablement une Étrangere n'est peut pas s'ÿ plaire ailleurs que dans une Republique; dans toutes les Cours (particulierement les petites) on est si occupé par mille Interêts de Haine ou d'Ambition, qu'on n'a pas le loisir de se divertir, ni de divertir les autres. Mais quoi qu'en effet je voye ici plusieurs personnes aimable, je vous jure que je ne voye rien qui approche de la Signora Chiara, et qu'il est impossible de la remplacer, ou de n'est pas la regretter tous les jours de ma vie; et je suis persuadé que tout le monde pense comme moi, qui a jamais eû l'honneur de joüir de vostre conversation delicieuse.

Je ne veux pas vous parler de nouvelles, dont vous etes (sans doute) mieux instruitte que moi, et que franchement ne m'intteresse guerre. Je me suis fait un plan de vie si éloigné du Tumulte du monde, que les plus grands évenemens me touchent, a peu pres, comme ceux que sont passé il y a cinq cens anns, et je suis ravy d'etre assez Maitresse de mon Destin, pour suivre le Goût que j'ai toujours eû pour la Tranquillité et l'obscurité. Pour vous, Madame, vous etes destinée a faire l'ornament d'une grande Cour; je vous y souhaitte toute sorte des plaisirs et d'agremens, mais malgre tous les amusemens que vostre état vous fournissent, je

[1] In June 1741 a British ship had violated Genoese neutrality by seizing a bark in the harbour. LM, in opposition to the British Consul, supported Genoa's protests (details in Halsband, *LM*, pp. 216–17).

pretends que vous trouviez quelque fois un quart d'heure pour m'écrire, et j'ai si bonne opinion de vostre Cœur q⟨ue je ne⟩ doute pas que vous voulez bien vous souven⟨ir⟩ d'une personne qui vous aime, et vous estime aussi parfaittement comme fait (Ma très chere Madame) de V. E. La tres humble et tres Obeissante Servante,

M. W. Montagu.

Juillet 6, Gènnes.

Addressez vos Lettres recommandez a Monsieur Birtles, Consul de Sa Majesté Britanique a Gènnes.

Text Bute MS   *Address* par Paris. A S. E. Madame La Signora Chiara Michielli Ambassadrice de la S. R. de Venise a la Cour de Madrid.[1]   *Postmark* D'ITALIE

To Wortley *15 July* [*1741*]

Genoa, July 15.

It is so long since I have heard from you, that thô I hope your silence is occasion'd by your being in the country, yet I cannot help being very uneasy and in some aprehension that you are indispos'd. I wrote you word some time ago that I have taken a House here for the remainder of the summer, and desir'd you would direct recomandé a Monsieur Birtles, Consul de S.M. Britanique.

I saw in the last news papers (which he sends me) the Death of Lord Oxford.[2] I am vex'd at it for the reasons you know, and recollect what I've often heard you say, that it is impossible to Judge what is best for our selves.

Text W MS ii. 15   *End. by W* [*Summary*] Ad 27 July.   Recd 20 July.

To Wortley *21 July* [*1741*]

Genoa, July 21. N.S.

I receiv'd halfe an hour ago yours of the 22nd of June. I wrote to give you thanks for the encrease of my allowance the

---

[1] Antonio Michiel did not present his credentials until 25 Oct. 1741.

[2] Edward Harley (b. 1689), 2nd Earl of Oxford, d. 16 June 1741.

first moment I had your Letter. I am not surpriz'd at delays or miscarriages of Letters in the present disturb'd state of Europe. I am very cautious what I write, and yet I find my Correspondance is not made secure by its Insignificancy. I will for the Future mark the Dates of my Letters,[1] but as I have not yet done it I cannot be particular as to those that are past, only I know that I have never been a fortnight without writeing.

I do not wonder at any change in the D[uchess] of Marlbrô's Court,[2] but have some small Curiosity to know if Mrs. Hammond keeps her Ground, which she got by routing Mrs. Dunch.[3]

I dare send you no News without the opertunity of a private conveyance, which is not very likely to fall in my way. I suppose you know our Freind the Procurator Grimani is chose Doge unanimously.[4] It is realy being Prisoner of State and I am very sorry for it, being sure that he is so.

Text W MS ii. 16–17   *Address* To Edwd Wortley Esqr in Cavendish Square London Angleterre   *Postmark* DE TURIN IY 27   *End. by* W [*Summary*] Ad 10 Aug.   Recd 27 Jul.

From Lord Hervey *27/16 July* [*1741*]

Grosvenor-Street, July 16. 17⟨41⟩

Dear Madam,

I have, according to your desire, deliver'd to Mr. Child the two Volumes of Dr. Middleton's Cicero, Mr. Cibber's Life, Pamela, and a Book you did not desire, which is the Memoirs of an Organist of

---

[1] In his letter of 22 June, W had enjoined LM to keep a list of the dates and subjects of her letters (W MS i. 124).

[2] Sarah (1660–1744), widow of 1st Duke of Marlborough.

[3] Mrs. Hammond, who in 1739 had tried to settle the Duchess's feud with her daughter the Duchess of Montagu (Stuart J. Reid, *John and Sarah Duke* *and Duchess of Marlborough*, 1914, pp. 428–9), was possibly Jane Clarges (d. 1749), widow of Anthony Hammond (1668–1738), and famous for her wit. Mrs. Elizabeth Dunch was related to the Duke (see above, p. 128, n. 2).

[4] Pietro Grimani was elected 30 June 1741 (Andrea da Mosto, *I Dogi di Venezia,* 1939, p. 298).

Ross,[1] all which Mr. Child has promised me to forward to Genoa or Leghorn by the first Oportunity. [*Passage omitted*]

The Genoese Affair has been under our Consideration and very proper Directions in my Opinion have been given for the termination of it, which I make no doubt will be comply'd with, and prevent your being anyway inconvenienced by a farther dispute between our Court and that Republic. I fear this is the only Squabble in Europe of which you will soon hear of any Conclusion; and wish rather than hope that you may not quickly hear of many important new ones breaking out.[2]

[*Passage in verse and prose omitted*]

Text Bristol MS ii. 113–14

To Wortley *29 July* [*1741*]

July 29. N.S., Genoa

I receiv'd yesterday the Bill for £250, for which I return you thanks.

If I wrote you all the political storys I hear, I should have a great deal to say. A great part is not true; and what I think so, I dare not mention in consideration of the various hands this paper must pass through before it reaches you.

Lord Lincoln and Mr. Walpole (youngest Son to Sir R[obert]) left this place 2 days ago. They visited me during their short stay.[3] They are gone to Marseilles and design passing some months in the South of France.[4]

Text W MS ii. 18   *End. by W* [*Summary*] Ad 10 Aug.   Recd 5 Aug.

[1] For *Cicero*, see above, p. 232; *Apology for the Life of Colley Cibber, Comedian* (1740); *Pamela; or, Virtue Rewarded* by Samuel Richardson (1740); and *The True Anti-Pamela; or, Memoirs of Mr. J. Parry* (1741). The last remains in her library (Sotheby Catalogue, 1 Aug. 1928, p. 96).

[2] The conclusion of the Genoese affair (see above, p. 242) was the Republic's vindication at the end of Aug. by an English law court.

[3] Horace Walpole, after having parted from his travelling companion, Thomas Gray, joined Lord Lincoln and Joseph Spence to continue his tour. On 19 July he wrote from Genoa to Mann that LM was there; and then after gossiping about her added: 'She has sent to desire to see us, and we shall go' (*Corr.* xvii. 91–92).

[4] From Genoa they sailed to Antibes, and continued by way of Toulon, Marseilles, and Aix to Paris; Walpole then returned directly to England (Walpole, 'Short Notes,' *Corr.* xiii. 10–11).

To Wortley *15 Aug.* [*1741*]

Aug't 15 N.S., Genoa.

I am sorry to trouble you on so disagreable a Subject as our Son, but I receiv'd a Letter from him last post in which he solicites your disolving his marriage, as if it was wholly in your power, and the reason he gives for it is that he may marry more to your satisfaction. It is very vexatious (thô no more than I expected) that time has no effect, and that it is impossible to convince him of his true Situation. He enclos'd this Letter in one to Mr. Birtles, and tells me that he does not doubt that debt of £200 is paid.[1] You may imagine this silly proceeding occasion'd me a Dun from Mr. Birtles. I told him the person that wrote the Letter was to my knowledge not worth a groat, which was all I thought proper to say on the subject.

Here is arriv'd a little while since, Count [*blank*],[2] who was President of the Council of War and enjoy'd many other great places under the late Emperor. He is a Spaniard. The next day after his arrival he went to the Doge[3] and declar'd him selfe his Subject, and from thence to the Arch Bishop[4] and desir'd to be receiv'd as one of his Flock. He has taken a great House at St. Pierre l'Arene where he sees few people, but what I think particular, he has brought with him 35 cases of Books.

I have had a particular account of Lord O[xford]'s death from a very good hand, which he advance'd by choice, refuseing all Remedys till it was too late to make use of them. There was a Will found dated 1728 in which he gave every thing to my Lady, which has affected her very much, notwithstanding the many reasons she had to complain of him.[5]

---

[1] See below, p. 270.

[2] Juan Antonio de Boixadors de Rocaberti (1673–1745), given by Charles VI the title of Count Savalla, was president of the Supreme Council of Flanders at Vienna (Alfred von Arneth, *Die Relationen der Botschafter Venedigs über Österreich*, 1863, p. 71). He died in Genoa. See also below, p. 254.

[3] Nicolò Spinola, Doge 1740–2.

[4] Nicolò Maria de Franchi (1657–1746), consecrated 1726.

[5] Henrietta Cavendish Holles (1694–1755) m. (1713) Lord Harley, later 2nd Earl of Oxford. His will, actually dated 1725, left his 'personalty', including his library, to his wife. Lord Orrery commented: 'The deceased earl has left behind him many books, many manuscripts, and no money: his lady brought

I allways thought there was more weakness than dishonesty in his actions, and is a confirmation of the Truth of that maxim of Mr. Rochefoûcault, un sot n'a pas assez d'étoffe pour estre honnête homme.[1]

Text W MS ii. 19–20   *Address* To Edwd Wortley Esqr in Cavendish Square London Angleterre   *Postmark* AV 19   *End. by W* [*Summary*] Ad 27 Aug.   Recd 19 Aug.

To Wortley 25 *Aug.* [*1741*]

Aug't 25. N.S.

I receiv'd yours of the 27th July this morning. I had that of March 19, which I answer'd very particularly the following post with many thanks for the encrease of my Allowance. It appears to me that the Letters I wrote between the 11th of April and 31st of May were lost, which I am not surpriz'd at. I was then at Turin, and that Court in a very great Confusion and extreme Jealous of me, thinking I came to examine their Conduct. I have some proofe of this, which I do not repeat least this should be stopp'd also.

The Manners of Italy are so much alter'd since we were here last, the alteration is scarce credible. They say it has been by the last War; the French being Masters introduce'd all their Customs, which were eagerly embrace'd by the Ladys and I beleive will never be laid aside, yet the Different Governments makes different manners in every state. You know, thô the Republic is not rich, here are many private Familys vastly so, and live at a great superfluous expence. All the people of the first Quality keeps Coaches as fine as the Speaker's,[2] and some of them 2 or 3, tho the streets are too narrow to use them in the Town; but they take the air in them, and their chairs carry them to the Gates. The Liverys are all plain, gold or silver being forbidden to be worn

him five hundred thousand pounds, four of which have been sacrificed to indolence, good-nature, and want of worldly wisdom: and there will still remain, after proper sales and right management, five thousand a year for his widow' (Swift,

Corr., ed. H. Williams, 1963–5, v. 206).
    [1] The maxim (No. 387 in Pléiade ed., 1957) ends: 'pour être bon'.
    [2] The Speaker of the House of Commons had a great gilded coach for his use on ceremonial occasions.

within the Walls. The Habits are all oblig'd to be Black, but they wear exceeding fine Lace and Linnen, and in their Country houses, which are gennerally in the Fauxbourg, they dress very rich, and have extreme fine Jewells. Here is nothing cheap but Houses; a Palace fit for a Prince may be hir'd for £50 per Annum, I mean unfurnish'd. All Games of chance are strictly prohibited, and it seems to me the only Law they do not try to evade. They play at Quadrille, Picquet etc., but not high.[1] Here are no regular public assemblys. I have been visited by all of the first Rank, and invited to several fine Dinners, particularly to the Wedding of one of the House of Spinola, where there was 96 sat down to Table, and I think the Entertainment one of the finest I ever saw. There was the night following a Ball and Supper for the same Company with the same profusion. They tell ⟨me all⟩ their great marriages are kept in the same public manner. No body keeps more than 2 Horses, all their Journeys being post. The expence of them includeing the Coachman is (I am told) £50 per Annum. A chair is very near as much; I give 18 franks[2] a week for mine. The Senators can converse with no Strangers during the Time of their Magistracy, which lasts 2 years. The number of servants are regulated and allmost every Lady has the same, which is 2 footmen, a Gentleman usher, and a page, which follow her chair.

Text W MS ii. 21–22   *Address* To Edwd Wortley Esqr in Cavendish Square London Angleterre   *Postmark* DE TURIN AV 31   *End.* *by W* L.M. 25 Aug. 1741.   Customs of Genoa. Ad 17 Sept. Recd 31 Aug.

[1] Charles de Brosses, who visited Genoa shortly before, also remarked that the nobles dressed in black, and that 'la dépense de ces gens-là qui n'ont ni habits, ni équipages, ni tables, ni jeux, ni chevaux, n'est pas considérable; cependant ils sont d'une richesse excessive' (*Lettres familières sur l'Italie*, ed. Y. Bezard, 1931, i. 55–56). In 1718 LM had remarked on several of these customs in Genoa (i. 430).

[2] About 15 shillings.

To Wortley *8 Sept.* [*1741*]

Sept 8. N.S., Genoa

It is a great pleasure to me to hear by yours of Aug't 8th (which I receiv'd this day) that you are in perfect Health. I should not be surpriz'd if our Son was sincerely an Enthusiast. Mr. Anderson[1] told me that at Troyes he had a fit of praying for 4 or 5 hours together, and that he was with difficulty hinder'd from going into a Convent, thô I think his last letter to me, of which I have given you an Account, does not look like it, since he desires to marry thô his Wife is alive. 'Tis true no Inconsistency is to be wonder'd at in such a Head as his. I expect nothing from him but going from one Species of Folly to another. Folly (as Mons. Rochefoûcault remarks) is the only incorrigible Fault.[2] This is a very nice subject for me to write on, but I think it my Duty to put you in mind that in so near a Relation as that of Father and Son, there is no medium between a thorough displeasure and a thorough Reconciliation. If you take the latter party, I am persuaded there is nothing you can do for him that he will not think very little, and that he will not [*sic*] find people to be of his mind. I very well know him; he is capable of making up a fine story to move pity, and can behave himselfe so to the Eye of a Stranger as to make a tolerable Figure even to a Man of Sense that does not give himselfe the trouble of a nice Observation, which very few people do in a matter that does not personally concern them. I have no regard to what Murray says.[3] He is a proffess'd Patron of Pope's, very likely to be prejudice'd by his Lyes, and not a sincere man, of which I know a very strong instance which perhaps I never told you, it being related to me in Confidence very little before I left England.

[1] John Anderson had been Montagu's tutor and companion since at least 1732, when they lived at Troyes (his letters to LM, W MS iv. 150–3). He was a Highland Scot (John Fleming, *Robert Adam and His Circle*, 1962, p. 226).

[2] LM apparently telescoped these two maxims of La Rochefoucauld: 'La folie nous suit dans tous les temps de la vie....' and 'La faiblesse est le seul défaut que l'on ne saurait corriger' (Nos. 207, 130, Pléiade ed., 1957).

[3] William Murray, famous jurist and later Earl of Mansfield. He was an adviser and close friend of Alexander Pope.

In General, most people are readily dispos'd to be (what they call) good natur'd and Generous at the Expence of another; add to this the lavish promises of Eternal Service and Freindship which your Son is ready to make to every body he sees. I am clearly of Opinion that whoever you send over to him, you will have no just information. I speak on this Subject without any Prejudice whatever. I hope and beleive I shall never know who is your Heir; consequently in regard to my selfe, it is a thing quite indifferent. But I should think I was guilty of breach of Trust to you if I conceal'd my real thoughts on this occasion. Anger and Compassion are equal weaknesses, and a Wise Man never suffers himselfe to be influence'd by either in a⟨ny⟩ Action of Consequence. I think your only Error ⟨has⟩ been too much lenity to him; if he had been forc'd again to Sea, when he first deserted it after making it his request to be place'd there, it had hinder'd a long train of succeeding Mischeife. Mr. Edgecombe takes the most prudent method with his Son in keeping him at a distance, thô he has not committed halfe the notorious Follys of ours, and is a youth of Bright parts. His allowance is no more than £300 per Annum.[1] If you are reconcil'd to him you must resolve to pay his debts etc.; if you are determin'd otherwise, I would hear no body speak on that Subject.

I desire you to forgive the Liberty I have taken in explaining my selfe so fully. My Intention is good, and if I mistake, it is a fault of Judgment. I wrote to him last post, and will do it often, as you direct.

Text W MS ii. 23–24   *Address* To Edwd Wortley Esqr in Cavendish Square London Angleterre   *Postmark* DE TURIN SE 14   *End. by W* [*Summary*] Ad 17 Sept.   Recd 14 Sept.

[1] As LM had pointed out before (p. 186 above).

To Mme Chiara Michiel *9 Sept.* [*1741*]

Sept. 9, Gennes

Excellenza,

J'ai reçeû avec tres grande plaisir (ma chere Madame) les nouvelles du vostre santé, de vostre heureuse arrivé a Madrid, et de la continuation de vos bontez pour moi, toutes des choses qui m'interesse infiniment. Mais que je vous plains! a la fleur de vostre age, charmante comme vous etes, de perdre trois annees de vostre Vie[1] parmi des Bêtes trop sot pour sçavoir vous admirer, et trop ignorant pour vous amuser: il faut esperer que Venus vous envoyra quelque Prince étranger digne de vous adorer; sans cela, je ne voye aucune resource pour vous. Vous ne pouvez pas perdre l'habitude de charmer; c'est un don naturel dont vous ne pouvez pas vous defaire, mais c'est bien triste de l'excercir sur des animaux tel que vous me les depeignez.

La vie de Gènnes est assez douce, mais je ne laisse pas de regretter Venise a tout moment. J'ai eû une Lettre de Mons. Mackinsie ou il me presse d'ÿ retourner, comme le seul sejour qui me convient; c'est un cœur d'Ange que celui de cet Garçon. Il me demande de vos nouvelles, et je ne suis pas surpris qu'on ne vous oublie jamais.

Je ne sçai ce que je deviendrois, et je suis toujours dans l'incertitude; je refflechi trop, et peutestre vos Dames espagnoles sont plus heureuse, qui ne reffiechissent jamais.

Mon Baggage est arrivé sain et sauf, et je passe des Journées entieres parmi la poussiere de mes Livres. Helas! Madame, pour quoy ne puis-je pas les conclure aupres de vous? Mais je ne veux pas vous ennuyer en poussant des Helas. Au bout de compte, chacun a son Fardeau, et il me prends quelque fois la fantaisie de me jetter a la mer, par curiosité pour voir si l'autre monde n'a pas quelques scenes pour [*sic*] divertisant que je ne trouve dans celui ci.[2]

---

[1] Antonio Michiel was evidently appointed ambassador for three years; he served until 4 Aug. 1744 (*Repertorium*, ii. 416).

[2] LM repeated this idea a few years later in an essay complaining that the boredom of Avignon (where she lived 1742–6) was so great that she wanted to throw herself into the Rhône (W MS viii; extracts in Halsband, *LM*, p. 232).

Pendant que j'ÿ suis, en quel endroit que je serois, vous aurois toujours de mes nouvelles; donnez moi des vostres, et tachons de nous consoler en nous communi⟨cant⟩ nos deplaisirs. Mon plus sensible sera toujours vostre absence, étant avec la plus tendre estime, Madame, de V. E. La tres humble et tres Obeissante Servante,

M. W. Montagu.

Text Bute MS   *Address* A S. Excellence Madame Madame l'Ambassadrice de la S. Republique de Venise a Madrid. *Postmark* GENOVA

To Wortley *18 Sept.* [*1741*]

Genoa, Sept 18. N.S.

I am frighted out of Italy by the encreasing of the report of the comeing of the Spaniards, who are now expected here daily.[1] I am not apt to credit Public report, but I perceive it is more generally beleiv'd than ever; the Imperial Minister retir'd from this place yesterday,[2] so that I think it would be imprudence to stay. I go to Geneva; if the circumstances alter I may return.

William and Mary[3] both declar'd that they will not pass the Alpes, which puts me to a great deal trouble, they not making this Declaration till halfe my things were pack'd up. The Truth is, they have both behav'd very ill for above a Twelve month in hopes to provoke me to turn them away, that I might be at the Expence of their Journey to England; but I have suffer'd all their Sauciness with the Temper of Socrates, knowing that a great many faults are to be overlook'd for the sake of having people about me that at least would not rob or murder me. But there being a Dutch ship arriv'd in Port, who has offer'd them a cheap passage, they

[1] In the War of the Austrian Succession Spain claimed the Habsburg possessions in Italy.

[2] Giovanni Orazio, Count Guicciardi, Austrian minister since 5 Nov. 1740; his last dispatch from Genoa is dated 19 Aug. 1741 (*Repertorium*, ii. 254). He came of a Modenese family that had moved to Austria early in the century.

[3] William and Mary Turner, her servants who had accompanied her from England.

have made the Bargain without giveing me any warning; in
short, I must do as well as I can. As to William, I can easily
enough find another in his Place, but I should be sorry to be
without an English maid that I could in some measure depend on in the case of Sickness or other Accidents. I therefore wish that Mary, the House maid who liv'd with me
when I left London, might be sent to Geneva. There are
great conveniencies of travelling cheap through France. I
desire you would take the charges of her Journey out of the
next Quarter's allowance. This vexation hinder'd my sleeping last night, and has discompos'd me so much that I am
afraid I have wrote a very sad Letter, but I hope it is In-
telligible. If Mary will not come, I do not desire any other
to be sent in her room. I think of her because I ⟨know⟩ her
to be sensible and handy.

Text W MS ii. 25–26   *Address* To Edwd Wortley Esqr in Cavendish Square London Angleterre   *Postmark* SE 21   *End. by W* [*Summary*] Ad 26 Oct.   Recd 21 Sept.

To Wortley *19 Sept.* [*1741*]

Genoa, Sept. 19 N.S.

I am realy asham'd to write you this Letter. You will
think me very changable in my Resolutions, but Mary and
William, finding that I would not ask them to stay (as I
suppose they hop'd), have repented their Folly, and on their
Tears and promises of a better behaviour for the Future, I
have forgiven them and shall take them along with me.

When I am at Geneva I shall write you my observations
on Italy in a freer manner.

Text W MS ii. 27   *End. by W* [*Summary*] Ad 26 Oct.   Rec. 24 Sept.

To Wortley *22 Sept.* [*1741*]

Sept. 22. N.S., Genoa

I receiv'd yesterday yours of Aug't 27th O.S. and send you the enclos'd according to your order.

The Spaniard that has establish'd himselfe in St. Pierre l'Arene is call'd Count Savilari. If I omitted his name when I mention'd him it was by mistake. He was President of the Council of Flanders and had many other great places under the late Emperor, to whom (they say) he was much a Favourite. He lives here very retir'd, but keeps 2 Coaches and has a great Family of servants. I have never seen him, he visiting no Ladys. He brought with him a Priest and 2 Abbés that are allmost all his Company. I propose setting out for Geneva next monday. The Weather is now very fine, thô we have had great Rains. I expect to pass my time in that little Town

> nunc veterum libris, nunc ⟨som⟩no, et inertibus horis,
> ducere sollicitæ jucunda oblivia vitæ.[1]

Text W MS ii. 28–29   *Address* To Edwd Wortley Esqr in Cavendish Square London Angleterre   *Postmark* DE TURIN SE 28   *End. by W* [*Summary*] Ad 26 Oct.   Recd 28.

To Lady Pomfret *2 Oct.* [*1741*]

Turin, October 2nd.

I had the honour of seeing Lord Lempster[2] yesterday, who told me to my great surprize your letter complains of my silence, while I was much mortified at yours, having never heard once from you since I left Leghorn, though I have wrote several times. I suppose our frequent removals have occasioned this breach in our correspondence, which it will

---

[1] . . . now with books of the ancients, now with sleep and idle hours, to quaff sweet forgetfulness of life's cares' (Horace, *Satires*, ii. vi. 61–62; transl. Loeb Library).

[2] Lady Pomfret's eldest son.

be a great pleasure to me to renew. I hear you are very well diverted at Bruxelles;[1] I am very much pleased here, where the people in general are more polite and obliging than in most parts of Italy.

I am told Lady Walpole is at present at Verona, and intends to pass the carnival at Venice. Mrs. Prat[2] passed this way last week; the Duchess of Buckingham is daily expected.[3] Italy is likely to be blessed with the sight of English ladies of every sort and size. I staid some time at Genoa, tempted to it by the great civilities I received there, and the opportunity of hiring a palace in the most beautiful situation I ever saw. I was visited there by Lord Lincoln and Mr. Walpole, who informed me that you hurried away from Venice, designing for England. I hope some good occasion has stopped you. I do not doubt you have heard Mrs. Goldsworthy's melancholy history; which is very comical.[4] I saw often Signora Clelia Durazzo, who was your friend and very much mine; and we had the pleasure of talking frequently of your ladyship, in many parties we had together.[5] I have thus given you a long account of my travels, I hope to have in return the history of yours.

I am told, since I began this letter, that Miss Windsor, who is very well married in Holland (I forget the name),[6] is

[1] From Rome Lady Pomfret had travelled through Bologna, Venice, Augsburg, and Frankfurt, reaching Brussels in July 1741 (Hertford, *Corr.* i. xxiii; iii. 311).

[2] Henrietta (1676–1769), da. of Sir John Brookes, widow of John Pratt. She travelled with the Duchess of Buckingham, from whom she inherited a considerable fortune (*Gentleman's Mag.*, 1769, pp. 461–2).

[3] Katherine Darnley (1682–1743), illegitimate daughter of James II, and widow of the 1st Duke of Buckingham. She was probably on her way home after visiting her half-brother the Pretender in Rome; and by the end of Dec. 1741 reached London (Walpole, 'Reminiscences', *Works*, 1798, iv. 316; *Corr.* xvii. 253–4).

[4] Philippia Vanbrugh (*c.* 1716–77) m. (1734) Burrington Goldsworthy,

British Consul in Leghorn 1736. She had been the mistress of Gen. Carl Franz von Wachtendonck, commander of the Emperor's Tuscan forces, their liaison lasting from about 1737 until his death in Aug. 1741. It was then discovered that the General had been paying her for her services (Warren H. Smith, 'La Belle Consulesse', *Originals Abroad*, 1952, pp. 34–5).

[5] When Lady Pomfret had visited Genoa two years before, 'la signora Durazzi, a woman of infinite wit, and agreeable conversation, always entertained' her (Hertford, *Corr.* i. 107).

[6] Catherine (1715–42), da. of 1st Viscount Windsor, m. (27 April 1741) Mattheus Lestevenon van Berkenrode (1715–97), diplomatist (*Nieuw Nederlandsch Biog. Woordenboek*, 1911–37, x. 599). She was Lady Pomfret's half-sister. To Horace Mann she seemed 'a little

gone to Naples. I think I was very unlucky not to meet with her; I should be very glad to have an opportunity of shewing my regard to your ladyship, in serving any of your relations; and perhaps my experience might be of some use to a stranger. If my intelligence from hence can be any way agreeable to you, you have a right to command it. I wish I could shew you more effectually how much I am Ever yours,

M.W.M.

Be pleased to direct, 'recommandé à Mons. Villette, Ministre de S.M. Britanique'.

Text 1837, ii. 256–7

To Wortley *12 Oct.* [*1741*]

Geneva, Oct. 12.

I arriv'd here last night, where I find every thing quite different from what it was represented to me. It is not the first time it has happen'd to me in my travells. Every thing is as dear as it is at London; 'tis true as all Equipages are forbidden, that Expence is entirely retrench'd. I have been visited this Morning by some of the Cheife people in the Town, who seem extreme good sort of people, which is their general character, very desirous of attracting strangers to inhabit with them, and consequently very officious in all they imagine can please them. The way of living is absolutely the reverse of that in Italy. Here is no shew and a great deal of eating. There is all the Magnificence imaginable, and no Dinners but on particular Occasions, yet the difference of the Prices renders the total Expence very near equal. As I am not yet determin'd whither I shall make any Considerable Stay, I desire not to have the money you intend me till I ask for it.

If you have any Curiosity for ⟨the⟩ present state of any of the States of Italy, I beleive I can give you a truer account than perhaps any other Traveller can do, having allways had

pert pretty patriot. . . . She is tired of Italy nor can conceive how her sister could like it' (Walpole, *Corr.* xvii. 200–1).

PLATE 5

Henrietta, Countess of Oxford, and her daughter, Lady Margaret Harley,
later Duchess of Portland

From a painting attributed to Michael Dahl

the good fortune of a sort of Intimacy with the first persons in the Governments where I resided, and they not guarding themselves against the Observations of a Woman as they would have done from those of a Man.

Text W MS ii. 30–31   *Address* To Edwd Wortley Esqr in Cavendish Square London Angleterre [*in another hand*] par Amsterdam *Postmark* OC 15   *End. by W* [*Summary*] Ad 26 Oct.   Recd 15 Oct.

To Wortley *22 Oct.* [*1741*]

Oct. 22. N.S., Geneva

I have this minute receiv'd yours of the 17th of Sept'r. I am not at all surpriz'd my Son should say that it is my Fault you are not reconcil'd to him. He told Lister[1] so, and I perceiv'd he had said the same thing to G[ibson], thô he did not tell it to me in so plain terms as the other. He had before said it to my selfe when he was hot headed at the Periwig maker's in St. Albans street, adding that every body was of that opinion. I thought then that this was put into his head by Forester[2] from Pope. I am very sorry you should have had any uneasyness on the account of my not writeing often to him. I wrote from Turin, which I do not find he receiv'd. Since that I have wrote twice from Genoa; I suppose he has receiv'd them. During the whole time I was at Genoa there was not one English merchant ship put into that Port. I have now left a Box for the Dutchess of Portland[3] in the hands of the Consul, who does not expect any opertunity of sending it till it is determin'd whither or no the Spaniards intend for Italy, which I hear differently spoke of here.

This Place is exactly like an English Country Town, The

---

[1] Not identified.

[2] The Rev. John Forster of Elstree, Montagu's tutor from the time of the boy's return from Gibralter, had been sent with him to the West Indies for a few years (Wh MS 439; Forster's account in *Public Ledger*, 25 Oct. 1777, reprinted in John Nichols, *Lit. Anecdotes of the 18th Century*, 1812–15, iv. 626–9).

[3] Margaret Cavendish Harley (1715–85) m. (1734) 2nd Duke of Portland. She was Lady Oxford's only daughter and a close friend of Lady Bute's. Since she was a great collector (the famous Portland Vase was acquired by her), the box may have contained *objets d'art* purchased for her.

Prospects very pretty to any Eye that had not seen Naples or Genoa. I should prefer the first to any other place of residence in consideration of the Beauty and climate, if the Customs were more agreable or our Nations on better Terms, but in all Arbitrary Courts the Subjects dare not have a long or familiar acquaintance with any Stranger that is not well with the Government. I beleive the Councils all over Europe change very often; a short time, however, must determine them. In General, it is a Melancholy Refflexion to see how far our National esteem is sunk in all foreign Courts; in particular, I have found every where more regard than I had reason to expect.

Your Busy time is now approaching;[1] I hope no Engagements whatever will occasion you to hazard your Health.

Text W MS ii. 32–33   *Address* To Edwd Wortley Esqr in Cavendish Square London Angleterre par Paris [*added in another hand*] franc pr Paris   *Postmark* GENEVE OC 22   *End. by* W [*Summary*] Ad 26 Oct   Recd 22 Oct.

To Wortley 5 *Nov.* [*1741*]

Geneva, Nov. 5. N.S.

I have now been here a month. I have wrote to you 3 times without hearing from you, and cannot help being uneasy at your silence. I think this air does not agree with my Health. I have had a return of many complaints from which I had an entire cessation during my Stay in Italy, which makes me encline to return thither, thô a Winter Journey over the Alps is very disagreable. The People here are very well to be lik'd, and this little Republic has an air of the Simplicity of Old Rome in its earliest Age. The Magistrates toil with their own Hands, and their Wives litterally dress their Dinners against their Return from their little Senate. Yet without dress or Equipage, 'tis as dear living here for a stranger as in Places where one is oblig'd to both, from the price of all sort of

---

1 W had been re-elected M.P. for Peterborough in May, and Parliament was to convene on 1 Dec. 1741.

provision, which they are forc'd to buy from their Neighbours, having allmost no Land of their own.

I am very impatient to hear from you. Here are many
reports concerning the English affairs, which I am sometimes
spleenatic enough to give credit to.

Text W MS ii. 34–35   *Address* To Edwd Wortley Esqr in Cavendish Square London Angleterre par Paris [*added in another hand*] franc
pr Paris   *Postmark* GENEVE   NO 5   *End. by W* [*Summary*] Ad
1 Dec.   Recd 4 Nov.

To Wortley *15 Nov.* [*1741*]

Chamberry, Nov. 15. N.S.

Your last Letter (which I receiv'd at Geneva) was dated
Sept. 17, since which I have not heard from you, which makes
me very uneasy. I have left that Town on the account of the
sharpness of the Air, which disagreed with me very much.

I find I was very rightly inform'd of the projected descent
of the Spaniards; what will be the Event is uncertain. I had
the good nature to tell it in private to the Consul (without
mentioning my Informer) but being a very wise Man he was
so positively assur'd of the Freindship of the French, he only
told me it was impossible.[1]

I am now at the door of Italy. You know this Town is old
and ill built,[2] but is wholly inhabited by the poor Savoyard
Nobillity, who are very well bred and extreamly carressing
to strangers.

I have wrote to you several times since I heard from you.
I had a letter last post from my Daughter,[3] who says she is
again with child. I have had no answer to the Letter I wrote
to my Son. I will write again.

Be pleas'd to direct your next recommandé a Monsieur

---

[1] John Birtles at Genoa was called by
Walpole 'as unlicked a poor cub as ever
I saw' (*Corr.* xvii. 92).

[2] Lord Orrery found it 'one of the
poorest, dirtiest, filthiest towns' he had
ever seen (1754, *Letters from Italy*, 1774,

p. 33). Other travellers concur, even as
late as Henry James in 1872: 'There is
shabbiness and shabbiness. . . .' (*Trans-
atlantic Sketches*, 1875, p. 72).

[3] No letters from Lady Bute to LM
can now be found.

Guillaume Boisier[1] a Geneve; I am told it is the safest method of conveying Letters hither. I beg you would write soon; when you are long silent I am so uneasy on the account of your Health that it affects mine.

Text W MS ii. 36–37   *Address* To Edwd Wortley Esqr in Cavendish Square London Angleterre par Paris   *Postmark* DE CHAMBERY NO 20   *End. by W* [*Summary*] Ad 1 Dec.

To Wortley 22 *Nov.* [*1741*]

Chambery, Nov. 22. N.S.

I wrote to you last post, but am afraid it has miscarry'd, not being frank'd as it ought to have been.

I left Geneva, finding the sharpness of that air did not agree with me. I am much better here, but in great uneasyness on account of your long Silence. I have not heard from you since I left Genoa, thô I have wrote many times. Till I hear from you I shall have no quiet in my Mind.

Direct to Mr. Guillaume Boissier a Geneve; I am told there is no other safe Direction.

Text W MS ii. 38   *End. by W* [*Summary*] Ad 1 Dec.

To Wortley 30 *Nov.* [*1741*]

Nov. 30. N.S., Chambery.

I receiv'd this morning yours of Oct. 26, which has taken me out of the uneasyness of fearing for your Health. I suppose you know before this, the Spaniards are landed at Different Ports in Italy etc. When I receiv'd early information of the Design I had the charity to mention it to the English Consul (without nameing my Informer). He laugh'd, and answer'd it was impossible. This may serve for a small specimen of the general good Inteligence our wise Ministry has of all Foreign affairs. If you were acquainted with the

[1] Boissier (1690–1759) (J.-A. Galiffe, *Notices généalogiques sur les familles genevoises*, 1830, i. 281).

people they employ, you would not be surpriz'd at it. Except Mr. Villette at Turin (who is a very reasonable Man) there is not one of them who know any thing more of the Country they inhabit than that they eat and sleep in it.

I have wrote you word that I left Geneva on the sharpness of the Air, which much disagreed with me. I find my selfe better here; thô the Weather is very cold at present, yet this situation is not subject to those terrible Winds which reign at Geneva.

I dare write you no News thô I hear a great deal.

Direct to me at Chambery, en Savoye, par Paris.

Text W MS ii. 39–40   *Address* To Edwd Wortley Esqr in Cavendish Square London Angleterre par Paris   *Postmark* DE CHAMBERY NO 30   *End. by W* [*Summary*] Recd 30 Nov. Ad 30 Nov.

To Lady Pomfret 3 Dec. [1741]

Chambery, December 3, N.S.

At length, dear madam, I have the pleasure of hearing from you; I hope you have found every thing in London to your satisfaction.[1] I believe it will be a little surprize to you to hear that I am fixed for this winter in this little obscure town; which is generally so much unknown, that a description of it will at least have novelty to recommend it. Here is the most profound peace and unbounded plenty, that is to be found in any corner of the universe; but not one rag of money. For my part, I think it amounts to the same thing, whether one is obliged to give several pence for bread, or can have a great deal of bread for a penny, since the Savoyard nobility here keep as good tables, without money, as those in London, who spend in a week what would be here a considerable yearly revenue. Wine, which is equal to the best Burgundy, is sold for a penny a quart, and I have a cook for very small wages, that is capable of rivalling Chloé.[2] Here are no equipages but chairs, the hire of which is about a crown

---

[1] The Pomfrets arrived in London on 20/9 Oct. (Walpole, *Corr.* xvii. 165, n. 5).

[2] The famous French cook employed by the Duke of Newcastle.

a week, and all other matters proportionable. I can assure you I make the figure of the Duchess of Marlborough, by carrying gold in my purse, there being no visible coin but copper. Yet we are all people that can produce pedigrees to serve for the Order of Malta. Many of us have travelled, and 'tis the fashion to love reading. We eat together perpetually, and have assemblies every night for conversation. To say truth, the houses are all built after the manner of the old English towns, nobody having had money to build for two hundred years past. Consequently the walls are thick, the roofs low, &c. the streets narrow, and miserably paved. However, a concurrence of circumstances obliges me to this residence for some time.

You have not told me your thoughts of Venice. I heartily regret the loss of those letters you mention, and have no comfort but in the hopes of a more regular correspondence for the future. I cannot compassionate the Countess, since I think her insolent character deserves all the mortifications Heaven can send her. It will be charity to send me what news you pick up, which will be always shewn advantageously by your relation. I must depend upon your goodness for this; since I can promise you no return from hence, but the assurances that I am Ever faithfully yours.

Be pleased to direct as before to Mons. Villette, as the super-direction. Here are no such vanities as gilt paper, therefore you must excuse the want of it.

Text 1837, ii. 258–9

To Wortley *22 Dec.* [*1741*]

Chambery, Dec. 22

I have not heard from you since I came to this place but I think it very possible the Letters may have miscarry'd. At this crisis all are suspected and open'd, and consequently often lost. I send this by way of Geneva, and desire you would direct thither for me, recommended to Monsieur Guillaume Boisier.

The Company here is very good and sociable, and I have reason to beleive the Air the best in the World, if I am to form a Judgment of it from the health and Long Life of the Inhabitants. I have halfe a dozen Freinds, male and female, who are all of them near or past fourscore, who look and go about as if they were but forty. The provisions of all sorts are extreme good, and the Wine is (I think) the most agreable I ever tasted; and thô the Ground is now cover'd with snow, I know no body trouble'd with colds, and I observe very few chronical distempers. The greatest Inconvenience of the Country is the few tolerable rides that are to be pick'd out, the roads being all Mountainous and stony. However, I have got a little horse, and sometimes amble about after the maner of the D[uchess] of Cleveland, which is the only fashion of rideing here.[1]

I am very impatient to hear from you, and hope your Busyness does not injure you Health.

Text W MS ii. 41–42   *Address* To Edwd Wortley Esqr in Cavendish Square London Angleterre par Paris [*added in another hand*] franc pr Paris   *Postmark* GENEVE   IA 5   *End. by W* [*Summary*] Rec'd 5 Jan.   Ad 7th.

To Lady Mar [*?1741*]

Birth of her Ladyship's grandchild.[2]

Text Summary in 19th-century hand; album among Mar and Kellie MS

[1] Although LM had sent for her side-saddle (above, pp. 141–2) she was riding astride, the manner customary for Italian ladies (Tobias Smollett, *Travels in France and Italy*, 1765, Letter 35). The Duchess who rode thus was evidently (see below, p. 393) wife of the 2nd Duke.

[2] This ambiguous phrase almost cer-tainly summarizes LM's letter to Lady Mar of 10 Aug. [1744], printed in vol. iii, Appendix II. Or possibly it refers to John Francis Erskine (d. 1825), son of Lady Frances Erskine, who had mar-ried her cousin the previous year; in 1824 he was restored to the Earldom of Mar forfeited by his grandfather.

To Wortley *21 Jan.* [*1742*]

Chambery, Jan. 21.

I have wrote to you from hence several times, and am inexpressibly uneasy at receiving no answer. I cannot imagine the reason of your silence and am in the utmost aprehensions for your Health. I beg in the most earnest manner you would let me hear from you, tho only 2 lines. I will not trouble you with a long letter, and am indeed too much disorder'd to write one.

Direct to Mons. Guillaume Boisier a Geneve, who will take care to send it to me.

Text W MS ii. 43   *End. by W* [*Summary*] Ad 28 Jan.   Recd 28 Jan.

To Wortley *9 Feb.* [*1742*]

Feb. 9, Chambery

I receiv'd Yesterday yours of the 7th of Jan., which brought me the good news of your Health. That which you mention of the 30th of November never came to my Hands, which is easy to be accounted for from the present disturb'd state of Europe, which intterupts Commerce of all sorts.

The news I have lately heard of the dreadfull Earthquake at Leghorn, which (I am told) has almost destroy'd the whole Town, will I fear be sensibly felt by our Merchants at London.[1] I have very fortunately withdrawn all my things from thence, as I luckily left Florence last year a fortnight before the great Inundation.[2] I have sent you so many accounts of this little Town I will not trouble you with a repetition of them. I am glad my Daughter will have the happyness of being with you.[3] I hope she will be sensible of your goodness to her by every instance of Duty and affection.

Text W MS ii. 44   *Address* [*cut off*]   *Postmark* ⟨?⟩ 11   *End. by W* [*Summary*] Ad 22.   Recd 12 Feb.

[1] The devastating earthquake at the end of Jan. was reported in detail by Mann (Walpole, *Corr.* xvii. 284, 303–5).

[2] Described on 4 Dec. 1740 by Lady Pomfret (Hertford, *Corr.* ii. 187–8) and by Walpole (*Corr.* xiii. 237).

[3] Lady Bute had evidently come to London for her lying-in and stayed at W's house in Cavendish Square. On 13 April 1742 she bore a daughter, Jane.

To Wortley *24 Feb.* [*1742*]

Chambery, Feb. 24. N.S.

I will not trouble you with long letters in your present hurry, which I am sensible hardly allows you time for reading them. I have receiv'd yours of Jan. 27. I very much fear the fatigue of your long attendances.[1] I have wrote this post to Mr. Child for money, as you order'd me.

Text W MS ii. 45   *End. by W* [*Summary*] Ad 21 Mar.   Recd 1 Mar.

To Lady Pomfret *4 March* [*1742*]

Chambery, March 4, N.S.

I know not whether to condole or congratulate your ladyship on the changes in England; but whatever they are, I hope they will no way turn to your disadvantage. The present prospect of war in Italy hinders my return thither; and I live here in so much health and tranquility, I am in no haste to remove. I am extremely glad to hear your affairs are settled to your satisfaction; I expect Lady Sophia shall be so very soon; at least, if my correspondents are not much mistaken in England, I shall have the honour of being her relation; and as I have had a long and familiar conversation with her lover, both at Rome and Genoa, I think he has a very uncommon merit, which may deserve her uncommon beauty;[2] which I am told is the admiration of her own country, as it was that of every other through which she passed. I know

[1] After Walpole's fall from power— he resigned 22/11 Feb.—W's activity in Parliament would be more vigorous. He had supported the unsuccessful impeachment proceedings in Feb. 1740 (Rich. Chandler, *Hist. and Proc. of the H. of C.*, 1742–4, XIII, ii. 181).

[2] In Florence Lord Lincoln—who was a distant relation of LM's—had fallen in love with Lady Sophia Fermor.

He wrote an eloquent account of his passion to his uncle the Duke of Newcastle (8 April 1741, Add. MS 33,065, ff. 405–7), and later talked to Horace Walpole of his determination to marry her in spite of her lack of fortune (*Corr.* xvii. 91). But by Sept. 1741, on his way home, he had given up hope of marrying her, as he informed his uncle (quoted in Walpole, *Corr.* xxx. 23, n. 14).

not whether to say Sir William Lemon was very unlucky in not dying two years before he had committed a folly which will make his memory ridiculous; or very fortunate in having time given him, to indulge his inclination, and not time enough to see it in its proper light.[1]

The Marquis of Beaufort[2] is one of my best friends here; he speaks English as well as if he had been born amongst us, and often talks to me of Miss Jefferys.[3] The finest seat in this country belongs to him; it is very near the town, finely furnished; and he has taken pleasure in making it resemble an English house. I have dined there several times. He has been married about seven years. His lady is a well-bred agreeable woman; and he has a little daughter about six years old, that is an angel in face and shape. She will be the greatest heiress of this province, and his ambition is to marry her in England.[4]

The manners and fashions of this place copy those of Paris. Here are two assemblies, always concluding with a good supper; and we have had balls during the carnival, twice a week; which, though neither so numerous nor magnificent as those in London, were perhaps full as agreeable. After having given your ladyship a sketch of this town, you may imagine I expect a return of intelligence from London; how you pass your time, and what changes and chances happen amongst our acquaintance. When you see Lady E. Spelman,[5] or Mrs. Bridgman,[6] I should be obliged to you if you told them I am still their humble servant. I hope you are persuaded that I am unalterably yours,

M.W.M.

Text 1837, ii. 259–61

[1] Sir William Leman (1685–22 Dec. 1741) m. (1737) Anna Margaretta Brett (d. 1745), who had been mistress to George I (John S. Burn, *The Fleet Registers*, 1833, p. 73).

[2] Charles-Antoine, marquis de Beauffort (d. 1744).

[3] Lady Pomfret's maiden name; hence he must have met her in London before 1720.

[4] His daughter, by his second wife Agnès de Croisilles, was Marie-Clothilde-Josèphe, who m. (1751) Philippe-François-Joseph d'Audenfort, seigneur de la Potterie.

[5] Lady Elizabeth (d. 1748), da. of 1st Earl Middleton, and wife of William Spelman of Wickmer, Norfolk.

[6] See above, p. 133.

To Jean-Robert Tronchin[1] *24 March* [*1742*]

Vous avez été trop bien employé (Monsieur) pour meriter des reproches de vostre silence. Il y a des occasions ou on seroit coupable de se souvenir mesme des ses amis; vous n'en avez point qui prends plus de part ⟨?⟩ vostre bonheur que moi. Je vous charge de mes complimens de felicitation a Madame vostre épouse;[2] c'est une peine que je vous impose pour vostre oubli. Je suis tres persuadé de son merite par le choix qu'elle a faite, et je croy vous connoistre trop pour douter de la durée de vostre felicité.

L'entrée d'Italie me paroist interdit, mais je n'ai pas encore fixé mon sejour. Vous m'accuserai peutestre de Legereté, mais a la verité ma Resolution depende necessairement sur une varieté de circonstances qui changent tous les jours, et je voye par un triste experience qu'il n'y a point de Liberté dans cet monde. On a beau se defaire des Passions et des Prejuges; on est toujours ésclave par quelque endroit. Ces Refflexions melancholique sont tres deplacé quand ils sont addressé a vous. Dans vostre situation presente vous avez peine a comprendre qu'il y a des difficultez et des embarras. Je souhaitte de tout mon Cœur la continuation de cett aimable Enthousiasm qui vaut mieux que toutes les veritez Philosophique.

Je suis, Monsieur, vostre tres humble et tres Obeissante Servante,

M. W. Montagu.

Chambery, Mars 24.

J'ose vous prier d'embrasser tendrement Mlle Franconi[3]

---

[1] This newly discovered correspondent, Jean-Robert (1710–93), was son of the *procureur-général* Jean Tronchin, of a prominent Genevese family. Trained as a lawyer, he was a member of the Council of Two Hundred, and in 1759 became *procureur-général* himself (Albert de Montet, *Dict. biog. des genevois et des vaudois*, 1878, ii. 580–1). This and LM's two other letters to Tronchin are printed in *Journal de Genève*, 2 Nov. 1941 (excerpts), and *La Suisse et ses amis* by Claire-Éliane Engel, [1943], pp. 55–59).

[2] On 11 March 1742 Tronchin married Élisabeth-Charlotte, da. of Gaspard Boissier (J.-A. Galiffe, *Notices généalogiques sur les familles genevoises*, 2nd ed., 1892, ii. 867).

[3] Probably Sara Franconis (1696–1768), who m. (1744) André Gallatin (ibid. ii. 700).

et de faire bien des complimens a toute vostre aimable Famille.[1]

Text MS at University of Geneva   *Address* A Monsieur Monsieur Tronchin Junior a Geneve

To James Stuart Mackenzie[2] 27 *March* [*1743*]

You have certainly forgot that I wrote you word long since, that I had desir'd from Lady Oxford preferment for your Freind in the strongest manner, and she answer'd me[3] that she had put his name in her table Book, and would certainly remember him the first occasion that offer'd, but knew of none likely to fall at Present. You may be assur'd of all my possible services as long as I live, and 'tis no complement to tell you, I have the most sincere esteem for you, and know in the whole world so few people that I can esteem, that I verily beleive I have more value for you than you have for your selfe, from the Comparisons I often make between your character and those I daily see and hear of.

Your Citation is so just and well apply'd, there is nothing to be added to it. It is not surprizing that at my Age I make those refflections, but 'tis a very uncommon merit, in all the bloom of youth and affluence of Fortune, that you should see through the tinsel glitter of the World, and despise the rotten Hearts under the gaudy appearances. I am afraid every year will confirm you in these melancholy notions, for which I know no remedy but the advice of Solomon and Epicurus. Let us eat and drink, for to morrow we dye, which last refflection I think far from Melancholy to any Honest mind, being fully persuaded, what ever future state is allotted for us, it cannot be worse than this. Perhaps we are to go the round of the planets, and then, do but imagine what lively

---

[1] LM's letters to Tronchin are translated in the Appendix below.

[2] This comes from a newly discovered correspondence (ten letters) from LM to Lord Bute's brother.

[3] Lady Oxford, recently widowed, had been a girlhood friend of LM's (i. 114). Of their voluminous correspondence, the earliest extant letters are Lady Oxford's of 28/17 Sept. 1743 and LM's of 13 April 1744.

Creatures we shall be in Mercury or Venus; I dare swear the inhabitants are entirely unacquainted with spleen and vapours. A French man drunk with champain is a dull animal to them. They have undoubtedly many sensations that raise them more above us, than we are above Trouts. For my part I am determin'd for my prese⟨nt⟩ satisfaction to hope to meet you there, if ⟨we⟩ are destin'd never to meet again here; and I expect to see you with some distinguish'd rays of Light as the due reward of your Virtue.

Avignon, March 27.[1]

Text Bute MS   *Address* To James Stewart Mackensie Esqr in Conduit Street near Hanover Square London Angleterre par Paris. *Postmark* MR 28   *End. by Mackenzie* Lady Mary Wortley Montague Avignon 27 March 1742. answered [*struck out* Recd March 28th]

From Wortley [*2 April*/*22 March 1742*][2]

Our Son embarked at Harwich on the 10th after having been in England about 3 months.[3] I hear he avoided coming near the Sharpers, and is grown a good manager of his money, but his weakness is such that Mr. Gibson with much difficulty prevailed with him to go back, and he writ a letter as if he was afraid he should come hither again unless he was soon advised what to do. He declares as if he wanted to be in the army unless something more for his advantage is proposed, and I have said to Mr. G[ibson] I will not oppose his going into the Army as a volunteer but that I believe he may take some course more to his advantage. I hear my Lord Carteret[4] (with whom he has been more than once) speaks well of his behaviour, but his obstinacy in staying here and what he writes incline me [to] think it will not be easy to persuade him to follow good Advice.

I can not imagine any one is so likely as your selfe to give an impartial account of him. Under this difficulty I can think of no better expedient than to advise him to apply to you for leave to come to some place where you may converse with him. I hope you may see him without

[1] The year 1742 was added in error by Mackenzie. LM did not settle in Avignon until May. (This letter belongs on p. 302 below.)

[2] The date from 1861, ii. 102.

[3] Montagu must have gone there from Ysselstein, Holland, where he had lived since 1737.

[4] Later Earl Granville; he became Secretary of State after on 12 Feb. 1742.

being disturbed by him. If you appoint him to be at a place 20 miles or further from that where you chuse to reside and order him to go by a feigned name, you may easily reach him in a Post chaise and come back after you have passed a week where he is, and this you may do more than once to make a full trial of him, and I wish he might stay within a certain distance of you till you have given me an account of him and I have agreed to what is fixed between him and you.

He declares he sets his heart on being in England, but then he should give me such proofes as I require that he is able to persevere in behaving himselfe like a reasonable man. These proofes may be agreed on between you and me, and I believe I shall readily agree to what you shall think right.

I think you shoud say nothing to him but in the most calme and gentle way possible, that he may be invited to open himselfe to you freely. He seems, I hear, shocked at your letter in which you complained of his not regarding the truth, tho I believe you made no mistake in it unless your saying his marriage coud not be dissolved. He knows very well it may by act of Parliament, which is what he means when he writes he wants to be quit of his wife. He denies that he knew Birtles to be nephew to Henshaw[1] who lent the £200. As he is commended by several here and by more in Holland (who perhaps flatter him) it may seem wrong to speak to him with any shew of warmth or Anger.

I incline to think he has been made an Enthusiast in Holland, and you woud do well to try throughly whether he is so in good earnest and likely to continue so. If he is, I need not mention how much caution shoud be used in speaking to him. I think (whatever his notions are) you woud do well to say nothing to him but what you woud say before any company.

I shall advise him by Mr. G[ibson] to go to Langres[2] or some place near it, where he may wait for your answer to such letter as he writes for leave to come to any place you appoint.

I shall give you fuller informations about him in a Post or two, if not by this. I hope this affair will not be very troublesome to you as you can retire from him whenever you please. He shall not have much more money than is sufficient to carry him to you. When you have furnished him with any it shall be made good to you.

[Passage omitted]

He may have more Cunning than is imagined to gain his Points, and perhaps is not made uneasy being abroad and may have little or no

---

[1] George Henshaw, Consul at Genoa, had died in 1724 (*Polit. State of G. B.*, xviii. 530; *Hist. Register*, p. 47); W probably meant John Bagshaw (d.

1737), Consul from *c.* 1727 until his death (*Gentleman's Mag.*, p. 701).
[2] Bar-le-Duc *struck out*.

inclination to go into the army, but thinks to prevent it I may give him some considerable advantage. If you seem not at all averse to his going, perhaps he will of himselfe quit that Scheme and go into some other that you may like better.

If you think it best he shoud make a Campagne, you will take care not to detain him too long. Perhaps you may recommend him to our minister at Turin, that he may serve in the Sardinian Forces, where if he shoud do wrong it will be less known than if he did it in Flanders.

Perhaps by another name he might meet you unobserved at Lyons or Pont-beauvoisin. I need not mention that whatever money you put into his hands shall [be] repaid you at Demand. If he goes back to Holland, I suppose £20 is enough for his charges.

I have yours of the 24 Feb. Lord and Lady Bute seem to live well together. They lost their son (who was above a year old) on the 16th.[1] He had Fits and a Feavour. The Surgeons say his brains were too large and occasioned the Fits.

They are both retired to Richmond for 10 days or a fortnight.

Text W MS i. 125–8 (draft)

To Wortley 6 *April* [*1742*]

April 6. N.S., Chambery

I receiv'd yesterday a note from Child for the Quarters of Michaelmass and Xmas, for which I return you many thanks, but am much mortify'd at your long silence. I have wrote so often without a return that I am afraid of importuning.

Lady Oxford writes me word my Daughter is with you. I have not heard from her since she left Scotland. I hope her obedience and affection for you will make your Life agreable to you. She cannot have more than I have had; I wish the success may be greater.

Text W MS ii. 46   *End. by W* [*Summary*] Ad 12 Apr.   Recd 5 Apr.

---

[1] For the child's birth, see above, p. 219.

From Wortley *23/12 April 1742*

12 Apr. 1742

[*Passage omitted*][1] Mine of the 22nd and 29 Mar. were about our Son at large. He shews a resolution to go into the Army and Lord Carteret has promised him to get him a Commission but did not tell me when he woud send it him. He may not do it soon. I am in doubt whether it is possible to hinder him from going into the army (unless I did something for him in present) and whether it woud be right to hinder him if I coud. I hope you will try him thoroughly, speak always mildly, gently and kindly to him and keep him within a reasonable distance of you till you and I have settled what is to be done about him. All commend his good behaviour in Company and Mr. G[ibson] says by his discourse one woud not think him the same man he was when in London before. Try whether he is an enthusiast or what turn of mind he has. He may have a good deal of art in hiding what he is. I hear he says what you writ to him open for Messrs. Clifford to see did him harm. I justified it as you will easily do. I coud not tell which way to get an impartial account of him but by you, and hope your seeing and conversing with him will give you little trouble. He does not know that he is advised to go near you for any reason but to be advised by you, who are more likely than any other to give him right advice. [*Passage omitted*]

Text W MS i. 129–30 (draft)

To Wortley *23 April* [*1742*]

Lions, April 23. N.S.

I have this minute receiv'd 4 Letters from you dated February 1, Feb. 22, March 22, March 29th. I fancy their lying so long in the post offices may proceed from your forgetting to Frank them, which I am inform'd is quite necessary.

I am very glad you have been prevail'd on to let our Son take a commission. If you had prevented it he would have allways said, and perhaps thought and persuaded other people, you had hinder'd his riseing in the World, thô I am

---

[1] The first part of this draft, in a secretary's hand, repeats W's suggestions for preventing the loss or delay of LM's letters.

fully persuaded that he can never make a tolerable Figure in any Station in Life. When he was at Morins on his first leaving France, I then try'd to prevail with him to serve the Emperor as Volunteer, and represented to him that a handsome behaviour one Campagne might go a great way in retreiveing his character, and offer'd to use my Interest with you (which I said I did not doubt would succeed) to furnish him with a handsome Equipage. He then answer'd, He suppose'd I wish'd him kill'd out of the Way. I am afraid his pretended Reformation is not very sincere; I wish time may prove me in the wrong. I here enclose the last Letter I receiv'd from him. I answer'd it the following post in these words:

'I am very glad you resolve to continue Obedient to your Father and are sensible of his goodness towards you. Mr. Birtles shew'd me your Letter to him in which you enclos'd yours to me, where you speak to him as your Freind, subscribeing your selfe his faithfull Humble Servant. He was at Genoa in his Uncle's house when you was there, and well acquainted with you, thô you seem ignorant of every thing relateing to him.[1] I wish you would not make such sort of Apologys for any errors you may commit. I pray God your future behaviour may redeem the past, which will be a great blessing to your affectionate Mother.'

I have not since heard from him. I suppose he knew not what to say to so plain a detected falsehood. It is very disagreable to me to converse with one from whom I do not expect to hear a word of Truth and who, I am very sure, will repeat many things that never pass'd in our Conversation. You see the most solemn assurances are not binding from him, since he could come to London in opposition to your commands after haveing so frequently protested he would not move a step but by your order. However, as you insist on my seeing him, I will do it, and think Valence the properest Town for that Interview. It is but 2 days Journey from this place; it is in Dauphiné.[2]

---

[1] See above, p. 270.

[2] Montagu had been befriended and subsidized by his father's first cousin Edward Montagu (1692–1775), for many years M.P. for Huntingdon, whom he kept informed of the negotia-

tions. When young Montagu first heard from Gibson that he would have to meet LM, he told his patron: 'She is my Mother, so my tongue is tied, but I leave you to think whether or no this is an agreable proposition' (Amsterdam, 12

I arriv'd here friday night, haveing left Chambery on the report of the French designing to come soon thither. So far is certain that the Governor had given command for repairing the Walls, etc., on which men were actually employ'd when I came away, but the Court of Turin is so politick and misterious it is hard to Judge, and I am apt to beleive their designs change according to circumstances.

I shall stay here till I have an Answer to this Letter. If you order your Son to go to Valence I desire you would give him a strict command of going by a feign'd Name. I do not doubt your returning me whatever money I may give him, but as I beleive if he receives Money from me he will be makeing me frequent visits, it is clearly my opinion I should give him none; whatever you think proper for his Journey you may remit to him.

I am very sorry for my Daughter's loss, being sensible how much it may affect her, thô I suppose it will be soon repair'd. It is a great pleasure to me when I hear she is happy. I wrote to her last post and will write again the next.

Since I wrote I have look'd every where for my Son's Letter, which I find has been mislaid in the Journey. There is nothing more in it than long professions of doing nothing but by your command, and a positive assertion that he was ignorant of Mr. Birtles' relation to the late Consul.

Direct your next recommendé a Monsieur Imbert,[1] Banquier a Lions.

Text W MS ii. 47–49   *Address* To Edwd Wortley Esqr in Cavendish Square London Angleterre par Paris   *Postmark* AP 21   *End.* by *W* [*Summary*] Ad 29 Apr.

April 1742, N.S., MS Mo 2835, Huntington Library). More discreetly, a few days later he informed his father (through Gibson): 'I should be certainly inexcusable if I doubted my Mother's capacity to advice [*sic*] me in my affairs and should be happy if I could have her council, but have never yet been able to obtain it but in general termes, viz: *to behave well*. . . .' At the same time he divulged his true feelings to his patron:

that he hoped Lord Carteret, who had promised him a company in the army, 'will not wait for and be determin'd by Lady Mary's consent or disapprobation, for as it certainly will be for my good I am sure she will do her utmost to hinder it' (Leyden, 17 April, MS Mo 2836).

[1] Probably Joseph-André Imbert, of the Provençal family, appointed in 1753 Trésorier Général en France en la Généralité de Provence.

To Wortley 25 *April* [*1742*]

April 25 N.S., Lions.

On recollection (however inconvenient it may be to me on many accounts) I am not sorry to converse with my Son. I shall at least have the satisfaction of makeing a clear Judgment of his behaviour and temper, which I shall deliver to you in the most sincere and unprejudice'd manner. You need not aprehend that I shall speak to him in Passion; I do not know that I ever did in my Life. I am not apt to be over heated in Discourse, and am so far prepare'd even for the worst on his side that I think nothing he can say can alter the resolution I have taken of treating him with calmness.

Both Nature and Interest (were I inclin'd to follow blindly the Dictates of either) would determine me to wish him your Heir rather than a stranger; but I think my selfe oblig'd both by Honor, conscience, and my regard for you, no way to deceive you, and I confess hitherto I see nothing but Falsehood and weakness through his whole Conduct. It is possible his person may be alter'd since I saw him, but his figure then was very agreable, and his manner insinuateing. I very well remember the proffessions he made to me, and do not doubt he is as lavish of them to other people. Perhaps Lord C[arteret] may think him no ill match for an ugly Girl that sticks upon his hands.[1] The project of breaking his marriage shews (at least) his Devotion counterfeit, since I am sensible it cannot be done but by false Wittnesses; his Wife is not young enough to get Gallants, nor rich enough to buy them.

I make choice of Valence for our interview as a Town where we are not likely to find any English, and he may (if he pleases) be quite unknown, which it is hardly possible to be in any capital Town either of France or Italy. Here are many English of the Tradeing sort of people, who are more likely to be inquisitive and talkative than any other. Near Chambery there is a little Colony of English who have undertaken the working of the mines in Savoy, in which they find

---

[1] Of Lord Carteret's three surviving daughters, only the youngest, Frances (d. 1788), was unmarried; she m. (1748) 4th Marquess of Tweeddale.

very pure Silver, of which I have seen se⟨ver⟩al cakes of about 80 ounces each.

Text W MS ii. 50–51 *Address* To Edwd Wortley Esqr in Cavendish Square London Angleterre par Paris *End. by W* [*Summary*] Recd 29 Apr. Ad 3 May.

To Wortley 2 *May* [*1742*]

Lions, May 2, N.S.

I receiv'd this morning yours of April 12 and at the same time the enclos'd which I send you, which is the first I have receiv'd since the Detection of that falsehood in regard to Mr. Birtles. I allways sent my Letters open that Mr. Clifford[1] (who has the character of sense and Honesty) might be wittness of what I said, and he not left at Liberty to forge orders he never receiv'd. I am very glad I have done so, and am persuaded that had his Reformation been what you suppose it, Mr. Clifford would have wrote to me in his favour. I confess I see no appearance of it; his last Letter to you and this to me seems to be no more in that submissive Style he has us'd, but like one that thinks him selfe well protected. I will see him (since you desire it) at Valence, which is a by Town, where I am less likely to meet with English than in any Town in France, but I insist on his going ⟨by⟩ a feign'd name and comeing without a Servant.[2] People of superior Fortunes to him (to my knowledge) have often travell'd from Paris to Lyons in the Diligence. The expence is but one 100 Livres (about £5 st.), all things paid. It would not be easy to me at this time to send him any considerable Summ; and whatever it is, I am persuaded, comeing from me, he would not be satisfy'd with it, and make his complaints to his Companions. As to the alteration of his temper, I see the same Folly through out. He now supposes (which is at best

---

[1] A member of the banking firm of that name in Amsterdam.

[2] Montagu begged his father (through Gibson) to be allowed a servant 'since that only in travelling can distinguish me from the meanest creature on the face of the Earth' (to Edward Montagu, Paris, 15 May 1742, N.S., MS Mo 2839, Huntington Library).

downright childish) that one hour's conversation will convince me of his Sincerity. I have not answer'd his Letter, nor will not till I have your orders what to say to him.

Be pleas'd to direct recommandé a Monsieur Imbert, Banquier a Lyon.

I receiv'd his Letter to Day.

Text W MS ii. 79–80   *Address* To Edwd Wortley Esqr in Cavendish Square London Angleterre par Paris   *Postmark* MA 3   *End. by W* [*Summary*] Ad 3 May   Recd 3 May.

To Wortley 6 *May* [*1742*]

May 6. N.S.

I here send you enclos'd the Letter I mention'd of your Son's. The pacquet in which it was put was mislaid in the Journey. It will serve to shew you how little he is to be depended on. I saw a Savoyard Man of Quality at Chambery who knew him at Venice and afterwards at Genoa, who ask'd me (not suspecting him for my Son) if he was related to my Family. I made answer he was some Relation. He told me several Tricks of his. He said that at Genoa he had told him that an Uncle of his was dead and had left him 5 or £6,000 per Annum, and that he was returning to England to take possession of his Estate. In the mean time he wanted Money and would have borrow'd some of him, which he refus'd. I made answer that he did very well. I have heard of this sort of Conduct in other places, and by the Dutch Letters you have sent me I am persuaded he continues the same method of Lying, which convinces me that his pretended Enthusiasm is only to cheat those that can be impos'd on by it. However, I think he should not be hinder'd accepting a Commission. I do not doubt it will be pawn'd or sold in a Twelve month, which will prove to those that now protect him how little he deserves it.

I am now at Avignon, which is within one day's Journey of Valence. I left Lions last Thursday, but I have taken care that whatever Letters come thither shall be sent to me. I came to this Place, not finding my selfe well at Lions. I thought this change of Air would be of service to my Health, and find I was not mistaken.

All the road is fill'd with French troops who expect orders to march into the King of Sardinia's Dominions.[1]

I am in great Pain for my Daughter's Situation, fearing that the loss of her Son may have some ill Effect in her present Condition. I beg you would let me know the minute she is brought to Bed.[2]

Text W MS ii. 52–53   *Address* To Edwd Wortley Esqr in Cavendish Square London Angleterre par Paris   *Postmark* MA 10   *End. by W* [*Summary*] 10 May.   24.

To Jean-Robert Tronchin [*May 1742*]

Je suis tres flatté (Monsieur) de l'honneur de vostre souvenir, et de tous les gracieuxetes dont vous m'asseurez de la part des Dames de Geneve. Je suis bien faschée que le destin m'entraine ailleurs, mais je suis si persuadé de l'impossibillité d'ÿ resister, que je me suis laissé aller sans Resistance par le Courant de la Rhosne jusqu'ici, ou effectivement j'ÿ trouve beaucoup d'agrement, des Belles Maisons, des jolis Jardins, des sociétés aimable, de la bonne chere, des Promenades charmantes. Mais (car les mais empoisonnent tous les biens de cet monde) il y a un vent capable de renverser tous mes projets, et si cette Bize cruelle dure encore quelques jours, je renonce a tous les plaisirs d'Avignon, et Dieu sçait ou j'addresserai mes pas.

Nous sommes ici inondé des Espagnols, mais ce sont des Ennemis poli qui me font mille honnetetez, et je ne me trouve pas mal de leur Conversation. Je commence mesme a pardonner a Mlle Franconi sa bien veillance pour eux; et si je pouvois regler les conseils d'Europe, ils seront nos alliez, et nous porterons de concert nos armes ailleurs. Et quoy que je me suis accoutumé depuis assez long temps de

---

[1] The King of Sardinia had thrown in his lot with Maria Theresa in the War of the Austrian Succession.

[2] She bore a daughter on 13 April O.S. (see above, p. 264, n. 3).

regarder les évenemens avec le sang froid d'un Spectateur, j'avoûe qu'il y a des momens ou je suis depité de voir des miserables Bœufs se faire des plaŷes (peutestre incurable) pendant qu'un Renard leche le sang que coule de deux costez. Je ne sçai comment ce triste Refflection m'est échapé; il est de mon Age d'en faire, et de la vostre de s'en moquer. Je vous le permets de tout mon Cœur; rejoüissez vous, Monsieur; profitez de tous les biens dont la Nature et la fortune vous ont comblé, et soyez persuadé qu'il n'ÿ a personne (mesme de vos plus proches) qui prend plus de part a vostre heureuse Situation que (Monsieur) vostre tres humble et tres Obeissante Servante,

M. W. Montagu.

Text MS at University of Geneva   *Address* A Monsieur Monsieur Tronchin Junior a Geneve

To Mme Chiara Michiel *20 May* [*1742*]

Avignon, Mai 20.

Excellenza,

Il me paroist cent anns depuis j'ai eu de vos Nouvelles, ma belle Ambassadrice,[1] mais je ne sçaurois jamais oublier les charmes de vostre Conversation, et toutes les Graces que j'ai admiré dans vostre personne.

Me voici établi pour quelque temps a Avignon. C'éstoit a grand regret que j'ai quitté l'aimable Italie, mais il va (dit-on) devenir la Theatre de la Guerre, et je n'ai pas osé y rester. J'ai du moins la Consolation d'etre sous la domination d'un Prince Italien, et (entre nous soit dit) du seul Prince pour qui j'ai de l'estime, parce qu'il est le seul qui me paroist regarder ses peuples comme étant sous sa protection, et il se fait un étude de les soulager,[2] pendant que les autres souverains les considerent uniquement comme des êtres crée pour servir leurs passions.

---

[1] LM's most recent known letter to Mme Michiel was written from Genoa on 9 Sept. [1741].

[2] Avignon was a Papal possession; and LM wrote in other letters of her very high regard for Benedict XIV.

J'ai quelques fois des Lettres du pauvre Monsieur Mackinsie, qui s'ennuye fort dans sa triste Patrie, et qui me parle
éternellement de Venise. Nous sommes ici toute entouré
des Espagnols; Dieu sçait ce qui en arrivera. J'avoûe
qu'exceptant mes amis (pour les quels je m'intteresse vive-
ment) la sort de genre humain m'est aussi indifferent que celui
des Papillons, que les bleus battent les verds, ou les Rouges
les jaunes. Tous ces évenemens me parroissent indigne de
consideration, et je m'envelope dans une Philosophie qui me
donne une grande Tranquillité malgre les Tumultes de
l'Europe. Mais cette quietude ne va pas jusqu'a me rendre
indifferente a vostre souvenir, et je se⟨rois⟩ au desespoir si
je ne me flattois pas que vous m'honorez quelque fois de
vos pensées, comme étant autant qu'on peut estre (Ma chere
Madame) de V. E. La tres humble et tres Obeissante
Servante,

M. W. Montagu.

Text Bute MS   *Address* A S. E. Madame Madame l'Ambassadrice
de la S. Republique de venise a la Cour de S. M. Catholique a Madrid

To Wortley *23 May* [*1742*]

Avignon, May 23. N.S.

I have receiv'd this morning yours of April 12 and 29,
and at the same time one from my Son from Paris dated the
4th Instant. I have wrote to him this day that on his answer
I will immediately set out to Valence and shall be glad to see
him there.[1] I suppose you are now convince'd I have never
been mistaken in his character, which remains unchang'd,
and what is yet worse, I think is unchangable. I never saw
such a complication of folly and Falsity as is in his Letter to
Mr. G[ibson]. Nothing is cheaper than living in an Inn in a
Country Town in France, they being oblig'd to ask no more

[1] On 1 May Montagu wrote from
Paris to his patron Edward Montagu,
'. . . I must needs own I wish I may have
something before I see Lady Mary, for
she is much to be fear'd as as [*sic*] woman
set upon a young man's ruin and much
more still as a woman of a superior
genius' (MS Mo 2838, Huntington
Library).

than 25 sous for dinner and 30 for supper and lodging of those that eat at the public Table, which all the young Men of Quality I have met have allways done. It is true I am forc'd to pay double because I think the Decency of my Sex confines me to eat in my chamber.

I will not trouble you with detecting a number of other falsehoods that are in his Letters. My Opinion on the whole (since you give me leave to tell it) is that if I was to speak in your place I would tell him: 'that since he is obstinate in going into the army, I will not oppose it, but as I do not approve, I will advance no Equipage till I know his behaviour to be such as shall deserve my future favour. Hitherto he has allways been directed either by his own Humour or the advice of those he thought better Freinds to him than my selfe. If he renounces the Army I will continu to him his former allowance, notwithstanding his repeated disobedience under the most solemn proffessions of Duty. When I see him act like a sincere honest Man I shall beleive well of him. The opinion of others who either do not know him, or are impos'd on by his pretences, weighs nothing with me.'

Text W MS ii. 54–55   *Address* To Edwd Wortley Esqr in Cavendish Square London Angleterre par Paris   *Postmark* MA 24   *End. by W* L.M. 23 May 1742.   Abt Son.   Ad 24th.

To Wortley *30 May* [*1742*]

Avignon, May 30. N.S.

I receiv'd this day yours of May 3rd.

I have wrote to let my Son know I am ready to meet him at Valence on the first notice of his setting out. I think it very improbable that Lord St[air] should make him any such promise as he told Mr. Anderson, or even give him hopes of it.[1] If he had any right notions, Paris is the last place he

---

[1] On 23 April Montagu had written from Antwerp to his patron that he wished to be one of Lord Stair's aides-de-camp, but that they were all chosen (MS Mo 2837, Huntington Library). In March Stair had been appointed Field-Marshal, and in April Commander-in-Chief of the armies in the war to support the Pragmatic Sanction.

would have appear'd in, since I know he owes Knight[1] money, and perhaps many other people.

I am very glad of my Daughter's Health, and hope you enjoy yours.

Text W MS ii. 56   *End. by W* [*Summary*] Ad 17 June.   Recd 31 May.

To James Stuart Mackenzie *1 June* [*1742*]

June 1. Avignon

'Tis allways with great pleasure I receive the news of your Health. If I learnt nothing else from your Letters, they would be ever agreable to me, but you are in the wrong to make apologys. I can assure you with truth, I should be glad to read them if they were address'd to another person and wrote by one I had never seen. You have a very uncommon and a very beautifull fault: you want a due sense of your own merit; you often think too favourably of others, and are unjust to your selfe. I allow you to undervalue your person or be difident of your understanding (tho any other man would be proud of both) but at least be just to your Virtue. The more you see of the World, you will be every day more persuaded that a Heart like yours is more valuable, and allmost as much alone as the great Di'mond the King of France wears in his Hat;[2] and do not deny your selfe the only recompence that perhaps you ever will receive:

> The secret praise of your own conscious mind.
> The Victor's shout not halfe that pleasure brings,
> Nor thanks from Senates, nor the smiles of Kings.
> These, in all ages, partially bestow'd,
> To Chance, or to Intrigue, are often ow'd.
> The calm applause of selfe-refflecting Thought
> No Art can gain, nor by no Bribe is bought.[3]

I beleive you will think me in the right to dress up in Poetry a thought that seems so romantick, but it is not less my

[1] Either Robert Knight the elder (d. 1744), cashier of the South Sea Company, who had fled to Paris to escape prosecution; or his son Robert (1702–72).

[2] The famous Pitt diamond was set in the French crown.

[3] Since Feb. 1742 Mackenzie had been M.P. for Argyllshire.

opinion in plain prose, and I think so highly of that inward aprobation that I look upon it as reserv'd for Heaven's peculiar Favourites.

> On meaner Men, their meaner Gifts they shower,
> To Walpole Riches,[1] and to Carteret Power.

I say nothing to you of my selfe, as a subject not worth speaking about. I am in every light so insignificant that I am often tir'd of being, thô my Existence is accompany'd with such strong health and spirits that if I had neither memory nor Looking Glasses, I should think I was endowed with perpetual Youth.[2]

Text Bute MS   *Address* To The Honble J Mackinsie Esqr in Conduit Street near Hanover Square London Angleterre par Paris   *Postmark* iv 6   *End. by Mackenzie* Lady Mary Wortley Montague. Avignon 1st June 1742.

To Lady Pomfret *1 June* [*1742*]

Avignon, June 1, N.S.

I have changed my situation, fearing to find myself blocked up in a besieged town; and not knowing where else to avoid the terrors of war, I have put myself under the protection of the Holy See. Your ladyship being well acquainted with this place, I need not send you a description of it; but I think you did not stay in it long enough to know many of the people.[3] I find them very polite and obliging to strangers. We have assemblies every night, which conclude with a great supper; and comedies which are tolerably well acted. In short, I think one may wile away an idle life with great tranquility; which has long since been the utmost of my ambition.

I never was more surprized than at the death of the Duchess of Cleveland; I thought her discretion and constitution made to last at least as long as her father's. I beg you

---

[1] On his retirement (in Feb. 1742) as Prime Minister, Sir Robert was created Earl of Orford and promised a pension of £4,000. He had amassed great wealth during his lengthy term of office, but died (in 1745) £40,000 in debt.

[2] LM's next surviving letter to Mackenzie dates from 1759 (iii. 196–7).

[3] In 1739 Lady Pomfret had stayed there one day (Hertford, *Corr.* i. 87).

to let me know what accident has destroyed that fine figure which seemed built to last an age.[1] You are very unjust to me in regard to the Marquis of Beaufort; he is too much an Englishman not to be inquisitive after the news of London. There has passed nothing there since he left it that he has not been informed of. Lord Lempster can tell you that before I came to Turin he had mentioned to him that he had had the honour of seeing his mother. He removed from Chambery with his whole family about the same time I left it; and for the same reason they passed into Italy; and if Piedmont proves the theatre of war, intend to refuge themselves at Lucca. I am much mortified that I can have no opportunity of giving him so great a pleasure as I know your compliment would be, his civilities to me deserving all possible gratitude. His daughter is but seven years old, a little angel both in face and shape. *A propos* of angels, I am astonished Lady Sophia does not condescend to leave some copies of her face for the benefit of posterity; 'tis quite impossible she should not command what matches she pleases, when such pugs as Miss Hamilton can become peeresses;[2] and I am still of opinion that it depended on her to be my relation.[3]

Here are several English ladies established, none I ever saw before; but they behave with decency, and give a good impression of our conduct, though their pale complexions and stiff stays do not give the French any inclination to imitate our dress.

Notwithstanding the dulness of this letter, I have so much confidence in your ladyship's charity, I flatter myself you will be so good as to answer it. I beg you would direct to me 'recommandé à Monsieur Imbert, Banquier à Lyon;' he will take care to forward it to, dear madam, Your faithful humble servant,

M.W.M.

Text 1837, ii. 261–3

[1] Henrietta Finch m. (1732) 3rd Duke of Cleveland; she d. 14 April 1742, after less than two days' illness, aged 37. Her father, Daniel (1647–1730), 7th Earl of Winchilsea, lived to the age of 82.

[2] Elizabeth (1720–1800), da. of Lord Archibald Hamilton, m. (15 May 1742)

8th Baron Brooke, later 1st Earl of Warwick. Walpole describes her as 'excessively pretty and sensible, but as diminutive' as her husband (*Corr.* xvii. 391).

[3] By marrying Lord Lincoln, a possibility long since evaporated (see above, p. 265, n. 2).

To Wortley 6 *June* [*1742*]

Avignon, June 6. N.S.

I have just receiv'd a Letter from my Son that he is at Montelimar waiting to see me.[1] I intend going thither to morrow, tho' I have little hopes from my visit. What ever is the Event you shall have a faithfull account of it.

Text W MS ii. 57   *End. by W* L. M. 6 June 1742.   fr. Avignon. Ad 17 June   Recd 7 June.

To Wortley *10 June* [*1742*]

Avignon, June 10 N.S.

I am just return'd from passing 2 days with our Son, of whom I will give you the most exact account I am capable of. He is so much alter'd in his person, I should scarcely have known him. He has entirely lost his Beauty, and looks at least 7 years older than he is.[2] The wildness that he allways had in his Eyes is so much encreas'd it is downright shocking, and I am afraid will end fatally. He is grown fat, but is still gentile and has an air of Politeness that is agreable. He speaks French like a French man and has got all the Fashionable expressions of that Language, and a volubillity of words which he allways had, and which I do not wonder should pass for Wit with inconsiderate people. His behaviour is perfectly civil, and I found him very submissive, but in the main no way realy improv'd in his understanding, which is exceeding weak; and I am convince'd he will allways be led by the person he converses with, either right or wrong, not being capable of forming any fix'd Judgment of his own. As to his

[1] From Montelimar on 5 June, Montagu wrote to Edward Montagu, his relation and patron: '. . . having heard Lady Mary is att Avignon I am come hitherto, and wait her orders with impatience tho I am much afraid our interview will not be advantageous to me. . . .' (MS Mo 2845, Huntington Library). The meeting actually took place at Orange, as LM informed W on 18 Oct. 1743.

[2] Montagu was almost exactly 29.

Enthusiasm, if he had it I suppose he has allready lost it, since I could perceive no turn of it in all his Conversation, but with his Head I beleive it is possible to make him a Monk one day and a Turk three days after. He has a flattering, insinuateing manner which naturally prejudices strangers in his favour.

He begun to talk to me in the usual silly Cant I have so often heard from him, which I shorten'd by telling him I desir'd not to be trouble'd with it, that proffessions were of no use where actions were expected, and that the only thing [that] could give me hopes of a good Conduct was regularity and truth. He very readily agreed to all I said (as indeed he has allways done when he has not been hot headed). I endeavor'd to convince him how favourably he has been dealt with, his allowance being much more than, had I been his Father, I would have given in the same case. The Prince of Hesse, who is now marry'd to the Princesse of England,[1] liv'd some years at Geneva on £300 per Annum. Lord Hervey sent his son at 16 thither, and to travel afterwards, on no larger pension than £200, and thô without a Governor he had reason enough not only to live within the compass of it, but carry'd home little presents for his Father and Mother, which he shew'd me at Turin.[2] In short, I know there is no Place so expensive but a prudent single man may live in it on one £100 per Annum, and an Extravagant one may run out ten thousand in the cheapest.

Had you (said I to him) thought rightly, or would have regarded the advice I gave you in all my Letters, while in the little Town of Islestein you would have laid up 150 per Annum. You would now have had £750 in your pocket, which would have almost paid your Debts, and such a management would have gain'd you the esteem of the reasonable part of Mankind. I perceive'd this Refflection, which he had never made him selfe, had a very great weight with him. He would have excus'd part of his Follys by saying

---

[1] See above, p. 123, n. 5.

[2] Hervey's eldest son (see above, p. 240) evidently required a larger allowance. On 2 April 1739 his grandfather, Lord Bristol, paid out £271. 10s. for 'the half year since he went from England to Geneva'; on 15 May 1740, £150 'to pay off his farther expenses at Geneva'; and two days later, an additional £150 'to answer other new drafts' John Hervey, *Diary 1688–1742*, 1894, p. 120).

Mr. G[ibson] had told him it became Mr. W.'s Son to
live handsomely. I made answer that whither Mr. G. had
said so or no, the good sense of the thing was no way
alter'd by it; that the true figure of a Man was the Opinion
the world had of his Sense and Probity, and not the Idle
expences, which were only respected by foolish or ignorant
people; that his case was particular, he had but too publickly
shewn his Inclination to Vanitys, and the most becomeing
part he could now act would be owning the ill use he had
made of a Father's indulgence and proffessing to endeavor
to be no farther expence to him, instead of scandalous
Complaints and being allways at his last shirt and last
Guinea, which any Man of Spirit would be asham'd to own.
I prevail'd so far with him that he seem'd very willing to
follow this advice, and I gave him a paragraph to write to
G[ibson], which I suppose you will easily distinguish from
the rest of his Letter.

He ask'd me if you had settle'd your Estate. I made
answer that I did not doubt (like all other wise men) you
allways had a Will by you, but that you had certainly not put
any thing out of your power to change. On that, he begun
to insinuate that if I could prevail on you to settle your
Estate on him, I might expect any thing from his Gratitude.
I made him a very clear and possitive answer in these words:
I hope your Father will outlive me, and if I should be so
unfortunate to have it otherwise, I do not beleive he will
leave me in your power; but was I sure of the contrary, no
Interest nor no Necessity shall ever make me act against my
Honor or Conscience, and I plainly tell you that I will never
persuade your Father to do any thing for you till I think you
deserve it. He answer'd by great promises of Future good
Behaviour and Oeconomy. He is highly delighted with the
prospect of going into the army, and mightily pleas'd with
the good Reception he had from Lord St[air], thô I find it
amounts to no more than telling him he was sorry he had
allready nam'd his Aids de Camp, and otherwise should have
been glad of him in that post. He says Lord C[arteret] has
confirm'd to him his promise of a Commission.

The rest of his Conversation was extreamly Gay. The
various things he has seen has given him a superficial

universal knowledge. He realy knows most of the modern Languages, and, if I could beleive him, can read Arabic and has read the Bible in Hebrew.[1] He said it was impossible for him to avoid going back to Paris, but he promis'd me to lye but one night there and go to a Town six posts from thence on the Flanders road, where he would wait your orders, and go by the name of Mons. Du Durand, a Dutch officer, under which name I saw him. These are the most material passages, and my Eyes are so much tir'd I can write no more at this time. I gave him 240 livres[2] for his Journey.[3]

Text W MS ii. 58–61   *Address* To Edwd Wortley Esqr in Cavendish Square London Angleterre par Paris   *Postmark* IV 14   *End. by* *W* L.M. 10 June 1742.   After having passed two days with our Son. Ad 17 June   Recd 14 June.

To Wortley 27 *June* [*1742*]

Avignon, June 27. N.S.

I receiv'd yesterday yours of the 24th of May O.S. I hope you have had a long letter in which I gave you a full account of our Son's behaviour. I have not since heard from him, thô he promis'd to write immediately and we parted very good Freinds, he protesting to follow my advice in all things.

I wish you would direct your next for me at this Place. I shall receive it some days sooner and I am told it will come equally safe, only adding *Par Paris*.

I am glad your Health is not injur'd by your Fatigues; I hope you will take care to preserve it.

Text W MS ii. 62   *End by* *W* [*Summary*] Recd 30 June.

[1] On 6 Sept. 1741 Montagu had enrolled at Leyden University as a student of Oriental languages (Edward Peacock, *Index to English Speaking Students at Leyden University*, 1883, p. 106).

[2] Approximately £12.
[3] In 1745 Walpole passed on gossip to Mann about LM's interview with her son, giving it an incestuous turn (*Corr.* xviii. 567).

To Wortley 9 *July* [*1742*]

Avignon, July 9 N.S.

I receiv'd yours of June 17 this morning. Nothing can be more pleasing to me [than] to hear my Daughter's behaviour is agreable to you.

When I parted with my Son, he promis'd to write to me from Paris. I have never heard from him since, neither do I know where to direct to him. I am very willing to do whatever you think can be of service to him, thô I fear it is to very little purpose, and my Sight is so much decaid that writeing long letters is painfull to me.

If you direct for me at Avignon, par Paris, I shall receive your Letters some days sooner.

Text W MS ii. 63   *End. by W* [*Summary*] Recd 12 July.

To Wortley *19 July* [*1742*]

N.S. July 19, Avignon

I was very glad to observe in yours of June 21st (which I receiv'd this morning) that every thing you think proper to be said to our Son, I have allready said to him in the most pressing manner I was able. I am very willing to repeat it over again in my letters to him as soon as I know where to direct. I never heard from him since we parted thô he promis'd over and over to write from Paris.

All the English without Distinction see the Duke of Ormond.[1] Lord Chesterfeild (who you know is related to him)[2] lay at his House during his stay in this Town, and to

---

[1] James Butler (1665–1745), 2nd Duke; a leader of the Jacobites in 1715, he fled abroad to join the Pretender's court, and had lived many years in Madrid before retiring to Avignon.

[2] Only by marriage. Chesterfield was grandson of the third wife of the 2nd

Earl, whose second wife was an aunt of Ormond's. Actually, although LM never mentioned it because of her antipathy to Chesterfield, she was related to him by blood—his mother Lady Elizabeth Saville having been a granddaughter of 'Wise' William Pierrepont.

say truth, nothing can be more insignificant.[1] He keeps an assembly where all the best Company go twice in the week. I have been there sometimes, nor is it possible to avoid it while I stay here. I came hither not knowing where else to be secure, there being at that time strong appearances of an approaching rupture with France, and all Italy being in a Flame. The Duke lives here in great Magnificence,[2] is quite inoffensive, and seems to have forgot every part of his past Life and to be of no Party. And indeed, this is perhaps the Town in the whole world where Politics are the least talk'd of.

I receive this minute a Letter from our Son dated from Senlis. He says you have order'd him to return. I know not whither he means to England or Holland; neither does he give any Direction to write to him. As soon as I have one I will not fail to do it.

Text W MS ii. 64–65   *Address* To Edd Wortley Esqr in Cavendish Square London Angleterre par Paris   *Postmark* IY 19   *End. by W* [*Summary*] Recd 21.

To Wortley *15 Aug.* [*1742*]

Avignon, Aug't 15 N.S.

You give Lord Bute the character I allways beleiv'd belong'd to him from the first of our Acquaintance, and the opinion I had of his Honesty (which is the most Essential Quality) made me so easily consent to the match.[3] The faults I observ'd in his temper I told my Daughter at that time. She made answer (as most people do while they are blinded with a passion) that she did not dislike them. I have nothing to desire of her; I never wish'd any thing but her affection, and if I was to owe the appearances of it to the

[1] In Sept. 1741 Chesterfield paid a visit to Ormond. According to Walpole his motive was political intrigue (*Corr.* xvii. 232, n. 18; also Samuel Shellabarger, *Lord Chesterfield and His World*, 1951, p. 190).

[2] Charles de Brosses estimated (in

1739) that the Duke managed to spend an income of 800,000 livres (£40,000) in Avignon, 'le séjour des vieux ruinés' (*Lettres familières sur l'Italie*, ed. Y. Bezard, 1931, i. 23).

[3] LM and W had reluctantly—rather than 'easily'—consented.

Solicitations of another, it would give me no pleasure. I am very glad she continues her Intimacy with the Dutchess of Portland,[1] whose Company will never injure her, either by Advice or Example. I have allways answer'd her Letters very regularly, and if she shews them to you, You will see in them nothing but kindness.

I do not doubt that in case of a War with France,[2] the notice you mention would be given to all the English, but I know enough of the nation to be persuaded it would be very disagreable living amongst them in such a circumstance.

I write this post to our Son, and will never omit my endeavors to set him right.

Text W MS ii. 66–67   *Address* To Edwd Wortley Esqr in Cavendish Square London Angleterre par Paris   *Postmark* AV 16   *End. by W* [*Summary*] Ad 26 Aug.

To Mme Chiara Michiel *1 Sept.* [*1742*]

Sept. 1, Avignon

Je suis charmé (aimable Ambassadrice) de tout ce que vous me dittes d'obligeant, et je vous asseure que je suis plus flatté d'un marque de vostre amitie que je serois de l'aprobation de l'academie. Moins je me trouve digne de vos Louanges, plus je me sens obligé a la partialité que vous avez toujours eû pour moi. Je vous plains d'etre dans un païs ou vous brillez aussi inutilement qu'une Lampe dans un Sepulchre. J'ose dire que vous trouverez assez de Gout dans ma patrie pour vous distinguer et vous admirer, quand nous n'aurons pas assez des charmes pour vous plaire.

Mons. Mackinsie m'a écrit une Lettre ou il me parle de son Intention de quitter l'Angleterre. S'il pouvoit se trouver a Madrid je conviens qu'il auroit de quoy remplacer toutes choses, mais comme c'est impossible, je suis persuadé que sa melancholie le suivroit par tout, et il feroit tres mal de se brouïller avec ses parens seulment pour se distraire. Je lui a écrit tres serieusement la dessus. Il a assez de merite pour être necessaire a sa Patrie, et je sacrifirois volontiers

[1] Lady Oxford's daughter.   [2] Officially declared in 1744

le plaisir de la voir au bien public, qui demande des honêttes hommes comme lui. Son Age est fait pour les affaires, et une retraitte qu'on appelle philosophique dans la viellessesse [*sic*] passe pour parresse dans un jeune homme. On doit ses premiers années a sa Famille, et un peu d'Ambition sied mieux qu'un Apparence de fainantise.

Adieu, Ma Belle Ambassadrice. Conservez moi toujours l'honneur de vostre souvenir; personne n'en connoist mieux le prix. Vos Lettres aimable ⟨et⟩ sensé valent infiniment mieux que tout le faux brillant des Conversations françoises.

Text Bute MS   *Address* A S. Excellence Madame Madame l'Ambassadrice de la S. R. de Venise a la Cour de Madrid

To Wortley *3 Sept.* [*1742*]

Avignon, Sept. 3. N.S.

I receiv'd a Letter yesterday from our Son, without either date or direction to answer it, in which he says he is in London at the desire of Lord Carteret. As I doubt the Truth of this assertion, knowing how little he regards what he says, I am afraid this Journey is only an effect of his Extravagancy, of which I never hope to see an end. I wrote a long Letter to him lately, enclos'd (as you desir'd) to Mr. Clifford, but know not whither he has receiv'd it.

Text W MS ii. 68   *End. by W* [*Summary*] Ad   Recd 6 Sept.

To Wortley *20 Sept.* [*1742*]

Sept. 20.

I suppose by this time you have had my Letter in which I gave you an Account of that I receiv'd from my Son. If ever he acts in a rational or a sincere manner I shall be much surpriz'd.

I receiv'd this day yours of Aug't 26. I am very glad to find your great Journeys do not disorder your Health.[1]

Text W MS ii. 69 *End. by W* [*Summary*] Ad

To Mme Chiara Michiel *15 Oct.* [*1742*]

Ma tres chere Madame,

Je viens de reçevoir vostre aimable Lettre, qui m'a fait un plaisir sensible. Je dois pardonner a mon Destin bien de choses pour m'avoir fait une Amie aussi charmante et aussi fidele que vous. Je suis ici depuis quelque jours pour voir Monsieur Mackinsie. Nous ne parlons que de vous, et vous pouvez estre persuadé de la maniere vive dont nous parlons. Il pense comme moi, que dans tous nos voiages nous n'avons rien connu de vostre merite, et nous regrettons sans cesse l'impossibillité de vous aller trouver. Il part demain pour Londres, ou il va joüer la Role de Senateur. Plût a Dieu qu'ils fussent tous aussi honnêtes Gens que lui; j'espererois renaitre dans ma Patrie l'honneur romaine. J'entends de l'ancienne Rome, car vous comprenez bien que je n'ai pas trop d'envie que nous imitons la moderne; et j'estime encore plus la vertu et la morale que la Peinture et la Musique. Je me contenterois mesme de nostre miserable partage du Soleil si je pouvois me vanter que le desinteressement et la Liberté Brilloient chez nous.

Je laisse a Monsieur Mackinsie de finir ma Lettre;[2] il vous diroit mieux que moi l'adoration qu'il a pour vous, mais non pas de meilleur cœur que, Ma tres chere Madame, vostre tres humble et Obeissante Servante,

M. W. Montagu.

Lyons, Oct're 15

[1] According to notes on his travels in 1742, W rode on horseback from Wharncliffe Lodge to London (171 miles) in twenty-eight hours, taking two days (Wh MS 110).

[2] In his letter to Mme Michiel, sent along with this, Mackenzie gives a farcically comic account of how LM has beaten him (dislocating her thumb) in order to force him to write at once instead of from Paris. He signs it as 'Innocence le premier', and adds: 'D'une petite cellule ou MiLady m'a enfermé'.

On m'a dit une nouvelle bien étonnante, que Mons. du Canges[1] a été inspiré de se faire Catholique.

Text Bute MS

To Lady Pomfret *4 Nov.* [*1742*]

Nov. 4, N.S., Avignon.

I am very much obliged to your ladyship for judging so rightly both of my taste and inclinations as to think it impossible I should leave a letter of yours unanswered. I never received that which you mention; and am not surprized at it, since I have lost several others, and all for the same reason; I mean, mentioning political transactions; and 'tis the best proof of wisdom that I know of our reigning ministers, that they will not suffer their fame to travel into foreign lands; neither have I any curiosity for their proceedings, being long ago persuaded of the truth of that histori-prophetical verse which says,

The world will still be ruled by knaves
And fools, contending to be slaves.[2]

I desire no other intelligence from my friends but tea-table chat, which has been allowed to our sex by so long a prescription, I believe no lady will dispute it at present. I am very much diverted with her grace's passion, which is perhaps excited by her devotion, being piously designed to take a strayed young man out of the hands of a wicked woman. I wish it may end as those projects often do, in making him equally despise both, and take a bride as charming as Lady Sophia; who, I am glad, has had a legacy from Mrs. Bridgman,[3] though I could have wished it had been more important. I hear the Duke of Cleveland will be happily disposed of to Miss Gage; who, I do not doubt, will furnish his family with a long posterity, or I have no skill in airs and graces.[4]

---

[1] LM had known him in Venice; he was a native of Dutch Flanders, born *c.* 1692 (van Berkhout MS letter to his brother, 3 June 1740).

[2] LM had used the same couplet in 1738 in No. VI of *The Nonsense of Common-Sense*.   [3] See above, p. 133.

[4] At the death of the young Duchess

This place affords us no news worth telling. I suppose you know Lady Walpole[1] has been near dying; and that Mrs. Goldsworthy being detected *flagrant de lit*, is sent back to England with her children; some of which I hear he disowns.[2] I think her case not unlike Lady Abergavenny's, her loving spouse being very well content with her gallantrys while he found his account in them, but raging against those that brought him no profit.[3] Be pleased to direct your next to Avignon, and I believe it will come safe to your ladyship's Faithful humble servant,

M.W.M.

Text 1837, ii. 266–7

To Wortley 7 *Nov.* [*1742*]

Nov. 7. N.S., Avignon.

I was very glad to receive this Day yours of Oct. 15, being in a great deal of pain on account of your long silence. I am surpriz'd you say nothing of my Son. Since I heard of his return to London, I know nothing of him,[4] having never

of Cleveland in April, Walpole remarked: 'So the poor creature her Duke is again to be let' (*Corr.* xvii. 398); but the Duke, William Fitzroy (1698–1774), did not remarry. Miss Gage was probably Teresa, da. of 1st Viscount Gage. His Grace thus remained without heirs.

[1] Margaret, Horace's sister-in-law.

[2] LM's gossip about the wife of the Consul at Leghorn (see above, p. 255) was probably not true. With her three children she left Leghorn in Aug. 1742 to further her husband's career in England—where she could also educate her children and economize by living with her father (Warren H. Smith, *Originals Abroad*, 1952, pp. 47–49, 55).

[3] Katherine Tatton (d. 1729), widow of 3rd Baron Abergavenny, m. (1725) his cousin William Neville (d. 1744), 4th Baron. 'She was taken en flagrant Delit by her Steward and her Butler (posted by her Lord for that Purpose)

on a Bed with one Mr. Lydal, a friend of her Husband's, who used to be perpetually with him and then lay in the House with them in the Country. . . . Upon this discovery Mr. Lydal was forced to give Bail for his appearance and my Lady was immediately sent to London with orders to the Servants if her Father would not recieve her, to sett her down in the Street' (Hervey to his mother, Bristol MS ii. 237). In Feb. 1730 her husband recovered damages of £10,000 from his adulterous friend (Egmont, *Diary*, i. 50).

[4] Montagu kept his relation Edward Montagu informed; on 3 Oct. 1742 he wrote from Hammersmith that he was much concerned with money problems, particularly his debts; and that while his father insisted that he leave England, Lord Carteret thought he should stay until he got an army commission (MS Mo 2840, Huntington Library).

had any answer to the letter I sent him through Mr. Clifford's hands.

It is still Summer here, and they tell me there is seldom above a month in the year colder Weather.

I dare write you no public reports; I suppose they would be stopp'd, as all are that come from London.

Text W MS ii. 70   *End. by W* [*Summary*] Ad 22 Nov.   Recd 9 Nov.

To Jean-Robert Tronchin *12 Nov.* [*1742*]

Avignon, Nov. 12.

Vous me faittes des reproches (Monsieur) que je ne croyois pas meriter. Si vous n'aviez pas reçeû la Lettre que je vous a écrite (il y a longtemps) de Lion, c'est la faute de la poste ou des Gens a qui je l'avois remise. Je vous asseure que je n'ai pas manquée d'estre sensible a l'honneur et l'agrement de vostre commerce. Il me sembloit que c'étoit vous qui l'avait discontinué, et je ne voulois pas vous importuner, sachant que trop l'impossibilité de vous amuser.

Je suis ici, non par Gout, mais par un espece de necessité formé par la tournure des choses; et la triste Experience m'aprend que la Liberté est aussi peu faite pour l'homme que l'immortalité. Nous avons beau nous servir des regimes et des remedes, ou faire des arrangements d'independance. Nous sommes né pour estre esclave et mortel. Le plus heureux parmi nous est un miserable qui tire sa consolation de la Comparaison. Vous trouverez cette morale d'une austerité ridicule. J'avoûe qu'elle est fort mal addressée; vostre Age et vostre Situation ne vous presentent que des Images riantes. Puisse telles vous durer des siecles! et je souhaitte de tout mon Cœur que vous soyiez d'humeur toute vostre vie de vous mocquer de mes sombres refflections, que je dois peutestre a l'air de mon Païs natale, que tout le soleil de Provence ne peut pas corriger.

Il y a plus de deux mois que je n'ai reçeû de nouvelles de l'Abbé de Lescheraine,[1] lui ayant envoyée une grande Lettre

---

[1] Probably Michel-Louis de Lescheraine (1697–1782), attached to the monastery at the Grande Chartreuse   (E.-A. De Foras, *Armorial et nobiliaire de l'ancien duché de Savoie*, 1893, iii. 256).

par le Comte de Loches.¹ Je suis incapable d'oublier ceux que j'estime; jugez donc si je ne serois pas toujours, Monsieur, vostre tres humble et tres Obeissante Servante,

M. W. Montagu.

Je prends la Liberté de faire mes compliments a toute vostre aimable Famille et a Mlle Franconi.

Text MS at University of Geneva   *Address* A Monsieur Monsieur Tronchin Junior a Geneve

To Wortley *12 Dec.* [*1742*]

Avignon, Dec. 12. N.S.

It is so long since I have heard from you, I cannot forbear importuning you with a Letter. I do not doubt the approaching meeting of the Parliament allows you very little Leisure,² but your silence gives me so much uneasyness, I beg of you to write, thô but one line, to assure me of your Health.

I have never heard from my Son, nor know not where he is.

Text W MS ii. 71   *End. by W* [*Summary*] Ad 20 Dec.

To Wortley *24 Dec.* [*1742*]

Avignon, Dec. 24. N.S.

I receiv'd this morning yours of Nov. 22 with great pleasure, from the account of your Health.

I am not surpriz'd at what concerns my Son; I expect never to hear any thing agreable relateing to him.

Every body is now expecting new Measures from the English Parliament. I hear a great deal said on that subject, but am afraid to write any thing that may prevent my Letters comeing to your Hands.

Text W MS ii. 72   *End. by W* [*Summary*] Ad 27 Jan.   Recd 28 Dec.

---

¹ Joseph de Loche (d. 1751), comte de Vanzy. He was related by marriage to Lescheraine (ibid., 277).

² After several prorogations, the second session of Parliament began on 16 Nov. 1742.

To Wortley *8 Jan.* [*1743*]

Avignon, Jan. 8. N.S.

I am very sorry to hear you complain of your health, particularly at the beginning of the Sessions. I hope you are by this time convince'd that the attendance in Parliament is not worth hazarding a Fever or even a Cold.

The month of Nov'r here was fine soft weather. Dec'r has been sharp cold, but allways clear till within this Fortnight that we have had a great fall of Snow, which lay some days on the ground. The oldest people say they never remember the like. But now we enjoy the usual Sun shine, yet the Air is cold and pierceing, which I am told will continue till February, which is commonly Spring. If the Soil here was as good as the climate we should have all the advantages of Italy, but the barren Sands afford little herbage, and often a Scarcity of Wheat, which makes bread dear, but excellent in its kind. Mutton [is] very good, Beef rare and bad, Wine good of various sorts. In general it is what the French call un Païs de bonne chere, but not so cheap as many others. The frequent high Winds are the most disagreable thing belonging to this Country, yet perhaps they contribute to purify the Air.

If you would know any other particulars, I shall be glad to satisfy your Curiosity in the best manner I am able.

Text W MS ii. 73–74   *Address* To Edwd Wortley Esqr in Cavendish Square London Angleterre par Paris   *Postmark* IA 18   *End. by W* [*Summary*] Ad 27 Jan   Recd 18 Jan.

To Mme Chiara Michiel *20 Jan.* [*1743*]

Avignon, Jan. 20.

J'etois si empressé de vous temoigner ma reconnoisance (ma tres chere Madame) pour vostre aimable Lettre que j'ai oublié la date de la mienne; je vous demande pardon de cette negligence. Vous m'avez rendu justice en étant persuadé que je ne serois pas sorti d'Avignon sans vous en avertir. Je connois trop le prix de vostre commerce pour hazarder de la perdre, et je puis vous asseurer avec verité qu'elle fait le principal plaisir de ma vie.

Je ne suis pas surpris de l'ignorance de vostre bon Danois;[1] il est d'un Païs ou la stupidité est permise, mais j'avoûe que je suis quelque fois étonné que sous un ciel aussi beau que celui ci je trouve tres souvent des Absurditez tout aussi fort. C'est l'esclavage qu'abrutisse les esprits, et il est seure que il n'y a que les hommes libre qui peuvent estre ou vertueux ou raisonables. S'il n'avoit eu des Republiques Grec et Romain, il n'y auroit eu ni Poetes, historiens, ni Orateurs, et nous n'aurons des meilleur memoires qui nous avons des Parthes et des Assyriens.

J'ai reçeû la poste derniere des nouvelles de Mons. Mackinsie. Il est absorbé dans les affaires. Il est vrai que c'est un attention digne d'un honnête homme, mais je crains que cet attachment nuise a sa Santé.

Pendant que le reste de l'Europe est rempli des Projets pour defendre ou étendre leurs differens états, nostre petite ville n'est occupé que des Plaisirs du Carnival, pas si brillant que ceux de Venise mais qui ne laissent pas d'avoir leur merite. Les dames et les cavaliers s'amusent a joüer des Pieces de Theatre; on donne des Bals; et si les incidens du Jeu ne meloit pas d' amertume parmi ces divertisments, nous pourions nous vanter d'une Tranquillité parfaitte.

Adieu, ma tres chere Madame. Je souhaitte a vous ⟨et⟩ vostre illustre Famille toute sorte de Joye et Contentement. Je ne doute pas que vous trouviez en tout Païs des personnes attaché a vous, mais jamais vous en verrez de plus sensible de vostre merite que, Madame, vostre tres humble et tres Obeissante Servante,

M. W. Montagu.

Text Bute MS *Address* A S. E. Madame Madame l'Ambassadrice de la S. Republique de Venise a S M Catholique a Madrid

---

[1] Count von Dehn, Danish Ambassador to Spain (see below, p. 302, n. 1).

To Wortley *8 Feb.* [*1743*]

Avignon, Feb. 8.

I have receiv'd yesterday the halfe year of Xmas last, for which I give you many thanks.

I am at present ill of a very great cold, which lyes so much in my head I am hardly able to write.

I hope your silence is not occasion'd by ill health. I think it a great while since I have heard from you.

Text W MS ii. 75   *End. by W* [*Summary*] Ad 24.   Recd 12 Feb.

To Wortley *18 Feb.* [*1743*]

Avignon, Feb 18. N.S.

I am now very well recover'd of the Epidemical Distemper which has been so universal in this Town. No Age or Sex has escap'd it, yet not one person dy'd of it. It has spread all over these Frontiers of France, and (they say) came from Italy. It has been very fatal at Marseilles and Lyons. The Duke of O[rmond] has recover'd sooner than most of those attack'd by it. I have observ'd that those which let blood have continu'd sick longer than the others. It was a fever accompany'd with pains in the Limbs and side. There are still many ill of it.

Since I began to write I have receiv'd yours dated 27 of Jan. O.S. I am very glad my Daughter is with you.[1] I hope her Conduct will never give you cause to repent your goodness to her.

If you please to add the ten Louis I gave my Son to my next Quarter's allowance, I had rather receive it in that manner than [have you] lay it out in Effects; carriage is very expensive and troublesome.

---

[1] On 24 March [O.S.] W informed LM that he planned to set out for Yorkshire on the 28th; 'I leave Lord and Lady Bute in my house, who propose to set out for Scotland a fortnight after I am gone' (W MS i. 131).

I recommend to you the care of your Health, which I wish you would make your first concern.

Text W MS ii. 76–77   *Address* To Edwd Wortley Esqr in Cavendish Square London Angleterre par Paris   *Postmark* FE 21   *End. by W* [*Summary*] Ad 24. Recd 21 Feb.

To Wortley *20 March* [*1743*]

March 20 N.S., Avignon.

I receiv'd yours of the 24th of Feb. this morning. I am glad your Health continues notwithstanding the Epidemical Distemper which has been felt in all parts of Europe.

The Sun here is now very warm, but the Weather rather cold from the North Winds which allways reign in this Season, and generally continu till May.

I receiv'd to day a very foolish Letter from our Son. I have answer'd it by this post in the best manner I am able. It is the first time I have heard from him since he left Holland.[1]

Text W MS ii. 78   *End. by W* [*Summary*] Recd 23 Mar.   Ad 24th.

To Mme Chiara Michiel *22 March* [*1743*]

Je n'ai jamais tant du plaisir que je trouve quand j'ai l'honneur de reçevoir de vos nouvelles, ma chere et aimable Ambassadrice, quoique je suis touché de la triste vie que vous mené, qui n'est pas seurement faite pour vous. Une merite comme la vostre ne doit pas être enseveli parmi des stupides et des Ignorants. Je me souviens d'avoir vû en Angleterre le Comte de Dehn, dont vous me parlez. Il étoit envoyé du Duc de Brunswic,[2] et se faisoit remarquer a Londres par des depenses ridicule. Il y etoit recherché par toutes les Coquettes qui vouloient a ses presents magnifique, et assez meprissée par les personnes d'une autre Caractere, qui ne le voyoit guerre. Voila le beau role qu'il a joué. Je m'imagine que

---

[1] But see above, p. 292.   [2] August Wilhelm (see i. 288, n. 3).

c'est quelque François qui vous a parlé si favourablement de lui; ils ne connoissent d'autre merite que le faste ou l'impertinence.[1]

J'en suis passablement ennuyé, et voudrois me retrouver sur le Canal de Venise. Mais helas! les desordres d'Italie me defend d'ÿ penser. Le seul bonheur que j'envisage, c'est de vous revoir quand vous repassez en France, et je veux me faire une affaire de me presenter sur vostre Roûte. On vous oublie jamais (ma belle Dame) et je suis persuadé que Mons. Mackinsie pense comme moi, quoy qu'il est si absorbé dans le Parlement qu'il y a longtemps que je n'ai eû de ses Lettres.[2] Milord Mareschalle est encore en France, mais tres éloigné d'ici; je ne sçai a quel desein, il s'est établi a Bologne sur mer, qui est une tres vilaine petite ville.[3]

Adieu, Ma tres chere et respectable Amie. Il n'y a personne qui vous rende plus de Justice que moi, et je suis ravÿ de connoitre dans vostre merite de quoy justifier l'inclination que j'ai d'etre toute ma vie a vous.

Avignon, Mars 22me.

Text Bute MS   *Address* A S. E. Madame Madame Clara Michielli Ambassadrice de la S. Republique de Venise a S. Majesté Catholique a Madrid

To Wortley 24 *April* [*1743*]

April 24.

I receiv'd yesterday yours of March 24. I am clearly of your opinion touching the Distemper that has reign'd all over Europe. The progress of it convince'd me long since

[1] Konrad Detlef, Count von Dehn (1688–1758), was Ambassador from Brunswick to England twice: from Oct. 1727 for five months, and from March 1729 for three (H. Ehrencron-Müller, *Forfatterlexikon Omfattende Danmark,* 1924–32, ii. 341; *Repertorium,* ii. 21). Karl Ludwig Pöllnitz describes him in terms similar to LM's—as ostentatiously rich (*Lettres et mémoires,* 3rd ed., 1737, i. 100–3). From 1740 to 1747 he served as Danish Ambassador to Spain (*Repertorium,* ii. 45).

[2] LM wrote to him on 27 March [1743] (printed above, pp. 268–9).

[3] George Keith (1693–1778), 9th Earl Marischal, had been an attainted Jacobite since 1716. Early in 1743 he settled near Boulogne to await the planned Jacobite invasion of England (Edith E. Cuthell, *The Last Earl Marischall,* 1915, i. 196).

that it has been entirely owing to Infection, and they say begun in Prague.¹

Mr. Boswell and his Lady, Sir Wm Wentworth's daughter, arriv'd here 2 days ago. I invited them to dinner and have shewn them all the Civillitys in my power. They desire their Complements to you. She is a pretty, agreable young Woman.² The Duke of Berwick³ pass'd here last week, and many other Spanish officers.

As to what regards my Son,⁴ I have long since fix'd my Opinion concerning him. I am not insensible of the misfortune, but I look upon it as on the loss of a Limb, which ceases to give Solicitude by being irretreivable.

Text W MS ii. 81–82   *Address* To Edwd Wortley Esqr in Cavendish Square London Angleterre par Paris   *Postmark* MA 2   *End. by* *W* [*Summary*] Ad 7 May.   Recd 5 May.

To Mme Chiara Michiel *4 May* [*1743*]

ce 4 de mai, Avignon.

Je suis toujours tres sensible (ma belle et chere Ambassadrice) de l'honneur de vostre souvenir. Je vous jure que l'impression de vos graces et vos bontez ne sera jamais

¹ In his letter W wrote: 'The Epidemical Distemper that was in Italy and the South of France is, I believe, here. Our Daughter and her eldest child [Mary (1738–1824)] have had it, and many persons are supposed ill of it in town. Some think it is from the Weather, but I take it to be from Infection' (W MS i. 131).

² Diana (1722–95), da. of Sir William Wentworth (1686–1763), m. (1739) Godfrey Bosville (1717–84), of Gunthwaite, Yorks. (J. Foster, *Pedigrees of the Co. Families of Yorks.*, 1874, i. *sub* Bosvile; ii. *sub* Wentworth). When they visited Florence, Horace Mann thought her provincial and 'extreme insipid' and her husband 'one of the greatest fools I ever saw' (Walpole, *Corr.* xviii. 238–9,

242, 286). But many years later in London she made a good impression on James Boswell as a 'stately sensible woman' (1766, *Boswell on the Grand Tour: Italy . . .*, ed. F. Brady and F. A. Pottle, 1955, p. 284); and after conversing with her, Dr. Johnson told Boswell, 'Sir, this is a mighty intelligent lady' (1772, *Life of Johnson*, ed. G. B. Hill and L. F. Powell, 1934, ii. 169).

³ James Francis Edward Stuart-Fitzjames (1718–85), attainted Duke of Berwick, appointed in 1743 brigadier-general in the Spanish service.

⁴ In his letter W wrote: 'I have heard nothing of our Son's Commission of late, and can send you no good news of him.'

effacé de mon Cœur, et je saisirai avec avidité toutes les occasions qui pourront se presentir de vous le prouver.

Je vous obeirai en vous parlant sincerement a l'égard de la Princesse di Ajaccio, que j'ai beaucoup vû a Naples.[1] Elle étoit alors si jeune qu'on peut esperer qu'elle s'est corrigé, mais c'etoit une petite impertinente françoise, toute petri des prejugez et des ridicules de son Païs, meprisant toute la magnificence de la famille de son Mari, quoy qu'elle n'avoit rien vû de plus beau qu'un Couvent pres de St. Denis, ou elle fût élevé; d'ailleurs assez joli de figure, avec de tres belle dispositions a la Coquettrie. Voici son portrait au juste, que je serois fasché de montrer a une autre que vous. Vous sçavez que le Prince di Ajaccio a beaucoup de merite; il m'a fait toutes les politesses imaginable durant mon sejour a Naples, et je serai ravy de lui rendre service. Il trouvera une grande resource dans vostre Maison a Madrid, et je ne doute pas que vous sera contente de sa Conversation, qui est fort aimable. Si j'osois je vous prierai de lui faire les compliments de ma part.[2]

J'ai reçeû la poste passé une Lettre de Monsieur Mackinsie, qui me paroist tres degouté de toutes les divisions de nostre malheureuse patrie. Si vous etiez a Venise, je suis persuadé qu'il y retournera, ce qui n'est pas surprenant. Ou trouve-t-on une Amie comme vous? Si je vous disois tout ce que je pense sur cet chapitre, vous m'accuserez peutestre de flatterie. Je puis pourtant vous asseurer hardiment que je tais encore plus que je ne dis, quand je vous proteste de vous estre fidellement et tendrement attaché a jamais.

Text Bute MS   *Address* A S. E. Madame Madame Chiara Michielli Ambassadrice de la S. Republique de Venise a Madrid

[1] See above, p. 220, n. 2.

[2] In May 1743 Prince Iaci was named Ambassador to Spain by the King of the Two Sicilies; he arrived in Madrid with his wife in June. She died in Dec.

'd'une fausse couche, par une peur qu'elle eut d'un chat, vingt-quatre heures après être accouchée d'un garçon' (Chenaye-Desbois, v. 346).

From Lord Hervey *31/20 May 1743*

May 20/31, 1743

I am to thank you, dear Madam, for a letter full of all those striking, judicious truths which the wisdom of the ancients taught us traditionally in theory, and the folly of our cotempor[ar]ys has manifested experimentally in practice. But tho' I agree with you in thinking the human species so worthless a race of animals that considering the present events of Europe in that light, I can feal no more concern for two or three hundred thousand of these animals destroyed by war than when I read of as many swept off by a plague in Smirna, or swallow'd up in an earth-quake in Sicily. . . . *[Passage omitted]*

Text Bristol MS ii. 139, 142   *Address* a Madame Madame de Montagu à Avignon (par Paris)   *Postmark* D'ANGLETERRE

To Wortley *1 June* [*1743*]

Avignon, June 1. N.S.

I hope you will take care not to return to London while it is in this unhealthy state; we are now very clear in these parts. Mrs. Bosville is gone to Turin, where they intend to reside. She had the good Fortune to meet an English man of War on the Coast, without which she would have found the passage very difficult.[1] She had so much her Journey at heart that she undertook to ride over the Mountains from Nissa to Savona, but I beleive (notwithstanding her Youth and Spirit) would have found the execution impossible. She has chose the most agreable Court in Europe, where the English are extreamly carress'd. But tis necessary to be young and Gay for such projects; all mine terminate in

---

[1] Mr. and Mrs. Bosville presumably sailed from Antibes or Nice to Genoa, and then continued north by land to Turin. But they never settled there: they spent the summer in Florence, after which Mrs. Bosville went to Genoa to await her naval lover while her husband returned home to England (Walpole, *Corr.* xviii. 238, 286, 309).

Quiet, and if I can end my Days without great Pains 'tis the utmost of my Ambition.

Text W MS ii. 83–84   *Address* To Edwd Wortley Esqr at his House in Cavendish Square London Angleterre par Paris   *Postmark* IV 6 *End. by W [Summary]* Ad 22 June.   Recd 6 June.

From Lord Hervey *29/18 June 1743*

Ickworth Park, June the 18th 1743[1]

The last stages of an infirm life are filthy roads, and like all other roads, I find the farther one goes from the capital the more tedious the miles grow, and the more rough and disagreeable the ways. I know of no turnpicks to mend them; medicine pretends to be such, but doctors, who have the management of it, like the comissioners for most other turnpikes, seldom execute what they undertake. They only put the toll of the poor cheated passenger in their pockets and leave every jolt at least as bad as they found it, if not worse. May all your ways (as Solomon says of wisdom) be ways of pleasentness, and all your paths peace; and when your dissolution must come, may it be like that of your lucky workman. Adieu.

Text Bristol MS ii. 143

To Wortley *16 July [1743]*

Avignon, July 16 N.S.

I receiv'd yours this morning of the 22nd of June with a great deal of pleasure, thinking it a long time since I had heard from you. The general course of the post is now often interupted. The last Courier from Paris was assassinated, and his packet riffled. It is hop'd the last Action, which is said to be very advantageous of our side, will facillitate a peace.[2] Every body seems weary of a War in which all partys suffer.

[1] This was one of the last things Hervey wrote; on 23 June he dictated his will because 'I was not Strong enough to write' (P.C.C. Boycott, f. 264). He died on 5 Aug. of this year.

[2] In the battle of Dettingen, on 27 June, the French were defeated by the allied army of the English, Hanoverians, and Austrians, led by George II.

I am told Admiral Mathews is dangerously ill of the Stone at Nice.[1]

I hope your Health continues, and that you will take care to preserve it.

Text W MS ii. 85–86   *Address* To Edwd Wortley Esqr in Cavendish Square London Angleterre par Paris   *Postmark* IY 18   *End. by W* Ad L.M. 16 July 1743. The Posts do not go regularly. The Action near Aschaffemberg.[2] Ad 25 July.

To Wortley *28 July* [*1743*]

Avignon, July 28 N.S.

I receiv'd last post a Letter from my Son dated from Bruxelles the 16th instant in which he says he is proceeding to the Army the next day. He does not mention whither it is with your permission, nor gives me no Direction to write to him. Perhaps the same rashness which has ruin'd him in other affairs may be Lucky to him there.

I am certainly inform'd that the Plague has penetrated from Messina[3] into Calabria, which spreads a great Terror to Naples and Rome. 15,000 are said to have dy'd of it at Messina. We have had hitherto a very mild Healthy Summer.

Text W MS ii. 87   *End. by W* [*Summary*] Ad 25 Aug.   Recd 1 Aug.

From Wortley *5 Aug./25 July* [*1743*]

25 July.

I have yours of the 16. The enclosed was, as you see, directed to my house. I imagine it comes from Lady Marr and may not be agreable

---

[1] Thomas Mathews (1676–1751) was Commander-in-Chief in the Mediterranean. During the summer he was ashore at Villefranche, by permission of the Duke of Newcastle, to recover his health (H. W. Richmond, *The Navy in the War of 1739–48*, 1920, i. 230–1).

[2] Aschaffenburg in Bavaria, near which the battle of Dettingen took place.

[3] The bubonic plague had begun in Messina in May. On 23 July Horace Mann estimated the dead at 30,000 though they actually amounted to 40,000 (Walpole, *Corr.* xviii. 252, 269 and n. 5; also 282, 288, 301–2).

to you, but as I cannot ghess what is in it, I thought it best to send it you.

Tho our son is said to set his heart upon a Commission, yet (as Mr. G[ibson] tells me) he coud not persuade him to go abroad without one when the King went. He did [not] resolve to go till about the 20th or the 21 of June, on which day Mr. G. told me of his resolution; but he did not set out from London till the 30th, which was just a week after the news of the Battle came to London.

He writ to Mr. G. a letter from Brussels 5 days after his setting out, in which he seemed pleased with his Expedition and determined to make the best of his way to Francfort. What Lord C[arteret] will advise him to, I cannot ghess. I suppose Mr. G. will from time to time inform me of his letters.

Text W MS i. 133 (draft)

To Wortley *19 Aug.* [*1743*]

Aug't 19th N.S.

This Letter which I receiv'd yesterday enclos'd in yours of July 25 has (as you see) nothing in it disagreable to me, on the contrary is the most rational I have receiv'd from my Sister since her Disorder. As she sends me no Direction, I beg you would take care of the Answer.

I have accidentally had (I beleive) a true information of my Son's behaviour at Paris, which was not at all better than in London 6 years ago. I wish Flanders may be more Lucky to him.

The Weather is here at present very hot, but agrees very well with me. I hope you have perfect Health in London.

Text W MS ii. 88   *End. by W* [*Summary*] Ad 25 Aug.   Recd 22 Aug.

To Mme Chiara Michiel *29 Aug.* [*1743*]

Trop chere et trop aimable Madame,

Je dois vous appeller ainsi puis que malgre les marques que vous me donnez de vostre amitie, dont je connois tout le prix, nous sommes et resterons dans un éloignment qui me permet pas de Jouïr de cette conversation charmante, capable de me consoler du tout; et (ce que me touche encore plus sensiblement) je sçai que malgre le brillant exterieur de vostre Situation, vous n'avez pas un bonheur fait pour un goût aussi juste et aussi delicat que la vostre.

Je serois trop heureuse si je pouvois partager vos ennuis; je les troquerois volontiers contre tous les plaisirs de France, qui sont aussi peu faittes pour moi que ceux de Madrid pour vous. On sçait aussi peu ce que c'est que la Conversation ici, que si on étoit poisson. Il est vrai qu'ils sont tres éloigné de la taciturnité de cet animal; c'est un caquet éternelle, mais avec moins de variation que celui des peroquets; toujours les Cartes a la main, les mesmes riens repeté à tout propos, et croyant que l'étourderie est vivacité d'esprit; si peu capable d'Amitie qu'ils ne regrettent ni n'estiment personne qu'a proportion de leur utilité a Quadrille, qui leur paroist le grand But de la Science Humaine. Vous serois un jour, je croy (ma belle Ambassadrice), a Paris, ou vous verrois, tel que je l'ai depeint, le grand Original de tous ces copies de province. Je vous avoûe que je suis excedé a un point que j'ai envie de me jetter en Italie, au travers tout le feu et le sang dont elle est menacée.

Il y a quelques temps que je n'ai pas reçeu des nouvelles de Monsieur Mackensie, mais je suis si bien persuadé de son Cœur et son goût, que je suis seure qu'il conserve toujours pour vous le respectueux admiration que vous étes faittes pour inspirer, mais dont personne est plus penetrée que, ma chere Ambassadrice, vostre fidelle et sincere amie et Servante,

                                   M. W. Montagu.
Avignon, Août 29me

Text Bute MS   *Address* A S. E. Madame Madame l'Ambassadrice de la S. Republique de Venise a la Cour de Madrid.

To Wortley *16 Sept.* [*1743*]

Avignon, Sept. 16 N.S.

I am very glad that your Health continues. I had a Letter from my Daughter last post, by which I am inform'd all her Family are well.

Several Scotch pass here often. I say nothing to you of public news, not being able to depend on any thing I hear. Several French Regiments are quarter'd round this Province in order (they say) to joyn D. Philip.[1]

Text W MS ii. 89–90   *Address* To Edwd Wortley Esqr at his House in Cavendish Square London Angleterre par Paris   *Postmark* SE 19   *End. by W* Ad   L.M. 16 Sept. 1743.   fr. Avignon. Ad 24 Oct. Recd 22d

From Lady Oxford[2] *28/17 Sept. 1743*

Welbeck,[3] Sept'r 17th 1743 O.S.

Dearest Madam,

I take the 1st oppertunity to beg your Ladyship's acceptance of my most Gratefull Thanks for your kind letter I received here the 15th O.S.[4] The share of Health you injoy is the most pleasing comfort I can meet with in your Absense,[5] and I constantly pray for the continuence of that Blessing and that you may not allways be deprived of every other, except what you have and ever will possess (a good Mind).

[Passage omitted]

[1] Don Philip (1720–65), son of Philip V of Spain, commanded the Spanish troops in northern Italy.

[2] Of Lady Oxford's correspondence the drafts of 57 letters to LM are extant among the Harley MS.

[3] In the Dukeries, Notts.; Welbeck Abbey was Lady Oxford's paternal home.

[4] LM's first surviving letter is that of 13 April [1744].

[5] Their friendship had been very warm before LM left England. In 1738 she engaged C. F. Zincke to paint her portrait in miniature, and presented it to Lady Oxford (miniature now owned by the Duke of Portland: see Frontispiece); the next year George Vertue made an engraving of this along with portraits of Lady Oxford's daughter and son-in-law (Victoria and Albert Museum; Princeton University Library). Before she went abroad LM sat for a large portrait in oils inscribed on the back 'done from life by Carolus De Rusca London 1739 Given by her Ladyship to Lady Oxford' (Plate 10 in Halsband, *LM*).

Lord Hervey's Will[1] is at this time the cheife Subject of Discourse, particularly 2 Paragraffs *I leave such a sum of Money to all my Younger Children born in Wedlock, so much to Lady Hervey because I can not help it.*[2] *My Youngest Daughter*[3] *to be brought to Mrs. Horner imediatly.*[4] I did not imagine he would write such expressions in a Will to be Published after his Death. It is thought the Duke of Argile is not like to last long in this World.

I had lately a letter from Lady Arran.[5] In it she mentions Mr. Butler[6] remembers you with Gratitude. I Think her sincere; I Hope he is so.

I am with the Greatest Esteeme, Affection and Gratitude, Dearest Lady Mary, Ever your Ladyship's Most Devoted Friend and Servant.

Text Harley MS (draft)   *End. by Lady Oxford* Welbeck Septr 17th 1743 O.S. Directed Par Paris   A Miledi Montagu   Laice Au Maitre de Post A Avignon

To Wortley [*18 Oct. 1743*]

I receiv'd yours of Sept 21 O.S. this day, Oct. 18 N.S., and am allways glad to hear of your Health.

I can never be surpriz'd at any sort of Folly or Extravagance of my Son. Immediately on leaving me at Orange after the most solemn promises of reformation, he went to Montelimart, which is but one day's post from thence, where he behav'd him selfe with as much vanity and Indiscretion as ever. I had my Intelligence from people who did not know my relation to him, and do not trouble you with the particulars, thinking it needless to expose his character to you who are well acquainted with it. I am persuaded whoever protects

---

[1] P.C.C. Boycott, f. 264.
[2] Except for annuities to his younger children, he left everything to his eldest son, and nothing to his wife except what he had to. He even required her to post bond.
[3] Carolina Hervey (1736–1819).
[4] Susanna (d. 1758), da. of Thomas Strangways, widow of Thomas Horner, was mother-in-law of Hervey's intimate

young friend Stephen Fox, 1st Lord, later Earl of, Ilchester. On 16/5 Dec. Lady Oxford wrote that Mrs. Horner had 'refused to take the Charge of Mis Hervey'.
[5] Elizabeth (1680–1756), da. of 2nd Baron Crew, m. (1705) 1st Earl of Arran.
[6] Probably James Butler (d. 1759), who later inherited Lord Arran's estate (*Gentleman's Mag.*, 1759, p. 242).

him will be very soon convince'd of the Imposibillity of his behaving like a rational Creature.

I know the young Lady Carlisle. She is very agreable, but if I am not mistaken in her Inclinations, they are very gay.[1] Lady Oxford wrote to me last post[2] that Lady Strafford was then with her. She informs me that the Duke of Argyle is in a very bad state of Health. I hope you will take care to preserve yours.

Text W MS ii. 91–92   *Address* To Edwd Wortley Esqr in Cavendish Square London Angleterre par Paris   *Postmark* OC 19   *End. by W* [*Summary*] Ad 24 Oct.   Recd 20 Oct.

To Wortley 4 *Nov.* [*1743*]

Nov. 4. N.S., Avignon

I receiv'd this post the enclos'd Letter. I send it to you in order to have your Direction in what manner to answer it. I think the style is rather better than ordinary and probably he was help'd in it, but the sense as usual, mistakeing civillity for aprobation in the behaviour of his commanders[3] and saying nothing has been done without him, when I know nothing he has done. If you think it proper, I will tell him of the Bond you mention'd as if I had heard of it from another Hand.

I am very sorry for the Death of the Duke of Argyle on the account of my Daughter, her Lord loseing a great support. He dy'd a young man in the account of this Country, where no body is old till fourscore years and ten.[4]

1 Isabella (1721–95), da. of 4th Baron Byron, m. (8 June 1743) 4th Earl of Carlisle, a recent widower 28 years her senior. She indulged her gay inclinations as an elderly lady, leading a busy amorous career on the Continent (Warren H. Smith, *Originals Abroad*, 1952, pp. 97–112).

2 In her letter of 28/17 Sept.

3 On 20 Sept. 1743 Montagu was commissioned a cornet in Cope's Dragoons (7th Hussars) (C. T. Atkinson in *Journal of the Soc. for Army Hist. Research*, xxvii, 1949, p. 160).

4 John Campbell (b. 1680), 2nd Duke of Argyll, died on 4 Oct., aged almost 63. He was Lord Bute's uncle. Because he had opposed Walpole and hastened his downfall he was given important posts by the new ministry, but resigned them after a few weeks because he thought them insufficient rewards. LM was apparently unaware that he had lost his power.

It is now such fine Weather that people walk every evening and 'tis impossible to bear a fire.

Text W MS ii. 93–94   *Address* To Edwd Wortley Esqr in Cavendish Square London Angleterre par Paris   *Postmark* NO 7   *End. by W* [*Summary*] Ad 24th

To Mme Chiara Michiel 7 *Nov.* [*1743*]

Avignon, Nov. 7.

Vous serois (je croy) tres surprize, ma chere Madame, d'entendre que Monsieur Mackinsie a passé par Lyon, que je ne l'ai point vûe, et qu'il a passé a Venise par le pas de St. Bernard, malgre la saison, malgre les Espagnols, et malgre le sens commun.[1] S'il est allé baiser le seuil de vostre porte, c'est un but qui lui fait honneur; d'ailleur je ne sçaurois m'imaginer aucune motif raisonable pour abondonner tous ses interests et tous ses amis, et j'en suis veritablement mortifiée par le part que je prends a tout ce qui luy regarde. Je voudrois qu'il s'estimoit autant que je l'estime; il auroit plus de soin de sa personne et de sa conduitte. Je ne doubte pas que vous ne l'ayez donné des conseils tres sage, mais vous voyez qu'il n'écoute que son goût. J'avoue que Venise a des charmes bien attraiante, et que si j'etois aussi vif que lui, je ferois la mesme chose, mais je suis d'une age ou on attend de trouver la Discretion, et a le sien on excuse la vivacité.

Je partage tous vos deplaisirs, ma charmante Amie; je conviens que le sejour des montagnes sterile n'est pas fait pour vous, et on peut dire que vous etes furieusement deplacé. Je ne sçaurois pourtant convenir que vostre esprit diminuroit; je suis persuadé qu'il est aussi incapable de s'affoiblir que les raions du soleil de se soüillir en éclairant un fumier. Il est vrai que c'est dommage de briller pour des

[1] Behind LM's cryptic remark lies a dramatic, romantic episode. In London that autumn Mackenzie had met the dancer Barberina Campanini (1721–99), and had become so infatuated with her that they fled to Venice intending to marry (Pierre Gaxotte, *Frederick the Great*, transl. R. A. Bell, 1942, p. 235; J.-J. Olivier and W. Norbert, *Barberina Campanini Eine Geliebte Friedrichs des Grossen*, 1909, pp. 41 ff.).

objets si indigne et si insensible. Je me flatte de vous voir dans une situation plus agreable; le plus ardent des mes souhaits vous accompagnent par tout, étant attaché a vous par l'amitie le plus tendre et l'estime le plus respectueux.

Text Bute MS   *Address* A S.E. Madame Madame Michielli Ambassadrice de la S. Republique de Venise a la Cour de Madrid.

To Wortley *20 Nov.* [*1743*]

Nov. 20. N.S.

I have just receiv'd yours of Oct'r 24 O.S. and am allways very glad to hear of the continuation of your Health.

As to my Son's behaviour at Montlimart, it is nothing more than a proofe of his weakness and how little he is to be depended on in his most solemn proffessions. He told me that he had made acquaintance with a Lady on the road who has an assembly at her House in Montelimart and that she had invited him thither. I ask'd immediately if she knew his name. He assur'd me no, and that he pass'd for a Dutch Officer by the name of Durand.[1] I advis'd him not to go thither, since it would raise a Curiosity concerning him, and I was very unwilling it should be known that I had convers'd with him, on many accounts. He gave me the most solemn assurances that no mortal should know it, and agreed with me in the reasons I gave him for keeping it an entire secret, yet rid strait to Montelimart, where he told at the assembly that he came into this Country purely on my orders and that I had staid with him 2 days at Orange, talking much of my kindness to him, and insinuateing that he had another name much more considerable than that he appear'd with. I knew nothing of this till several months after, that a Lady of that Country[2] came hither, and meeting her in Company, she ask'd me if I was acquainted with Monsieur Durand. I had realy forgot he had ever taken that name, and made answer no, and that if such a person mention'd me, it was probably some Chevalier d'indus⟨trie⟩[3] who sought to introduce

---

[1] As ordered by LM (p. 288 above).   LM names her on 29 Dec [1744].
[2] Probably Madame St. Auban, as   [3] Swindler.

himselfe into company by a suppos'd acquaintance with me.
She made answer, the whole Town beleiv'd so by the improbable Tales he told them, and inform'd me what he had said, by
which I knew what I have related to you.

I expect your orders in relation to his Letter.

Text W MS ii. 95–96   *Address* To Edwd Wortley Esqr in Cavendish Square London Angleterre par Paris   *Postmark* NO 23   *End.*
by W [*Summary*] Recd 23 Nov. Ad 24.

To Wortley 20 Dec. [1743]

Avignon, Dec. 20. N.S.

I receiv'd yours of the 24 of Nov. O.S. yesterday. I send
you the enclose'd for my Son, not knowing where to direct
to him. I have endeavor'd to write it according to your
minutes, which are entirely just and reasonable.

You may perhaps hear of a triffle which makes a great
noise in this part of the World, which is that I am building,
but the whole expence which I have contracted for is but £26 st.

You know the situation of this Town is on the meeting
of the Rhosne and Durance. On one side of it within the
Walls was formerly a Forteresse built on a very high rock.[1]
They say it was destroy'd by Lightning. One of the Towers
was left part standing, the Walls being a yard in Thickness.
This was made use of sometime for a public mill, but the
height makeing it inconvenient for the carriage of meal, it
has stood useless many years. Last summer in the hot evenings I walk'd often thither, where I allways found a fresh
breeze and the most beautifull land prospect I ever saw
(except Wharncliffe),[2] being a view of the windings of two
great Rivers, and overlooking the whole County, with part
of Languedoc and Provence. I was so much charm'd with it
that I said in Company that if that old mill was mine I would

---

[1] The Rocher-des-Doms, the wind-
swept acropolis of Avignon.
[2] Lady Louisa Stuart described
Wharncliffe (in 1778) as placed 'like an
eagle's nest, upon the very summit of a
steep rock, which is entirely covered
with wood, and the trees grow almost
close to the walls' (*Letters,* ed. R. B.
Johnson, 1926, p. 30).

turn it into a belvedere. My words were repeated, and the 2 Consuls waited on me soon after with a donation from the Town of the Mill and the land about it.[1] I have added a Dome to it, and made it a little rotunda, for the foresaid summ. I have also amus'd my selfe with patching up an Inscription, which I have communicated to the Arch Bishop,[2] who is much delighted with it; but it is not pl⟨a⟩c'd and perhaps never shall be.

> Hic O Viator sub Lare parvulo
> Maria hic est condita, hic jacet
> Defuncta humani Laboris
> sorte, supervacuaque vita.
> Non indecora pauperies [*sic*] nitens
> et non inerti nobilis otio,
> vanoque dilectis popello
> Divitiis animosus hostis.
> Possis ut illam dicere mortuam
> En terra jam nunc Quantula sufficit!
> Exempta sit curis Viator
> Terra sit illa levis precare.
> Hic sparge Flores, sparge breves rosas,
> Nam vita gaudet mortua Floribus,
> Herbisque odoratis Corona
> Vatis adhuc cinerem calentem.[3]

---

[1] At the meeting of the town council on 18 Oct. 1743 '. . . a eté exposé par Mons. Le premier Consul que Miledy Montaigu luy a fait connoitre qu'elle seroit bien aise d'avoir a sa disposition une des tours que la ville a sur la Roche pour en pouvoir jouir de la beauté de la vue et se reposer quand elle y va, et que Le Conseil luy feroit palisir s'il luy en accordoit la jouissance sa vie durant, ce qu'entendu par le Conseil celuy a unaniment agrée la demande de la d[ite] Dame, et luy a accordé la jouissance d'une des dites tours pour tout le temps qu'elle restera dans cette ville, sans préjudice de la propriétée de la ville sur celle' (Conseils, xxxxi. 446, Archives, Palais des Papes, Avignon).

[2] Joseph de Guyon de Crochant (1674–1756), appointed to Avignon in 1742.

[3] Adapted by LM from Abraham Cowley, 'Epitaphium. Vivi Authoris', *Poemata Latina*, 1668, p. 420. In the second line she substituted her own name (Maria) for 'Couleius'. The epitaph, as translated by Joseph Addison:
From life's superfluous cares enlarged,
His debt of human toil discharged,
Here Cowley lies! beneath this shed,
To every worldly interest dead;
With decent poverty content,
His hours of ease not idly spent;
To fortune's goods a foe profest,
And hating wealth by all carest.
'Tis true he's dead; for oh! how small
A spot of earth is now his all;
Oh! wish that earth may lightly lay,
And every care be far away;
Bring flowers; the short-lived roses bring,
To life deceased fit offering:
And sweets around the poet strow,
While yet with life his ashes glow
(*Works*, Bohn ed., 1856, vi. 536).

You will know how I pick'd up these Verses,[1] thô the Arch Bishop did not.

Text W MS ii. 97–98   *Address* To Edwd Wortley Esqr in Cavendish Square London Angleterre par Paris   *Postmark* DE 26   *End. by W* Ad L.M. 20 Dec. 1743/4.   Verses.   Ad 19 Jan.

To Wortley *12 Jan.* [*1744*]

Jan. 12. N.S., Avignon

I have receiv'd yours of the 22nd of December halfe an hour ago. I allways answer your Letters the same post I receive them if they come early enough to permit it; if not, the post following. I am much mortify'd you have not receiv'd two I have wrote, and in the last a Letter enclos'd for my Son. I cannot help being very much concern'd at the continual trouble he is to you, thô I have no reason to expect better from him. I am persuaded the Flattery of G[ibson] does him a great deal of harm. I know G.'s way of thinking enough not to depend on any thing he says to his advantage, much less on any Account he gives of himselfe. I think 'tis an ill sign that you have had no Letter from Sir J. Cope concerning him.[2] I do not doubt he would be glad to commend his Conduct if there was any room for it. It is my Opinion he should have no Distinction in Equipage from any other Cornet, and every thing of that Sort will only serve to blow his Vanity and consequently heighten his Folly. Your Indulgence has allways been greater to him than any other parent's would have been in the same circumstances. I have allways said so and thought so. If any thing can alter him, it will be thinking firmly that he has no dependance but on his own conduct for a future maintenance.

Text W MS ii. 99–100   *Address* To Edwd Wortley Esqr in Cavendish Square London Angleterre par Paris   *Postmark* IA 16 *End. by W* Ad   L.M. 12 Jan. 1743/4.   Son.   Recd 17 Jan. Ad. 19 Jan.

---

[1] In their early courtship letters W had mentioned Cowley to LM; and her library sent abroad in 1739 included a two-volume edition of Cowley's works (Wh MS 135).

[2] Lt.-Gen. Sir John Cope (1690–1760), colonel of the 7th Hussars, in which Montagu was a cornet.

To Mme Chiara Michiel *15 Jan.* [*1744*]

Je vous asseure, ma tres chere et charmante Ambassadrice,
que je n'ai pas douté un moment a l'égard de la noblesse de
vos sentiments. Je sçais que vostre Cœur est digne de vostre
naissance, et plût a dieu que Monsieur Mackinsie voulut se
laisser toujours diriger par des Conseils aussi sages et aussi
respectables que les vostres. Il a quitté Londres dans le temps
que le Duc d'Argyle mouroit, pour ne le pas voir expirer; il
me paroit tres touché de sa perte. Je croi que cet malheur a
mis le comble a son degoût pour l'Angleterre; et je ne suis
pas surprise (quoy que fasché) que se trouvant son Maitre,
il a cherché son plaisir au depens de l'ambition qu'on doit
avoir a son Age. Enfin il est pressé de vivre, et on doit le
regarder comme un Philosophe prematuré.[1]

Je me flatte tres agreablement de l'Idée que vous me
donnez de vostre retour en sept mois.[2] Si je suis vivante je
vous verrois a vostre passage, et le plaisir de vous embrasser
me dedomagera des chagrins que vostre éloignment m'a
causé. Vous verrez par la vivacité de ma joie a quel point je
suis (Aimable Ambassadrice) vostre tres humble etc. etc.

Avignon, Jan. 15.

Il faut addresser les Lettres a Mons. Mackinsie recommandé a Mons. Smith, Consul d'Angleterre.[3]

Text Bute MS   *Address* A S. E. Madame Madame de Michielli
Ambassadrice de la S. Republique de Venise a la Cour de Madrid

[1] Although LM must have known
that Mackenzie had eloped from England with the dancer Barberina (see
above, p. 313, n. 1), she puts forward
instead a less scandalous reason for his
departure, the death of his uncle.

[2] Cav. Michiel's three-year appointment would then be terminated. He left

Madrid on 4 Aug. 1744 (*Repertorium,*
ii. 416).

[3] Joseph Smith was apparently acting
consul; his official appointment was not
announced until March 1744 'in room
of Neil Brown, Esq; dec.' (*Gentleman's
Mag.*, p. 169). Browne had died in 1740.

To Wortley 5 *Feb.* [*1744*]

Avignon, Feb. 5. N.S.

I think it a great while since I heard from you. I have wrote 3 times since I receiv'd your last letter. Here is a Comet which is very bright and covers a great part of the Horizon.[1] If it will give you any pleasure I will send you an account of its progress as taken by the Jesuits.

Chance has occasion'd a secret of great importance to come to my knowledge. I dare not write it, fearing that my Letter will not come to your hands if I should mention it.[2]

Text W MS ii. 101   *End. by W* L.M. 5 Feb. 1743/4.   The Comet. A Secret.   Ad 20th Feb.

To Wortley *17 Feb.* [*1744*]

Avignon, Feb. 17. N.S.

I am very sorry you have given your selfe so much trouble about the Inscription.[3] I find I express'd my selfe ill if you understood by my Letter that it was plac'd. I never intended it without your Aprobation, and then would have put it in the inside of the Dome. The word *pauperie* is meant as is shewn by the whole line

Non indecora pauperie nitens

to be a Life rather distant from Ostentation than in poverty, and which answers very well to my way of living, which thô decent is far from the shew which many Familys make here.

The nobillity consists of about 200 houses; amongst them are 2 Dukes, that of Crillon[4] and of Guadagna,[5] the last an Italian Family, the other French. The Count of Suze[6] (who

---

[1] In England the comet was judged the most spectacular since 1680 (*Gentleman's Mag.*, Feb. 1744, p. 86).

[2] She sent it on 25 March.

[3] In her letter of 20 Dec. [1743].

[4] François-Félix de Balbe-Berton, duc de Crillon.

[5] Spreti (iii. 598) mentions a branch of this Florentine family settled in Provence.

[6] Louis-Michel de Chamillart (1709–74), comte de la Suze.

also values himselfe very much on his pedigree) keeps a constant open Table, as does several others. You will judge by that, the provisions are exceeding cheap, but it is otherwise, the price of every thing being high for Strangers; but as all the Gentlemen keep their land in their own hands and sell their Wine, Oyl, and Corn, their housekeeping looks very great at a small Expence. They have also all sort of Gibier from their own Lands, which enables them to keep a splendid Table. Their Estates have never been Tax'd, the Pope drawing (as I am assur'd) no Revenue from hence. The Vice Legate[1] has a Court of Priests, and sees little other Company, which I beleive is partly owing to the little respect the nobillity shew him, who despise his want of Birth. There is a new one expected this Spring, Nephew to the Cardinal Acquaviva.[2] He is young, and they say intends to live with great Magnificence.

Avignon was certainly no Town in the time of the Romans,[3] nor is there the smallest remains of any Antiquity but what is entirely Gothic. The Town is large, but thinnly people'd. Here are 14 large Convents, beside others. It is so well situated for Trade and the silk so fine and plentifull that if they were not curb'd by [the] French not permitting them to trade, they would certainly ruin Lyons; but as they can sell none of their manufactures out of the Walls of the Town, and the Ladys here (as every where else) preferring foreign stuffs to their own, the Trades people are poor and the Shops ill furnish'd. The people of Quality all affect the French manner of living, and here are many good Houses. The climate would be as fine as that of Naples if we were not persecuted by the North Wind, which is allmost a constant plague. Yet by the great age and surprizing Health I see many of them enjoy, I am persuaded the Air is very wholesome. I see of both Sexes past 80 who appear in all the assemblys, eat great suppers and keep late Hours, without any visible infirmity. It is to day Shrove Tuesday. I am invited to sup at the

---

[1] Niccolò Lercari, a Genoese patrician, Vice-Legate 1739–44 (Gaetano Moroni, *Dizionario di erudizione storico-ecclesiastica*, 1840–61, iii. 376).

[2] Cardinal Trojano Acquaviva (1694–1747), of the family of the Dukes of Atri; his distant cousin Pasquale Acquaviva (1719–88) was appointed Vice-Legate to Avignon in 1743 (Moroni, i. 74, 75).

[3] As Avenio it was a leading city of Gallia Narbonensis.

Dutch⟨esse o⟩f Crillon's,[1] where I do not doubt I shall see near 50 Guests who will all of them, young and old (except my selfe), go mask'd to the Ball that is given in the Town house. It is the sixth given this Carnival by the Gentlemen gratis. At the first there was 1,200 Tickets given out, many comeing from the Neighbouring Towns of Carpentras, Lisle, Orange, and even Aix and Arles, on purpose to appear there.

D[on] Philip is expected here the 22nd. I beleive he will not stay any time, and if he should, I think (in the present situation) it would be improper for me to wait on him.[2] If he goes into Company, I suppose I may indifferently see him at an Assembly.

Text W MS ii. 102–4   *Address* To Edwd Wortley Esqr in Cavendish Square London Angleterre par Paris   *Postmark* FE 24   *End. by W* Ad   L.M. 17 Feb. 1743/4   Acct of Avignon   Don Philip expected the 22d.   The Word Pauperie.   Ad 22 Mar.

To Wortley 25 *March* [*1744*]

I take this opportunity of informing you in what manner I came acquainted with the secret I hinted at in my Letter of the 5 of Feb. The Society of Free Masons at Nismes presented the Duke of Richlieu,[3] Governor of Languedoc, with a magnificent Entertainment. It is but one day's post from hence, and the Dutchess of Crillon with some other Ladys of this Town resolv'd to be at it, and allmost by force carry'd me with them, which I am tempted to beleive an act of providence, considering my great reluctance and the service it prov'd to be to unhappy innocent people. The greatest part of the Town of Nismes are secret Protestants, which are still severely punish'd according to the Edicts of

[1] Marie-Thérèse Fabry-de-Moncault, da. of the Governor of Besançon, m. (1715) the duc de Crillon.

[2] England was at war with Spain.

[3] Louis-François-Armand du Plessis (1696–1788), grand-nephew of Cardinal Richelieu; since 1738 the King's Lieu-tenant-General of Languedoc. He was successful in pacifying, temporarily at least, the rebellious religious factions in that stronghold of Protestantism (H. Noel Williams, *The Fascinating Duc de Richelieu*, 1910, pp. 129–30).

Lewis 14th whenever they are detected in any public worship. A few days before we came, they had assemble'd; their minister and about a dozen of his Congregation were seiz'd and imprison'd.[1] I knew nothing of this, but I had not been in the Town 2 hours when I was visited by two of the most considerable of the Huguenots, who came to beg of me with Tears to speak in their Favour to the Duke of Richlieu, saying none of the Catholics would do it and the Protestants durst not, and that God had sent me for their Protection, the Duke of Richlieu was too well bred to refuse to listen to a Lady, and I was of a Rank and Nation to have Liberty to say what I pleas'd. They mov'd my Compassion so much I resolv'd to use my endeavors to serve them, thô I had little hope of succeeding.

I would not therefore dress my selfe for the Supper, but went in a Domine to the Ball, a Masque giving oppertunity of talking in a freer manner than I could have done without it. I was at no trouble in engageing his Conversation. The Ladys having told him I was there, he immediately advanc'd towards me, and I found from a different motive he had a great desire to be acquainted with me, having heard a great deal of me. After abundance of Compliments of that sort, I made my request for the Liberty of the poor Protestants. He with great freedom told me that he was so little a Bigot, he pity'd them as much as I did, but his orders from Court were to send them to the Gallys. However, to shew how much he desir'd my good Opinion, he was returning and would solicite their Freedom (which he has since obtain'd).[2] This obligation occasion'd me to continue the Conversation, and he ask'd me what party the Pretender had

[1] Confirmed by a document dated 2 Feb. 1744: 'Copie du jugemen rendu... sur une Assemblée tenue près de Nismes' condemning a group of Protestants for a clandestine meeting (TT 438, § 118, Archives Nationales, Paris).

[2] Richelieu's memoirs, drawn from his notes and not completely reliable, tell of his going to see the prisoners in Nîmes: 'Je m'y transportai, affectant la plus grande colère et la résolution de sévir contre ces malheureux; je les interrogeai moi-même; je vis plus d'égarement et de fanatisme que de crime, et j'engageai les femmes les plus distinguées de la ville à me demander leur grâce.' The prisoners threw themselves at his feet, promising to abide by the law against meetings. 'Alors je leur fais donner leur parole qu'ils rentreront dans leur devoir; et paraissant céder aux instances des dames, je leur accorde leur pardon et la liberté' (*Mémoires historiques et anecdotiques*, 1829, v. 290–1).

in England. I answer'd, as I thought, a very small one.—We are told otherwaies at Paris (said he); however, a Bustle at this time may serve to facilitate our other projects, and we intend to attempt a descent. At least it will cause the Troops to be recall'd, and perhaps Admiral Mathews will be oblig'd to leave the passage open for D[on] Philip.[1]

You may immagine how much I wish'd to give you immediate notice of this;[2] but as all Letters are open'd at Paris, it would have been to no purpose to write it by the post and have only gain'd me a powerfull Enemy in the Court of France, he being so much a favourite of the King's, he is suppos'd to stand Candidate for the ministry. In my Letter to Sir R[obert] W[alpole] from Venice I offer'd my service, and desir'd to know in what manner I could send Intteligence if any thing happen'd to my knowledge that could be of use to England. I beleive he imagin'd that I wanted some Gratification, and only sent me cold thanks.[3]

I have wrote to you by the post an account of my servants' leaving me; as that is only a domestick affair I suppose the Letter may be suffer'd to pass.

I have had no Letter from my Son, and am very sure he is in the wrong when ever he does not follow your direction, who (apart from other considerations) have a stronger Judgment than any of his Advisers.

Avignon, March 25.

Text W MS ii. 105–7   *Address* To Edwd Wortley Esqr   *End. by W*
L.M. 25 Mar. 1744.   Brt by William.[4]   Intelligence.   Ad 21 May.

---

[1] That is, the British fleet blockading Italy would be diverted to prevent an invasion of England. Marshal Saxe had been making preparations at Dunkirk for a Jacobite invasion, but this was known to the English Ministry as early as 12/1 Feb. 1744 (Basil Williams, *The Whig Supremacy 1714–1760*, 2nd ed., 1962, p. 248 and n. 4).

LM's interview was confirmed twenty years later by Richelieu's niece; as reported by Horace Walpole, 'a great mas-

querade being made at Marseilles [*sic*] for Duc de Richelieu, Lady Mary Wortley set out from Avignon, went to it in a dirty domino, talked to him for 3 hours, then said she had satisfied her curiosity and returned without unmasking' ('Paris Journals for Dec. 1765', *Corr.* vii. 281).

[2] France declared war against England on 31 March [N.S.].

[3] See above, p. 195.

[4] Her servant (see next page).

To Wortley *26 March* [*1744*]

Avignon, March 26. N.S.

I am afraid this Letter will be wrote to no purpose. However, it is possible, as it only relates to domestic affairs, it may arrive safe, thô having had no answer to several I have wrote gives me reason to apprehend the Contrary. My English Servants leave me to morrow.[1] I have done every thing in my power to retain them, thô they have been all along very troublesome and expensive, but thinking my selfe assur'd of their Honesty made me very unwilling to part with them in a Country where there is no body I can thoroughly confide in. William was struck with the Palsey the first Winter I came here, and lay several months on my Hands bed rid. I sent him last summer to the Waters of Baluruc,[2] 3 days journey from hence, which did him great service, yet he has still one hand lame. I did not trouble you with the account of it, thinking it would give you some concern. She also lay in a second time. Notwithstanding all this, their Fidelity made me easy with the expence, but they have such an Aversion to living out of England, he says wisely he had rather be a chimney sweeper in London than a Lord in France, and they have undertaken this Journey with their 2 children at their own Expence. However, as they have serv'd me faithfully, I beg you to order her a present of 5 guineas out of my allowance. They intend living in Yorkshire; their Honesty deserves your favour.

This is the 4th Letter I have sent since I have heard from you.

William fancys the Air of this place occasion'd his sickness, but I am persuaded it was caus'd by the strong Wines of this Country and eating the same Quantity of meat here that he did in England. I caution'd him against it, but I perceiv'd he thought I spoke to save expences, and I realy beleive his neglect of my advice is the real cause of his misfortune. I do not accuse him of drunkeness, having allways

---

[1] William and Mary Turner, who had accompanied her from England.   [2] Balaruc-les-Bains, with mineral hot springs, about 60 miles from Avignon.

seen him sober, but the Heat here makes more abstinence necessary than English Servants can easily comply with.

Text W MS ii. 108–9   *Address* To Edwd Wortley Esqr in Caven-dish Square London Angleterre Par Paris   *Postmark* AP 23   *End.* *by W* [*Summary*] Recd 23 Apr.   Ad 21 May.

To Lady Oxford[1] *13 April* [*1744*]

April 13 N.S., Avignon

It is 2 posts since I had the Honnour of your Ladyship's obliging Letter,[2] which is a longer time than I have ever yet been without returning thanks for that Happyness, but the post is now stopp'd, and I should not have ventur'd to write at present if I had not an oppertunity of sending by an English Family which is leaving this place, thô I think a Correspond-ance so inoffensive as ours might be permitted in the midst of War. There would be neither Party nor contest in the World if all people thought of Politics with the same Indifferency that I do, but I find by experience that the utmost Innocence and strictest silence is not sufficient to guard against Suspi-cion, and I am look'd upon here as capable of very great Designs at the same time that I am, and desire to be, ignorant of all Projects what ever. It is natural, and (I think) just, to wish well to one's Religion and Country, yet as I can serve neither by Disputes, I am content to pray for both in my Closet, and avoid all Subjects of Controversie as much as I can. However, I am watch'd here as a dangerous Person, which I attribute cheiffly to Mrs Hay, who, having chang'd her own Religion, has a secret Hatred against every one that does not do the same.[3]

My Health, which your Ladyship enquires after so kindly, is extreme good; I thank God I am sensible of no Distemper or Infirmity. I hope all your Complaints are vanish'd. I saw

[1] This is the earliest extant letter from LM to Lady Oxford.
[2] Of 14/3 March 1744 (Harley MS).
[3] Mrs. Hay was a rabid Jacobite (see above, p. 228, n. 4). Lady Oxford, who was related to her by marriage, replied to LM's aspersions: 'Mrs. Hay, I Beleive, will not quite forget My civili-ties to Her before she went by Yond Sea' (18/7 May 1744, Harley MS).

Lord Goring at Venice; he appear'd to me a very well dispos'd young Man.[1] I hear Miss F. Levison has made a silly
match, which I am sorry for, thô I hope it may turn out
better than is expected.[2] I am concern'd for poor Miss Cole's
distresses; her merit deserves better Fortune.[3]

Dearest Madam, take care of your selfe; while you live,
there is allways a great Blessing allow'd to Your Ladyship's
most faithfull Devoted Servant,

M. W. Montagu.

Text Wh MS 507   *Address* To The Rt Honble the Lady Henrietta
Countess of Oxford in Dover Street near St James's London
Postmark MA 2   *End. by Lady Oxford* R: at Dover Street Tuesday
May 2d O:S:

To Lady Mar *14 April* [*1744*]

Avignon, Ap. 14 N.S.

I am very much oblig'd to you (Dear Sister) for your kind
Letter. I am sorry for Miss F. Levison's Distresse; I am
afraid she will find more uneasyness in a narrow fortune than
she yet apprehends. If I was in England I would use all my
endeavors to serve her. Perhaps her marriage may turn out
better than is expected. I hope your Health is mended. I
heartily pray for it and the prosperity of all your Family. Pray
make my Compliments to Lady Fanny,[4] and be assur'd that
I am ever, Dear Sister, you most affectionate Sister,

M. W. Montagu.

Text MS at Princeton University

[1] On 14/3 March Lady Oxford had
written: 'It is said Lord Goreing is to
marrie Lord Northampton's Daughter;
he is much commended' (Harley MS).
Actually John Fitzpatrick (1719–58),
2nd Baron Gowran, later 1st Earl of
Upper Ossory, m. (30 June 1744)
Evelyn Leveson-Gower, a niece of LM's.

[2] Frances Leveson-Gower (d. 1788) m.
(1744) Lord John Philip Sackville

(1713–65), M.P., 2nd son of 1st Duke
of Dorset.

[3] Grace, da. of John Merick Cole,
lived in Chelsea in poor circumstances.
'They very often mention you with
thorough Gratitude', Lady Oxford had
reported to LM on 14/3 March.

[4] Lady Frances Erskine, Lady Mar's
daughter, with whom she lived.

To Wortley [*6 May 1744*]

I receiv'd but this morning, May 6 N.S., yours dated March 22nd. I suppose this delay has been occasion'd by the present disturbances. I do not doubt mine have had the same fate, but I hope you will receive them at length.

I am very well acquainted with Lady Sophia Fermor, haveing liv'd 2 months in the same house with her.[1] She has few equals in Beauty or Graces. I shall never be surpriz'd at her Conquests. If Lord Carteret had the design you seem to think,[2] he could not make a more proper choice, but I think too well of his understanding to suppose he can expect his happyness from things unborn, or place it in the chimerical notion of any pleasure ariseing to him from his name subsisting (perhaps by very sorry representatives) after his Death. I am apter to imagine that he has indulg'd his Inclination at the expence of his Judgment, and it appears to me the more pardonable weakness. I end my Refflections here, fearing my Letter will not come inviolate to your Hands.

I am extreamly glad my Account of Avignon[3] had any thing in it entertaining to you. I have realy forgot what I wrote, my sight not permitting me to take copys. If there are any particulars you would have explain'd to you, I will do it to the best of my power. I can never be so agreably employ'd as in amuseing you.

You say nothing of my Son; I guess you have nothing good to say.

Text W MS ii. 110–11   *Address* To Edwd Wortley Esqr in Cavendish Square London Angleterre par Paris   *Postmark* MA 12 *End. by W* [*Summary*] Ad 21 May.   Recd 12 May.

---

[1] LM had visited the Pomfret family in Florence from 22 Aug. to 16 Oct. 1740. On 14 April 1744 Lady Sophia married Carteret, a widower thirty years her senior. Walpole called it a 'drawing-room conquest' (*Corr.* xviii. 424); it 'furnished the town with conversation in abundance' (Delany, *Corr.* ii. 295).

[2] Evidently the 'design' of producing sons. That summer Walpole reported: 'There is hurry for a son: his only one [Robert Carteret (1721–76)] is gone mad' (*Corr.* xviii. 501).

[3] On 17 Feb. [1744].

To Wortley *15 May* [*1744*]

May 15. N.S.

I have this morning receiv'd yours of Ap. 23 and am very much vex'd none of mine have come to your hands, having wrote several times since the date you mention. I suppose they have been stopp'd in France. I hear the posts are now open, and I hope by this time you have receiv'd them. I am particularly acquainted with the young Lady Carteret. She is Beautifull and engageing, and has reason to think her selfe much oblig'd to me, but I have so often seen prosperity cause an entire oblivion that I do not expect she should either remember or acknowledge it.[1] I could say many things on this subject, which I forbear, fearing the opening of Letters, which is the practise of all Countries.

I am sorry but not surpriz'd at the conduct of my Son,[2] being fully persuaded he is incapable of acting right on any occasion. I have never heard from him since the Letter for him I sent enclos'd to you.

The Weather here has had some similitude with that in England, being more rainy than has been known for several years, Drougth being the usual Complaint of this Climate. We find the benefit of this uncommon Weather in the goodness of the Garden stuff, which is very delicious but of a very short duration, the heat of the Sun soon burning it. Fruit (excepting olives, Grapes and figs) is allways very scarce, the spring Winds generally destroying the Blossoms. Upon the Whole, this Town was very agreable to me till of late, that I am very coldly look'd upon on the Account of the late Disturbances,[3] Mrs. Hay (who is here call'd Lady Inverness)[4] whispering that I am a Spy, which I see makes some afraid to converse with me, and others drop Speeches on purpose to hear my Reply, in which they are allways disapointed by my being

[1] After her marriage Walpole found her just as he expected: '*très grande dame*; full of herself' (*Corr.* xviii. 442; also 483).

[2] Montagu was in London in the spring of 1744. In Feb. and April he attended meetings of the Divan, or Turkish Club, to which he had been elected (club minutes, entitled *Al-Koran*, owned by the Earl of Sandwich).

[3] Attempts by the French to launch a Jacobite invasion.

[4] Col. Hay had been created by the Pretender Earl and (in 1727) Duke of Inverness.

invincibly silent. However, it makes my residence so uneasy that if I knew where to go, I beleive I should quit the
Town. But France is now forbidden, and a Journey to Italy
impracticable while the Spaniards are ⟨eve⟩ry where on
the Frontiers.

Text W MS ii. 112–13　　*Address* To Edwd Wortley Esqr in
Cavendish Square London Angleterre par Paris　*Postmark* MA 17
End. by W [*Summary*] Ad 21 May.　Recd 18 May.

To Lady Oxford *1 June* [*1744*]

June 1. N.S.

Dearest Madam,

I have many thanks to give you for the agreable news of
your Health (which is allways in the first place regarded by
me) and the safe delivery of the Dutchesse of Portland, whose
little Son will, I hope, grow up a blessing to you both.[1] I
heartily congratulate your Ladyship on this encrease of your
Family; may you long enjoy the Happyness of seeing their
Prosperity.

I am less surpriz'd at Lady Sophia's marriage than at
the Fortune Lord Pomfret has given her; she had charms
enough to expect to make her Fortune, and I beleive the
raising of such a Summ must be uneasy in his present Circumstances.[2] By the Accounts I have receiv'd of Lady John
Sackvile, I think the young Couple are much to be pity'd,
and am sorry to hear their Relations treat them with so much
severity. If I was in England, I would endeavor to serve
them.[3]

[1] Lady Oxford had written: 'My
Daughter was brought to Bed of a Son
31st March. She is quite Recover'd and
the Boy Thrives very well' (18/7 May
1744, Harley MS). He was the second
son, Lord Edward Charles Cavendish
Bentinck (d. 1819).

[2] 'Lord Pomfret gave her £5,000
Portion' (ibid.).

[3] 'I wish Mis F. Levison had own'd
her Marriage before she fell in Labour'

(ibid.). The details are given by
Mrs. Delany: 'she fell ill, and in the
midst of her pains told [her sister] the
Duchess of Bedford (who they say was
ignorant of her condition till that
moment), that she had been married a
year to Lord John Sackville. A wretched
couple I fear they will prove; he is ill-
natured and a man of no principle, and
she has shewn the world that she has
little prudence' (*Corr.* ii. 263).

Mrs. Hay has behav'd to me with a great deal of Impertinence; there is no Principle to be expected from a Woman of her character. Your Ladyship need not mention your Command of continuing our Correspondance;[1] it is the only Comfort of my Life, and I should think my selfe the last of human beings if I was capable of forgetting the many obligations I have to you. If you could see my Heart, you would never mention any thing of that kind to me. It is impossible to have a more tender and gratefull sense of all your Goodness, which added to the real esteem I have of your merit, binds me to be eternally and invio[l]ably your Ladyship's most Sincere and devoted Servant,

M. W. Montagu.

Your Ladyship will permit me to offer my compliments to the Duke[2] and Dutchess of Portland.

Text Wh MS 507   *Address* To The Rt Honble the Lady Henrietta Countess of Oxford in Dover Street near St James's London Angleterre par Paris   *Postmark* IV 4   *End. by Lady Oxford* R: at Dover Street Monday June 4th 1744 O:S:

To Wortley *12 June* [*1744*]

Avignon, June 12. N.S.

I beleive William may tell truth in regard to the expences of his Journey, makeing it at a Time when the passage of the Troops had double'd the price of every thing, and they were detain'd 10 days at Calais before they had permission to pass over. I represented these inconveniencies to them before they set out, but they were in such a hurry to go, from a Notion that they should be forc'd to stay after the Declaration of War, that I could not prevail on them to stay a week longer, thô it would probably have sav'd a great part of their Expence. I would willingly have kept them (with all Faults),

---

1 'I hope you will forgive my Renewing My Request to Continue me the Happiness of your Corespondence, the only consolation I can have for your Absence' (Lady Oxford, 18/7 May).

2 William Bentinck (1709–62), 2nd Duke.

being persuaded of their Fidelity, and that in case of any accident happening to me, you would have had a Faithfull account of my Effects, but it was impossible to make them contented in a Country where there is neither Ale nor salt Beef.

This Town is considerably larger than either Aix or Montpellier, and has more Inhabitants of Quality than of any other sort, having no Trade, from the Exactions of the French, thô better situated for it than any Inland Town I know. What is most singular is the Government, which retains a sort of Imitation of the old Roman. Here are 2 Consuls chose every year, the first of which from the cheife noblesse, and there is as much struggling for that Dignity in the Hotel de ville as in the Senate. The Vice Legate cannot violate their Priveleges, but as all Governors naturally wish to encrease their Authority, there are perpetual factions of the same kind as those between Prerogative and Liberty of the Subject. We have a new Vice Legate arriv'd a few days since, nephew to Cardinal Acquaviva, Young, rich, and handsome, and setts out in a greater Figure than has ever been known here.[1] The Magistrate next to him in place is call'd the Viguier, who is chose every year by the Hotel de ville,[2] and represents the person of the Pope in all Crimnial [*sic*] Causes, but his Authority so often clipp'd by the Vice Legate's,[3] th⟨ere⟩ remains nothing of it at present but the ho⟨nor⟩ of Precedence during his Office and a Box at the Playhouse Gratis, with the surintendance of all public diversions. When Don Philip pass'd here he begun the Ball with his Lady, which is the Custom of all the Princes that pass. The beginning of Avignon was probably a Colony from Marseilles, there having been a temple of Diana[4] on that very spot where I have my little Pavillion. If there was any

---

[1] See above, p. 320, n. 2.

[2] The town council, of 48 members, was presided over by the consuls and an assessor (in charge of the police). The *viguier*, assisted by two judges, was in charge of civil and criminal cases (Louis de Laincel, *Avignon, le comtat et la principauté d'Orange*, 1872, pp. 303–4).

[3] 'Le vice-légat était encore intendant-général des armes de sa sainteté en cet État, et juge par appel de toutes les affaires ecclésiastiques, civiles et criminelles de la ville d'Avignon et du Comtat' (J. B. M. Joudou, *Avignon, son histoire, ses papes, ses monumens, et ses environs*, 1842, p. 258).

[4] LM had earlier denied Avignon its Roman beginnings (see above, p. 320). The temple to Diana had been built by Augustus on the Rocher-des-Doms (Joudou, p. 454).

Painter capable of drawing it, I would send you a view of the Landschape, which is one of the most Beautifull I ever saw.

Text W MS ii. 114–15   *Address* To Edwd Wortley Esqr in Cavendish Square London Angleterre par Paris   *Postmark* IV 18 *End. by W* [*Summary*] Recd 18 June   Ad 24 June.

To Lady Oxford 2 *July* [*1744*]

Avignon, July 2 N.S.

I am extreamly glad to find by your Ladyship's of the 7th of June that your Health is amended, and as I am persuaded that there is nothing more conducive to it than Amusements, I think it extreme reasonable you should take that of embellishing your Paternal Seat,[1] which on many Accounts I think one of the most rational, as well as agreable, you can take. It is indeed a sort of Duty to support a Place which has been so long dignify'd and distinguish'd by your Ancestors, and I beleive all People that think seriously or justly will be of that Opinion. As for others, their Censure ought to be wholly disregarded, as it is impossible to be avoided. There are many in the World incapable of any other sort of Conversation except that of remarking the mistakes of others, and are very often so much mistaken themselves, they blame the most praise-worthy Actions, and are so unacquainted with Virtue, they do not know it when they see it.[2]

I hope your Ladyship will live to see finish'd, and enjoy many years, the Beautifull Improvements you are makeing. If I am permitted to see them in your Company, I shall esteem my selfe very happy; if I am so unfortunate to survive you, I have no more prospect of any pleasure upon Earth.[3]

---

[1] Welbeck Abbey, about four miles from LM's paternal seat at Thoresby.

[2] In her letter of 18/7 June, Lady Oxford wrote: 'I conffess I retard the payment of the Great Debts by indevouring to incline my Family to reside at the only Habitable Seat of my Ancesters, it being my oppinion the Estate reduced will still bear mantaining one

House upon it. I will not conceal from you what the Generality of the World calls part of my Foly but give you some account of my Proceedings at that Place'—which she then does (Harley MS).

[3] An answer to Lady Oxford's remark, 'I hope some time either before or after my Death you will see what I have

It is a very great Truth, that as your Freindship has been the greatest Blessing and Honor of my Life, it is only that which gives me any pleasing view for those years that remain, which, be they few or many, are entirely devoted to you by, Dear Madam, your Ladyship's most faithfull Obedient Servant,

M. W. Montagu.

Text Wh MS 507   *Address* To The Rt Honble the Lady Henrietta Countess of Oxford in Dover Street near St James's London Angleterre par Paris   *Postmark* IY 9   *End. by Lady Oxford* R: at Dover Street Monday July 9th O:S: 1744

To Mme Chiara Michiel *3 July* [*1744*]

Avignon, ce 3 de Juillet

Vous ne voulez pas permettre (ma chere Madame) que je vous donne les Titres qui vous sont deû, et ils doivent étre absorbé dans le souvenir des vos Graces et vostre merite, et je suis prêt d'oublier vostre rang et vous considerer simplement comme la plus aimable Dame du monde. C'est un hommage de Cœur que je rende, et que vous estes faitte pour exiger en tout Païs, independamment de vostre Naissance et de tous les autres honneurs. Il y a et il aura toujours de Femmes de Qualité et des Ambassadrices, mais la belle Signora Chiara est unique dans cet monde, et moi qui a tant voyagé je n'ai jamais rien veû que vous ressemblâtes.

My Lord Mareschalle est parti d'ici depuis quinze jours pour chercher son pain en Moscovie.[1] Effectivement c'est un homme d'esprit et de merite, et un vraie Martyr de sa Probité. Dans sa premiere jeunesse il a sacrifié un haut rang et des grands biens a un Idée de Fidelité a son Prince, mal entendu a la verité mais qui partoit d'un bon Cœur; et, a l'heure qu'il est, il refuse des établissements considerable

done or Propose to be done. . . .' (ibid.). Her extensive alterations are summarized in A. S. Turberville, *A History of Welbeck Abbey and Its Owners*, 1938–9, i. 393–8).

[1] Lord Marischal (see above, p. 302) had retired to Avignon before the abortive Jacobite invasion in the spring of 1744. He did not go to Russia, though he tried to in the summer of 1746 (Edith E. Cuthell, *The Last Earl Marischall*, 1915, i. 211, 223–4). His brother, James Keith, was in the Russian military service 1728–47.

pour garder le Culte des ses Ancestres. Il y a peut estre des prejugez a tout cela, mais aussi il y a un droiture et un desinteressement qu'on ne sçauroit assez respecter. Il m'a beaucoup parlé de la Cour ou vous etes, et je croy la connoitre a peu pres comme elle est.

Je suis ici dans l'azyle contre les tumultes de la Guerre qui allarment toute l'Europe; je pense quelque fois qu'ils seront en peu de temps dissipé. Vous étes plus a portée de juger des evenemens; je ne les voye que de loin, et vous etes dans le centre de l'Intteligence.

Mes Sentiments ne peuvent jamais se refroider a vostre égard, et le titre d'Amie que vous m'avez permis est trop glorieux pour moi, pour que je neglige aucune occasion de vous prouver que je suis par la plus tendre attachement, pour toute ma vie, vostre tres humble et tres Obeissante Servante,

M. W. Montagu.

Text Bute MS   *Address* A S. E. La Signora Chiara Michielli Ambassadrice de la Serenissima Republique de Venice a la Cour de S. M. Catholique Madrid.

To Mme Chiara Michiel *12 July* [*1744*]

Avignon, ce 12 de Juillet.

Je ne vous a pas fait mon Compliment (ma chere et charmante Amie) sur le renouvellement de nostre Alliance.[1] Comme je croi tout l'avantage pour nous, c'est a moi de recevoir les felicitations. J'étois toujours honteuse de nostre sotte brouillerie;[2] (entre nous soit dit) je regarde quasi tout les querrelles de princes sur le mesme pied; et je ne voye

[1] In 1737 England had broken diplomatic relations with the Republic because of 'extraordinary distinctions and honours paid to the Pretender's son at Venice'. In the spring of 1744 relations were resumed with the appointment of the Earl of Holdernesse as Ambassador Extraordinary and Sir James Gray as Secretary of the Embassy (Walpole, *Corr.* xviii. 431–2; D. B. Horn, *Brit. Dipl. Rep. 1689–1789,* 1932, pp. 84–85).

[2] According to Horace Mann LM had [in 1740] 'promised the Doge and Senate to bring the King to, and convince him how wrong he had been to be so angry with 'em. She told me herself she had wrote to Sir Robert [Walpole] and others and assured them that the Pretender's son was not received as had been represented but that the old consul [Niel Browne] was a fool and doted with age' (Walpole, *Corr.* xvii. 98).

rien qui marque si positivement la deraison de l'homme que la Guerre. Effectivement quel extravagance de s'entretuer pour des interests tres souvent imaginaire, et toujours pour le plaisir des personnes qui ne se croyent pas mesme obligé a ceux qui se sacrifient pour eux! Si les Rois voulurent jouer a la Bassette pour des villes et des provinces, Patience! Comme de Maitre a Maitre il n'ÿ a que la main, je ne serois pas trop fasché de voir la Reine d'Hongrie et ses Alliez tenir la Banque, et l'Empereur avec le siens ponter.[1] On verroit peutestre Munich sur une carte; un paroli emportera Prague, Linzt, et Passau, sans ces terrible masacres et Incendies, qui font horreur a tout ceux qui veulent du bien au genre humain en general. Si j'étois plenipotentinaire je ferois cet proposition au premier Congres qui se tiendroit; mais helas, je crains que je trouverois peu des personnes aussi pacifique que moi.

Que je serois aise (ma belle Ambassadrice) de vous voir a Londres! Vous reusirez par tout, mais j'ose me flatter que vous trouverez de Gens chez nous qui sçaurons ce que vous valez, et par consequence seront plus empressé de vous faire leur Cour que par tout ailleurs. Mais jamais on aura plus de plaisir a vous rendre justice que (ma tres chere Dame) vostre tres humble etc.

Text Bute MS *Address* A S. E. Madame Madame l'Ambassadrice de la S. R. de Venise a la Cour de Madrid

To Lady Pomfret *12 July* [*1744*]

Avignon, July 12, N.S.

It is but this morning that I have received the honour of your ladyship's obliging letter of the 31st of May; the other you mention never reached me, and this has been considerably retarded in its passage. It is one of the sad effects of war, for us miserable exiles, the difficulty of corresponding with the few friends who are generous enough to remember the

[1] Referring to the War of the Austrian Succession, then being fought; its main antagonists were Maria Theresa and the newly elected Emperor Charles VII (Elector of Bavaria).

absent. I am very sorry and surprized to hear your good constitution has had such an attack. In lieu of many other comforts I have that of a very uncommon share of health, in all my wanderings, having never had one day's sickness, though nobody ever took less care to prevent it. If any marriage can have a prospect of continued happiness, it is that of Lord and Lady Carteret. She has fortunately met with one that will know how to value her, and I know no other place where he could have found a lady of her education; which in her early youth has given her all the advantages of experience, and her beauty is her least merit. I do not doubt that of Lady Charlotte will soon procure her a happy settlement.[1] I am much pleased with my niece's meeting with Lord Goreing;[2] he visited me at Venice, and seemed one of the most reasonable young men I have seen.

I endeavour to amuse myself here with all sorts of monastic employments, the conversation not being at all agreeable to me, and friendship in France as impossible to be attained as orange-trees on the mountains of Scotland;[3] it is not the product of the climate; and I try to content myself with reading, working, walking, and what you'll wonder to hear me mention, building. I know not whether you saw when you were at Avignon the rock of Douse,[4] at the foot of which is the Vice Legate's palace; from the top of it you may see the four provinces of Venaisin, Provence, Languedoc, and Dauphiné, with the distant mountains of Auvergne, and the near meeting of the Durance and Rhone which flow under it; in short, it is the most beautiful land prospect I ever saw. There was anciently a temple of Diana, and another of Hercules of Gaul, whose ruins were turned into a fort, where the powder and ammunition of the town were kept, which was destroyed by lightening about eighty years since. There remained an ancient round tower, which I said in presence of the Consul I would make a very agreeable

---

[1] Lady Charlotte Fermor (1725–96), Lady Pomfret's second daughter, m. (1746) William Finch (d. 1766), brother of 7th Earl of Winchilsea. Even Walpole, who ridiculed her family, thought her capable of making any man happy (*Letters*, ed. Mrs. P. Toynbee, 1903, ii. 110).

[2] Lord Gowran (see above, p. 326).

[3] LM expressed her boredom in an untitled French essay addressed to Margaret of Navarre (W MS viii; excerpts in Halsband, *LM*, p. 232).

[4] Probably a misreading of 'Doms'.

belvidere if it was mine. I expected no consequence from this accidental speech of mine; but he proposed to the Hotel de Ville, the next day, making me a present of it; which was done *nemine contradicente*.[1] Partly to shew myself sensible of that civility, and partly for my own amusement, I have fitted up a little pavilion, which Lord Burlington would call a temple, being in the figure of the Rotunda;[2] where I keep my books and generally pass all my evenings.

If the winds were faithful messengers, they would bring you from thence many sighs and good wishes. I have few correspondents in England, and you that have lived abroad know the common phrases that are made use of; 'As I suppose you know every thing that passes here;' or, 'Here is nothing worth troubling you with;' this is all the intelligence I receive. You may judge then how much I think myself obliged to you, dear madam, when you tell me what passes amongst you. I am so ignorant, I cannot even guess at the improper marriages you mention. If it is Lady Mary Grey that has disposed of herself in so dirty a manner, I think her a more proper piece of furniture for a parsonage-house than a palace;[3] and 'tis possible she may have been the original product of a chaplain.

I believe your ladyship's good-nature will lament the sudden death of the poor Marquis of Beaufort,[4] who died of an apoplectic fit. He is a national loss to the English, being always ready to serve. . . .[5]

Text 1837, ii. 263–6

[1] See above, pp. 315–16.

[2] Richard Boyle (1694–1753), 3rd Earl of Burlington, noted as an enthusiast for Palladian architecture. LM probably had in mind Chiswick House, his villa described by Hervey as 'too little to live in, and too large to hang to one's watch' (James Lees-Milne, *Earls of Creation*, 1962, p. 154).

[3] Lady Mary Grey (1720–62), da. of 1st Duke of Kent, m. (March 1744) the Rev. Dr. David Gregory (1696–1767), a canon of Christ Church, Oxford, and first professor of modern history and languages there (*London Magazine*, 1744, p. 152). Walpole described her as deformed but very rich (*Corr.* xx. 133, n. 3). She was something of a bluestocking; she and Mrs. Carter read aloud Cicero and Molière (Elizabeth Carter and Catherine Talbot, *A Series of Letters 1741–1770*, 3rd ed., 1819, i. 34).

[4] See above, p. 266.

[5] *Sic* in text.

To Wortley [*16 July 1744*]

I receiv'd this morning, July 16th N.S., yours of June 24th.
I hope my daughter has only misreckon'd,[1] which often
happens without any ill Consequence, of which I know many
examples, amongst others the Dutchesse of Portland. I
think my Son should shew me the common Civillity of
answering my Letter.

I hear Pope is dead.[2] I can scarce beleive it, you not
having mention'd it.

I pity W. Turner and his Wife, as I think they are both
honest people.[3] Since they went, I beleive I have heard the
true reason of their leaving me, being told she is 6 months
gone with child and I haveing said to her, after her second,
that if she was with child again I would keep neither of them.
She promis'd, as she had done before, very solemnly that it
should not happen again, and I suppose was asham'd to own
it, not hopeing another pardon.

Text W MS ii. 116–17   *Address* To Edwd Wortley Esqr in
Cavendish Square London Angleterre par Paris   *Postmark* IY 19
End. by W [*Summary*] Ad 23 July.   Recd 18 [*sic*] Jul.

To Lady Mar *10 Aug.* [*1744*]
[*This letter is printed in vol. iii, Appendix II*]

To Lady Oxford *10 Aug.* [*1744*]

I am very glad your Ladyship has been at Bulstrode,[4]
being fully persuaded the good Air and good Company
there will very much contri⟨bute⟩ to your Health. Your
Satisfaction is the most agreable News I can hear, thô I am
very well pleas'd that one of my Neices is so happily dispos'd

[1] For the birth of this child, see LM's
letter of 14 Aug.
[2] Pope died on 10 June/30 May 1744.
[3] Her servants (p. 324 above).
[4] The Duke and Duchess of Port-

land's seat in Buckinghamshire.
[5] Elizabeth Leveson-Gower (d. 1784)
m. (1751) John, later 3rd Earl Waldegrave. Lady Oxford had confused her
with her sister who m. Lord Gowran.

of, but I was told it is Miss Evelyn and not Miss Betty[5] that is now Lady Goreing. I am much oblig'd to Miss Cole for her remembrance, and am sorry the troubles of that good Family are not at an end.[1] There is very seldom Merit without Persecution; a good Conscience is the most valuable of all Blessings and the only one that is beyond the power of Fortune.

I hear that Pope is dead, but suppose it is a mistake since your Ladyship has never mention'd it. If it is so, I have some small curiosity for the Disposition of his affairs, and to whom he has left the Enjoyment of his pretty house at Twict'nam, which was in his power to dispose for only one year after his Decease.[2]

Dear Madam, I know not in what words to thank you for your kind Intentions for me in the Lottery.[3] I have had so many occasions of the same nature, it is not strange I want Expressions to signify my Gratitude. You interest your selfe too much for one that I fear is unlucky enough to render useless all your Generous Endeavors, and can never make you any return, notwithstanding the sincere and inviolable attachment with which I am (Dearest Madam) Your Ladyship's most faithfull Devoted Servant,

M. W. Montagu.

Avignon, Aug't 10. N.S.

Text Wh MS 507   *Address* To The Rt Honble the Lady Henrietta Countess of Oxford in Dover Street near St James London Angleterre par Paris   *Postmark* AV 13   *End. by Lady Oxford* d: Avignon Augst 10th N:S: came to Dover Street Monday Augst 13th O:S: 1744   R: at Welbeck Thursday—16th O:S:

---

[1] On 23/12 July Lady Oxford called the Cole family 'some of the few of the most sincere and Gratefull of your Servants and well wishers. Bad Health and hard Usage do constantly attend those Honest People' (Harley MS).

[2] In her answer, on 29/18 Aug., Lady Oxford wrote: 'It is true Pope is Dead. I did not mention it, knowing the Contempt you have for worthless People. It's said by some he died worth £9,000, others say £7,000. His Will is odly stiled and is likely to be disputed at Law between Pattee Blunt and his Sister. Pattee

is the largest Legatee. I dare not trust my Memory to repeat it. If I can get the News Paper in which it is Printed, you shall have it. As to his House in Twite'-ham, I am told he did not performe his covenants he made with Mr. Vernon, consequently Mr. Vernon's Children claime some recompence' (Harley MS).

[3] On 23/12 July Lady Oxford wrote: 'I have made up 3 Tickets for you for this Year's Lottery. I decline sending you the choice of Numbers, and hope you may have better luck because you can scarce have worse.' (See below, p. 353).

To Wortley *14 Aug.* [*1744*]

Avignon, Aug't 14 N.S.

I had a Letter the last post from Lord Bute with an Account of my Daughter's happy delivery of a Son.[1] I have wrote to return him thanks and wish Joy.

No English papers have come here since the declaration of War, and as I have no correspondants but Lady Oxford and your selfe, I am allmost totally ignorant of whatever happens at London, she seldom speaking of any thing but her own affairs.

Here has been for this eight days last past, and still continues, a constant North Wind that makes a sort of Winter.

I am curious to know if William [Turner] has recover'd his Limbs in England. His opinion that his Native Air would restore his health was the reason he gave for leaving me.

Text W MS ii. 118–19   *Address* To Edwd Wortley Esqr in Cavendish Square London Angleterre par Paris   *Postmark* AV 20 *End. by W* [*Summary*] Recd 21 Aug.   Ad 26 Aug.

To Mme Chiara Michiel *20 Aug.* [*1744*]

Avignon, ce 20 d'Août

Ma tres chere et aimable Amie,

Le mesme jour que j'eus l'honneur de reçevoir vostre aimable Lettre, Le Cardinal Barni est arrivé ici.[2] Il m'a dit que vous deviez partir peu de jours apres lui de Madrid,[3] et que necessairement vous passera par Nismes, qui n'est que quatre postes d'ici. J'ai depeché sur le champ un Courier avec une Lettre pour vous attendre, et ordre de m'avertir de vostre arrivée; et j'ai preparée ma chaise de poste, en me flattant au moins de l'esperance de passer quelques heures

---

[1] John Stuart (30 June 1744–1814) succ. his father as 4th Earl; later 1st Marquess of Bute.

[2] Giambattista Barni (1676–1754),

Cardinal (1743), and since 1739 Nuncio to Madrid; he left that city on 20 June 1744 (*Repertorium*, ii. 266).

[3] Mme Michiel left Madrid on 4 Aug.

PLATE 6

.... qu'un mariage si disproportioné de toute
façon, que la vertu la plus scrupuleuse .... se
contentera d'un engagement clandestin en pareil cas,
& si elle agissoit d'une autre manière, c'estoit, &
ne pouvoit estre que par des motifs interessés dont
il étoit le dupe. je ne scai si cette remonstrance
a eü un bon effet, n'ayant rü aucune reponse.

    vous me pardonnerez (ma Belle dame) cette
grande detail, je ssai que vous avez le .....
assez genereux pour estre touché des malheurs
de vos amis, croyez que le mien est tout penetré
des sentiments d'estime et d'amitie pour vous,
& que toute expression me paroist foible quand
je voudrois vous dire a quel point je suis
vostre tres humble & tres Obeissante Servante.

vous avez un Ambassadeur
anglois de grande Naissance
d'ailleurs - pas trop brillant ni
par l'esprit ni pla figure.
ceci est dit pour vous seule

                                    M. W. Montagu

*Letter of Lady Mary Wortley Montagu to Mme Chiara Michiel, dated
20 Aug. [1744]*
Bute MSS

avec vous. Enfin je suis forcée d'abandonner ces agreable Idees. Vous avez pris sans doute une autre route, et il faut me contenter de vous renouveller de loin les asseurances d'une tendre attachment que ne finira qu'avec ma vie. Mais pourquoy m'avez vous pas fait sçavoir le chemin que vous avez pris? J'aurois fait volontiers cent leius pour avoir le plaisir de vous entretenir.

J'avois aussi mille choses a vous dire sur le sujet du Malheureux Mackinsie.[1] Il m'a écrit de Berlin pour tacher de donner des raisons pour la plus deraisonable conduitte qui fût jamais.[2] J'ai eû pitié de son égarement, et j'ai taché a mon tour de ramener son esprit en douceur, sans lui disputer le merite miraculeux de la merveille dont il est enchanté. Je lui prié uniquement de faire refflections que si elle avoit une veritable passion pour lui, elle sera la premiere a lui detourner d'une pensée si funeste qu'un marriage si disproportioné de toute façon, que la vertu la plus scrupuleuse se contentera d'un engagement clandestin en pareil cas; et si elle agissoit d'une autre maniere, c'estoit et ne pouvoit estre que par des motifs interressez dont il étoit le dupe. Je ne scai si cette remonstrance a eû un bon effet, n'ayant eû aucune reponse.[3]

Vous me pardonnerez (Ma Belle Dame) cette grande detail; je sçai que vous avez le ⟨cœur⟩ assez genereux pour estre touché des malh⟨?eurs⟩ de vos amis. Croyez que le

[1] In Venice the lovelorn Mackenzie had been parted from Barberina (see above, p. 313, n. 1) because Frederick the Great insisted that she fulfil her contract to dance at his Court. She was forcibly conducted to the Prussian border, Mackenzie followed by another route, and in May 1744 both were in Berlin.

[2] As Lady Louisa Stuart relates: 'He announced his good fortune to my grandmother, Lady Mary Wortley, in a letter which she preserved, informing her that he had reason to think himself the most lucky of men: he was about to marry a woman whose preference did him the highest honor—one infinitely his superior in every particular excepting birth. What his family might say to it he could not tell, and did not care; he only knew they ought to be proud of the connection. But he really thought a man of his age was fully competent to judge for himself, and provide for his own happiness. To the last sentence Lady Mary affixed this pithy marginal note, "*The poor boy is about nineteen*" ' [He was about twenty-five.] (*Selections from Her Manuscripts*, ed. J. Home, 1899, pp. 53–54.

[3] Although LM did not know it, by this time the situation had been resolved. Through the efforts of the British Ambassador in Berlin, Mackenzie was expelled from Prussia, while Barberina was forced to remain; and in July he was back in England, though he continued to write ardent love-letters to her (J.-J. Olivier and W. Norbert, *Barberina Campanini Eine Geliebte Friedrichs des Grossen*, 1909, pp. 51–70 *passim*).

mien est tout penetrée des sentiments d'estime et d'amitie pour vous, et que toute expression me paroist foible quand je voudrois vous dire a quel point je suis vostre tres humble et tres Obeisante Servante,

M. W. Montagu.

Vous aurez un Ambassadeur anglois de grande Naissance, d'ailleurs pas trop brillant ni par l'esprit ni par la figure.[1] Ceci est dit pour vous seule.

Text Bute MS   *Address* A S. E. Madame La Signora La Signora Chiara Michielli Bragadini a Venezia Italia

To Lady Oxford *14 Sept.* [*1744*]

The Disorder of your Ladyship's Health, which you mention,[2] gives me the highest concern, thô I hope it is now over, and that the good air of Welbeck will wholly establish it. I beg of you with the utmost earnestness, that you would be carefull of your selfe; I can receive no proofe of your Freindship so obliging to me, thô I am yours by every Tye that can engage a gratefull Heart.

Mr. Wortley has said nothing to me of his visit to your Ladyship, nor can I guess on what Account it was, but suppose it relateing to some Country Interest. I know so well your Just way of thinking, that I am sure you allways act right.[3] Mrs. Massam[4] inform'd me of the hard Fortune of

[1] Robert Darcy, 4th Earl of Holdernesse. He received his credentials as Ambassador Extraordinary on 21 June and arrived in Venice on 17 Oct. 1744 (D. B. Horn, *Brit. Dipl. Rep. 1689–1789*, 1932, pp. 84–85). LM's opinion is similar to that of Walpole: 'that formal piece of dullness' (*Corr.* xx. 202).

[2] In her letter of 29/18 Aug. 1744 (Harley MS).

[3] Lady Oxford had written: 'The Day before I came out of Town I was sirpriz'd with a Messidge from Mr. Wortley for an Appointment, which I fix'd, and I hope he did not disaprove of my Behaviour, which I meant civily and to answer his Purpose.' On 4 Oct./24

Sept. she told the reason for his visit: 'He said he understood I was going to sell the Manuscripts and that your Ladyship had show'd him some Poems in which his Grand Father, his Mother and his Brother were all Reflected on, and he desired they might not be sold. I answer'd I would appoint Mr. Hocker who is making a Catilogu to attend him at Dover Street the next Morning, and if he found the Book it should be set a side for me. What become of this Affair I know not, I not having heard from Mr. Wortley or Hocker since.' The poems could not be found (see below, p. 354).

[4] Probably Henrietta Winnington (d. 1761), who m. (1736) Samuel, later

poor Lady Euston.[1] I very much pity Lady Burlington, but should do it yet more if there had not been some Circumstances in her marrying her Daughter which makes her in some measure blamable for the Event.[2] However, there can be no Excuse for the Brutal behaviour of her worthless Husband. Your happy Disposition of the charming Dutchess of Portland secures you from all Sorrows of that kind, and I pray to God you may live to see your Grand children as happily settle'd. Your Life is the Greatest Blessing that can be bestow'd on your Family. I am fully persuaded they all think so, and I hope that consideration will be of force to make you carefull to preserve it. I need not add how dear it is to me, being to my last moment, Dearest Madam, with the tenderest Affection, your Ladyship's Devoted Servant,

M. W. Montagu.

Avignon, Sept. 14. N.S.

Text Wh MS 507   *Address* To The Rt Honble the Lady Henrietta Countess of Oxford in Dover Street near St James's London Angleterre par Paris *Postmark* SE 17   *End. by Lady Oxford* d: Avignon Septr 14th N:S: came to Dover Street Tuesday Sept. 18 O:S: R: Welbeck Thursday 20th Septr 1744 O:S:

Baron Masham. She had seen LM in Avignon; after her return to London, as Lady Oxford related, 'She said she was extreamly obliged to you and she indulged her selfe with staying a day longer then she intended on your account' (16/5 Dec. 1743, Harley MS).

[1] Dorothy Boyle (b. 1724), da. of 3rd Earl of Burlington, m. (10 Oct. 1741) George Fitzroy (1715–47), styled Earl of Euston, eldest son of 2nd Duke of Grafton; she died of smallpox on 2 May 1742. In her letter of 29/18 Aug. 1744 Lady Oxford wrote: 'You seem to hear so little what is done in your native climate, it is possible you may be a stranger to Lord Burlington's Daughter's Death,

generally said to be occasion'd by the quite undeserv'd Barbourous Behaviour of her Husband, Lord Euston.' He was noted for his brutality and ill-temper; his bride had been 'of the softest temper, vast beauty, birth and fortune!' (Walpole, *Corr.* xvii. 175).

[2] Lady Burlington could be blamed for several possible reasons: although the bride was deeply in love with Euston he was indifferent to her (Sir Charles Hanbury Williams, *Works*, 1822, i. 252–3); and even before his marriage to Lady Dorothy he had behaved with brutal rudeness to her as well as to her mother (Walpole, *Corr.* xvii. 174; Hertford–Pomfret, *Corr.* ii. 162–5).

To Wortley *14 Oct.* [*1744*]

Oct'r 14, Avignon

I receiv'd yours of Aug't 24 but this morning. These delays of the post are occasion'd by the present situation of affairs, in which all things move irregularly. I have had the Comfort of a Letter from my Daughter in which she tells me her little Son is a fine thriving child.

I do not attempt to inform you of any News, least my Letter should be stopp'd. I receiv'd last post one from my Son, but no direction in it where to send an Answer, nor any thing worth repeating. I hope your Health continues good; it is allways a pleasure to me to hear of it.

Text W MS ii. 120   *End. by W* L.M. from Avignon 14 Oct.   Rec. 3 Aug. 1748 [*sic*]

To Lady Oxford *15 Oct.* [*1744*]

Oct. 15 N.S., Avignon

Dearest Madam,

I have receiv'd but this day your Ladyship's of Aug't 29th. This length of passage is, I suppose, occasion'd by the cessation of correspondance between Dover and Calais; all Letters must now go round by Holland, which is a great Greife to me, since I must now content my selfe to be some weeks longer before I can hear from my Dearest Lady Oxford, whose kindness was the greatest Comfort of my Life. Every thing that relates to you is of Importance to me; I am therefore very much concern'd that you have fall'n into ill Hands in your Building.[1] The World is so corrupt it is difficult to meet with Honesty in any station, and such good Hearts as yours, which are not naturally inclin'd to Suspicion, are often Lyable to be impos'd on. If I could think my selfe capable

---

[1] On 9 Sept./29 Aug. 1744 Lady Oxford had written: 'I am so much Hurried with my Works within and without Doors and with endevouring to extricate my selfe out of the Hands of one that has cheated me of some Thousand Pounds that I can scarce get time to write these few lines' (Harley MS).

of being any way usefull to you, it would make this distance between us doubly painfull to me.

I am surpriz'd Lord Burlington is unmention'd in Pope's will; on the whole it appears to me more reasonable and less vain than I expected from him.[1] I cannot conclude my Letter without repeating my most earnest desire that you would consider your Health in the first place, and let no busyness whatever interupt your care of it. There is no expression can tell you how dear it is to Your Ladyship's most faithfull and affectionate Servant,

M. W. Montagu.

Text Wh MS 507   *Address* To The Rt Honble the Lady Henrietta Countess of Oxford in Dover Street near St. James's London Angleterre   *Postmark* OC 27   *End. by Lady Oxford* came to Dover Street Saturday O:S: Octor 27th   R: Welbeck Monday Octor 29th 1744 O:S:

To Wortley *16 Oct.* [*1744*]

N.S. Oct. 16, Avignon

I wrote to you the last post, but have been told since that my Letter will not be suffer'd to pass, and all future correspondance to England must be by way of Holland. I send this to a Banker at Paris.

I have receiv'd a Letter from my Son, but no direction how to answer it. I forbear sending you any news, neither can I depend on any thing of that sort that is said here. The War has double'd the price of all provision.

Text W MS ii. 121   *End. by W* [*Summary*] Ad 30 Nov.   Recd 1 Novr

---

[1] In answer to LM's request of 10 Aug., Lady Oxford sent a transcript of Pope's will copied from a newspaper, on 9 Sept./29 Aug. 1744. In his will, drawn on 12 Dec. 1743, Pope left the bulk of his estate in trust to Martha Blount, and after her death to his next of kin (printed in *Gentleman's Mag.*, 1744, pp. 313–14).

To Wortley 29 *Oct.* [*1744*]

Avignon, Oct. 29. N.S.

I have wrote twice to you this month but fear you may not have had either of them. I send this by Geneva. I receiv'd yours of Sept. 29th this morning.

I am very much concern'd for the ill state of poor Lady Oxford's Health.[1] She is the only Freind I can depend on in this World (except your selfe). She tells me she stays at Welbeck, having been cheated of some thousands [*sic*] by one she employ'd in her Building there, and is very troublesomely engag'd in setting things in order.

I have had a Letter from my Son of a very old date, but no direction where to answer it. There is nothing in it worth repeating.

We have had unusual Rains, but they are allways welcome here, Drougth being the general Complaint of this province.

Text W MS ii. 122–3   *Address* To Edwd Wortley Esqr in Cavendish Square London Angleterre [par Hollande *struck out*]   *Postmark* NO 19   *End. by W* [*Summary*] Ad 30 Nov.   Recd 20 Novr

To Lady Oxford 29 *Oct.* [*1744*]

Dearest Madam,

I receiv'd your Ladyship's obliging Letter of Sept. 24 this morning, and sometime since that in which was a Copy of Pope's Will, for which I return'd you my Immediate thanks, but fear that Letter miscarry'd, since I hear they should all be directed through Holland. These redouble'd attacks of your cholic, which must necessarily weaken any Constitution, give me inexpressible pain. I had at the same time a Letter from Mr. Wortley that tells me your Health is very uncertain. If I am so unhappy to survive you, I shall look upon my selfe as a Widow and an Orphan, having no

---

[1] On 4 Oct./24 Sept. 1744, Lady Oxford wrote that she was taken 'violently Ill last Saturday with the Cholick in my Stomack and Bowells' (Harley MS).

Freind in this World but your selfe. If you saw the Tears with which these lines are accompany'd, you would be convince'd of the Sincerity of them. Let me beg you upon my knees to take care of your Life, and let no other regard whatever occasion the neglect of it. I fear the omission of the Bath Waters this Autumn season may be attended with ill Consequences. For God's sake (Dear Madam) leave all things when it is necessary [to] think of your own Preservation. Mr. Wortley tells me Lady Peterborough is with you, which I am glad of for both your sakes.[1] He adds that your Alterations at Welbeck are in the best taste. I pray Almighty God you may live many comfortable years to enjoy them, and that some part of the reward of your vertue may be in this World. These are the daily and most earnest Prayers of your Ladyship's most faithfull and devoted Servant,

M. W. Montagu.

Avignon, Oct. 29.

Text Wh MS 507   *Address* To The Rt Honble the Lady Henrietta Countess of Oxford in Dover Street near St James's London [Par Hollande *struck out*]   *Postmark* NO 19   *End. by Lady Oxford* came to Dover Street Tuesday 20th Novr O:S: R: Welbeck Thursday 22d Novr 1744 O:S:

To Wortley *29 Dec.* [*1744*]

N.S. Dec. 29, Avignon.

Yours which I receiv'd this morning, dated the 30th of Nov., releiv'd me out of a great deal of pain occasion'd by your long silence. I have wrote 4 times since I heard from you. I hear every body complain of Letters lost, and am not surpriz'd I suffer the same misfortune.

I saw in the Dutch prints the Death of the Dutchess of Marlbrô, but with a very imperfect account of her Will. I should be glad to hear something of it, particularly if she has left Legacys to Mrs. Dunch and Mrs. Hammond.[2]

---

[1] LM had last seen Lady Peterborough in France in 1739 (see above, p. 143).

[2] Sarah, Duchess of Marlborough, died on 18 Oct. 1744. Twenty-six wills which she drew up still survive: 'These had to be altered continually as her relations and friends either died or were cut out of them owing to quarrels' (now

I am very glad if my Son can act reasonably, thô I own I very much doubt it, after his behaviour at Montlimart against his word solemnly given, and without any reason to induce him to such a conduct but downright Levity and Folly. I have lately seen Madam St. Auban,[1] who inform'd me of all the Circumstances of his nonsense. He told her his whole History (mixing, however, some notorious Lyes in it) [and] shew'd her my Letters to convince her he was the person he pretended to be, which she very much doubted by his extravagant discourse.[2] If you think the enclos'd[3] proper to be sent to him, I leave it to your discretion.

Text W MS ii. 124–5   *Address* To Edward Wortley in Cavendish Square London   *Postmark* ⟨?⟩   *End. by W* [*Summary*] Ad 22 Jan.   Recd 10 Jan.

To Edward Wortley Montagu, junior, *29 Dec.* [*1744*]

Dec. 29 N.S., Avignon

You mention in your Letter of Aug't 7 many that you have wrote to me; I have never receiv'd any other.

I shall be very glad to hear of your good behaviour, and that you know how to value your character. I cannot help distrusting it when I refflect on the many solemn promises you made me at Orange of takeing care to keep your selfe conceal'd. You saw how much precaution I us'd to that purpose, and pretended to be very well satisfy'd with the reasons I gave you (thô I think my Commands ought to have been sufficient) why I thought it would be disadvantageous to me you should be known in this Country. Yet after all this, on your leaving me, at only a halfe day's journey distant you show'd my Letters to Madame St. Auban, and told her a long story of your selfe and Family, with several Falsehoods

among Earl Spencer's MS, HMC *Bull. of the National Reg. of Archives*, No. 13, 1964, p. 23). In her final will (P.C.C. Anstis, f. 259), drawn on 11 Aug., with a codicil 15 Aug. 1744, there is no mention of either her relation Mrs. Dunch or

of Mrs. Hammond (see above, p. 244).
   [1] Not identified.
   [2] LM had related this to W on 20 Nov. [1743] (pp. 314–15 above).
   [3] Printed as next letter.

mix'd in it. It will be very fruitless to deny this; I had it from her own Mouth with so many circumstances I can make no doubt of it. I wish you would consider that there is nothing meaner or more unworthy a Gentleman than breach of promise, and that tatling and lying are Qualitys not to be forgiven even in a chambermaid. I speak to you plainly as one more interested in your welfare than any of your Companions can be, and tis the best proofe I can give you that I am your affectionate Mother,

M. Wortley.

Text W MS iii. 7–8   *End. by W* L.M. to Son.   29 Dec. 1744. Copy [*i.e. in LM's hand*].

To Wortley 27 *Jan.* [*1745*]

Avignon, Jan. 27. N.S.

I receiv'd this day yours of the 28th of December. I hope you have had before this time two of mine. In my last I enclos'd a Letter to my Son, if you think it proper to be sent.

In these changing times every day presents something of new difficulty. It is reported here that the takeing of Mareschall Bell lisle[1] will make the residence of France very unsafe to all the English. I am very secure here, which is all the recommendation of this place. I should have chang'd it long since if I had known where to remove, but I know no part of Europe except this little spot and the Isle of Malta which is not likely to be disturb'd by the ravage of Troops.[2] The Pope's state in Italy has suffer'd so much that I am inform'd it is allmost ruin'd. We feel some part of the Inconvenience by the dearness of Provision. The Winter has been severer than I have yet known it in this part of the World. We have had violent north Winds continu'd a whole Month, which I think the most troublesome sort of ill Weather.

---

[1] Charles-Louis-Auguste Fouquet (1684–1761), marquis de Belle-Isle. On 20 Dec. 1744, en route from Cassel to Berlin with his brother and a large suite, he was arrested at a Hanoverian post and taken to England (Walpole, *Corr.* xviii. 562–3).

[2] The Knights of the Order of St. John had occupied Malta since the 16th century.

As your Health is my first wish, the hearing of it is my greatest Pleasure.

Text W MS ii. 126–7   *Address* To Edwd Wortley Esqr in Cavendish Square London Angleterre   *Postmark* FE 7   *End. by W* [*Summary*] Ad 19 Feb.   Recd 8 Feb.

To Wortley *1 March* [*1745*]

March 1. N.S.

I have but now receiv'd yours of Jan. 22nd. These delays and miscarriages of the post are very disagreable. I have not heard from Lady Oxford this three months; I have that dependance on her character and Freindship, I complain only of the post for this interuption in our Correspondance.[1]

As to my Son, if you positively command me, I will certainly write to him, but my own Opinion is so perfectly fix'd in regard to him, I had much rather have nothing to do with him. I seldom receive a character of any one from the opinion of others, and never judge but by Facts of any body, and as yet have known none to his advantage.[2]

We hear of nothing here but vigorous preparations for War, and an animosity against the English that makes this Town very disagreable.

Text W MS ii. 128   *End.* [*by W* [*Summary*] Recd 8 Mar.   Ad Apr. 8.

To Wortley *22 March* [*1745*]

March 22 N.S.

I have receiv'd this Day yours of the 19th of Feb. I am very glad your Health continues. I have little to write from

[1] The post was not to blame; Lady Oxford did not write between 24 Nov. 1744 and 23 Feb. 1745 [O.S.], as she stated on 5 May/24 April 1745 (Harley MS).

[2] In Feb. Montagu was garrisoned in Bruges with his regiment; and he confided to his cousin that his father was 'absolutely deaf to all considerations, att least pecuniary', and that he was anxious to borrow money to pay off some of his debts and get a licence to return to England (to Edward Montagu, 17 Feb. 1745, N.S., MS Mo 2841, Huntington Library).

hence but an account of mine, the news here being not at all to be depended on. I was told by an English Gentleman some very extravagant Weddings in England, which appear so incredible I cannot beleive them.[1] As to public affairs, I seldom enquire after them, and if I did, should only have false informations.

It is now a sort of Summer, but the Cold returns sometime in May.

Text W MS ii. 129   *End. by W* [*Summary*] Recd 25.   Ad 9 May.

To Lady Oxford *13 April* [*1745*]

Dearest Madam,

It is so long since I have had the happyness of a Letter from your Ladyship, thô I have done my selfe the Honor of writeing to you several times, that my impatience makes me send this by a private hand as far as Paris, fearing that the others have miscarry'd. I think my selfe so well acquainted with the goodness of your Heart, and a long experience has so perfectly assur'd me of the firmness of your Freindship, that I cannot suppose it is in the power of Time or Distance to occasion your forgettfullness. I only accuse my ill Fortune for this intteruption of our Correspondance, which deprives me of the only Consolation I have in this Life. I am often in pain for your Health; in short, my uneasyness is beyond Expression. I hope this will reach your hands, and am persuaded that you will be so good to let me hear from you. I have no pretensions to that Honor but the sincerest attachment and affection with which I shall be to the last moment of my Life (Dearest Madam) Your Ladyship's most Faithfull and Obedient Servant,

April 13.   M. W. Montagu.

Text Wh MS 507   *Address* To The Rt Honble the Lady Henrietta Countess of Oxford in Dover Street near St. James's London Angleterre par Hollande   *Postmark* ⟨AP 20⟩   *End. by Lady Oxford* d April 13th N:S: I supose wrote from Avignon   R: Welbeck Monday April 22d O:S: 1746 [*altered from* 1745]

[1] She refers to them more specifically in 1748 (see below, p. 400).

To Wortley *20 May* [*1745*]

May 20 N.S.

It is so long since I heard from you, I am in a great deal of pain, thô I hope the negligence or infidelity of the post is the only cause of your silence. It is reported here that the English have extreamly suffer'd in a late action.[1] I cannot so far forget I am a Mother as not to be under concern for my Son, notwithstanding all the reasons he has given me to be indifferent about him. I am impatient for a true account, which is not to be expected here where all news is partially related.

This is the third Letter I have wrote since I heard from you.

Text W MS ii. 130   *End. by W* [*Summary*] Ad 18 June.

To Lady Oxford *1 June* [*1745*]

June 1, Avignon

Dearest Madam,

It is but this Day I have receiv'd the pleasure of your Ladyship's obliging Letter. It is impossible to tell you the joy it gave me after so long a silence, thô very much abated by the account of your ill Health. I pray with the utmost fervency that your Journey may contribute to your recovery, and am persuaded that it is the safest and most probable method of mending a constitution.[2] I could wish it southward, not in regard to my own Interest, but as a Removal to a better air. I have often repeated to you how exceeding dear your Life is to me; if you valu'd it as much, all other

[1] In the battle of Fontenoy, on 11 May, the Austrian allies were severely beaten by a much larger French army. For England it was a 'glorious defeat', with a large number of officers killed or wounded.

[2] In her letter of 5 May/24 April 1745, Lady Oxford wrote: 'I have very little time, being just going into the Coach towards Northumberland, and if my Health permits me from thence in to Scotland. I am farr from well but I Think if the Journey is not too much for me, it will mend it' (Harley MS).

considerations would be laid aside when your preservation was in question.

I beleive the Interuption of our Correspondance may be partly owing to your Ladyship's having forgot to direct your letter enclos'd to Monsieur Pierre de Vos a Rotterdam, Hollande.

What ever good Fortune happens to me must allways come through your Hands. This is the first prize that ever came to my share, and it is owing to your Ladiship in all senses.[1]

My Daughter wrote me word the last post that Thoresby is utterly destroy'd by Fire.[2] I cannot help feeling some concern, and at the same time making many Refflections on the Vanity of all Worldly Possessions. I thank God my Heart is so entirely detach'd from them that I never desire more than the small portion I enjoy.

I finish my Letter with the most earnest recommendations to your Ladyship to take care of your Health, and the assurances of the most unalterable Gratitude and affection from, Dearest Madam, Your most Faithfully Devoted Humble Servant,

M. W. Montagu.

Text Wh MS 507   *Address* To The Rt Honble the Lady Henrietta Countess of Oxford in Dover Street near St James London Angleterre   *Postmark* IV 8   *End. by Lady Oxford* R: Welbeck Monday June 10th 1745 O:S: came to Dover Street—8th O:S:

[1] Lady Oxford had informed her: 'Your Ladyship had a Prize came up of £50 in the last Lotery and 2 Blanks which, if I live to return, I will give you an Account what I have done with it' (Harley MS). This lottery (see above, p. 339) was for Joint-Stock Annuities: closing date 5 Oct., drawing on 26 Nov. 1744 (C. L'E. Ewen, *Lotteries and Sweepstakes*, 1932, pp. 148–9).

[2] On 4 April, Thoresby, the Pierrepont seat then occupied by LM's nephew, burned down (*Gentleman's Mag.*, p. 218). In her reply to this letter Lady Oxford reported: 'The Duke of Kingston's loss is great. He saved all his Papers, most of the best Furniture, and all his Plate. He was on the Spot, and behaved mighty well. He dined after with me . . . and spoke very prudently about ingageing in Expences for rebuilding it, and that [for the] time He Intended to content himselfe with fitting up the Offices which were not injured, till he had more Money' (23/12 June 1745).

To Wortley *8 June* [*1745*]

N.S. June 8, Avignon

I have this day yours of the 8 of April O.S. and at the same [time] one from Lady Oxford, who has not receiv'd (as she says) any from me since November, thô I have wrote several times.

I perfectly remember carrying back the Manuscript you mention and delivering it to Lord Oxford. I never fail'd returning to himselfe all the Books he lent me. It is true I shew'd it to the Dutchess of Montagu, but we read it together, and I did not even leave it with her. I am not surpriz'd in that vast Quantity of manuscripts some should be lost or mislaid, particularly knowing Lord Oxford to be careless of them, easily lending them, and as easily forgetting he had done it.[1] I remember I carry'd him once one very finely illuminated, that when I deliver'd, he did not recollect he had lent to me, thô it was but a few days before. Where ever this is, I think you need be in no pain about it;[2] the verses are too bad to be printed excepting from Malice, and since the Death of Pope I know no body that is an Enemy to either of us.

I will write to my Son the first opertunity I have of doing it; by the post [it] is impossible at this time. I have seen the French list of the dead and wounded, in which he is not mention'd, so that I suppose he has escap'd. All Letters, even directed to Holland, are open'd, and I beleive those to the army would be stopp'd.

I know so little of English affairs I am surpriz'd to hear Lord Granville has lost his power.[3]

Text W MS ii. 131–2   *Address* To Edwd Wortley Esqr in Cavendish Square London Angleterre   *Postmark* iv 8   *End. by W* Ad L.M. 8 June 1745.   has mine of 8 Apr.   Abt Ld Oxfords Manuscript book of Poems.   Recd 8 June.   Ad 18 Ju[ne]

[1] Respectable persons were allowed to consult and even take out books and manuscripts provided that Lord Oxford's librarian approved their credentials (James Lees-Milne, *Earls of Creation*, 1962, pp. 178–9).

[2] For W's attempt to secure the verse, see above, p. 342, n. 3.

[3] Earl Granville—Carteret's title after the death of his mother in Oct. 1744—had been forced to resign as Secretary of State in Nov. 1744.

To Wortley [*16 June 1745*]

I receiv'd yours of May 9th this Day, June 16th N.S., in which you mention Lady Oxford's Letter to me. I have receiv'd it (as I beleive), it being dated April 24th. From the beginning of this War I have sent all my Letters enclos'd to Mr. Pierre de Vos at Rotterdam, to whom I was directed by Mr. Child's Correspondant at Paris, who wrote to me to desire I would pass no more Letters through his hands. I suppose the expence is deducted from the money remitted to me, it being much diminish'd since the Declaration of War. I am very much oblig'd to you for the trouble you have taken about my Letters; every body complains of the post.

I heard from my Daughter 3 days ago. She informs me Thoresby is burnt down to the Ground, a piece of news that furnish'd me with many Refflections.

The Conversation here is wholly on the Events of the War, which I think you are better and sooner acquainted with than I am. I have yet had no account of the English kill'd or wounded in the last action, which gives me a good deal of uneasyness.[1]

Text W MS ii. 133–4   *Address* To Edwd Wortley Esqr in Cavendish Square London Angleterre   *Postmark* IV 19   *End. by W* [*Summary*] Ad 18 July

From Wortley *29/18 June 1745*

18 June 1745.

My letter to L. M. in which I send Extracts of our Son's letter and explain some Passages in them. I also send her an Extract of

[1] W informed their son of LM's solicitude; and he responded in a letter to Gibson (to be transmitted to W): 'I am extreamly glad to hear my Mother is Anxious about me, not only as 'tis a mark of Her Affection, than which nothing can be more dear to me, but as it also assures me that she Herself is well, for as I told You in my last I was very uneasy about her, and since I know Her Ladyship is still att Avignon I will do myself the Honour to write to Her immediately. . . . ' (17 July 1745, W MS v. 69).

Gen. St. Clair's letter.[1] I mention how he was recommended by the Duke of Montagu[2] and Lord Carteret and that he is commended by several of the General Officers. I mention those of the H[ouse of] Commons. I add thus.

I think it may not be amiss to advise him in a gentle way to be sure never to break a promise, never to assert what is not strictly true, never to justify his past behaviour but to be the first to condemn it. Our Son is now on a very publick Stage. He was recommended by the Duke of Montagu to the Duke of Cumberland.[3]

Hers of 8th of June N.S. came hither 8th of June O.S.

Letters to Holland must be recommended.

I writ to her 9th and 17th of May.

Text W MS i. 134 (memorandum)   *End. by W* Extracts to L.M. 18 June 1745.

To Wortley 7 *July* [*1745*]

July 7. N.S.

I am much oblig'd to you for the Account you have given me of my Son. If I could depend on his relation, I should hope that his behaviour in the proffession he has chose would in some measure re-establish his character, but as I have a too long experience of his Idle vain way of talking of himselfe, I do not much regard what he says on any subject. I have heard the Wind of a Cannon will dismount a Man and that may be his meaning,[4] thô it is possible that it may be

[1] In the battle of Fontenoy, Montagu had apparently acquitted himself with credit. According to his own account, written the day after the battle, the Duke of Cumberland had appointed him aide-de-camp to Gen. James Sinclair (d. 1762), of the Royal Scots, who commanded the second line at Fontenoy and acted as Quartermaster-General (Montagu to Gibson, 12 May 1745 N.S., W MS v. 77–78; printed by C. T. Atkinson in *Journal of the Soc. for Army Hist. Research*, xxvii, 1949, pp. 163–4). Montagu's commission as captain-lieutenant in the Royal Scots is dated 29 May 1745 (ibid., p. 160).

[2] John Montagu (1690–1749), 2nd Duke, was Master-General of the Ordnance.

[3] William Augustus (1721–65), son of George II, was Commander-in-Chief in Flanders.

[4] In his letter of 12 May to Gibson (transmitted to LM by W) Montagu had written: 'I was twice dismounted by the Cannon but ⟨ ?got⟩ my horse again; I receiv'd a shot in my cloaths and had my shoulder knot shot off but have no other hurt than a contusion in my back from the two falls I got. . . .' Montagu later explained that the cannon might not have caused his falls (to Gibson, W MS v. 78, 69).

entirely invented. However, it is something that he has not behav'd him selfe as ill as several of the French. Here are two men of Quality in this Neighbourhood who ran away while their Companys fought. I have seen no Account of the battle that I could rely on.

I receiv'd this post a letter from Mrs. Chenevix, who charges me with a triffleing Debt which she says I left unpaid.[1] I do not remember it, but as the Summ is but 7 pound, I had rather pay it than have her make a noise about it. I desire you would be so good to order the payment out of the Money you send me.

We have had very unusual Rains here for a long while together.

Text W MS ii. 135–6   *Address* To Edwd Wortley Esqr in Cavendish Square London Angleterre   *Postmark* IY 13   *End. by W* [*Summary*] Recd 13 July.   Ad 18 July.

To Wortley *19 July* [*1745*]

July 19. N.S.

I was very agreably surpriz'd by the extracts you were so good to send me of my Son's Letters. His style is very much mended; I hope his conduct may be so too. As you seem to wish I should write to him, I have done it in a manner according to your Intention. This is the Copy.

'I am very well pleas'd with the accounts I have had of your behaviour this Campaign. I wish nothing more than that your future conduct may redeem your past. You are now in a station where you will be observ'd, and may have opertunity of acquiring a character that may cause your Indiscretions to be forgotten or forgiven. I have allways heard that the best and worst Company in the World are to be found in the Army; I hope you will take care to choose the first. Your Collonel, Sir John Cope, is a Man of sense and honnor;[2] I should be glad to hear you had obtain'd his

---

[1] Elizabeth (Deard), wife of Paul Daniel Chenevix, keeper of a toyshop (Walpole, *Corr.* xviii. 366, n. 12). Toyshops at this time also sold jewellery and bric-à-brac.

[2] LM was apparently unaware of Montagu's promotion and transfer to Gen. Sinclair's regiment.

aprobation and Confidence. I hope experience will correct that Idle way of talking that has done you so much injury. I have not heard from you since your arrival in Flanders, thô I have wrote more than once. Your welfare is allways wish'd by your affectionate etc.'

I have directed this to Rotterdam to the banker,[1] who I do not doubt will take care of it if he receives it, but my Letters are all open'd here, and many stopp'd. 'Tis one of the reasons makes this place disagreable, but I know not where or how to remove. They are all here enthusiastically devoted to the Interest you may guess,[2] and notwithstanding my real indifference and perfect silence on all Political accounts, I am look'd upon as a very deep Polititian that has very great designs, and am watch'd on all occasions.

Text W MS ii. 137–8   *Address* To Edwd Wortley Esqr in Cavendish Square London Angleterre   *Postmark* IY 23   *End. by W* Ad L.M. 19 July 1745.   Abt Son.   Ad 4 Mar. Recd at Amsterdam[3] 15 Aug. N.S.

To Lady Oxford *21 July* [*1745*]

Dearest Madam,

Your Ladyship's Letters are allways greatly agreable to me, but doubly so when they bring the news of your Health. Change of air and exercise are the best remedys I know; I am very glad you have experience'd them, and hope you will on no account neglect the care of your selfe. I cannot express to you how many uneasy moments I have had on that subject. 'Tis the only way you can be wanting to your Freinds and Family, but it is their greatest as well as tenderest interest, that you should take care to preserve a Life so valuable as yours. I pass my time very disagreably at present amongst the French; their late Successes have given them an Air of Triumph that is very dificult for an English Heart to suffer.[4]

---

[1] Pierre de Vos.
[2] Jacobite intrigue.
[3] On 2 Aug./22 July W left England for the Continent (W to LM, 15/4 March 1746, W MS i. 135).
[4] After their victory at Fontenoy, the French under Marshal Saxe continued their victorious sweep through Flanders.

I think less of Politics than most people, yet cannot be entirely insensible of the misfortunes of my Country. I am very sorry for the Duke of Kingston's;[1] I beleive, in his place, I should renounce building on a spot of Ground that has been twice so unfortunate.[2]

I suppose you are now in the midst of your deserving Family, and sincerely pertake of all the blessings you enjoy in them. Your Happyness cannot exceed your merit or my wishes. You will give me leave to present the Dutchess of Portland with my Respects at the same time that I assure your Ladyship that I am with the truest and most tender affection, Dearest Madam, inviolably Yours,

M. W. Montagu.

Avignon, July 21. N.S.

Text Wh MS 507   *Address* To The Rt Honble the Lady Henrietta Countess of Oxford in Dover Street near St James's London Angleterre   *Postmark* IY 29   *End. by Lady Oxford* d: Avignon July 21 N:S: came to London July 29 O:S: R: Welbeck Thursday Augst 1st O:S: 1745

To Wortley *25 Aug.* [*1745*]

Aug't 25 N.S.

I receiv'd this Day yours of the 18th of July. I have allready answer'd that in which you give me a particular account of my Son, and enclos'd in it the Copy of the Letter I sent to him, which I hope is wrote according to your Intention. I am willing to flatter my selfe that better company may give him a better way of thinking.

I am stunn'd here every day with a Succession of ill news. The insecurity of the post hinders me from giving you any particular account.

I am sorry for the distresses of my poor servants,[3] being persuaded they are very honest people, thô their Pride and

---

[1] The fire at Thoresby.

[2] Thoresby, built about 1683, had been gutted by fire in 1686 and restored

(John Harris in *Architectural History*, iv, 1961, pp. 11, 13).

[3] William and Mary Turner.

folly made them very troublesome to me. William said when he went away, he had rather be a chimney sweeper in England than a Lord in France. My Conscience is very clear of their misfortunes, since I made them all the representations of the Folly they were about that I could do, and in as kind a manner. The very morning they went I offer'd them to stay, but they were obstinate, as most people are when they are endeavoring their own Ruin. I am very well satisfy'd (hitherto) with those that have succeeded them. It is scarce possible to keep English servants abroad; I have met with no English in my travels that have [not] been oblig'd to part with theirs.

I will give you no farther trouble with any little accounts I may have. I give you many thanks for those that are past.

Text W MS ii. 139–40   *Address* To Edwd Wortley Esqr in Cavendish Square London Angleterre [*added in another hand*] at Mr Houghtons opposite Sir John Oldcastles¹ Cold Bath Feilds *Postmark* AV 31   *End. by W* [*Summary*] Ad 4 Mar.

To Wortley *10 Jan.* [*1746*]

Avignon, Jan. 10. N.S.

I return you many thanks for the trouble you have taken in sending me Miss Fielding's books.² They would have been much welcomer had they been accompany'd with a Letter from your selfe. I receiv'd at the same time (which was but two days ago) one from Mr. Muilman,³ who inform'd me that you were at the Waters of Pyrmont.⁴ The date is so old I suppose you are long since return'd to England.⁵ I hope your journey has been rather for Pleasure than necessity of

---

¹ A tavern in Coldbath Fields, Clerkenwell (R. Thurston Hopkins, *This London: Its Taverns, Haunts and Memories*, [1927], p. 111).

² Sarah Fielding (1710–68) had by now published *The Adventures of David Simple*, vols. i and ii (1744). This was not the first time LM had asked for books to be sent from England; in 1741 she requested several from Lord Hervey (see above, p. 241).

³ Henry Muilman, of the Dutch banking family in Amsterdam. He earns his mention in the *DNB* (xv. 1099) through his marriage to the courtesan Teresia Constantia Phillips.

⁴ A spa in Germany.

⁵ W had apparently returned in Dec. 1745 (W to LM, 15/4 March 1746, W MS i. 135–6).

Health. I suppose your travelling (of which I never had any notice from you) has occasion'd the miscarriage of the many [letters] I have wrote to you. I directed them all to Cavendish Square (which perhaps you have left)[1] excepting the last, which I enclos'd to my daughter. I have never heard from her since, nor from any other person in England, which gives me the greatest uneasyness; but the most sensible part of it is in regard of your Health, which is truly sincerely the dearest concern I have in this World.

I am very impatient to leave this Town, which has been highly disagreable to me ever since the beginning of this War; but the impossibillity of returning into Italy, and the law in France which gives to the King all the Effects any Person deceas'd dyes possess'd of,[2] and I own that I am very desirous my Jewells, and some little necessary Plate that I have bought, should be safely deliver'd into your Hands, hopeing you will be so good to dispose of them to my daughter.[3] The Duke of Richlieu flatterd me for sometime that he would obtain for me a permission to dispose of my goods,[4] but has not yet done it, and you know the uncertainty of Court promises.

I beg you to write, thô it is but two lines. 'Tis now many months since I have had the pleasure of hearing from you.

Text MS[5] formerly at Drexel Institute, Philadelphia   *Address* Edward Wortley Esq. [*added in another hand*] at Messrs Samuel Child, Backwell & Co. London. *Postmark* IA 21   *End. by W* [*Summary*] Recd 22 Jan   Ad 4 Mar.

[1] For the years 1744 and 1745 W is unlisted as a rate-payer in Cavendish Square; in 1746 he again paid rates, evidently for a smaller house (Rate Books, Marylebone Town Hall).

[2] The *droit d'aubaine*: 'All the effects of strangers (Swiss and Scotch excepted) dying in France, are seized by virtue of this law, though the heir be upon the spot—the profit of these contingencies being farm'd, there is no redress' (Laurence Sterne, *A Sentimental Journey*, 1768, chap. i, n. 1).

[3] W replied to this incomplete sentence: 'As to the Jewels, if that accident should happen I shall dispose of them as you mention' (15/4 March 1746).

[4] She had conversed with the Duke at least once: at Nîmes in 1744 (see above, pp. 322–3).

[5] Printed in *Gentleman's Mag.*, 1851, pp. 485–6.

To Lady Oxford *21 Jan.* [*1746*]

Dearest Madam,

It is so many months since I have had the Honor of hearing from your Ladiship (or indeed from any one in England) thô I have wrote several times, I can suppose nothing else but that my Letters, or the Answers to them, are lost. It is the most pleasing Conjecture I can make, however disagreable, your ill Health being a cause that I am very unwilling to beleive. I know none that would so sensibly afflict me, not even your forgetting me, thô I should lose by it the greatest comfort of my weary Life. I hope, by what I see in the news papers, that all the troubles in the North are at an end.[1] I need not add the concern it has given me, being often frighted with false reports which are daily rais'd in this place, which I know not how to quit, since there are few others that I can remain in with Safety during the present state of Europe, which is overwhelm'd with all the fatal Consequences of War. I hope your Ladyship's Estate has no way suffer'd in the late disturbances.[2] I pray God continue to you and your deserving Family a long series of Prosperity. It is the daily and fervent prayer of (Dearest Madam) your Ladyship's most Gratefull and Faithfull Humble Servant,

M. W. Montagu.

Avignon, Jan. 21. N.S.

Text Wh MS 507   *Address* To The Rt Honble the Lady Henrietta Countess of Oxford in Dover Street near St James's London Angleterre   *Postmark* FE ⟨?3⟩   *End. by Lady Oxford* d: Avignon Jan. 21st N:S: came to Dover Street Feb. 4th O:S: 1745   R: at Welbeck Thursday Feb: 6th: O:S: 1745

[1] The Jacobite rising, begun in the summer of 1745, was still making headway in Scotland; not until April was it decisively crushed.

[2] In her answer Lady Oxford wrote: 'My Estate is doubtless the worse for these Publick disturbances in the Nation in the North and added loss from the Distemper among the Catle in the South.

I wish I cou'd guess when we shall find Peace and Quietness. The Highland Army was no nearer me then Derby and I do not find they had much reason to complain of injury. All Notts. fled with great Precipitation. I chose to remain here [at Welbeck]' (19/8 Feb. 1746, Harley MS).

To Lady Oxford 7 *Feb.* [*1746*]

Feb. 7. N.S.

Dearest Madam,

It is impossible to express my uneasyness from your silence. I trouble'd your Ladyship not many days ago with a long account of it, not foreseeing the present opertunity of sending this by one of the late Duke of O[rmond]'s servants[1] who has desir'd me to give a certificate of his behaviour to Lord Arran.[2] In justice to him I cannot refuse saying that I think I saw none in that large Family (where there was as much Faction and ill management as in any Court in Europe) that seem'd to serve with so much Fidelity and attachment. I have that opinion of his Honesty, if it was suitable to my little affairs I would retain him in my own service. Your Ladyship (who is allways ready to do good) will mention this to Lady Arran.[3] I say nothing of many other things relateing to that Family, which do not concern me. To say truth, the Melancholy Letters I have from my Daughter dispirit me so much I am hardly capable of thinking on any thing else, excepting your selfe, who is allways first in my thoughts and will be last in my praiers when ever it pleases God to dismiss from this troublesome world Your Ladyship's most Faithfull Obedient Servant,

M. W. Montagu.

Text Wh MS 507   *Address* To The Rt Honble the Lady Henrietta Countess of Oxford in Dover Street near St James London   *End. by Lady Oxford* came to Dover Street[4] Saturday May 17th O:S: 1746 R: Welbeck Monday May 19th O:S:

---

[1] The Duke of Ormond died on 16/5 Nov. 1745; the servant was named Wilson.

[2] Charles Butler (1671–1758), 1st Earl of Arran, the late Duke's brother.

[3] A correspondent of Lady Oxford (see above, p. 311).

[4] Delivered by Wilson, as Lady Oxford wrote to LM on 1 June/21 May 1746 (Harley MS).

To Wortley *11 Feb.* [*1746*]

Avignon, Feb. 11. N.S.

I receiv'd but this morning yours of Jan. 10. O.S. It gave
me so much pleasure that I cannot too soon return thanks
for it, having suffer'd for some months past all the uneasyness imaginable from your silence, having wrote very often
without receiving any answer, thô I have sent my Letters
by different ways. I directed one to Mons. Muilman at
Amsterdam, he having accompany'd the books with one in
which he offer'd me his service very obligeingly. I perceive
Lady Oxford's Letters and mine have had the same Destiny.
I was in great pain for her Health, being fully persuaded
that neither time nor distance can alter her Freindship. I
shall write to her this post, and will not fail letting her know
that you have sent me her Message. I am willing to flatter
my selfe that the way is now open for the post. It is certain
that all private Correspondance has been intterupted for
some time. Here is an English young Lady (who stays here
on account of her Health) who has had no news from her
Relations since September last.

I sent you a Copy of my Letter to my Son, but I know not
whether you ever receiv'd that, or He the original. I am as
totally ignorant of all English Affairs as if I was the Inhabi-
tant of another Planet. There is nothing interests me equally
to your Health; therefore I beg you would let me often
have an account of it, tho it be but by two lines.

Text W MS ii. 141–2   *Address* To Edwd Wortley Esqr   *End.*
by W [*Summary*] Recd 17 Feb   Ad 4 Mar.

To Lady Oxford *15 Feb.* [*1746*]

Avignon, Feb. 15 N.S.

Dearest Madam,

I receiv'd by the last post an account from Mr. Wortley
of your Ladiship's kind Enquirys after me. Tis the first time

I have heard from him of many months, thô he has wrote many times, and I find all my Letters have miscarry'd. I never receiv'd that which he tells me you was so good to send by Child,[1] nor any other since September, which I answer'd immediately. I have address'd several others to you by different ways, but I fear with equal ill Fortune. The last I sent was by a servant of the late Duke of O[rmond] who accompanys his Corps.[2] I flatter my selfe (by having now heard from England, and that one of mine to my Daughter is come to her hands) that the post is now open. I can assure you (Dearest Madam) that during all my uneasyness on the Interuption of our Correspondance, I fear'd for your Health, but never once suspected your forgetting me. I have had too many proofes of your unweary'd Freindship to think you capable of changing, and however insignificant I am, I am perfectly persuaded that you will ever retain the goodness you have allways had for me, which whenever I forfeit, I must forfeit my reason, since only the loss of that can make me unmindfull of your Virtue and Merit.

I beleive Lord Arran has been much abus'd in the Disposition of his Brother's affairs. I cannot help hateing the sight of Injustice so much, it is with difficulty I restrain my selfe from meddling, notwithstanding the experience I have of its being a very thankless office in that Family.

I cannot express to your Ladiship what a comfort it is to me to hear of your Health, nor how much I have suffer'd by the uncertainty of it. I hope Your Civil broils are now over, and that I may once more have the Satisfaction of assuring you frequently that I am ever, Dearest Madam, inviolably Your Ladyship's Obedient Faithfull Servant,

M. W. Montagu.

My Complements and good wishes attend your Family.

Text Wh MS 507   *Address* To The Rt Honble the Lady Henrietta Countess of Oxford in Dover Street near St. James's London   *Postmark* FE 22   *End. by Lady Oxford* came to Dover Street Saturday Febry 22 OS   R: at Welbeck Monday Febry 24th O:S: 1745

[1] Samuel Child, the London banker.
[2] The Duke, who had died in Avignon, was buried in Westminster Abbey on 22 May 1746.

To Lady Bute[1] *3 March* [*1746*]

Avignon, March 3. N.S.

My Dear Child,

I will not trouble you with repetitions of my concern for your uneasy Situation, which does not touch me the less from having foreseen it many years ago;[2] you may remember my thoughts on that subject before your marriage.—God's will be done. You have the blessing of happiness in your own Family, and I hope time will put your affairs in a better condition.

The mortality of Cattle was in this Country the last year, but as to milk and butter, I have long learn'd to live without them, the Cows in this part of the World being too ill fed to afford either.

I am flatter'd here with the hopes of Peace. I pray heartily for it, as what can only put an end to your troubles, which are felt in the tenderest manner by your most affectionate Mother,

M. Wortley.

My Complements to Lord Bute. I am sorry if I have occasion'd him any trouble in asking for the Book; I fancy'd he might have had it in his own Library. I beg him to take the money for it at the same time he sends it to Mr. Child.

Text W MS iii. 255–6   *Address* [*missing*]   *Postmark* MR 10

To Lady Oxford *10 March* [*1746*]

Avignon, March 10. N.S.

I have at length the honor of a Letter from your Ladiship; 'tis the first I ever receiv'd from you that gave me pain, but I own that I cannot without a very sensible affliction find that you can suppose me capable of being in any way wanting

---

[1] This is the earliest letter remaining of the voluminous series from LM to her daughter.

[2] No doubt LM means Lord Bute's poverty, which forced him and his family to live in Scotland.

to that sincere and tender Freindship which I have so often profess'd and which you so well deserve.¹ I can assure you (Dear Madam) with great truth that you are never absent from my thoughts, and your Correspondance [is] the greatest pleasure of my Life. I have wrote to you many times, without any answer; the same thing has happen'd to my Letters to Mr. Wortley, and I hear every body that corresponds with England make the same Complaint. I hope the post is now settled in the usual manner, and we shall have no more Interruptions in our Commerce, but whatever happens, let me beg you, Dearest Madam, never to imagine I can be so stupidly ungratefull to forget one moment the many tyes by which I am ever bound to be yours. I have little to boast of but an honest gratefull Heart, and I should hate my selfe if any Length of time or distance of Place could diminish any part of that Zeal with which I am most faithfully and inviolably Your Ladyship's most devoted humble Servant,

M. W. Montagu.

Text Wh MS 507   *Address* To The Rt Honble the Lady Henrietta Countess of Oxford in Dover Street near St. James's London *End. by Lady Oxford* came to Dover Street   R: Welbeck Saturday March 22d 1745 O:S:

To Wortley 20 *March* [*1746*]

Avignon, March 20

I have not heard from you so long that I should be in great pain for your Health if I had not had this post a Letter from my Daughter, who informs me that you are well. I am afraid my Letters have all miscarry'd for some months past, thô I have sent them by various ways, and I am sure there is never any thing in them that should give occasion for their being stopp'd. I had a Letter from my Son the last post, very much to his own Advantage (if he tells truth). He says that

---

¹ Lady Oxford had written, on 14/3 Feb., 'If constancy, Faithfullness and Affection merits Friendship, I have a just claime to the continuance of the Hapyness of yours as long as I live in this World' (Harley MS).

the Governor (to whom he was aid de Camp)[1] has wrote to
P[rince] C[harles][2] in his favour. I have sent him a very kind
Letter, beleiving it proper to give him some encourragment
if his behaviour deserves it.

The King of France has employ'd a great Number of
Workmen to remove the Earth round the ancient Temple
of Diana that is near Nismes. They have made great discoverys, particularly the Foundation of a very large Palace
which is suppos'd that of Agrippa when he was Governour
of Gaul Narbonese.[3] They have found many medals and
other pieces of Antiquity. The greatest part are carry'd to
the King, and some privately sold in this Country. A Peasant
brought me a very curious piece of a mix'd metal, on which
are the Figures of Justice, a Roman officer, and several other
Groupes. I have shown it several persons who cannot guess
for what use it was design'd. I will send it to you by the first
opertunity. I will not pretend to decide the value, but I
think I can be sure it was realy found very deep amongst the
ruins of the Palace I have mention'd.

I am falln into the same distress that gave me so much
trouble in Italy. The man and maid servant who I had taken
in place of William and Mary have follow'd their Example.
They are marry'd and she big with child. I find it impossible
to have a Family small enough to consist of reasonable
Creatures.

Text W MS ii. 143–4   *Address* To Edwd Wortley Esqr in Cavendish Square London Angleterre   *Postmark* ⟨MR⟩ 31   *End. by W*
[*Summary*] Recd 1 Apr.   Ad 15 Apr.

¹ In the autumn of 1745 Montagu
had been appointed aide-de-camp to
Gen. Sir John Ligonier (1680–1770),
Governor of Kinsale, Commander-in-
Chief (since Jan. 1746) of the British
troops and mercenaries in the Austrian
Netherlands. Neither W nor LM yet
knew that on 4 March their son, with the
garrison in Brussels, had been captured
by the French. On that day Montagu
wrote to the Duke of Newcastle: 'I am
comprehended among the Austrian prisoners, having been the Governor's Aide-
de-camp during the Siege' (4 March/21

Feb. 1746, Add MS 32,805, f. 23). He
then set out for Liège, where he was to
remain prisoner.
² Prince Charles of Lorraine (1712–
80), Governor-General of the Low
Countries, 1744.
³ The Temple of Diana had been
known earlier; and a stone inscription
naming Marcus Agrippa (63–12 B.C.),
governor of Gallia Narbonensis, was
thought to be part of the public baths
(J. D. Maucomble, *Histoire abrégée des
antiquités de Nismes*, 1789, pp. 12–17,
41–42).

To Wortley 2 *April* [*1746*]

Avignon, Ap. 2. N.S.

I have just receiv'd yours of March 4 O.S. The news it brought me of your Health gave me a great deal of pleasure, thô I am (at the same time) much mortify'd to find my Daughter has not follow'd your opinion in every thing.[1] I wrote to her some time since, adviseing her very strongly to consult you on all occasions as her surest and best Freind, thô I did not then know she had been indiscreet enough to neglect doing it. However, I am persuaded it is not her Fault, but of those by whom she is directed.[2] I will speak to her again on the same subject if you think it proper, not otherwise.

I return you a great many thanks for complying with my request in relation to my Jewells.[3] She knows nothing of it, nor do I desire she should.

I gave you an account in my last of the Letter I receiv'd

[1] W had informed her: 'Lord and Lady Bute came out of Scotland after she had asked my opinion, which I gave against their coming. They chose to be at Twickenham without asking my opinion, and have for the next year taken the house that was Mr. Stoner's for £45 a year, which you will think extremely cheap. She tells me they design to lay down their coach, and that Scotch Estates bring little to London' (15/4 March 1746, W MS i. 135).

[2] LM did not know that her daughter was being 'directed' by Lady Frances Shirley (1706–78), Earl Ferrers's daughter who lived in Twickenham. From the beginning of 1744, she tried to persuade W to bring the Butes to London. In Feb. 1745 she related to Lady Bute her conversation with W: 'I . . . ask'd him if he had heard from you. Yes, was my Answer. I then said the Duchess of Portland had told me Lord Bute was tired of his retirement and talk'd of coming to England. He did not wonder at it, he said. I then wish'd

you some agreable place near Twickenham, as I knew nobody either more agreable or more deserving, and ask'd him if he knew any pretty place near. No, he said. In short I had some dificulty to command my self. . . .' A week later Lady Frances wrote again: 'So far am I from thinking your commands any way troublesom that I am determin'd to persue as far as posible my desire of serving you. After Your Father left me, he went up to Lady Anne [perhaps her sister], and in conversation told her, he wonder'd every body did not like best living upon their own Estates, for his part he never was so happy as in Yorkshire.' She then promised Lady Bute to see him again in a day or two: 'I will then make Your London Scheme intirely my own and beg him to approve. . . . I fear he is pretty steady where he is to part with his money' (8 Jan. 1744, 5 Feb., 12 Feb. 1745, Bute MS).

[3] That after her death they be given to Lady Bute.

from my Son. I suppose you may easily enquire the Truth
of the Relation he sent me. I did not seem to doubt it in my
Answer.

I hope you will take [care] of your Health preferably to all
other concerns; nothing can be so important.

Text W MS ii. 145–6   *Address* To Edwd Wortley Esqr in Cavendish Square London Angleterre   *Postmark* AP 7   *End. by W* [*Summary*] Ad 15 Apr.   Recd 8 Apr.

To Lady Oxford [*11 April 1746*]

Dearest Madam,

I receiv'd the Happyness of your Ladyship's of Feb. 26
but this morning, April 11 N.S. It has been a long time on
the road, but since I have it at length I ought to be contented. The news here is, in general, Peace, which seems
wish'd by all sides. When it is settled, I hope our Correspondance will meet with no future Interuption. It is the
greatest comfort of my Life, and doubly so when I am
inform'd of the recovery of your Health. I beleive the air of
Welbeck (which was that of your Infancy) will agree better
with you than any other, which makes me wish your Ladyship would continue in it as long as your affairs permit.

I wrote a letter to you by a Servant of the late Duke of
O[rmond] who ask'd me a sort of Certificate of his Honesty,
I suppos'd in order to justify him to Lord Arran, to whom
he had (as he said) been misrepresented. I said to you what
I realy thought at that time. I have since heard that the poor
Man is disorder'd in his Head, and that he is parted from
the other Servants with whom he travell'd. I know not what
is become either of him or my Letter. However, there was
nothing in it that can be of any prejudice, containing only
my constant assurances of the tenderest Freindship for you,
and complaints of your silence, which was then so painfull
to me I was glad to snatch at any occasion where there
appear'd a possibillity of conveying a Letter to you, not
doubting but those by the post had been lost. Dearest
Madam, while I have life I shall ever be, with the highest

sense of Gratitude, Your Ladyship's Most Faithfull Affectionate Servant,

M. W. Montagu.

Text Wh MS 507   *Address* To The Rt Honble the Lady Henrietta Countess of Oxford in Dover Street near St. James's London Angleterre   *Postmark* AP 18   *End. by Lady Oxford* d: I supose fr: Avignon April 11 N:S: came to London Fryday April 18th 1746 O:S: R: Welbeck Monday April 21st 1746 O:S:

To Lady Oxford *3 June* [*1746*]

Dearest Madam,

I had the Happyness of receiving two of your Ladyship's ever kind Letters this day, June 3 N.S. I need not repeat my Gratitude, which is allways in the highest degree, and yet I think it far below what I owe you, as the best and truest Freind that I ever was blest with.

If I am to beleive the public accounts I have reason to hope our intestine troubles are now over. I wish one article in your Ladyship's of Ap. 23rd may prove certain; it cannot fail being to our Advantage.[1] I will say nothing more of affairs, that may occasion my Letter being stopp'd; I am persuaded they are all open'd more than once.

I hear the Dutchess of Manchester is marry'd, but I cannot learn to whom.[2] No News interests me so much as that of your Health; it is the highest Obligation you can lay on me, to take care of it. I am quite asham'd of the trouble you

---

[1] Lady Oxford had 'received a letter last post from London which mentiond a Report in Town that a person of Great distintion was arrived there from Spain with an Offer to make a Separate Peace with England and exclude France, and that Lord Chesterfeild is sent for over from Ireland to go as our Embasador to Spain.' On 29/18 June she told LM the news was false (Harley MS).

[2] 'I was told [the] Duchess of Manchester was to marry Mr. Hussey, but I

have not heard it is or is likely to be', Lady Oxford wrote on 29/18 June; but on 13/2 Aug. that the Duchess 'owns her marriage'. It was 'declared' by Hussey's friends on 2 July 1746 (Walpole, *Corr.* ix. 36), and a son was born to them in Jan. 1747; they had been married secretly *c.* 1743. Edward Hussey (1721–1802) took his wife's name of Montagu, and later became 1st Earl Beaulieu.

give your selfe in relation to the Lottery.[1] You will not be thank'd, or I should say more on that Subject. You will permit me to make my Acknowledgments to the Duke and Dutchess of Portland for their obliging remembrance; may they long continue Blessings to you and each other.

We have had such long and surprizing Rains in this Country, there has been an inundation in this Town that hinder'd many people from stiring out of their Houses. Mine happens to be situated so high that I suffer'd nothing from it; the Consequences would, however, have been very bad if it had lasted, but it was over in two days. I cannot conclude without renewing my solicitations for the care of your selfe, with my earnest prayers for your Welfare, which are utter'd with the greatest Zeal by, Dearest Madam, Your Ladiship's most faithfull and affectionate Servant,

M. W. Montagu.

Text Wh MS 507   *Address* To The Rt Honble the Lady Henrietta Countess of Oxford in Dover Street near St. James's London Angleterre   *Postmark* IV 12   *End. by Lady Oxford* came to Dover Street Thursday June 12th 1746 O:S: R: Brodsworth[2] Sunday June 15th O:S:

To Wortley *3 June* [*1746*]

June 3. N.S., Avignon

I receiv'd this day yours of April 15th. I hope by this time you have had mine in which I gave you an account of that which I wrote my Son in answer to one from him dated from Liege. I said nothing in it but what was obliging to him. I wish he may turn out at length such as may be agreable to you.[3] I am very willing to flatter my selfe on that Subject. My Daughter writes me word that she is again with child.[4] I have

---

[1] In her letter of 4 May/23 April Lady Oxford listed lottery tickets she had bought for LM.

[2] Broadsworth Hall, Yorks., residence of Lady Oxford's sister-in-law, Lady Kinnoull.

[3] Montagu, a prisoner of the French,

wrote to his cousin Edward Montagu on 15 March that he would like a diplomatic post, but would have to remain at Liège until ransomed (MS Mo 2842, Huntington Library).

[4] Lady Anne, born 14 Sept. 1746, in St. James's parish (Bute MS). For her

not mentioned to her any thing like supposing that she has any way fail'd in the Duty she owes you. I find some of her Letters are lost, and I hear in general that the Correspondance with England is again very strictly search'd into. I never write Public news of any kind; however, I perceive that does not secure my Letters, which are often lost, and oftener retarded.

I have made a little journey (on the account of Exercise) into the high Languedoc, and find my Health much mended by it. I have seen Tholouse, Montpellier, and several other Towns in my Way, and met with great civillitys every where. The ArchBishops of Narbonne and Tholouse[1] invited me to Supper the first night of my arrival. It is impossible to travel unknown in France, there is such strict enquiry in every Town of passage.[2]

As you make no Complaint of your Health I hope it is perfectly good. It is the sincere wish of my Heart.

Text MS in Pierpont Morgan Library   *Postmark* ⟨?⟩ 12   *End. by* *W* L.M. 3 June 1746.   has made a Tour in Languedoc.

To Lady Oxford 20 *July* [*1746*]

                             Avignon, July 20. N.S.

Dearest Madam,

I sincerely beg your Ladyship's pardon for what I said in regard to Wilson, since I perceive it has occasion'd you some trouble. It was only an attestation of what I thought due to an Honest Man, that appear'd to me hardly dealt with by a pack of Knaves. I am neither surpriz'd nor offended at

extravagant amatory and marital career (as Countess Percy; d. ?1818) see Warren H. Smith, *Originals Abroad*, 1952, pp. 141–54.

[1] Jean-Louis de Balbe-Berton-Crillon (1684–1751), Archbishop of Narbonne since 1739; Charles-Antoine de La Roche-Aymon (1692–1777), Archbishop of Toulouse since 1740.

[2] Starting on her journey in April, and unattended by a servant, LM travelled on a passenger barge down the great canal of Languedoc. Additional details about her tour are in the letters of a young Irishman she met, Sir James Caldwell (c. 1720–84), who also wrote to Montesquieu about her (Halsband, *LM*, pp. 233–5).

Lord Arran's conduct.[1] He has suffer'd so much in his own Interest by misplaceing his Confidence, no body ought to be angry at his mistakes towards others.

.This is the first time of my Life I have been two posts without making my acknowledgments for your Ladyship's ever kind Letters, which are the Comforts of my Life. Nothing could have hinder'd my doing it but an Indisposition in my Eyes, which are still too bad to suffer me to write long, but I fear your tenderness would be in pain for my Health if I delaid giving you some account of it. God preserve yours, and add to it every other blessing. I can say no more but the constant repetition of my being ever, Dearest Madam, Your most Faithfully Affectionate humble Servant,

M. W. Montagu.

Text Wh MS 507   *Address* To The Rt Honble the Lady Henrietta Countess of Oxford in Dover Street near St James's London Angleterre   *Postmark* IY 29   *End. by Lady Oxford* came to Dover Street Tuesday July 29th O:S: 1746   R: Welbeck Thursday July 31st O:S:

To Wortley *20 July* [*1746*]

July 20 N.S., Avignon

This is the first time of my Life I have been 2 posts without answering a Letter from you, but I have been this fortnight past afflicted with a Fluxion on my Eyes, which hardly permits me to read a Letter, much less to write one. It is now something abated but still too bad to suffer me the pleasure of writeing many lines. I am exceedingly pleas'd that my Daughter's behaviour has your aprobation; I hope she will never do any thing to forfeit it. I wish my Son may

<hr>

[1] Lady Oxford had written that she was 'ready to obey any command of yours except recomending a Servant', and then told why: 'I send you Lady Arran's answer. *I received the Honour of your Ladyship's letter which I show'd My Lord imediatly.* I did not expect a civiler answer from Lord Arran. Folly and ingratitude is a plentifull Weed. I do not suspect Lady Arran to be in the least to blame' (29/18 June 1746, Harley MS). Wilson was the servant of the late Duke of Ormond, Lord Arran's brother.

374

at length give you the same satisfaction. I can say no more; I am not able to read what I have allready written.

Text W MS ii. 147   *End. by W* [*Summary*] Ad 31 Jul. Recd at Scarborough 31 Jul.

To Wortley *23 Aug.* [*1746*]

Brescia, August 23 N.S.

You will be surpriz'd at the date of this Letter, but Avignon has been long disagreable to me on many Accounts, and now more than ever from the concourse of Scotch and Irish Rebells that choose it for their Refuge, and are so highly protected by the Vice Legat that it is impossible to go into any Company without hearing a Conversation that is improper to be listen'd to and dangerous to contradict. The War with France hinder'd my settling there for reasons I have allready told you, and the difficulty of passing into Italy confin'd me, thô I was allways watching an opertunity of returning thither.¹ Fortune at length presented me one.

I beleive I wrote you word when I was at Venice that I saw there the Count of Wackerbarth (who was Governour to the Prince of Saxony, and is Favourite of the King of Poland) and [of] the many Civillitys I receiv'd from him as an old Freind of his Mother's.² About a month since came to Avignon a Gentleman of the Bedchamber of the Prince, who is a man of the First Quality in this Province, I beleive charg'd with some private Commission from the Polish Court.³ He brought me a letter of recommendation from

¹ LM had complained to Sir James Caldwell about 'the Jacobites, priests and gamesters of Avignon' (Caldwell to LM, [July 1746]); and he then wrote to another friend, 'I am now determined to go to Italy, having made the Party with Lady Mary Wortley Montague' (B 3/15/104, B 3/7/1, Bagshawe MS, John Rylands Library). But he did not go.

² See above, p. 166.

³ Count Ugolino Palazzi (b. 1716). He was eldest son of Federico (1687–1731), who m. (1714) Giulia (1697–

1751), da. of Count Ottavio Fenaroli (Antonio Fappani, 'Lady Montagu ed il conte Ugolino Palazzi' in *Commentari dell'ateneo di Brescia*, 1961, p. 102). In the 'Italian Memoir', a document LM dictated *c*. 1756 to explain her financial involvement with Palazzi for a ten year period (1746–56), she states that she had been introduced to him in Venice in 1740 (Wh MS 510, f. 1). The 'Memoir' is written in Italian; all excerpts here are translated.

Count Wackerbarth which engag'd me to shew him what civillitys lay in my power. In Conversation I lamented to him the impossibillity of my attempting a Journey to Italy, where he was going. He offer'd me his protection, and represented to me that if I would permit him to wait on me, I might pass under the notion of a Venetian Lady. In short, I ventur'd upon it, which has succeeded very well, thô I met with more impediments in my Journey than I expected.

We went by Sea to Genoa, where I made a very short stay and saw no body, having no passport from that state and fearing to be stopp'd if I was known. We took post chaises from thence the 16th of this month, and was very much surpriz'd to meet on the Bo[c]chetta[1] the Baggage of the Spanish Army with a prodigious number of sick and wounded soldiers and officers, who march'd in a very great Hurry.[2] The Count of Palazzo order'd his Servants to say we were in haste for the Service of D[on] Philip,[3] and without farther examination they gave us place every where, notwithstanding which the multitude of carriages and loaded mules which we met in those narrow roads made it impossible for us to reach Seravalle till it was near Night. Our Surprize was great to find coming out of that Town a large body of Troops surrounding a body of Guards, in the midst of which was Don Philip in person, going a very round trot, looking down and pale as ashes. The Army was in too much Confusion to take notice of us, and the night favouring us we got into the Town, but when we came there it was impossible to find any Lodging, all the Inns being fill'd with wounded Spaniards. The Count went to the Governour and ask'd a chamber for a Venetian Lady, which he granted very readily, but there was nothing in it but the bare Walls, and in less than a Quarter of an hour after, the whole House was empty both of Furniture and people, the Governor flying into the Citadelle and carrying with him all his goods and Family. We were forc'd to pass the night without Beds or Supper.

About Day Break the Victorious Germans enter'd the Town. The Count went to wait on the Generals (to whom I

---

[1] A term for a mountain pass in the Apennine region.

[2] The Spanish army was in retreat before the Austrians and Sardinians, who were England's allies.

[3] Commander of the Spanish army.

beleive he had a commission). He told them my name, and there was no sort of Honor or Civillity they did not pay me. They immediately order'd me a Guard of Hussars (which was very necessary in the present disorder) and sent me refreshments of all kinds. Next day I was visited by the Prince of Baden Dourlach, the Prince Loüestien,[1] and all the principal officers, with whom I pass'd for a Heroine, shewing no uneasyness thô the Cannon of the Citadelle (where was a Spanish Garrison) play'd very briskly. I was forc'd to stay there two days for want of post horses, the post master being fled with all his servants, and the Spaniards having seiz'd all the horses they could find. At length I set out from thence the 19th instant with a strong escorte of Hussars, meeting with no farther accident on the road except at the little Town of Vogherra, where they refus'd post horses till the Hussars drew their Sabres.

The 20th I arriv'd safe here. It is a very pretty place, where I intend to repose my selfe (at least) during the remainder of the Summer. This Journey has been very expensive, but I am very glad I have made it. I am now in a neutral Country under the protection of Venice. The Doge is our old Freind Grimani, and I do not doubt meeting with all sort of Civillity. When I set out I had so bad a Fluxion on my Eyes I was realy afraid of loseing them. They are now quite recover'd and my Health better than it has been of some time. I hope yours continus good and that you will allways take care of it.

Direct for me at Brescia by way of Venice.

Text W MS ii. 148–51   *Address* To Edward Wortley Esqr in Cavendish Square London Angleterre   *End. by* W [*Summary*] Ad 31 Oct.   Recd Sept. 25.

To Mme Chiara Michiel [*Sept. 1746*]

Ne croyez pas, ma tres charmante et respecta⟨ble⟩ Amie, que les impressions que vous faittes s'effacent jamais. Je n'ai

---

[1] Christof, Prince of Baden-Dur-lach (1717–89); Karl Thomas, Prince of   Löwenstein (1714–89) (Isenburg, i. 86, 90).

jamais manquée un moment a l'amitie que je vous ai vouée toute ma vie, mais les desordres de l'Italie a coupée toute commerce des Lettres, et les vostres et les miennes on été egalement perdues. Je n'ai reçeû celle ci qu'aujourduy, parce [que] Monsieur de Martinigo[1] a voulu me la rendre en mains propre, et il y a quinze jours que je suis au lit avec la Fievre. J'ÿ suis encore, et je vous écris d'une main foible mais d'un Cœur tout penetré de vos bontez. J'ai franchi mille perils pour me retrouver a la cara Italia. Que j'ai des choses a vous dire! Il faut attendre le retablissement de ma santé pour avoir le plaisir de vous embrasser. Je n'ai pas la force d'écrire davantage. Je suis toute a vous, ma belle Madame, et sera eternellement de V. E. la tres humble et tres devouée amie et servante,

M. W. Montagu.

Je vous prie de me dire ce que devenu l'abbé Conti.[2]

Text Bute MS   *Address* A S. E. La Signora La Signora Chiara Michielli

To Wortley 24 Nov. [1746]

Brescia, Nov. 24 N.S.

I bragg'd too soon of my good Health, which lasted but two days after my last Letter. I was then seiz'd with so violent a Fever that I am surpris'd a Woman of my Age could be capable of it. I have kept my Bed 2 months, and am now out of it but a few hours in the Day. I did not mention in my last (thinking it an insignificant circumstance) that Count Palazzo had wrote to his mother (without my knowledge) to advertise her of my Arrival. She came to meet me in her Coach and six, and it was impossible to resist her Importunity of going to her House,[3] where she would keep me till I had found a Lodging to my likeing. I had chose one

---

[1] Probably of the Brescian family Martinenghi.

[2] Antonio Conti, an old friend.

[3] On the present Piazza del Foro (Antonio Fappani in *Commentari dell'ateneo di Brescia*, 1961, p. 104).

when I wrote to you and counted upon going there the beginning of the week following, but my violent illness (being as all the Physicians thought in the utmost danger) made it utterly impossible. The Countess Palazzo has taken as much care of me as if I had been her Sister, and omitted no Expence or trouble to serve me.[1] I am still with her, and indeed in no condition of moving at present. I am now in a sort of milk Diet which is prescrib'd me to restore my strength. From being as fat as Lady Bristol,[2] I am grown leaner than any body I can name. For my own part, I think my selfe in a natural decay. However, I do what I am order'd. I know not how to acknowledge enough my Obligations to the Countess, and I reckon it a great one from her, who is a Devote, that she never brought any Priest to me. My Woman, who is a zealous French Hugonote, I beleive would have tore his Eyes out; during my whole illness it seem'd her cheife concern. I hope your H⟨ealth⟩ continues good.

Text W MS ii. 152–3   *Address* To Edwd Wortley Esqr in Cavendish Square London Angleterre   *Postmark* DE 20   *End. by W* [*Summary*] Ad 26 Dec.[3]   Recd 23 Dec.

To Lady Oxford 24 Nov. [1746]

Nov. 24. N.S., Brescia

Dearest Madam,

I have thought never to have the Honor of writeing to you again. I have been 2 months in my Bed with a Fever, which every body as well as my selfe thought mortal, but I am now in my great chair by the Fire side, still so weak I am not able to move farther. This is the first use I make of my Hand and I cannot employ it in a greater truth than assuring your

[1] In 1743 the widowed Countess Palazzi, pleading her poverty, had applied for permission to sell some property in Gottolengo (Cancelleria Prefetti, Sup. Comune Gottolengo, c. 26, Archivio di Stato, Brescia). The Count's hospitality, LM later emphasized in her 'Italian Memoir', was distinctly mercenary. Although he played an important if

puzzling role in her life for the next ten years, his name does not appear again in any of her known letters to England.

[2] Wife of the 1st Earl.

[3] Cf. LM's date, 25 Dec. (p. 384). Evidently W's memoranda sometimes bore different dates from those on his letters.

Ladyship I shall ever be to my last moment Your Faithfull affectionate Humble Servant,

M. W. Montagu.

Text Wh MS 507   *Address* To The Rt Honble the Lady Henrietta Countess of Oxford Dover Street near St. James's London   *End.* *by Lady Oxford* R: Welbeck Janu: 15th 1746 O:S: Thursday

To Mme Chiara Michiel *31 Dec. 1746*

l'ultimo giorno de l'anno 1746

Excellenza,

Il y a certainement un sort jetté sur nostre amitie; toutes les fois que je tache de vous en donner des marques, quelques maudit Genie les detournent, et veut me faire passer aupres de vous pour la personne la plus ingratte et la plus insensible qui fût jamais.

J'ai repondu (ma chere et charmante amie) a vostre stima-tissima folgio [*sic*] dans le moment mesme que je l'ai reçeûe, quoy que j'etois dans un état a ne pouvoir presque soutenir ma plume, brulant au lit d'une fievre ardent. Dieu sçait si ma Lettre vous ettes parvenue; je n'ai point eû de reponse.

Quand je me portai un peu mieux je vous a écrite encore pour vous temoigner a quel point j'etois mortifiée du retarde-ment de l'honneur de vous voir. Les Medicins m'ont mis au ⟨lit⟩, et c'est tout ce que je puis esperer de vous embrasser a l'Ascension.

On vient de me dire que le Païsan a qui on avoit donné ma Lettre pour porter a la poste l'avoit perdu, et on a pas osé me le dire, de peur de me chagriner, étant encore assez foible. Jugez de ma fureur! Je demandée du papier dans le moment, et je tente pour la troisieme fois de vous faire sçavoir que mon Cœur est toujours le même pour vous, et je suis persuadée que ceux qui vous sont attachez ne vous échappent jamais. Mais parmi cet nombre, j'ose me vanter qu'il n'ÿ a pas un plus penetré de vostre merite et de vos agremens que celui de, Excellenza, vostre tres fidelle A⟨mie⟩, et tres humble et tres Obeissante Servante,

M. W. Montagu.

Je vous prie, mia Carissima, de me dire de nouvelles de l'Abbé Conti et Monsieur du Cange.[1]

Text Bute MS   *Address* A S. E. La Signora La Signora Chiara Michielli Bragadini Venezia.[2]

To Wortley *18 Jan.* [*1747*]

N.S. Jan. 18, Brescia

I receiv'd yours of Oct. 31 but yesterday. I know not if you have had a long one from me giving you an Account of my late severe fit of sickness, of which I am not now quite recover'd, being still very weak.

It has froze hard this several days past, but there is allways a clear fine Sun.

I own I was much surpriz'd at the Dutchess of Manchester's Extravagant match, and yet more at her Journey to Ireland.[3]

I return you thanks for the news you have taken the trouble to send me; I am allways pleas'd to hear of my English Acquaintance.

My Eyes are too weak to say more.

Text W MS ii. 154   *End. by W* [*Summary*] Ad 20 Feb.   Recd 5 Feb.

To Lady Oxford *1 March* [*1747*]

Dearest Madam,

Your Ladyship's obliging Letter of Jan. 17 O.S. came to me yesterday. It gave me great pleasure, and at the same time mortification, on refflecting that you should suffer so much uneasyness on my Account. I am now (I think I may say) quite recover'd, which is allmost a miracle; I beleive few people of my Age ever did, of so severe and so long a fit of

---

[1] LM knew him in Venice in 1740.
[2] For LM's next surviving letter to Mme Michiel, in 1756, see iii. 111.

[3] Edward Hussey, the Duchess's husband, was an Irishman. For their marriage, see above, p. 371.

sickness. I hope you think me in the right in leaving Avignon,[1] which is now all full of miserable Refugees. France I should not have been permitted to stay in, and I am quiet in a Republique that is in our Alliance, which is all the present Aim that I have. Your Ladyship says nothing of your own Health; I flatter my selfe it is good. I beg of you that you will never give your selfe any concern about mine. My Life is useless to the World, and (allmost) tiresome to my selfe.

I did not know Mrs. Stanton was dead;[2] I have so few Correspondants in England that every thing from thence is news to me. I never receiv'd your Ladyship's Letter of Aug't 23, which I suppose was owing to my Removal. That part of Italy I pass'd in comeing hither has suffer'd so much by the War that it is quite different from when I left it. I wish every English man was as sensible as I am of the terrible Effects of Arbitrary Government, some of the most Plentifull parts of the World being reduce'd to near a Famine. This province, which is free from Troops, enriches it selfe by the poverty of its Neighbours, which occasions all provisions to be as dear as in England. The Carnival here has been very gay and Magnificent; I had no share of either, being at that time confin'd to my chamber, and having no tast for Diversions of that Nature. In all situations I am ever (Dearest Madam) with the tenderest affections of my Heart, Your Ladyship's most Faithfull and most Obedient Servant,

M. W. Montagu.

Bres[c]ia, March 1 N.S.

Text Wh MS 507   *Address* To The Rt Honble the Lady Henrietta Countess of Oxford in Dover Street near St James's London *Postmark* ⟨AP ?⟩   *End. by Lady Oxford* d: Bresia March 1. N:S: came to London Tuesday April 14th 1747 O:S: came to Welbeck Thursday April 16th 1747 O:S:

[1] 'Your leaving Avignon was certainly right,' Lady Oxford assured her, and added significantly, 'I wish you could with Ease live in your Native Country' (6 May/25 April 1747, Harley MS).

[2] On 28/17 Jan. Lady Oxford had written: 'One Peice of News came by chance to me, which is, Mr. Stanton it is ⟨who⟩ is married to A Widow Peck of Essex worth 12 Hundred a year that she has or will give Mr. Stanton.'

To Wortley [*17 March 1747*]

Yours of the 26th of Dec. came to me but this Day, March 17 N.S. The passage by Genoa is now clos'd and all Letters oblig'd to go a great way about. My Health is much mended. I ride out every morning, which has very much contributed to my Recovery. I am at present in a little house I have taken some miles from Brescia for the sake of the Air.¹

I wish good Company may reform my Son, as bad debauch'd him.² I have not heard from my Daughter of some time; I do not doubt our Letters are often lost.

Here is a great pen'north to be had if the Dutchess of Marlbrô was living to take advantage of it, the purchase being 100 thousand Guineas, for which I am ⟨tol⟩d the investiture of Guastalla is to be bought.³

Text W MS ii. 155–6   *Address* To Edwd Wortley Esqr in Cavendish Square London Angleterre   *Postmark* AP 4   *End. by* W [*Summary*] Ad 10 Apr.   Recd 6 Apr.

---

¹ This house was in Gottolengo, about eighteen miles south of Brescia. In her 'Italian Memoir' LM relates that after her illness (in Nov. 1746), the doctors said 'that the country air was absolutely necessary for the restoration of my health. The Count [Palazzi] suggested to me one of his country houses; I consented to go there, although so weak that I had to be carried in a litter. . . . I found the house so dilapidated and ruined that if I had known the state it was in, I would never have gone there . . . a few days later he returned, and told me that . . . I was mistress of his house and of all that belonged to him. . . . Meanwhile I found that the country air was very salubrious for me, and I hoped to recover completely in a short time' (Wh MS 510, ff. 3–5: transl.).

² Montagu, a prisoner of the French since March 1746, had been freed in Sept., not by ransom but by exchange with French prisoners. He then went to Breda to join the staff of his kinsman Lord Sandwich, who was Minister Plenipotentiary in the truce talks with the French (Jonathan Curling, *Edward Wortley Montagu*, 1954, pp. 107–9).

³ Guastalla was an Imperial fief lying between Parma and Mantua; and after the death of the last Duke of Guastalla (in Aug. 1746) without issue, it was occupied by Austrian troops in the name of Maria Theresa. In April 1748 it was incorporated into Parma and Piacenza (Ireneo Affò, *Istoria della città e ducato di Guastalla*, 1785–7, iv. 90, 93). In Aug. 1748 the furniture of the ducal palace was sold at auction (see below, p. 409).

To Wortley 9 *April* [*1747*]

Brescia, Ap. 9. N.S.

I receiv'd yours of Feb. 20 last post. I have answer'd that of December 25, which was much longer on the road. The late War has harrass'd Italy to such a degree it is not to be known to be the same Country I saw 5 year ago.

I beleive the Duke and D[uches]s of Montagu[1] cannot help being mortify'd at the Dutchess of Manchester's Folly. It is generally fatal to Women to be at their own Disposal.

My Health is much mended; I endeavour to confirm it by useing Exercise.

Text W MS ii. 157   *Postmark* ⟨?⟩   *End. by W* [*Summary*] Ad 19 May.   Recd 28 Apr.

To Wortley *18 May* [*1747*]

May 18. N.S.

I receiv'd yours dated April 10 yesterday. Tis a quicker passage than I have yet had of any Letter since my arrival in this Country.

The Weather is so surprizingly cold that I have had a fire this morning. I begin to credi⟨t⟩ the old Tradition of Herodotus.[2]

I wish nothing more than the Reformation of my Son, but I own I cannot yet beleive it from any of the appearances that I know. His leaving Lord S[andwich][3] is a plain proofe to me that he is not much in his favour or has lost that part of it he has had. I know my Son; he is a showy companion and may easily impose on any one for a short time. I am persuaded that if Lord S. had a good opinion of his character

---

[1] Parents of the Duchess of Manchester, whose remarriage had been made public the previous summer.

[2] See below, p. 475.

[3] John Montagu (1718–92), 4th Earl; his grandfather was W's first cousin.

he would have wrote to you in his favour. As to the Civillitys of the great men, I look upon them as meer Court nothings.[1]

Text W MS ii. 158–9   *Address* To Edwd Wortley Esqr in Caven- dish Square London Angleterre   *Postmark* IV 2   *End. by W* L.M. 18 May 1747.   Abt our Son.   Recd 2 June.   Ad 9 June.

To Lady Oxford *1 July* [*1747*]

July 1, Brescia

Dearest Madam,

'Tis so long since I have had the Honor of hearing from you that I cannot help being in concern for your Health; mine is much mended by the Country Air and the great regularity with which I live. I flatter my selfe it is the Fault of the Post that I have not the happyness of hearing from you. I pray for Peace on many Accounts, but cheiffly that our Correspond- ance may become more certain. I can say with Truth, 'tis the only pleasure of my Life, and 'tis no small one to think I have a Freind of your Merit.

I am told Lord Cook is marry'd to Lady M[ary] Camp- bell; I knew him when he was at Venice, and beleive her Oeconomy will be a very necessary allay to the expensiveness of his temper.[2] Mr. Wortley (who is the only Correspondant I have in London except my Daughter) tells me you have made Welbeck a very delightfull place.[3] It was allways so by the situation; I do not doubt of the improvement by your

---

[1] Montagu was in England in the spring of 1747 as the protégé of Sand- wich, to whom Chesterfield wrote: 'I received your separate letters by your kinsman Captain Wortley, who seems to be a very sensible clever young fellow. I am sorry that the ill usage of his father and mother should have reduced him to such shifts and variety of situations, as have vilified him, and must necessarily obstruct his advancement in any but the military walk' (27 March O.S. 1747, *Letters*, ed. B. Dobrée, 1932, iii. 890). Montagu wanted to leave the army, but Chesterfield strongly advised him against

it (ibid. 926).

[2] Edward (1719–53), styled Viscount Coke, only son of 1st Earl of Leicester, m. (1 April 1747) Lady Mary Camp- bell (1727–1811), da. of 2nd Duke of Argyll. He was a notorious profligate, addicted to drinking and gambling.

[3] Lady Oxford replied: 'I am glad Mr. Wortley approves of the improve- ments I have made here, and still Hope some convenient opportunity will bring you into your Native Country, and that you may inhabit it with Ease' (22 July 1747 [O.S.], Harley MS).

good Taste. If Wishes had the power of conveying the person, your Ladyship would soon see me there, but I fear there is not so much felicity in store for me. God's will be done. Where-ever I am, I can never be other than, with the tenderest affection, Your Ladyship's most Faithfull Devoted Servant.

M. W. Montagu

Text Wh MS 507   *Address* To The Rt Honble the Lady Henrietta Countess of Oxford in Dover Street near St James's London *Postmark* ⟨?⟩ 15   *End. by Lady Oxford* came to London Wensday July 15th O:S: came to Welbeck Saturday July 18th O:S: 1747

To Wortley *1 July* [*1747*]

July 1. N.S.

I receiv'd yours of May 19 this morning. I am not surpriz'd to hear the D[uches]s of Manchester has ill success in her adventure. I never knew it happen otherwise in such disporportionate [*sic*] Matches, thô some can better dissemble their disquiet than others. Lord Cook visited me when I was at Venice, and I think I know enough of his Temper to beleive him very happily marry'd to a Lady whose Oeconomy may correct his expensive Humour.

My Health is much mended by the Country Air, thô I am still weak. I hope yours is perfectly good, since you say nothing to the Contrary. I should [be] extreamly glad to hear of our Son's reformation. I had a Letter from him at the same time with yours, and shall answer it this post.

Text W MS ii. 160–1   *Address* To Edwd Wortley Esqr in Cavendish Square London Angleterre   *Postmark* IY 15   *End. by W* [*Summary*] Ad 25 Jul.   Recd at the Lodge [Wharncliffe] 18 July

From Wortley 5 *Aug.*/25 *July 1747*

Wortley, 25 July 1747

Yours of the 1st came hither on the 18th. I mentioned to you in my last that Lord Sandwich proposed to bring our Son into Parliament.

He then seemed not determined whether to bring him in for the Town or County. My Lord's brother served before for the County.[1] As he thought it not proper his brother should be chosen again, our Son was named as the next of the family to his brother, except myselfe, who woud not have quitted Peterborough.[2] He was chosen without opposition for the County on the 18th.[3] As my Lord's brother is Captain of a man of war, and has been lucky in Prizes,[4] perhaps my Lord may think it more for his interest that he should not be in Parliament because he will be in less danger of being unemploy'd. Some think, but I do not know, that he has some way disobliged my Lord. When he mentioned to me his intention to bring in our Son he seemed to think he might depend on his discretion and shoud not repent of his having done him that favour.

Text W MS i. 137–8   *Address* [*in another hand*] A Madame Madame Marie Wortley Montagu a Brescia par Venise   *Postmark* JB

To Lady Oxford *1 Sept.* [*1747*]

Brescia,[5] Sept. 1. N.S.

Dearest Madam,
    This is the fourth Letter I have wrote since I have had the Honor of yours, and am in so much pain for your Health that I have little Enjoyment in the recovery of my own. I am willing to flatter my selfe that your silence is occasion'd by the irregularity of the post, which this unhappy war often intterupts. The Fear of this never reaching you puts a great damp on my writeing, yet I could not be easy without

[1] At the death of the M.P. for Huntingdonshire in 1745, Capt. William Montagu (1720?–57), Sandwich's brother, was elected (*Returns of Members of Parliament*, 1878, ii. 88).

[2] W had sat for Peterborough (Northants.) in the Parliaments of 1734 and 1741. In 1747 he was elected for both Peterborough (26 June) and Bossiney, a notorious pocket borough in Cornwall (2 July); he chose to sit for the former, and assigned Bossiney to William Ord (ibid. 98).

[3] In a subsequent letter to Sandwich,

W justified his not having supported Capt. Montagu for re-election in Huntingdonshire (6 Nov. 1747, MS owned by the Editor); on 18 July his son had defeated Capt. Montagu for that seat.

[4] As commander of the *Bristol*, Capt. Montagu captured a rich Spanish ship in 1745 (Collins, iii. 470).

[5] Although LM lived mostly in the village of Gottolengo she headed her letters from this nearby post-town (see below, p. 406).

endeavouring (at least) to give you my repeated assurances of that everlasting affection I shall allways Feel for your Ladyship, which you so highly deserve, and have by so many obligations acquir'd.

I have liv'd this 8 months in the Country, after the same manner (in little) that I fancy you do at Welbeck, and find so much advantage from the Air and Quiet of this retreat that I do not think of leaving it. I walk and read much, but have very little company except that of a neighbouring Convent. I do what good I am able in the village round me, which is a very large one, and have had so much success that I am thought a great Physician and should be esteem'd a Saint if I went to Mass. My House is a very convenient one, and if I could have your Ladyship's dear Conversation, I may truly say my Life would be very comfortable. That is a melancholy thought when I refflect on the impossibillity of that Happyness being obtain'd by (Dearest Madam) Your most Faithfully devoted Humble servant,

M. W. Montagu.

Be pleas'd to direct to Brescia par Venise.

Text Wh MS 507 *Address* To The Rt Honble the Lady Henrietta Countess of Oxford in Dover Street near St James's London Angleterre *Postmark* oc 12 *End. by Lady Oxford* came to London Monday Octor 12th O:S: 1747 R: Welbeck Thursday Octor 15th O:S:

To Wortley *10 Sept.* [*1747*]

Sept. 10 N.S., Brescia

I have just receiv'd yours of June [*sic*] 25th.[1] I am very glad of my Son's good Fortune, and wish his future behaviour may be such as may give him a just title to your pardon for his past Follys. He will be now in a light to shew how far he is capable of makeing a good Figure, at least such a one as not to be a reproach to his Family. I have had no answer to my last letter to him. I directed it as he desir'd, to Lord Sandwich's at the Hague.

1 W's letter of 5 Aug./25 July, printed above.

I hope your Health continues good, since you say nothing to the contrary.

Text W MS ii. 162–3   *Address* To Edward Wortley Esqr in Cavendish Square London Angleterre   *Postmark* OC 12   *End. by W* [*Summary*] Ad 1 Dec.   Recd 9 [*sic*] Oct.

To Lady Oxford 29 *Nov.* [*1747*]

Nov'r 29 N.S.

Dearest Madam,

I receiv'd yesterday the most sensible pleasure by your obliging Letter. It is impossible to tell you what joy the sight of your Ladiship's hand gave me, which was very much heighten'd by the account of your Health and continu'd goodness to me. I beleive the air you are in is the best in England, and I do not doubt but the Tranquillity and regularity of your Life will re-establish your Constitution, which is naturally a very good one, and only hurt by Melancholy Refflections, which I hope you will never more have any occasion for. It is no Dimunition [*sic*] of the Dutchess of Portland's merit to say you deserve what ever affection she can pay, since those who do their Duty can never be too much valu'd. I sincerely share in the satisfaction you have in seeing that she performs hers to you; it is the clearest proofe of her good sense and good mind. May you long be happy in one another. I am glad my Daughter enjoys her Conversation, which is in every sense an honor and advantage.[1]

I have bought the House I live in, which I suppose you will imagine little better than a House of office when I talk of my purchaseing, and indeed it has cost me little more than the price of one; but to say Truth it is not much more than the shell of a Palace, which was built not above 40 year ago, but the Master of it dying before it was quite finish'd, and falling into Hands that had many others, it has been wholly

---

[1] Lady Oxford had written: 'Lady Bute . . . with Lord Bute are much with my Daughter and her Husband' (17 Oct. 1747 [O.S.], Harley MS); and the Duchess of Portland found Lady Bute 'a most agreeable friend in all respects' (24 July 1747, Eliz. Montagu, *Corr. 1720–1761*, ed. E. J. Climenson, 1906, i. 244).

neglected; but being well built the walls are perfectly sound, and I amuse my selfe in fitting it up. I will take the Liberty of sending your Ladyship a plan of it, which is far from magnificent, but I beleive you will be of my Opinion, that it is one of the most convenient you ever saw.[1] The owners of it, looking upon it as only an expence to them, were pleas'd to part with it for a Triffle.[2] I won't make you any excuses for troubling you with this long account of my little affairs. Your Freindship and good nature, I know, gives you a concern in all that regards Your Ladyship's ever faithfull and affectionate humble Servant,

M. W. Montagu.

Text Wh MS 507   *Address* To The Rt Honble the Lady Henrietta Countess of Oxford in Dover Street near St James's London *Postmark* IA 18   *End. by Lady Oxford* came to London Jan: 18th O:S: Monday   R: Welbeck Jan: 21st O:S: 1747 Thursday

To Lady Bute *17 Dec.* [*1747*]

Dec. 17. N.S., Brescia.

Dear Child,

I receiv'd yours of October 14 but yesterday. The negligence of the post is very disagreable. I have at length had a Letter from Lady Oxford by which I find mine to her has miscarry'd, and perhaps the answer which I have now wrote may have the same Fate.

I wish you joy of your young Son.[3] May he live to be a

---

[1] A rough description of the house is given by Antonio Fappani in *Commentari dell'ateneo di Brescia*, 1961, pp. 109–10.

[2] In her 'Italian Memoir' LM testifies that after renting (or borrowing) the house in Gottolengo she put locks on the doors and glass in the windows; then, although still uncertain of where to settle: 'Insensibly I grew accustomed to the solitude of Gottolengo, the walks pleased me, the air was refreshing, and I let myself be induced to remodel the old house.... The Count [Palazzi] sold

me his house in Gottolengo, with a deed signed in the presence of witnesses, and I repaired and enlarged it, and filled it with my furniture' (Wh MS 510, ff. 11–12: transl.). When she discovered (nine years later) the full extent of the Count's swindles, she was told that the house was entailed, and that it was hers only as long as she occupied it (f. 34).

[3] James Archibald (19 Sept. 1747–1818), second son. He ultimately inherited the Wortley estates, and was father of 1st Baron Wharncliffe.

blessing to you. I find I amuse my selfe here in the same
Manner as if at London, according to your account of it;
that is, I play at Whist every night with some old Priests
that I have taught it to, and are my only Companions. To
say truth, the decay of my sight will no longer suffer me to
read by Candle light, and the evenings are now long and
dark, that I am forc'd to stay at home. I beleive you'll be
perswaded my Gameing makes no body uneasy, when I tell
you that we play only a penny per Corner. 'Tis now a year
that I have liv'd wholly in the Country, and have no design
of quitting it. I am entirely given up to rural Amusements,
and have forgot there are any such things as Wits or Fine
Ladys in the World. However, I am pleas'd to hear what
happens to my acquaintance. I wish you would inform me
what is become of the Pomfret Family,[1] and who Sir Francis
Dashwood has marry'd. I knew him at Florence. He seem'd
so nice in the choice of a Wife, I have some Curiosity to
know who it is that has had charms enough to make him
enter into an Engagement he us'd to speak of with fear
and trembling.[2]

I am ever, Dear Child, your most affectionate Mother,
M. Wortley M.

My service to Lord Bute and blessing to my Grand
children.

Text W MS iii. 41–42   *Address* To The Rt Honble the Countess
of Bute [at Twickenham *struck out*] London Middlesex Angleterre
[*in another hand*] in New Burlington Street Burlinton Garden   *Postmark* IA 18   20 IA

[1] The brilliant marriage of Lady
Pomfret's eldest daughter Sophia to
Carteret (Secretary of State), in 1744,
had been of short duration; she died a
year later. For Lady Pomfret's next
daughter, Charlotte, see above, p. 336,
n. 1. In July 1745 Lord Lempster had
been reported taken prisoner by the

French at Ghent (Walpole, *Corr.* xix.
71–72).

[2] Dashwood (see above, p. 207) m.
(1745) Sarah (d. 1769), da. of George
Gould, widow of Sir Richard Ellis.
Walpole called her 'a poor forlorn Pres-
byterian prude' (*Corr.* xix. 224).

To Wortley *18 Dec.* [*1747*]

Dec. 18. N.S., Brescia

It is so long since I have had the pleasure of hearing from you that I begin to fear all my Letters have miscarry'd, and should be in pain for your Health if I had not had a Letter from my Daughter last post which assures me that you are well. I wrote to my Son (as I have allready told you) directed, as he desir'd, to Lord Sandwich, but have had no Answer. I am afraid that the Messengers I sometimes send to Bres[c]ia put the money that should Frank my Letters into their pockets, and throw them away.

I walk very much, and find the benefit of it in my Constitution, which is much mended by exercise and a very exact regularity. I hope and heartily wish the continuance [of] your Health and that you take care not to injure it by parlimentary Fatigues.

Text W MS ii. 164   *End. by W* [*Summary*] Ad   Recd 18 Jan.

To Lady Bute *5 Jan.* [*1748*]

Dear Child,

I am glad to hear that your selfe and family are in good Health. As to the alteration you say you find in the World, it is only owing to your being better acquainted with it. I have never, in all my various Travels, seen but two sorts of people (and those very like one another); I mean Men and Women, who allways have been, and ever will be, the same. The same Vices and the same Follys have been the fruit of all ages, thô sometimes under different Names. I remember (when I return'd from Turkey) meeting with the same affectation of youth amongst my acquaint⟨an⟩ce that you now mention amongst yours, and I do not doubt but your Daughter will find the same twenty years hence, amongst hers. One

of the greatest happiness of Youth is the Ignorance of Evil,
thô it is often the ground of great Indiscretions; and sometimes the active part of Life is over before an honest Mind
finds out how one ought to act in such a World as this. I am
as much remov'd from it as it is possible to be on this side
the Grave, which is from my own Inclination, for I might
have even here a great deal of Company, the way of living
in this province being what I beleive it is now in the sociable
part of Scotland and was in England a hundred years ago.

I had a visit in the beginning of these Holidays of 30 Horse
of Ladys and Gentlemen with their servants (by the way, the
Ladies all ride like the late D[uches]s of Cleaveland).[1] They
came with the kind Intent of staying with me at least a
fortnight, thô I had never seen any of them before; but they
were all Neighbours within ten mile round. I could not avoid
entertaining them at supper, and by good Luck had a large
Quantity of Game in the House, which with the help of my
Poultry furnish'd out a plentifull Table. I sent for the
Fiddles; and they were so obliging to dance all Night, and
even dine with me next day, thô none of them had been in
Bed, and were much disapointed I did not press them to
stay, it being the Fashion to go in troops to one anothers'
houses, hunting and danceing together, a month in each
Castle. I have not yet return'd any of their visits, nor do not
intend it of some time, to avoid this expensive Hospitality.
The trouble of it is not very great, they not expecting any
Ceremony. I left the ⟨room about⟩ one o' clock, and they
continu'd their Ball in the Saloon ⟨above⟩ stairs without
being at all offended at my ⟨departure⟩. The greatest
Diversion I had was to see a ⟨lady⟩ of my own age comfortably
danceing wi⟨th her⟩ own Husband some years older, and
I can ass⟨ure you⟩[2] she jumps and Gallops with the best of
them.

May you allways be as well satisfy'd with your Family
as you are at present, and your children return in your age
the tender care you have of their Infancy. I know no greater

---

[1] Ladies rode astride (see above, p. 263, n. 1). A curious Scots traveller in 1744 was surprised to see Italian ladies ride in this way (Alexander Drummond, *Travels*, 1754, p. 54).

[2] MS torn; missing text (except last insertion) from 1861, ii. 158.

Happiness that can be wish'd for you by your most affectionate Mother,

M. Wortley.

Brescia, Janu. 5.

My complements to Lord Bute and blessing to my Grand children.

Text W MS iii. 15–16   *Address* To The Rt Honble the Countess of Bute [at Twictnam near *struck out*] London [Middlesex *struck out*] Angleterre [*in another hand*] in Newburlington Street Burlington Garden   *Postmark* IA 20   25 IA   *End. by* W L.M. to L B. 5 Jan. 1747/8

To Wortley [*2 Feb. 1748*]

Yours of the 1st of December O.S. came to me this morning, Feb. 2 N.S. I hope your Health continues good, since you say nothing to the contrary.

I think the D[uches]s of Manchester['s] silence is the most reasonable part of her conduct. Complainers are seldom pity'd, and boasters yet seldomer beleiv'd. Her Retirement is, in my opinion, no proofe either of her Happiness or discontent, since her appearance in the World can never be pleasing to her, having sense enough to know 'tis impossible for her to make a good Figure in it.

I was show'd at Genoa the ode on Ch[arles] Ch[urchill][1] as a production of Dr. Broxholm.[2] I own I thought it much in his Style and am apt to beleive (from what I know of Sir Ch[arles] H[anbury Williams]) he is more likely to have the Vanity to father it than the Wit to write it.[3] I have seen heaps

---

[1] In Sir Charles Hanbury Williams's *Works* is an imitation of an ode of Horace's, entitled 'General Churchill's Address to Venus'. The editor, dating it Dec. 1739, states that it was 'the first production that made Sir C. H. Williams known as a Poet' (1822, i. 234–6). Horace Walpole, whose notes are used in that edition, may have shown the verses to LM when they met in Genoa in July 1741.

[2] Noel Broxholme (1689?–1748), physician and wit. Walpole admired his Latin odes, apparently unpublished (*Corr.* ix. 66).

[3] Hanbury Williams (1708–59) was a diplomatist and satiric poet. LM expressed her contempt for him more fully in her letter to Lady Bute of 7 July [1757] (iii. 131).

of his Poetry, but nothing to distinguish him from the Tribe of common Versifyers. The last I saw was an ode address'd to Mr. Dodington on his courtship to the late D[uke] of Argyle.¹ Those two you mention have never reach'd me. I should be very much oblig'd to you if you would send me copys of them.

The Winter here begun with the last month. The snow is still on the Ground in some places, but the air much soften'd, and we reckon the Spring begun. I hear the new Opera at Brescia much aplauded, and intend to see it before the end of the Carnival. The people of this province are much at their ease during the miseries which the War occasions their Neighbours, and employ all their Time in Deversions.

Text W MS ii. 165–6   *Address* To Edwd Wortley Esqr in Cavendish Square London Angleterre   *Postmark* FE 16   *End. by W* [*Summary*] Ad 23 Mar.   Recd 16 Feb.²

To Lady Bute *3 Feb.* [*1748*]

My Dear Child,

I return you thanks for the News you send me. I am allways amus'd with the changes and chances that happen amongst my acquaintance. I pity the D[uches]s of Devonshire and admire the greatness of mind that makes her refuse an addition to her own Estate, but am surpriz'd she can relinquish the care of her children who are yet unsettle'd.³ Lady Thanet's behaviour has allways been without any regard to public censure, but I am ever astonish'd (thô I have frequently seen it) that Women can so far renounce all Decency

¹ 'An Ode to the Duke of Argyle, as from Mr. Doddington, (Written in June 1740.)', *Works*, 1822, i. 14–16.

² From this year on, W kept a record of LM's letters in a document (now lost) entitled 'Mr. Wortley's own Abstract of the Letters which he received from Lady Mary, between 1748 and 1755' (sold at Southgate's Auction Rooms, 22 Jan. 1828).

³ Catherine Hoskins (d. 1777) m.

(1718) William Cavendish, later 3rd Duke of Devonshire (1698–1755). According to Walpole the Duke parted from her 'by breaking a promise he had given her of not marrying his son [Lord Hartington] to Lady Burlington's daughter'; but they were reconciled the next year (*Corr.* xx. 66 and n. 24). Of their seven children, three sons and one daughter were still under age.

as to endeavour to expose a Man whose name they bear.[1] Lady Burlington has made a lucky choice for her Daughter. I am well acquainted with Lord Hartington and do not know any Man so fitted to make a Wife happy, with so great a Vocation for matrimony that I verily beleive if it had not been establish'd before his Time, he would have had the Glory of the Invention.[2]

I hear the Carnival is very bright at Brescia. I have not yet been to pertake of it, but intend to go see the Opera, which I hear much commended. Some Ladies in the neighbourhood favour'd me last week with a visit in Masquerade. They were all dress'd in white like Vestal Virgins, with garlands on their Heads. They came at night with Violins and Flambeaux, but did not stay more than one Dance, persuing their way to another castle some miles from hence.

I suppose you are now in London. Where ever you are, you have the good wishes of your most affectionate Mother,

M. Wortley M.

Feb. 3. N.S.

My C⟨omp⟩lements to Lord Bute and blessing to my Grand children.

Text W MS iii. 300–1   *Address* To The Rt Honble the Countess of Bute at [Twictnam near *struck out*] London Middlesex Angleterre [*in another hand*] New Burlington Street Burlington Gardens *Postmark* FE 15   19 FE

---

[1] Mary Saville (1700–51), da. of 2nd Marquess of Halifax, m. (1722) Sackville Tufton (1688–1753), 7th Earl of Thanet. Their separation had been rumoured in 1745 (HMC *Denbigh MSS*, v, 1911, p. 146).

[2] William (1720–64), Marquess of Hartington and later 4th Duke of Devonshire, m. (27 March 1748) Lady Charlotte Elizabeth Boyle (1731–54), only surviving daughter of Lady Burlington, Lady Thanet's sister. LM had

known him in Venice, where he and Jan Teding van Berkhout visited her on 1 June 1740 (van Berkhout MS diary). His friend Lord Mansel, who had been in Venice at the same time, wrote to LM after returning to England: 'I am surprized that Hartington, who has always made it his business to dangle after all the fine Ladies in Italy, and wheresoever he has been, shoud know so little of Weomen' (18/7 July 1740, W MS iv. 181).

To Wortley *24 April* [*1748*]

Brescia, April 24. N.S.

I return you many thanks for yours of March 21, in which were the Copys of Sir Ch[arles] H[anbury Williams]'s poetry, which extremely entertain'd me. I find Tar Water succeeded to Ward's drop.[1] 'Tis possible by this time that some other Quackery has taken place of that. The English are easyer than any other Nation infatuated by the prospect of universal medicines, nor is there any Country in the World where the Doctors raise such immense Fortunes. I attribute it to the Fund of Credulity which is in all Mankind. We have no longer faith in Miracles and Reliques, and therefore with the same Fury run after receits and Physicians. The same Money which 300 years ago was given for the Health of the Soul is now given for the Health of the body, and by the same sort of people: Women and halfe witted Men. In the Countries where they have shrines and Images, Quacks are despis'd, and Monks and Confessors find their account in mannageing the Fear and Hope which rule the actions of the Multitude.

I should be extremely pleas'd if I could entirely depend on Lord Sandwich's account of our Son.[2] As I am wholly unacquainted with him, I cannot judge how far he may be either deceiv'd or interested.[3] I know my Son (if not much alter'd) is capable of giving Bonds for more than he will ever be worth, in the view of any present Advantage.

Lord Bute and my Daughter's conduct may be owing to the advice of the Duke of Argyle.[4] It was a Maxim of Sir

[1] The universal nostrum sold by Joshua Ward (1685–1761), widely used from the 1730's until his death. Hanbury Williams had written a satire on it (*Works*, 1822, ii. 1–2); but LM refers to his 'Tar-Water, A Ballad' (ibid. 21–24), about the nostrum enthusiastically advocated by the philosopher George Berkeley.

[2] Having resigned from the army (on 7 Jan. 1748) Montagu was now at Aix-la-Chapelle assisting Sandwich, pleni-

potentiary in the peace negotiations.

[3] W had written to Sandwich, 'Your Approbation of my son's Conduct does him much Honour, and in persevering to shew his Gratitude for your goodness, he will pursue his own Interest' (2 April/22 March 1748, MS owned by the Editor).

[4] Bute's uncle, the 3rd Duke of Argyll (formerly Lord Islay) was respected by LM for his intelligence (see iii. 20). In 1747 Bute had met the Prince of

R[obert] Walpole's that whoever expected advancement should appear much in public.[1] He us'd to say, whoever neglected the World would be neglected by it, thô I beleive more Familes have been ruin'd than rais'd by persuing that Method.

If I was not afraid of tireing you with the length of my Letter, I would give you the History of an Irish Conquest at Avignon, more extrodinary (all circumst⟨ances⟩ consider'd) than Mr. Hussy's,[2] the irresistable Lover being some years past threescore. I own the vexation of that foolish Adventure gave the finishing stroke to my dislike of that Town, having a real kindness for the young Lady that flung her selfe away. She was Daughter to Mr. Carter[3] who I think you knew, a Relation of Lady Bellasis.[4]

Text W MS ii. 167–8   *Address* To Edwd Wortley Esqr in Cavendish Square London Angleterre   *Postmark* MA 21   *End. by W* [*Summary*] Recd abt 21 of May.   Ad 7 June.

To Lady Oxford *27 April* [*1748*]

Brescia, Ap. 27. N.S.

Dearest Madam,

It is so long since I have had the Happiness of hearing from you I cannot forbear writeing, thô perhaps this letter may have the same fate of those that have preceded it. I receiv'd one from my Daughter but a few days ago that was dated in September. Mr. Wortley writes me word that she has chang'd her retir'd way of Life, and is much in Public; I wish it may be to her Advantage. I hope the Dutchess of Portland and her Family continue in perfect Health; I do not fear your Ladiship's receiving any trouble from her, if

Wales by chance, and they soon became close friends.

[1] LM had earlier admired Walpole's aggressiveness (see i. 226).

[2] Of the Duchess of Manchester.

[3] Not identified.

[4] Probably Susan Armyne (1644–

1713), who m. (1662) Sir Henry Belasyse (1639–67); created (1674) Baroness Belasyse. W had known her, for Addison wrote to him in 1711: 'Lady Bellasis is very much your humble servant' (*Letters*, ed. W. Graham, 1941, p. 264).

she gives you none by her sickness. The real part I take in every thing that concerns you gives me a share in every branch of your Prosperity; I have a pleasure in all your improvements at Welbeck, when I hear them commended, thô I shall never see them. 'Tis allmost the only attachment I have in this World, being every day (as it is fit I should) more and more wean'd from it. I hope your silence is only occasion'd by the irregularity of the post, which I cannot expect to see reform'd while the War continues. Notwithstanding my Indifference for other things, your Freindship and Health will ever be tenderly dear to, Madam, Your Ladyship's most faithfull Obedient Servant,

M. W. Montagu.

Text Wh MS 507   *Address* To The Rt Honble the Lady Henrietta Countess of Oxford in Dover Street near St James's London *Postmark* MA 21   *End. by Lady Oxford* came to London May 21st O:S: Saturday   R: Welbeck 23d O:S: 1748 Monday

To Lady Bute [*6 May 1748*]

I am very much oblig'd to you (Dear Child) for yours of Feb. 20th, which came to my hands but yesterday, May 5th, N.S. I am glad to hear that you are so well diverted, and that Lady Jane has got so well over the small pox.[1] I think Lady L[ucy] Wentworth is better marry'd than I expected.[2] She is of an age to be wean'd from the Vain part of Life, and with a prudent conduct may be very happy in a moderate Fortune. I have seen General Howard's name very often in the news paper and suppos'd him to be Brother to Lord Carlisle, but he was not marry'd (at least did not declare himselfe so) when I left England.[3] The Death of the Duke of Bridgewater will make Lord Trentham's marriage yet more advantageous.[4] I

---

[1] Lady Jane Stuart (1742–1828), Lady Bute's second daughter.

[2] Lady Lucy (d. 1771), da. of 1st Earl of Strafford, m. (Feb. 1748) Col., later Sir George Howard (1720?–96) (*London Mag.*, 1748, p. 92).

[3] Carlisle's brother, Brig.-Gen. the

Hon. Charles Howard, died in 1765 unmarried.

[4] Granville Leveson-Gower (1721–1803), LM's nephew, styled Viscount Trentham (1746), m. (28 March 1748) Lady Louisa Egerton (1723–61), da. of 1st Duke of Bridgewater. Her brother

heard at Avignon that the young Duke had marry'd himselfe very unluckily,[1] as also the Duke of Chandos, Lord
Salisbury, and Lord Bristol, but have had no Confirmation
of it.[2]

I am surpriz'd you mention Lady Townshend's giving a
Ball. I thought she was parted from her Lord and not in
Circumstances of giving public Entertainments.[3] I pray
for a peace, which may make Correspondance more regular
and give me more frequent oppertunities of telling you that
I am ever (Dear Child) your most affectionate Mother,

M. Wortley.

My Complements to Lord Bute and blessing to my Grand
children.

Text W MS iii. 288–9   *Address* To The Rt Honble the Countess
of Bute at Twictnam near London Middlesex Angleterre   *Postmark* SE 12

To Lady Bute *10 May* [*1748*]

I give you thanks (Dear Child) for your entertaining account of your present Diversions. I find the public Calamities
have no Influence on the pleasures of the Town. I remember
very well the play of The Revenge, having been once acquainted with a party that intended to represent it (not one

John (b. 1727), 2nd Duke, died unmarried on 4 March 1748, and was succeeded by his only surviving brother,
Francis (1736–1803), who never married
and at his death left his enormous estate
to his nephew—thus ultimately fulfilling
LM's prediction.

[1] In 1745 the 2nd Duke of Bridgewater had been rumoured as married to
his tutor's niece (Egmont, *Diary*, iii.
308).

[2] Henry Brydges (1708–71), 2nd
Duke of Chandos, m. (1744) as his
second wife Anne Jefferies, who had been
his mistress; Egmont calls her an inn-

keeper's maid (iii. 307–8). James Cecil
(1713–80), 6th Earl of Salisbury, m.
(1745) Elizabeth Keet, described by
Egmont as 'daughter to a barber and
shewer of the tombs in Canterbury'. The
1st Earl of Bristol was falsely rumoured
in 1745 as having married his late wife's
maid. Egmont called it 'a lucky season
for low people's marrying' (ibid.).

[3] Lord and Lady Townshend had
long been estranged; on 19 March 1741
[O.S.] W had written to LM that 'Lady
Townshend and my Lord agreed to live
separately about a fortnight or 3 weeks
ago' (W MS i. 122).

of which is now alive).[1] I wish you had told me who acted
the principal parts. I suppose Lord Bute was Alonzo by
the magnificence of his Dress.[2] I think they have mended
their choice in The Orphan.[3] I saw it plaid at Westminster
School, where Lord Ereskine was Monimia, and then one
of the most Beautifull Figures that could be seen.[4]

I have had here (in low life) some amusements of the same
sort. I beleive I wrote you word I intended to go to the
Opera at Brescia, but the Weather being cold and the roads
bad prevented my Journey, and the people of this Village
(which is the largest I know—the Curate tells me he has
two thousand communicants) presented me a petition for
leave to erect a Theatre in my Saloon. This House had stood
empty many years before I took it, and they were accustom'd
to turn the stables into a Playhouse every Carnival. It is now
occupy'd by my Horses, and they had no other place proper
for a stage. I easily comply'd with their request, and was
surpriz'd at the Beauty of their scenes, which thô painted by
a country painter are better colour'd and the perspective
better manag'd than in any of the second rate Theatres in
London. I lik'd it so well, it is not yet pull'd down. The
performance was yet more surprizing, the actors being all
peasants, but the Italians have so natural a Genius for
Comedy, they acted as well as if they had been brought up
to nothing else, particularly the Arlequin, who far surpass'd
any of our English, thô only the Taylor of the Village, and
I am assur'd never saw a play in any other place. It is pity
they have not better poets, the pieces being not at all
superior to our Drolls. The music, Habits and illumination
were at the expence of the Parish, and the whole Entertainment (which lasted the 3 last Days of the Carnival) cost me

[1] Edward Young, author of the tragedy *The Revenge*, had been patronized
by LM in 1724 (see above, p. 34). Young
had met Lady Bute before her marriage
(HMC *Bath MSS*, i, 1904, p. 294).

[2] Walpole said of Bute that in 1748
he 'had fallen in love with his own
figure, which he produced at masquerades in becoming dresses, and in plays
which he acted in private companies
with a set of his own relations' (*Mem. of
George II*, 1822, i. 40–41). Bute's daughter describes these productions of *The
Revenge* and *The Orphan* (Lady Louisa
Stuart, *Selections from Her Manuscripts*,
ed. J. Home, 1899, p. 40).

[3] Thomas   Otway's   *The   Orphan*
(1680), one of the most popular tragedies
of the time.

[4] In 1720 Erskine, Lady Mar's stepson, had acted this part 'mighty well'
(HMC *Portland MSS*, v, 1899, p. 593).

only a Baril of Wine, which I gave the actors, and is not so dear as small Beer in London. At present, as the old song says,

> —— all my whole care
> Is my farming affair,
> To make my Corn grow, and my apple Trees bear.

My improvements give me great pleasure, and so much profit that if I could live a hundred years longer I should certainly provide for all my Grand children; but alas, as the Italians say, h'o sonato vingt e quatro 'ora; and it is not long I must expect to write my selfe your most affectionate Mother,

M. Wortley.

My Compliments to Lord Bute and blessing to your little ones.

May 10 N.S.

Text W MS iii. 92–93   *Address* To The Rt Honble the Countess of Bute at Twictnam near London Middlesex Angleterre   *Post-mark* ⟨?⟩ 12

To Lady Bute [*10 July 1748*]

Dear Child,

I receiv'd yours of May the 12th but yesterday, July the 9th. I am surpriz'd you complain of my silence. I have never fail'd answering yours the post after I receiv'd them, but I fear, being directed to Twictnam (having no other direction from you), your servants there may have neglected them.

I have been this six weeks, and still am, at my Dairy house, which joins to my Garden.[1] I beleive I have allready told you it is a long mile from the Castle, which is situate in the midst

---

[1] In her 'Italian Memoir' LM relates how Palazzi told her that 'an old dying priest wanted to sell his small property in order to pay his debts, that I could have it at a bargain price, allowing the priest to occupy the house during his lifetime, that there was a large garden which could be arranged to my taste, that it was close enough to the castle [her house in Gottolengo] to serve all my needs. . . . I went myself and found the place very lovely, and I bought it for 800 sequins [£400] cash. I amused myself by planting it, and must have spent another 200 sequins on the place. That was in the year 1747' (Wh MS 510, f. 11: transl.).

of a very large village (once a considerable Town, part of the walls still remaining) and has not vacant ground enough about it to make a Garden, which is my greatest amusement; and it being now troublesome to walk or even go in the chaise till the Evening, I have fitted up in this farm house a room for my selfe, that is to say, strewd the floor with Rushes, cover'd the chimney with moss and branches, and adorn'd the Room with Basons of earthern ware (which is made here to great perfection) fill'd with Flowers, and put in some straw chairs and a Couch Bed, which is my whole Furniture.

This Spot of Ground is so Beautifull I am afraid you will scarce credit the Description, which, however, I can assure you shall be very litteral, without any embellishment from Imagination. It is on a Bank forming a kind of Peninsula rais'd from the River Oglio 50 foot, to which you may descend by easy stairs cut in the Turf, and either take the air on the River, which is as large as the Thames at Richmond, or by walking an avenu two hundred yards on the side of it you find a Wood of a hundred acres, which was allready cut into walks and rideings when I took it. I have only added 15 Bowers in different views, with seats of Turf. They were easily made, here being a large quantity of under Wood, and a great number of wild Vines which twist to the Top of the highest Trees, and from which they make a very good sort of Wine they call Brusco. I am now writeing to you in one of these arbours, which is so thick shaded the Sun is not troublesome even at Noon. Another is on the side of the River, where I have made a camp Kitchin, that I may take the Fish, dress and eat it immediately, and at the same time see the Barks which ascend or Descend every day, to or from Mantua, Guastalla or Pont de vic,[1] all considerable Towns. This little Wood is carpetted (in their succeeding seasons) with violets and strawberrys, inhabited by a nation of Nightingales, and fill'd with Game of all kinds excepting Deer and wild Boar, the first being unknown here, and not being large enough for the other.

My Garden was a plain Vineyard when it came into my hands not two year ago, and it is with a small expence turn'd into a Garden that (apart from the advantage of the climate)

[1] Pontevico.

I like better than that of Kensington. The Italian Vineyards
are not planted like those in France, but in clumps fasten'd
to Trees planted in equal Ranks (commonly fruit Trees) and
continu'd in festoons from one to another, which I have
turn'd into cover'd Gallerys of shade, that I can walk in the
heat without being incommoded by it. I have made a dineing
room of Verdure, capable of holding a Table of 20 Covers.
The whole ground is 317 feet in length and 200 in Breadth.
You see it is far from large, but so prettily dispos'd (thô I say
it) that I never saw a more agreable rustic Garden, abounding
with all sort of Fruit, and produces a variety of Wines. I
would send you a piece if I did not fear the custom would make
you pay too dear for it. I beleive my Description gives you
but an imperfect Idea of my Garden.

Perhaps I shall succeed better in describing my manner of
life, which is as regular as that of any Monastery. I generally
rise at six, and as soon as I have breakfasted put my selfe at
the head of my Weeder Women, and work with them till
nine. I then inspect my Dairy and take a Turn amongst my
Poultry, which is a very large enquiry. I have at present 200
chicken, besides Turkys, Geese, Ducks, and Peacocks. All
things have hitherto prosper'd under my Care. My Bees and
silk worms[1] are double'd, and I am told that, without
accidents, my Capital will be so in two years time. At 11
o'clock I retire to my Books. I dare not indulge my selfe in
that pleasure above an hour. At 12 I constantly dine, and sleep
after dinner till about 3. I then send for some of my old
Priests and either play at picquet or Whist till tis cool
enough to go out. One Evening I walk in my Wood where I
often Sup, take the air on Horseback the next, and go on the
Water the third. The Fishery of this part of the River belongs
to me, and my Fisherman's little boat (where I have a green
Lutestring Awning) serves me for a Barge. He and his Son
are my Rowers, without any expence, he being very well
paid by the profit of the Fish, which I give him on condition
of having every day one dish for my Table. Here is plenty
of every sort of Fresh Water Fish, excepting Salmon, but we
have a large Trout so like it that I, that have allmost forgot
the taste, do not distinguish it.

---

[1] For LM's raising of silkworms, see below, p. 421.

We are both plac'd properly in regard to our Different times of Life: you amidst the Fair, the Galant and the Gay, I in a retreat where I enjoy every amusement that Solitude can afford. I confess I sometimes wish for a little conversation, but I refflect that the commerce of the World gives more uneasyness than pleasure, and Quiet is all the Hope that can reasonably be indulg'd at my Age.

My Letter is of an unconscionable length. I should ask your pardon for it, but I had a mind to give you an Idea of my passing my time. Take it as an instance of the affection of, Dear Child, your most affectionate Mother,

M. Wortley.

My Compliments to Lord Bute and blessing to my Grand children.

Text W MS iii. 96–99   *Address* To The Rt Honble the Countess of Bute at Twictnam near London Middlesex Angleterre   *Postmark* SE 5

To Lady Oxford *17 July [1748]*

Dearest Madam,

I have wrote so often to your Ladyship without ever having the Happiness of an Answer, that I own my Spirits quite sink under the misfortune of your silence, which is more touching to me as it was more unexpected than any other. The fix'd esteem I have for you will not suffer me to doubt the continuation of your Freindship, thô I am very conscious of not deserving it. I know not what to say more; if I am importunate I have allready said too much, but I can never cease to be, Dearest Madam, Your Ladiship's most faithfull and sincerely devoted Humble Servant,

M. Wortley Montagu.

Brescia, July 17 N.S.

Text Wh MS 507   *Address* To The Rt Honble the Lady Henrietta Countess of Oxford in Dover Street near St James's London Angleterre   *Postmark* SE 5   *End. by Lady Oxford* d: fr: Brescia July 17th N:S: R: Dover Street Monday Septr 5th O:S: 1748

To Wortley *17 July* [*1748*]

July 17 N.S.

Yours of June 7th O.S. came to my hands but yesterday. I am very much vex'd and surpriz'd at the miscarriage of my Letters. I have never fail'd answering both yours and my Daughter's the very next post after I receiv'd them. I begin to suspect my servants put the franking money in their pockets and throw away the Letters. I have been in the Country this year and halfe, thô I continu'd to date from Brescia as the place to which I would have directed, being (thô not the nearest) the safest post town. I send all my pacquets thither, and will for the Future enclose them to a Banker there, who I hope will be more carefull in the forwarding them.

I am glad my Daughter's conduct justifys the Opinion I allways had of her understanding. I do not wonder at her being well receiv'd in sets of Company different from one another, having my selfe preserv'd a long Intimacy with the Dutchesses of Marlbrô and Montagu, thô they were at open War and perpetually talking of their complaints.[1] I beleive they were both sensible I never betraid either, each of them giving me the strongest proofes of Confidance in the last Conversations I had with them, which were the last I had in England. What I think extrodinary is my Daughter's continuing so many years agreable to Lord Bute, Mr. Mackensie telling me the last time I saw him that his Brother frequently said amongst his companions that he was still as much in Love with his Wife as before he marry'd her. If the Princesse's favor lasts, it may be of use to her family.[2] I have often been dubious if the seeming Indifference of her H[ighness]'s behaviour was owing to very good sense or

---

[1] LM corresponded with both mother and daughter. Three of the Duchess of Marlborough's letters to her remained among the W MS: 25 Sept. [1729], W MS iv. 183–4 (1861, ii. 9–10); 18 Sept. 1731, lot 572 (now at Harvard Univ.); 12 March [n.y.], lot 573 in Sotheby sale of 25 July 1903. Two letters to LM from the Duchess of Montagu in [1724] are W MS iv. 204–7.

[2] The Prince of Wales m. (1736) Princess Augusta (1719–72), da. of the Duke of Saxe-Gotha. After the Prince's death in 1751 her intimacy with Lord Bute was viewed with suspicion by their political enemies.

great insensibillity;[1] should it be the first, she will get the better of all her Rivals, and probably one day have a large share of power.

I sent you my Son's Letter and a copy of my answer to it; I should be glad to hear you approv'd it. I am very much pleas'd that you accustom your selfe to Tea, being persuaded that the moderate use of it is generally wholesome. I have planted a great deal in my Garden, which is a fashion lately introduce'd in this Country, and has succeeded very well. I cannot say it is as strong as the Indian, but has the advantage of being Fresher and at least unmix'd.

Text W MS ii. 169–70   *Address* To Edwd Wortley Esqr in Cavendish Square London Angleterre   *Postmark* SE 5   *End. by W* [*Summary*] recd 5 Sept.   Ad 29 Sept.

To Lady Bute *26 July* [*1748*]

Dairy House, July 26. N.S.

I am realy as fond of my Garden as a young Author of his first play when it has been well receiv'd by the Town, and can no more forbear teizing my Acquaintance for their aprobation. Thô I gave you a long account of it in my last, I must tell you I have made 2 little Terrasses, rais'd 12 steps each, at the end of my great walk. They are just finish'd and a great addition to the Beauty of my Garden. I enclose to you a rough draught of it, drawn (or more properly, scrawl'd) by [my] own hand, without the assistance of Rule or Compasses, as you will easily perceive. I have mix'd in my espaliers as many Rose and Jessamin Trees as I can cram in, and in the squares design'd for the use of the Kitchin have avoided puting any thing disagreable either to sight or smell (having another Garden below for Cabbage, Onions, Garlick ⟨et⟩c.). All the walks are garnish'd with beds of Flowers, beside the parterres which are for a more distinguish'd sort. I have neither Brick nor stone walls; all my Fence is a high Hedge,

[1] When the Princess first came to England (in 1736), her discreet conduct seemed to most people an indication of good sense but to Lady Stafford of great stupidity (Hervey, *Memoirs*, ii. 551).

mingle'd with Trees, but fruit so plenty[ful] in this Country nobody thinks it worth stealing. Gardening is certainly the next amusement to Reading, and as my sight will now permit me little of that, I am glad to form a taste that can give me so much employment, and be the plaything of my Age, now my pen and needle are allmost useless to me.

I am very glad you are admitted into the Conversation of the Prince and Princess. It is a favor that you ought to culti-vate for the good of your Family, which is now numerous, and it may one day be of great advantage. I think Lord Bute much in the right to endeavor the continuance of it, and it would be imprudent in you to neglect what may be of great use to your children. I pray God bless both you and them; it is the Daily prayer of your most affectionate Mother.

M. Wortley M.

Now the sea is open,[1] we may send pacquets to one another. I wish you would send me Campbel's book of Prints of the English Houses,[2] and that Lord Bute would be so good to chuse me the best Book of practical Gardening extant. I shall trouble you with some more commissions but insist on it that you would take from Child whatever money they may come to. If ⟨you⟩ consign them to the English Consul at Venice directed to me, they will come very safe.

Text W MS iii. 108–9   *Address* To The Rt Honble the Countess of Bute at Twictnam near London Middlesex Angleterre   *Post-mark* 10 SE

To Wortley *18 Aug.* [*1748*]

Aug't 18 N.S.

I receiv'd yours of July 12 this morning. It gave me great pleasure by informing me of your Health, but a large portion of vexation to find all my Letters both to you and my

---

[1] Preliminaries for a treaty had been signed at Aix-la-Chapelle on 30 April.
[2] Colin Campbell's *Vitruvius Britan-nicus; or the British Architect*, containing plans of public and private buildings in Great Britain, three volumes (1717–25).

PLATE 7

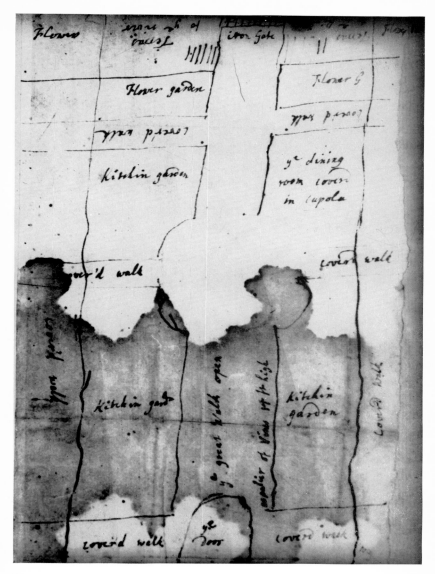

*Plan of garden near Gottolengo, from letter of Lady Mary Wortley Montagu
to Mary, Countess of Bute,* [10 July 1748]

Wortley MSS iii. 110

Daughter are lost. I have never fail'd answering any receiv'd
from either, the same or the next post after they came to my
Hands, and have wrote such long Letters I was afraid of
tireing you both with reading them. I have sent them all to
Mr. Pierre de Vos at Rotterdam, according to Mr. Child's
direction. I am sure I would not spare any money; I can lay
out none to give me so much pleasure as secureing our
Correspondance. If I owe any thing it is Child's fault in not
informing me better. I write to him this post concerning it.
I sent you the last Letter I receiv'd from my Son, with the
Copy of my Answer to it.

The apprehension that what I write may never reach you
is so discourraging that it takes off all the satisfaction I should
otherwaies find in writeing. I gave you thanks for the Poetry
you sent me, in a long Letter which I do not find you ever
receiv'd, and I have sent my Daughter such particular accounts of my Country Amusements and way of Life, she
could not know more of it if she was in the Neighbourhood.
I am very glad she passes her time so agreably and in a
manner that may be one day advantageous to her Family.
We are both properly scituated according to our different
times of Life, she in the Gaitys of a Court, I in a Retirement
where my Garden and Dairy are my cheife Diversions.

Here has been the finest Auction, 15 mile from hence,
that has been known of a long time, being the whole Furniture of the Palace of Guastalla.[1] I could not forbear going
to see it. There were several pictures of the first masters
that went off for a Song, and a Crucifix of Silver said to be
the Work of Michael Angelo sold for little more than
the Weight.[2] The greatest part fell into the hands of the
Jews.

I am very much oblig'd to you for the offer of the London
Pamphlets and shall write to my Daughter about it. I should
be glad to see the Apology for a Late Resignation.[3] Now the
sea is open I may easily have things by way of Venice. If you

---

[1] See above, p. 383.

[2] This crucifix may have been a copy
of the lost bronze by Michelangelo, who
is not recorded as having made a silver
one (Charles de Tolnay, *Michelangelo*,
1943–60, v. 172–3).

[3] Published anonymously at the
beginning of April 1748, it defended
Chesterfield for resigning as Secretary
of State in Feb. (*Letters*, ed. B. Dobrée,
1932, i. 159–62).

would order me six dozen of Nottingham ale[1] directed to me, consign'd to Mr. Daniel Amman, merchant at Venice, it would be very acceptable amongst my Neighbours. Be pleas'd to take the money due for it out of my allowance.

Text W MS ii. 171–2   *Address* To Edwd Wortley Esqr Cavendish Square London   *End. by W* [*Summary*] Ad 29 Sept.   recd 18 Sept.

To Wortley *10 Sept.* [*1748*]

Sept. 10. N.S.

I saw in the news paper last week that our Son is one of the Secretarys to the Embassy of Lord S[andwich].[2] I ⟨wish⟩ he may succeed in that business bett⟨er⟩ than he has yet done in the proffessions he has undertaken. I know not whether he has had the answer I made to the last letter I receiv'd from him. I sent it to you with a copy of my return to it, which I fear never reach'd you. I will therefore repeat it as near as I can remember it. I may be mistaken in some expressions, but I am very sure the cheif heads are exactly the same.

'I am very glad to hear of your Health, but sorry to find you still continue in the vain way of thinking that has been your Ruin. I will not ask your Father to encrease your allowance; it is amply sufficient for all the show you ought to make. Your past extra⟨vaganc⟩ies are known to all that know yo⟨u and⟩ me. A modest behaviour and a frugal expence are necessary to persuade the World you are convince'd of the Folly of your former Conduct. The very reasons you give for desireing a larger income prove you do not want it, since Lord Sandwich's presenting you as his Relation entitles you to more respect than an embrodier'd Coat or a rich Livery, which gain no Esteem but amongst the weakest of both sexes, and only serves to draw the Eyes of the Mob and even by them is oftner ridicule'd than admir'd. The true Figure a Man makes is in proportion to the Opinion people have of

---

[1] W agreed to her request the next year, but she then withdrew it (see below, p. 433).

[2] Montagu's commission as a Secretary to the Congress at Aix-la-Chapelle is dated 22/11 July 1748 (Add MS 36,121, f. 194).

his Honesty and understanding. Your Father's example ought to have the greatest weight with you. His real Generosity and perfect disinteressedness has gain'd him the applause of all those whose applause is worth having. Public Tables and great Equipage are only becomeing in those who bear public characters. Prudence and Decency will recommend you to the thinking part of Mankind, and make you a Blessing, as you ⟨have⟩ hitherto been a misfortune, to your affectionate ⟨Mother⟩.'

His letter to me I cannot litteraly rem⟨ember⟩; it was very long and childish.

Text W MS ii. 173–4   *Address* To Edwd Wortley Esqr in Cavendish Square London Angleterre   *Postmark* OC 22   *End. by W* Ad L.M. 10 Sept. 1748.   Sons writing abt an increase of his Allowance. Ad 27 Oct.   Recd 24 Oct.

To Lady Oxford *23 Oct.* [*1748*]

Oct. 23. N.S.

Dearest Madam,
    I cannot help continuing to write thô 'tis many Months since I have had the Happyness of hearing from your Ladyship. I will not endeavor to represent to you the uneasyness it gives me; I know your Goodness but too apt to share all the sufferings of your Freinds. I hope you are convince'd of that unalterable affection you so well deserve from me, and then I need not say how painfull your silence is to, Dearest Madam, Your most faithfully Devoted Servant,

M. W. Montagu.

Text MS in Dreer Collection, Historical Society of Pennsylvania *Address* To The Rt Honble the Lady Henrietta Countess of Oxford in Dover Street near St James's London   *End. by Lady Oxford* R: Welbeck Thursday Novr 24th OS 1748   sent by Mr Child Banker

To Lady Bute *23 Oct.* [*1748*]

Oct. 23. N.S.

Dear Child,

I verily beleive I have wrote you ten Letters since I have had the pleasure of hearing from you. I am persuaded it is not your Fault but that of the post, which I know not how to remedy. I send this with as little hope as a Sally of Enfans perdus,[1] but I cannot refuse my selfe the satisfaction of continuing to assure you that I am ever your most affectionate Mother.

M. Wortley

My Complements to Lord Bute and blessing to my Grand children.

Text W MS iii. 281

To Wortley *23 Oct.* [*1748*]

Oct. 23. N.S.

I have wrote so many Letters in vain that I realy grow weary of writeing, and cannot find in my Heart to write three sides of paper once a week to no manner of purpose. I have directed in different ways, and all ends in the same thing. You must forgive me a little peevishness on this occasion, thô I do not at all mean it by way of reproach, being convince'd it is no more your fault than mine, but wholly that of the post. I beg of you, be so good to mark in your next those you have receive'd of mine, particularly whether you had that which I wrote to return you thanks for the entertaining poetry you sent me, another with some account of Mrs. Bosvil,[2] one with my Son's Letter and a Copy of my Answer, a duplicate of which I sent you the last time I wrote. There are many others to which I have no return, a great number to my Daughter and allmost as many

---

[1] A military term meaning forlorn hopes.

[2] LM had met Diana Bosville in Avignon in 1743 (see above, p. 303).

to Lady Oxford. It is impossible to represent to you how much I am mortify'd at this Interuption of my Correspondance with England; it realy embitters all my Days. Till I know you receive what I send, I have not Spirits enough to try at amuseing you. When I can depend on my Letters reaching you I shall with great pleasure obey your commands in sending you accounts of my passing my time. It can never be employ'd so agreably to my selfe as in endeavoring to entertain you.

Text W MS ii. 175–6　　　*Address* To Edwd Wortley Esqr in Cavendish Square London Angleterre　　*End. by W* [*Summary*] Recd 23 Nov.

To Wortley *23 Oct.* [*1748*]

Oct. 23 N.S.

If all my Letters come to your Hands you will certainly be tir'd with reading them. I send three this post, three different roads, to try which of them is most certain to reach you.

There is still great impediments on the side of Genoa, and I beleive will continue till the Total Evacuation of the Troops, which cannot now be expected till the Spring. When I can hope our Correspondance regularly fix'd, I shall not fail to write long Letters.

Text W MS ii. 179–80　　　*Address* To Edwd Wortley Esqr in Cavendish Square London Angleterre　[*in another hand*] Franca per Venezia　　*Postmark* NO 10　　*End. by W* L.M. 23 Oct. 1748. Sends three letters this Post. By Venice.　　Recd 10 Nov.

To Wortley *23 Oct.* [*1748*]

Oct. 23. N.S.

The Interuption of our Correspondance is so disagreable to me that if I cannot alter it any other way I shall realy change my Situation, notwithstanding the Inconveniencies attending a Winter journey, but every thing is more supportable to me than being accus'd of neglecting a commerce which is the greatest Comfort of my Life.

Text W MS ii. 177–8   *Address* Edwd Wortley Esqr in Cavendish Square London   *Postmark* NO 10   *End. by W* L.M. 23 Oct. 1748 The Commerce of letters the greatest Comfort of her life. Recd 10 Nov.

To Lady Bute 6 *Dec.* [*1748*]

Brescia, Dec. 6. N.S.

Dear Child,

I have not had the pleasure of hearing from you of several months, notwithstanding I have continu'd to write many long Letters. I need not mention the pain your silence gives me. I know not to what to attribute this Interuption of our Correspondance. I cannot beleive you would willingly give so much uneasiness to your most affectionate mother,

M. Wortley.

Text W MS iii. 263–4   *Address* To The Rt Honble the Countess of Bute [at Twictnam near *struck out*] London Middlesex Angleterre [*in another hand*] In Grosvenor Street   *Postmark* DE 27 30 DE

To Wortley 25 *Dec.* [*1748*]

Dec. 25. N.S.

I hope I have now regulated our Correspondance in a manner more safe than by Holland. I have sent a large Collection of Letters to you and my daughter which have all miscarried; neither have I had one line from either of some months. I am now assur'd by one of the principal Merchants here that all those directed to Signor Isaac M. de Treves, a Venetia, shall be carefully remitted, and I beg you would make use of that Direction.

I was surpris'd not many days ago by a very extrodinary Visit. It was from the Dutchess of Guastalla (who you know is a princess of the House d'Armstadt, and reported to be near marriage with the King of Sardinia).[1] I confess it was an Honor I could easily have spar'd, she comeing attended with the greatest part of her Court, her Grand Master, who is Brother to Cardinal Valenti,[2] the first Lady of her Bed-chamber, 4 pages and a long etc. of inferior Servants, beside her Guards. She enter'd with an easy French air, and told me since I would not oblige her by comeing to her Court she was resolv'd to come to me and eat a salad of my raising, haveing heard much Fame of my Gardening. You may imagine I gave her as good a supper as I could. She was (or seem'd to be) extremely pleas'd with an English sack posset of my ordering. I own'd to her freely that my House was much at her service, but it was impossible for me to find Beds for all her suitte. She said she intended to return when the moon rose, which was an hour after midnight. In the mean time I sent for the violins to entertain her attendants, who were very well pleas'd to dance while she and her Grand Master and I plaid at Picquet. She press'd me extremely to return with her to her Jointure House, where she now resides (all the Furniture of Guastalla being sold). I excus'd my selfe on not daring to venture in the cold night 15 mile, but promis'd I would not fail to pay her my Acknowledgments for the great Honor her Highness had done me, in a very short time, and we parted very good Freinds. She said she intended this Spring to retire into her native Country. I did not take the Liberty of mentioning to her the report of her being in treaty with the King of Sardinia, thô it has been in the news paper of Mantua; but I found an opertunity of hinting it to Signor Gonzaga, her Grand Master, who told me the Dutchess would not have been pleas'd to talk of it, since perhaps there was nothing in it more than a Freindship

---

[1] The older of the two Duchesses of Guastalla was Theodora (1706–84), da. of the Landgrave of Hesse-Darmstadt, widow of Duke Anton Ferdinand since 1729; L M probably means the younger Duchess, Eleonore (1715–60), da. of Duke Leopold of Holstein-Wiesenburg, widow of Duke Josef only since 1746 (Isenburg, ii. 129). The King of Sardinia, Charles Emanuel (1701–73), already thrice a widower, did not marry again (ibid. 114).

[2] For the Cardinal, see above, p. 227, n. 2; his brother is not identified.

that had long been between them, and since her Widowhood
the King sends her an express every day.[1]

I beleive you'l wish this long Story much shorter, but I
think you seem'd to desire me to lengthen my Letters, and
I can have no greater pleasure than endeavoring to amuse
you.

Text W MS ii. 181–2   *Address* To Edwd Wortley Esqr   *End. by W*
[*Summary*] Recd 18 Jan.   Ad 25 Jan.

To Lady Bute *25 Dec.* [*1748*]

Dec. 25. N.S.

Dear Child,

I find all my long letters to you have miscarry'd, neither
have I heard from you of many Months. I know not where
the fault lies, but have resolv'd to change the Method of our
Correspondance to try at least if it be possible to fix it in a
more regular manner. I wish you would let me know the
cheife heads of those you have last receiv'd, being unwilling
to trouble you with repetitions.

Since the Peace is concluded,[2] I suppose you may safely
send me the Book of Campbell's Vitruvius Brittanicus. I
desire Lord Bute would be so good to chuse for me the best
book of practical Gardening and at the same time a little
Windsor chair, no larger than a play thing. You may imagine
I design it as a model, haveing a mind to place some in my
Garden and not knowing how to explain to the Workmen
here what I mean. I insist upon it that you take money from
Child for whatever commissions I trouble you with. Direct
whatever you send me, to me through the hands of Signor
Isaac M. de Treves at Venice, who will take care to send it
to me. I wish you would also direct your Letters recommended to him, and I hope they will for the future come safe
to your most affectionate mother,

M. Wortley Montagu.

[1] The King, a widower only seven
years, could not have courted the older
Duchess for nineteen.
[2] At Aix-la-Chapelle in Oct. 1748.

My Compliments to Lord Bute and blessing to my Grand children. I am asham'd to have promis'd Lady Mary a Token so long without performance.[1] The first safe hand shall bring it to her.

Text W MS iii. 284–5

To Lady Oxford *1 Jan.* [*1749*]

January 1. N.S.

Dearest Madam,

It is now a year (and it appears to me a thousand) since I have had the Happiness of a Line from your Ladyship. I have, however, never discontinu'd writeing, being still persuaded that it is my ill Fortune and not any change of your Freindship which occasions your silence. I own I never deserv'd so great a blessing, but yet I am conscious of doing nothing to forfeit it since you so generously bestow'd it on me, and I think I know your Heart too well to beleive that Time and Distance can have any effect to my Disadvantage. I have now chang'd the direction of my Letters in hopes of re-establishing our Correspondance, and beg your Ladyship would address your next to Signor Isaac M. de Treves a Venetia. He has promis'd to forward them carefully to me, and now the peace is settle'd I flatter my selfe I shall no longer suffer the uneasyness that this long Interuption of our Commerce has given me, being ever with the tenderest Affection, Dearest Madam, Your Ladyship's most faithfull Obedient Servant,

M. W. Montagu.

Text Wh MS 507   *Address* To The Rt Honble the Lady Henrietta Countess of Oxford in Dover Street near St James's London *End. by Lady Oxford* R: Welbeck Monday Janry 23d 1748 O:S:

---

[1] LM was to continue harping on this promise to her godchild.

To Lady Oxford [*2 Feb. 1749*]

Dearest Madam,
   I receiv'd this day, the 2nd of Feb. N.S., the Happyness of your Ladiship's obliging Letter of December 17th. It has releiv'd me from the great anxiety I was under in regard to your Health. I have ever done you the Justice (during this long Interuption of our Correspondance) of being persuaded you was incapable of forgetting me, or if sometimes my Melancholy, join'd with a consciousness of my own unworthyness, suggested to me a contrary thought, I presently corrected it as not suited to that Esteem you so well deserve from me. I hope the good air of Welbeck has entirely re-establish'd your Health. I should be ungratefull to Heaven to complain of mine, which is indeed better than I have reason to expect. I walk very much; I sometimes ride; I amuse my selfe with a little Garden that I have made out of a Vineyard; and if I could enjoy your Ladyship's Conversation I should not regret a World in which I never had great pleasure, and have so little Inclination to return to, that I do not even intend to see the new Court which is expected at Parma, thô it is but ten mile from Hence.[1] Dearest Madam, continue to me the Honor of writeing to me, and be assur'd that you can bestow your Favours on no person who is more sensible of their value than Your Ladyship's most faithfully Devoted Humble Servant,

M. Wortley Montagu.

Text Wh MS 507   *Address* To The Rt Honble the Lady Henrietta Countess of Oxford in Dover Street near St James's London *End. by Lady Oxford* d: 2d Feby NS   R: Welbeck Monday Feby 27th 1748 O:S:

---

1 LM must have been away from her home in Gottolengo (see next letter), which is forty miles from Parma—as she writes to Lady Bute on 6 March [1749].

To Lady Bute [*Feb. 1749*]

Dear Child,

I have wrote you so many Letters without any return that if I lov'd you at all less than I do I should certainly give over writeing. I receiv'd a kind Letter last post from Lady Oxford, which gives me hopes I shall at length receive yours, being persuaded you have not neglected our correspondance, thô I am not so happy to have the pleasure of it.

I have little to say from this solitude, having allready sent you a description of my Garden,[1] which, with my Books, takes up all my time. I made a small excursion last week to visit a Nunnery 12 mile from hence, which is the only Institution of the kind in all Italy. It is in a Town in the state of Mantua, founded by a Princesse of the House of Gonzagua,[2] one of which (now very old) is the present Abbesse.[3] They are dress'd in black, and wear a thin cypress veil at the back of their heads, excepting which they have no mark of a religious habit, being set out in their Hair and having no guimpe, but wearing des collets montez, for which I have no name in English, but you may have seen them in very old pictures, being in Fashion both before and after ruffs. Their House is a very large handsome building, thô not regular, every sister having liberty to build her own Apartment to her Taste, which consists of as many rooms as she pleases. They have each a separate Kitchin and keep Cooks and what other servants they think proper. Thô there is a very fine public refectory, they are permitted to dine in private whenever they please. Their Garden is very large, and the most adorn'd of any in these parts. They have no Grates, and make what visits they will, allways two together, and receive those of the Men as well as Ladys. I was accompany'd when I went with all the Nobility of the Town, and they shew'd me

---

[1] On 10 and 26 July [1748].

[2] Margarita Gonzaga (1564–1618), da. of the Duke of Mantua and wife of the Duke of Modena and Ferrara; in 1599, two years after her husband's death, she founded the Convent of Saint Ursula in the country called Le Borre (Federigo Amadei, *Cronaca universale della città di Mantova*, 1957, iii. 181–2, 202–3, 350–1).

[3] Probably Clara Clarina (1686 ?– 16 Nov. 1749), illegitimate daughter of the last Duke of Mantua (ibid. v. 362).

all the House without excludeing the Gentlemen; but what I think the most remarkable privelege is a Country House which belongs to them, 3 mile from the Town, where they pass every vintage, and at any time any four of them may take their pleasure there for as many days as they choose. They seem to differ from the Channonesses[1] of Flanders only in their vow of Celibacy. They take pensioners, but only those of Quality. I saw here a niece of General Broun.[2] Those that proffess are oblig'd to prove a descent as noble as the Knights of Malta.

Upon the whole I think it the most agreable community I have seen, and their behaviour more decent than that of the cloister'd Nuns, who I have heard say themselves that the Grate permits all Liberty of speech since it leaves them no other, and indeed they gennerally talk according to that maxim. My House at Avignon joyn'd to a monastery, which gave me occasion to know a great deal of their conduct, which (thô the convent of the best Reputation in that Town, where there is 14) was such as I would as soon put a Girl into the playhouse for Education as send her amongst them.

My paper is at an end, and hardly leaves room for my Complements to Lord Bute, blessing to my Grand children and assurance to your selfe of being your most affectionate Mother.

M. Wortley

Text W MS iii. 113–14   *Address* To The Rt Honble the Countess of Bute at Twict'nam near London Middlesex [*in another hand and struck out*] Free S. Child

---

[1] In almost secular convents; several in the Low Countries accepted English girls, who were permitted to leave and marry.

[2] Maximilian Ulysses von Browne, of Irish descent and in the Austrian service (Christopher Duffy, *The Wild Goose and the Eagle: A Life of Marshal von Browne 1705–1757*, 1964). His aunt Barbara O'Neillan (d. 1752) lived in Mantua, and had five children (ibid., p. 22).

To Lady Bute *6 March* [*1749*]

March 6. N.S.

Dear Child,

I had this day the Happiness of a Letter from [your] Father, in which I had the additional pleasure of being inform'd that you are safely deliver'd of a Daughter.[1] I pray God make her a blessing to you. I did not even know you were with child, not having had any Letter from you of many Months. I do not doubt you have sent me several and I know not how to account for the loss of them. I desire you would direct your next recommandé al' Signor Isaac M. de Treves, a Venezia. You are in a place that every day may furnish you with a new subject to write. I have little to say from hence (having allready sent you the description of my Garden). My time passes as regularly as that of a Clock, the returning seasons bringing with them their Country busyness, which is all the variety of my Life. I am now employ'd with the care of my silk worms' eggs. The silk is gennerally spun the latter end of May. I wish you would tell me the price it bears at London,[2] and that you would send me (by sea, directed to the care of the same Signor Isaac at Venice) Collen Campbell's Book of English seats. These two articles I have often mention'd, but I beleive my Letters have miscarry'd. I desire Lord Bute would be so good to chuse for me a Book of practical Gardening. If there is any thing come out that you think would amuse me, you may put it in the same pacquet, takeing the price of Mr. Child, which I insist on your doing.

I saw in the news paper the Death of Lord Monson. I should be glad to know if my Sister continues in his Family[3] and what other changes happen amongst my acquaintance.

[1] Lady Augusta Stuart (10 Jan. 1749–78).

[2] Raw and spun silk, the principal article of commerce in Brescia, was exported throughout Europe (J. J. de Lalande, *Voyage en Italie*, 3rd ed., 1790, vii. 239; E. Pariset, *Les Industries de la soie*, 1890, p. 163).

[3] Monson (d. 18 July 1748), as a trustee of the 1st Duke of Kingston's estate, had supervised the 2nd Duke's education and administered LM's legacy. In 1728, when Lady Mar's custody was being arranged, he declined to serve as a trustee (see above, p. 88). Why Lady Mar lived in his house is puzzling; she was under the care of her daughter Lady Frances Erskine.

I suppose Miss Rich is now a great Fortune[1] and probably marry'd to some body or other.

The Ladies of my Neighbourhood are (most of them) prepareing cloaths and Equipage to assist at the Entry of Don Philip into Parma,[2] which is 40 mile from hence. However, I do not intend to give my selfe the trouble and expence of the Journey to see a ceremony which I guess will not differ much from the many I have seen. My Curiosity is not only lessen'd but almost abolish'd, and peasants as agreable to me as Princes. This sounds very oddly to you, but my Age will give you the same sentiments. We that stand on the Threshold of Life (as Mr. Waller calls it)[3] see every thing in a very different Light from what they appear in Youth and vigour.

I should excuse the Length of this Letter (duly considering the dullness of it) but I hope you can forgive it, as it comes from your most affectionate Mother.

M. Wortley

My complements to Lord Bute and blessing to all your little ones.

Text W MS iii. 294–5   *Address* To The Rt Honble the Countess of Bute at Twict'nam near London Middlesex

To Wortley 6 *March* [1749]

March 6. N.S.

I receiv'd yours of Jan. 23rd this morning with more Satisfaction than I can express, having been long in pain for your Silence. I never had that you mention of Dec. 12th nor

---

[1] Probably Elizabeth (1716–95), only daughter of Sir Robert Rich; when she m. (10 Aug. 1749) George Lyttelton, her dowry was £20,000. LM thought her brother was dead (see iii. 17).

[2] By the Treaty of Aix-la-Chapelle, Don Philip of Spain was awarded Parma, Piacenza, and Guastalla.

[3] Leaving the old, both worlds at
  once they view,
That stand upon the threshold of
  the new
(Edmund Waller, *Works in Verse and Prose*, ed. 1730, p. 201). LM's library in 1739 contained a copy of 'Waller's Works' (Wh MS 135).

any other since the Month of Aug't, thô I have wrote six Letters since that time, which convinces me that there is no other safe method of corresponding but through the hands of a Banker at Venice, and therefore beg of you to continue to direct in the same manner as your last. It will be a few days later, and with a little more expence, but I hope to receive them more punctually, and there is nothing I would not pay for that pleasure.

I am very glad my Daughter is safely deliver'd. I did not so much as know she was with child, having not heard from her of many months. I do not question she has sent many Letters, but I have been so unfortunate to receive none of them. I suppose mine to her (which have been very long and frequent) have also miscarry'd.

We have hitherto had no Winter, to the great Sorrow of the people here, who are in fear of wanting Ice in the Summer, which is as necessary as Bread. They also attribute a malignant fever, which has carry'd off great numbers in the neighbouring Towns, to the uncommon warmth of the air. It has not infected this Village, which they say has ever been free from any contagious Distemper. It is very remarkable that when the Disease amongst the Cattle rag'd with great violence all round, not one dy'd or sicken'd here.

The method of treating the Physitian in this country, I think should be the same every where. They make it his Interest that the whole Parish should be in good health, giving him a stated pension, which is collected by a Tax on every House, on condition he neither demands nor receives any fees, nor ever refuses a visit either to rich or poor. This last Article would be very hard if we had as many Vapourish Ladies as in England, but those imaginary ills are entirely unknown here. When I recollect the vast Fortunes rais'd by Doctors amongst us, and the eager persuit after every new piece of Quackery that is introduce'd, I cannot help thinking there is a fund of Credulity in Mankind that must be employ'd some where, and the money formerly given to Monks for the health of the Soul is now thrown to Doctors for the health of the Body, and gennerally with as little real prospect of Success.

I suppose the Sir Charles Wyndham you mention is

younger Son of Sir W[illia]m. I think I have heard the eldest nam'd John, who had no very good character.[1]

Text W MS ii. 183–4   *Address* To Edwd Wortley Esqr in Cavendish Square London   *End. by W* [*Summary*] Recd at Newbold[2] 30 Mar.   Ad 20 Apr.

To Wortley *24 April* [*1749*]

C. Mutius Sex. F.
P. Papilius M. F.
Q. Mutius P. F.
M. Cornelius P. F.
II II vir. Turrim Ex. DD.
Ad Augendas Locaver.
Idemque Probavere.

This is a very fair inscription in large Characters on a large stone found in the pavement of the old Church, and makes now a part of the Wall of the new one which is now building.[3] The people here, who are as ignorant as their Oxen and live like them on the product of their land without any Curiosity for the History of it, would infer from thence that this Town is of Roman Foundation, thô the Walls, which are yet the greatest part standing (only the Towers and battlements demolish'd), are very plainly Gothic, and not one Brick to be found any where of Roman Fabrick, which is very easily distinguish'd. I can easily beleive their Tradition that the old church (which was pull'd down 2 year ago, being ready to drop) was a pagan Temple; and do not doubt it was a considerable Town founded by the Goths when they over ran Italy. The Forti[fi]cations were strong for that Age, the Ditch still remaining without the Walls being very broad and

---

[1] Sir William Wyndham (1687–1740), Tory politician and friend of Bolingbroke, had two sons: the elder, Charles (1710–63), later 2nd Earl of Egremont; and Percy (*c.* 1723–74), later 1st Earl of Thomond.

[2] An estate recently inherited by W (see below, p. 427).

[3] The inscription is also recorded in C. L. P. Marinoni, *Lady Montagu Wortley e la sua decennale dimora alle rive del lago d'Iseo*, 1904, p. 17. The new church was consecrated in 1765 (Antonio Fappani in *Commentari dell'ateneo di Brescia*, 1961, p. 127).

deep, in which ran the little River that is now before my House, and the moat turn'd into Gardens for the use of the Town, the name of which being Gotolengo is a confirmation of my Conjecture.[1]

The castle which certainly stood on the spot where my House now does, being on an Eminence in the midst of the Town, was probably destroy'd by Fire. When I order'd the Court to be levell'd, which was grown uneven by long neglect, there was found such quantitys of burnt bricks that plainly shew'd the remains of a considerable Fire, but whether by the Enemy or accidental I could get no information. They have no records or Parish books beyond the time of their comeing under the Venetian Dominion, which is not much above three hundred years ago, at which time they were, as they now are, a large village, being 2 mile in circuit, and contains at present (as the Curate told me) two thousand communicants.

The Ladies of this neighbourhood that had given themselves the trouble and expence of going to see D[on] Philip's entry into Parma[2] are return'd, according to the French saying, avec un pied de nez. As they had none of them ever seen a Court before, they had figur'd to them selves prodigious Scenes of Galantry and Magnificence.[3] If I did not write by the post I would tell you several particulars that I beleive would make you laugh. He is retir'd into the Country till the arrival of his Princess,[4] who is expected in May next. I take the Liberty of encloseing this to Lord Bute, not knowing where to direct to him in London.

April 24. N.S.

Text W MS ii. 185–6 *Address* To Edwd Wortley Esqr in Cavendish Square London *End. by* W Ad L.M. 24 Apr. 1749 makes no

---

[1] This etymology is also given in Giovanni Flechia, *Di Alcune Forme de' nomi locali dell'Italia superiore*, 1871, p. 98).

[2] Don Philip, prevented by floods from making his entry on 7 March, arrived in Parma two days later (Federigo Amadei, *Cronaca universale della città di Mantova*, 1957, v. 341–2).

[3] Horace Mann in Florence reported on 18 April that the new Duke of Parma 'has disgusted all his new subjects; he is so horridly French that they cannot please him and . . . so horribly poor that they are quite disappointed and disgusted' (Walpole, *Corr.* xx. 45).

[4] Don Philip m. (1739) Elisabeth (1727–59), da. of Louis XV of France.

mention of my last of 20 Apr. nor of that of 13 Mar.   Abt an Inscription in the Church Wall of Gotolengo   Ad 25 May.   Recd 19 May.

To Lady Oxford [*26 April 1749*]

Dearest Madam,

Thô I have received the Happyness of yours of the 25th of January very late, it being now the 26th of April, yet it gave me so much pleasure by the assurance of your Health and continu'd goodness to me that I can scarce complain of the Delay. My Letters have no value but as comeing from a Heart sincerely yours, truly gratefull and sensible of your merit. I have had some fits of an Ague this spring, which Distemper has been epidemical in this Country from the uncommon Rains we have had. I am now very well recover'd, thô I have not yet venture'd out of the House, the Weather being still wet and raw. I beleive it will be safest to send the Letters your Ladiship honors me with, in a Cover to Signor Isaac M. de Treves, a Venise.

I hope your Flourishing Family still continues in perfect Health and prosperity. I hear mine encreases every Year, and that my Daughter is much distinguish'd by Her Royal Highness. I flatter my selfe that she is allways happy in the Dutchess of Portland's Freindship, which I look upon as the greatest Advantage that she can enjoy in this World. I am entirely a Stranger to all other news in England. There is none in which I am so much interested as that of your Health, of which I beg to hear often, being ever (Dearest Madam) with the tenderest affection your Ladiship's most faithfull Devoted Servant,

M. W. Montagu.

Text Wh MS 507   *Address* To The Rt Honble the Lady Henrietta Countess of Oxford in Dover Street near St James's London   *End. by Lady Oxford* d: 26th April NS   R: Welbeck Monday June 5th 1749 OS

To Wortley *1 May* [*1749*]

May 1. N.S.

I wish you joy of your new seat. I have been told that the Gardens and Plantations are in the best taste of any in that Country.[1] Long may you enjoy it in Health and Happiness!

I give you many thanks for the Ale,[2] which is in great esteem here, by Reputation, for it is otherwise quite unknown. I would send you some Wine of my own makeing in return if I thought it would arrive good and be worth paying the Custom.

I cannot readily answer your Question concerning the passage of Letters, being 18 mile from Brescia, and there is no body in this Neighbourhood that has any foreign Correspondance. I will not fail to enquire the first Opertunity, and let you know it. I have allways dated my Letters from Brescia, being the nearest post Town, but have been there but twice, and that only for a few days, since my recovery from that terrible fit of sickness at my arrival. I find this air agree very well with me, and amuse my selfe with my little Country busyness.

I am very glad my Daughter's Conduct answers the Opinion I ever had of her understanding. I do not say it to lessen the praise she deserves, but I realy think there is some due to Lord Bute. It is seldom that the affections of a Man of his age continue so many years. May she allways possess them and every other blessing. I think her much in the right to cultivate the Princesse's Favor, but in genneral have no great Faith in Court Freindships, and remember Lord Bathurst's[3] Epigram, that Princes are the Sons of Kings.

Text W MS ii. 187–8   *Address* To Edwd Wortley Esqr in Cavendish Square London   *End. by W* Ad L.M. 1 May 1749   Wishes me

[1] From his cousin James (son of Charles Montagu), who died on 30 Oct. 1748, W inherited the estate of Newbold Verdon, Leics. Elizabeth Montagu thought it (in 1744) 'one of the most charming and pleasant' she had ever seen (*Corr. 1720–1761*, ed. E. J. Climen-son, 1906, i. 262, 190).

[2] Evidently promised by W in answer to LM's request of 18 Aug. 1748; but he later decided it would be too difficult to send (see below, p. 433).

[3] A friend in the 1720's (see above, p. 53).

joy of Newbold Thanks for what I have sd abt the Ale. [*Summary*]
Ad 8 July Recd 1 June

To Lady Bute 7 *May* [*1749*]

May 7 N.S.

Dear Child,

I have allready wish'd you Joy of your new Daughter and wrote to Lord Bute to thank him for his Letter. I don't know whither I shall make my Court to you in saying it, but I own I can't help thinking that your Family is numerous enough, and that the Education and disposal of 4 Girls is employment for a whole Life.

I remain in a Retirement where my amusements are confine'd to my Garden and Dairy. However, I should be glad to know now and then what is doing amongst my Acquaintance at London, and beg you would enquire of the Price raw silk bears. I have ask'd this Question very often but suppose my Letters have miscarry'd, having never had any answer. Your Father has been so obliging to promise me some ale. If you would send at the same time Colin Campbell's book of architecture consign'd to Signor Isaac M. de Treves, it would come safe to me.

I imagine the Duke of Kingston is now building.[1] I was told he intended it on the same Ground where the last House stood, which I think an ill fancy, being the lowest part of the Park, and he might chuse others with a prospect more agreable, which is in my opinion the first thing to be consider'd in a Country Seat. I have given you a large Description of that of my Dairy House, which is the most Beautifull of any in this province. If I knew it was lost I would repeat it.

This Letter is so dull I am asham'd to set my name to it.

Text W MS iii. 19–20   *Address* To The Rt Honble the Countess of Bute at Twict'nam near London Middlesex

[1] Lady Oxford later informed her the 'Duke of Kingston has not built at Thoresby but turn'd the stables into Rooms' (30/19 Sept. 1749, Harley MS). He did not build a new house until 1768 (H. M. Colvin, *Biog. Dict. of English Architects 1660–1840*, 1954, p. 123). The old one had burned down in 1745.

To Lady Oxford *26 May* [*1749*]

Dearest Madam,

I can never thank you enough for the Happyness I receive from your kind Letters, the continuation of your unweary'd Freindship being the consolation of my Life. I have had but a melancholy spring, having been long afflicted with an ague of which I am scarcely recover'd. It has gone through the greatest part of my Family, and been almost epidemical in this Country. My Retirement is so great that were my Spirits better than they are, it is impossible my Letters should have any thing to recommend them but the Sincerity of the Heart they come from. Your Ladiship's figure in the World does not suffer you to live so much out of it, thô I know your Taste so well, to be sure that you avoid the Hurry of it and pity those that are condemn'd to it. My Praiers and wishes allways attend your flourishing Family; may they ever be worthy your Vertue and repay with Duty the tenderness you have for them. While I am, I am with the most faithfull affection Your Ladiship's most devoted Humble Servant,

M. W. Montagu.

May 26. N.S.

Text Wh MS 507   *Address* To The Rt Honble the Lady Henrietta Countess of Oxford in Dover Street near St James's London   *End. by Lady Oxford* d: May 26th N:S: R: Welbeck Saturday Decr 30th 1749 O:S:

To Lady Bute *27 May* [*1749*]

May 27. N.S.

Dear Child,

I had the pleasure of your Letter 2 days ago, in which you tell me of the marriage of Mr. Mackensie, which I was extremely glad to hear, wishing him happyness who I think well deserves it from an uncommon share of Honor and good nature, of which even his indiscretions are proofes.[1] The Dutchess of Argyle has acted (in my opinion) with equal Generosity and prudence.[2] Her ill success in the Disposal of Lady Mary has shewn her the mistake of interested Matches, which are gennerally unfortunate.[3]

This Spring has been very melancholy to me, having been tormented with a Quotidian Ague, of which I am scarcely recover'd, and my Woman (who is the most necessary Servant in my Family) still afflicted with a Tertian, which puts ⟨my⟩ whole House in Disorder, and hinders my remove to my Dairy, to my great mortification now the Heats are begun. If my Garden and my House stood together I would not change this seat for Lord Tilney's[4] or the Marquis of Rockingham's,[5] but alas, they are some miles asunder.

Your new fashion'd game of Brag was the Genteel amusement when I was a Girl.[6] Crimp succeeded to that, and Basset and Hazard employ'd the Town when I left it to go to Constantinople. At my Return I found them all at Commerce, which gave place to Quadrille and that to Whist, but the rage of Play has been ever the same, and will ever be so amongst the Idle part of both Sexes. It is the same in every great Town, and I think more particularly all over France. Here is a young man of Quality 4 mile from hence, just of

[1] For Mackenzie's amorous 'indiscretions', see above, pp. 200, 341. On 16 Feb. 1749 he married his cousin Lady Betty Campbell (d. 1799), da. of 2nd Duke of Argyll.

[2] Jane Warburton (1683–1767) m. (1717) 2nd Duke of Argyll; she had been Maid of Honour to Queen Anne and to Caroline, Princess of Wales: a 'good natured, plain, honest, ill-educated woman' (GEC).

[3] Lady Mary Coke's match had been very unfortunate (see above, p. 385); in 1749 she swore the peace against her brutal husband, and won a legal separation the following year. Actually, the Duchess had not approved of the match because of Coke's notorious character (Charles W. James, *Chief Justice Coke: His Family and Descendants at Holkham*, 1929, p. 235).

[4] Wanstead, the 1st Earl Tylney's estate in Essex, had been purchased in 1673 by his father, who went to 'a prodigious cost in planting walnut trees and making fish ponds, many miles in circuit' (GEC). The house, built 1715–22, was designed by Colin Campbell; Christopher Hussey calls it 'the first great Palladian-Whig "palace" ' (*English Country Houses: Early Georgian 1715–1760*, 1955, p. 16).

[5] Wentworth-Woodhouse, the 1st Marquess of Rockingham's seat in Yorkshire, begun in 1725 but not completed until 1768, is an enormous Palladian house, its east front 200 yards long (ibid., pp. 147–54).

[6] Perhaps 'brag' had an earlier name; the *OED*'s first reference is 1734.

age (which is ⟨ 1 ?⟩ through all the Venetian State), who lost
l⟨ast⟩ Carnival at Brescia ten thousand pound, being all the
money his Guardians had laid up in his minority, and as his
estate is entail'd he cannot raise one farthing on it, and is
now a sort of Prisoner in his castle, where he lives upon
Rapine; I mean running in debt to poor people who perhaps
he will never be able to pay.

I am afraid you are tir'd with this insignificant Letter. We
old Women love tatling. You must forgive the Infirmitys of
your most affectionate Mother,

M. Wortley.

My Complements to Lord Bute and blessing to all yours.

Text W MS iii. 21–22   *Address* To The Rt Honble The Countess
of Bute [*in another hand*] in Great Grosvenor Street

To Wortley *11 June* [*1749*]

June 11. N.S.

Here has been a Prodigy without any Mixture of Fraud.
A Woman in this Village was deliver'd a few days since of a
child with two distinct Heads and necks, both entirely perfect and Beautifull. Their Countenances seem'd Male and
Female, joyn'd to one body without any defect, the Sex male.
It dy'd on its comeing into the World. The Mother is in
good Health, it being produce'd with the feet forwards,
otherwise she must have been kill'd in Labour. The Physician
here disected it, but having not proper instruments nor (I
beleive) overmuch skill, could not make such nice Observations as might have been done. He only told me he found
the Heart twice the bigness that is usual, but all the rest (as
far as he could perceive) of the naturall size and figure. In the
Time of ancient Rome, this Accident would have given
employment to the whole Senate.

I am amaz'd at my Sister Carolina's absurd match; with

her great Fortune,[1] it shows she has a great deal of Dutch in her Composition.[2]

I have obey'd you in writeing this in a large character. I have not yet us'd any Glasses, nor indeed would it be easy to find one in this Country, and I think it would be in vain to send for one, since it is necessary it should be fitted to the sight of the person that is to use it. I am of opinion that without absolute necessity it is better to forbear them.

The present Weather may be put into the Number of Prodigies; it is now cold enough to sit by the Fire.

Text W MS ii. 189–90   *Address* To Edwd Wortley Esqr in Cavendish Square London   *End. by W* [*Summary*] Ad 8 July.

To Wortley [*14 July 1749*]

I receiv'd yours of May 29th this day, July 14 N.S. I have never fail'd answering every one that has come to my Hands the same post or the immediate succeeding one. I do not doubt the Interuption in our Correspondance is often occasion'd by the negligence or infidelity of my Messengers, but your last came to me open'd, with the mark of the Sanita, which shews me that the Venetians are at present under a real or pretended fear of some Contagious Distemper,[3] but I have heard of no such thing. There are often Quarentains set up on Disputes with the Neighbouring States, especially in the time of the Fairs.

I am sorry I have given you so much trouble on the

---

[1] Of LM's two half-sisters, Lady Anne Pierrepont (the younger) died in 1739; thereupon her portion of £15,000 was cancelled by the trustees of her father's estate, and £10,000 added to her sister's portion (memorandum dated 6 May 1739, Monson MS, xliii.). Lady Caroline (1716–53) m. (9 Jan. 1749) Thomas Brand (*c.* 1717–70). He was an M.P. with settled estates worth £1,716 p.a. (History of Parliament, *House of Commons 1754–1790*, ed. L. Namier and J. Brooke, 1964, ii. 112).

[2] From her maternal grandfather, the 1st Earl of Portland. LM believed that her half-sister had married for money but despite her disapproval the marriage was very successful: 'they were infinitely happy and lived in the most perfect friendship' that Horace Walpole ever saw (*Corr.* ix. 150).

[3] The Sanitary Office was set up to prevent the spread of infectious disease (Pompeo Molmenti, *Venice*, transl. H. F. Brown, 1908, III. i. 97–98).

Account of the Ale, since you are not of Opinion it will come good. If it is not yet sent, I beg you to let it alone. I am far more solicitous for Lord Bolingbroke's Book.¹ All the writeings I have ever seen of his appear'd to me copy'd from the French Eloquence, I mean a poor or trite thought dress'd in pompous Language.

I wish I could write, as you desire, on better paper, but this is the best to be had in this place.

The last Letter I had from my Daughter was dated Feb. 27. I am persuaded she has wrote since, but I have never been so happy to receive any one.

The Inundations of the Rivers (by the uncommon Rains that have falln this year at the time of the melting of the Snow) have done a great deal of mischeife. I have been in the number of the sufferers.

Text W MS ii. 191–2   *Address* To Edwd Wortley Esqr in Cavendish Square London   *End. by W* [*Summary*] Ad 21 Sept. N.S.   Recd at Paris² 18 Aug.

To Lady Bute *24 July* [*?1749*]³

Louviere,⁴ July 24 N.S.

Dear Child,

I am now in a place the most beautifully Romantick I ever saw in my Life. It is the Tunbridge of this part of the World, to which I was sent by the Doctor's order, my Ague⁵ often returning notwithstanding the Loads of Bark I have taken. To say truth I have no reason to repent my Journey,

---

¹ *Letters, on the Spirit of Patriotism: on the Idea of a Patriot King: and On the State of Parties, At the Accession of King George the First,* 1749 (reviewed in May).

² W was on a visit to France with his son, whom he apparently considered sufficiently reformed. They were presented at Versailles on 23 Sept. 1749 (Duc de Luynes, *Mémoires sur la cour de Louis XV,* 1860–5, ix. 505). W stayed abroad until Feb. 1750.

³ The year may be 1747 (see below, p. 435, n. 2); but for other reasons (given in the footnotes) 1749 seems more plausible.

⁴ Lovere, at the northern end of Lago d'Iseo, was recommended by Brescian doctors for its salubrious air and mineral waters (C. L. P. Marinoni, *Lady Montagu Wortley e la sua decennale dimora alle rive del lago d'Iseo,* 1904, p. 22).

⁵ LM first mentions this recurring ailment on [26 April 1749].

thô I was very unwilling to undertake it, it being 40 mile, halfe by Land and halfe by Water, the Land so stony I was almost shook to pieces; and I had the ill luck to be surpriz'd with a storm on the Lake that if I had not been near a little port (where I pass'd a night in a very poor Inn) the Vessel must have been lost. A fair Wind brought me hither next morning early.

I found a very good Lodging, a great deal of good Company,[1] and a Village in many respects ressembling Tunbridge Wells, not only in the Quality of the Waters (which is the same) but in the manner of the buildings, most of the Houses being separate at little Distances, and all built on the sides of Hills, which indeed are far different from those of Tunbridge, being six times as high. They are realy vast Rocks of different figures cover'd with green moss or short grass, diversify'd by Tufts of Trees, little Woods, and here and there Vineyards, but no other Cultivation except Gardens like those on Richmond Hill. The whole lake, which is 25 mile long and 3 broad, is all surrounded with these impassable Mountains, the sides of which, towards the bottom, are so thick set with villages (and in most of them Gentlemen's seats) that I do not beleive there is any where above a mile distance one from another, which adds very much to the Beauty of the Prospect.

We have an Opera here which is perform'd three times in the Week. I was at it last night, and should have been surpriz'd at the neatness of the Scenes, goodness of the Voices, and justness of the actors if I had not remember'd I was in Italy. Several Gentlemen jump'd into the orchestre and joyn'd in the consort, which I suppose is one of the freedoms of the Place, for I never saw it in any great Town. I was yet more amaz'd (while the Actors were dressing for the Farce that concluded the Entertainment) to see one of the principal amongst them (and as arrand a petit Maitre as if he had pass'd all his Life at Paris) mount the stage and present us with a Cantata of his own performing. He had the Pleasure of being allmost deafen'd with applause. The Ball begun afterwards, but I was not Witness of it, having accustom'd

---

[1] In the summer of 1747 LM remained at Gottolengo in quiet retirement (see above, p. 388).

my selfe to such early hours that I was halfe asleep before the Opera finish'd. It begins at ten o' clock, so that it was one before I could get to bed, thô I had supp'd before I went, which is the custom.

I am much better pleas'd with the Diversions on the Water, where all the Town assembles every night, and never without Music; but we have none so rough as Trumpets, kettle Drums, and French Horns; they are all Violins, Lutes, Mandolins and Flutes doux. Here is hardly a man that does not excell in some of these instruments, which he privately addresses to the Lady of his affections, and the public has the advantage of it by his adding to the number of the Musicians. The Fountain where we drink the Waters rises between 2 hanging Hills, and is over shadow'd with large Trees that give a freshness in the hotest time of the Day. The provisions are all Excellent, the Fish of the Lake being as large and well tasted as that of Geneva, and the Mountains abounding in Game, particularly black Cocks, which I never saw in any other part of Italy.

But none of the amusements here would be so effectual to raiseing my Spirits as a Letter from you. I have receiv'd none since that of Feb. 27.[1] I do not blame you for it but my ill Fortune that will not let me have that Consolation. The news paper informs me that the Chevalier Grey (so he is styl'd) is appointed minister at Venice.[2] I wish you would let me know who he is, intending to settle our Correspondance through his hands. I did not care to ask that Favour of Lord Holderness.[3]

Dear child, I am ever your most affectionate Mother.

M. Wortley M.

My Complements to Lord Bute and blessing to all your little ones. Direct as usual.

Text W MS iii. 11–14   *Address* To The Rt Honble The Countess of Bute

[1] On [14 July 1749] LM had told W about this same letter.

[2] Sir James Gray (*c.* 1708–73), previously Secretary of the Embassy, presented his credentials as Resident in May 1746. He was absent on leave from May 1748 to Sept. 1749 (D. B. Horn, *Brit. Dipl. Rep. 1689–1789*, 1932, p. 85).

[3] Ambassador since 1744, Holdernesse had left Venice in Aug. 1746 (ibid.).

To Lady Bute *11 Aug.* [*1749*]

Louvere, Aug't 11. N.S.

Dear Child,

Thô I receive no Letters from you, and consequently do not know whether mine ever come to your hands, yet I cannot forbear writeing. The very next day after I wrote my last, my Fever seiz'd me again, which has now tormented me 4 months, off and on. My Woman's return'd also the same day, who has had it 8 months. I was recommended to the Physician of this place,[1] with much said in his praise as Master of several secrets, of which I did not beleive one word. However, I was prevail'd on to take his advice. He gave both her and me a small doze of powder, which is a preparation of the Bark of his Invention, how compos'd I cannot tell, but so it is that after once takeing neither of us have had any return of the Ague, on the contrary are restor'd to Health and strength as if by miracle. 'Tis true we continu'd to take one doze per day, 12 days together, but without any confinement, having allways been abroad pertakeing of all the Diversions.

I cannot help giving you this Information, thô I am afraid you will think it like Ward's drop or Tar Water, but 'tis certainly true that since I have been here I have seen such miraculous success of his Med'cines in various cases that I think I ought to let you know it, particularly of a mouth Water for the Scurvy in the Teeth, which I have seen experience'd by an Abbé past 50, who came from Ferrara on purpose to be under his care, and who had not one Tooth that did not shake, and his Gumms seem'd perish'd. They are come again and all his Teeth firm. The Doctor says this Water will keep its virtue 2 or 3 years, and bear Transportation, which if true might be of great use in England, where that Distemper is almost Epidemical. The Tryal can hurt no body, since the Water is not to be swallow'd. I beleive you will think I have been very long on this subject.

I intend staying here the remainder of this Month. 'Tis

---

1. Dr. Baglioni, as LM names her Lovere doctor ('Italian Memoir', Wh MS 510, f. 17). For her full description of him in 1754, see iii. 52–53.

impossible to be in a more agreable place in regard of the Situation, goodness of provisions, and abundance of the most excellent Fruits of all kinds. 'Tis true I could wish there was less Company, being heartily weary of the Eternal Hurry of Operas, puppet shews etc. Here is a gameing room, but I have never been at it, nor do I know any Ladys that go there, being a rendezvous of mix'd Company.

My paper is at an end or you would be trouble'd with more tattle from your most affectionate Mother.

M. Wortley

My Complements to Lord Bute and blessing to my Grand children.

Text W MS iii. 296–7   *Address* To The Rt Honble The Countess of Bute

To Lady Oxford *20 Aug.* [*1749*]

Louvere, Aug't 20. N.S.

I receiv'd this morning your Ladyship's obliging Letter of June 8th; the sight of your hand gave me great Pleasure, but the complaints you make of ill Health equally alarm'd and greiv'd me. I beg of you, dearest Madam, not to write when it is troublesome to you. God knows my Heart; I would not purchase any Happyness at the expence of the least Inconvenience to you. I have been here this month drinking the Waters, by Advice, having had many returns of the Ague, but have found great benefit from these Waters, and am now in hopes I am entirely quit of it.

I think Lady F. Meadows pays very dear for whatever advantages she may gain. But Interest is so commonly preferr'd to Honor, I do not doubt her conduct will be applauded by many people.[1] I suppose Thoresby is (at least in part) rebuilt, or I know not where so many can lodge. My

[1] In her letter (of 8 June [O.S.], Harley MS) Lady Oxford wrote that the Duke of Kingston 'lives cheifly in this Country [Notts.], thô He is now in Town. His Sister [Lady Frances], Mr. Medows, and all their children came lately from London to Thoresby with Madame, as she is call'd in this Country' ('Madame' was the Duke's mistress, for for whom see below, p. 459).

Daughter writes me word she has fitted up that House[1] near Hampstead which I once had the Honor to see with your Ladiship; I hope it is a proofe she is in no Want of Money.

I propose staying here but a few days longer; my love of Retirement grows upon me, and 'tis my opinion whoever knows the World cannot be very fond of it. It is impossible for me to conclude my Letter without recommending to you the care of your selfe. It is no complement, but a plain truth, when I say that your Ladyship is the only true Freind I ever had in my Life; judge therefore how dear you are to (Dear Madam) your most affectionate and Faithfull Servant,

M. W. Montagu.

Text Wh MS 507   *Address* To The Rt Honble the Lady Henrietta Countess of Oxford in Dover Street near St James's London   *End. by Lady Oxford* R: Welbeck Thursday Septr 7th 1749 O:S:

To Lady Bute *22 Aug.* [*1749*]

Louvere, Aug't 22nd N.S.

Dear Child,

I receiv'd yours of the 30th of May but yesterday, to my great Vexation, fearing I may lose the Box of Books and (what is more dear to me) your Letter, by the delay of the post, not bringing me the bill of Loading in the proper time. I have sent a messenger to Venice, but would not defer giving you thanks till his return. You say nothing of the Price, but I insist on it. You should take it from Child, with order he should deduct it in the next bill he sends to me.

We are now very quiet here, all the Beau monde being hurry'd away to the Fair of Bergamo,[2] which is esteem'd the best in Italy, after that of Sinigallia. Our Theatres are all shut up, the performers being also gone thither. I was much press'd to go by several partys, but would not fatigue my selfe with a Journey of 30 mile. I have sent my Woman to

---

[1] Cane Wood (now Ken Wood) House.
[2] The fair, from late Aug. to early Sept., was held in an elaborate structure (with 600 shops), with a theatre nearby (J. J. de Lalande, *Voyage en Italie*, 3rd ed., 1790, vii. 245).

buy pen'norths, hearing that there are merchants from all parts of Europe.

I am surpriz'd at the account you give of London, yet can hardly suppose there is not some rational Creatures in it. The D[uches]s of Portland must be much alter'd if she is never content out of a Croud, and by the character of Lady Middlesex (who I am told is your most intimate Companion),[1] I should guess her to be another that would prefer an easy conversation to the noise of an Assembly.

I very well remember Cane Wood House, and cannot wish you in a more agreable place. It would be a great pleasure to me to see my Grand children run about in the Gardens. I do not question Lord Bute's good Taste in the Improvements round it, or yours in the choice of the Furniture.[2] I have heard the Fame of paper Hangings, and had some thoughts of sending for a suit, but was inform'd that they are as dear as Damask here, which put an end to my Curiosity.

I beleive you think it a long time since I promis'd my God Daughter[3] ⟨a⟩ Token. I still wait an oppertunity of sending it, and engage it shall improve by the delay.

I am ever (Dear Child) your most affectionate Mother,

M. W. Montagu.

My Complements to Lord Bute and blessing to your little ones.

Text W MS iii. 23–24   *Address* To The Rt Honble the Countess of Bute [*in another hand*] in grosvenors Street

[1] In her letter of 8 June [O.S.] Lady Oxford had remarked that the Princess of Wales and Lady Middlesex were 'ingaging' Lady Bute. Grace Boyle (d. 1763), da. of 2nd Viscount Shannon, m. (1744) the Earl of Middlesex, son and heir of 1st Duke of Dorset. Since 1743 she had been Mistress of the Robes and a Lady of the Bedchamber to the Princess, and was reputed to be the Prince's mistress. Horace Walpole describes her as 'very short, very plain, and very yellow: a vain girl, full of Greek and Latin, and music, and painting, but neither mischievous nor political' (*Mem. of George II*, 1822, i. 65–66).

[2] Lady Oxford reported her daughter's impression of Kenwood as 'genteely fitted up' (30/19 Sept. 1749, Harley MS). It had been conveyed to Bute in 1746 by his uncle the 3rd Duke of Argyll (L.C.C., *Survey of London*, xvii, 1936, p. 130).

[3] Lady Bute's eldest daughter, Lady Mary.

To Wortley [*4 Sept. 1749*]

I receiv'd yours of July 8 this morning, Sept. 4 N.S. I beleive I have seldom fail'd mentioning the date of all the Letters that have come to my Hands, but as I have wrote many when I had none to acknowledge, 'tis possible that may have occasion'd your thinking that I neglected the Dates.

It was Miss Carter (Daughter of Mr. Carter who I have heard you speak of as a Relation of Lady Bellasis) that gave me the Description of Newbold Hall. I know not what is become of her since her foolish Marriage, that I sent you a long account of.[1]

I seldom saw Mr. Hewet[2] at Venice. I fancy he was displeas'd with me for not introduceing him to the noble Ladys, which was out of my power. They look on all Governours as Servants and will not receive their visits.

If it was possible to transport Houses, I could send you very fine Palaces which you might purchase at ten per Cent. I was offer'd the other day one of the most agreable Houses I ever saw, in a Delightfull Situation, for nothing if I would buy the Land about it, valu'd at 20,000 Crowns, and I beleive they would have thrown me in the Furniture into the Bargain, thô it is allmost new, with some good Pictures.

I am still at Louvere, thô the high Season for drinking the Waters is over, but my Health is so much mended by them that I intend to stay some time longer. There is a Constant Courier goes between this place and Brescia, which is more secure for Letters than when I am at Gottolengo, where they must allways come by a private Messenger, and I beleive are often lost from that reason.

Text W MS ii. 193–4   *Address* To Edwd Wortley Esqr [*in another hand*] At Mr. George Waters Junr Banker at Paris   *Postmark* ⟨?⟩
End. by W [*Summary*] Ad 20 Nov. N.S.

---

[1] See above, p. 398.   [2] Lord Granby's tutor (see above, p. 165).

To Lady Bute 5 *Sept.* [*1749*]

Dear Child,   Louvere, Sept. 5 N.S.

I have once more recover'd my Health by the use of these
Waters, and can say I am at this present writeing in a better
State of Health than I have been for some years. I rise early,
take the air on the Water every Evening, and generally land
at some part of its banks and allways find some new Walk
amongst the Mountains, which are cover'd with Vines and
fruit trees, mix'd with several natural Cascades, and embellish'd with variety of Beautifull prospects. I think I have
allready describ'd this place to you. It realy answers all the
delightfull Ideas of Romance. I could not be persuaded to
leave it for the Fair of Bergamo, thô halfe engag'd to do so.
I play at Whisk an hour or two every afternoon. The fashion
here is to play for the collation; the losers have at least the
Consolation of eating part of their money.

I am extreamly pleas'd with your Father's kindness to
you. I do not doubt of your Gratitude and affection. He
speaks to me much of the Beauty of your Sons.[1] I cannot help
wishing it had fallen to the share of your Daughters, but I
beleive it is the Destiny of Lord Bute's Family. I never heard
his mother's[2] much celebrated, thô both her Brothers have
been remarkable for their Figure.[3]

My Dear Child, God Bless you and yours. I am ever your
most affectionate Mother,

M. Wortley.

My Complements to Lord Bute. I hope you will remember ⟨to send me⟩ the 3rd Vol. of Architecture[4] with any other
amuseing Books. Direct them to the English Minister at
Venice, Sir James Gray.

Text W MS iii. 279–80 *Address* To The Rt Honble The Countess
of Bute [*in another hand*] in Grosvenor Street

[1] John was 5, and James Archibald
nearly 2 years old.

[2] Anne Campbell (d. 1736), da. of
1st Duke of Argyll, m. (1711) 2nd Earl
of Bute.

[3] Bute's two maternal uncles were the
2nd and 3rd Dukes of Argyll; the former was thought to be very handsome
and graceful, but the latter 'slovenly in
his person' (Walpole, *Mem. of George II*,
1822, i. 240).

[4] Apparently LM had received only
the first two volumes of Colin Campbell's *Vitruvius Britannicus* (1717–25).

To Lady Oxford *24 Sept.* [*1749*]

Sept. 24. N.S.

I receiv'd yesterday your Ladyship's obliging Letter.[1] It was a great Comfort to me to see your hand, thô the account of your Indisposition much abated that pleasure. I have receiv'd great Benefit from drinking of Steel Waters, and am apt to beleive they would be usefull to you, since I find Dr. Sydenham (who is my Oracle in Physic) recommends them generally to all Women at a certain time of Life.[2]

You do me Justice (Dearest Madam) in thinking I can never be wanting in my Expressions of Affection for you; 'tis all I can return for your unweary'd Freindship, and I should be the most unworthy and most ungratefull Creature living was I capable of omitting the assurances of my being ever yours, thô I can offer you nothing but fruitless wishes, and sincere Praiers for your Health and Happiness. The Dutchess of Portland allways shares in them, both for your sake and her own uncommon Merit. 'Tis impossible to pay too much to such a Parent as you, yet Justice and Gratitude are so seldom seen in this World, it is no small Desert where they are found. God preserve you long for one another.

I am glad your Ladyship amuses your selfe with building,[3] and hope you will advantage to your health, as well as diversion. My Daughter writes me word she is wholly taken up with Court Attendance; I wish her better success with it than many others have had, but have observ'd (Generally) so much disapointment follows it that I shall not be surpriz'd if she also experiences it. I am ever, Dearest Madam, Your Ladyship's most Faithfull and Eternally oblig'd humble Servant,

M. W. Montagu.

[1] Dated 2 Aug. [O.S.] 1749 from Cavendish Lodge (Harley MS).

[2] Steel water was a popular remedy containing iron. Dr. Thomas Sydenham (1642–89), noted physician, prescribed it for hysteric disorders (*Works,* 11th ed., 1740, pp. 315–22). LM expresses her admiration for him again in a letter to Sir James Steuart (5 Sept. 1758).

[3] In her letter of 21 Jan. 1747/8 [O.S.] Lady Oxford had described in detail the small house called Cavendish Lodge, which she had built for retirement and economy. It stood in Clipstone Park, five miles from Welbeck.

Text Wh MS 507   *Address* To The Rt Honble the Lady Henrietta Countess of Oxford in Dover Street near St James's London   *End. by Lady Oxford* R: Welbeck Saturday Decr 16th 1749 O:S:

To Lady Bute *1 Oct.* [*1749*]

Oct. 1. N.S.

My Dear Child,

I have at length receiv'd the Box with the Books enclos'd, for which I give you many thanks, as they amus'd me very much. I gave a very ridiculous proofe of it, fitter indeed for my Grand daughter than my selfe. I return'd from a party on Horseback and after have [*sic*] rode 20 mile, part of it by moon shine, it was ten at night when I found the Box arriv'd. I could not deny my selfe the pleasure of opening it, and falling upon Fielding's Works was fool enough to sit up all night reading. I think Joseph Andrews better than his Foundling.[1] I beleive I was the more struck with it, having at present a Fanny in my own House, not only by the Name, which happens to be the same,[2] but the extrodinary Beauty, joyn'd with an understanding yet more extrodinary at her age, which is but few months past sixteen. She is in the post of my Chambermaid. I fancy you will tax my Discretion for takeing a Servant thus qualify'd, but my Woman, who is also my Housekeeper, was allways teizing me with her having too much Work, and complaining of ill Health, which determin'd me to take her a Deputy; and when I was at Louvere (where I drank the Waters) one of the most considerable merchants there press'd me to take this Daughter of his. Her mother has an uncommon good character, and the Girl has had a better Education than is usual for those of her Rank. She writes a good hand and has been brought up to keep accounts, which she does to great perfection, and had her selfe

---

[1] *Joseph Andrews* had been published in Feb. 1742, and *Tom Jones, A Foundling* on 28 Feb. 1749.

[2] Chechina, a diminutive of Francesca. In her Commonplace Book LM noted '. . . went [to] Louvere, took Chechina, staid 3 months with me; ⟨? at⟩ G[ottolengo], her Father sent for her Nov. 1. . . . 1750, Louvere, Brescia, Checinna's marriage' (MS f. 22, Fisher Library, University of Sydney).

such a violent desire to serve me, that I was persuaded to take her. I do not yet repent it from any part of her behaviour; but there has been no peace in the Family ever since she came in to it—I might say the Parish, all the Women in it having declar'd open War with her, and the Men endeavoring at Treatys of a different sort. My own Woman puts her selfe at the Head of the first Party, and her spleen is encreas'd by having no reason for it, the young creature never stirring from my Apartment, allways at her needle, and never complaining of any thing. You will laugh at this tedious account of my Domesticks (if you have patience to read it over), but I have few other subjects to talk of.

I am sorry you did not take the money for the Books from Child. I write him this post to pay it to you, but you will wait longer for it than I could wish.

I am much pleas'd at your account of your children. May they ever be as agreable to you as they are at present!

The Waters have very much mended my Health. I endeavor to preserve it by constant rideing, and am a better horse Woman than ever I was in my Life, having compli'd with the fashion of this Country, which is every way so much better than ours I cannot help being amaz'd at the obstinate Folly by which the English Ladys venture every day their Lives and Limbs.[1]

My paper only allows me to add I am your most affectionate Mother,

M. W.

My Complements to Lord Bute and blessing to your little ones.

Text W MS iii. 17–18   *Address* To The Rt Honble the Countess of Bute [*in other hands*] opposite Dr Trebecks[2]   in Great Grosvenor Street   *Postmark* PENY POST PAYD   TFR

---

[1] LM rode astride (see above, p. 263).

[2] Andrew   Trebeck   (1681–1759), Rector of St. George's, Hanover Square,

1725–58 (J. Venn, *Alumni Cantab. to 1751*, iv. 262; *Gentleman's Mag.*, 1759, p. 442).

To Lady Oxford *27 Nov.* [*1749*]

Dearest Madam,

I am inexpressibly greiv'd that of at least ten Letters I I have done my selfe the Honor of addressing to your Ladyship this Year, only two have reach'd you; I know not what method to take to secure them better for the Future. It is a great addition to the Pain of Absence, when the only Consolation of it is thus intterupted. I am very much oblig'd to the Dutchesse of Portland for remembering so insignificant a Servant. I have the most gratefull Sense of her Goodness, and Esteem for her Merit, which I beleive no body denys her. I do not wonder her Conversation contributes to your Health; I hope you will contrive to enjoy it often, and am persuaded you will find more benefit from that than any other med'cine. I am very glad my Daughter is still happy in an Intimacy every way so advantageous to her.

I left Louvere in September, and have had no return of my Ague since. I intend to repeat drinking the Waters next season, and beleive they are very necessary for me, and have also a great Opinion of the Physician of the Place.[1] Your Ladiship knows I have no partiality to that proffession, but I have realy seen such wonderfull Success on many Occasions from his prescriptions that I cannot help thinking he has some valuable secrets. I could wish it possible you could consult him, but all written cases are so liable to mistakes I know not how to advise it. My constant Praiers and wishes for your Health and Happyness daily attend you; 'tis all that can be offer'd by, Dearest Madam, Your Ladyship's most faithfully affectionate Humble servant,

M. W. Montagu.

Nov. 27. N.S.

Text Wh MS 507   *Address* To The Rt Honble the Lady Henrietta Countess of Oxford in Dover Street near St James's London   *Postmark* PENY POST PAYD ⟨?⟩   *End. by Lady Oxford* d: Novr 27th NS R: Cavendishe Lodge Thursday Decr 21st 1749 OS

[1] Dr. Baglioni.

To Lady Bute 27 *Nov.* [*1749*]

Nov. 27. N.S.

Dear Child,

By the account you give me of London, I think it very much reform'd. At least you have one sin the less (and it was a very reigning one in my time); I mean Scandal. It must be litterally reduce'd to a Whisper since the Custom of living alltogether. I hope it has also banish'd the fashion of talking all at once (which was very prevailing when I was in Town) and may perhaps contribute to Brotherly Love and unity, which was so much declin'd in my memory that it was hard to invite six people that would not, by cold looks or piqueing Refflections, affront one another. I suppose Partys are at an end, thô I fear it is the Consequence of the old Almanack prophecy, Poverty brings Peace; and I fancy you realy follow the French mode, and the Lady keeps an assembly, that the assembly may keep the Lady, and card money pay for Cloaths and Equipage as well as Cards and Candles.[1] I find I should be as Solitary in London as I am here in the Country, it being impossible for me to submit to live in a Drum,[2] which I think so far from a cure of uneasynesses that it is, in my opinion, adding one more to the heap. There are so many attach'd to Humanity, 'tis impossible to fly from them all, but Experience has confirm'd to me (what I allways thought), that the persuit of pleasure will be ever attended with Pain, and the study of ease be most certainly accompany'd with Pleasures.

I have had this morning as much delight in a Walk in the Sun as ever I felt formerly in the crouded Mall even when I imagin'd I had my share of the admiration of the place, which was generally sour'd before I slept by the Informations of my female Freinds, who seldom fail'd to tell me it was observ'd I had shew'd an inch above my shoe heels, or some other criticism of equal weight, which was construe'd

---

[1] When visiting Paris in 1739 Walpole observed that 'it is no dishonour to keep public gaming houses: there are at least an hundred and fifty people of the first quality in Paris who live by it' (*Corr.* xiii. 164).

[2] An assembly at a private house.

affectation, and utterly destroy'd all the Satisfaction my vanity had given me. I have now no other but in my little Hus-wifery, which is easily gratify'd in this Country, where (by the help of my receipt Book) I make a very shineing Figure amongst my Neighbours by the Introduction of Custards, Cheesecakes and mince'd Pies, which were entirely un-known in these Parts, and are receiv'd with universal ap-plause, and I have reason to beleive will preserve my Memory even to Future ages, particularly by the art of Butter makeing, in which I have so improv'd them that they now make as good as in any part of England.

My paper is at an end, which I do not doubt you are glad of. I have hardly room for my Complements to Lord Bute, blessing to my Grand children, and to assure you that I am ever your most affectionate Mother.

M. W.

Text W MS iii. 111–12   *Address* To The Rt Honble the Countess of Bute [*in another hand*] in Great Grosvenor Street   *Postmark* PENY POST PAYD   TMO

To Wortley 25 Dec. [1749]

Dec. 25. N.S.

I receiv'd yours from Paris dated Nov. 20 but this morn-ing, and never had that you mention of Sept. 21, which would have sav'd me a great deal of uneasyness which I have suffer'd ⟨from⟩ your imagin'd Silence, not knowing where to direct, my Daughter having told me you had left England.[1] I hope you have found Advantage to your Health from your Travels. Lady Sandwich is one Example (amongst many others) that there is no Rule certain for the attainment of Long Life. She has not Sought it by Abstinence or Regu-larity, and yet enjoys a happier old Age than is common to Mankind.[2]

[1] W had been abroad since the sum-mer (see above, p. 433, n. 2).

[2] Elizabeth Wilmot (1674–1757), da. of 2nd Earl of Rochester, the famous poet and wit, m. (1689) 3rd Earl of Sandwich, and was thus related to W by marriage. After her husband's death in 1729 she resided in Paris, where she shone in the brilliant salon society.

I know not whether you ever receiv'd the Letter in which I gave you my Opinion (as you desir'd) of Lord Boling-broke's Pamphlet.[1] I am unwilling to trouble you with Repetitions, and yet I am afraid do it very often, from the uncertainty I am in of my Letters coming safe. I direct this as you order'd, to Paris, but as it is possible you may have allready left it, I shall send another to Mr. Child. It is very hard if neither of them reach you.

I beg your Pardon for this bad Paper, but have no better at present and would not delay writeing till I could get a finer sort.

Text W MS ii. 197–8   *Address* A Monsieur Monsieur Wortley Montagu recommendé a Monsieur G. Waters le jeune Banquier[2] a Paris per Venezia   *Postmark* DE LIO⟨NE⟩   *End. by W* [*Summary*] Ad 2d Apr. 1750.   Recd at Paris 17 Jan. 1750.

To Wortley 25 *Dec.* [*1749*]

Dec. 25. N.S.

I have allready wrote you one Letter directed (as you order'd) to Paris but, fearing you may be gone from thence, I send this to Mr. Child, which I hope will reach you. I never had that you mention of Sept. 21, which has occasion'd me great uneasyness from your suppos'd Silence. I lose so many Letters that I have lost all my Correspondants, amongst others Lady Pomfret. I am sorry she does not intend for Italy. Her Conversation is more entertaining than the Gene-rality of Ladys', but I fancy her Circumstances will not permit her to live here. The Country Towns in France are much cheaper, and the Journey shorter if she designs to return to England.[3]

I would write you what Account I hear of the little Courts round us, but am afraid of the Security of my Letter.

---

[1] *Letters, on the Spirit of Patriotism,* etc; her critique is lost.

[2] George John (b. 1705), son of George Waters (see above, p. 22).

[3] On 8 Oct. 1749 [O.S.] Lady Pom-fret set out from London for the south of France for the recovery of her health (*Daily Advertiser,* 12 Oct.).

I hope the Waters have been usefull to your Health. The Continuance of it is my Sincere and Zealous Wish.

Text W MS ii. 195–6   *Address* To Edwd Wortley Esq: [*added in other hands*]...The Honble...Montagu...to the care of Mr George Waters Junr Banker in [Paris *struck out*] a Calais chez Monsieur Carpentier a Calais   *Postmark* RJ   *End. by W* [*Summary*] Recd at Calais 11 Feb. N.S.   Ad 2 Apr. 1750.

To Lady Bute [*Jan. 1750*]

My Dear Child,

I am extremely concern'd to hear you complain of ill Health at a Time of Life when you ought to be in the Flower of your strength. I hope I need not recommend to you the care of it. The tenderness you have for your children is sufficient to inforce you to the utmost regard for the preservation of a Life so necessary to their well being. I do not doubt your Prudence in their Education, neither can I say any thing particular relateing to it at this Distance, different Tempers requiring different management. In General, never attempt to govern them (as most people do) by Deceit; if they find themselves cheated (even in Triffles) it will so far lessen the Authority of their Instructor as to make them neglect all their future admonitions. And (if possible) breed them free from Prejudices; those contracted in the Nursery often influence the whole Life after, of which I have seen many Melancholy Examples.

I shall say no more of this Subject, nor would have said this little if you had not ask'd my advice. 'Tis much easier to give Rules than to practise them. I am sensible my own Natural Temper is too Indulgent. I think it the least dangerous Error, yet still it is an Errour. I can only say with Truth that I do not know in my whole Life having ever endeavor'd to impose on you or give a false colour to any thing that I represented to you. If your Daughters are inclin'd to Love reading, do not check their Inclination by hindering them of the diverting part of it. It is as necessary for the Amusement of Women as the Reputation of Men;

but teach them not to expect or desire any Applause from it.
Let their Brothers shine, and let them content themselves
with makeing their Lives easier by it, which I experimentally
know is more effectually done by Study than any other way.
Ignorance is as much the Fountain of Vice as Idleness, and
indeed generally produces it. People that do not read or work
for a Livelihood have many hours they know not how to
imploy, especially Women, who commonly fall into Vapours
or something worse. I am afraid you'l think this Letter very
tedious. Forgive it as comeing from your most affectionate
mother,

M. W.

My Complements to Lord Bute and Blessing to my
Grand Children.

Text W MS iii. 61–62   *Address* To The Rt Honble the Countess
of Bute [*in another hand*] in Grosvenors Street

To Lady Bute *19 Feb.* [*1750*]

Feb. 19. N.S.

My Dear Child,

I gave you some general Thoughts on the Education of
your children in my last Letter, but fearing you should think
I neglected your request by answering it with too much
conciseness, I am resolv'd to add to it what little I know on
that Subject, and which may perhaps be usefull to you in a
concern with which you seem so nearly affected.

People commonly educate their children as they build
their Houses, according to some plan they think beautifull,
without considering whither it is suited to the purposes for
which they are design'd. Allmost all Girls of Quality are
educated as if they were to be great Ladys, which is often as
little to be expected as an immoderate Heat of the Sun in the
North of Scotland. You should teach yours to confine their
Desires to probabillitys, to be as usefull as is possible to
themselves, and to think privacy (as it is) the happiest state
of Life.

I do not doubt your giving them all the instructions

necessary to form them to a Virtuous Life, but tis a fatal mistake to do this without proper restrictions. Vices are often hid under the name of Virtues, and the practise of them follow'd by the worst of Consequences. Sincerity, Freindship, Piety, Disinterestness, and Generosity are all great Virtues, but persu'd without Discretion become criminal. I have seen Ladys indulge their own ill Humour by being very rude and impertinent, and think they deserv'd approbation by saying, I love to speak Truth. One of your acquaintance made a Ball the next day after her Mother dy'd, to shew she was sincere. I beleive your own refflection will furnish you with but too many Examples of the ill Effects of the rest of the Sentiments I have mention'd, when too warmly embrace'd. They are gennerally recommended to young People without limits or distinction, and this prejudice hurrys them into great misfortunes while they are applauding them selves in the noble practise (as they fancy) of very eminent Virtues.

I cannot help adding (out [of] my real affection to you) I wish you would moderate that fondness you have for your children. I do not mean you should abate any part of your Care, or not do your Duty to them in its utmost extent, but I would have you early prepare your selfe for Disapointments, which are heavy in proportion to their being surprizing. It is hardly possible in such a number that none should be unhappy. Prepare your selfe against a misfortune of that kind. I confess there is hardly any more difficult to support, yet it is certain Imagination has a great share in the pain of it, and it is more in our power (than it is commonly beleiv'd) to soften what ever ills are founded or augmented by Fancy. Strictly speaking, there is but one real evil; I mean acute pain. All other Complaints are so considerably diminish'd by Time that it is plain the Greife is owing to our Passion, since the sensation of it vanishes when that is over.

There is another mistake I forgot to mention usual in mothers. If any of their Daughters are Beauties, they take great pains to persuade them that they are ugly, or at least that they think so, which the Young Woman never fails to beleive springs from Envy, and is (perhaps) not much in the wrong. I would, if possible, give them a just notion of their Figure, and shew them how far it is valuable. Every advantage has its Price, and may be either over or undervalu'd. It is the common Doctrine of (what are call'd) Good Books to inspire a contempt of Beauty, Riches, Greatness etc., which has done as much mischeife amongst the young of our Sex as an over eager desire of them. They should look on these things as Blessings where they are bestow'd, thô not necessarys that it is impossible to be happy without. I am persuaded the ruin of Lady F[rances] M[eadows] was in great measure owing to the Notions given her by ⟨the s⟩illily good people that had the care of ⟨her⟩.[1] 'Tis true her Circumstances and your Daughters' ⟨are⟩ very different. They should be taught to be content with privacy, and yet not neglect good Fortune if it should be offer'd them.

I am afraid I ha⟨ve⟩ tir'd you with my Instructions. I do not give them as beleiveing my Age has furnish'd me with Superior Wisdom, but in compliance with your desire, and being fond of every oppertunity that gives a proofe of the tenderness with which I am ever Your affectionate Mother,
M. Wortley.

I should be glad you sent me the 3rd Vol. of Architecture, and with it any other entertaining Books. I have seen the D[uches]s of M[arlborough]'s, but should be glad of the Apology for a Late Resignation.[2] As to the Ale, tis now so late in the year it is impossible it should come good.

You do not mention your Father. My last Letter from him told me he intended soon for England.[3] I am afraid several of mine to him have miscarry'd, thô directed as he order'd.

I have ask'd you so often the price of raw silk that I am weary of repeating it. However, I once more beg you would send me that Information.

Text W MS iii. 82–85   *Address* To The Rt Honble The Countess of Bute

[1] Lady Frances Pierrepont, LM's niece, had lived with her grand-aunt Lady Cheyne (d. 1732) after her grandfather's death (see above, p. 62). After 1732, though nominally under the care of her brother (the 2nd Duke of Kingston), she lived with LM until her elopement in April 1734.

[2] LM had already requested the third volume of Campbell on architecture (5 Sept. [1749]) and the *Apology* (18 Aug. [1748]); the Duchess's political testament, written with the help of Nathaniel Hooke and published in 1742, was *An Account of the Conduct of the Dowager Duchess of Marlborough, from her first coming to Court, to the year 1710.*

[3] On 11 Feb. 1750 W was at Calais, no doubt on his way home.

To Lady Oxford 2 *March* [*1750*]

March 2nd N.S.

Dearest Madam,

I receiv'd this Day the Happiness of two Letters you have honour'd me with, dated Dec. 23 and January 6th. I am very glad your Health is mended; thô it is not so well re-establish'd as I could wish, yet I hope time will perfect it. I have pass'd this Winter without any Complaint, which I attribute to the Waters of Louvere, and am resolv'd to drink them again in the Season. I beg of you, Dearest Madam, let not your tenderness for me give you any uneasy moments. I could wish indeed my Destiny had plac'd me near Welbeck, but then I remember that could not be, without being also near another Place,[1] from whence I should often hear accounts that would embitter even your Ladyship's conversation. I am more sensible (perhaps) than I ought to be of the Figure my Family makes, and often refflect on the Happyness of my Father, who dy'd without seeing any of the misfortunes that have since happen'd.

I heartily congratulate the Satisfaction you express in your Hopefull growing Children;[2] I pray God continue it, and every other Blessing. I think you have a fair Prospect in the good sense and good Nature of the Duke and Dutchess of Portland; they cannot give better proofe of both than in a right behaviour to you. It is no more than your Due, but in this Age 'tis an uncommon merit to be just. I hope my Daughter will be so far her own Freind as to shew her selfe on all occasions one of the Dutchesse's humble servants. She sends me such a Description of London as would cure me of desireing to see it, if it was my Inclination, which since your Ladyship is not there, is no way my wish. Public Life is what I was never fond of, and would now become me less than ever; I have allways been amaz'd at the Passion for it continuing, as in the late Dutchess of Marlbrô, and can only attribute it to the Flatterers round her, who nourish'd in her that Desire of Applause which is as Vain as the

---

[1] Thoresby, where LM's nephew the Duke of Kingston lived with his French mistress.

[2] Lady Oxford's grandchildren.

endeavors of Children that run to catch the Rainbow. I need not say this to your Ladyship, who in highly deserving it has allways shunn'd it, but you have the goodness to permit me to communicate my thoughts to you, and tis a pleasure to me to shew my selfe eternally, Dearest Madam, your Ladyship's Devoted Humble Servant.

M. W. Montagu

Text Wh MS 507   *Address* To The Rt Honble the Lady Henrietta Countess of Oxford in Dover Street near St James's London   *End. by Lady Oxford* R: Welbeck Thursday April 5th O:S: 1750

To Lady Oxford *24 May* [*1750*]

May 24 N.S.

For the first time of my Life I have had a kind Letter from dear Lady Oxford lye by me 4 days unanswer'd. It found me on a sick bed, from which I can scarce say I am risen, since I am up but a few hours in the Day, and this is wrote (God knows) with a feeble hand, but I am impatient to thank your Ladyship for your unweary'd Goodness to me. I have had the severest illness I ever had, and heard Sentence of Death pronounce'd against me. I am now told I am out of Danger; I will not hurt your tenderness (which I am well acquainted with) by a recital of my Sufferings.[1]

Since Lady N[assau] Pawlet would take a Boy,[2] I am surpriz'd she has found one with so good an Estate; I

[1] In her next letter to Lady Oxford (23 June) she recited them more fully. In her 'Italian Memoir' she wrote: 'In the month of March 1750 I caught cold while walking; I was taken with fever and very troublesome complications. I had doctors come from Brescia and from Cremona, and recuperated with great difficulty very slowly' (Wh MS 510, f. 14: transl.).

[2] Isabella Tufton (d. 1763), a cousin of Lady Oxford's, widow of Lord

Nassau Powlett since 1741, m. (8 March 1750) Francis Blake Delaval (1727–71). LM's information came from Lady Oxford, who noted the great disproportion in the ages of the couple (7 April 1750 [O.S.], Harley MS). The strange story of this marriage between the rich, mad, middle-aged widow and the handsome young rake is fully related in Francis Askham, *The Gay Delavals*, 1955, pp. 35–51 *passim*.

suppose his Father has many other Sons, or is not fond of Posterity.[1]

May God continue every Blessing to you; my weakness obliges me to finish my Letter, with the assurance of my being ever, Dearest Madam, Your faithfull obedient Servant,

M. W. Montagu.

I will write again soon if it please God to restore my Health.

Text Wh MS 507   *Address* To The Rt Honble the Lady Henrietta Countess of Oxford in Dover Street near St James's London   *End. by Lady Oxford* R: Cav: Lodge Thursday June 21st O:S: 1750

To Wortley *28 May* [*1750*]

May 28 N.S.

I receiv'd yours of the 2nd of April O.S. 2 days ago. I was then on a sick Bed and am now scarce recover'd of a very severe illness. It was a great Comfort to me to hear of your Health, for which I was much in pain. I have not had any Letter from my Daughter of a long time, and am sorry she breeds so fast,[2] fearing it will impair her Constitution.

I wonder you do not imitate at London the wise conduct of this State, who, when they found the rage of play untameable, invented a method to turn it to the Advantage of the Public; now Fools lose their Estates, and the Government profits by it.[3]

I have wrote several long Letters to my Daughter but know not whither she has receiv'd any of them.

I must shorten this from the weakness both of my Head and Hand.

Text W MS ii. 199–200   *Address* To Edwd Wortley Esqr in Cavendish Square London Angleterre   *Postmark* PENY POST PAYD TMO   *End. by W* [*Summary*] Ad 24 June   Recd 18 June.

[1] On the death of his father (Francis Blake Delaval, 1692–1752), he inherited an estate of £9,000 a year (*Gentleman's Mag.*, p. 584). His motive for marrying was purely mercenary; and as for posterity, his father had six other sons (Askham, pp. 2, 51).

[2] Since 1738 Lady Bute had borne eight children and was again pregnant.

[3] Since 1638 the Venetian government had regulated the Ridotto, where immense sums were gambled away (Pompeo Molmenti, *Venice*, transl. H. F. Brown, 1908, III. ii. 171).

To Angelo Maria Contarini[1] *10 June 1750*

Excellenza,

Je suis infiniment obligée a vostre Bonté qui s'interresse pour moi. Mais cet Homme[2] dont vous parlé est un Fou et un Imposteur. Je sors d'une Maladie tres dangereuse, dont je suis a peine convalescente. Quand il est venu ici vestu d'Abbé, sans se nommer, j'étois encore trop malade pour voir personne. Je lui a envoyée ma Femme de chambre pour demander ce qu'il vouloit de moi. Il la donnoit une Lettre qui veritablement étoit a mon addresse, mais dont la signature etoit d'une Dame qui je ne connoisois pas (et qui peut estre n'est pas au monde), et tout rempli des Follies, qui montroit clairment qu'elle estoit forgée. Je lui fis rendre sa Lettre, en le priant de se retirer; sur cela il a eû la Hardiesse de tirer un Pistolet contre mes Gens.[3]

Si j'étois en etat de sortir je ne manquerai pas de venir en personne informer Vostre Excellence de ces faits. Je vous demande pardon de cette mauvaise Griffonage, mais j'ai encore la main et la Tête bien foible. J'ai entendu dire que cet extravagant s'est donné pour mon Parent, sans qu'il m'apartient d'aucune façon. Il a été dejà enfermé en France par ordre de Son Pere,[4] qui est veritablement un homme respectable, fort a plaindre d'avoir un tel enfant.

Je suis, Monsieur, avec l'estime deûe a vostre Merite et

---

1 Contarini (1693–1772) (Archivio di Stato, Venice). As *Podestà* of Brescia, he was sent by the Venetian Republic to administer the province.

This letter is translated on p. 529 below.

2 François-Zacharie de Quinsonas Lauberivière (1719–59), a Knight of Malta (C.-É. Engel, *L'Ordre de Malte en Méditerranée*, 1957, p. 291). He had apparently met LM in Avignon. This involvement is a newly discovered episode in LM's biography.

3 On 8 June the Chevalier made a deposition to Contarini that when he went to Gottolengo to pay his respects

to LM and to deliver a letter entrusted him by John Anderson, his way was blocked by servants; and that when he reached her house he was intercepted and threatened by armed thugs led by Palazzi, to whom he finally surrendered the letter. The next day (9 June) Contarini wrote to LM asking whether he could see her about the Chevalier's complaint. Her answer to him is this letter of 10 June, brought back by his messenger.

4 Claude-Joseph de Pourroy, Seigneur de Lauberivière, Quinsonas, Guillemières.

vostre Caractere, de Vostre Excellence la tres humble Servante,

M. W. Montagu.

Juin 10. 1750.

J'espere, Monsieur, de vostre Justice qu'au moins cet Homme soit chassé du Païs.[1]

Text MS in Archivio di Stato, Venice[2]

To Lady Bute 22 *June* [1752][3]

My dear Child,

Since you tell me my Letters (such as they are) are agreable to you, I shall for the Future indulge my selfe in thinking upon paper when I write to you.

I cannot beleive Sir John's advancement is owing to his merit, thô he certainly deserves such a Distinction, but I am persuaded the present disposers of such dignitys are neither more clear sighted or more disinterested than their Predecessors.[4] Ever since I knew the World, Irish Patents have been hung out to Sale like the lac'd and embrodier'd Coats

---

[1] The aftermath was this: on 16 June the Chevalier wrote again to Contarini protesting that LM's denials were the result of her ill health and her subjection by Palazzi; and he wrote to her himself (*c.* 27 June) explaining his solicitude for her safety and freedom, and protesting that his honour had been besmirched. In a final report to the Venetian government (on 12 July) Contarini concluded that LM was not held against her will. In her 'Italian Memoir' LM relates how she contradicted accusations of Palazzi's imprisoning her, though she omits any mention of the Chevalier (Wh MS 510, ff. 14–15; Halsband, *LM*, p. 248).

Gossip of the investigation reached Walpole and Mann (*Corr.* xx. 272, 279); and Voltaire sent Frederick the Great a coarse quip about the Chevalier and LM (*Corr.*, ed. T. Besterman, 1953–64, xx. 121).

[2] This letter and the other 17 documents in the case are classified as Dispacci dei Rettori agl'Inquisitori, Brescia, Busta 235; Lettere degl'Inquisitori ai Rettori, Brescia, Busta 21. The relevant documents, including LM's letter translated into Italian, are printed in Antonio Fappani, 'Lady Montagu ed il conte Ugolino Palazzi' in *Commentari dell'ateneo di Brescia*, 1961, pp. 113–24.

[3] In previous editions incorrectly dated 1750; its chronological place in this edition is iii. 13.

[4] Sir John Rawdon (1720–93), created in 1750 Baron Rawdon of Moira, in the Irish Peerage. Walpole remarked that he was being rewarded for his 'boasted loyalty of having been kicked down stairs for not drinking the Pretender's health, though even that was false' (*Corr.* xx. 136).

in Monmouth Street,[1] and bought up by the same sort of
people; I mean those who had rather wear shabby Finery
than no Finery at all, thô I don't suppose this was Sir John's
case. That good Creature (as the country saying is) has not
a bit of Pride in him. I dare swear he purchas'd his Title for
the same reason he us'd to purchase Pictures in Italy; not
because he wanted to buy, but because some body or other
wanted to sell. He hardly ever open'd his mouth but to say
—What you please, Sir—At your service—Your humble
servant—or some gentle expression to the same effect. It is
scarce credible that with this unlimited complaisance he
should draw a blow upon himselfe, yet it so happen'd that
one of his own Country Men was Brute enough to strike
him. As it was done before many Witnesses, Lord Mansel
heard of it, and thinking that if poor Sir John took no notice
of it he would suffer daily insults of the same kind, out of
pure good nature resolv'd to spirit him up, at least to some
show of Resentment, intending to make up the matter afterwards, in as honorable a manner as he could for the poor
patient. He represented to him very warmly that no Gentleman could take a Box o' th'ear. Sir John answer'd with great
calmness: I know that, but this was not a Box o' th'ear, it was
only a slap o' th'Face. I was as well acquainted with his two
first Wives as the difference of our ages permitted. I fancy
they have broke their Hearts by being chain'd to such a
companion.[2]

'Tis realy terrible for a well bred virtuous young Woman
to be confin'd to the conversation of the Object of their
contempt. There is but one thing to be done in that case,
which is a method I am sure you have observ'd practis'd with
success by some Ladies I need not name. They associate the
Husband and the Lapdog, and manage so well that they
make exactly the same figure in the Family. My Lord and

[1] Where, in the 18th century, second-
hand clothes were sold (H. B. Wheatley,
London Past and Present, 1891, ii.
554).
[2] His first wife was Helena Perceval
(1718–46). Her father, 1st Earl of Egmont, held a very high opinion of
Rawdon's good nature, sobriety, prudence, calm temper, and sincere Christianity (*Diary*, iii. 228, 229); more disinterested observers had an opinion
closer to LM's (Walpole, *Corr.* xx. 136).
As his second wife, Rawdon m. (1746)
Anne Hill (1716–51), da. of 1st Viscount
Hillsborough; and as his third he m.
(26 Feb. 1752) Elizabeth Hastings
(1731–1808), da. of 9th Earl of Huntingdon.

Dell tag after Madam to all Indifferent places, and stay at home together whenever she goes into Company where they would be troublesome.

I pity Lady F. M[eadows] if the Duke of K[ingston] marrys.[1] She will then know that her mean Compliances will appear as despicable to him as they do now to other people. Who would have thought that all her nice notions and pious meditations would end in being the Humble Companion of M[adame] de la Touche?[2] I do not doubt she has been forc'd to it by Necessity,[3] and is one proofe (amongst many I have seen) of what I allways thought, that no body should trust their Virtue with Necessity, the force of which is never known till it is felt, and it is therefore one of the first Dutys to avoid the Temptation of it. I am not pleading for Avarice, far from it; I can assure you I equally contemn Lady Carol: B[rand], who can forget she was born a Gentlewoman for the sake of Money she did not want.[4] That is indeed the only Sentiment that properly deserves the name of Avarice. A prudential care of one's affairs, or (to go farther) a desire of being in Circumstances to be usefull to one's Freinds, is not only excusable but highly laudable, never blam'd but by those who would persuade others to throw away their money in hopes to pick up a share of it. The greatest declaimers for disinterestness I ever knew have been capable of the vilest actions on the least view of profit, and the greatest instances of true Generosity given by those who were regular in their Expences and superiour to the vanitys in Fashion.—

I beleive you are heartily tir'd of my dull moralitys. I confess I am in very low spirits. It is hotter weather than has

[1] Lady Frances, the Duke's sister, lived with him and his mistress at Thoresby.

[2] Marie Thérèse de Fontaine (1712–65), illegitimate daughter of a Paris banker, m. (1729) Nicolas Vallet de La Touche. In 1736 she abandoned her husband to join the Duke in England; their liaison aroused much comment (Hélène Monod-Cassidy, *Un Voyageur-Philosophe au XVIIIe. Siècle: L'Abbé Jean-Bernard Le Blanc*, 1941, pp. 42–43; HMC *Denbigh MSS*, 1911, p.

120; *Lord Hervey and His Friends*, ed. Lord Ilchester, 1950, p. 258; HMC *15th Report*, iii, 1896, p. 158). In 1741 she renounced the Church of Rome for that of England, and became a naturalized British subject (Manvers MS 4098–4100).

[3] Philip Meadows, with whom Lady Frances had eloped in 1734, had an annual income of less than £900 (GEC, viii, 394, n. *e*).

[4] For her half-sister Lady Caroline's marriage, see above, p. 432, n, 1.

been known for some years, and I have got an abominable cold, ⟨which⟩ has drawn after it a troop of complaints I will not trouble you with reciteing. I hope all your Family are in good Health. I am humble Servant to Lord Bute. I give my Blessing to my Grand children and am ever your most affectionate Mother,

M. Wortley.

June 22. N.S.

Text W MS iii. 186–8   *Address* To The Rt Honble the Countess of Bute recommended to S. Child Esqr near Temple Bar London Angleterre [*in another hand*] Grosvenor Street

To Lady Oxford *23 June* [*1750*]

June 23rd N.S.

Dearest Madam,

I wrote a Letter to your Ladyship not long since; 'tis the first that I wish might never come to your hands, but as my Wishes seldom succeed I fear it will not fail to arrive safe, and give your good nature pain by imagining me in a worse state than I am. To say truth I was very unfit for writeing at all at that time, but my Impatience to express my Gratitude for yours would not suffer me to wait till my Health was more confirm'd, thinking also that perhaps it would never be so.

My illness was a Defluxion fallen on my Teeth and Gums, which I neglected at first as what I had us'd to be trouble'd with (thô never since I was abroad) and contented my selfe with the little remedys common for the Tooth ach, which had no effect. The pain daily encreasing for above a Month, in all which time I could eat nothing but spoon meat, I was at length persuaded to let the Surgeon of the village examine my Mouth. He happen'd to be an honest Man and of more skill than is usualy found in the Country. I saw him turn pale, which gave me a bad opinion of my Case, thô he did not explain it to me, but went away, and told every body he met that the Gangreen was already form'd, and he thought my recovery impossible.

One of my Neighbours (without my knowledge) took post Horses, and fetch'd from Cremona (a Large Town 25 mile from hence) the most celebrated Surgeon in all these parts. He arriv'd in a few hours. They then told me the Danger I was in, and I consented to let him use what Operations he pleas'd. He immediately apply'd red hot Irons to my Gumms, but said he could not have hopes of my Cure till 24 hours were past, my Tongue being infected and so swell'd that I could not utter one word, thô I was in perfect Memory and Senses.

It pleas'd God I slept very well that night, the pain being moderated as the Danger encreas'd. The Surgeon was much surpriz'd to find me next morning without any Fever, which he expected the apprehension would give me, in which case, he said, he thought it impossible to save me, but he now beleiv'd I should be able to bear the Caustics he was oblig'd to apply. I was under his Hands several days; he had left me but one before I wrote to your Ladyship. I am now able to eat every thing, and every day gathering strength. While God continues me in this World I shall ever be, Dearest Madam, your Ladyship's faithfully Devoted Servant,

M. W. Montagu.

Text Wh MS 507   *Address* To The Rt Honble the Lady Henrietta Countess of Oxford in Dover Street near St James's London Angleterre *End. by Lady Oxford* R: Bulstrode Sunday July 29th O:S: 1750

To Lady Bute *23 June* [*1750*]

June 23rd N.S.

Dear Child,

I have not heard from you a long Time, which gives me great uneasyness. Your Father wrote me word you expect to lye in this month.[1] I hope it is now over, but till I hear it is, I cannot be out of pain. I am recover'd of a very dangerous illness, in which I have suffer'd very much, but I thank God am now in good Health. I intend drinking the Waters again this Season, by which I found so much benefit the last year.

---

[1] Lady Caroline Stuart (d. 1813) was born on 28 May 1750, O.S.

I know not whither you have receiv'd some long Letters I have sent to you. It is very disagreable to be allways in doubt about them; and it is that Thought makes me tell you so soon that I am your affectionate Mother.

M. W. Montagu

My Compliments to Lord Bute and blessing to my Grand children.

Text W MS iii. 290–1   *Address* To The Rt Honble the Countess of Bute London [*in another hand*] in Grosvenors Street   *Postmark* PENY POST PAYD ⟨?⟩

To Lady Bute *13 July* [*1750*]

Brescia,[1] July 13. N.S.

Dear Child,

I am very uneasy at your continu'd Silence, fearing it is occasion'd by ill Health and hearing from your Father that you expected to lye in in June, of which I have yet had no account, thô I have wrote you many Letters. I have had a very severe sickness my selfe, but am now very well recover'd and intend in a few Days to drink the Waters of Louvere, from which I found so much benefit the last Year.

I send this by Mr. Anderson, hoping that it cannot fail comeing safe to you.[2] I shall repeat in it some things which I have allready said, but suppose my Letters have miscarry'd, having never had any Answer. I have often desir'd you to

[1] An aftermath to the investigation by the *Podestà* of LM's alleged imprisonment by Palazzi is recorded in her 'Italian Memoir': 'The Count went to Brescia, and returned two days later with a closed carriage that his mother sent me, begging me to come to her house to quieten all the false rumours which were still circulating, and which only my presence could suppress. The doctor assured me that I could make the journey without danger, and I made it, so weak that my maid held me up in the carriage. . . . So I was visited by a num-

ber of ladies and gentlemen; I laughed at the idea of being kept in Gottolengo by force, and it seemed very natural to me that a woman of my age should seek retirement, and so I told everyone I saw' (Wh MS 510, f. 15: transl.).

[2] John Anderson, formerly her son's tutor (see above, p. 249), arrived in Brescia about 10 July and was received by LM while she was staying in the Palazzi house (Contarini's report of 12 July 1750, Archivio di Stato, Venice).

enquire and let me know the price raw silk bears at London.
I also beg you would send me the third Volume of Campbel's
Architecture, accompany'd by any other Books that you think
will entertain me. My cheife Amusement is reading. I thank
God (notwithstanding so much illness) my Eyes yet serve me
very well without the help of Glasses. But I am much shock'd
at an accident that has happen'd in my own Family within
this few days. My Steward (who is a very faithfull good
Servant) had a defluxion falln on one of his Eyes, and without any Consultation was so indiscreet as to let blood, at one
time 32 ounces, which the Doctors say is the reason of the
Cataracts which are now suddenly form'd on both his Eyes,
and I fear he will be soon totally Blind. I am as much afflicted
from Compassion to the poor Man, as by the Inconvenience
I shall find in loseing his service. He is not much above forty
and may live long miserable. I think it impossible to be other
in that Circumstance, thô I shall take care for his subsistance.
   This minute I have receiv'd a Letter from you dated
March 20th. This is very provokeing; however, I beg you
would not be discourrag'd from writeing, no more than my
selfe. Mr. Anderson says 'tis the common Fate of Letters
wrote from Italy, and to say truth I begin to despair of seeing
it otherwaies. However, I shall never omit any oppertunity
of telling you ⟨that I⟩ am, Dear Child, Your most affectionate Mother,

M. Wortley.

My service to Lord Bute and blessing to my Grandchildren. Your Father speaks much of the Boys' Beauty.

Text W MS iii. 298–9   *Address* To The Rt Honble The Countess
of Bute

To Lady Oxford *13 July* [*1750*]

July 13

Dearest Madam,
   My last was so tedious a Melancholy Epistle I wish it
may have miscarry'd. Being now perfectly recover'd, I think

my selfe to blame for having trouble'd you with a Relation that may give pain to your Ladyship's good nature. The Doctors tell me I may expect a long continuance of good Health after so severe an illness. I cannot say I have great Confidence in their foresight, but at present I have no reason to complain.

I send this by one that was formerly Governour to my Son, who I hope will take care it is safely convey'd to your Ladyship.[1] He tells me that my Complaints of the post are common to all the Strangers in Italy. We live in a Country so expos'd, and for that reason so suspicious, that I beleive no Letters pass, till after several Examinations, through the different States, which occasions their being often lost and allways delaid. This day I have receiv'd one from my Daughter dated the 20th of March.

I intend in a few days to go to Louvere, having found so much benefit from drinking the Waters the last Year. I hope the Good air of Nottinghamshire contributes to your Ladyship's Health; that and every other Blessing to you is my most Zealous wish. I am very glad my Lord Titchfeild is so deserving a Youth; God long preserve him to you, and you to him.[2] This [is] the daily Praier of, Dearest Madam, Your Ladiship's ever faithfull and Obedient Humble Servant,

M. Wortley M.

Text Wh MS 507   *Address* To The Rt Honble the Lady Henrietta Countess of Oxford in Dover Street near St James's London   *End. by Lady Oxford* R: Welbeck Saturday Feby 16th O:S: 1750

To Wortley *13 July* [*1750*]

Brescia, July 13 N.S.

I came hither 2 days ago in my Journey to Louvere, where I intend to drink the Waters from which I receiv'd so much Benefit the last Year.

[1] Anderson delivered it to her London house (Lady Oxford to LM, 13/2 March 1751, Harley MS).

[2] William Henry Cavendish Bentinck (1738–1809), Marquess of Titchfield, later 3rd Duke of Portland, was Lady Oxford's grandson. In her letter of 18/7 April 1750 Lady Oxford had written of his recovery from a serious illness and of his 'industry and quickness at his Book'.

Mr. Anderson came to see me as he pass'd through this Town with a young Pupil. I was very glad to have an opportunity of writeing to you and my Daughter by a safe hand. I am out of Patience at the Irregularity of the post. I have this morning receiv'd one from her dated the 20th of March, in which she mentions several others that have never come to my Hands, and complains of my Silence, when I write at least once in a Fortnight. I am afraid all of mine to you have the same Fate, which Mr. Anderson tells me is common in Italy. I wrote you a long Criticism on Lord Bolingbroke's book, which I fear you never receiv'd. I do not mention it from the value I have for it, but as I would not neglect any desire of yours, you having seem'd Curious to know my Opinion of it.

I am very glad to hear of your good Health and heartily wish the long Continuance of it.

Text W MS ii. 201–2   *Address* To Edwd Wortley Esqr in Cavendish Square London Angleterre   *End. by W* Ad L.M. 13 Jul. 1750 brought by Mr. Anderson.   12 Feb. 1750/1 Recd

To Wortley *3 Sept.* [*1750*]

Louvere, Sept. 3. N.S.

I receiv'd yesterday yours dated June 24. I am very well persuaded that the delay of all my Letters and the loss of many is occasion'd by the posts in Italy. I receive none but what are carelessly reseal'd, and some of them quite open. I am not surpris'd at it, considering the present circumstances, of which I would give you the Detail if it was safe to do it. I have now chang'd the method of conveyance, sending this to the English Minister at Venice, who I have desir'd to put it in his pacquet.

On the Top of one of the highest Hills with which this Place is surrounded, here has been, 2 months since, accidentally discover'd a remarkable piece of Antiquitity [*sic*]: a stone Vault in which was the remains of a Human Body, a Table, a spoon and a knife, and about a Hundred pieces of coin, of a mix'd Metal, in none of which there is any legible Inscription.

Most of them with the rest of the things I have mention'd
are in the possession of the Parish Priest. I am endeavouring
to get them into mine. If I do, and you have any Curiosity to
see them, I will send them to you. It is certain there is no fraud
in this Discovery, the People here haveing no Notion of the
Value of any thing of this kind. I am of opinion it is a Gothic
antiquity, there being no Trace of any Inscription haveing
ever been on the Stone.

Direct your next recommandé au Chevalier James Gray,
Ministre de S[a] M[ajesté] Britanique a Venise.

Text W MS ii. 203–4   *Address* To Edwd Wortley Esqr in Cavendish Square London Angleterre   *End. by W* [*Summary*] Ad 3 Oct.
Sent from London 22 Sept.

To Lady Oxford *11 Oct.* [*1750*]

Oct. 11. N.S.

Dearest Madam,

I did not receive my usual Pleasure from the Honor of
your Ladyship's Letter,[1] finding in it that you are still tormented with returns of Cholical Pains; the Bath has been
generally a remedy for them, and I hope you will now try it.
Your Life may find much Happyness in the Society of your
deserving Family, and is so justly dear to them that I flatter
my selfe you will omit no care for the preservation of it. Mine
is too insignificant both to my selfe and others to be worth
much looking after; I would willingly avoid Pain, and I
thank God the Waters of Louvere have remov'd all my
Complaints and restor'd me to a degree of Strength I did not
expect. I have been retir'd to my Country Habitation allmost
a month, it being necessary to make that Journey before the
rains render it impracticable. Louvere is certainly one of
the prettyest places in the World, but the road to it one of the
worst I ever pass'd, being all over precipices, which I beleive
is one reason that makes it unknown to Travellers, thô very
well worthy their Curiosity.[2]

[1] Dated 22 Aug. 1750 [O.S.] (Harley
MS).
[2] LM has been called 'the discoverer
of the Lake of Iseo' (Evelyn Martinengo
Cesaresco, *Lombard Studies*, [1902],
p. 182).

I take the Liberty to beg your Ladyship would give my gratefull thanks to the Dutchess of Portland for her kind remembrance of me, with my best wishes for her continu'd Health and Prosperity; I hope you will both live to [see] all her young Family happily establish'd. I rejoice to hear Lord Titchfield's character so much to your Satisfaction; may every hour improve it! It is the Sincere and earnest Praier of, Dearest Madam, your Ladyship's ever faithfully Devoted Servant,

M. W. Montagu.

Text Wh MS 507   *Address* To The Rt Honble the Lady Henrietta Countess of Oxford in Dover Street near St James's London   *End. by Lady Oxford* R: Welbeck Saturday Novr 10th 1750 O:S:

To Lady Bute [*17 Oct. 1750*]

Dear Child,

I receiv'd yours of Aug't 25 this morning, Oct. 17 N.S. It was every way welcome to me, particularly finding you and your Family in good Health. You will think me a great Rambler, being at present far distant from the date of my last Letter. I have been persuaded to go to a Palace near Salo, situate on the vast Lake of Gardia, and do not repent my Pains since my arrival, thô I have pass'd a very bad road to it. It is indeed (take it altogether) the finest place I ever saw. The King of France has nothing so fine, nor can have in his Situation. It is large enough to entertain all his Court, and much larger than the Royal Palace of Naples, or any of those of Germany or England. It was built by the G[reat] Cosmo Duke of Florence, where he pass'd many months for several years, on the account of his Health, the Air being esteem'd one of the best in Italy.[1] All the offices and conveniencies are suitably magnificent, but that is nothing in regard to the Beauties without doors.

---

[1] On Lago di Garda. It was built in 1556 by the marchese Sforza Pallavicino —and not by Cosimo III, who visited it in 1668; by then it had come into the Martinenghi family (Cesaresco, *Lombard Studies,* pp. 91, 104, 112–14).

It is seated in that part of the Lake which forms an Amphitheatre, at the Foot of a Mountain near three mile high, cover'd with a Wood of Orange, Lemon, Citron and Pomgranate Trees, which is all cut into Walks, and divided into Terrasses, that you may go into a several garden from every Floor in the House, diversify'd with Fountains, Cascades, and Statues, and joyn'd by easy marble Staircases which lead from one to another. Here are many cover'd Walks, where you are secure from the Sun in the hottest part of the Day by the Shade of the Orange Trees, which are so loaded with Fruit you can hardly have any Notion of their Beauty without seeing them. They are as large as Lime trees in England. You will think I say a great deal; I will assure you I say far short of what I see, and you must turn to the Fairy Tales to give you any Idea of the real charms of this Enchanting Palace, for so it may justly be call'd. The Variety of the Prospects, the natural Beauties, and the Improvements by Art, where no cost has been spar'd to perfect it, render it the most compleat Habitation I know in Europe, while the poor present Master of it (to whose Ancestor the G[rand] Duke presented it, having built it on his land), having spent a noble Estate by Gameing and other Extravagance, would be glad to let it for a Triffle, and is not rich enough to live in it. Most of the fine Furniture is sold. There remains only a few of the many good pictures that adorn'd it, and such goods as were not easily to be transported, or for which he found no chapman.

I have said nothing to you of the magnificent Bath embellish'd with Statues, or the Fish ponds, the cheife of which is in the midst of the Garden to which I go from my Apartment on the first Floor. It is circle'd by a marble Balister and supply'd by Water from a cascade that proceeds from the Mouth of a Whale, on which Neptune is mounted, surrounded with Reeds. On each side of him are Tritons which from their Shells pour out Streams that augment the Pond. Higher on the Hill are 3 Collosal status of Venus, Hercules, and Apollo. The Water is so clear you see the numerous Fish that inhabit it, and 'tis a great pleasure to me to throw them bread, which they come to the surface to eat with great greediness. I pass by many other Fountains, not to make my Description too tedious.

You will wonder, perhaps, never to have heard any mention of this Paradice either from our English Travellers or in any of the printed Accounts of Italy. It is as much unknown to them as if it was guarded by a flameing Cherubim. I attribute that Ignorance in part to its being 25 mile distant from any post Town, and also to the Custom of the English of herding together, avoiding the Conversation of the Italians, who on their side are naturally reserv'd and do not seek Strangers. Lady Orford could give you some knowledge of it, having past the last six months she staid here in a House she hir'd at Salo,[1] but as all her time was then taken up with the melancholy Vapours her distresses had thrown her into, I question whither her Curiosity ever engag'd her to see this Palace, thô but halfe a mile from it.

Oct. 25.

I was intterupted in this part of my Letter by a visit from Count Martinenghi (master of this House) with his Son and 2 Daughters.[2] They staid till this morning, being determin'd to show me all the fine Places on this side the Lake to engage me to grow fond of staying here, and I have had a very pleasant progress in viewing the most remarkable Palaces within ten mile round. 3 from hence is the little Town of Maderna, where the last Duke of Mantua built a retreat worthy a Sovereign.[3] It is now in the Hands of a rich merchant who maintains it in all its Beauty. It is not halfe so large as that where I am, but perfectly proportion'd and uniform, from a Design of Palladio's, the Garden in the Style of Le Nôtre, and the furniture in the best Taste of Paris. I am allmost ready to confess it deserves the preference to this, thô built at far less expence. The Situations are as different as is possible when both of them are between a Mountain and the Lake. That under which the Duke of Mantua chose to build is much lower than this, and allmost steril. The prospect of it is rather melancholy than agreable; but the Palace,

---

[1] On the death of her father-in-law in 1745, Lady Walpole had become Countess of Orford. She had visited Salo in 1741 (Walpole, *Corr.* xvii. 196).

[2] By the will (1690) of Camillo Martinengo Cesaresco, the palazzo was entailed, and each heir had to bear or assume the name of Camillo (Cesaresco, pp. 107–8).

[3] The last Duke of Mantua, at whose death the duchy was annexed by Austria, was Ferdinando Carlo Gonzaga (1652–1708). But the palazzo at Maderno was built in 1660.

being plac'd at the foot of it, is a mile distant from the lake, which forms a sort of Peninsula halfe a mile broad, and 'tis on that is the delightfull Garden, adorn'd with Parterres, Espaliers, all sort of Exotic Plants, and ends in a Thick wood cut into rideings. That in the midst is large enough for a Coach and terminates at the lake, which appears from the Windows like a great canal made on purpose to beautify the prospect. On the Contrary, the Palace where I lodge is so near the Water that you step out of the Gate into the Barge, and the Gardens being all divided you cannot view from the House above one of them at a Time. In short, these two Palaces may in their different Beauties rival each other, while they are neither of them to be excell'd in any other part of the World.

I have wrote you a terrible long letter, but as you say you are often alone, it may serve you for halfe an hour's amusement. At least receive it as a proofe that there is none more agreable to me than giving assurances of my being (Dear Child) your most affectionate Mother,

M. Wortley M.

My Complements to Lord Bute and blessing to my Grand children.

Yours of Sept. 23rd is just this minute brought to me. I heartily wish you and my Lord Bute joy of his Place, and wish it may have more advantageous Consequences, but am glad you do not too much found Hopes on things of so much uncertainty.[1] I have read S[arah] Fielding's works, and should be glad to hear what is become of her.[2] All the other Books would be new to me, excepting Pamela, which has met with very extrodinary (and I think undeserv'd) success. It has been translated into French and into Italian.[3] It was all the Fashion at Paris and Versailles, and is still the Joy of the Chambermaids of all Nations.

[1] On 30 Sept. Bute 'kiss'd hands' as Lord of the Bedchamber to the Prince of Wales [at £600 p. a.] (George Bubb Dodington, *Political Journal*, ed. J. Carswell and L. A. Dralle, 1965, p. 280).

[2] LM had asked W to send Sarah Fielding's works (10 Jan. [1746]); and she is listed among the subscribers to Miss Fielding's *Familiar Letters between the Principal Characters in David Simple* (1747).

[3] *Pamela* was translated into French in 1741, and into Italian in 1744–6.

Direct the Books to the care of Sir James Gray, the English Minister at Venice.

Text W MS iii. 27–32   *Address* To The Rt Honble The Countess of Bute to be left wth Samuel Child Esqr near Temple Bar London Angleterre

To Lady Oxford *20 Nov.* [*1750*]

Dearest Madam,

I am extremely pleas'd I have at length found a method of hearing from your Ladyship in a shorter time than I have hitherto done, but am sorry to hear that you return to Welbeck without passing some time at the Bath, which us'd to be so advantageous to your Health. I need not repeat how dear that is to me. I wish you would be persuaded how valuable and necessary your Life is to your Family and all that know you. I am very glad my Lord Titchfield proves so much to your Ladyship's Satisfaction;[1] may every Year encrease it. I hear Lord Bute is of the Bed Chamber to the Prince; I hope it may prove yet more fortunate in its Consequence, thô Court Favor is as little to be depended on as fair weather at Sea. I begin to incline to your Ladyship's opinion that the Air of Gotolengo is not proper for me, and am seeking for some other place to reside, at least some part of the Year. I am at present in one of the finest places in Europe, which is to be let for a small Rent. I intend to morrow to go see another that is recommended me. Where-ever I am, I can never be other than, Dearest Madam, Your Ladyship's most oblig'd and most faithfull Humble Servant,

M. W. Montagu.[2]

Salo, Nov. 20. N.S.

Text Wh MS 507   *Address* To The Rt Honble the Lady Henrietta Countess of Oxford in Dover Street near St James's London   *End. by Lady Oxford* R: Welbeck Monday Decr 31st O:S: 1750

---

[1] In her letter of 22 Sept. O.S. Lady Oxford had written that her grandson was coming from Westminster School to dine in Dover Street (Harley MS).

[2] LM's next known letter to Lady Oxford is dated 1 June [1753] (vol. iii).

To Wortley *20 Nov.* [*1750*]

Nov. 20th N.S.

I receiv'd yours of Oct. 3rd much sooner than I have done any others of late, thô it had been also open'd. If I find any proper opertunity, I will write you a long letter, which I do not care to hazard by the post.

The great difference between this State and that of the Church has been slightly mention'd in the news papers. It is not yet thoroughly accomodated, thô much soften'd since I wrote.[1]

I am very glad of Lord Bute's good Fortune. I have wish'd my Daughter Joy in a long letter. I do not write so copiously to you, fearing it should be troublesome to your Eyes. I sent her some Italian Poetry that is much admir'd here.

The Continuation of your Health is my most fervent Desire and the news of it my greatest Pleasure.

Text W MS ii. 205–6   *Address* To Edwd Wortley Esqr in Cavendish Square London Angleterre   *Postmark* PENY POST PAYD ⟨?⟩ *End. by W* [*Summary*] Ad 31 Dec   Recd 29 Dec.

To Lady Bute [*24 Dec. 1750*]

Dear Child,

I receiv'd yours of Oct'r the 28th this morning, Dec. 24 N.S. I am afraid a letter of 2 sheets of paper that I sent you from Salo never came to your hands, which I am very sorry for; it would have been perhaps some entertainment, being the Description of Places that I am sure you have not found

---

[1] The controversy between Venice and the Papacy arose when the Pope agreed (in Nov. 1749) that an Austrian should be nominated bishop for the Austrian territory in the Venetian patriarchate. Considering this a loss of jurisdiction, Venice broke off diplomatic relations with Rome in Sept. 1750. The next month France agreed to mediate with the suggestion that the disputed region be divided into two separate bishoprics. Venice and the Papacy resumed relations in Feb. 1751 (Ludwig von Pastor, *The History of the Popes*, transl. E. F. Peeler, 1938–53, xxxvi. 98–103).

in any Book of Travels. I also made my hearty congratulations to Lord Bute and your selfe on his place, which I hope is an earnest of future advantages.

I desir'd you to send me all the Books of which you gave a catalogue, except H. Fielding's and his Sister's, which I have allready. I thank God my Taste still continues for the Gay part of reading; wiser people may think it triffling, but it serves to sweeten Life to me, and is, at worst, better than the Generallity of Conversation.[1]

I am extremely pleas'd with the account you give me of your Father's Health. His Life is the greatest Blessing that can happen to his Family.

I am very sincerely touched with the D[uches]s of Montagu's misfortune, thô I think it no reasonable cause for locking her selfe up.[2] Age and ugliness are as inseparable as heat and Fire, and I think it all one in what shape one's Figure grows disagreable. I remember the Princesse of Moldavia at Constantinople[3] made a Party of Pleasure the next day after loseing one of her Eyes, and when I wonder'd at her Philosophy, said she had more reason to divert her selfe than she had before. 'Tis true our climate is apt to inspire more melancholy Ideas. The enlivening Heat of the Sun continues the cheerfullness of Youth to the Grave with most people. I receiv'd a visit not long since from a Fair young Lady that had new lain in of her 19th child. In reality she is but 37, and has so well preserv'd her fine shape and complexion she appears little past twenty. I wish you the same good Fortune thô not quite so numerous a posterity. Every Happyness is ardently desir'd for you by (Dear Child) your most affectionate Mother,

M. Wortley M.

My Complements to Lord Bute and blessing to all your

---

[1] In Oct.–Nov. 1740 Lady Walpole remarked to Joseph Spence, 'I wonder how anybody can find any pleasure in reading the books which are Lady Mary's chief favourites! [romances and novels]' (*Anecdotes*, ed. J. M. Osborn, 1966, § 1559). Both ladies had been in Florence the summer of 1740.

[2] The Duchess had been at the 'Point of Death' in the summer of 1749, soon after the Duke's death (*Daily Advertiser*, 8 July 1749). Apparently she lost her eyesight (see below, p. 479).

[3] The reigning Prince of Moldavia from 1716 to 1725 was Michael Racovitza.

little ones. I am asham'd not to have sent my token to my God Daughter; I hope to do it in a short time.

Text W MS iii. 43–44   *Address* To The Rt Honble the Countess of Bute recommended to the care of Samuel Child Esqr near Temple Bar London Angleterre [*in another hand*] Grosvernors Street   *End. by W* L.M. to La. Bute 24 Dec. 1750.   On Ld Butes being made of the Princes Bedchamber.   Ds of Montagu's not appearing and an Old La. in Italy [*sic*] that lost an Eye.

To Lady Bute *11 Feb.* [*1751*]

Feb. 11. N.S.

Dear Child,

Thô I have not heard from you of a long time, I attribute it to the badness of the roads, which I suppose retards the post. If the Weather is proportionably severe in England, you must be halfe froze to Death. I repent very much leaveing of Salo, where the Snow never lyes two days, having been bury'd in it here this two months. I must now depend on you for all the English news I shall hear, the Dutch papers being no longer distributed. In the last I saw the Melancholy account of the Duke of Montross having lost his sight, a terrible misfortune to so young a Man![1] I bless God mine serves me yet without Glasses, and I still find my greatest Amusement in reading. This Carnival has afforded none at all, every body being confin'd where chance found them before Xmas.

I wish you would direct your Letters for me to Sir James Gray, the King's Minister at Venice. I beleive they will come sooner and safer to your most affectionate Mother,

M. Wortley M.

My Complements to Lord Bute and blessing to my Grand children.

Text W MS iii. 261–2   *Address* To The Rt Honble the Countess of Bute to be left with Samuel Child Esqr near Temple Bar London Angleterre [*in other hands*] Grosvenors Street [? Keandwood] *Postmark* PENNY POST PAID ⟨?⟩

[1] William Graham (1712–90), 2nd Duke of Montrose. Walpole also pitied him for his untimely blindness (*Letters*, ed. Mrs. P. Toynbee, 1903, xiii. 312).

To Wortley 11 Feb. [1751]

Feb. 11. N.S.

I have not heard from you of a long time. I hope your silence is not occasion'd by any Indisposition. My Daughter gave me the Satisfaction of letting me know you return'd from the North in good Health. I do not give you the trouble of long letters, fearing that reading of them might be uneasy to your Sight, but I write very largely to my Daughter, supposing she will communicate them to you.

The Snow that begun to fall here the last days of November is not yet off of the Ground. The roads are now scarce passable. This Weather is esteem'd a Prodigy in this Country. I begin almost to credit the Tradition in Herodotus, and beleive the World will once again change its Position, and Italy change Situation with Moscovy.[1] I have not stir'd out of my Apartment this two months, thô I have no reason to complain of my Health. The Continuation of yours is my most earnest wish.

Text W MS ii. 207–8   *Address* To Edwd Wortley Esqr in Cavendish Square London Angleterre   *Postmark* PENY POST PAYD TMO *End. by W* [*Summary*] Recd 26 Feb.

To Wortley [2 March 1751]

I receiv'd Yours of Dec. 31 but this morning, March 2nd N.S. I suppose the uncommon Severity of the Weather has occasion'd this long delay of its arrival. We have been bury'd in Snow near three months. The people here are as much surpriz'd at it as you could be at the Earthquake at London.[2] There was (for some time) no passing from one Market to Another, nor no possibillity of my setting a foot out of the

---

[1] Herodotus actually wrote: 'But were the stations of the seasons changed, so that the south wind and summer had their station where now the north wind and winter are set . . . the sun . . . would pass over the inland parts of Europe as he now passes over Libya' (*History*, transl. Loeb Library, i. 303–5).

[2] On 8 March 1750 (*Daily Advertiser*, 9 March).

House, which made me often repent my leaving Salo, where the Soil permits walking after any Rain. We are here in a deep Clay which thô very Advantageous to the Farmer is very dirty on the least Wet. I beleive Virgil had seen a storm on the Lake, by his Description,[1] which is terrible when ever it happens, but the Watermen are seldom mistaken in fore-seeing it, and being not naturally over venturesome, ill Accidents are rarer than on the Thames, thô the Body of Water being so large there is allwaies some little Swell like that on the Sea. It beats against the Wall of the Court belonging to the House where I lodg'd, and I did not think the noise of it disagreable.

I wish Lord Bute good Success in all his persuits. You and I know enough of Courts not to be amaz'd at any Turns they may take. Your Advice will be his best Guide, and I hope he will allwaies take it.

Text W MS ii. 227–8   *Address* To Edwd Wortley Esqr in Cavendish Square London Angleterre   *End. by W* [*Summary*] Recd 28 Mar. Ad 9 May.

To Lady Bute 2 *March* [*1751*]

March 2. N.S.

Dear Child,

I had the Happiness of a Letter from your Father last post, by which I find you are in good Health, thô I have not heard from you of a long time. This frequent Interuption of our Correspondance is a great uneasyness to me. I charge it on the neglect or irregularity of the post. I sent you a Letter by Mr. Anderson a great while ago,[2] to which I never had any Answer. Neither have I ever heard from him since, thô I am fully persuaded he has wrote concerning some little commissions I gave him. I should be very sorry he thought I

---

[1] Virgil describes the storm on Bena-cus (Lago di Garda) in the *Georgics*, ii. 159–64. Addison quoted and translated this passage in his *Remarks on Italy* (1705) and added: 'This lake perfectly resembles a sea, when it is worked up by storms' (*Misc. Works*, ed. A. C. Guthkelch, 1914, ii. 41).

[2] On 13 July 1750.

neglected to thank him for his Civillitys. I desire Lord Bute would enquire about him. I saw him in Company with a very pretty Pupil, who seem'd to me a promising Youth.[1] I wish he would fall in Love with my Grand Daughter. I dare say you laugh at this early design of provideing for her. Take it as a mark of my affection for you and yours, which is without any mixture of selfe Interest, since with my age and Infirmitys there is little probabillity of my living to see them establish'd. I no more expect to arrive at the Age of the Dutchess of Marlbrô[2] than to that of Methusalem, neither do I desire it. I have long thought my selfe useless to the World. I have seen one Generation pass away, and it is gone, for I think there are very few of those left that Flourish'd in my Youth.

You will perhaps call these melancholy Refflections; they are not so. There is a Quiet after the abandonning of Persuits, something like the rest that follows a Laborious Day. I tell you this for your Comfort. It was formerly a terrifying view to me that I should one day be an Old Woman; I now find that Nature has provided pleasures for every State. Those are only unhappy who will not be contented with what she gives, but strive to break through her Laws by affecting a perpetuity of youth, which appears to me as little desirable at present as the Babies do to you, that were the delight of your Infancy.—I am at the end of my paper, which shortens the Sermon of, Dear Child, your most affectionate Mother,

M. Wortley M.

Text W MS iii. 137–8 *Address* To The Rt Honble the Countess of Bute [*struck out*] to be left with Samuel Child Esqr near Temple Bar London Angleterre [*in another hand*] Grosvenor Street

To Lady Bute *2 April* [*1751*]

April 2.

My dear Child,

I am sorry for the uneasyness you were under on the account of Lord Bute's health, thô I hope it was over long

---

[1] Not identified.   [2] 84 years old at her death in 1744.

before I receiv'd the news of it. I wish many years continuance of the Happiness you possess in one another. It is what sweetens all the Accidents of Life, and can be made up by no other advantage where it is wanted. I dare swear you have examples enough amongst your Acquaintance to convince you that the greatest Affluence of Fortune is but a splendid wretchedness where there is no satisfaction at home.

I bought not long since the Pictures of the Prince and Princess which now adorn my Gallery. Hers does not do her Justice, but his represents him as naturally as a Looking Glass. They belong'd to a Gentleman Lately dead, who had been a sort of Favourite to the Duke of Saxa Gotha, who made a present of them to him, being copys of those sent from England to that Court.[1]

I have lately lost a Freind,[2] I may say the only one I had in this Country, to whom I had uncommon Obligations, having been sick two months in her House, in all which time she serv'd me with as much care as if I had been her Sister. This accident has touch'd me very sensibly. She was carry'd off in three days illness; thô I think it much happier than a lingering sickness, yet there is something shocking in observing the short interval between Life and Death.—These Refflections give a melancholy turn to my Letter, which should hasten the conclusion of it, being but an ill way of entertaining where I rather wish to give pleasure. In all humours I am your most affectionate Mother,

M. Wortley M.

My Complements to Lord Bute and blessing to our Children.

Direct your next recommendez a Mons. le Chevalier James Gray, Ministre de S[a] M[ajesté] Britanique a Venise.

Text W MS iii. 253–4   *Address* To The Rt Honble The Countess of Bute

---

[1] Augusta, Princess of Wales, was daughter of Frederick II (1676–1732), Duke of Saxe-Gotha (Isenburg, i. 49).

[2] Countess Palazzi, mother of LM's mysterious cavalier (see above, p. 375, n. 3).

To Wortley *15 April* [*1751*]

April 15. N.S.

I have receiv'd no Letter from you since that dated Dec. 31, which I answer'd immediately. The last I had from my Daughter gave me an Account of Lord Bute's illness. I hope he is recover'd, and am in pain about it, beleiving his Life in every sense necessary to her Happyness. My Health is better this Spring than it has been for some years past. The Doctors tell me I may expect it to continue so a considerable time after the severe illness I suffer'd the last Year. I hope you enjoy a more settle'd Health, and that you will find no ill consequence from that complaint of your Eyes which you mention. I extremely pity the Dutchess of Montagu for the loss of Hers. I wonder if any body is malicious enough to refflect the Duke of Shrewsbury lost one of his exactly in the same manner, as I have heard.[1]

I will send you a long letter of my Observations here the first convenient Oppertunity. In the mean time perhaps it will be some amusement to you to hear of a Phenomenon which I think really deserves that name. It was a single blast of Wind which overturn'd some houses, damag'd several others, and rooted up near a hundred large trees, almost in a direct Line, without ⟨to⟩uching any thing on either hand, ⟨and⟩ lasted so short a time that ⟨the⟩ People who had their Houses unroof'd had not time to be frighten'd, it being over almost as soon as they perceiv'd it, and the rest of the Town did not so much as know it. It happen'd at noon. I will send a particular account of all its effects if you are curious to know it.

Text W MS ii. 209–10   *Address* To Edwd Wortley Esqr in Cavendish Square London Angleterre   *Postmark* PENNY POST PAID TR⟨?⟩
End. by W [*Summary*] I omitted to mention the Receipt of this in mine of 24 June.   Recd 11 May

[1] Charles Talbot (1660–1718), 1st Duke of Shrewsbury, had been very handsome, but as a young man contracted a disease of the eyes, and lost one of them (T. C. Nicholson and A. S. Turberville, *Charles Talbot, Duke of Shrewsbury*, 1930, p. 20). He was rumoured to have been a lover of the Duchess's mother (ibid., p. 43, n. 1).

To Lady Bute [*April 1751*]

My Dear Child,

'Tis impossible to tell you to what degree I share with you in the misfortune that has happen'd.[1] I do not doubt your own reason will suggest to you all the alleviations that can serve on so sad an occasion, and will not trouble you with the common place Topics that are us'd (gennerally to no purpose) in Letters of Consolation. Disapointments ought to be less sensible at my Age than yours, yet I own I am so far affected by this that I have need of all my Philosophy to support it. However, let me beg of you not to indulge a useless Greife to the prejudice of your Health, which is so necessary to your Family. Every thing may turn out better than you expect. We see so darkly into Futurity, we never know when we have a real cause to rejoice or lament. The worst appearances have often happy Consequences, as the best lead many times into the greatest misfortunes. Human prudence is very straitly bounded. What is most in our power (thô little so) is the disposition of our own Minds. Do not give way to melancholy; seek amusements. Be willing to be diverted, and insensibly you will become so. Weak people only place a merit in affliction. A gratefull remembrance, and what ever honor we can pay to their memory, is all that is owing to the Dead. Tears and Sorrow are no Dutys to them, and make us incapable of those we owe to the living.

I give you thanks for your care of my Books. I yet retain, and carefully cherish, my taste for reading. If relais of Eyes were to be hir'd like post horses, I would never admit any but silent Companions. They afford a constant variety of Entertainment, and is allmost the only one pleasing in the Enjoiment and inoffensive in the Consequence. I am sorry ⟨your⟩ Sight will not permit you a great use of it. The prattle of your little ones and Freindship of Lord Bute will supply the place of it. My Dear Child, endeavor to raise your Spirits,

---

1 Frederick, Prince of Wales, died on 31/20 March 1751; this ended Bute's appointment and power as First Lord of the Bedchamber.

and beleive this advice comes from the tenderness of your most affectionate Mother,

M. Wortley.

My complements and sincere condoleance to Lord Bute.

Text W MS iii. 68–69   *Address* To The Rt Honble the Countess of Bute recommended to the care of Samuel Child Esqr near Temple Bar London Angleterre

To Wortley *8 May* [*1751*]

I am very much concern'd for the Death of the Prince, which I fear will have an ill effect on my Daughter's affairs. Many people will be sufferers on this occasion, perhaps a great Number of Creditors.[1] If Mr. Littleton remembers his Dispute with me on the first separation of the Roial Family,[2] he will now think my Opinion not so absurd, that all Debt should be avoided, it being possible for a young Man to die before his Father. I suppose Prince George[3] will have a Household fix'd, and methinks his Father's Servants should have the Preference. However that is, the Disapointment must still be great to Lord Bute; I do not doubt his Hopes were very high.

Nescia Mens hominum fati, sortisque futuræ.[4]

As I have a good opinion of his Honesty, I think it a national misfortune that he has lost the prospect of having a share in the Confidence of a King. My Daughter will probably regret the pleasures of a Court, and yet more the advantages she might expect for her Children. I am very sorry she is going to encrease their Number, being persuaded it cannot be without Danger to her. I return you many thanks for your Generosity to her, which she has acquainted me with. Above all things, I recommend to you the Care of your own Health.

[1] The Prince had accumulated vast debts in the expectation of his succession.

[2] George Lyttelton, later 1st Baron, supported the Opposition centred on the Prince of Wales. In 1737 the Prince was evicted from St. James's Palace by his parents for disobeying them.

[3] The future George III (1738–1820).

[4] 'O mind of man, knowing not fate or coming doom' (*Aeneid*, x. 501; transl. Loeb Library).

I beleive your own Judgment preferable to any Physician's. We see daily instances of their mistakes. Here is now a reigning Distemper they know not what to make of. People are taken with a pain in the side and car⟨ried⟩ off in a few Days. I fancy it is owing to the uncommon Rains, which still continue. The Inundations of the Rivers have done great Damage, and are yet unpassable in most places.

May 8. N.S.

Text W MS ii. 211–12   *Address* To Edwd Wortley Esqr recommended to the care of Samuel Child Esqr near Temple Bar London Angleterre   *End. by W* [*Summary*] Ad 23 June.   Recd 17 June.

To Wortley *24 May* [*1751*]

May 24 N.S.

I can no longer resist the desire I have to know what is become of my Son. I have long suppress'd it, from a beleife that if there was any thing of good to be told, you would not fail to give me the pleasure of hearing it.[1] I find it now grows so much upon me that whatever I am to know, I think it would be easier for me to support than the Anxiety I suffer from my Doubts. I beg to be inform'd, and prepare my selfe for the worst with all the Philosophy I have. At my time of Life I ought to be detach'd from a World which I am soon to leave. To be totally so is a vain Endeavor, and perhaps there is Vanity in the Endeavor. While we are Human we must

[1] As secretary to his cousin Sandwich at Aix-la-Chapelle, young Montagu had not been of much help because of his poor handwriting and untrustworthy character (Richard Lodge, *Studies in Eighteenth-Century Diplomacy 1740–1748*, 1930, pp. 325, 363). After visiting Paris to meet his father, he returned to London, where as an M.P. he was immune from arrest for debt. He was nominated on 1 March, and elected on 31 May 1750, to the Royal Society (R.S. MS Certificates 1731–50, f. 422). After another excursion to France, in Feb. 1751 he made a sensational reappearance in London, duly reported by Walpole: 'Our greatest miracle is Lady Mary Wortley's son, whose adventures have made so much noise: his parts are not proportionate, but his expense is incredible. His father scarce allows him any thing: yet he plays, dresses, diamonds himself, even to distinct shoe buckles for a frock, and has more snuff-boxes than would suffice a Chinese idol with an hundred noses' (*Corr.* xx. 226).

Submit to Human Infirmitys, and suffer them in Mind as well as Body. All that Refflection and Experience can do is to mitigate, we can never extinguish, our passions. I call by that Name every Sentiment that is not founded upon Reason, and own I cannot justifye to mine the Concern I feel for one who never gave me any view of Satisfaction.

This is too melancholy a Subject to dwell upon. You complement me on the continuation of my Spirits. 'Tis true I try to maintain them by every Art I can, being sensible of the terrible Consequences of loseing them. Young People are too apt to let theirs sink on any Disapointment. I have wrote to my Daughter all the considerations I could think on to lessen her Affliction. I am persuaded you will advise her to Amusements, and am very glad you continue that of Travelling, as the most usefull for Health.[1]

I have been Prisoner here some Months by the Weather. The Rivers are still unpassable in most places. When they are abated I intend some little Excursions, being of your Opinion that Exercise is as necessary as Food, thô I have (at present) no considerable Complaint. My Hearing and, I think, my Memory are without any Decay, and my Sight better than I could expect. It still serves me to read many hours in a day. I have appetite enough to relish what I eat, and have the same sound unintterupted Sleep that has continu'd through the Course of my Life, and to which I attribute the Happyness of not yet knowing the Head Ach. I am very Sorry you are so often trouble'd with it, but Hope from your care and temperance that if you cannot wholly overcome it, yet it may be so far diminish'd as not to give you any Great Uneasyness or affect your Constitution.

Text W MS ii. 213–14   *Address* To Edwd Wortley Esqr recommended to the care of Samuel Child Esqr near Temple Bar London Angleterre   *End. by W [Summary]* Ad 29 Sept./10 Oct.   Recd 28 Aug./8 Sept. at Vienna.

[1] On this journey, as his endorsement shows, W went to Vienna.

To Lady Bute *19 June* [*1751*]

June 19 N.S.

My dear Child,

I receiv'd yesterday yours of May 16th, in which was enclos'd the Captain's bill for the Box. I am much oblig'd to Lord Bute for thinking of me so kindly. To say truth, I am as fond of Baubles as ever, and am so far from being asham'd of it, it is a Taste I endeavor to keep up with all the art I am mistrisse of. I should have despis'd them at twenty for the same reason that I would not eat Tarts or cheese cakes at 12 year old, as being too childish for one capable of more solid Pleasures. I now know (and alas, have long known) all things in this World are almost equally triffling, and our most serious projects have scarce more Foundation than those Edifices that your little ones raise in cards. You see to what Period the vast Fortunes of the Duke and D[uches]s of Marlbrô and Sir R. Walpole are soon arriv'd. I beleive, as you do, that Lady Orford is a joyful Widow, but am persuaded she has as much reason to weep for her Husband as ever any Woman has had, from Andromache to this day. I never saw any second Marriage that did not appear to me very ridiculous. Hers is accompany'd with Circumstances that render the Folly compleat.[1]

Sicknesses have been very Fatal in this Country as well as England. I should be glad to know the names of those you say are deceas'd. I beleive I am ignorant of halfe of them, the Dutch News being forbid here. I would not have you give your selfe the trouble, but order one of your Servants to transcribe the Catalogue. You will perhaps laugh at this Curiosity. If you ever return to Bute, you will find that what happens in the World is a considerable Amusement in Solitude. The people I see here make no more impression on my Mind than the Figures in the Tapestry. While they are directly before my Eyes, I know one is cloath'd in blue and another in red, but out of sight they are so entirely out

[1] Within two months of the death of her estranged husband, Lady Orford m. (25 May 1751) Sewallis Shirley, with whom she had been living. They separated three years later.

of memory I hardly remember whither they are Tall or short. I sometimes call my selfe to account for this Insensibillity, which has something of Ingratitude in it, this little Town thinking themselves highly honnour'd and oblig'd by my residence. They intended me an extrodinary mark of it, having determin'd to set up my Statue in the most conspicuous Place. The marble was bespoke and the Sculptor bargain'd with before I knew any thing of the matter, and it would have been erected without my knowledge if it had not been necessary for him to see me to take the Resemblance. I thank'd them very much for the Intention, but utterly refus'd complying with it, fearing it would be reported (at least in England) that I had set up my own Statue. They were so obstinate in the Design, I was forc'd to tell them my Religion would not permit it. I seriously beleive it would have been worshipp'd (when I was forgotten) under the name of some Saint or other, since I was to have been represented with a Book in my Hand, which would have pass'd for a proofe of canonization.

This complement was certainly founded on reasons not unlike those that first fram'd Goddesses, I mean being usefull to them, in which I am second to Ceres. If it be true she taught the art of sowing Wheat, it is sure I have learn'd them to make Bread, in which they continu'd in the same Ignorance Misson complains of (as you may see in his Letter from Padua).[1] I have introduce'd French rolls, custards, minc'd Pies, and Plumb pudding, which they are very fond of. 'Tis impossible to bring them to conform to Sillabub, which is so unnatural a mixture in their Eyes, they are even shock'd to see me eat it. But I expect Immortality from the Science of Butter makeing, in which they are become so skillfull from my Instructions, I can assure you here is as good as in any part of Great Brittain. I am afraid I have bragg'd of this before,[2] but when you do not answer any part of my Letters I suppose them lost, which exposes you to some repetitions. Have you receiv'd that I wrote on my first notice of the Prince's Death?

[1] 'Le pain est comme de la terre, quoique fort blanc & de bonne farine: c'est qu'on ne le sçait pas faire. . . .' (Maximilien Misson, *Voyage d'Italie*, 1691, ed. 1743, i. 191). LM owned a copy of the 5th ed., 1722 (Sotheby Catalogue, 1 Aug. 1928, p. 92).

[2] Above, p. 447.

I shall receive Lord Bute's china with great Pleasure.

The Pearl Necklace for my God Daughter has been long pack'd up for her; I wish I could say sent. In the mean time give her, and the rest of yours, my Blessing. With Thanks and Compliments to Lord Bute from your most affectionate Mother,

M. Wortley M.

I desire you would order the china to be pack'd ⟨and sent by a⟩ skillfull Man of the Trade, or I shall receive it in pieces.

Text W MS iii. 49–51   *Address* To The Rt Honble the Countess of Bute recommended to Samuel Child Esqr near Temple Bar London Angleterre

To Wortley *20 June* [*1751*]

June 20th N.S.

I receiv'd yours of May the 9th yesterday with great Satisfaction, finding in it an Amendment of your Health. I am not surpris'd at Lady Orford's Folly, having known her at Florence.[1] She made great Court to me. She has parts and a very engageing manner; her Company would have amus'd me very much, but I durst not indulge my selfe in it, Her Character being in universal Horror. I do not mean from her Galantrys, which no body trouble'd their Heads with, but she had a Collection of Free thinkers that met weekly at her House to the Scandal of all Good Christians.[2] She invited me to one of those Honorable Assemblys, which I civilly refus'd, not desiring to be thought of her Opinion, nor thinking it right to make a Jest of Ordinances that are (at least) so far Sacred as they are absolutely necessary in all Civiliz'd Governments, and it is being in every sense an Enemy to Mankind to endeavor to over throw them.

Tar Water is arriv'd in Italy. I have been ask'd Several

---

[1] Lady Pomfret's diary during the two months that LM stayed with her in Florence (in 1740) records more than ten visits with Lady Walpole, either at the Palazzo Ridolfi or at Lady Walpole's house (Finch MS).

[2] For her character as a free-thinker, see iii. 4 and n. 3.

Questions concerning The use of it in England.¹ I do not find it makes any great progress here. The Doctors confine it to a possibillity of being usefull in the Case of inward ulcers, and allow it no farther merit. I told you sometime ago the method in this Country of makeing it the Interest of the Physician to keep the Town in good Health.² I wish that, and the Roman Law concerning last Testaments,³ were imported for the good of England. I know no foreign Fashion or Quackery that would be so usefull am⟨ong⟩st us. I have wrote a long Letter to my Daughter this post. I cannot help fearing for Her. Time ⟨and⟩ Distance has encreas'd and not diminish'd my tenderness for her. I own it is stronger than my Philosophy; my reason agrees with Atticus, but my passions are the same with Tully's.⁴

Text W MS ii. 215–16   *Address* To Edwd Wortley Esqr recommended to Samuel Child Esqr near Temple Bar London Angleterre *End. by W* [*Summary*] Ad 29 Sept./10 Oct.   Recd 28 Aug./8 Sept. at Vienna.

To Lady Bute [*23 July 1751*]

Dear Child,

I receiv'd yesterday, July 22 N.S., yours of June 2nd. I own I could not help regretting the D[uchess] of Montagu⁵ (with whom I have pass'd many agreable hours) thô I think I am in the wrong in so doing, being persuaded her Life was grown burdensome to her, and I beleive she would not own her selfe in danger to avoid the remedys that would have been press'd upon her. I am not surpriz'd at Lady Orford's marriage. Her money was doubtless convenient to Mr. Shirley,⁶ and I dare swear she piques her selfe on not being

---

¹ LM mentions it above, p. 397.

² See above, p. 423.

³ All children, male and female, had equal rights in family property under early Roman law.

⁴ The published correspondence between Atticus and his friend Cicero reflects their contrasting temperaments. LM elsewhere expresses her admiration

for Atticus (iii. 64).

⁵ She died on 14 May 1751.

⁶ Sewallis Shirley (1709–65), son of 1st Earl Ferrers (*Stemmata Shirleiana*, 1873, p. 173). They separated because she refused to allow him 'something independant' (George Bubb Dodington, *Political Journal*, ed. J. Carswell and L. A. Dralle, 1965, p. 280).

able to refuse him any thing; it has been her way with all her Lovers. He is the most creditable of any she ever had. His Birth and sense will induce him to behave to her with Decency, and it is what she has not been much us'd to. As it is a true saying, *Cowards more blows than any Hero bear*,[1] it is as certainly true, Ladies of pleasure (very improperly so call'd) suffer more mortifications than any Nun of the most austere order that ever was instituted. Lady O[rford] is a shineing instance of that Truth; the most submissive Wife to the most Tyranic Husband that ever was born, is not such a slave as I saw her at Florence.[2] I have hardly ever seen Engagements of that sort on another footing. Contempt is joyn'd with Satiety in those Cases, and there are few Men that do not indulge the Malignity that is in Human Nature, when they can do it (as they fancy) justifiably.

I have had a return, thô in a less degree, of the Distemper I had last year, and am afraid I must return to the Waters of Louvere. The Journey is so disagreable I would willingly avoid it, and I have little taste for the Diversions of the place.

Aug't 1. Thus far of my Letter was wrote at Gotolengo, and it is concluded at Louvere, where the Doctors have dragg'd me. I find much more company than ever I have done by these Waters, as I formerly did by those at Islington.[3] You may remember when I first carry'd you there we scarce saw any but our selves, and in a short time we could hardly find room for the croud. I arriv'd but last night, so can say nothing of my Success in relation to my Health. I must end my Letter in a Hurry. Here is Company, and I can only say I am ever your ⟨most⟩ affectionate Mother,

M. Wortley.

Text W MS iii. 52–53   *Address* To The Rt Honble the Co⟨untess of Bute⟩ recommended to the ⟨care of⟩ Samuel Child Esqr near Te⟨mple Bar London⟩ Angleterre [*in another hand*] Grosvenor Street

---

[1] John Sheffield, Duke of Buckingham's *Essay on Satire* (1675), line 232.

[2] Her lover in Florence was comte de Richecourt (1694–1759), vice-president of the Council of Regency there (Walpole, *Corr.* xvii. 24, n. 9). Richecourt snubbed her publicly in a manner Walpole called 'shocking, brutal, and villainous'; Mann remarked that she didn't mind (*Corr.* xvii. 45, 53).

[3] A spa since the 1680's.

To Wortley *1 Aug.* [*1751*]

Louvere, Aug't 1.

I have not heard from You of sometime, thô I have wrote twice or thrice. I hope your Silence is not occasion'd by ill Health, my Daughter not mentioning it in a Letter I receiv'd from her. She tells me Lord Bute designs me a present of English China. I would not refuse it, fearing he might take [it] ill, and yet I would not receive a Letter [or] a present from him without returning it. I wish you would tell me what would be acceptable.

The Doctors have forc'd me to these Waters. I arriv'd but last night, so can say nothing of their Effect in regard to my Health. I think the Journey has done me some service.

I am forbid to write much. I hope you continue well, which is my most earnest Wish.

Text W MS ii. 217–18   *Address* To Edwd Wortley Esqr in Cavendish Square   recommended to S. Child Esqr near Temple Bar London Angleterre   *End. by W* [*Summary*]Recd at Vienna 27 Sept./8 Oct. Ad 29 Sept./10 Oct.

To Lady Bute *10 Sept.* [*1751*]

Louvere, Sept. 10. O.S.

Dear Child,

I am much oblig'd to your Father for showing you my Letter,[1] being persuaded he meant kindly to me, thô it was not wrote with the intention of being shown. It is not the first time I have made him the same declaration of my Opinion of Lord Bute's Character, which has ever been my Sentiment, and had I thought differently I would never have given my consent to your marriage, notwithstanding your Inclination, to which (however) I thought it just to pay a great regard.[2] I have seldom been mistaken in my first

---

[1] Probably that of 8 May [1751].   was similar (see above, p. 290).
[2] In 1742 LM's opinion, sent to W,

judgment of those I thought it worth while to consider, and when (which has happen'd too often) Flattery or the persuasions of others has made me alter it, Time has never fail'd to show me I had done better to have remain'd fix'd in my first (which is ever the most unprejudice'd) Idea.

My Health is so often disorder'd that I begin to be as weary of it as mending old Lace; when it is patch'd in one place it breaks in another. I can expect nothing better at my time of Life, and will not trouble you with talking any more about it.

If the new Servant of the Princesse is the Misse Pit I knew, I am sorry for it. I am afraid I know her very well; and yet I fancy 'tis a younger sister, since you call her Anne, and I think the name of my Acquaintance was Mary. She I mean left France a small time before I went thither.[1]

I have some Curiosity to know how pious Lady Ferrers[2] behaves to her new Daughter-in-law. My Letter is cut short by the Arrival of Company. They wait while I tell you I am allwaies Your most affectionate Mother.

M. Wortley

My Complements to Lord Bute and blessing to your little ones, who I hope are recover'd by this time of their troublesome distemper.

I recollect my selfe; I was mistaken in Mrs. Pit's name; it is Anne. She has Wit but———[3]

Text W MS iii. 309–10   *Address* To The Rt Honble the Countess of Bute recommended to the care of Samuel Child Esqr near Temple Bar London Angleterre

[1] Mary (1725–82) was the youngest of the Pitt sisters. Anne (1712–81) was appointed, in June 1751, Keeper of the Privy Purse to the Princess of Wales and superintendent of the education of Princess Augusta. She had lived in France in the early 1740's (Lord Rosebery, *Lord Chatham, His Early Life and Connections,* 1910, pp. 47–48, 79).

[2] Selina Finch (1681–1762) m. (1699) 1st Earl Ferrers (d. 1717). Her son Sewallis Shirley had recently married the Dowager Lady Orford.

[3] As Walpole summarized her earlier career at Court: 'being of an intriguing and most ambitious nature, she soon destroyed her own prospect by an impetuosity to govern her mistress, and by embarking in other Cabals at that Court. Her disgrace followed' (*Mem. of George III,* 1845, i. 66).

To Wortley *10 Sept.* [*1751*]

Louvere, Sept. 10. N.S.

The same day I receiv'd yours of June 23 I had one from my Daughter that tells me you are set out for Lorrain. I heartily wish your Journey may have a good Effect on your Health. Mine is very infirm at present, thô (as I am told) not at all in a dangerous State, but I have a complaint which is entirely new to me, and if I did not hope to get rid of it, my Life would be burdensome to me. I mean Deafness, of which I never had the least degree till within these few weeks. They call it Vapours and say Steel Waters are the only remedy for it. Hitherto I have found little benefit from them. I am forbid writeing, which shortens your trouble in reading this Dull Letter.

Text W MS ii. 219–20   *Address* To Edwd Wortley Esqr recommended to the care ⟨of⟩ Samuel Child Esqr near Temple ⟨Bar⟩ London Angleterre   *End. by W* [*Summary*] Ad 25 Nov. O.S.   Recd on my Arrival from Abroad 12 Nov. O.S.

To Lady Bute *1 Nov.* [*1751*]

Louvere, Nov. 1.

Dear Child,

I receiv'd yours of Aug't 25, and my Lord Bute's obliging notice of your safe delivery, at the same time. I wish you joy of your young Son,[1] and of every thing else. You do not mention your Father, by which I suppose he is not return'd to England, and am in pain for his Health, having heard but once from him since he left it, and know not whither he has receiv'd my Letters. I dare say you need not be in any doubt of his good opinion of you. For my part, I am so far persuaded of the goodness of your Heart, I have often had a mind to write you a consolatory epistle on my own Death, which I

---

[1] Frederick (17 Sept. 1751–1802), no doubt named after the late Prince of Wales. He became the black sheep of the family (History of Parliament, *House of Commons 1754–1790*, ed. L. Namier and J. Brooke, 1964, iii. 500).

beleive will be some affliction, thô my Life is wholly useless
to you. That part of it which we pass'd together you have
reason to remember with Gratitude, thô I think you misplace
it. You are no more oblig'd to me for bringing you into the
World than I am to you for comeing into it, and I never
made use of that common place (and like most common
place, False) argument, as exacting any return of affection.
There was a mutual necessity on us both to part at that time,
and no obligation on either side. In the care of your Infancy
there was so great a mixture of Instinct, I can scarce even
put that in the number of the proofes I have given you [of]
my Love; but I confess I think it a great one, if you compare
my after conduct towards you with that of other Mothers,
who generally look on their children as devoted to their
Pleasures, and bound by Duty to have no Sentiments but
what they please to give them: playthings at first, and afterwards the Objects on which they may exercise their Spleen,
Tyranny, or ill Humour. I have allways thought of you in
a different manner. Your Happiness was my first wish and
the persuit of all my Actions, divested of all selfe interest. So
far I think you ought, and beleive you do, remember me as
your real Freind. Absence and Distance have not the power
to lessen any part of my tenderness for you, which extends to
all yours, and I am ever Your most affectionate Mother,

M. Wortley.

I send no Complements to Lord Bute, having wrote to
him this post.

Text W MS iii. 33–34   *Address* To The Rt Honble the Countess of
Bute recommended to the care of Samuel Child Esqr near Temple
Bar London Angleterre

To Wortley *10 Nov.* [*1751*]

Nov. 10th N.S.

I receiv'd yours of Oct. 10 this day, which is much
quicker than any I ever had from England.

I will not make any refflections on the conduct of the

person you mention; 'tis a subject too melancholy to us both.[1] I am of opinion taillying at Bassette is a certain revenue (even without cheating) to those that can get constant punters, and are able to submit to the Drudgery of it, but I never knew any one persue it long and preserve a Tolerable Reputation.

The news of the recovery of your Health makes me amends for the displeasure of hearing his ill Figure. I have often read and been told that the Air of Hungary is better and the Inhabitants in general longer liv'd than in any other part of Europe. You have given me a very surprizing Instance of it, far surpassing in Age the old Woman of Louvere, thô in Some circumstances I think her story as extrodinary. She dy'd but ten years ago and is well remember'd by the Inhabitants of that Place, the most Creditable of which have all assur'd me of the Truth of the Following Facts. She kept the greatest Inn there till past 50; her Husband then dying and she being rich, she left off that Trade, and having a large House with a great deal of Furniture, she let Lodgings, which her Daughters (2 maids past 70) still continue. I lodg'd with them the first year of my going to these Waters. She liv'd to 100 with good Health, but in the last 5 years of it fell into the decays common to that Period, dimness of Sight, loss of Teeth and Baldness; but in her Hundreth Year her sight was totally restor'd, she had a new set of Teeth and a fresh Head of Brown Hair. Her Daughters assur'd me she had also another mark of youth that generally happens to Girls of 15. This last Article I never heard from any but them. I mention'd it to several Ladys who none of them had heard it, but the rest was confirm'd to me by every body. She liv'd in this renew'd vigour ten years, and had then her Picture drawn, which has a vivacity in the Eyes and Complexion that would become five and twenty, tho' by the Falls in the Face one may discern it was drawn for a very old Person. She dy'd meerly of an Accident which would have kill'd any other, tumbling down a very bad stone staircase

---

[1] In his letter (from Vienna) W evidently wrote about their son's new exploits: after going about London that summer with a young woman of questionable reputation he married her (bigamously) in July, and then with her and two men went to Paris, where he set up as a gambler (Jonathan Curling, *Edward Wortley Montagu*, 1954, pp. 123–30).

which goes into the Cellar. She broke her Head in such a manner she liv'd but two days. The Physician and Surgeon that attended her told me her Age no way contributed to her Death.

I enquir'd whither there was any Singularity in her Diet, but heard of none, excepting that her Breakfast was every Morning a large Quantity of Bread sopp'd in cold Water. The common Food of the Peasants in this Country is the Turkish Wheat you mention,[1] which they dress in various manners, but use little milk, it being chieffly reserv'd for cheese or the Tables of the Gentry. I have not observ'd either amongst the poor or rich that in General they live longer than in England. This Woman of Louvere is allways spoke of as a Prodigy, and [I] am surpriz'd she is neither call'd Saint nor Witch, being very prodigal of those Titles. I return you many thanks for the length of your entertaining Letter, but am very sorry it was troublesome to you. I wish the reading of this may not be so.

I will seek for a picture for Lord Bute.[2]

Text W MS ii. 221–4   *Address* To Edwd Wortley Esqr to be left with Samuel Child Esqr near Temple Bar London Angleterre   *End. by W* Sons Tallying at Bassette. [*Summary*] Recd 9 Dec. O.S. Ad 30 Jan.

To Lady Bute 8 Dec. [1751]

Dec. 8.

My Dear Child,

I receiv'd yours of Oct. 24 yesterday, which gave me great pleasure by the account of the good Health of you and yours; I need not say how near that is to my Heart. I had the Satisfaction of an Entertaining Letter from your Father out of Germany, by which I find he has had both Benefit and amusement from his Travells. I hope he is now with you.

I find you have many wrong notions of Italy, which I do

---

[1] Indian corn made into flour (Smollett, *Travels through France and Italy*, 1766, Letter 8).

[2] Apparently W's suggestion for repaying Bute for his intended present of English china (see above, p. 489).

not wonder at. You can take your Ideas of it only from Books
or Travellers. The first are generally antiquated or confin'd
to Trite Observations, and the other yet more superficial.
They return no more instructed than they might have been
at home by the help of a Map. The Boys only remember
where they met with the best Wine or the prettyest Women,
and the Governors (I speak of the most learned amongst
them) have only remark'd Situations and Distances, or at most
Status and Edifices. As every Girl that can read a French Novel
and Boy that can conster a Scene in Terence fancys they
have attain'd to the French and Latin Languages, when God
knows it requires the Study of a whole Life to acquire a
perfect knowledge of either of them, so after a Tour (as they
call it) of three years round Europe, people think themselves
qualify'd to give exact accounts of the Customs, Policys and
Interests of the Dominions they have gone through post,
when a very long stay, a diligent Enquiry, and a nice Observation are requisite even to a moderate degree of knowing a
Foreign Country, especially here, where they are naturally
very reserv'd.

France indeed is more easily seen through, the French allways talking of themselves; and the Government being the
same, there is little difference from one province to another.
But in Italy the Different Laws make different customs and
manners, which are in many things very particular here from
the singularity of the Government. Some I do not care to
touch upon, and some are still in use here, thô obsolete in
almost all other places, as the Estates of all the great Familys
being unalienable, as they were formerly in England. This
would make them very potent if it was not balance'd by
another Law that divides whatever land the Father dyes
possess'd of amongst all the Sons, the eldest having no
advantage but the finest House and best Furniture.[1] This
occasions numerous Branches and few large Fortunes, with
a train of Consequences you may imagine.

But I cannot let pass in Silence the prodigious alteration since
Misson's writeing in regard to our Sex.[2] This Reformation

---

[1] For these practices in Venice, see
James C. Davis, *The Decline of the
Venetian Nobility*, 1962, pp. 68–69.

[2] In the *Voyage d'Italie*, Misson
writes, 'L'Amour & la jalousie sont les
deux fureurs qui répandent le plus de

(or if you please, depravation) begun so lately as the year 1732, when the French over run this part of Italy, but it has been carry'd on with such fervor and Success that the Italian go far beyond their Patterns, the Parisian Ladies, in the extent of their Liberty. I am not so much surpris'd at the Women's conduct as I am amaz'd at the change in the Men's sentiments. Jealousie, which was once a point of Honor amongst them, is exploded to that degree it is the most infamous and ridiculous of all characters, and you cannot more affront a Gentleman than to suppose him capable of it.[1]

Divorces are also introduce'd and frequent enough. They have long been in fashion in Genoa, several of the finest and greatest Ladies there having two Husbands alive. The constant pretext is Impotency, to which the Man often pleads guilty, and thô he marrys again and has children by another Wife, the plea remains good by saying he was so in regard to his first; and when I told them that in England a complaint of that kind was esteem'd so impudent, no reasonable Woman would submit to make it, I was answer'd we liv'd without Religion, and that their Consciences oblig'd them rather to strain a point of Modesty than live in a state of Damnation. However, as this method is not without inconvenience (it being impracticable where there is children) they have taken another here: the Husband deposes upon Oath that he has had a commerce with his Mother in law, on which the marriage is declar'd Incestuous and nullify'd, thô the children remain legitimate. You will think this hard on the old Lady who is scandaliz'd, but it is no scandal at all, no body supposeing it to be true without circumstances to confirm it; but the marry'd couple are set free, to their mutual content, for I beleive it would be difficult to get a Sentence of Divorce if either side made opposition; at least I have heard no example of it.

I am afraid you will think this long letter very tedious, but you tell me you are witho⟨ut⟩ company, and in solitude any thing amuses, thô yours appears to me a sort of paradise.

sang en Italie. Les Italiens sont jaloux, dit-on, pour un rien, & le moindre soupçon leur excite un accès de rage'; and he gives examples of how women are guarded (ed. 1743, iii. 183–4).

[1] LM's observation is closely corroborated by Alexander Drummond (*Travels,* 1754, p. 84).

You have an agreable Habitation, a pleasant Garden, a Man
you love and that loves you, and are surrounded with a
numerous hopefull Progeny. May they all prove comforts
to your age; that and all Blessings is daily wish'd you by,
my Dear Child, your most affectionate Mother,

M. Wortley.

My Complements to Lord Bute and blessing to your
little ones.

Text W MS iii. 191–3   *Address* To The Rt Honble the Countess of
Bute recommended to the care of Samuel Child Esqr near Temple
Bar London Angleterre

To Miss —— —— [17??]

[A spurious letter, printed in: Philip Thicknesse, A Narrative
of what passed between General Sir Harry Erskine and
Philip Thicknesse, Esq; In consequence of a Letter written
by the latter to the Earl of B——— ———, Relative to the Publication of some Original Letters and Poetry of Lady Mary
Wortley Montague's, Then in Mr. Thicknesse's Possession,[1]
1766, pp. 24–25][2]

[1] Thicknesse's account is uncritically
accepted by his recent biographer:
Philip Gosse, *Dr. Viper, The Querulous
Life of Philip Thicknesse*, 1952, p. 302.
  [2] Reprinted in William Cole, *A*

*Journal of My Journey to Paris in the
Year 1765*, ed. F. G. Stokes, 1931, pp.
87–88; Cole copied it, he states, from
The Whitehall Evening Post of 3 May
1766.

Appendix

TRANSLATION OF FRENCH CORRESPONDENCE

From Jean-Baptiste Rousseau *23/12 Feb. 1726*

Brussels, 23 February 1726

It is true, Madam, that I have profited as much as I could from the chance that made me find here a friend worthy of You. Nobody is a better judge of merit than Madame Cantillon, and it would be difficult indeed for Yours to escape notice in conversations with her. I cannot return enough gratitude for the goodness that she had in not forgetting me and in reminding you of the feelings of respect and admiration which I have retained for you. Since your letter came, I thought I should lose the only friend in this Country who shares them with me; the Duke d'Aremberg had an attack of pleurisy last Sunday which endangered his life. He is much better since yesterday, and I have been asked to assure you on his behalf that no one honours you as much as he does.

The changes made at your Court hold nothing to surprise me, and would indeed distress me only slightly if I were sure that my Friends knew how to make good use of what the vulgar call disgrace. To oust a Courtier from his place is to restore him his liberty, and it seems to me that when one has paid his contribution to the Public and sufficiently established his fortune and reputation, he should no longer think of anything but enjoying in peace the fruits of his labours and resting on his laurels. For myself, I regard men in favour as the Spartans regarded the Greeks, and on close consideration most of them are more to be pitied than envied. We are in hopes that Faustina will pass through here this Lent before going to London. I am convinced she will reawaken the taste of the English for opera. Great changes are spoken of at the

498

Court of France. Your Spectator would have matter to try his strength on if the manners of politics were his province like those of morality.

Adieu, Madam; if you have still some pity for a man who considers himself exiled wherever you are absent, condescend to give me news sometimes of your health and that of your charming friend, whom I take the liberty of greeting here. Nobody in the world is with as much respect as I am, Madam, your most humble and most obedient Servant,

Rousseau.

Text (p. 59 above)

From Jean-Baptiste Rousseau 6 *July*/25 *June 1726*

Brussels, 6 July 1726.

Nothing is more humiliating for me, Madam, than the modesty with which you speak of yourself, and if I were a man to pride myself on writing fine letters, I should be abashed at the slight account you seem to make of your own. But what else would happen? I should write to you no more and in consequence [have] no reply, and then I should soon have to sink back into the lethargy from which you have drawn me. What a fine blessing God has given me in curing me of Vanity and the infatuation of wit! For a long time I have ceased to lay claim to it, but I still lay claim in a small way to the merit of discernment, and on that subject you will permit me, if you please, Madam, to admire you for ever no matter what you do to dissuade me. My faith is unshakeable, and I will persist in my Religion even to the point of martyrdom.

I understand how you can be so indifferent to the news which attracts the notice of the generality of mankind. When the Kings behaved stupidly, the Greeks who bore the brunt of it were right to be concerned. As for us, to whom their stupidities are neither here nor there, we should be very wrong to become enraged with a Scene which is performed only for our amusement. The allusion of Sir [John] Falstaff, which I have had explained to me, makes me understand the good use you can make of it, and I am convinced that it is on that level that you should consider all the other Theatrical Productions which are played in the different courts of that part of the world we inhabit.

Wisdom would suffer too much if everyone were wise. Folly is its nourishment and fools its providers. Giddiness and sadness are two extremes which are equally opposed to it, and I could find no better way of proving this truth to you, Madam, than by the little fable with which I am going to end this letter.

Folly, having taken it into her head to travel, left France one day and arrived in England. There she found Good Sense, and the astonishment they felt at a meeting so new to them was followed by a curiosity which led them to become acquainted. It was not long before they noticed that each of them had a merit which the other lacked. There they were united in a friendship that soon developed into love. They were married; and from this Alliance, more reasonable than that of Hanover, was born Wisdom, whose perfection consists in the reconciliation of the good qualities of her Father and her mother, which, mingled according to a carefully proportioned pattern, form in her that cheerful reason which makes true Philosophers.

The Duke d'Aremberg leaves in five or six days for Paris, where he wishes very much that you were still Ambassadress. As for me, Madam, I wish for nothing in the world so much as to be able to convince you of the respectful attachment with which I am for ever devoted to you.

Text (p. 67 above)

From Charles de Montesquieu 11 *March* 1731

I have the honour, Madam, of asking a favour of you; It is to be so good as to send as many of your friends as you can to Lincoln's Inn Fields at eight on Monday the 22nd of the month. It is for Mlle Sallé's benefit night. She has been strongly recommended to me by M. de Fontenelle and the Marquise de Lambert, and Lady Stafford also patronizes her. As she is very virtuous no one is obliged to her. You will therefore greatly please me, Madam, if you will use your interest for her. I have the honour to be with every kind of respect, Madam, your very humble and obedient servant:

Montesquieu.

London, 11 March 1731

Text (p. 94 above)

To Francesco Algarotti [*Aug. 1736*]

I no longer know how to write to you. My feelings are too ardent; I could not possibly explain them or hide them. One would have to be affected by an enthusiasm similar to mine to endure my Letters. I see all its folly without being able to correct myself. The very Idea of seeing you again gave me a Shock while I read your Letter, which almost made me swoon. What has become of that philosophical Indifference that made the Glory and the tranquillity of my former days? I have lost it never to find it again, and if that passion is healed I foresee nothing except mortal ennui.—Forgive the absurdity that you have brought into being, and come to see me.

Text (p. 103 above)

To Francesco Algarotti [*Sept. 1736*]

How timid one is when one loves! I am afraid of offending you by sending you this note though I mean to please you. In short I am so foolish about everything that concerns you that I am not sure of my own thoughts. My reason complains very softly of the stupidities of my heart without having the strength to destroy them. I am torn by a thousand conflicting feelings, that concern you very little, and I don't know why I confide this to you. All that is certain is that I shall love you all my life in spite of your whims and my reason.

Text (p. 103 above)

To Francesco Algarotti [*10 Sept. 1736*]

Friday, past midnight

. . . I am a thousand times more to be pitied than the sad Dido, and I have a thousand more reasons to kill myself. But since until now I have not imitated her conduct, I believe that I shall live either by cowardice or by strength of character. I have thrown myself at the head of a foreigner just as she did, but instead of crying perjurer and villain when my little Æneas shows that he wants to leave me, I consent to it through a feeling of Generosity which Virgil did not think women capable of. In truth I admire myself for such extraordinary disinterestedness, and you should be happy to be loved in so singular a manner. The pure love which M[onsieu]r de Cambrai speaks of so eloquently is not so perfect as mine, and I have a devotion for you more zealous than any of the adorers of the Virgin has ever had for her. I believe that all these men have had a little vanity in their devotion, or they hoped for great rewards for their prayers. Here am I praying to you without hope that you will give me any credit at all for it, and I spend whole hours in my Study absorbed in the contemplation of your perfections. I remember the least of your words, your puerilities, your follies, even your very impertinences; I like everything in you, and I find you so different from the rest of mankind (who yet have the insolence to think themselves of the same species) that it does not surprise me that you have inspired sentiments which until now have not been inspired in anybody.——

Perhaps it is bad French that I write, but as my letters are in your hands to burn the moment that they bore you, I write whatever comes into my head. I haven't the vanity to dare hope I please you; I have no purpose except to satisfy myself by telling you that I love you,——and who will not love you? I invited Mademoiselle —— to supper last night. We drank to your health, and she said naively that she had never seen anybody so attractive as you. I did not answer, but these few words made her conversation so charming to me that I kept the poor girl until two o'clock in the morning, without speaking further of you, but happy to be with somebody who had seen you—what a bizarre pleasure! One must have a Heart filled with a strong passion, to be touched by trifles which seem of such little importance to others. My reason makes me see all its absurdity, and my Heart makes me feel all its importance. Feeble Reason! which battles with my passion and does not destroy it, and which vainly makes me see all the folly of loving to the degree that I love without hope of return. Yet you were sorry to leave; I saw it in your eyes, and there was no pretence at all in the chagrin which showed in your manner. I do not delude myself about the impossible; it was not me that you were sorry to leave, but surely you were sorry to leave London. So I could have held on to you, and it was a false delicacy which prevented me from making the proposal to you, and so I lost, through false shame, fear, and misplaced nobility, all the pleasure of my life.——

I don't know whether you understand anything of this Gibberish, but you must believe that you possess in me the most perfect friend and the most passionate lover. I should have been delighted if nature permitted me to limit myself to the first title; I am enraged at having been formed to wear skirts. . . .

This is the 2nd letter that I write. It is the only pleasure which is left to me. How mixed with bitterness that sad pleasure is!

Text (p. 104 above)

To Francesco Algarotti *20 Sept.* [*1736*]

Sept. 20. O.S.

Is it possible that I have no news from you? It seems to me that you promised to write to me from Calais. I think only of that, and while I wait everything bores me, everything displeases me, and I am in a state which would draw pity even from the People who hate me most. It seems to me that it ought to have cost you less to write three or four lines to me than to spend as many hours talking to me. Philosophically, an exchange of letters with me ought to give you a kind of Pleasure. You will see (what has never been seen till now) the faithful picture of a woman's Heart without evasion or disguises, drawn to the life, who presents herself for what she is, and who neither hides nor glosses over anything from you. My weaknesses and my outbursts ought at least to attract your curiosity, in presenting to you the accurate dissection of a female Soul. It is said that Montaigne pleases by that naturalness which reveals even his faults, and I have that merit if I have no others in your eyes. So it is not possible that my letters bore you to the extent that you renounce them so brusquely.

It would be very much worse if some accident had happened to you. —We have not heard of storms or vessels lost.—I must be enlightened at whatever cost.—I will see Lord Hervey; he should have had news of you. Ingrate though you are, I should have a moment of pleasure in knowing that you have arrived safely in Paris, where you would make fun of my letters with some beautiful Parisienne. No matter, I shall always write to you, in order to please you if you love me, or to enrage you if you wish to forget me. How unhappy I am! and what a stroke of Mercy a stroke of Lightning would be at this moment!

This is the fourth Letter I send you. You must be thoroughly bored with my complaints, but is it my duty to protect your repose when you have so little concern for mine?

Text (p. 106 above)

To Francesco Algarotti *15 June* [*1738*]

It is more than a month since I have heard from you; however, I hasten to answer your letter by the first postal courier after I receive it. I realise well enough the folly of such conduct, but it is a pleasure I could not possibly refuse myself. It seems to me that Fortune refuses me enough [pleasures], without my taking the trouble to scold myself. So I abandon myself to my inclination and recall all my pleasant phantoms, disdaining all that surrounds me, and I choose to abandon myself to the sweet illusion which tells me that you think of me sometimes, distant as you are, and uncertain as I am when I shall see you. It is the only Idea that can please me. I confess I am surprised to find in myself such extraordinary Feelings. I have a Heart made to sustain a Sylph, and if you were one of those intelligences who read the depths of the soul, you would be charmed to see mine so filled with delicate and unselfish tenderness.

Seriously, if your affairs prevented your plan of coming to England, and if I were fully persuaded that I should truly please you in retiring to Venice, I would not hesitate to settle in the States of the Signory for the rest of my life, I assure you in good faith. This tells you well enough that I am entirely yours.

June [?Jan. (1739)] 15 O.S.

Text (p. 115 above)

To Francesco Algarotti *11 July* [*1738*]

Is it possible that you believe I received the most amiable Letter which has ever been written, from you, without answering it? No; you do not believe it at all, and you hide from me your having received two of my Letters since yours from Milan, in order to excuse your silence. I forgive you this artifice, as I forgive you everything, for the sake of merit and graces as unusual as yours. I have been the Penelope of your absence, neglecting all the objects that I saw in order to dwell every moment on the charms of a fugitive whose abode I did not even know, and whose existence I sometimes doubted. In spite of these cruel uncertainties, that dear remembrance constituted the only pleasure of my life. Judge then of your Injustice when you accuse me of having forgotten you. I have read, I have re-read, and I shall re-read your book. I shall always find new beauties; none of its charms escapes me. You would be too fortunate if you could find my taste and my sentiments in a person who would appeal to your Fancy. . . .

July 11. O.S.

Text (p. 116 above)

To Francesco Algarotti *24 July* [*1738*]

I could not keep myself from answering you the first moment that I received your letter, although I am afraid that you are not yet in Paris, and perhaps M. Robert will not bother saving it for you. I am quite accustomed to the loss of Letters to you; nevertheless I cannot possibly console myself for two I addressed to Milan which you say you did not receive. Your indifference, even your forgetfulness (for all its cruelty), is more bearable than your Injustice. I could not suffer for a moment that you should believe me capable of not being devoted to you for my whole life. No, you don't know me at all. I have a constancy and an integrity which should take the place of charms and graces; and in spite of the suddenness with which you pleased me, I am rather difficult to please, and consequently incapable of changing the object of my attachment.

I write in a bad humour, made horrible by the fear that you may not have my letter. This is the second that I have addressed to Paris. If I were sure that you would receive it, I would speak to you at greater length, but never with more tenderness and sincerity.

July 24 O.S.

Text (p. 117 above)

To Francesco Algarotti *20/9 Aug.* [*1738*]

I am losing patience. It is a great proof of this that I am running the risk of writing to you by a route which I infinitely dislike. I have sent you two Letters to Milan and two others at M. Robert's, without hearing anything from you. I dare not go into detail about my feelings. Imagine what I have to say to you, crushed as I am by your silence.

20 August N.S.

Text (p. 119 above)

To Francesco Algarotti [*Nov. 1738*]

I am too much affected by your ways of treating me. What have you seen so disobliging in my last Letter? Would to God that I might receive similar marks of your attachment for me! But I am not made to inspire the tenderness that I am capable of feeling, and am wrong to be offended. You have too much wit to need any explanation. If you wish to quarrel with me, it is because you wish it. You know only too well that you are the only object in the world which pleases me. I have done everything until this moment to prove it to you, and I shall always be the same towards you; and I have so little Notion of finding anything else agreeable, I would wish with all my heart, if I lose the hope of seeing you, to lose my life at the same Moment.

Text (p. 129 above)

To Francesco Algarotti *8 Jan.* [*1739*]

I have sworn not to write to you any more until I hear news from you. One swears in vain when Inclination leads. I am horribly silly, however, to let myself be swept away by that Demon, while you forget me before the eyes of some Idol of a Parisienne, painted and gilded, who receives (perhaps without appreciation) the homage that would make all my happiness. I no longer wish to feed on chimeras, and I shall unfailingly return to my sad good sense if you do not furnish me soon with new matter for delicious visions by a kind little Letter.

Jan. 8. O.S.

Text (p. 132 above)

To Francesco Algarotti [*Feb. 1739*]

You do me justice in believing I am in every way sincere with you. I am that naturally with everybody; and to make up for the charms that you will not find, you will always find the rarest and most perfect good faith.

You can believe that I am much happier to facilitate your return than your departure, although I confess I tremble and my philosophy leaves me when I think that I shall perhaps see you seeking other attachments,—

But let us forget these Reflections; I wish to blind myself to all that. I do not know too well how to go about sending you a bill of exchange. I believe the best way is that you draw for the agreed sum on Mr. Trible in Lichfield Street near Soho Square. He is my Jeweller, and I have a good opinion of his discretion, although I don't know any proof of it. When I see you, I shall tell you many things.

Text (p. 134 above)

To Francesco Algarotti *12 March* [*1739*]

How unjust you are, and how little you know me! But are you obliged to know me? You have seen me too little, but yet it seems to me that a tenderness proved by absence and silence ought to produce more confidence. Could I imagine that what I proposed to you would offend you? No matter; you shall be served in your own manner. I send you the bill of exchange as you desire. Perhaps I express myself badly, but my Heart reproaches me with nothing except the Weaknesses for which you owe me gratitude.

Here is the bill in the form which I am told is required. I should have liked it better another way.

March 12. O.S.

I received your Letter yesterday.

Text (p. 137 above)

To Francesco Algarotti *16 July* [*1739*]

I am leaving to seek you. It is not necessary to accompany such a proof of an eternal Attachment with an embroidery of words. I shall meet you in Venice. I had intended to meet you on the road, but I believe it is more discreet, and even more certain, to wait to see you at the end of my pilgrimage. It is for you to grant my prayers and to make me forget all my fatigues and chagrins.

Do not write to me any more in London. I shall not be there, and a Letter found might have very unfortunate consequences.

July 16. O.S.

I hazard this Letter by another way, not being sure that you received the one which I addressed to Mr. Rondeau. I hope it is not necessary to beg you not to stay in London, if you arrive there.

Text p. 139 above)

To Francesco Algarotti [*24 July 1739*]

At last I depart tomorrow with the Resolution of a man well per-suaded of his Religion and happy in his conscience, filled with faith and hope. I leave my friends weeping for my loss and bravely take the leap for another world. If I find you such as you have sworn to me, I find the Elysian Fields, and Happiness beyond imagining; if—But I wish to doubt no more, and at least I wish to enjoy my hopes. If you want to repay me for all that I am sacrificing, hurry to me in Venice, where I shall hasten my arrival as much as possible.

Text (p. 140 above)

To Francesco Algarotti [*c. 6 Sept. 1739*]

Here I am at the feet of the Alps, and tomorrow I take the step which is to lead me into Italy. I commend myself to you in all perils like Don Quixote to his Dulcinea, and I have an imagination no less inflamed than his. Nothing frightens me, nothing diverts me a moment; absorbed in my own thoughts, neither the fatigues of the road nor the pleasures offered me in the towns have distracted me for an instant from the sweet contemplation in which I am immersed. . . .

Text (p. 147 above)

To Francesco Algarotti *24 Dec.* [*1739*]

Dec. 24 N.S.

I can hardly believe that all my letters, which I sent by different routes, have missed you; but even if that should have happened, it seems to me even more extraordinary that you could imagine that I travel about the world in order to see carnivals and Festivals. You must remember that you agreed with me to live in the Venetian states, and I cannot think of a single new Reason for you to turn aside from this design. I have arranged all my affairs on this plan, and it is not possible for me to go to Paris, even if I had a Desire to, which I am very far from having.

I have done enough to prove that I wish to pass my life with you.

It is certain that if I cannot make your happiness you cannot make mine. I do not intend to constrain you.

I have received here many more civilities and even honours than I deserve; and I should lead a peaceful enough life if it were not troubled by the remembrance of an ingrate who has forgotten me in an Exile which he caused.

Text (p. 164 above)

To Francesco Algarotti *12 March* [*1740*]

Why so little Sincerity? Is it possible that you could say that you remonstrated with me against Italy? On the contrary, I still have one of your letters, in which you assure me that whatever town I establish myself in you will not fail to go there yourself, and I chose Venice as that which suited you the most. You know that the least of your desires would have led me to decide even on Japan. Provence or Languedoc would have pleased me perfectly, and saved me much Fatigue and Expense. Recall, if you please, the Conversations which we had together, and you will confess that I should naturally have believed that the journey I have made was the one to bring me closest to you. Geneva is always full of English people, consequently hardly suitable for my Sojourn, Holland even less because of its proximity.

I am settled here where I have found pleasures which I had not at all expected. The Procurator Grimani (whose merit and importance you doubtless know) is so very much a Friend of mine that he has made it a point of pride to render Venice agreeable to me. I am sought out by all the most considerable Ladies and Gentlemen here. In brief, I am miraculously much better off than in London. I should certainly leave all the conveniences of my life a second time to make the happiness of yours if I were persuaded I was necessary to it. Be honourable enough to think about this seriously. Consult your Heart; if it tells you that you would be happy near me, I sacrifice all for that. It is no longer a sacrifice; your Friendship and your conversation will make the delights of my life. It is not possible for us to live in the same house, but you could lodge close to mine, and see me every day if you should want to. Tell me your thoughts frankly. If it is true that your inclination persuades you to choose this plan, I would return to France and settle in some provincial town where we could live in Tranquillity.

March 12. N.S.

Text (p. 175 above)

To Francesco Algarotti [*July 1740*]

. . . Here is the pastime that I occupy myself with in your absence.
I fear that your great visit is doomed to be a great folly. In that case,
I shall see you late. But I shall wait with so much patience and sub-
mission that they should deserve extraordinary rewards.

Text (p. 198 above)

To Francesco Algarotti *11 Oct.* [*1740*]

I shall write you little because I fear you will not receive my Letter.
I don't want to believe that you would not wish to answer it. Do me
the favour of letting me know your Intentions. I have left Venice and
am ready to go where you wish. I await your orders to regulate my
life. Remember that I have been undecided a long time, and that it is
assuredly time for me to make up my mind.

Oct. 11. N.S.

Address your Letter in Care of the English Resident in Florence. I
am leaving that city to make a small tour, while awaiting news of you.

Text (p. 206 above)

To Mme Chiara Michiel *28 Dec.* [*1740*]

I could not possibly express too soon (my dear Madam) my gratitude
for a Letter as obliging and as kind as that I had the honour to receive
from you. It would have given me pleasure by its charm if it had been
addressed to someone else; judge therefore to what extent I am touched
by the marks of your kindness to me, who feel no merit save that of
being very sensible of yours, which certainly I only share with all those
who have the good fortune to come near you. I am delighted that Mr.
Mackenzie is of that number; he is not unworthy of your regard. I
have never known a better formed mind or a better placed Heart. I

shall never forget his offer to come as far as Bologna to meet me if I wanted to return to Venice. I should be only too pleased if I could find an opportunity of proving to him the esteem that I have for his attention towards me. Meanwhile, I recommend him to you, Madam; you see that I dare to trust you to pay my debts, and I am persuaded that I shall not be deceived in the confidence that I have in your kindness. Indeed it is only ugly women and feeble minds that ought to be feared, and you have too many charms to lack any Generosity. Truly I find no fault in that Gentleman save being a little too Young; it seems to me one can excuse that pretty fault, if only because he will correct it all too rapidly.

Although I found several agreeable people in this Country, I am on the point of leaving it. My presence is absolutely required near my Baggage, which I will have transported only to the place where I shall settle; and it is impossible for me to find salvation in a Monarchy, so much do I find occasions to complain against Providence which suffers it on the earth. I don't doubt, Madam, that you have often thanked God for the advantage of your birth, but if you were established in a Court, I answer for it that you would be so sensible of the Good fortune of Independence that you would daily offer prayers of Thanksgiving. I see here poor Prince Iaci in slavery almost as harsh as that of Count Wackerbarth, obliged to rise at the crack of dawn, whatever the weather, to walk 3 or 4 leagues to share with the King the Glory of massacring Snipe. This work has no intermission except for Sundays, which he says he awaits with more impatience than the poorest Artisan. Yet these are the blessings with which princes overwhelm their favourites. I don't speak to you at all of the inside of the Palace, which you will see at Madrid, of which this one is only the Miniature.

My Letter is becoming too long, and it is not fair that, in recompense for the pleasure that yours has given me, I should kill you with tedious Reading. Adieu, my very dear Madam; be assured that in every Country where my Destiny may lead me, you will always have someone entirely devoted to your service, and I will be all my life Your Excellency's very humble and very Obedient Servant,

M. W. Montagu.

Address your letter in care of Mr. Goldsworthy, English Consul at Leghorn.

Dec. 28.

Text (p. 217 above)

To Mme Chiara Michiel *25 Feb.* [*1741*]

Leghorn, Feb. 25.

I arrived here yesterday evening, where I had the honour of finding your kind Letter. I do not want to delay a moment in showing my gratitude, although I am quite surrounded with packages, and confounded by merchants' bills etc. Despite all the obliging things that you tell me, I must reproach you for your forbidding me to dwell upon your Praises. You want then, Madam, to deprive me of my most acute pleasure, but it is no use, and I will speak well of you everywhere, even if you should be angry.

I am delighted that Mr. Mackenzie is making himself worthy of your kindness; and frankly I think I have spent my life with vulgar prejudices about people of his age. I had Preconceptions that they were all thoughtless and should well be avoided, which I have always done, until my travels forced me to keep company with them; and I assure you that I have found among them good Faith and honour, which is rare enough elsewhere, and naturally it must be thus. There are few People endowed with a strong enough virtue to preserve themselves in the dealings of the world; Young people still have a remnant of sincerity, which, joined to the maxims of a noble Education, renders them more estimable than people of an advanced age, who are ordinarily corrupted by bad Examples. You see that it is not my own praise that I sing; as for you, Madam, you enjoy that Brilliant season at which the mind has matured without the face's suffering from it. I would that Heaven might perform a miracle in your favour, and that you could be such as you are, for two or three hundred years to come.

I do not know what my wandering destiny will require of me; one way or another my Heart tells me that we shall see each other again. I come from Rome, which I have seen in all its charms during the last days of the Carnival, but the Embroiderers and Bath-keepers are wasted on those people. Perhaps it is a Grace that St. Peter accords to the State of the Church, but I have never seen faces so formed to inspire chastity. Indeed the city is so sparsely peopled that one understands it endures only through pure conjugal duty.

Allow me, Madam, to beg you to pay very cordial and very sincere compliments to the Procurator Grimani on my behalf; and be convinced that in all countries where I shall be, I am inviolably, My very dear Madam, Your Excellency's very humble and very Obedient Servant,

M. W. Montagu.

Text (p. 229 above)

To Mme Chiara Michiel *15 April* [*1741*]

Madam,

I have received through Mr. Mackenzie the kind Letter that you did me the honour of writing me. The poor Boy left yesterday, quite overcome with sorrow at leaving Italy. He supped with me, we drank your health, and he urged me at least ten times to tell you everything that his Gratitude and his admiration could inspire. Truly he has the best Heart I have ever known, and I am well pleased with his Taste, since he assures me he has never seen anything so charming and estimable as you.

I am very flattered by the Remembrance which the Procurator Grimani has honoured me with. So far my travels have offered me nothing to equal my friends in Venice, but you are leaving it, Madam, and you are taking with you a very great part of the charms which I found there. I do not doubt that you will find in every Country people sensible of your merit; but I dare add that your Admirers in London would be more worthy of you than those in Madrid. Beauty is the true universal Language; justice will be done to yours everywhere, but you have a thousand charms that will escape the Spanish and delight the English. After staying with us twenty years, you would still have enough to efface all the Beauties of Spain. Your Senate (whose wise Administration is the admiration of Europe) ought to think seriously of this matter; it seems to me that such an expense is as useless as if they sent a garrison of a hundred thousand men to the Island of Corfu.

Adieu, Madam. I was about to bore you still further; happily for you, unhappily for me, visits force me to tell you in haste that I am inviolably, Madam, Your Excellency's very humble and very Obedient Servant,

M. W. Montagu.

Ap. 15, Turin

Text (p. 235 above)

To Francesco Algarotti [*May 1741*]

Yes, I would spend the morning writing to you even if you should be furious. I have begun to scorn your scorn, and in that vein I no longer wish to restrain myself. In the time (of foolish memory) when I had a frantic passion for you, the desire to please you (although

I understood its entire impossibility) and the fear of boring you almost stifled my voice when I spoke to you, and all the more stopped my hand five hundred times a day when I took up my pen to write to you. At present it is no longer that. I have studied you, and studied so well, that Sir [Isaac] Newton did not dissect the rays of the sun with more exactness than I have deciphered the sentiments of your soul. Your eyes served me as a Prism to discern the Ideas of your mind. I watched it with such great Intensity that I almost went blind (for these prisms are very dazzling). I saw that your soul is filled with a thousand beautiful fancies but all together makes up only indifference. It is true that separately—divide that Indifference (for example) into seven parts, on some objects at certain distances—one would see the most lively taste, the most refined sentiments, the most delicate imagination etc. Each one of these qualities is really yours. About manuscripts, statues, Pictures, poetry, wine, conversation, you always show taste, Delicacy, and vivacity. Why then do I find only churlishness and indifference? Because I am dull enough to arouse nothing better, and I see so clearly the nature of your soul that I am as much in Despair of touching it as Mr. Newton was of enlarging his discoveries by means of Telescopes, which by their own Powers dissipate and change the Light rays.

Text (p. 237 above)

To Mme Chiara Michiel 6 *July* [*1741*]

Excellency,

I hope (my very dear Madam) that you have arrived safely in Madrid, where I do not doubt you shine in every way. I am settled for this summer in Genoa, where I have found a rather fine Palace, charmingly situated, with a view of the sea and the land that appears made to inspire Dreams. The Ladies are very polite, and have shown me all possible civilities. Indeed a Foreigner cannot be happy elsewhere than in a Republic; in all Courts (especially the small ones) one is so taken up with a thousand Concerns of Hate or of Ambition that one has no leisure to amuse oneself or to amuse others. But although I actually see several agreeable people here, I swear to you that I see nothing that approaches Signora Chiara, and that it is impossible to replace her, or not to miss her every day of my life; and I am sure that everyone thinks as I do who ever had the honour of enjoying your delightful conversation. I do not want to speak to you of news, of which you are (no doubt) better informed than I, and which indeed hardly interests me. I have planned for myself a life so remote from the Tumult of the world that the greatest events concern me about as little as those that happened five hundred years ago, and I am delighted at being sufficiently Mistress of my Destiny to follow the Taste I have always had for Tranquillity and obscurity. As for you, Madam, you are destined to be the ornament of a great Court; I wish you all sorts of pleasures and charms in it, but despite all the amusements that your position brings you, I claim that you should sometimes find a quarter of an hour to write to me, and I have so good an opinion of your Heart that I don't doubt that you are willing to remember someone who loves you and esteems you as completely as does (My very dear Madam) Your Excellency's very humble and very Obedient Servant,

M. W. Montagu.

July 6, Genoa.

Address your Letters in care of Mr. Birtles, Consul of His Britannic Majesty at Genoa.

Text (p. 242 above)

To Mme Chiara Michiel 9 *Sept.* [*1741*]

Sept. 9, Genoa

Excellency,

I have received with very great pleasure (my dear Madam) the news of your health, your safe arrival in Madrid, and your continued kindnesses to me, all of which interest me infinitely. But how I pity you! in the flower of your age, charming as you are, to lose three years of your Life among Brutes too stupid to be able to admire you, and too ignorant to amuse you: one must hope that Venus will send you some foreign Prince worthy of adoring you; otherwise I see no resource for you. You cannot lose the habit of charming; it is a natural gift which you cannot relinquish, but it is very sad to use it on such animals as you describe to me.

Life at Genoa is pleasant enough, but I do not cease missing Venice for a moment. I have had a Letter from Mr. Mackenzie urging me to return there, as the only place suitable for me to stay; that Boy has the heart of an Angel. He asks me for news of you, and I am not surprised that you are never forgotten.

I do not know what will become of me, and I am still in doubt; I think too much, and perhaps your Spanish Ladies, who never think, are happier.

My Baggage has arrived safe and sound, and I spend whole Days in the dust of my Books. Alas! Madam, why can I not end them at your side? But I do not want to bore you with uttering Alas. After all, everyone has his Burden, and sometimes the fancy takes me to throw myself into the sea, through curiosity to see if the other world has not some [more] amusing scenes than I find in this.

While I am in this one, wherever I may be, you shall always have my news; give me yours, and let us try to console ourselves by telling each other of our sorrows. My most acute one will always be your absence, being with the most tender esteem, Madam, Your Excellency's very humble and very Obedient Servant,

M. W. Montagu.

Text (p. 251 above)

To Jean-Robert Tronchin *24 March* [*1742*]

You have been too well employed (Sir) to deserve reproaches for your silence. There are some occasions when it would be culpable to remember even one's friends; you have none who shares your happiness more than I. I entrust you with my felicitations to Madam your wife; that is a penance I lay on you for your forgetfulness. I am firmly convinced of her merit by the choice she has made, and I believe I know you too well to doubt the continuance of your felicity.

To enter Italy seems forbidden, but I have not yet decided where to live. Perhaps you will accuse me of Frivolity, but truly my Decision depends of necessity on a variety of circumstances that change every day, and I see by sad experience that there is no Liberty in this world. In vain we divest ourselves of Passions and Prejudices; we are always enslaved in some way. These melancholy Reflections are badly misplaced when addressed to you. In your present situation you can hardly understand that difficulties and annoyances exist. I wish with all my Heart for the continuance of that pleasing Enthusiasm which is worth more than all Philosophic truths.

I am, Sir, your very humble and very Obedient Servant,

M. W. Montagu.

Chambéry, March 24.

I presume to beg you to embrace Mlle Franconis tenderly and to make many compliments to all your charming Family.

Text (p. 267 above)

To Jean-Robert Tronchin [*May 1742*]

I am most flattered (Sir) by the honour of your remembrance, and by all the courtesies you make me on behalf of the Ladies of Geneva. I am much annoyed that destiny drags me elsewhere, but I am so convinced of the impossibility of resisting it that I have let myself drift without Resistance on the Current of the Rhône to this place, where indeed I find many attractions, Fine Houses, pretty Gardens, pleasant society, good living, charming Walks. But (because 'buts' poison all good things in this world) there is a wind capable of upsetting all my plans, and if this cruel North Wind lasts a few days longer, I shall renounce all the pleasures of Avignon, and God knows where I shall move to.

We are inundated with Spaniards here, but they are polite Enemies who pay me a thousand courtesies, and I find myself none the worse for their Conversation. I even begin to forgive Mlle Franconis her partiality for them; and if I could rule the councils of Europe, they should be our allies, and we would bear arms together somewhere else. And although I have accustomed myself for long enough to contemplate events with the detachment of a Spectator, I confess there are moments when I am vexed to see miserable Oxen wounding each other (perhaps fatally) while a Fox licks the blood that flows on both sides. I don't know how this sad Reflection has slipped from me; it fits my Age to make it, and yours to make fun of it. I give you permission with all my Heart; enjoy yourself, Sir; make the most of all the benefits that Nature and fortune have heaped upon you, and be sure that there is no one (even among those nearest to you) who takes more pleasure in your happy Situation than (Sir) your very humble and very Obedient Servant,

M. W. Montagu.

Text (p. 278 above)

To Mme Chiara Michiel 20 *May* [*1742*]

Avignon, May 20.

Excellency,

It seems to me a hundred years since I had News of you, my beautiful Ambassadress, but I could never forget the charms of your Conversation, and all the Graces that I have admired in your person.

Here I am settled for some time at Avignon. It was with great regret that I left delightful Italy, but it is going (they say) to become the Theatre of War, and I did not dare remain there. I have at least the Consolation of being under the dominion of an Italian Prince, and (between us let it be said) of the only Prince whom I esteem, because he is the only one who appears to me to consider his subjects as being under his protection, and he makes an effort to relieve them, whilst the other sovereigns consider them solely as beings created to serve their passions.

I sometimes have letters from poor Mr. Mackenzie, who is very bored in his dreary Country, and who speaks to me eternally of Venice. We are here entirely surrounded by Spaniards; God knows what will happen. I confess that except for my friends (in whom I have a lively interest) the fate of mankind is as indifferent to me as that of Butterflies, whether the blue beat the green, or the Red the yellow. All these events seem to me unworthy of consideration, and I wrap myself up in a Philosophy that gives me great Tranquillity despite the Tumults of Europe. But this quietude does not go so far as to make me indifferent to your memory, and I should be in despair if I did not flatter myself that you honour me sometimes with your thoughts, as being as much as it is possible to be (My dear Madam) Your Excellency's very humble and very Obedient Servant,

M. W. Montagu.

Text (p. 279 above)

To Mme Chiara Michiel *1 Sept.* [*1742*]

Sept. 1, Avignon

I am charmed (kind Ambassadress) with all the obliging things you tell me, and I assure you that I am more flattered by a sign of your friendship than I would be by the approbation of the academy. The less I believe myself worthy of your Praises, the more I feel indebted to the partiality that you have always had for me. I pity you for being in a country where you shine as uselessly as a Lamp in a Sepulchre. I dare say you will find enough Taste in my country to discern your value and admire you, even if we do not have enough charms to please you.

Mr. Mackenzie has written me a Letter in which he tells me of his Intention to leave England. If he could get to Madrid I am certain that he would find something to make up for all else, but as that is impossible, I am persuaded that his melancholy would follow him everywhere, and he would do a very bad thing to quarrel with his relations merely in pursuit of diversion. I have written to him very seriously about this. He has sufficient merit to be necessary to his Country, and I would willingly sacrifice the pleasure of seeing him for the benefit of the public, which needs good men like him. His Age is made for action, and a retirement that is called philosophic in old age passes for laziness in a young man. One owes one's early years to one's Family, and a little Ambition looks better than the Appearance of sloth.

Adieu, My Beautiful Ambassadress. Always keep for me the honour of your remembrance; no one knows its value better. Your kind and sensible Letters are worth infinitely more than all the false glitter of French Conversation.

Text (p. 291 above)

To Mme Chiara Michiel *15 Oct.* [*1742*]

My very dear Madam,

I have just received your kind Letter, which has given me a lively pleasure. I must pardon my Destiny many things for having given me a Friend as charming and as faithful as you. I have been here several days to see Mr. Mackenzie. We speak only of you, and you may be assured of the enthusiastic manner of our talk. He thinks as I do, that in all our travels we have known nothing equal to your merit, and we regret endlessly the impossibility of going to join you. He leaves tomorrow for London, where he goes to play the Role of Senator. Would to God that they were all as honourable Men as he; I should hope to see Roman honour reborn in my Country. I mean that of ancient Rome, for you well understand that I am not too desirous that we should imitate the modern; and I esteem virtue and morality even more than Painting and Music. I should be content even with our miserable share of Sun if I could boast that disinterestedness and Liberty Shone among us.

I leave it to Mr. Mackenzie to finish my Letter; he will tell you of his adoration for you better than I, but not with more goodwill than, My very dear Madam, your very humble and Obedient Servant,

M. W. Montagu.

Lyons, October 15

I have been told a very astonishing piece of news, that M. du Canges has been inspired to turn Catholic.

Text (p. 293 above)

To Jean-Robert Tronchin *12 Nov.* [*1742*]

Avignon, Nov. 12.

You reproach me (Sir), which I did not believe I deserved. If you had not received the Letter I wrote you (long ago) from Lyons, it is the fault of the post or of the People I had entrusted it to. I assure you that I have not failed to be conscious of the honour and the delight of your correspondence. I thought that it was you who had discontinued it, and I did not wish to importune you, knowing only too well the impossibility of amusing you.

I am here not by Choice but by a kind of necessity caused by the turn of events; and sad Experience teaches me that Liberty is as little made for man as immortality. In vain we employ systems and remedies, or make plans for independence. We are born to be enslaved and mortal. The happiest amongst us is a miserable creature who draws his solace from the Contrast. You will find this philosophy ridiculously severe. I admit that it is very badly directed; your Age and your Situation present you only with smiling Views. May such remain to you for centuries! and I wish with my whole Heart that all your life you may have the disposition to make fun of my sombre reflections, which I perhaps owe to the air of my native Country, which all the sun of Provence cannot correct.

It is more than two months since I received news from the Abbé de Lescheraine, having sent him a long Letter by the Comte de Loche. I am incapable of forgetting those I esteem; judge then if I shall not be for ever, Sir, your very humble and very Obedient Servant,

M. W. Montagu.

I take the Liberty of making my compliments to all your charming Family and to Mlle Franconis.

Text (p. 296 above)

To Mme Chiara Michiel *20 Jan.* [*1743*]

Avignon, Jan. 20.

I was so eager to prove to you my gratitude (my very dear Madam) for your kind Letter that I forgot to date mine; I beg your pardon for this negligence. You have done me justice in being convinced that I would not have left Avignon without informing you. I prize your

friendship too much to hazard losing it, and I can assure you truth-
fully that it is the main pleasure of my life.

I am not surprised at the ignorance of your good Dane; he is from
a Country where stupidity is permitted, but I confess that I am sometimes astonished that under a sky as fine as this one I very often find
just as great Absurdities. It is slavery that stupefies the mind, and it is
certain that only free men can be either virtuous or reasonable. If the
Greek and Roman Republics had not existed, there would have been
neither Poets, historians, nor Orators, and we should not have any
better memorials [of them] than we have of the Parthians and Assyrians.

I received by the last post news from Mr. Mackenzie. He is absorbed
in his duties. It is true that this is an activity worthy of a good man,
but I fear this zeal may harm his Health.

While the rest of Europe is full of Projects to defend or extend their
various states, our little town is concerned only with the Pleasures of
the Carnival, not as brilliant as those of Venice but which do not fail
to have their merit. The ladies and gentlemen amuse themselves in
performing Plays; Balls are given; and if Gambling arguments did not
mingle bitterness with these diversions, we could boast of a perfect
Tranquillity.

Adieu, my very dear Madam. I wish you and your distinguished
Family every kind of Joy and Happiness. I do not doubt that you would
find in all Countries persons attached to you, but never will you see
one more sensible of your merit than, Madam, your very humble
and very Obedient Servant,

                                                    M. W. Montagu.

Text (p. 298 above)

To Mme Chiara Michiel *22 March* [*1743*]

I never have so much pleasure as I find when I have the honour of
receiving your news, my dear and amiable Ambassadress, although I
am touched by the sad life that you lead, which is certainly not made
for you. A merit like yours ought not to be buried among the stupid
and the Ignorant. I recollect having seen in England the Count von
Dehn, of whom you speak. He was envoy of the Duke of Brunswick,
and made himself noticed in London by his ridiculous extravagance.
He was sought after by all the Coquets who wanted his magnificent
presents, and quite scorned by persons of another Character, who
hardly saw him. Such was the fine role that he played. I imagine that

it is some Frenchman who spoke to you so favourably of him; they know no other merit than ostentation or impertinence.

I am fairly bored with them, and would like to be back on the [Grand] Canal of Venice. But alas! the disorders of Italy forbid my thinking of it. The only good fortune that I envisage is seeing you again when you come back through France, and I want to make a point of meeting you on your Route. You are never forgotten (my beautiful Lady) and I am persuaded that Mr. Mackenzie thinks as I do, although he is so absorbed in Parliament that for a long time I have not had any Letters from him. Lord Marischal is still in France, but very far from here; he has settled, I do not know for what purpose, at Boulogne-sur-mer, which is a very ugly little town.

Adieu, My very dear and revered Friend. There is no one who does you more Justice than I, and I am enchanted to recognize in your merit that which can justify my inclination to be yours all my life.

Avignon, March 22nd.

Text (p. 301 above)

To Mme Chiara Michiel *4 May* [*1743*]

4 May, Avignon.

I am always very sensible (my beautiful and dear Ambassadress) of the honour of your remembrance. I swear to you that the impression of your graces and your kindnesses will never be effaced from my Heart, and I shall avidly seize all the opportunities that may present themselves to prove it to you.

I will obey by telling you in all sincerity about Princess Iaci, whom I saw a great deal of in Naples. She was then so young that one may hope she has improved, but she was a little impertinent French girl, all full of the prejudices and absurdities of her Country, contemptuous of all the magnificence of her Husband's family, although she had seen nothing finer than a Convent near Saint Denis, where she was brought up; apart from that, a pretty enough face, with very fine inclinations towards Coquetry. That is her portrait exactly, which I would be vexed to show to anyone other than you. You know that Prince Iaci has a great deal of merit; he paid me all the civilities imaginable during my stay in Naples, and I should be delighted to do him some service. He will find a great resource in your House in Madrid, and I do not doubt that you will be pleased with his

Conversation, which is very agreeable. If I dared I would beg you to give him my compliments.

I received last post a Letter from Mr. Mackenzie, who seems to me very disgusted with all the divisions in our unhappy country. If you were in Venice, I am sure he would return there, which is not surprising. Where can one find a Friend like you? If I told you all I think on this subject, you would perhaps accuse me of flattery. I can, however, assure you boldly that I keep unsaid much more than I say, when I protest to you that I am faithfully and tenderly attached to you for ever.

Text (p. 303 above)

To Mme Chiara Michiel *29 Aug.* [*1743*]

Too dear and too kind Madam,

I must address you thus since in spite of the proofs you give me of your friendship, whose value I know well, we are and will remain at a distance that does not let me Enjoy that charming conversation, capable of consoling me for everything; and (what touches me still deeper) I know that despite the brilliant outward appearance of your Situation, you do not have a happiness made for a taste as sound and as delicate as yours.

I should be too happy if I could share your vexations; I would willingly exchange for them all the pleasures of France, which are as little made for me as those of Madrid for you. People here know as little what Conversation is, as if they were fish. It is true that they are very far removed from the taciturnity of that creature; there is an eternal chatter, but with less variety than that of parrots; always with Cards in hand, the same trifles repeated continually, and thinking giddiness is vivacity of wit; so little capable of Friendship that they miss or esteem people only in proportion to their usefulness at Quadrille, which seems to them the great Object of Human Knowledge. Some day you will be, I think (my beautiful Ambassadress), at Paris, where you will see, just as I have depicted it, the great Original of all these provincial copies. I confess to you that I am bored to the point where I long to fling myself into Italy, through all the fire and blood that threaten her.

It is some time since I had any news from Mr. Mackenzie, but I am so convinced of his good Heart and his taste that I am sure he always retains the respectful admiration for you that you were made to inspire, but with which no one is more imbued than, my dear Ambassadress, your faithful and sincere friend and servant,

M. W. Montagu.

Avignon, August 29th

Text (p. 308 above)

To Mme Chiara Michiel 7 *Nov.* [*1743*]

Avignon, Nov. 7.

You will be (I think) very surprised, my dear Madam, to hear that Mr. Mackenzie has passed through Lyons, that I did not see him at all, and that he has gone to Venice by the St. Bernard Pass, in spite of the season, in spite of the Spaniards, and in spite of common sense. If he has gone to kiss the threshold of your door, that is a goal that does him honour; otherwise I could not imagine any reasonable motive for abandoning all his interests and all his friends, and I am truly mortified by the concern I have for everything that affects him. I wish he would esteem himself as much as I esteem him; he would take more care of his person and of his conduct. I don't doubt that you have given him some very sound advice, but you see he only follows his inclination. I admit that Venice has very attractive charms, and that if I were as lively as he, I should do the same thing, but I am of an age when one expects to find Discretion, and at his age liveliness is to be excused.

I share all your displeasures, my charming Friend; I am convinced that a sojourn among barren mountains is not for you, and one may say that you are frightfully misplaced. However, I cannot possibly agree that your wit would diminish; I am persuaded it is as incapable of being weakened as the sun's rays of being soiled in shining on a dunghill. Truly it is a pity to shine for objects so unworthy and so insensitive. I flatter myself that I shall see you in a more agreeable situation; my most ardent wishes accompany you everywhere, being attached to you by the most tender friendship and the most respectful esteem.

Text (p. 313 above)

To Mme Chiara Michiel *15 Jan.* [*1744*]

I assure you, my very dear and charming Ambassadress, that I have not doubted for a moment the nobility of your sentiments. I know that your Heart is worthy of your birth, and would to God that Mr. Mackenzie was always willing to let himself be directed by Counsels as wise and as respectable as yours. He left London at the time the Duke of Argyll was dying, to avoid seeing him expire; he seemed to me very much moved by his loss. I believe that this misfortune completed his disgust for England; and I am not surprised (although sorry) that, finding himself his own Master, he has sought his pleasure at the expense of the ambition one ought to have at his Age. In short, he is in a hurry to live, and must be considered a premature Philosopher.

I flatter myself very agreeably with the Idea that you give me of your return in seven months. If I am alive I will see you on your journey, and the pleasure of embracing you will make amends for the griefs your absence has caused me. You will see by the liveliness of my joy to what extent I am (Kind Ambassadress) your very humble etc. etc.

Avignon, Jan. 15.

Letters to Mr. Mackenzie must be addressed in care of Mr. Smith, English Consul.

Text (p. 318 above)

To Mme Chiara Michiel *3 July* [*1744*]

Avignon, 3 July

You will not allow me (my dear Madam) to give you the Titles which are your due, and they must be absorbed in the recollection of your Graces an dyour merit, and I am ready to forget your rank and to consider you simply as the most amiable Lady in the world. It is tribute from the Heart that I render, and which you are made to exact in all Countries, independently of your Birth and of all other honours. There are and always will be Women of Quality and Ambassadresses, but the beautiful Signora Chiara is unique in this world, and I who have travelled so much have never seen anything resembling you.

Lord Marischal left here a fortnight ago to seek his bread in Muscovy. Indeed he is a man of spirit and of worth, and a real Martyr to his Integrity. In his early youth he sacrificed a high position and extensive property to an Idea of Fidelity to his Prince, a mistaken intention indeed, but which arose from a good Heart; and at present he refuses considerable rewards to follow the Creed of his Ancestors. There are perhaps some prejudices in all this, but there is also a rectitude and a disinterestedness that cannot be sufficiently respected. He spoke to me a great deal of the Court where you are, and I think I know it more or less as it is.

I am here in a refuge from the tumults of War that alarm all Europe; I think sometimes that they will be dispelled shortly. You are in a better position to judge events; I see them only from afar, and you are in the centre of Intelligence.

My Sentiments can never cool towards you, and the title of Friend that you have granted me is too illustrious in my eyes for me to neglect any opportunity to prove to you that I am by the most tender attachment, for all my life, your very humble and very Obedient Servant,

M. W. Montagu.

Text (p. 333 above)

To Mme Chiara Michiel *12 July* [*1744*]

Avignon, 12 July.

I have not Congratulated you (my dear and charming Friend) on the renewal of **our** Alliance. Since I believe all the advantage ours, it is for me to receive the felicitations. I was always ashamed of our silly disagreement; (between us be it said) I regard almost all quarrels of princes on the same footing; and I see nothing that marks man's unreason so positively as War. Indeed what folly to kill one another for interests often imaginary, and always for the pleasure of persons who do not think themselves even obliged to those who sacrifice themselves for them! If Kings wanted to play at Basset for towns and provinces, Patience! As between Master and Master there is only the hand [of cards], I should not be too angry to see the Queen of Hungary and her Allies hold the Bank, and the Emperor punt with his. One would perhaps see Munich on one card; a double-stake would bring Prague, Linz, and Passau, without these terrible massacres and Fires, which horrify all those who wish well to mankind in general. If I were a plenipotentiary I would make this proposition to the first Congress that was held; but alas, I fear that I should find few people as peace-loving as I.

How pleased I should be (my beautiful Ambassadress) to see you in London! You will succeed everywhere, but I dare flatter myself that you will find People among us who will know your value, and consequently will be more assiduous to pay you Court than anywhere else. But never will anyone take more pleasure in doing justice to you than (my very dear Lady) your very humble etc.

Text (p. 334 above)

To Mme Chiara Michiel *20 Aug.* [*1744*]

Avignon, 20 August

My very dear and kind Friend,

The same day that I had the honour of receiving your kind Letter, Cardinal Barni arrived here. He told me that you were to leave Madrid a few days after him, and that you would have to pass through Nîmes, which is only four posts from here. I immediately sent out a Messenger with a Letter to await you, and an order to notify me of your arrival; and I prepared my post-chaise, flattering myself at least with the hope of passing a few hours with you. At last I have been forced to abandon these agreeable Ideas. No doubt you have taken another route, and I must be content with renewing to you from afar the assurances of a tender attachment that will end only with my life. But why did you not let me know the road you took? I would willingly have travelled a hundred leagues for the pleasure of talking with you.

I also had a thousand things to say to you on the subject of the Unfortunate Mackenzie. He wrote to me from Berlin in an endeavour to justify the most unreasonable conduct that ever was. I took pity on his waywardness, and I sought in my turn to restore his sense gently, without disputing the miraculous merit of the wonder by which he is enchanted. I only begged him to reflect that if she had a real passion for him, she would be the first to turn him from so disastrous an idea as a marriage so disproportionate in every way, that the most scrupulous virtue would be content with a clandestine engagement in such a case; and if she acted otherwise, it was, and could only have been, from interested motives of which he was the dupe. I do not know if this remonstrance has had a good effect, not having had any reply.

You will pardon (My Beautiful Lady) these details; I know that you have a heart generous enough to be touched by the misfortunes of your friends. Believe that mine is entirely pervaded with feelings of esteem and of friendship for you, and that any expression seems feeble when I want to tell you to what extent I am your very humble and very Obedient Servant,

M. W. Montagu.

You will have an English Ambassador of high Birth, in other respects not too brilliant either in wit or appearance. This is said for you alone.

Text (p. 340 above)

To Mme Chiara Michiel [*Sept. 1746*]

Do not believe, my very charming and revered Friend, that the impressions you make are ever effaced. I have never failed for a moment in the friendship that I vowed to you for all my life, but the disorders of Italy have cut all communication by Letters, and yours and mine have alike been lost. I received this one only today because Monsieur Martinengo wanted to put it into my own hands, and for a fortnight I have been in bed with a Fever. I am still there, and I write to you with a weak hand but with a Heart entirely moved by your kindnesses. I have overcome a thousand perils to return to dear Italy. How many things I have to tell you! I must await the recovery of my health to have the pleasure of embracing you. I have not the strength to write any more. I am entirely yours, my beautiful Madam, and will be eternally Your Excellency's very humble and very devoted friend and servant,

M. W. Montagu.

I beg you to tell me what has become of the Abbé Conti.

Text (p. 377 above)

To Mme Chiara Michiel *31 Dec. 1746*

the last day of the year 1746

Excellency,

There is certainly a spell cast on our friendship; every time I try to give you some signs of it, some accursed Genie diverts them, and wants to make me appear to you as the most ungrateful and unfeeling person that ever was.

I replied (my dear and charming friend) to your most esteemed letter the very moment that I received it, although I was in such a state as to be almost unable to hold my pen, in bed, burning with an intense fever. God knows if my Letter reached you; I have had no reply at all.

When I was a little better I wrote to you again to show you how much I was mortified by the postponement of the honour of seeing you. The Doctors have put me in bed, and all that I can hope is to be able to embrace you at Ascension.

I have just been told that the Peasant to whom my Letter had been given to carry to the post had lost it, and they did not dare tell me, for fear of vexing me, being still very weak. Imagine my fury! I demanded some paper that instant, and I am trying for the third time to let you know that my Heart is still the same towards you, and I am convinced that those who are attached to you never forget you. But among that number, I dare boast that there is not one more deeply aware of your merit and your charms than, Excellency, your very faithful Friend, and very humble and Obedient Servant,

M. W. Montagu.

I beg you, my Dearest, to give me news of the Abbé Conti and M. du Canges.

Text (p. 380 above)

To Angelo Maria Contarini *10 June 1750*

Excellency,

I am infinitely obliged to you for your Kind interest on my behalf. But that Man of whom you speak is a Lunatic and an Impostor. I am just getting over a very serious Illness, which I have hardly recovered from. When he arrived here dressed as an Abbé, without giving his name, I was still too ill to see anyone. I sent my Chambermaid to ask him what he wanted of me. He gave her a Letter that was indeed addressed to me, but signed by a Lady whom I did not know (and who perhaps does not exist), and quite full of Madness, that showed clearly it was forged. I had his Letter returned to him, and asked him to leave; whereupon he had the Effrontery to draw a Pistol against my Servants.

If I were in a condition to go out I should not fail to come in person to tell Your Excellency these facts. I ask your pardon for this poor Scribble, but I still have a very weak hand and Head. I have heard it said that this madman, with whom I am not connected in any way, has passed himself off as my Relation. He has already been confined in

France by order of His Father, who is truly a respectable man, much to be pitied for having such a son.

I am, Sir, with the esteem due to your Merit and your Character, Your Excellency's very humble Servant,

M. W. Montagu.

June 10. 1750.

I trust, Sir, in your Justice, that at least this Man may be expelled from the Country.

Text (p. 456 above)

PRINTED IN GREAT BRITAIN
AT THE UNIVERSITY PRESS, OXFORD
BY VIVIAN RIDLER
PRINTER TO THE UNIVERSITY